THE
CHINESE
HERITAGE

THE
CHINESE
HERITAGE

K. C. WU

CROWN PUBLISHERS, INC.
New York

Printed in the United States of America

Published simultaneously in Canada by General Publishing Company Limited

Library of Congress Cataloging in Publication Data

Wu, Kuo-Cheng, 1903–
    The Chinese heritage.

    Bibliography: p.
    Includes index.
    1. China—Civilization—To 221 B.C.   I. Title.
DS741.65.W8   1981   931   80-28846
ISBN: 0-517-54475X

10 9 8 7 6 5 4 3 2 1

First Edition

Book design by Elaine Golt Gongora

To my late father and mother
and also
To my wife

CONTENTS

GENEALOGICAL CHARTS

MAPS

PREFACE

The Chinese Heritage is intended both for the general reader and for specialists.

For the general reader, it is hoped that the reading of the book will enable him to appreciate more fully the origins and quintessence of the Chinese ethos in its entirety and thus to understand more precisely the rationale and the social and political outlook of the Chinese both as a people and as individuals. For this purpose, the main text provides sufficient information. The general reader, unless he chooses to, need not concern himself too much with the notes, though both they and the Bibliography have been prepared with him in mind.

For specialists, however, every statement or assertion made in the text is documented with references or explanatory notes. And for their convenience, while the Pinyin system of romanization is used throughout, in the Bibliography the names of authors and books published in Chinese are also given in Chinese characters as well as in Wade-Giles transliterations.

I would like at this time to gratefully acknowledge the assistance of Dr. H. K. C. Yee, who, through his expertise in astronomy, has helped me to reaffirm the authenticity of the earliest Chinese written historical document on record, *yaodian,* which described the events of the 23rd century B.C.

I am also greatly indebted to Sir Yue-Kong Pao of Hong Kong for his generous contribution to my work.

I wish also to express my deep appreciation to my son, Dr. H. K. Wu, for his varied, sustained, and unfailing support, and to my daughter-in-law, Dr. Kathleen Johnson Wu, for having read through several drafts of my manuscript and given me many a valuable criticism and suggestion.

K.C.W.

July 1981

THE
CHINESE
HERITAGE

CHAPTER I

INTRODUCTION: DISTINCTIVE FEATURES OF THE EARLY CHINESE HERITAGE

· 1 ·
POVERTY OF MYTHOLOGY

If we look for distinctive features that characterize the early Chinese cultural heritage, our attention may very well be drawn first to its apparent poverty of mythology. The Sumerians had *Gilgamesh;* the Hindus, *Mahabharata* and *Ramayana;* the Greeks, the *Iliad* and *Odyssey;* the Romans, the *Aeneid;* the Scandinavians and the Germans, *Volsungasaga* and *Nibelungenlied;* and the Egyptians, though they did not seek to express themselves through epics, had a body of myths as rich and fanciful as any. These are tales about their heroes, both human and divine, told and retold none knows how many times, each time with new adornments, additions, or alterations—tales that were remembered and cherished when the written word was yet to be born, when men still felt they could communicate directly and freely with gods and demons, when neither gods nor demons deported themselves much differently from men. These are, of course, not the stuff of which histories are made. But they are beautiful flashbacks to mankind's early life on earth, teetering between infancy and childhood, that have made these various peoples' cultural heritage fascinating and colorful.

But not so with the Chinese. Despite the acknowledged antiquity of their race, what the modern Chinese have inherited from their proverbially honorable ancestors in this field is so shabby and scant that it borders almost upon the ludicrous. Their mythology, if it deserves to be called by that name at all, boasts of no lengthy, episodic narratives. Instead, it consists of only a handful of broken and isolated anecdotes, abruptly told without any sense of organization or artistry, whose characters seem to have entered from nowhere, and then exited into the same nothingness. Putting them side by side with those famed epics or sagas of other peoples, they look like crude oddities.

If one should ask a Chinese on the street to tell of his native mythological tales, very likely he would tell of two. He would begin with the story that the first man who lived on Earth was named Pangu and that he separated earth from heaven. Before him, these two bodies were joined together in one vast nebulosity in the shape of an egg, which Pangu managed to rend asunder. The lighter part ascended above and became heaven, while the heavier part settled below and became earth. And, believe it or not, this is the beginning and the end of the story.

There are some varied versions about how he did the rending. Some would say he did it by applying an ax, and others simply by his growing taller and taller and thus keeping the two bodies farther and farther apart. Still others would have it that when Pangu passed away, his head was transformed into mountains, his eyes became the sun and the moon, his veins and arteries seas and rivers, and his hair and skin vegetables and plants. But nothing was said about his origins: whether he had been created by some unknown force or had just been born of that nebulosity itself. Nor was there an account of whether he had mated, or who his mate had been, or how he had succeeded in populating the earth afterward. All these notwithstanding, somewhere in modern Guangdong province in southern China there is a mount in which the remains of Pangu are supposed to be buried.

The second story the Chinese on the street would probably tell would be equally abrupt, though more romantic. Yi, the great archer, was given a drug capable of prolonging life indefinitely by Xiwangmu, Queen Mother of the West, a lady of mystery.[1] But before he could partake of the drug, his beautiful wife, Changwo, swallowed it. Forthwith she flew straight to the moon to abide ever after, leaving her husband in despair, unable to follow her. And Changwo has since remained in the eyes of the Chinese the Maiden of the Moon, forever enjoying her immortal beauty and forever suffering her inconsolable loneliness—a fitting subject for poets to pour forth their rhymed commiserations without end.

Very likely, the telling of the two stories would have exhausted the mythological repertoire of the Chinese on the street. And likely too, if he should claim that these stories are descended from time immemorial, he would be mistaken. For, so far as research can ascertain, they both seem to have been invented quite later. The Maiden of the Moon story was first related in a book compiled in the 2nd century B.C., which is far from ancient to the Chinese.[2] And the tale of Pangu did not make any intrusion into Chinese literature until about the 3rd century A.D.[3] Besides, we have the best evidence we can possibly have that neither of these stories ever obtained currency before 299 B.C. In that year one of the greatest Chinese poets of all time, Qu Yuan, drowned himself. But shortly before committing suicide, he visited the temple of his royal ancestors and viewed all the murals on which were painted the best-known myths and legends of his day. Viewing those pictures, he wrote beneath each of them his inquisitive comments in rhyme. After his death, his countrymen collected these, put them in the form of a poem, and called it *Inquiries to Heaven*. The first lines may be roughly translated as follows:

> We talk about the very beginning of Antiquity,
> Who had been there to tell us that it was so?
> Neither the Upper nor the Nether Sphere assumed definitive shape then;
> On what grounds could anybody this know?
> While light was yet darkness and darkness light,
> Who could see through it all, his eyes however bright?
> Then the separation came; and day follows night, as night follows day.
> Thus was Time begun. But for what purpose? I say!
> It takes the male and the female to join together in order to create three;
> From where did this principle spring? And from it why cannot we be free?
> The heavenly sphere is round and has levels nine;
> Who had measured it up and built it so fine?
> It is rotating and revolving night and day,
> How can its axle be suspended at nowhere, by the way?
>
> . . .
>
> The sun and the moon, to what or to whom do they belong?
> And the myriads of stars, how did these come along?
> The sun rises from the east and sets in the west;
> How much distance does it cover before taking its daily rest?
> The moon wanes and waxes, as a man dies and is then born again;
> A rabbit is seen inside it; hiding there, what advantage can it gain? [4]

From these passages the popular belief in those days is very clear. Before heaven and earth were separated, there was an infinite nebulous vastness where light was darkness and darkness light. And the poet wondered who could have been there to tell that it was so. Certainly neither he nor the mural artists appeared to have any idea about the existence of Pangu. As to the moon, he observed a rabbit hiding inside—which, by the way, is still what many Chinese, looking at the moon from the ground of China, fancy they see in the silver reflections on its surface. The artists did not paint the flight of the maiden Changwo to the moon, nor did the poet say so much as a word about it, a subject which would have seemed far more appealing to the artistic or poetic mind than a simple rabbit in hiding.

This poem of undisputed authenticity puts into serious doubt, if it does not completely disprove, the possibility that the two popularly accepted mythical tales described above had been transmitted from the earliest times. But a question that should be of more interest to us is, Does the poem reveal any other tales? To be sure, it makes reference to many things. But before we answer our question, we must first make a distinction between *myth* and *legend*. Though the two words have often been used interchangeably, we suggest that whereas legends are woven around historical events that are known to have actually happened, myths are embroidered about occurrences which, so far as human intelligence can tell, could not have happened at all. If we proceed from this differentiation, the poem, while disclosing many legends to which we may have occasion to refer later on, nevertheless bears witness to the currency of only three myths prior to the 3rd century B.C. One of the three myths is that the earth, after its separation from heaven, had not remained level, but had inclined toward the southeast. This was said to have occurred at the time of one of the early emperors. A powerful minister then in charge of public labor, by the name of Kang Hui, had tried to seize the throne for himself but was defeated in the struggle for power. In anger he dashed all his might against the Uncircumscribed Mountain, and the earth's slanting resulted. This is of course an attempt of a primitive people to explain why the rivers of China, as they knew them, are all flowing either eastward or southward; why the west and northwest of China are higher in altitude than the eastern and southern plains.[5]

The second myth is that during the early reign of Emperor Yao, ten suns appeared in the firmament, leading to a severe drought. So Yao commanded the great archer Yi to destroy the suns that were spurious. (Was Yi the husband of the famous Maiden of the Moon? No indication of whatever nature is given here or elsewhere.) But he did shoot nine suns down; the one he could not is, of course, the true sun that still shines today.

If these two myths are short and abrupt, the third one is even more so. It is about one divine ruler named Nuwa (Lady Wa), who could transform her body into different shapes many times a day. Commenting on this particular mural, the poet asked,

> Nuwa was endowed with such a body;
> Who could have conceived and wrought such a wonder?

This is all we have from the poem. To have something more like a story about her, we have to wait another century and a half for the same source that gave us the Maiden of the Moon. Here it is further stated that in the days of Nuwa the sky was found gaping in the northwestern corner. No explanation is given about how the breach had been brought about, nor any description of how it looked. We are only told that Nuwa collected and refined stones of five colors with which she repaired the damage without much ado.[6]

The above account nearly exhausts the repertoire of early Chinese myths. There may be a few more, very few, that can be garnered from books of dubious authority, or doubtful antiquity.[7] But a further review of them would be profitless. For they are all like the stories given here—stories involving only isolated and disconnected incidents and told in a most desultory and artless manner.

However, to make this discussion even more exhaustive, we shall expand it to include the somewhat mythical impressions the early Chinese had formed about four species of animals, which they called the "Four Intelligents" *(si ling)*.[8] These are *long,* the dragon; *feng,* the phoenix; *lin,* the unicorn; and *gui,* the tortoise. Not that they were considered to be superior to man. The early Chinese, like their present-day descendants, were conceited enough to think that man is the most intelligent of all creatures.[9] But they believed nonetheless that these four species of animals were each endowed with some particular virtues of their own that made them admired, respected, and even sometimes venerated.

In China's first dictionary, produced by Xu Shen in the early 2nd century A.D., we find this definition of the character *long:* "Head of all animals that swim or crawl; it can be visible or invisible, tiny or huge in size, short or long in dimensions; in springtime it can ascend to the heavens; in autumn it can sink into the depths of waters. This character is designed after the picture of a flying body of flesh." Many fabulous stories have been told about the dragon in China, but most of them were invented after 49 B.C. when the then emperor chose to call his reign year the Year of the Yellow Dragon. From that time on, the Sons of Heaven have been fond of identifying themselves with that supernatural animal; and in the eyes of the common people it has also assumed more and more incredible features of divine dignity. But in the earlier days this was not exactly so. In reliable history books we learn of a family who made it their profession to raise dragons, so to speak, on a sort of dragon farm. And actually, at one time, a female dragon was slaughtered and eaten.[10] But on the whole the dragon was credited with unusual intelligence. Thus after Confucius had met with Lao Tzu, he was said to have compared this great Taoist[11] philosopher with the dragon.[12] Hence the popular saying, now used when one wishes to pay the highest tribute to another man's intellect: "He is like a divine dragon. One can see only his head, not his tail." Moreover, the Chinese dragon, unlike its Western counterpart, was seldom venomous or malicious; it was supposed to be a creature of generally benevolent inclinations. Thus in the later days a custom grew up of worshiping dragons as rain gods, dispensers of heaven's most precious gift to agricultural China.

If the Chinese emperors liked to be identified with the dragon, the Chinese empresses liked to be identified with the phoenix. The Chinese phoenix, however, has no such legend as the Egyptian phoenix that could resurrect itself from ashes. Instead, we meet with this description in Xu Shen's dictionary: "*feng*: a divine bird. According to Tian Lao [a famous minister of the Yellow Emperor, circa 2700 B.C.], viewed from the front, it looks like a swan; from the rear, like a unicorn; it has the serpent's neck, the fish's tail, the dragon's scales, the tiger's back, the swallow's jowl, the rooster's beak. . . . If it appears, the world will be enjoying great peace and ease."

The Chinese character *lin*, which is translated here as "unicorn," is described by the same dictionary as "an animal of benevolence, having the body of an antelope, the tail of an ox, and a single horn." And according to some commentaries, the horn is flesh-tipped so that though it looks like a weapon ready for use in self-defense, it is never intended to do injury to others.[13] Also, the animal is supposed to appear only when there is a benevolent rule in the realm. It was therefore the untimely appearance of a unicorn and its being killed in a ducal hunt in 481 B.C. that caused Confucius, lamenting this tragic occurrence, to lay down his pen and write no more.[14] He died two years later.

The last of the "Four Intelligents" is the tortoise. This reptile is certainly no mystery to us. But from the very ancient times the Chinese seemed to have ascribed to it, or rather to its shells, the special faculty of being able to forecast the future. In one of the earliest historical documents of China, which is supposed to have been written around the 23rd century B.C. and which describes the different levies collected from the various regions of the empire, a mid-southern region where nine rivers meet (probably the present-day Jiangxi province) was ordered to pay tribute of large tortoises with shells over one foot and two inches in length, wherever such could be caught.[15] Besides divination, tortoiseshells were also used as currency of great value.[16]

The above is all that can be said about Chinese mythology. In comparison with others, how paltry and lackluster it must look! But in view of the undoubted antiquity of Chinese culture as well as the acknowledged richness of its heritage, how can there have existed such an apparent anomaly? Those critical of the Chinese may attribute it to a deficiency in imagination; and those partial to them may aver that they are possessed of a higher degree of realism or rationality. But to search for more solid reasons, we must look elsewhere. As mythology is closely linked with religion, let us now turn our attention to the early religious concepts of the Chinese, which seem to be also quite different from those of other peoples.

· 2 ·

RELIGION WITHOUT PRIESTHOOD

There is no question that the ancient Chinese believed in one almighty God. All the records, from the earliest times, testify to this. They called Him *di*, "the Lord," or *shangdi*, "the Lord Above." As God abides above, and above is heaven, *tian*, so they also called Him *tian*, "Heaven." [17] Unlike other peoples, however, they never endowed their God with human attributes or with any kind of physical image. From all records prior to the 2nd century B.C., there is no indication that they had ever worshiped idols. Idol worship appeared only in the reign of the brilliant but superstitious *wudi*, "the Martial Emperor" (144–88 B.C.), of the Han dynasty, who had some particular deities whom he worshiped specially portrayed in painting in a palace built for them.[18] And when in 120 B.C. one of his great cavalry commanders captured from the northern nomadic hordes a "golden man used in sacrifice to Heaven," such a sculpture had never been seen before and was recorded as an item of interest and rarity.[19] In fact, idol worship was introduced to China only after the advent of Buddhism in the 1st century A.D.

But the early Chinese, although believing in one almighty God, were not strictly monistic. In the very first document preserved by Confucius in the *Book of History,* it is stated that when Emperor Shun first took over the reins of government (circa 23rd century B.C.), after having worshiped the Lord Above, he also paid reverence to the Six Venerables (which are believed by some scholars to be Light, Darkness, and the Four Directions between heaven and earth), to the spirits of major mountains and rivers, and to all other deities. Mozi, or Micius, as some Western scholars like to call him, who lived after Confucius (551–479 B.C.) but before Mencius (371–289 B.C.), was the only Chinese philosopher who attempted to formulate a sort of religion out of the concepts of his day. In his book there are found three chapters entitled "On the Understanding of Spirits," *ming gui.* He used the word "spirits" to include deities, and he maintained that there are three—heavenly deities, the deities of rivers and mountains, and deities which worthy men have become after death. But all these deities are under the direction of the supreme Lord Above, more or less like the hierarchy of the mundane imperial regime which Mozi knew, with all the princes, dukes, and other feudal lords owing their allegiance to the emperor.

Among the lesser deities, two were of special significance to the ancients. The first one was almost equated with the Lord Above, though considered slightly inferior. For while the Lord Above is often referred to as Heaven, the first lesser deity was none other than Earth itself. Thus in the olden days, when people made solemn supplications, they usually called on both Heaven and Earth together *(huangtian houtu)* as their witness.[20] This concept of

Earth as inseparable companion of Heaven, however, went through a subtle change because of a problem created by the feudal system that gradually developed. It was acknowledged that only the emperor could worship Heaven and Earth. But how about the feudal lords who owed their allegiance to the emperor but were also rulers in their own delimited domains? The heavens, of course, are an indivisible whole; but the earth may be said to be divided in this respect. Could not each of the lords be allowed to worship a surrogate of the deity Earth, so to speak, as a sort of guardian angel for his own particular division of land? Thus the idea of *she* was born. In each feudal state an altar was built so that the lord could worship his own *she*. Presently this became the tradition for the emperor also, for, while claiming overlordship of all, he had also an imperial realm of his own to take care of. Thus it was that whereas a feudal lord need worship only his own *she*, the emperor must worship, besides Heaven and Earth, the *she* of his personal domain too. And when an imperial dynasty was overthrown by another or when a feudal state was abolished or conquered, the first thing to be done was to have that particular *she* removed or destroyed.[21] Then the concept of *she* was further expanded. Sometime during the Zhou dynasty a custom was established to permit a village with more than one hundred households to have a *she* of its own.[22] This is probably the beginning of the "local joss" idea. And after Buddhism was introduced into China, the josses became small idols enclosed in tiny shrines which dotted the land.[23]

The second deity of special significance is an example of a worthy man who was apotheosized after death. This was Emperor Shun's minister of agriculture *(ji)*, who helped save people from starvation during the years of the Great Flood in the 23rd century B.C. by teaching them how to plant a variety of grains to suit different soil and terrain. Although *ji* was the title of his office, and not his name, he was consecrated as god of agriculture and called simply Ji. Now, in the life of an agricultural society, nothing could be more important than land and farming; so these two deities—She and Ji—became the most revered of all, next only to Heaven and Earth. Indeed, in the period of the Warring States, 468–221 B.C., the two words were usually spoken together to form one single term, *sheji*, representing the spiritual entity of a state in its entirety. After the abolition of feudalism, the term was no longer so frequently used.

As to the rites of worship, these were quite simple. The elaborations came in later days. In worshiping the Lord Above at the time of Shun, the ceremonies were held outside the city limits, wherever the imperial capital might be, in an open field to its south. A bonfire would be burned so that flames could be sighted from afar going upward toward heaven; and the sacrifice would be an ox—the utmost token of reverence.[24] Human sacrifice did not seem to have ever been considered. Not that the Chinese never indulged in that kind of atrocity. In 531 B.C. there was a record of such an incident.[25] But that was due to the cruelty of an upstart tyrant of a southern kingdom who wanted to flaunt his power before his peers by sacrificing a prince to a mountain; his action was denounced immediately and widely. There were also instances of an order being left upon a ruler's death that many of his capable lieutenants as well as favorite concubines commit suicide and be buried with him to keep him company in the next world.[26] But that, perhaps, could be more appropriately attributed to malice, jealousy, or even statecraft than to superstition or sheer inhumanity. In fact, this practice can be traced even further back. In the Anyang excavations it was discovered that in the imperial burial grounds of the Shang dynasty between the 14th and 12th centuries B.C. there were slain and buried along with the dead sovereign not only ministers, concubines, attendants, and guards but also hundreds of others, mostly in their twenties and thirties and lined up in rows. But this suggests the killing of captives in order to throw fright into other nations at the time of the transfer of imperial authority—a motivation more political than superstitious. At any rate, so far as worshiping Heaven and Earth is concerned, there is no indication that human sacrifice had ever been practiced.

The worship of Heaven and Earth was usually held at the capital of the empire. But when the reigning emperor thought that he had accomplished something especially commendable, then he would perform a ceremony out of the ordinary, called *fengchan*, which was more often than not held at Taishan, the sacred mountain of the East. Supposedly there were five sacred mountains in China, with one in each of the four directions and a fifth at the center. Somehow the sites of the four others were changed from one mountain to another in successive ages, but throughout Chinese history Taishan has always maintained its position as the sacred mountain of the East. *Feng* was the ceremony conducted at the top of the mountain, the word literally meaning "to increase height by piling up earth." As Taishan is much nearer to heaven than the plains, the idea was to pile up more earth on its highest peak to symbolize man's desire to be even closer to the Lord Above. After this ritual was completed, the emperor would descend to one of the chosen sites at the foot of the mountain, where the ground had already been cleared and an altar constructed. And here he would preside at the ceremoy *chan* in order to worship Earth. According to one source, before the 7th century B.C. there had already been some seventy-two rulers who had performed this special service at Taishan, of whom twelve were still distinctly remembered at that time.[27] However, in 219 B.C., the third year after the so-called First Emperor had united China by force, he wanted to conduct *fengchan* at Taishan and consulted scholars about the necessary and proper rituals to follow. But the scholars, having no records to rely upon, could not agree among themselves. The First Emperor was of course not a man to be de-

terred by such trifles; he ascended the sacred mountain and pursued a ritual
of his own. It was recorded that he erected a stone monument on its top in
commemoration of his own achievements, increased the height of the peak
by adding to it more earth, and worshiped.[28] But as to the exact rituals he
had improvised, he kept them secret and unknown to the public.[29]

It may be wondered why the scholars had not kept any records of the
ceremonies performed by no less than seventy-two rulers before the First
Emperor. Though many explanations can be ventured, the real answer may
be a very simple one. China never had anything like institutionalized religion, as other peoples had. The Chinese had formed religious concepts
about the Lord Above and a sort of spiritual hierarchy under Him, but they
had never organized a formal religious establishment on the basis of that
belief. There were ceremonies performed on definite occasions, and even at
regular intervals, but the men who officiated at them would invariably be
those who were important in the community by virtue of their achievements
in nonreligious fields and not because of their preeminence in any religious
structure. In other words, to use modern parlance, these men were laymen,
not clerics. Or simply, China did not have, and never had, a priesthood.

In the studies made on other early peoples, we usually find that in their
society the lords spiritual seemed to enjoy greater prestige, if not wield
greater power, than the lords temporal. Thus in India, the Brahmans held
precedence over Kshatryas; in Egypt, the priests often dominated the kings;
and in African tribes, the witch doctors almost controlled the chieftains. But
in China there are no records whatever to that effect. This is evidenced by
the book *Zhou Li,* which detailed the organization of the imperial government of the Zhou dynasty, founded in the 12th century B.C. Under the
minister of the imperial household, *zongbo,* there were three offices whose
functions might be considered to have religious or supernatural bearings.[30]

The first office consisted of diviners. The ancients believed that the future
could be foretold through the use of the so-called Eight Trigrams, which
were later expanded into sixty-four hexagrams. By applying heat to a tortoiseshell or an ox bone, or by arranging milfoil stalks in accord with a
prescribed procedure, lines, broken or unbroken, would be formed; and the
diviners' principal duty was then to read the lines, consult the books, find in
which situation which hexagram would be applicable, and thus to tell what
kind of future could be anticipated regarding the question that had been
raised. Their position would have been a powerful one if the diviners could
have kept the books on the trigrams and hexagrams secret among themselves. But the books seemed to be common property to all who were literate
at the time. And often it appeared to be the wise, or clever, nonreligious men
who had contributed more to the making of the comments of the hexagrams.
For instance, the founder of the Zhou dynasty, Wen Wang, and his son,

Zhougong, are considered chiefly responsible for the composition of the *Book of Changes, Yi Jing,* which had become the standard book on the explanation of the mysteries of the hexagrams to the exclusion of all others since the 12th century B.C. , and which, also, has recently gained so much popularity in the West. Thus the influence of the diviners in interpreting the future was very much restricted; and their office became a comparatively mechanical one, downgraded to taking care of the precious tortoiseshells and milfoil stalks and going through the proper motions of applying heat to the former or arranging the latter in the prescribed manner.

The second office consisted of invocators. Their duties were threefold: to be familiar with all sorts of invocations and prayers that had been spoken in the past and to be able to compose new ones when required; to categorize and differentiate the various deities concerned and to know or to recommend what kind of fitting sacrifice should be offered to each of them; and to serve as masters of ceremony on formal occasions, somewhat like present-day protocol officers. The whole office does not seem to suggest much opportunity for its occupants to exercise significant influence, occult or otherwise.

The third office consisted of men called *wu.* If one looks up the character *wu* in any Chinese-English dictionary, it is invariably translated as "witch" or "sorcerer." So here one is tempted to think that at last we have run into the Chinese counterpart of the African witch doctor, if not that of the Western priest. And this hypothesis appears to be further strengthened by the fact that there did exist two Wu, father and son, who were great and powerful ministers in the Shang dynasty in the 16th or 17th century B.C.[31] But upon closer examination, we find little substantiation for this supposition. On the one hand, we can never be sure that the *wu* of this father-and-son team was not just a family surname rather than a title that symbolized the craft they had practiced. On the other, they were remembered only for their wisdom and virtue, not for any fame in black magic or dark powers. At any rate, even if this bit of evidence is inconclusive either way, there is no question that an analysis of the office of *wu,* as given in the book *Zhou Li,* can lead to only one conclusion.

The office of *wu* consisted of two chief *wu* who supervised a number of male and female *wu.* Their main duty seemed to be to dance the rain dance in the event of a drought. Except for that, their functions were manifestly trivial, such as guarding buried sacrifices, or accompanying their masters or mistresses to a house of mourning to extend condolences. Nor were their persons accorded much respect or consideration. In 639 B.C. in the state of Lu, after the performance of the rain dance had brought no relief to a severe drought, the disappointed duke wanted to burn all the *wu* concerned forthwith and was only dissuaded from doing so by a wiser and less superstitious counselor.[32] Moreover, the office of *wu* was deemed much lower than that of the invocator or diviner. The ancient bureaucracy was divided into six grades. While the senior diviners and senior invocators were ranked in the fourth grade and the other diviners and invocators in the first to the third, the two chief *wu* were ranked in the second grade and the other *wu* were not ranked at all, apparently regarded as mere retainers, or servants.

There is another proof of the scant regard the ancients held for *wu*.[33] As noted before, one of the duties of the chief *wu* was to accompany his lord or lady to extend condolences to a house where death had occurred. In the procession, the *wu* was supposed to walk ahead with the funeral invocator and brandish a peachwood broom to fend off sickness and evil spirits. But when the procession reached the destination, only the invocator was allowed to enter the house with his master, not the *wu*, who was left behind standing outside the gate. This was said to be a way of showing respect to the house visited. And from this one can perceive the entire attitude of the ancients toward those who claimed to possess occult powers. They were superstitious enough to avail themselves of their services, but they were also too skeptical to give much weight to their pretensions.

Were the Chinese ancients always like that? Had their society never been dominated by priests or witch doctors? There is a curious passage in the *Lore of Chu (chuyu)* which deserves to be quoted here at length.[34] Chu was a kingdom that had flourished in southern China (the present-day Hubei, Hunan, and Jiangxi provinces) from the 12th to the 3rd century B.C., and because of its proximity to the undeveloped areas farther south, had been regarded as more or less troublesome and barbarous by the Chinese who dwelt in the central plains. The passage is very difficult to comprehend even in the original text; we shall, however, endeavor to translate it literally as follows:

> In the ancient times the ways of men and of gods were not confused with each other. When there were people who possessed concentrated and undivided minds; who were at the same time reverent and upright; whose intelligence was such as to be invariably able to find out what was fitting and proper for things both above and below; whose wisdom was enough to light up and shine in remote and dark places; who were as penetrating in seeing as they were thorough in hearing—when there were such people, then illustrious gods would descend on them. If this happened to men, these men were called *xi;* if it happened to women, these women were called *wu*.[35]
>
> These *xi* and *wu*, therefore, could recognize the gods each in their various places, classify them, and rank them. Also, they could ascertain and regulate what animals, what utensils, what time, and what ceremonial dresses should be used in offering sacrifices to them. These men being themselves brilliant descendants of past sages, from them were chosen those who had knowledge of the names of rivers and mountains, of the lineage of distant ancestors, of the management of the ancestral temple, of the proper ranking of different generations; and, also, who were of diligent reverence, of ritualistic appropriateness, of dignified appear-

ance, of lofty countenance, of solid integrity, and of immaculate apparels; all these for the purpose of paying veneration to the illustrious gods—from such men were chosen those who would serve as *zhu,* "invocators."

In addition, from the descendants of famous surnames were chosen those who had the knowledge of cultivation and growth in the four seasons, of the diversified nature of animals, jades, and silks, of the designs of dresses, and of the measurements of the utensils that were required in various ceremonies; and the knowledge of the positions in which the different ancestors should be placed as well as those in which the venerators should place themselves; and also the knowledge of where the altars or holy grounds should be located, of the many gods above and below, and of the origins of the different houses and surnames; all these with a mind dedicated to the pursuit of past tradition—such men should be made *zong,* "elders." [36]

It was from this origin that we began to have officers dealing with sacred affairs pertaining to Heaven, Earth, and gods as well as officers dealing with mundane affairs pertaining to men, animals, and things. And thus were developed the five departments of government, which could conduct their businesses respectively in good order and would not be confused with one another.[37]

Therefore, the people could keep to their integrity and loyalty, while the gods gloried in granting the people blessings and causing them no harm. The gods and the people each followed their own ways: The latter showed due respect for the former without bothering them with ceaseless entreaties. And as the gods gave the people bountiful growths, so the people requited the gods with fitting sacrifices. Hence disasters and calamities were not visited upon men; all that men needed was given them without deficiency.

At the time of the decline of Shaohao,[38] the tribes of Jiuli created a state of disorder, in which the ways of gods and of men were indiscriminately thrown together, and no more direction of things could be discerned. Each man had a different god to worship, and each house its own *wu* to prescribe the ceremonies. There was simply no true understanding any more. The people offered one sacrifice after another without end, became impoverished in consequence, and yet had no idea as to what actual blessings they gained. There was no standard regulation for worship, and men put themselves in places where gods should be. They had no awe for gods any longer, and violated their pledges and oaths without fear. And the gods, having become familiar with men, knew how evil men's ways were. Thus no more bountiful growths were awarded to men, which in turn caused a shortage of things that could be used for sacrifices to gods. Hence disasters and calamities kept on rising and increasing, yet the evil atmosphere remained unexhausted.

When Zhuanxu [39] received the empire, he ordered the Lord of the South named Zhong to take charge over all the affairs pertaining to heaven and the gods, and the Lord of the North named Li to take charge over all the affairs pertaining to this earth and the humans. The purpose was to return to the ancient tradition so that the ways of gods and men would not again encroach upon each other. This is called "stopping the communication between heaven and earth."

Sometime later, the tribes of Sanmiao reverted to the ways of Jiuli. So Emperor Yao reappointed the descendants of Zhong and Li, who had not forgotten the old tradition, and made them take charge again in their respective fields. This continued through the dynasties of Xia and Shang.

The above passage has baffled many a Chinese scholar in the past. But now, equipped with an understanding of Western priesthood and African witch doctors, we may have a better comprehension of its significance. From this passage we may gather that in remote antiquity the Chinese did also have a class of persons called *xi* and *wu,* who claimed to be able to communicate directly with gods, and who consequently enjoyed a great deal of prestige and importance in their society. This was true, if not throughout China, at least in some parts of South China. But the system ran amok when each tribe began to set up its own gods, boast of the prowess of its *wu,* and strive to impose its beliefs upon others, which naturally resulted in turmoil and chaos.

This situation was regarded as unwholesome by the people dwelling in the northern plains, who had always claimed a sort of overlordship over the south, and whose own religious views were also different. So they subjugated those southern tribes again and again, and compelled them to adopt their beliefs, which, in contrast, were easy and simple to follow. In the first place, they believed in one almighty God, the Lord Above, with a hierarchy of gods under Him, such as Earth, the gods of the mountains, the rivers, and so forth. But their gods were all imageless, including the Lord Above. Asked what He looked like, they would just point at the blue heaven. And, secondly, they believed that the two worlds, spiritual and mundane, should be kept apart. It was the will of the Lord Above to sustain and provide for men, to keep them in the path of righteousness by rewarding the good and punishing the evil. It was the duty of men to pay due respect to Him and to His host of subordinate gods by offering regular, appropriate sacrifices; and, above all, to obey His wishes and concentrate on developing sound and proper relations among men themselves, not to bother the gods with incessant demands and entreaties. Thus when one of Confucius's disciples asked the Master what constituted wisdom, he answered, "Give yourself earnestly to the duties due to men; render reverence to spiritual beings, but keep aloof from them—this may be called Wisdom." [40] Though the sage's answers to questions were as a rule so worded as to suit the individual character of each questioner (this one was probably given as a caution against the disciple's oversuperstitious nature), there can be no doubt that the sentiment as expressed here represents the prevailing Chinese attitude toward religion in general, which has been passed down to the present day from time immemorial, long before Confucius

This being so, it can be easily seen why the *wu,* whatever influence they might have had in the gray hours of the dawning of Chinese culture, had lost almost all of it in a very short time. Except for a few occasions of worship, communication between the gods and humans was distinctly discouraged. There was thus little room left for the exercise of their talents as constant go-betweens. And inasmuch as all rituals involved were simple formalities, any person could officiate who had some knowledge of past tradition as well as a certain presence of mind. As a result, there was no necessity, and therefore no real opportunity, for the growth of an institutionalized priesthood. To be sure, the Chinese are known for their ceremoniousness. But their ceremonies—and there was an abundance of them even in the early days—were concerned mostly with human relations, such as betrothals, weddings, funerals, mournings, community functions, and court activities, which far outnumbered religious rites.

From this, along with some other factors which we shall presently discuss, it may also be understood why the Chinese never developed much of a mythological lore. The gods are all nameless and imageless. If it could be said that they possess any particular characteristics, it is through their identification with physical entities completely visible. *Shangdi* is Heaven, *houtu* is Earth. What we can say of heaven is that it covers us all; what we can say of earth is that it bears us all. One may describe many things one sees in them or on them; but one cannot weave many fabulous stories about them. The same applies to mountains and rivers. Take Taishan. One may imagine its guardian deity helping a good man to climb up its peak without hazard, or throwing all sorts of obstacles in the way of a bad man. But however interesting one might make such stories, what Taishan could be said to have done would not be much more than what any other mountain could do. To attribute to Taishan more would make the storyteller himself unbelievable.

And this, perhaps, is one of the principal reasons why throughout her long history China has never had a religious war (that is, unless the subjugation of the Jiuli and Sanmiao tribes by the northerners, as recounted above, may be considered an exception to the rule). Moreover, the Chinese language never had a word for "religion" until contact with the West and Christianity. Before that, the Chinese had only the word *jiao*, which means "teaching." Thus there are *kongjiao*, the teachings of Kongzi, or Confucius; *daojiao*, the teachings of the Way, as formulated by Lao Tzu; and *fojiao*, the teachings of Buddha. And the Chinese belief was, and still is, that all these teachings teach men to be good: Though their practices may be different, their aims are all the same. Even the coming of Islam did not seem to make much difference. But after the advent of Christianity, the Chinese had to coin a new word for religion. They did this by linking two characters together to form one term, *zongjiao*. While *jiao* is "teaching," *zong* is the same word used in the passage of the *Lore of Chu*, quoted above, signifying "elder" or "household." So the term *zongjiao* means "teachings of an elder or a household," with the implication that these teachings are to the exclusion of those of other elders, or other households. Prior to this, when Buddhism began to develop sects, the Buddhists also used the character *zong* to signify "sect." So *zongjiao* can also be translated as "sectarian teaching." But since the turn of this century, with the continuing impact of the West, the Chinese have become so accustomed to this term that not many of them now realize that before the 18th century it was not widely known at all.

· 3 ·
ANCESTRAL VENERATION

But the desire of man to have some communication with the divine is deeply rooted in his nature. The priests, the witch doctors, or the *wu* got their start by offering a service. Whereas ordinary men cannot see the gods and talk to them, the priests, the witch doctors, and the *wu* claim they can. And whether or not men believe them wholeheartedly, there is no question but that they find a source of great comfort in them. But now that the early Chinese had denigrated the value of the *wu*, how were they to satisfy the needs of their spirtual yearnings? In other words, to whom or to what else could they turn as a more acceptable medium between themselves and the spiritual world?

The Chinese answer to this question was simple and direct. None could fulfill this function better than their own deceased ancestors. They believed, like most of humanity, that human existence consists of two components, flesh and spirit; and that death occurs when the spirit departs from the flesh. Hence it was recorded that in the earliest times when a person passed away, his kith and kin would climb up to the housetop and cry out: "So and so, do return!" It was only after the spirit failed to return that the remains would be buried.[41] Later, the belief was further expanded. While the flesh component remained the same, the spirit component was again divided in two parts, namely, *hun* and *po*. *Hun* is the finer part of the spirit, purely aerial, almost divine, and *po* the baser part, the animal essence that gives man his carnal appetites. After death occurs, while *po* will keep near the flesh remains, *hun* will rise above and away from them.[42] Thus, while interment might satisfy *po*, it gave no satisfaction to *hun*. Now the Chinese at this time did not have any idea of heaven or hell, paradise or limbo; these concepts were brought in later through Buddhism. To leave the *hun* of the deceased abandoned, forever wandering and forever lost, would be unthinkable to any conscientious descendant. Moreover, it was feared that because of such negligence, the *hun* might well turn into a sinister force causing serious harm to the living.[43] To find an abode of rest for the purely aerial elements of the dead became therefore a matter of necessity; and it was for this purpose that ancestral temples came into existence. Also, it was hoped that, once thus sheltered, the spirits would continue watching over the interests of their descendants as zealously as they had while alive. Indeed, to the ancients, their interests were exactly identical: If the descendants prospered, the sacrifices offered to the ancestors would be in abundance; but if their fortunes declined, let alone the exiguity of sacrifices, even the temple might be ruined and the spirits left utterly homeless.

And to be sure, the spirits, it seemed, could do much for their descendants. Being unearthly, they should have easy access to the gods, even to the Lord Above Himself. It was in this vein that an emperor was recorded to have addressed a deceased relative: "Uncle, thou hast ascended reverentially, and art now on the right or the left side of our imperial ancestors, helping them attend upon the Lord Above." [44] From such a conception of the spirits, it is natural that the next idea to develop was that of requesting them to intercede with the Lord Above, or with the other gods, whenever occasion required. This was especially true in the Shang dynasty (circa 18th to 12th century B.C.), whose people were known for paying special attention to the veneration of spirits.[45] Among the divination shells and bones excavated at the turn of this century, proof of this practice abounds. A number of the prayers addressed to the spirits were petitions for good harvest, for rain, for cure of ailment, or for the birth of a son and heir. And conversely, when rain did not fall in time, or when there was some sickness, the Shang believed that they had incurred the wrath of some ancestors who must be appeased. But it should be noted that throughout there was no indication that the Shang people thought their ancestors could accomplish these things by themselves. They could only intercede with the divine powers on their behalf. If they were pleased with their sacrifices, they would do their best; if they were not, they would not intercede at all.

The inscriptions on these so-called oracle bones, as we shall discuss later, are necessarily very limited. If we should attribute too much significance to them, we would be stepping beyond facts into fancy. Moreover, all the bones excavated so far are derived from the 14th to the 12th century B.C. Thus both in the matter of contents and in the matter of antiquity, they are not to compare with the document on Pangeng, which preceded them.[46] Pangeng was the Shang emperor, 1401–1374 B.C., who foresaw the eventual destruction of the old capital by flood, and moved it to a new safer site. But accustomed to the ease and luxury of the old city, the people did not at first share his farsighted apprehensions. In the document he was recorded to have harangued the people repeatedly. He coaxed them to remember how their forefathers had faithfully served his great ancestor, the founder of Shang; and he threatened them that unless they served him well, his great ancestor would inflict drastic punishment upon them, and their own forefathers would also "cut them off, abandon them, and see them die without succor." [47] This sounded almost like endowing the spirits with divine powers. Yet it was not. For in a previous harangue, referring to the founder of the

dynasty, he had said, "In everything our imperial ancestor did, he had reverentially obeyed the commands of Heaven." [48] And in a later harangue delivered after the capital had been moved to the new site, he again declared: "It
is because the Lord Above intends to restore to us the virtues of our great
ancestor that we have been successful in moving to this new city where we
can abide permanently." [49]

At any rate, if there had existed any confusion on the powers of the spirits
in the time of Shang, by the early Zhou this was all cleared up, as is evidenced by another document, known as the *Golden Coffer*.[50] The founder of
the Zhou dynasty was taken gravely ill. He had only very recently overthrown the Shangs and established his control over the empire, 1111 B.C. His
son and heir was then but a small boy, and the entire country was still
restive, in need of a firm and prestigious master at the helm. People dreaded
to think what might happen in case of his death; and none realized the
explosive nature of the situation more than his trusted brother, the Duke of
Zhou. So the latter, without the knowledge of the dying monarch, performed a private ceremony of his own and addressed an earnest petition to
their mutual deceased father, grandfather, and great-grandfather, which may
be briefly paraphrased thus: "Your own primal offspring is now being afflicted with this severe illness—the offspring that has received the mandate
from the Lord Above to pacify the four quarters! You owe Heaven, therefore, a duty to protect him. Pray, intercede, and take my own life instead as
a substitute for his!" And from then on the Chinese have always called to
their ancestors in the same spirit as the Duke of Zhou did. When they meet
with a shocking surprise, they will as often cry out in dismay, "My father!
My mother!" as they will exclaim, "My Heaven!" or "My God!" And if
they pray to their ancestors to grant blessings or to avert calamities—and
they do this only too often—they do it not in the belief that the spirits can
themselves fulfill the requests, but in the hope that the spirits will intercede
with the powers that can fulfill them. Hence, strictly speaking, these should
not be regarded as prayers in the Western sense. These are just favors they
ask of their forebears, treating them as if they were still alive, though dead.

Thus from the very outset of their recorded history, the Chinese seem to
have venerated, rather than worshiped, their ancestors side by side with
shangdi and the other gods. In the very first document of the *Book of History*,
the decree by which Emperor Yao named Shun his heir apparent, circa 2285
B.C., was said to have been transmitted to the latter at the former's ancestral
temple. It was only after the holding of this ceremony that Shun went
outside the city limits to worship *shangdi* in an open field.[51] Again, after
Shun had made his first inspection tour of the empire, he reported to the
temple immediately upon his return. Also, when Yao died and Shun succeeded to the throne, it was at the ancestral temple that he announced his

succession. This practice continued as still other ways of showing veneration developed. Shortly after Shun's death, in the Xia dynasty, 2205–1767 B.C., a custom appears to have emerged to venerate the most renowned early progenitor of the imperial house at the ceremony outside the city limits along with the worshiping of Heaven.[52] When Shang displaed Xia in the 18th century B.C., the development took one more step. In addition to the most renowned early progenitor, the Shang emperors sought to do equal honor to the founder of their dynasty.[53] And by the time Zhou succeeded Shang in the 12th century B.C., the practice had become established tradition. When the Zhou emperor worshiped Heaven in the open field outside the city, he would also venerate his most renowned early progenitor. Then almost immediately afterward, in another service at the ancestral temple, he would venerate the actual founder of the empire. In both cases, the early progenitor and the founder of the dynasty were venerated as "company for *tian* (Heaven)." [54] To the Chinese, this was not blasphemy. For they pretended nothing more than that the spirits of these ancestors were at the side of the Lord Above, to keep Him company, to wait upon Him, to intercede with Him on their behalf whenever necessary.

Such a conceptualization naturally leads to many questions. For instance, acknowledging that it was fitting and proper for a ruler to venerate his own ancestors, could he also venerate others along with them in his ancestral temple? The ancients early on gave an affirmative answer. From the oracle-bone inscriptions it is discovered that the Shang emperors venerated the first prime minister of the empire, who had helped found the dynasty, and who later had actually ruled the country in an interregnum.[55] And in the document on Pangeng, that persuasive ruler was recorded to have said to his people, "Now, I am offering the great sacrifice to our former emperors; your forefathers are also invited to follow and share in the same." [56] By the time of the Zhou dynasty, a firm rule on this point seems to have been established: "With regard to veneration, the sage-sovereigns have thus regulated: The persons that ought to be venerated are those whose laws and teachings have prevailed among the people; those who have laid down their lives in pursuance of duties and services; those who have brought benefits on the land with hard toil; and those who have warded off grave dangers or disasters. Anyone who does not belong to these categories is outside the book for veneration." [57] One can see that it is from an extension of this principle that the later dynasties consecrated Confucius as the sage-teacher to be venerated.

A second question arose: The spirits of the dead being aerial, what recognizable forms could be given each of them so that they could be distinguished one from another in ceremonies? The ancients used two methods. The first method seems to have obtained only in the early Zhou. This was to use a live person, formally called *shi*, to act in the place of the dead.[58] Now this character *shi* literally means "cadaver"; but inasmuch as the ancients did not imply anything unwholesome, we take the liberty of translating it here into "the departed." In any ceremony that was held in his honor, or in which he participated, the departed would be installed in his place of dignity, treated with reverence, and offered food and wine as though he were the real person still alive. And the departed, with the help of protocol officers, would conduct himself just as the real person would, except that he must not speak under any circumstances. As one can imagine, such a practice could become at times very cumbersome and impractical; it was later discontinued.

The second method to represent the dead was to use wood. It is not known when the custom first began. But according to the funeral rites prescribed in the early Zhou (12th century B.C.), shortly after a man breathed his last, a wooden pole three feet high would be planted erect in the courtyard, upon which would be hung a piece of cloth with the name of the deceased written on it. The pole was called *zhong,* meaning "weight." [59] From the choice of the word, we can conceive its significance. The ancients were afraid that the spirit, being aerial, might fly off to nowhere, and so they erected the pole for it to anchor itself with. However, after the remains were buried, the pole was interred too.[60] So as a new anchorage for the spirit, so to speak, they had another wooden tablet made, this time only one foot long, but much more elaborate in design, and also with the name of the deceased written on it. This they called *zhu,* meaning "host," or *shenzhu,* meaning "spirit-host," or "where the spirit itself is host." [61] The ancients would with due ceremony convey such a tablet into the ancestral temple, where it was supposed to abide permanently. And this use of wooden tablets has lasted with the Chinese unto today.

But once the tablet was conveyed into the temple, the ancients were confronted with a problem even more complex: where to place this particular tablet. For there were many ancestors to venerate, and seniority and protocol became important questions. The Shang, before the 12th century B.C., tried to give the matter a simple solution. We do not know if they had built a temple for every deceased emperor; but we do know that they had offered sacrifices to each and every one of them the year round.[62] However, toward the end of the Shang dynasty, with some thirty deceased emperors on the roll, and with their numerous spouses to boot, this practice had manifestly become quite a burden. So the Zhou decided to build ancestral temples no more than seven in total,[63] with a few especially distinguished ancestors having permanent temples of their own, and with the others sharing the honor in subordinate positions. But then which were entitled to permanent temples, and which should be subordinated? These questions often arose to give trouble to later dynasties.

· 4 ·
FAMILY SYSTEM AND INNOVATION OF SURNAMES

From this general review, we can see how much emphasis the Chinese ancients laid on the veneration of ancestors. And it is this selfsame belief of theirs—that the well-being of the ancestors and that of the descendants were directly linked to each other, and that their interests were mutually dependent and inseparable—that led them gradually to build up a family system unique and distinct from those of other nations.

This tendency is evidenced by the early appearance of surnames in China. For surnames are instruments designed to separate and distinguish people from one another in accordance with their parentage. Without surnames, it would be exceedingly difficult, if not impossible, for men to trace back their lineal descent. But with the help of surnames, men may even recognize the similarity, or dissimilarity, in lineage between themselves and other men at the very first encounter. Such recognition would not be a matter of importance to societies which did not lay much stress upon blood relationships. This is apparently why in many cultures surnames did not appear until only a few hundred years ago, whereas the Chinese seem to have used them even before the very beginning of their recorded history, which is some twenty-seven centuries before the Christian era.

Many sociologists believe that primitive societies started with a matriarchal form of family. This appears to be borne out in China by the fact that the earliest surnames all had their characters formed with the pictorial symbol "woman" as a radical.[64] Chinese recorded history, however, begins with the so-called Yellow Emperor, whose surname stands out pointedly as an exception to the rule. As related in the authoritative *Historical Records,* his surname is Gongsun, which literally may be translated as "Duke's grandson." [65] Although it may be too rash to attach much significance to this single fact, yet it seems not unreasonable to infer that about this time, or prior to it, the matriarchal family system had already been, or was being, displaced by the patriarchal. And this assumption appears to be supported by an additional account in the same *Historical Records:* "The Yellow Emperor had twenty-five sons; of these, fourteen received surnames." This succinct statement raises several questions: Why did not all the sons continue to use the surname Gongsun? If new surnames must be given to some sons, why not to all of them? What had the fourteen sons done to be treated differently? No ancient records have provided the answers, so we have to venture our own. The Yellow Emperor lived in an age when China was going through a transition from the way of nomadic life to that of agrarian settlements. He himself pursued the old practice of the nomad, and eleven of his twenty-five sons must have followed him to the end of his life. But fourteen

others, either prompted by their own independent-mindedness or encouraged by their father for his own reasons, were bent on moving elsewhere to
settle or to roam. This state of things is confirmed by a later recording of
sundry remote places to which some of these sons migrated. Thus on the
point of their departure it may have been deemed necessary by the astute
parent to award them new surnames so that when the descendants of the
same bloodline met with one another later, they would at once be able not
only to recognize their common kinship, but also to tell from which one of
the sons each had descended. And the wonder of this record is that of the
fourteen new surnames, four have actually survived through all these millennia to the present day.[66]

This practice, either originated by the Yellow Emperor or reinforced by
him, spread after his death, especially among the tribes that maintained close
association with his own. Thus by the time of Yao, his great-great-grandson,
a document purporting to give an account of that monarch's reign makes
mention of these tribes as "the hundred surnames." [67] But by the same
document it is also clear that only a moiety of the people had adopted the
practice, for, in contrast, there was mentioned too "a myriad of nations"
who apparently did not. Shortly afterward, however, a bold attempt was
made to apply the system to the then known world in its entirety. It was
during the reign of Yao that the Great Flood occurred. Emperor Yu, who
began his career as the principal officer entrusted by Yao's co-emperor,
Shun, with the gigantic task of controlling the flood, devoted a dozen years
of his life to the work and traversed the entire country from one end to the
other several times. After his tireless labors had finally brought the mission to
a successful conclusion, he reported back to Shun thus: "The fields were all
classified, and all revenues were established with reference to the three characters of the soil. The Central Nation then conferred lands and surnames so
that all professed a foremost love of virtue and would not act in any manner
contradictory to imperial action." [68] This last remark shows unmistakably
that the Central Nation as represented by Yao, Shun, and Yu had tried to
use surnames as a means to achieve an effective unification of the empire.
Where there were people or tribes without surnames, they would confer
surnames on them so that all the peoples could be distinguished one from
another. And to each people or tribe bearing the same surname the Central
Nation would assign an allotment of land, clearly delimited, so that disputes
with other peoples or tribes bearing different surnames could be avoided.
Without this system, one can hardly imagine how China, with the vast
territory that Yu had traversed, could have been effectively united at so early
a date.

This ambitious scheme, however, was too much ahead of its time. Not
long after Yu's death, a widespread reversion to nomadism seems to have

occurred, and the usage of surnames was substantially disrupted. From there on we lose the track of its development. But by the middle of Zhou, the pendulum appears to have definitely swung back—and with a vengeance. We come across an authoritative statement made in 715 B.C. to this effect: "When a man is born, he is given a *xing* on the basis of his descent; when he is enfeoffed, he is given by decree a *shi* on the basis of his fief." [69] Thus when a man was made a feudal lord of sorts, he and his descendants became possessors of not only one surname but two, a *xing* and a *shi*. However, while this practice might have served as a source of pride for some at first, it was just too redundant to endure. By the close of the period of the Warring States (468-221 B.C.), it was all but discarded. The people who could boast of a *xing* and a *shi* contented themselves with using only one of the two and called it their *xing*. And because of the special reverence they held for their ancestors, Chinese seldom like to change their surnames; so most of the *xing* adopted during this period or afterward have descended down to the present day. Thus unlike those of the West, the surnames in China are very limited in number.[70] And such is the latent strength of heritage that the Chinese today, when they intend to say "we the common people," still use the 4,000-year-old expression "we, the old hundred surnames."

The institutionalization of the Chinese family system, as a result of the early heritage, will be discussed in the concluding chapter of this volume. For the present, it behooves us to return to some of the primary circumstances that surrounded, or helped to mold, that heritage. With the transition from matriarchy to patriarchy, polygamy apparently entered into the scene. Yet, as a rule, it was only the patriarch of a large patriarchy, or a few who had the power and the means to do so, who engaged in the practice; the custom does not seem to have been observed by the people at large. However, as nomadism was still the prevailing condition, it was adjudged unsafe for womenfolk to live or roam by themselves. So out of this necessity came a generally accepted social convention: "It befits a woman to follow a man's lead three ways: While unmarried, she should follow her father; after marriage, she should follow her husband; in the event of her husband's death, she should follow her son." [71] While this was no doubt sound and prudent advice suited to the then particular environment, it has served nonetheless as a convenient pretext for men of later generations who believe in tighter control over women's movements to impose more restraint upon them.

Yet, reduced as their freedom was later to become, Chinese women were never at any time so severely segregated as some of their sisters in India or in the Middle East. Nor have they ever been regarded as intrinsically inferior to their men. For pitted against this aspect of their common heritage, there is still another aspect which is even stronger and more basic in the Chinese mind—the reverential regard for ancestors. The Chinese believed that it was the primal duty of descendants to sustain the needs of their ancestral spirits through sacrifices; consequently, there could be no injury done to the spirits greater than discontinuing those sacrifices, and therefore there could be no unfilial act worse than failure to produce posterity to make the continuation of such sacrifices possible.[72] Moreover, as no ancestors may be expected to relish being venerated by supposed descendants who are not truly of their own blood, so purity and chastity in women are highly treasured; and for this reason wives are always chosen with the greatest care, and treated by their husbands as equal partners in upholding the sanctity of their lineage. Hence the ancient maxim: "A son is honored because of his mother; and a mother is honored because of her son." [73] And from very ancient times, as evidenced by the oracle-bone inscriptions, the Chinese have always venerated their male and female ancestors alike.[74]

With the advent of patriarchy, there also arose the inevitable question of succession after a patriarch's death. This was a matter of especial importance to the ancients, for the patriarch of the ruling house was also acknowledged as the sovereign of the then known world. There seem to be only three methods usable under the circumstances, and the ancients appear to have tried all of them. The first was to choose the successor through consensus obtained among the elders. But what if no consensus could be reached? And what, especially, if the dying patriarch should want to name his own choice? The second method was probably derived from the nomadic background, when the roaming bands were ever in need of strong and vigorous leadership. Thus a practice was adopted for brother to succeed brother in the order of seniority of birth. So long as there were brothers to go the round, smoothness in the transfer of power appeared to be ensured. But the danger point was reached when the last of the brothers died. Should the position of authority go then to the oldest son of the oldest brother, who passed away long before, or to the oldest son of the brother who has just died? To make the latter the rule was obviously unfair to the scions of the older brothers; but to make the former the rule might be putting the very lives of those scions in jeopardy while they were still young and the last of their uncles was in the full enjoyment of undisputed sway. The third alternative was to have the eldest son of a patriarch succeed his father, or what is known as the rule of primogeniture. This is perhaps the best method to avert confusion or contention. Yet it is not foolproof. For trouble lurks again, when the heir and successor happens to be but a child and disputants are not lacking in desire to wield power on his behalf. Thus none of the three methods is free of defect; and indeed, as we shall see, it is on the jagged rocks of these questions that the ship of ancient China ran aground quite a few times.

But no matter which of the methods of succession was used, the inviolate principle was that the successor must be of the same blood as his predecessor. This pervasive preoccupation with lineal purity perhaps also helps to explain why the Chinese have almost no mythology to speak of. One may revere one's ancestors, but one knows that they were human beings just like oneself, not gods or demigods. One may brag about the physical prowess or mental alertness or moral rectitude of these ancestors, but one does not ascribe miracles to them. And even if one does, one can hardly expect others to believe in one's extravagance. Thus the only thing the Chinese ancients could possibly do to glorify their own lineage was to weave fanciful but not too incredible stories about the birth of the founder of their house in order to make him stand out from other people.

The history of ancient China, except for a short prelude of the so-called Five Premier Emperors, is a history of three dynasties—the Xia, the Shang, and the Zhou. The Xia were the only people who did not have to make up such stories. This is not because they were above such self-indulgence, but because the founder of their house happened to be none else than Yu, whose subjugation of the Great Flood was recognized by all as a human feat more marvelous than any ordinary miracle. The progenitors of the Shang and the Zhou were both associates of Yu; but their achievements, however worthy, were no match for Yu's. So the house of Shang had it that their early ancestor was conceived by his mother after she had swallowed an egg of a mysterious black bird.[75] And this started the custom of worshiping the spirit of the black bird as a deity of fertility, to whom sacrifices would be offered to pray for the blessing of posterity.[76]

Not to let the Shang monopolize the field, the house of Zhou went even further in this sort of embroidery. They claimed that their founder's mother became pregnant after she had trod in the footsteps of an unseen giant. She considered the conception unpropitious. When the baby was born, she abandoned him in a narrow alley. But the animals driven past would not step on him. Then the mother had the baby left in a forest and on the ice, but the birds gathered to cover him with wings to give him warmth. Marveling at this, the mother took him back and named him "the Abandoned One." And he grew up to become Emperor Shun's famous minister of agriculture, whom latter-day China consecrated as Ji.[77] How much does this story resemble that of Romulus and Remus! Yet, while mindful of the similarity between two legends which originated in different corners of the earth, we must not overlook one significant dissimilarity. The Chinese never made any pretense that "the Abandoned One" was descended from a god, but the Romans would have us believe that Romulus and Remus were fathered by Mars. Moreover, except for these stories about their births, all the written records about both the Shang and the Zhou progenitors are accounts of their meritorious deeds as human beings, deeds that eventually laid the basis for the founding of the two successive dynasties, without the slightest suggestion that either of them might have received assistance in his endeavors from supernatural sources.

· 5 ·
DEVELOPMENT OF WRITTEN LANGUAGE

Still, there appears to be another factor contributing to the poverty of mythology in China. And this is the early development of her written language. Like an infant that can never recall the circumstances of its own birth, perhaps man, too, can never adequately discover in what manner, through what process, or at what time he was able to bring written language into existence. The Chinese records have done what they could to trace their own development. In the *Book of Changes* it is definitely stated: "In remote antiquity reckonings were made by the knotting of ropes. This was changed by latter-day sages into written words." [78] Then, based on the same source, it was further alleged: "When Paoxi ruled the world, he first drew the Eight Trigrams and invented the written word as a substitute for reckoning by knotting ropes. From this are derived literature and records." [79]

However, as the time of Paoxi is so remote and obscure, it is natural that none can be sure exactly what he achieved. While all ancient writings agreed that he was the inventor of the Eight Trigrams, many did not believe that he had actually devised written characters. When Xu Shen compiled his dictionary in the early 2nd century A.D., he followed another tradition that also went back to remote times. Thus he stated in his own preface: "The reckoning by knotting ropes was used by the House of Divine Husbandman (*shennong*) as a basis for government. But affairs were getting more and more copious and complex, and there was much deception and chicanery. The record keeper (*shi*) of the Yellow Emperor, Cangxie, saw the marks and prints left by the claws and paws of birds and animals, and found that these could be differentiated in tracings. He became the first to invent written characters that could be carved on wood, to be used by the multitude of officers for the clarification of myriads of matters." Thus the invention of the written language was placed at the time of the Yellow Emperor. Although the exact years of the Yellow Emperor's reign are still being disputed, traditionally they are believed to be in the 27th century B.C.

This narrative about Cangxie's invention explains why the Chinese written language has been generally described as pictorial writing. Nevertheless, this is far from the truth. If we but pause a moment and ponder on the question of how many pictures we can draw and then present them each as a distinct word the meaning of which will be instantaneously understood by all, we shall soon be disappointed with the meagerness of our own accomplishment. And, for that matter, we need not blame ourselves for wanting in ingenuity or inventiveness. For even in Xu Shen's dictionary, which listed 9,353 entries, according to one count the genuine picture characters number only 242.[80] So picture writing forms only a very minor part in the composition of Chinese words. And to make up a workable and viable vocabulary, the Chinese ancients had to develop other methods for inventing characters.

For instance, how could the significance of "up" and "down" be symbolized? They drew one horizontal line and then added to it an upward vertical stroke, like ⊥ to represent "up"; and then another horizontal line with a downward vertical stroke like ⊤ to represent "down." This method they called "pointing to the matter." [81] Another method they used was "combining substance with sound." They first had a character picturing an open mouth in the shape of uttering the sound "huo." Then they put by its side the character portraying a flowing body of water. The combination suggests therefore a stream that carries enough water to make the continual sound "huo" while flowing—in short, a river. These two methods still convey some images or pictures. Yet there are purely abstract thoughts, to give expressions to which was a real challenge. The ancients, however, met these problems head on; and in giving those abstract thoughts formal expressions they also, consciously or unconsciously, inserted in them their own thinking or beliefs. For example, the character for "honesty" was composed by placing a man beside a symbol signifying "speech." Thus, while coining the word for "honesty," the coiner also implied that it is the obligation of a man always to stand by what he has spoken. Again, there is the character *wu,* which the ancients were especially proud of, and which is very difficult to translate into English, but which means something like "triumphant in war." In its invention, the inventor also gave it a belief of his own. This seemed to be widely known in the ancient world, as it was quoted by a prince just after he had won a decisive victory that secured his own position of hegemony in the empire in 597 B.C.[82] When pressed to build a monument in commemoration of his feat of arms, he refused, saying, "In writing, *wu* is formed by laying the spear at rest." And indeed it is. For the inventor of the character clearly asserted his peace-loving belief that the best use of a spear, or of any military weapon for that matter, is not to use it at all. Such, as we can see from the above, is the ingenuity and resourcefulness required for the formation of Chinese written words. There are still some other methods which space does not permit us to describe here; but they all appear to have their limitations. So the ancients came up with one last method—borrowing. When they ran into the necessity of coining a new character, and yet try as they would they could not find a proper way of doing so, then they just contented themselves with borrowing another character which came closest to its meaning or its sound, and used it for the time being, until a more fitting one could be coined later. This is how some Western scholars mistakenly thought that the Chinese called China "Flower Kingdom," because the Chinese character *hua,* which means "splendor" or "glory" as in this case, was once borrowed to mean "flower."

Casual and cursory as this survey is, one can yet conceive from it what a gargantuan task it was for the ancients to create so many characters. Moreover, the difficulties were aggravated by another problem. The first characters might very well have been sketched out on sand or on earth. But unless these could be preserved on a more solid base, it would be extremely hard, if not impossible, to ask others to imitate them and to disseminate them. The Chinese ancients undertook to solve this problem by carving the characters first on bark, or on blocks of wood. Later, they more or less replaced wood with bamboo, which they found to be more suitable. Though silk was discovered quite early, and though by the middle of the Shang dynasty the people had already learned to use hair brushes to paint characters,[83] silk was too expensive and bamboo was still depended upon, except in divination, when tortoiseshells and cattle bones were used. Now, carving on such materials as wood, bamboo, shell, or bone is not an easy matter; and to make the carvings of each and every character stand out distinctly and legibly must have presented difficulties we moderns may never fully appreciate.

Furthermore, the Chinese written language has an inherent complication which only a few languages have. It is monosyllabic. To their own inconvenience, the Chinese did not develop an alphabetic system in the past; and as a matter of fact, until very recent times they never tried to. Whether they actually began their spoken language in its present monosyllabic form, of course no one can tell. Monosyllables are but isolated sounds, the variations of which are quickly exhausted. In order to enlarge the range so as to forge a vocabulary ample enough for an ongoing society, many artifices have to be employed, such as the use of inflections by means of which the Chinese give at least four different tones to one sound—even, rising, falling, and abrupt. One doubts if primitive man in China had either the patience or the perseverance, both of which are clearly required for such an undertaking, to start developing his language in this manner. One wonders, also, if all humans are not prone to speak in polysyllables rather than in monosyllables. So far as the neighboring peoples of the Chinese are concerned, the Mongols, the Koreans, and the Japanese all have polysyllabic languages. Recently, a theory has been advanced that the Chinese and the Mongols originally spoke the same polysyllabic language, but unfortunately this supposition has not been fully explored.[84]

But whether the original spoken language of the Chinese ancients was polysyllabic or monosyllabic, the lack of an alphabetic system inevitably made the construction of the written language, especially in the matter of increasing its vocabulary, a very slow and laborious process. With an alphabet, the coining of new words would be just a matter of spelling out whatever novel sounds one had formed. But without an alphabet, besides the novel sounds, one had to create fresh symbols to represent them as separately recognizable characters. Moreover, with an alphabet, words can have as many syllables as one likes. But without an alphabet, the only practice possible is to limit one character to one syllable; else, endless confusion would have resulted. Thus even if the Chinese had not begun with a purely monosyllabic spoken language, the adoption of their writing system would have eventually compelled them to make their language monosyllabic. And the more characters they formed, the more they became committed to their own writing system, and the less incentive they had to create an alphabet.

Meanwhile, what the Chinese written language lacks in convenience is, many Chinese think, made up for by other characteristics. For one, there is true beauty in Chinese calligraphy. For another, there are quite a few types of Chinese belles-lettres which convey an aesthetic sense that seems to be possible only with a monosyllabic language. Then there is an additional value that the Chinese have discovered in their long history. Their written language is the one conservational force that has served to unite China through many a period of turmoil and division and to preserve her culture unscathed. And the Chinese people have noted with pride that even though the Korean and Japanese languages are polysyllabic, the Koreans adopted the Chinese written language as early as the 12th century B.C., and the Japanese followed suit in the 3rd century A.D. Not that these peoples lacked the inventiveness to devise a phonetic system. The Japanese formulated their own *kana* and used it in vernacular fiction as far back as the 10th century A.D., but they kept the Chinese as their official written language until the latter part of the 19th century, and would have continued doing so if it had not been for the impact of the West. And today even though Japan has been modernized for more than a century, the Japanese government still allows the use of 1,850 Chinese characters in newspapers and other publications; and of these, 891 have been labeled essential characters and are taught in the first six grades of public schools.[85] Likewise, in 1446 the Koreans invented their *han'gul*, which has been hailed by many modern scholars as a simple and almost perfect system of phonetic writing. But for five centuries thereafter the Koreans ignored it almost totally and continued using the Chinese written language. It is only since the end of World War II, in this era of nationalism, that *han'gul* has come into its own.

Also, the Chinese people remember that both the Mongols and the Manchus, leading at first a sort of nomadic life, had no written language of their own. When Genghis Khan determined to conquer China, he had an alphabet invented for his people. The Mongols did conquer China in 1279; but before their dynasty was overthrown in 1367, nearly all the Mongols in China had adopted Chinese as their written language. The Manchus took a lesson from this. When they began conquering China in 1644, they prepared themselves against that kind of assimilation. Having also devised a new alphabet for their language, they commanded that all official documents must be written both in Chinese and in Manchu side by side. But at the turn of this century, even most Manchu officials themselves could not read their own written language.

Now, to return to the Chinese written language itself, can we say that the somewhat legendary account of its invention by Cangxie, so far as its dating is concerned, is accurate? In other words, can we say that it really started from the time of the Yellow Emperor, who ruled in the 27th century B.C.? If not, what other estimates can we make? If so, what bases can we offer other than this legendary one? Indeed, until very recently no one would have dared venture even a supposition.

Of course, the Chinese traditional, recorded history goes back as far as the Yellow Emperor. But because of the rise of modern historiography, doubts have been cast upon the veracity of these accounts. As regards archaeological findings, China naturally has its share of fossils, pottery, and skeletal and other remains; but these reveal hardly anything about the language the people used. The earliest artifacts that bear some relevance to the subject under discussion are the bronze objects the Shang left us. These are products of a marvelous technique, and often carry inscriptions that testify to an advanced stage of linguistic development. But unfortunately for our purpose, the words found in those inscriptions are not numerous enough: They do not provide us with sufficient material to make a reasonable estimate about the vocabulary used by the people in the Shang dynasty.

At the turn of this present century, however, the oracle bones began to make their appearance. And from 1928 on, repeated excavations have taken place under government supervision at several sites of the ancient Shang capital, Anyang, which have resulted in our being given new insight into the written language of Shang. The oracle bones are so called by Western scholars because the bones were used for divination. The Chinese call them simply *jiagu*, "shells and bones." For actually not only collarbones of cattle, and sometimes of horses and of deer, were used, but also tortoiseshells, both upper and nether—indeed, the shells were more prized than bones. It seems that the ancients liked to have the future predicted through some kind of divination. And the Shang emperors were particularly addicted to this practice. Their favorite method when they had a question to ask was to have diviners bore holes through well-selected shells or bones, apply heat to them, and then watch the cracks shape about the holes, and make the predictions accordingly. The one who asked the question (usually the reigning monarch), the principal diviner who officiated at the ritual, the question asked, and the answer given—all these were carefully inscribed on the two sides of the cracks. The characters of the inscriptions were first written on the shell or bone with brush and colored ink, and then carved with a knife. Many of these shells or bones so inscribed were kept in storage as a sort of divination archive. Altogether, the excavations have unearthed some 100,000 pieces, intact or broken, invaluable or worthless. The period in which these shells and bones were used runs from 1384 to 1111 B.C.[86]

What is important for our discussion here, however, is that from the inscriptions archaeologists have learned that the total of the written vocabulary of this period stands at some 3,000 characters.[87] Now, when Xu Shen compiled his first dictionary of Chinese in the 2nd century A.D., the number of characters rose to 9,353. Thus it took some fourteen centuries for the vocabulary to grow threefold. The rate of growth is about 10 percent a century, computing cumulatively. In the 18th century A.D., the *Kangxi Dictionary* was published, containing 42,174 entries. Taking Xu Shen's dictionary as a base, it took therefore some sixteen centuries to grow more than fourfold; and interestingly enough, the rate of growth is again a cumulative 10 percent for every century. So now let us use this formula and compute backward, starting from the 14th century B.C., when the Shang vocabulary is understood to have reached 3,000. For the 15th century B.C., we should have 2,700; for the 16th century B.C., 2,430; and so on. By the time we arrive at the 27th century B.C., we should find that the number of characters stands at 766.

Admittedly, this is approximation at its broadest and crudest. Nevertheless, to anyone who is familiar with the requirements of so-called Basic English, the significance of this approximation must be inescapable. For it is generally conceded that if one knows some 800 words, one can go about one's daily business without much trouble. If this is the case, then we have approximated the time the Chinese had the use of 800 characters precisely at the time of the Yellow Emperor. As we have noted before, according to one Chinese tradition, it is under the Yellow Emperor that his record keeper Cangxie made the first breakthrough in the writing system and invented enough characters to satisfy the needs of an ongoing society. Consequently, this is the time when China began to have her recorded history.

· 6 ·

INVENTION OF THE *GANZHI* SYSTEM OF CHRONOLOGY

However, no history can be written without a system of chronology. In fact, our modern world is so accustomed to Christian-era dating that we hardly appreciate its immeasurable value. All ancient cultures experienced great difficulties in this regard. The Egyptians at first resorted to naming the years after the most important events that happened in each of them, such as the year in which a great battle had been fought, or the year in which a severe drought had occurred. But which year preceded which was left in doubt except in the minds of those who remembered them. The

Sumerians numbered the years by their kings; but unless one is certain about the sequence of the kings, one's understanding of Sumerian history often ends up in confusion. Very likely the Chinese ancients had also muddled away many centuries with methods like the Sumerians' or the Egyptians'. By the time of the Yellow Emperor, however, an endeavor was made to establish a system, which, though not too accurate at the beginning, became later (as it was continually improved upon) quite dependable. It is still being used today not only by the Chinese, but also by many other peoples in the Far East.

The Chinese apply the system to their lunar calendar, naming the years, the months, and the days alike. They call it the *ganzhi* system, which some Western scholars translate as the system of cyclic characters. Altogether there are twenty-two characters used for this purpose—ten known as *tiangan* ("celestial trunk") and twelve as *dizhi* ("terrestrial branch"). Originally, these seem to have been invented just as symbols, without any particular meaning attached to any of them. But as it is far easier to remember symbols with meanings than without them, meanings were eventually ascribed to these characters. Again, as the system was intended for popular use, so the meanings chosen were familiar to the people at large. Thus of the twelve terrestrial-branch characters, each came to be associated with a particular animal in the following order: rat, ox, tiger, hare, dragon, serpent, horse, sheep, monkey, cock, dog, and pig. But if the ancients were satisfied with this arrangement with respect to terrestrial-branch characters, what meanings could they attach to the celestial-trunk ones with which the people would feel equally at home? And presently they hit upon the five elements which the Chinese then believed to be the basic components of the universe: metal, wood, water, fire, and earth. Since there were only five elements but ten celestial-trunk characters, the ancients divided each of the five elements into two kinds: Metal became rough metal and refined metal; wood, hard wood and soft wood; water, sea water and rain water; fire, sun fire and kitchen fire; and earth, mountain earth and sand earth. The Chinese differentiations are really much subtler and more sophisticated. But this explanation, crude as it is, may perhaps help Western readers understand the development of these cyclic characters.

So now we have two lists of characters as follows:

A. *Tiangan,* "celestial trunk." For our purpose here we also use numerals to represent them.

1. *jia* (hard wood)   6. *ji* (sand earth)
2. *yi* (soft wood)   7. *geng* (rough metal)
3. *bing* (sun fire)   8. *xin* (refined metal)
4. *ding* (kitchen fire)   9. *ren* (sea water)
5. *wu* (mountain earth)   10. *gui* (rain water)

B. *Dizhi,* "terrestrial branch." For our purpose we now use alphabetic letters to represent these.

a.	*zi* (rat)	e.	*chen* (dragon)	i.	*shen* (monkey)
b.	*chou* (ox)	f.	*si* (serpent)	j.	*you* (cock)
c.	*yin* (tiger)	g.	*wu* (horse)	k.	*xu* (dog)
d.	*mao* (hare)	h.	*wei* (sheep)	l.	*hai* (pig)

The system is to place one of the celestial-trunk characters on top of one of the terrestrial-branch characters and keep on permutating, beginning with *jiazi* (hard wood rat), followed by *yichou* (soft wood ox), and so on. Now, as there are ten trunk characters and twelve branch characters, it will take sixty permutations to complete a cycle, ending in *guihai* (rain water pig). And once a cycle is completed, a new one will be commenced immediately with another *jiazi* leading the permutations. And the cycles can go on forever just like the centuries in the Christian era.[88]

Who devised this system? Some ancient sources attributed it to Danao, an adviser to the Yellow Emperor.[89] Perhaps it would be more appropriate for us to assume that this development, like that of the written language, is evolutionary in nature. If Danao was given the distinction, it may be because he was assigned by that famed monarch to put the system, or rather systems, that had been evolving before him in a final and finished form. And as is usual with such evolutionary processes, the early operations of the system were far from perfect. To begin with, the ancients seem to have outsmarted themselves. Like the philosopher who felt it necessary to make two separate openings in his wall to allow his two cats of different sizes to pass through, they developed for the same system not one set, but three sets of names—one set for naming the years, the second set for the months, and the third set, which is what we have described above, for the days.[90] And, strangest of all, the names for the years are not monosyllabic, but polysyllabic! Take for instance *jiazi* (hard wood rat). This is of course the name for the first day in a sixty-day cycle, as we have already explained. But for the first month of a sixty-month cycle (though the permutations follow the same principle), the name is *bizou.* And for the first year of a sixty-year cycle (still using the same principle of permutation), the name becomes *yanfeng kundun!*

Perhaps the different nomenclatures represent three different systems that had actually been evolving previously; and Danao, or the group of men who were asked to unify and coordinate these systems, simply decided to adopt only one principle for permutation but to retain all three sets of names, each for a separate measurement of time. However, if their motivation was not political compromise but a genuine desire to avert possible confusion in the usage, then they failed. Though the names for the years and for the months were apparently remembered by erudite scholars,[91] they were hardly put into actual use by the ancients themselves, who seemed to have preferred other alternatives they had probably employed all along. For the numbering of years, they continued, like the Sumerians, counting every ruler's reign from the year of his accession. As to the months, since there are only twelve months to number, they just followed the serial order of the numerals. So it seems to have been only with the days that the system found spontaneous following at the outset. For there being some thirty days to a month, it is far easier to remember them by the names of animals than by mere numbers. At any rate, from the oracle-bone inscriptions, we have learned for certain that this was still the practice observed by the Shang people, though the triple-named system, had supposedly been introduced thirteen centuries before. And, in fact, China had to wait another thirteen centuries to decide finally to use only one set of names—the *jiazi* set—for numbering the days, the months, and the years alike.[92]

Apart from this, the chronological system of ancient China had other difficulties. One of the simplest sources of confusion came from mixing up the year in which one ruler died with the year in which his successor acceded to the throne. It was, of course, the same year; but by counting it both as the last year of the deceased and as the first year of the successor, it increased the chronology by one year. Inasmuch as ancient Chinese records involve tens upon tens of centuries, or score upon score of generations, such mistakes could have happened none knows how many times, and awareness of this must have cast an endless shadow of doubt upon the accuracy of the chronology.[93]

Had the *ganzhi* system been perfected at the time it was introduced by the Yellow Emperor, such doubts would have been easily dispelled. For example, if an emperor died in the year of hard wood tiger, *jiayin,* and his successor acceded in the same year, no matter whether one counted the year as the last year of the old reign or the first year of the new, as long as it was recorded to be the year of hard wood tiger, no duplication would be possible. But unfortunately the system could not be perfected immediately. It may be said to have been born with a congenital deficiency, which only time, long time, could manage to mend; in effect, it was invented too far ahead of the astronomical knowledge of the times to be effective.

Like many other primitive peoples, the Chinese ancients obtained their first inspiration about measuring time from the moon. Watching that body wax and wane, they got the idea of a month. And observing that it took twelve months to cover the four seasons, they formed the notion of a year. But these simple calculations were not, and could not be, exact. Between a new moon and the next it is not 29 days or 30 days, but 29½. And 12 times 29½ is only 354 days, 11¼ days shorter than the 365¼ days of a full year. So for a lunar calendar to become accurate, it is necessary to insert once in every two or three years a leap month, like the leap day of the solar calendar, to catch up with the motions of the earth. And in order to know when to insert the leap month so that all the seasons are as properly proportioned as they should be, it is essential first to ascertain the summer and winter solstices as well as the vernal and autumnal equinoxes. The ancients, however, could not come by such knowledge easily; it had to take them centuries. One example suffices to show the exceeding slowness of progress. As noted before, the *ganzhi* system was said to have been invented at the time of the Yellow Emperor. Yet the Chinese did not learn the simple fact that intercalation of a month was absolutely necessary to make their calendar more accurate (let alone learn when to intercalate it) until the reign of Yao, the Yellow Emperor's great-great-grandson, some three centuries later.[94]

· 7 ·
BEGINNING, AND PRESERVATION, OF RECORDED HISTORY

Notwithstanding the imperfections of the *ganzhi* system of chronology, there seems to be no doubt that at the time of the Yellow Emperor, conditions were growing favorable for the commencement of a recorded history. Besides the breakthrough achieved in the written language, there was the development of the institution of *shi*, the very office Cangxie is said to have held. If Cangxie was indeed the father of the Chinese writing system, or had contributed substantially to the increase of the written vocabulary and hence brought about the breakthrough, then the word *shi* would have been one of his own making. Originally, the duties of that office might have been just those of record keeping, whether by knotting ropes or by carving figures on bone or wood. But now, conceivably, Cangxie could have given the word *shi* a new meaning—which may very well have formed the basis for its being defined later in Xu Shen's dictionary as "a person, or persons, who put down matters in writing." And soon afterward, it was said that wherever a ruler went, as a rule he would be accompanied by two *shi*, "the left *shi* to record his utterances, the right *shi* to record his actions."[95] So the word *shi* may be variously translated as "scribe," or "secretary," or "official historian."

Of course, the records kept by the *shi* in those early days must have been in very simple and crude form—the earlier the days, the simpler and cruder the form. But because of the special reverence the Chinese people held for their ancestors, the lineal descent of successive rulers appears to have been carefully registered generation by generation. There is no ancient record disclosing by what names those registrations were originally called. But when Sima Qian wrote his famous *Historical Records* in the 2nd century B.C.,

he called them *pudie,* "lineage tablets." Along with the *pudie,* there were
other tablets on which the *shi* of old inscribed cryptic notations, numbering
the years of the then ruler's reign, or giving an account of sorts about what
occurred in those years. These were called by Sima Qian *dieji,* "tablet
records." [96] Thus the recorded history of China may be said to have begun
with these tablets.

As the written language advanced, naturally both the rulers and the *shi*
became more desirous of expressing themselves. But the art of composition,
the technique of forming new characters, and the craft of carving them on
hard materials, whether bamboo, wood, or bone, were all in their infancy
state; and understandably, the capacity of those men to transform desires
into realities was severely restricted by such extraneous factors. Moreover,
the dozen or so centuries following the Yellow Emperor was a period in
which the pendulum of Chinese society was swinging back and forth between the nomadic and agrarian ways of life. While literary plants might
hope to find favorable soil in the settlements of an agricultural populace, their
growth was only too often recklessly trampled and scattered by the returning rampages of nomadism. Thus attempts at composition that may be dignified by the term "documents" are exceedingly few and far between. If the
works of those bygone *shi* were preserved at all through all the vicissitudes of
this uncertain era, thanks are again due to the special regard the Chinese
people had for their ancestors. Not only did they venerate the spirits of their
own forebears, but they seem to have also venerated some select spirits of the
rival houses they had toppled [97]—if for no other reason, perhaps out of a
desire to appease them for the injuries they had already done to their descendants. In any event, such records as *pudie, dieji,* and other compositions,
from the Yellow Emperor down, were apparently passed on not only from
generation to generation but also from dynasty to dynasty.

By the early Zhou, we know for certain that an officer in the imperial
court called *waishi* ("outside secretary" or "outside historian") was put in
specific charge of "books relating to *sanhuang* and *wudi.*" [98] *Sanhuang* was
the term used for the three rulers who went by the title *huang* and who were
known to have ruled in the earliest antiquity; and *wudi* was the term for the
five others who went by the title *di* and who came after *sanhuang.* (Inasmuch
as it is the combination of *huang* and *di* that forms the title *haungdi,* which,
since the end of the 3rd century B.C., the Chinese have used to address their
emperors, for simplicity we shall hereafter translate *sanhuang* as "Three
Primeval Emperors" and *wudi* as "Five Premier Emperors.") And around
the 6th century B.C., according to the *Historical Records,* the man who served
as the *shi* in charge of the storage of books was none else than Lao Tzu,
founder of Taoism.[99] So apparently all ancient records and writings were
reasonably well kept and well guarded down to that date. Moreover, by the

middle of the Zhou dynasty, all such materials seem to have been lumped together as one collection known to the public outside as *sanfen wudian basuo jiugiu,* "Three Tombs, Five Canons, Eight Cords, Nine Mounds." The Three Tombs and Five Canons may be assumed to be records pertaining to the above-mentioned Three Primeval Emperors and Five Premier Emperors. The Eight Cords are said to be discourses on the Eight Trigrams, and the Nine Mounds descriptions of the nine regions of the realm.[100] Although the language in which most of these materials had been written was manifestly becoming quite archaic, yet as late as 529 B.C., scholars who could read them could still be found.[101]

Meanwhile, the art of composition was progressing side by side with the increase of written vocabulary, which by the time of the founding of the Zhou dynasty had reached around 3,000 characters.[102] And the craft of carving characters on hard materials had become much more skilled and efficient too, as evidenced by the inscriptions on the oracle bones. Also, the technique of bookmaking began to emerge. From the discovery of the oracle bones, modern archaeologists are able to report: "Some of the tablets were provided at the edge with small perforations which were probably meant for stringing the inscribed tablets into bundles for storage as well as for reference. These constitute the earliest form of book in China, and have been found stacked in the archives in layers." [103] If this was the case with shell and bone tablets, it must also have been the case with wooden blocks or bamboo tablets, which by their nature could be more easily handled in this manner. In fact, ancient Chinese writings give more detailed information on this matter than recent archaeological findings. It seems that the ancients had long had conventions regarding the use of wooden blocks and bamboo tablets. When they had less than a hundred words to record, they used wooden blocks; when they had more, they used bamboo tablets.[104] Moreover, they appear to have standardized the size of the blocks and tablets as well as the number of words that should be written or carved on each of them. In A.D. 281 a thief robbed an ancient royal grave and unearthed a collection of books that had been buried there since about 299 B.C. All the books were made up of bamboo tablets fastened together in separate volumes with white silk, each tablet being "two feet and four inches long," [105] and having forty characters on it in ink.[106]

With so much technological advance to make writing an easier task, there was bound to be a general improvement in the cultural atmosphere. We have no information about conditions prior to Zhou. But by the time of Zhou we know that not only did the imperial court have its *shi* and its official annals, but large feudal states had theirs too.[107] Moreover, these *shi* seem clearly to have jointly developed a sort of professional tradition, which they upheld with one accord. Though their office could boast of little political power, they all appear to have wielded their pen always in the cause of truth, independently and fearlessly. There are quite a few instances when they did so at the risk of their own lives, such as putting down bluntly on record that so and so had murdered his liege lord, even though the murderer had now become the tyrant in power.[108] Also, they evidently made it a rule that they should never record anything unless they were absolutely sure of the facts. Said Confucious admiringly, "When I was young, I was still able to see a *shi* leave a blank in his text." [109] By this he meant that so rigidly careful were those official historians that they would rather leave blanks in their texts than put down something for which they might later be accused of inaccuracy or untruthfulness.

All this progress notwithstanding, such information as could be had from the *pudie, dieji,* historical compositions, and even official annals remained kept or stored in government archives or libraries, accessible only to a limited, select group of persons. It had to wait for Confucius, 551–479 B.C., to open up this vast hoard of knowledge to the public. Early in his life, under the sponsorship of his liege lord, the Duke of Lu, he took a special trip to the imperial capital to study the institutions of Zhou as well as those of previous dynasties.[110] He was recorded to have met Lao Tzu there and studied under him,[111] perusing, no doubt, all the books and documents in the latter's charge and probably taking copious notes of them. Later in his life, because his native state did not live up to his expectations, he left Lu and lived abroad in self-imposed exile for some fourteen years, traveling from one state to another.[112] Consequently he had ample opportunity to make himself also well acquainted with their archives and libraries. As a result of these studies, upon his return to Lu in old age, he was able to produce those works which are known as the Confucian Classics.[113] Although all of his works may be said to contain elements of historical significance, and one of them is even a detailed chronicle of China from 721 to 482 B.C.,[114] a discussion of them one by one is beyond the scope of our present study, which is concerned only with the initial portions of China's recorded history, that is, from the earliest times to the founding of the Zhou in the 12th century B.C.

For our purpose here, we need only discuss the two contributions Confucius made in this connection. The first contribution, strange as it may seem, was made by Confucius rather in spite of himself. It consists of two discourses (contained in *Dadai Liji*) he delivered in answer to a disciple's inquiry, which have since been known under the titles *wudide (Virtues of the Five Premier Emperors)* and *dixixing (Genealogy of the Premier Emperors)*. Now, these discourses appear to be nothing more than a recounting of what the earliest *pudie* and *dieji* may have recorded. As Confucius prided himself on being a transmitter of worthy ideas rather than a mere recounter of events, however memorable, we can read from the first of the two discourses itself that he was initially quite reluctant to respond to the request. More-over, the disciple who raised the question was one Zai Wo, not particularly noted either for his understanding [115] or for his industry.[116] For these rea-sons, Confucius apparently never put much value on the two discourses; nor did his many disciples other than Zai Wo.

However, his second contribution is a different matter. All the historical materials he had studied were buried in the imperial or state archives and not readily available to the people at large. Besides, the characters inscribed on those ancient tablets were becoming archaic and not easily comprehensible even to the few who had access to them. So, with a view to remedying these deficiencies for the benefit of the public, out of these materials he selected some one hundred most noteworthy compositions, converted their archaic characters into up-to-date ones, and assembled them together in chronolog-ical order. The first documents so chosen go back to Yao and Shun, the fourth and fifth of the Five Premier Emperors, approximately in the 23rd century B.C., and the last document is a public speech made at 627 B.C. by the famed Duke Mu of Qin, forefather to the man who was to conquer all China by force about 250 years after Confucius's death and assume the title "the First Emperor." In addition, Confucius wrote an introductory note for each of these documents, giving a brief explanation of its origin or back-ground. The compilation, when it first appeared, was known simply as *Shangshu*, "Ancient Writings." [117] But since the 2nd century B.C., after Confucius's teachings were elevated above those of all other schools, it has been called *Shujing*—the *Book,* or the *Classic, of History.*

The importance of Confucius to Chinese civilization, however, is to be found not only in his preserving and popularizing so many ancient records for posterity, nor in his transmitting what he considered to be worthy ideas from time immemorial down to his day, nor in his kneading them, molding them, consolidating them into one social, ethical system which he adjudged to be best for mankind. It is to be found also—and perhaps, more especially—in his making himself the primal agent to stir up the latent genius of the common people and cause an undreamed-of catalysis in the Chinese intellec-tual world. Before him, nobody, except for men in positions of power and authority, ever wrote and published a book; but he did—and at that, a series of books. Before him, no private individual ever opened a school and taught a system of thought of his own; but he did, with disciples finally numbering around some three thousand. And once he set off this trend, it soon turned into a torrent. Between Confucius's death and the First Emperor's conquest of all China, the two centuries and a half, 479–221 B.C., may truly be said to be an era in which the Chinese creative genius blossomed to unprecedented splendor with "a hundred schools" literally contending in thought.[118] We have no precise information as to how many books were actually produced in this period; we know, however, of a person living some two hundred years after Confucius who, though only a scholar of minor reputation, yet could boast of traveling about with five carts fully loaded with books.[119]

Had all those works been preserved, how much richer the Chinese heritage would have been! But as the matter stands, what had taken the Chinese creative genius so long to create was almost totally ruined in a brief moment of frenzy and aberration. In 221 B.C., the so-called First Emperor of Qin conquered all China. In 213 B.C., he slaughtered hundreds of scholars and ordered that all books, except for those on medicine, divination, and agriculture and forestry, be surrendered and burned. In 210 B.C. he died, and widespread rebellion immediately broke out. And in 207 B.C., rude and unruly insurgents captured the Qin capital and set to flames all the imperial palaces, along with the archives and libraries in which the last and official copies of so many forbidden books were stored.[120]

This series of disasters is usually referred to by later scholars as "the Fires of Qin." How much loss China has suffered through them no one really knows. In the field of ancient history alone, the famed collection of "Three Tombs, Five Canons, Eight Cords, Nine Mounds" is heard of no more. Also, the *Book of History* was totally lost—fortunately for a short time. Early in the 2nd century B.C., twenty-nine documents were found in private possession. And less than a hundred years later, another score or more documents were rediscovered, along with the introductory notes attributed to Confucius. But because of the troubled political condition of the time, this second batch was not at once submitted to the imperial court, which would have had the texts verified and officially taught to students by court-appointed instructors, like the first batch. This improvidence inadvertently opened the door to interpolations and forgeries; consequently, authenticity controversies arose before long and have since lasted for centuries.[121] So, strictly speaking, out of the original one hundred and some documents Confucius compiled to form the *Book of History*, only twenty-nine have been saved for posterity.

The two discourses of Confucius, however, are preserved intact (perhaps because they are simple restatements of long-past events that could give no offense to the First Emperor). Thus, about a hundred years after the Fires of Qin, when the great historian Sima Qian began planning to write a comprehensive history of China,[122] after having read all of the "ancient writings" obtainable in his day,[123] he found that the two discourses constituted the only source which gave him some consistent information about the Five Premier Emperors. Notwithstanding, he hesitated to use them. Not that he lacked faith in Confucius, but he had express reservations about Zai Wo, the disciple who transmitted the discourses.[124] His own family being descended from several generations of *shi* in the Zhou dynasty, Sima Qian was determined not to put down anything in writing unless or until he could verify the facts for himself. So in order to ascertain the truth about the Five Premier Emperors, he did something truly remarkable. He traversed vast distances in the empire to retrace the footsteps of those ancient personages. He traveled to every place where they were said to have been. He talked with anyone and everyone who had something to tell about them. Finally he was satisfied that the information he gathered was all supportive of Confucius's two discourses.[125] Then he was appointed by the Han court to the office of senior historian, *taishiling;* and, in his own words, he now had access to the "books stored in metal cabinets inside stone chambers." [126] And there he found the *pudie* and *dieji* derived from the remotest antiquities; and by these lineal tablets and tablet records, the genealogy and accounts of the Five Premier Emperors, as given in the two discourses, were once again confirmed.[127]

Moreover, as it happened, besides the twenty-nine documents of the *Book of History* already current in his time, Sima Qian had the opportunity to study at first hand the second batch of lost-and-found documents from the very scholar who had come into possession of them shortly after their rediscovery, long before any interpolations could have been introduced into their texts.[128] Thus the earliest recorded history of China, as represented by the *pudie* and *dieji* and some fifty-seven original documents, was put in its final and present form as the opening chapters of Sima Qian's famous *Historical Records.*

But the great historian's endeavor is not an unqualified success. To quote directly from him:

> When I studied *dieji,* I found that, beginning from the Yellow Emperor, the years of all the monarchs are numbered. But when I compared them with other *pudie* tablets and examined them against the chronology that goes by the system of the rotation of the five elements,[129] I found that these ancient writings disagree and conflict with one another. . . . Hence I have undertaken only to make a genealogical chart out of the divers materials.[130]

So, as explained in the preceding section, the *ganzhi* system, invented for chronological purposes at the time of the Yellow Emperor, had not worked well in the beginning. It was encumbered with too many innate weaknesses, which could not be cured except by the gradual accumulation of human knowledge through slow passage of time. The system, however, had improved considerably by the early Han. Himself a trained astronomer, Sima Qian was able to use it to make several chronological charts, year by year, cycle after cycle, to supplement his long narrative text, the earliest chart beginning with the year *gengshen* (rough metal monkey) in the Zhou dynasty, which is now computed to be 841 B.C.[131] He would have liked to do the same for the period from *gengshen* onward to the Yellow Emperor. But though the ancient tablets carried the numbers of the years of all the monarchs throughout this period, these were recorded by many *shi* of different generations, each using his own method of intercalation and some not using any intercalation at all, to say nothing about their other disparities. He knew that if he tried to make a chronological chart out of such tangled materials, it would never be accurate. So he discarded the idea and made only a genealogical chart instead.

Such is the high standard of Sima Qian's historiography. Yet, despite his efforts, the credibility of China's recorded history seems to have suffered from two factors. He himself had scrupulously avoided using the chronology of *pudie* and *dieji*. But once he had called attention to these sources, there were others who came after him, and studied them, and thought differently. And where a rigid historiographer had feared to tread, more venturesome but less cautious souls did not hesitate to rush in. Thus several versions of chronology going back to the Yellow Emperor have since been produced. The earliest one was worked out about a century after the *Historical Records* was written, by a father-and-son team who had access to the same materials that Sima Qian had had.[132] It is from this that the traditional chronology the Chinese have used for their ancient history is derived, though it underwent many a revision and modification over the centuries. After the discovery of the oracle bones in recent years, fresh attempts have been made to formulate different chronologies.[133] Although each of these several versions may be said to have its individual merits, all of them seem haplessly to share one characteristic in common—lack of indubitable certainty. In writing this book, we would have preferred to follow the example of Sima Qian, using only the reigns of various rulers for the narration of events, had we not been deterred by the thought that it would be overtaxing the reader's patience and perseverance to ask him to memorize so many strange Chinese names and, also, more important, to remember their correct historical sequence. We are therefore driven to adopt a chronology of sorts for the text, not because we think it is accurate beyond doubt, but because it affords a convenient, reasonable measurement of time for rough reference.[134] Although the occurrences of events and the failure to give precise dates for them are two different things, yet it must be admitted that the wanting of exactitude in all versions of Chinese chronology prior to the year 841 B.C. has not helped to establish the credence of the early recorded history of China.

In the meantime, the good name of the recorded history has undoubtedly suffered a more substantive injury from another cause. While the *pudie* and *dieji* remained safely "stored in metal cabinets inside stone chambers" in the Han palace, they served well a twofold purpose. On the one hand, they provided a ready means by which the veracity of the *Historical Records* could be confirmed. On the other, they served as an effective restraint upon those who would like to fabricate wild and incredible tales about so remote an antiquity. But unfortunately these invaluable tablets were irretrievably lost, probably at the end of the Eastern Han dynasty in the 2nd century A.D. as a result of a great political upheaval.[135] Shortly afterward, a crop of pseudo-historical works mushroomed, all purporting to derive their information from those original sources, and each vying with the others in bedecking itself with novel additions.[136] As Sima Qian's *Historical Records* begins only with the Yellow Emperor, first of the Five Premier Emperors, and gives no account whatever about the Three Primeval Emperors, this unfilled void became an open field for these pseudo-historians to let their imagination roam. One instance will suffice to show what they are like. Several of them made so bold as to go back to the first of the Three Primeval Emperors, calling him *tian huang*, "the Heavenly Emperor," and alleging that he was possessed of one body with twelve heads and ruled the world for eighteen thousand years.[137] Although no thinking Chinese has ever taken these pseudo-historical works seriously, yet inasmuch as they all claim to have originated from those vanished ancient tablets, they do special damage to the credibility of the real recorded history of China.

It is therefore no wonder that when Westerners first came into contact with China, their admiration for the antiquity of Chinese culture was mixed with disbelief in the early Chinese recorded history. Not only were those pseudo-historical works brushed aside as worthless, but Sima Qian's *Historical Records,* especially its opening chapters, also became suspect. And, indeed, there seemed to be justification enough for this occidental skepticism. For, to begin with, this part of the *Historical Records* in question is itself interspersed with some gaps quite inexplicable to the Chinese themselves. And, what is more, with the loss of the original *pudie* and *dieji,* Chinese scholars could produce nothing substantive with which to authenticate the names of fifty and more monarchs who were said to have ruled their country, from the Yellow Emperor down to the founders of Zhou, let alone their historical sequence. Thus Western sinologues, at the utmost, would only concede that credible Chinese history could go back as far as the late Shang (or Yin) dynasty, circa 14th to 12th century B.C., but not farther. And this concession is made not so much because any credence is given to the accounts of that dynasty as narrated in the *Historical Records* as because the Shang people have left many bronze artifacts that, though providing little clue to their origins, testify to the high technological level they had attained. Under the pressure of such Western impact, modern Chinese historians also began to express doubts about the authenticity of their own ancient records.

At the turn of this century, however, the so-called oracle bones were discovered. Though nothing like *pudie* or *dieji* has been found among them, yet from the standpoint of historiography, these oracle bones are almost as valuable as those lost lineal tablets and tablet records. For from their inscriptions we have learned anew of the thirty rulers of the Shang dynasty as well as their relations to one another. And the marvel is that they correspond entirely with the narrative text and the genealogical chart of the *Historical Records* both in the matter of names and in the order of historical sequence. Moreover, the *Historical Records* has traced back the lineal descent of Tang, founder of the Shang dynasty, to the foremost ancestor of his house, Di Ku, fourteen generations in all. And from the oracle bones we have again learned almost exactly the same, from Tang back to Di Ku, who is none other than the third of the Five Premier Emperors, father of Yao, and a great-grandson of the Yellow Emperor.[138] The reliability of much of early Chinese recorded history is therefore reaffirmed.

In addition, from a close study of the oracle bones, some of the gaps in the *Historical Records* which were formerly inexplicable seem now to have become explicable.[139]

However, because of past skepticism, this part of Chinese history has never been fully, or properly, told in the West. If now Westerners sometimes complain that they find it difficult to understand the character of the Chinese as a people, it may be, perhaps, simply due to their lack of perception about this particular area of the Chinese historical background. For the one and a half millennia between the Yellow Emperor and the founding of the Zhou dynasty constitute the earliest formative period of Chinese society. And remote as that period is, it is what happened in it that has set the Chinese on a course of cultural development apart and different from others, and that has built up for them a heritage which is still influencing their social and political behavior, their motivations and rationalizations, their moral and ethical compulsions and inhibitions. When the Chinese speak of their ancient sages, besides Confucius and before him, they usually mention seven names: Yao, Shun, Yu, Tang, Wen Wang, Wu Wang, and Zhougong.[140] And all of the seven lived and made their mark within those fifteen centuries.

This book is therefore a history of that period. It is also a study of the lives of those seven men, especially of their beliefs and of their practices in point of human relations, which, later, Confucius undertook to transmit to posterity.

NOTES

Page numbers following See above *refer to text pages.*

1. Some sources allege that *Xiwangmu*, translated here as Queen Mother of the West, was a man. See *Shan Hai Jing, xishanjing.*

2. *Huainanzi, lanming xun.*

3. See *Taiping Yulan*, 2, quoting from *Sanwu Liji* by Xu Zheng, who lived in the period of Three Kingdoms (A.D. 220–280). The story of Pangu bears a resemblance to that of Purusa in the *Rig-veda* and therefore suggests a Hindu origin.

4. *Chu Ci, tianwen.* Also see *Historical Records, quyuan liezhuan.*

5. The story is also told in *Liezi, tangwen.*

6. *Huainanzi, lanming xun.*

7. See *Shan Hai Jing* and *Liezi.*

8. *Li Ji, liyun.*

9. *Book of History, taishi,* 1.

10. *Historical Records, xia benji;* also see *Zuozhuan,* Duke Zhao, 29th year. The dragon this family claimed to have raised might have been a sort of dinosaur or some other kind of extinct reptile.

11. "Lao Tzu" and "Taoist" are here spelled according to the Wade-Giles system of transliteration. We use these spellings because they are more familiar to Western readers.

12. *Historical Records, laozi liezhuan.*

13. See Duan Yucai, *Shuowenjiezi Zhu.*

14. *Chunqiu,* Duke Ai, 14th year. Also see *Kongzi Jiayu,* chap. 16.

15. *Book of History, yugong.*

16. *Book of Changes, sun* hexagram.

17. See Ma Duanlin, *Wenxian Tongkao, jiaoshekao,* 1. Herrlee G. Creel, in *The Origins of Statecraft in China,* 1, pp. 493–506, has a special Appendix C, "The Origin of the Deity T'ien." He maintains that Tien (i.e., *tian*) was a Zhou deity and was identified with *di* or *shangdi* only after Zhou's conquest of Shang. But exhaustive as his research apparently was, he does not seem to have taken into account such documents as *gaoyaomo, ganshi, tang-shi, pangeng,* and *gaozong tongri*—all pre-Zhou documents in which *tian* is frequently used as substitute for *di* or *shangdi.* Of course, some scholars have expressed doubts about the authenticity of some of these documents; but so far in my own researches I have found none questioning that of *pangeng* or *gaozong tongri.* Also see Yang Rong-

guo, *Zhongguo Gudai Sixiangshi,* p. 4; and Gu Jie-gang, *Zhongguo Gushi Yanjiu,* 11, pp. 20–32.

18. *Historical Records, fengchan shu.*

19. *Historical Records, huoqubing liezhuan.*

20. *Zuozhuan,* Duke Xi, 15th year. Also see *Chu Ci, jiubian.*

21. See *Book of History, shuxu.* Also see Ma Duanlin, *Wenxian Tongkao, jiaoshekao,* 15.

22. Ban Gu, *Baihu Tongyi, sheji.*

23. Before Buddhism was introduced, the *she* was simply represented by an altar.

24. *Li Ji, jiaotesheng.*

25. *Zuozhuan,* Duke Zhao, 11th year. There are two other incidents mentioned also in *Zuozhuan* (Duke Xi, 19th year, and Duke Zhao, 10th year). But these two seem to connote public executions for certain explicit political or military purposes rather than human sacrifice. For the practice of meting out death penalties at *she* altars, see "the Gan Address" in Chap. III, Sec. 3.

26. See *Historical Records, qin benji.*

27. *Guanzi, fengchan.*

28. *Historical Records, qinshihuangdi benji.*

29. *Historical Records, fengchan shu.*

30. *Zhou Li, chunguanzongbo: taibu, taizhu,* and *wu,* etc.

31. *Book of History, junshi.*

32. *Zuozhuan,* Duke Xi, 21st year.

33. *Li Ji, tangong,* 11, and *sangdaji.* Also see *Yi Li, shisangli.*

34. *Guo Yu, chuyu.*

35. The character *xi* is a combination of two characters, with the character *wu* on the left and the character meaning "sight" on the right. *Wu,* however, is the generic term usually used for both.

36. *Zong* is a very difficult word to translate. In the sense it is frequently used, it is usually translated as "household," or "ancestry." According to *Zhou Li,* there was a minister in the imperial court called *zongbo,* which is usually translated as "minister of the imperial household." It may be also aptly translated as "chief of imperial household elders."

37. Obviously, the invocators were intended to take care of praying to the gods, leaving all the

mundane affairs to the elders. The five departments are said to be (1) civil affairs, (2) imperial household, (3) war, (4) justice, and (5) public works.

38. Son of the Yellow Emperor, circa 26th century B.C.

39. Grandson of the Yellow Emperor, circa 26th and 25th centuries B.C.

40. *Confucian Analects, yongye.*

41. *Li Ji, liyun.*

42. *Zuozhuan*, Duke Zhao, 7th year.

43. Ibid.

44. Ibid.

45. Ban Gu, *Baihu Tongyi, sanjiao.* Also see *Li Ji, biaoji.*

46. *Book of History, pangeng.*

47. Ibid., II. The quotation is a paraphrase.

48. Ibid., I.

49. Ibid., III.

50. *Book of History, jinteng.*

51. See above, p. 8.

52. *Zuozhuan*, Duke Zhao, 7th year.

53. *Guo Yu, luyu,* I.

54. See *Book of Poetry*, introductory note to the ode *siwen;* also, *Li Ji, jifa.*

55. See Chap. III, Sec. 6, and Chap. IV, Sec. 3.

56. *Book of History, pangeng,* I.

57. *Guo Yu, luyu,* I.

58. *Yi Li, shisangli,* and *Li Ji, zengziwen.*

59. *Yi Li, shisangli, shezhong,* and *Li Ji, tangong.*

60. *Chunqiu, Gongyangzhuan* and *Guliangzhuan,* Duke Wen, 2nd year.

62. Dong Zuobin, *Yin Lipu,* vol. II, book II, *sipu.*

63. *Li Ji, wangzhi.*

64. Examples are Si, Gui, Ji, and Jiang.

65. *Historical Records, wudi benji.*

66. The four surnames are Qi, Teng, Ren, and Xun.

67. *Book of History, yaodian.*

68. *Book of History, yugong.*

69. *Zuozhuan*, Duke Yin, 8th year.

70. Popular Chinese surnames are not much more than 500 (see the popular book *Baijiaxing*). According to the census of Taiwan taken September 16, 1956, there are altogether 1,195 surnames on that island. In the author's estimation, the number of Chinese surnames in mainland China cannot be too much larger.

71. *Yi Li, sangfu (zhuan).*

72. See *Mencius, lilou,* I.

73. *Chunqiu, Gongyangzhuan,* Duke Yin, 1st year.

74. See Dong Zuobin, *Yin Lipu, sipu.* When the Shang emperors offered sacrifices to their male ancestors, they also offered the same to their spouses.

75. *Historical Records, yin benji.*

76. *Li Ji, yueling.* The author often wonders if there is any link between this story and the Western belief about the stork.

77. *Historical Records, zhou benji.* Also see above, p. 8.

78. *Book of Changes, xici,* II, chap. 2.

79. Kong Anguo, *Shangshuxu.* Also see Chap. II, Sec. 1.

80. Xie Yunfei, *Zongguo Wenzixue Tonglun,* p. 86.

81. For a discussion of all the ancient methods, see Xu Shen's preface to his dictionary.

82. *Zuozhuan*, Duke Xuan, 12th year.

83. Dong Zuobin, *Jiaguxue Liushinian,* p. 101.

84. See Zhao Chizi, *Meng Han Yuwen Bijiaoxue Juyu.*

85. John W. Hall and Richard K. Beardsley, *Twelve Doors to Japan,* p. 204.

86. Dong Zuobin, *Jiaguxue Liushinian,* pp. 9–13. The dates given above are Mr. Dong's. According to traditional computation, 1111 B.C. should be 1122 B.C.

87. Ibid., p. 11.

88. If we substitute the Chinese characters with the numeral signs and alphabetic letters, we have the following table of a complete cycle:

1a	2b	3c	4d	5e	6f	7g	8h	9i	10j
1k	2l	3a	4b	5c	6d	7e	8f	9g	10h
1i	2j	3k	4l	5a	6b	7c	8d	9e	10f
1g	2h	3i	4j	5k	6l	7a	8b	9c	10d
1e	2f	3g	4h	5i	6j	7k	8l	9a	10b
1c	2d	3e	4f	5g	6h	7i	8j	9k	10l

Now, take the year 1975. According to the system, it is *yimao* (soft wood hare), or 2d on our table above. If we wish to know what animal a friend happens to be, he being born in 1956, then we just count back nineteen years and we have 3i, which is *bingshen* (sun fire monkey). Or if we want to know what the year 1900 is, we can do it in a very simple way. Because the year of 1975 is 2d, so sixty years before, the year 1915, also must be 2d. We count from there, on the above table, fifteen years back, and we get 7a, *gengzi* (rough metal rat). Or if we wish to find out what the year 2000 will be, we just move twenty-five years ahead, finishing our present cycle and starting a new one, and arrive at 7e, or *gengchen* (rough metal dragon). It is thus the first year A.D. is computed to be *xinyou* (refined metal cock) in the 33rd cycle, counting back from the present one.

89. See *Historical Records, lishu* (commentaries by Sima Zhen).

90. See *Er Ya, shitian;* and *Historical Records, lishu.* In the celebrated poem *lisao* (in *Chu Ci*), written in the 4th century B.C., the poet Qu Yuan used the three sets of names to give the year, the month, and the day of his birth.

91. See *Historical Records, lishu;* and *Er Ya, shitian.*

92. This practice was adopted in the reign of Guangwu, emperor of the Later Han dynasty, A.D. 25–57.

93. This source of confusion was finally corrected by Confucius, when he wrote *Chunqiu.* He established a rule that the year in which a ruler died would be invariably counted as the last year of his reign, while the new reign of his successor would begin only with the next year, not earlier. But *Chunqiu* only begins with the first year of Duke Yin of Lu, i.e., 721 B.C.

94. See *Book of History, yaodian.* Also see Chap. II, Sec. 3.

95. Ban Gu, *Qian Han Shu, yiwenzhi.*

96. See *Historical Records, sandai shibiao* and *shier zhuhou nianbiao.*

97. See *Zuozhuan*, Duke Zhao, 7th year. The Shang overthrew the Xia, founded by Yu. Yet the Shang also made it a practice to sacrifice annually to Gun, Yu's father.

98. *Zhou Li, chunguanzongbo: waishi.*

99. *Historical Records, Laozi liezhuan.* In Pinyin romanization, Lao Tzu is Laozi.

100. See Kong Anguo, *Shangshuxu.*

101. *Zuozhuan,* Duke Zhao, 12th year.

102. See above, p. 31.

103. Cheng Te-k'un, *Archaeology in China,* II, p. 134.

104. *Yi Li, pinli,* III, *ji.*

105. This is by the measurement used in the 3rd century A.D. By modern measurement, it is less than one half of a meter.

106. See Xun Xu, *Mutianzi Zhuan Xu.*

107. *Mencius, lilou,* II, mentions that three feudal states—Jin, Chu, and Lu—each had official annals. From *Guo Yu,* we may assume that besides these three, Qi, Zheng, Wu, and Yue had theirs too. The *Bamboo Chronicles* unearthed by the graverobber in A.D. 281 appear to be the official annals of Wei, one of the three states that emerged after the partition of Jin.

108. See *Zuozhuan,* Duke Xuan, 2nd year. The *shi* of Jin recorded that the prime minister "Zhao Dun had his lawful lord murdered." Also see *Zuozhuan,* Duke Xiang, 25th year. In a similar case that occurred in Qi, the murderer-minister had two *shi* killed in succession for the same kind of offense. But when a third *shi* recorded the same as his two predecessors, the tyrant gave up.

109. *Confucian Analects, weilinggong.*

110. *Historical Records, kongzi shijia.* The Chinese word *li* is here translated as "institutions." Reasons for this will be made clear in the concluding chapters of this book.

111. Ibid., and *laozi liezhuan.*

112. Ibid., *kongzi shijia.*

113. An enumeration of the important Confucian Classics can be found in Chap. IX, Sec. 2.

114. This is *Chunqiu, Spring and Autumn Annals.*

115. *Confucian Analects, bayi.*

116. Ibid., *gongyechang.*

117. Kong Anguo, *Shangshuxu.*

118. In *Qian Han Shu, yiwenzhi,* written by Ban Gu in the 1st century A.D., for philosophical works besides those of the Confucian school, there are listed 189 *jia* (schools or authors) with 4,324 *pian* (articles, treatises, chapters, or volumes), not counting books on divination, calendar-making, belles-lettres, weaponry, and medicine, etc. Most of these 189 *jia* seem to have originated in the period mentioned above. But this does not give us a measure to estimate how many unlisted books may have been lost.

119. *Zhuangzi, tianxia.* The man's name was Hui Shi.

120. See *Historical Records, qinshihuangdi benji* and *xiangyu benji.*

121. See Ban Gu, *Qian Han Shu, yiwenzhi* and *rulin liezhuan.* This matter is more fully discussed in the Appendix.

122. The *Historical Records* was completed around 104 B.C. Sima Qian began planning the work with his father some twenty years before. See *Historical Records, taishigong zixu.*

123. Ibid.

124. See ibid., *wudi benji.* In his concluding remarks Sima Qian stated that many Confucianists did not have confidence in Zai Wo.

125. Ibid.

126. Ibid., *taishigong zixu.*

127. See ibid., *sandai shibiao.* Sima Qian did not relate how the *pudie* and *dieji* could have survived the Fires of Qin. A possible explanation may be found in his biography of the first premier of the Han dynasty, *xiaoxiangguo shijia.* Xiao, the premier, served early as adviser to Liu Bang, leader of a band of insurgents, who was eventually to rise to become the founder of the Han dynasty. Liu's band was the first to enter the Qin capital. Before other insurgent bands could set fire to the palaces, Xiao was recorded to have had the farsightedness to stow away all Qin's *luling tushu,* "laws, regulations, charts, books," and save them for future use.

128. See Ban Gu, *Qian Han Shu, rulin liezhuan.* The scholar was Kong Anguo, a lineal descendant of Confucius. The lost documents were presented to him almost immediately after discovery because of his lineage.

129. By this he meant the *ganzhi* system. See above, pp. 32–33.

130. *Historical Records, sandai shibiao.*

131. Ibid., *shier zhuhou nianbiao.*

132. Ban Gu, *Qian Han Shu, lulizhi.* The father is Liu Xiang, and the son Liu Xin. Based on the father's work, the son produced *santongli,* tracing the years from the Han back to the Yellow Emperor and beyond. Liu Xiang is said to have also produced *Diwang Zhuhou Shipu,* which comprises genealogical tables of ancient monarchs and feudal princes.

133. One complete chronology for this period is produced by Dong Zuobin, who published his *Zhongguo Nianli Jianpu,* vol. I, in Taipei, Taiwan, 1960. Another chronology, a very brief and incomplete version, appears as an appendix in *Xiandai Hanyu Cidian,* Hong Kong, 1970. The differences of these chronologies can be illustrated by the fall of the Shang (or Yin) dynasty. The traditional version has it at 1122 B.C.; Dong, at 1111 B.C.; and Xiandai, at 1066 B.C. The last date is also adopted by Fan Wenlan, *Zhongguo Tongshi,* I, p. 375.

An independent attempt has been made by the Swedish sinologist Bernard Karlgren to pinpoint the fall of Yin at 1027 B.C. See his "Some Weapons and Tools of the Yin Dynasty," pp. 116–20. And independently of him, Professor Lei Haizong seems to have reached the same conclusion, according to Ping-Ti Ho, in *The Cradle of the East,* p. 5, n. 8.

134. We use the traditional chronology for almost the entire period covered by this book, that is, from the Yellow Emperor to Di Xin, the last emperor of the Shang (or Yin) dynasty. Not that we think it is more accurate than the other versions; but in our opinion, none of the other versions has conclusively proved its accuracy either. Where all appear to be not accurate, it seems less rash to use the one that has been the longest in use. However, from Di Xin to the end of the book, we more or less follow Dong Zuobin's chronology, again not because we are fully convinced of its accuracy, but because it gives a better accounting of the crowded events that occurred within those some fifty years. See Dong Zuobin, *Yin Lipu,* vol. I, part IV, chap. 3, *yinzhouzhiji nianlikao.*

135. See Fan Ye, *Hou Han Shu, rulin liezhuan,* II. Ban Gu, in his *Qian Han Shu, simaqian liezhuan,* did not use the names *pudie* and *dieji,* as Sima Qian had; but called them *shiben,* "generation roots." It might be conjectured that when Sima Qian examined those tablets in the 2nd century B.C., they were rather loosely kept. But as Ban Gu saw them later in the 1st century A.D., they were apparently collected together and given the title *shiben.* The collection was probably well kept until it vanished

at the end of the Eastern Han dynasty, when the tyrannical dictator Dong Zhuo, faced with mounting opposition, decided to move the capital from Luoyang to Changan.

136. Examples of such books are Xu Zheng's *Sanwu Liji* and Huangfu Mi's *Diwang Shiji;* and also the present version of *shiben.*

137. See *Taiping Yulan,* 1 and 71.

138. For a detailed discussion, see Chap. IV, Sec. 4.

139. See Chap. IV, Sec. 4.

140. For example, see Sun Yat-sen, *Sanmin Zhuyi,* Lecture 1.

CHAPTER II

FROM THE YELLOW EMPEROR TO YAO AND SHUN

(27th–23rd Century B.C.)

· 1 ·

LEGENDARY OR HISTORICAL PERSONALITIES BEFORE THE YELLOW EMPEROR

The *Historical Records,* through which the recorded history of ancient China is transmitted to us, begins its narrative with the Yellow Emperor, not earlier. This decision was made by its author, Sima Qian, after careful consideration.

Perhaps the best way to judge the reliability of a history is to examine what materials the author has known and yet decided not to use. We know that Sima Qian had studied all the "ancient writings" that had come down to his day [1] (which was the 2nd century B.C.); and we know, too, that not all the ancient writings he studied have come down to us. So what we can do is find out all the information which can be had from those writings that are yet with us, and single out the materials which Sima Qian had chosen not to include in his work. Such a method, of course, may not do full justice to that great historian, for, after all, we still have no idea about how many other ancient writings he might have studied and not used, but which are now lost to us. Nevertheless, the method seems to have its advantages. On the one hand, it may help the reader to have a better understanding of Sima Qian as a historiographer. On the other, it will also give him some information about what the Chinese people themselves believe may have happened in China before the time of the Yellow Emperor.

To begin with, there is the legend of the Three Primeval Emperors *(sanhuang).* As noted before, there was a special collection of records or documents known to the ancients as "Three Tombs, Five Canons, Eight Cords, Nine Mounds," Three Tombs being supposedly those pertaining to *sanhuang*.[2] Although this collection seems to have been irretrievably lost before Sima Qian's day, he could not but have been keenly aware of the significance of the Three Primeval Emperors as probable historical figures. In fact, he even had occasion to mention them in his own *Historical Records* in a particular context: The First Emperor of Qin, having conquered all China, commanded his advisers to consider what title would befit his own unprecedented power and dignity. The advisers, in their formal reply, submitted this statement: "In the ancient times there were *tianhuang* (Heavenly Emperor), *dihuang* (Terrestrial Emperor), and *taihuang* (Primal Emperor). Among these, *taihuang* was the most distinguished." [3] Though Sima Qian offers no explanation in his text for this allusion, the First Emperor's advisers must have had some basis for their statement. Presumably, this could have been found in the so-called Three Tombs; and the First Emperor, a man known to be both hard to deceive and hard to forgive, if he so wished, could have had it verified. However, about a century later, when Sima Qian, in the course of writing the *Historical Records,* examined "the books stored in metal cabinets inside stone chambers" in the imperial palace, apparently he found only *pudie* (lineal tablets) and *dieji* (tablet records) which began with the Yellow Emperor. Presumably again, those tablets bore no records about the Three Primeval Emperors. And consequently, except for this one occasion cited above, the great historian never referred to them again throughout his long, comprehensive history.

And strange as it may seem, as the matter stands now, there is simply no definitive information as to who those Three Primeval Emperors could be and what each of them might have done. All suggestions about their identities, such as have appeared in works after the *Historical Records,* are mere speculations.[4] As for the ancient writings that antedate Sima Qian, a number of them have indeed given quite a few names of those who were supposed to have ruled China before the Yellow Emperor.[5] But they have identified none of them as the Three Primeval Emperors; and what is worse, most of them have just mentioned those names as names, without providing any accompanying facts to substantiate their existence. And one of the names is Nuwa—the lady divine ruler, who could transform her body into many shapes,[6] and who therefore darkly indicates an origin more mythical than historical. So, after screening all those names carefully, we find that there are only four left that deserve our brief attention. These are (1) Youchao ("Have Nest"), (2) Suiren ("Fire Maker"), (3) Paoxi or Fuxi ("Animal Domesticater"), and (4) Shennong ("Divine Husbandman"). From a cursory look at these four names, one cannot help having a feeling that this is neither mythology nor history, but some systematic imaginings of an ancient sociologist trying to describe in a fanciful manner the successive stages of development in the evolution of primitive society.

Take "Have Nest" and "Fire Maker." The following is an account given about them in the 3rd century B.C.:

> In the ancient times there were fewer people and more animals. The people were victimized by beasts and reptiles. Then there came a sage who taught them how to build nests with wood in order to avoid harm; and the people were happy. So they made him their ruler and called him Youchao, "Have Nest."
>
> However, the people continued to eat fruits, berries, fish, clams, which were raw, fetid, malodorous, and causing so much injury to the digestive organs that they were ill most of the time. So there came another sage who taught them how to obtain fire by drilling wood and then cure the food of its stench and decay. And the people were happy and made him their ruler and called him Suiren, "Fire Maker." [7]

Clearly this befits a book of sociology.

Notwithstanding, Paoxi and Shennong present a different problem. For there is evidence to indicate that these two could very well have been genuine historical personages. Paoxi was known also as Fuxi. Paoxi suggests that he taught the people how to make meat always available for the kitchen; and Fuxi, more directly, that he taught the people how to domesticate animals. So both of these names seem to tell the same story about the man. However, if he were paid only with such a tribute as this, he would hardly be more real than "Have Nest" or "Fire Maker." But then he was credited with two achievements truly out of the ordinary. In the *Book of Changes* it is expressly stated:

> When Paoxi ruled the world, he looked up, observing the phenomena of the heavens, and he looked down, observing the ways of the earth. Also, he observed the styles of the birds and animals as well as the conditions of land and soil. He learned lessons from near and from afar, from his own person and from things outside. And he began to form the Eight Trigrams in order that men may communicate with divine enlightened virtues, and also categorize the nature of ten thousand matters. [8]

Now, the *Book of Changes* was of special importance to Sima Qian's family, for his father was known to have taken the trouble to study it under a master of great renown. [9] Moreover, it was considered to be one of the oldest and most authoritative books in their time. For while all other Confucian classics were ordered to be burned by the First Emperor of Qin, this book was made an exception because of its usefulness in divination. [10] And so it was reputed to have been preserved in its pristine form, free from blemish or alteration. Furthermore, it was generally believed at the time that "when Paoxi ruled the world, he first drew the Eight Trigrams and invented the written word

as a substitute for reckoning by knotting ropes. From this are derived literature and records." [11] Even if Sima Qian had been skeptical of the account,
surely he could not have missed the historic importance of the first attempt at
the invention of the written word.

Again, the *Book of Changes* makes this statement: "Out of the River
appeared the Scheme; and out of the Luo, the Script. From these the sages
took their lessons." [12] There is of course no mystery about the River and the
Luo, the River being the Yellow River, and the Luo one of its tributaries in
the present-day Henan province. But there is much mystery surrounding
the Scheme and the Script, which since then have been known as the River
Scheme and the Luo Script. Traditionally, the plans of the River Scheme
and the Luo Script are given as follows:

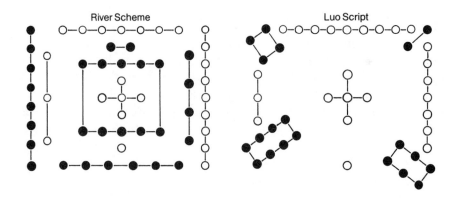

And, traditionally, the River Scheme is attributed to Paoxi and the Luo
Script to Yu, the great flood controller in the 24th century B.C. And later
legends would have it that it was a dragon-horse that bore the Scheme on its
back out of the Yellow River and presented it to Paoxi; and a tortoise that
performed a similar service with respect to the Script to Yu. Such fanciful
embellishments, we may safely assume, were alien to the critical mind of
Sima Qian. Yet there is one factual evidence which he could not very well
ignore as a historian. Upon the accession of the third Emperor of the Zhou
dynasty, circa 1067 B.C.,[13] an august ceremony was held at which all the
treasures of the court were displayed. Among these the River Scheme was
especially mentioned.[14]

Thus, so far as Paoxi is concerned, there is sufficient evidence that he
could have been a very real historical personality. And supported by the
documentation above, we may even visualize his attempt at inventing the
written word somewhat as follows: After having taught the people how to
domesticate animals, Paoxi was resting on the banks of the Yellow River.

Watching the waves rush forth like galloping horses or dragons, his attention was drawn to the traces that the subsiding waters had left on the sands. Being of an inventive mind, with a little assistance from himself, he soon arranged these traces into disparate specks, from one to ten, and placed them in different positions in a square—which presently became known as the River Scheme. This is perhaps a symbolic beginning of man's first undertaking to probe into the mysteries of numbers.

Now, more fascinated than ever with his own scheme, he considered a speck but a part of a broken line; and he started forming lines on the sands, making the lines into two kinds—unbroken and broken. He superimposed one line on another; but the combinations of double lines, even of two different kinds, are very limited. So he tried new combinations with three lines, and he obtained the Eight Trigrams, to wit:

But there is no way to tell these trigrams one from another in speech, unless a name is assigned to each of them. Yet it seems futile to create new names with unfamiliar sounds, which people may find it hard to remember and differentiate; it is better to associate the trigrams with things with which they are already familiar. He looked up to heaven and dedicated to it the trigram of three unbroken lines ☰; he looked down to earth and dedicated to it the one of three broken lines ☷. He looked toward water in the stream, and he found a resemblance in ☵. This being settled, he gave the opposite trigram ☲ the meaning of fire. Now, he was looking for an appellation for ☶, and he saw a mountain in the distance; and as he was searching for the same for ☳, he heard a clap of thunder. And he ended by making ☴ represent wind and ☱ represent metal. So the naming of the Eight Trigrams was completed. And he suddenly came to a realization that he had now entered a world vast and unexplored by men. For by making symbols and ascribing to each of them distinct meanings, the idea of the written word was born.

Of interest, however, is not how Paoxi may have made this invention, but how Sima Qian was to treat this matter historically. The temptation must have been truly great for him to include an account of Paoxi in his *Historical Records*. But he chose not to do so.

Of course, in the case of Paoxi, Sima Qian might have excused himself on grounds of exceeding antiquity and the consequent lack of certainty. But if this were the excuse, it could not be applied to Shennong, "Divine Husbandman." For the house of Shennong had ruled immediately before the Yellow Emperor; and this fact was recorded by Sima Qian himself in the very first chapter of the *Historical Records*. Moreover, the principal achievements of the first Shennong had been already described by several books antedating the great historian. Says one of them:

> In the ancient times the people ate and drank whatever and wherever they could, gathering fruits and berries from trees and plants and feeding on beasts and reptiles. And they were most of the time afflicted with disease, poison, and injuries. Then came Shennong, who taught the people to plant and cultivate the five cereals, to observe the differences of soil, to take note of what grains are suited to what kind of land, dry or wet, rich or poor, high or low. He himself tasted hundreds of plants as well as spring waters, both sweet and bitter, so that the people might know what to avoid. Once in this experiment, in a single day, he took in poison seventy times.[15]

This, also, was authenticated by no less an authority than the *Book of Changes:*

> At the end of the house of Paoxi, the house of Shennong rose. The latter bent wood to make a plow, and cut it to make a rake; with the plow and the rake he taught the whole world.[16]

All these showed how he had come to be known as "Divine Husbandman" (Shennong). But he seemed to have done even more. According to the same authority, it was he who first introduced systematic barter in China; or, at least, it was during his time that trade began to be institutionalized:

> The noontime was set as market time. At that time all people would meet with one another carrying their produce or merchandise. After making exchanges, they would each go their own ways satisfied.[17]

And it appeared too that Shennong had not gained the empire without some sort of struggle. This is noted in another book: "The people of Shusha attacked their own prince and joined with Shennong." [18] As to how long the house of Shennong had ruled China, there is also a definitive account. It was said "to have had the world for seventeen generations." [19]

Scanty as these materials are, conceivably Sima Qian must have had more, not less. But even with these, there seems to be ground to maintain that Shennong and his house are true historical figures that had played a very important role before the rise of the Yellow Emperor. Notwithstanding, Sima Qian chose not to make any mention of them, except for a brief reference to the last of the line, whom the Yellow Emperor had fought and vanquished. In the matter of historiography, therefore, he appears to have strictly and determinedly followed the tradition of the ancient official historians *(shi)*, so much admired by Confucius that he would sooner leave a blank in his text than put down something for which he himself was not absolutely sure he could vouch for its truthfulness or accuracy.[20]

THE YELLOW EMPEROR AND HIS IMMEDIATE SUCCESSORS

Before Sima Qian obtained access to the "books stored in metal cabinets inside stone chambers" of the Han palace, for information on the Yellow Emperor and his immediate successors, he relied principally on Confucius's two discourses—*Virtues of the Five Premier Emperors (wudide)* and *Genealogy of the Premier Emperors (dixing)*. As noted before, these discourses were delivered by Confucius in response to a disciple's question, not of his own volition. In fact, it may almost be said that he was more or less compelled to give answer because he did not want such misrepresentations about the Yellow Emperor as were apparently implied in the inquiry to continue uncorrected.

> Zai Wo inquired of Confucius: "Formerly I heard from Rongyi [21] that the Yellow Emperor had three hundred years. May I ask about Yellow Emperor? Was he human, or not human? How could he have three hundred years?"

Confucius was at first reluctant to answer the question, declaring that the times of the Yellow Emperor were of exceeding antiquity and it was all but impossible to give a full and authentic account of him. But at the disciple's insistence, he delivered a brief sketch of the Yellow Emperor's virtues and achievements, and then added:

> While he lived, the people enjoyed the advantages he gave them for some one hundred years; [22] after he died, the people continued to be awed by his presence for another hundred years; and when his presence was no longer felt, the people still used his teachings for another hundred years. This is why it is said that he had three hundred years.

Now, Zai Wo began to press further inquiries about the Yellow Emperor's successors, especially regarding the four of them who had enjoyed preeminent reputations. Confucius again showed some hesitation, stating that those Five Premier Emperors were different from the founders of the Three Dynasties which followed after them. [23] With regard to the latter, there were the works and words of these men themselves to fall back upon. But concerning the former, there was nothing to rely on except what had been told about them. Then, after outlining a skeleton narrative about those rulers, he concluded, "Yu, [24] the major virtues and achievements of the Premier Emperors are as I have told you. However, what the people have been saying about them has become extreme. But, Yu, you should not be that kind of a person!"

From this, Confucius's estimate of the Five Premier Emperors' position in antiquity can be clearly seen. He himself had studied all the records relating to them in the imperial archives; he was able to give the lineal descent of each of them; and he had no doubt that they were true historical figures who had played significant roles in shaping early China. But then more than two thousand years had elapsed between the Yellow Emperor and his own time. What with the lack of an adequate written language in the beginning, what with the exceeding exiguity of material in consequence, what with the proneness of human nature to hero worship and to exaggeration, it was unavoidable that incredible legends had mushroomed to shroud those emperors in even greater obscurity and mystery. Confucius never cared to be a historian, but he was always mindful of truth and accuracy. So he confined his own accounts of them to what he knew for certain. And that was very meager indeed. As to the *Historical Records,* Sima Qian lived some four centuries later than Confucius. Although he was able to confirm Confucius's accounts by his own independent studies, by his extensive travels, and, especially, by his close examination of the *pudie* and *dieji* derived from the earliest times, he was not able to find much more material to add to them substantially. So, all in all, these accounts are in the sketchiest form possible, full of unfilled and unexplained gaps. Indeed, had it been otherwise, we would have adjudged them unreliable.

At the time the Yellow Emperor appeared on the scene, the Chinese people seemed to be still largely nomadic, roaming mostly about the Yellow River Valley. Some five hundred years earlier,[25] the "Divine Husbandman," Shennong, had emerged teaching people to cultivate crops in order to produce staple food. But the nation as a whole still had a long way to go to become agricultural. However, as a result of his discovery, the house of Shennong became better equipped than others to cope with shortages both in winter and in famine; and it grew more and more populous and powerful. In the meantime, people were not lacking who wanted to share in the benefits of his knowledge and experience; and in order to learn from him, they were not averse to humbling themselves. Thus from that time on, Shennong and his descendants began to claim a sort of ascendancy over the other houses or tribes, calling their elders or chiefs *hou,* "princes," but styling themselves *yandi,* "Flame Emperors"—this very likely because they taught the people that before land could be cultivated, the ground must be first cleared by burning its wild growth. But whether this is what had actually happened, we can never ascertain. The written language had barely begun to develop, and even to the end of the last of the Flame Emperors, the knotting of ropes was used as the principal means of reckoning [26]—a means that is hardly qualified to transmit a coherent narrative.

At the time the Yellow Emperor appeared—which happened to be also the time the development of the written language was just about to make a gigantic breakthrough—the ancient Chinese world was in a state of frightful chaos. Whatever imperial pretensions the house of Shennong might have attempted, it was apparent that they had never exercised much physical control beyond a limited territory north of the Yellow River,[27] which formed the bases of their operations. Then, as the population grew, so houses and tribes multiplied, who were as slow to acknowledge a superior authority as they were quick to fight among themselves. Still, these houses or tribes were known more or less to each other through one affinity or another. But presently a new power rose under one Ciyou, who threatened, if not to absorb them all, to waste every one of them by plunder. He was not one of the recognized princes, his lineage being quite obscure.[28] And he seemed to have hailed from south of the Yangtze, generally considered at that time to be the habitat of barbarians, with a culture inferior to that of the north. But having discovered metal in some area under his control, he availed himself of the advantage and forged it into all sorts of weapons of war.[29]

The Yellow Emperor, whose surname was Gongsun and given name Xuanyuan, was then chieftain of a house based in the central part of the present-day Henan province.[30] He found himself, therefore, squeezed in between two conflicting forces: the one from the then reigning Flame Emperor trying to reassert a more rigorous control over the various princes, and the other from Ciyou bent on rapine and destruction. Thus threatened, the Yellow Emperor was compelled to take up arms. Perhaps because the danger from the north was nearer or more imminent, or perhaps because he thought that if he could gain ascendancy over the dominant imperial house he could the better unite the other princes of similar cultural affinity against their common enemy, the barbarian intruder from the south, he marched northward and fought against the last of the Flame Emperors in the wild plains on the borders of modern China proper and Inner Mongolia, about 150 kilometers northwest of Peking.[31] Both Confucius's discourse and the *Historical Records* use the same language in describing the conclusion of the contest: "It was only after three battles that he was able to proceed in accord with his will." Indeed, this could have occurred no sooner, for Ciyou was dogging his steps fast from behind. Now he summoned the other princes and lords to rally to his standard, and they came willingly. Together they met with Ciyou on another plain close to the one where he had won his recent victory.[32] Ciyou was captured and put to death. Then all the princes and lords hailed him as the Son of Heaven and honored him with the title *huangdi*, "Yellow Emperor." [33]

As to why this particular title was chosen, Confucius did not offer an explanation. But it is believed by later scholars [34] that according to the theory of the rotation of the five elements, earth is born out of fire. Since fire was the symbol of the Flame Emperor, the one who displaced him must be a representative of the virtues of earth; and as the color of earth is generally yellow, so the name Yellow Emperor was thought fitting and proper. But whatever the derivation of the title, there is no question but that the Yellow Emperor was the first man to have unified China, or a very large part of it, by military force. As is noted by the *Historical Records*,[35] "Wherever under heaven there were people who disobeyed him, he would go after them; but as soon as they were pacified, he would leave them. He crossed mountains and opened roads, never stopping anywhere to rest for long. On the east he went as far as the ocean and ascended the venerable Taishan. On the west he went as far as the Kongtong mountains and ascended the Rooster-Head Peak.[36] On the south he went as far as the Yangtze and ascended the Bear and the Xiang ranges.[37] On the north he chased away the Hunzhou barbarians[38] and convoked a meeting of the lords and princes at Mount Fu.[39] He based his headquarters on the plains of Zhuolu (where his celebrated victory over Ciyou was won); but he himself always wandered from place to place, living in camps accompanied by guards." (See Map I.)

He was probably also the first man who introduced a sort of supervisory governmental system in China. For, according to the *Historical Records*, "he established offices and named them after clouds, each cloud headed by a director. He also appointed two senior supervisors—one left, one right—to supervise the ten thousand nations." And tradition has also preserved for us some names who were reputed to be his ablest assistants.[40]

Apparently the Yellow Emperor reigned for a long time. But neither Confucius nor Sima Qian gave a date for his death, though some later scholars, claiming to base their information on the lost *pudie* or *dieji,* maintained that he had ruled exactly a hundred years. He died probably while making one of his incessant perambulatory tours. He was buried at Qiaoshan (Bridge Mountain) in northern Shaanxi province,[41] where later rulers of China were wont to make pilgrimage to sacrifice to him, acknowledging him as the Father of the Chinese Nation.

Perhaps because his was the period when the written language breakthrough occurred, he has been credited with more than is his due. For a language to have arrived at such a degree of development, hundreds or even thousands of years might have been needed for the nurturing of its growth. But the Chinese, generally speaking, have come to believe that it was Cangxie, his official historian *(shi),* who invented the Chinese writing system under his orders. Again, making a calendar and devising a system for counting the years must have preoccupied men long, long before the Yellow Emperor; yet the Chinese are given to think that it was Danao, a teacher or adviser to him, who invented the *ganzhi* system at his bidding. Besides these two, there are many "firsts" attributed to him. For instance, the Chinese usually regard Luozu, the Yellow Emperor's principal wife, as the first to

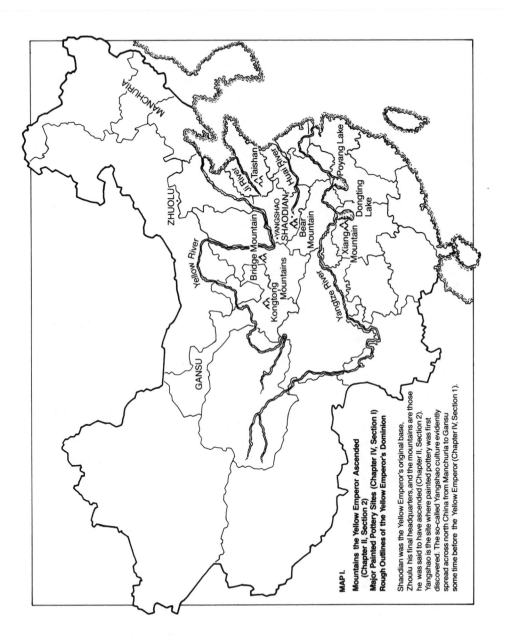

MAP I.

**Mountains the Yellow Emperor Ascended
   (Chapter II, Section 2)
Major Painted Pottery Sites (Chapter IV, Section I)
Rough Outlines of the Yellow Emperor's Dominion**

Shaodian was the Yellow Emperor's original base,
Zhoulu his final headquarters, and the mountains are those
he was said to have ascended (Chapter II, Section 2).
Yangshao is the site where painted pottery was first
discovered. The so-called Yangshao culture evidently
spread across north China from Manchuria to Gansu
some time before the Yellow Emperor (Chapter IV, Section 1).

produce silk from silkworms.[42] Moreover, Chinese military historians believe that the reason why the Yellow Emperor could have bested Ciyou, who had forged so many new weapons, was his successful use of mass archery for the first time in warfare.[43] But human progress, in the main, is by nature evolutionary and not revolutionary; and so we are inclined to think that the fame of the Yellow Emperor was benefited more than harmed by the state of the language at that time.

The Yellow Emperor practiced polygamy, which was probably the custom of the times. As noted before, he had twenty-five sons; and out of these twenty-five, fourteen were awarded surnames different from his own. According to the genealogy given by Confucius and confirmed by the *Historical Records,* the Yellow Emperor seems to have had only two sons by his principal wife, Luozu. However, as we shall see in the following table, all his successors were descended from her. So even though we cannot find the existence of such a rule in any of the ancient writings, there seemed nonetheless to be a sort of vague yet unmistakable impression favoring the issue or issues of the principal wife for succession.

The Yellow Emperor was succeeded by Shaohao.[44] But his rule was so feeble and ineffective that he did not qualify to be included among the famed Five Premier Emperors. However, from one of the most reliable ancient authorities we have a curious passage concerning an aspect of his administration.[45] When he acceded to the imperial dignity, there appeared at that time a phoenix. So he changed the names of government offices from Clouds, as his father had designated them, to Birds. Thus there were the Phoenix-Bird in charge of the calendar in general; the Swallow-Bird, of the equinoxes; the Shrike-Bird, of the solstices; the Green-Bird, of the "opening"; and the Carnation-Bird, of the "closing." [46] In addition, there were five Pigeon-Birds entrusted with the management of the people: the first somewhat resembling the minister of interior or minister of education in later days; the second, minister of war; the third, minister of works; the fourth, minister of justice; and the fifth, minister of miscellaneous affairs. Besides these, there were five Pheasant-Birds who superintended works in the production of implements and measurements; and nine Jay-Birds whose duty was to encourage people to engage in agriculture in the nine regions of the empire. However, because of the lack of further substantiation, we should not read too much meaning into this passage. But it is obvious that calendar-making was considered the most important function of the imperial court.

How long Shaohao had reigned we are not at all certain. But toward the close of his reign, there arose a disturbance in the south of the empire.[47] From where Ciyou had formerly raised his rapacious hordes, now Jiuli tribes again staged a rebellion.[48] One of the first things they did by way of show-

THE SUCCESSORS OF THE YELLOW EMPEROR [49]

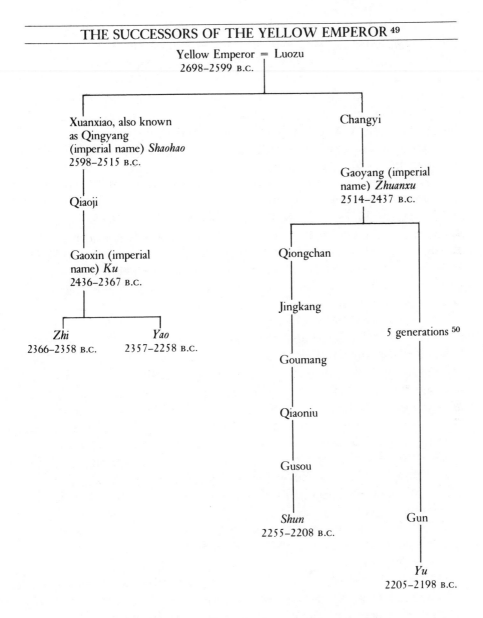

Yellow Emperor = Luozu
2698–2599 B.C.

Xuanxiao, also known
as Qingyang
(imperial name) *Shaohao*
2598–2515 B.C.

Qiaoji

Gaoxin (imperial
name) *Ku*
2436–2367 B.C.

Zhi
2366–2358 B.C.

Yao
2357–2258 B.C.

Changyi

Gaoyang (imperial
name) *Zhuanxu*
2514–2437 B.C.

Qiongchan

Jingkang

Goumang

Qiaoniu

Gusou

Shun
2255–2208 B.C.

5 generations [50]

Gun

Yu
2205–2198 B.C.

ing defiance was to refuse to abide by the calendar issued by the reigning
monarch—a token of submission which since then has always been required
by later dynasties of their feudal lords or tributary states. Whether Shaohao
died shortly after the outbreak or just abdicated in favor of a stronger replacement, we are again left in doubt. But there is no question about the
ability of the man who was named to succeed him either by his own choice

or by a general agreement among the princes of the empire. This was Zhuanxu, Shaohao's nephew, who has been recognized by both Confucius and Sima Qian as the first of the Yellow Emperor's four preeminent successors.

Zhuanxu was effective in quashing the rebellion and restoring peace and order throughout the country. Inasmuch as most of the territories south of the Yangtze were still very sparsely populated, the subjugation of the Jiuli tribes probably enabled him to claim dominion over all of the land in that direction. It was thus said that his sway extended as far as Jiaozhi, the present-day Vietnam. This pretension is of course inaccurate, but perhaps not inexcusable.

The victors from the north had always considered the southern tribes less advanced in culture than themselves. For one thing, the northerners had already developed a workable written language, and the southerners had not. For another, the southerners were given to animism, with each tribe having its own gods and some sort of priests or witches to speak for them, which the northerners, with their idea of an imageless Lord Above, had always looked down upon as primitive superstition. Therefore, as much for political as for religious reasons, Zhuanxu was determined to extirpate those animistic beliefs in the land which had given so much trouble to the imperial house. For any tribal god, if allowed to thrive independently, might very well aspire to challenge the supreme Lord Above by inciting its worshipers to rebel against the authority of the emperor. And such priests or witches as the tribes used to boast of would likely be the first to instigate and the last to discourage them to do so. So as soon as the Jiuli tribes were subdued, Zhuanxu gave command to two of his ablest ministers to conduct a campaign which he called "Stopping Communication Between Heaven and Earth," [51] banning those superstitious practices and forbidding any human to presume to speak in the name of gods or spirits.

Moreover, as calendar-making was regarded as a principal imperial function, the two ministers were also entrusted with the additional duty of working out an improved method of computation. The original calendar, though supposedly devised by the Yellow Emperor, must have been in a very crude and inaccurate form. By the time of Shaohao, as can be seen from the bare government structure he had created, attention was already focused on fixing the equinoxes and solstices. The best way to fix these, in the simple thinking of the ancients, was to station men in the southern and northern limits of the empire to make close observations. But because of the disturbance of the Jiuli, this scheme must have been rudely disrupted at its very inception. So as soon as the south was pacified, the two ministers were ordered anew to make the necessary rectifications relating to the calendar. Thus the titles of these two ministers were officially recorded as the Southern Rectifier and the Northern Rectifier.[52] The results of their labor must be adjudged to be quite successful. For we know for a fact that the Zhuanxu calendar, along with the original Yellow Emperor calendar, was still preserved in the first century A.D.[53] Though Zhuanxu's successors made additional improvements, and though the Three Dynasties that followed each adopted a different calendar of its own, in the main it is the method of computation used in the Zhuanxu calendar that has been continuously accepted for general guidance.[54] And this influence was eclipsed only some twenty-four centuries later by a calendar issued in 104 B.C.[55]

At the death of Zhuanxu, the throne reverted to Shaohao's grandson Ku, usually recorded as Di Ku (Emperor Ku). Was this reversion effected because Ku was exceedingly precocious, as indeed he was said to have been?[56] Or was it a fulfillment of a previous agreement made between Shaohao and Zhuanxu, when the former abdicated in favor of the latter? Or was it an act in compliance with a general understanding among the elders of all the houses descended from the Yellow Emperor, or among the lords and princes of the empire, whether related to the imperial house or not, that the throne should be passed on to the eldest son or to the eldest son's eldest son whenever possible? And if so, would whether or not the eldest son was born of a principal wife make a difference? We confess we are again at a loss for conjecture. But it seems that the ancients themselves at this time were also groping rather confusedly for an answer to this question of succession, as the story of Di Ku would appear to testify.

Di Ku ruled well and effectively; under him the empire manifestly enjoyed a long period of continued tranquillity. And consequently he was remembered as another of the Yellow Emperor's preeminent successors, that is, the third of the Five Premier Emperors. As the records have it, he married four wives, each of whom bore him a son. Di Ku then asked by divination which of the four sons would be destined to inherit the empire, either in his own person or through his descendants. And the answer was that all of the four would.[57] The very fact that Di Ku had posed such a question for divination seems to indicate that there was no fixed rule for succession at the time. And the events that followed also tend to confirm that assumption. Upon Ku's decease, he was succeeded by Zhi, the son by the fourth wife. And as we shall relate later, shortly afterward, Zhi had to yield the throne to Yao, the son by the third wife, who was then barely sixteen years old.[58] And all this, despite the fact that both the second and especially the first or principal wife were not barren of male issue. Why this order of succession? The one possible logical explanation is that at the time of Ku's death, the only son old enough to assume the reins of the empire was Zhi, Yao being then less than sixteen and the other two sons even younger. So the imperial honors fell on Zhi because there was no alternative; and later on Yao, for the same reason. But, as destiny would have it, the other two sons were not to be denied their birthrights either. They grew up to become renowned ministers to Yao's successor, Shun; and each of them, through their descendants generations later, was able to found a dynasty to rule China, the Shang and the Zhou. As to the stories of their births, these have already been told before. The son of the second wife was the one conceived after the mother had swallowed a black bird's egg; and that of the first or principal wife was none else than "the Abandoned One," whose misadventures in infancy resemble so much those of Romulus and Remus.[59]

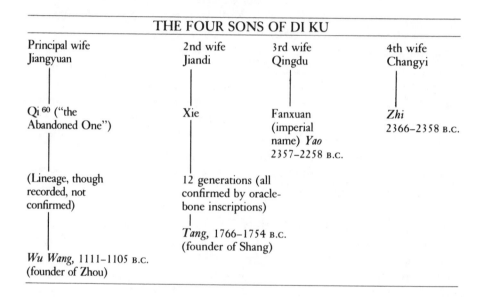

THE FOUR SONS OF DI KU

Principal wife Jiangyuan	2nd wife Jiandi	3rd wife Qingdu	4th wife Changyi
Qi [60] ("the Abandoned One")	Xie	Fanxuan (imperial name) *Yao* 2357–2258 B.C.	*Zhi* 2366–2358 B.C.
(Lineage, though recorded, not confirmed)	12 generations (all confirmed by oracle-bone inscriptions)		
	Tang, 1766–1754 B.C. (founder of Shang)		
Wu Wang, 1111–1105 B.C. (founder of Zhou)			

Could the genealogy of the two dynasties in question have been fabricated to satisfy dynastic vanity? The names of the descendants of these two men, however, have been recorded in the *Historical Records;* and in the case of the Shang dynasty at least, the recent discovery of the oracle bones has verified the accuracy of the lineage, generation by generation, that traced back to Di Ku, almost in every detail except for two very minor discrepancies.[61]

As mentioned before, Di Ku was succeeded by Zhi. But how Zhi lost the throne to Yao is again not clearly understood. Like Shaohao, Zhi was not mentioned at all in *Virtues of the Five Premier Emperors.* And in the *Historical Records* there is but a short and cryptic passage: "Di Zhi acceded. He was no good. He died. His younger brother Fangxuan acceded. This is known as Di Yao." [62]

· 3 ·
YAO

With the accession of Yao, Chinese history enters into a new phase. So far, from the Yellow Emperor to Di Ku, we have based our account strictly on Confucius's two discourses and Sima Qian's *Historical Records*. But from Yao on we have more sources equally dependable. The foremost of these is of course the *Book of History*, which, though compiled by Confucius, was not written by him. In fact, the very first document of this book is the one called *yaodian, Canon of Yao*,[63] which gives an outline of the major events that happened during Yao's reign. However, this document has one shortcoming. Nearly all the other documents that follow in the book are pronouncements or edicts that were made by those directly responsible for them, and presumably recorded by official scribes or historians *(shi)* either right on the occasion or shortly afterward. But this is not the case with the *Canon of Yao*, which begins with these words: "As can be told by examination into the past, Di Yao was named Fangxuan," and so on and so forth. So it is clear that the canon was composed not by Yao himself, not even during his lifetime, but was written by some official historian some time later, the exact date unknown.[64] No doubt the official historian or historians who wrote the canon had researched carefully into the records of the past as they themselves had professed. But to Confucius, as is evidenced by his answer to his disciple Zai Wo, all he learned about Yao and Shun [65] through this document was still "what had been told about them"; and he deplored that, because of exceeding antiquity, no pronouncements or edicts directly attributable to these two emperors whom he admired so much had been left to enable him to have a better understanding of them.

In spite of his youth, when Yao ascended the throne, he soon won over all the people. Thus the canon sang his praise: "He made shine his own illustrious virtues so as to attach himself to the nine branches of blood relations.[66] When the nine branches of blood relations were harmonized, he regulated the hundred surnames with an open and even hand. After the hundred surnames became enlightened with his wise rule, he united and pacified the myriad of nations. Thus all the black-haired people were transformed and lived in tranquillity."

From this description we may somewhat visualize the progressive steps of sound statesmanship Yao had practiced. The society of his time was still one of houses or clans. The emperor, or *di*, was head of the principal house, and as the Yellow Emperor's direct descendant, was also generally recognized as the overlord of the empire by all other houses or tribes. His main support therefore came from his own kith and kin, the so-called nine branches of blood relations. Unless these were united behind him, he would have no solid base to fall back upon. Perhaps it is because Zhi, Yao's older half brother, had been found wanting in this capacity that he was adjudged to be "no good"; and Yao, apparently taking a lesson from him, had remedied the situation quickly. As to the hundred surnames, these were of course not exactly a hundred in number; by the expression it is meant the numerous houses who were possessed of surnames, whether related to the imperial house or not. Very likely all of these enjoyed a degree of political and cultural affinity with the ruling house and with one another so that they constituted the second line of supporters whose allegiance and friendship it was for the overlord to cultivate and solidify. As regards the myriad of nations, these were the divers tribes or nations that were culturally different, or less advanced. As the times were still half nomadic and half agricultural, these tribes must have been largely nomadic, living or roaming side by side with "the hundred surnames" either right within the dominion or on the outskirts of the then vaguely defined confines of the empire. The aim of the imperial regime toward these tribes or nations was chiefly to pacify them, to make them acknowledge its authority wherever possible, or at least to see to it that none of them would become a potential or real force of such proportions as to threaten the general peace and order of the realm, as Ciyou and the Jiuli tribes did. And in all of these three objectives, Yao appears to have succeeded superbly.

Moreover, Yao carried out the traditional imperial function of calendar-making with fresh vigor. Zhuanxu, as noted before, had stationed a Rectifier in the north and another in the south to make close observations of the solstices and equinoxes. Yao did not find this arrangement sufficient. Now that his entire domain had been pacified, he had four ministers, brothers from two families, stationed in the limits of the four directions of the empire, each with a specific instruction to keep watch on a particular star at his post in order to determine the equinoxes and solstices the better. In the canon, he concluded his instructions with a summary command: "A round year consists of some 366 days. By the use of a leap month the four seasons can be determined and the year go a complete round. So fix this exactly so that all offices can be regulated in accord with it and all the works of the year may be satisfactorily performed." This statement shows plainly that at Yao's time the people were still not aware that a year is 365¼ days. But it is also clear that under Yao the system of using an intercalary month for calendar-making was at last definitely adopted.

Yao's astronomical instructions struck Dr. W. H. Medhurst, a 19th-century sinologist, with special significance. James Legge, who translated the *Book of History* into English at that time, quoted him in a note as follows:

If Cor Hydra culminated at sunset on the day of the vernal equinox in the time of Yaou, the constellation on the meridian at noon of that day must have been

Pleiades in Taurus. Now as by the retrocession of the equinoxes the stars of the zodiac go back a whole sign in 2,000 years, it would take 4,000 years for the sun to be in Pleiades at the time of the vernal equinox, which is about the time when Yaou is said to have flourished, and affords a strong confirmation of the truth of Chinese chronology. For Pleiades is 56 degrees and one third from the point where the ecliptic crossed the equinoctial A.D. 1800, and as the equinox travels backwards 50 seconds and one tenth per annum, it would take about 4,000 years for Pleiades to be in the zenith at noon of the vernal equinox. Referring to Chinese records, we find that Yaou's reign closed 2254 years before Christ, which added to 1800 makes 4054; and a retrocession of 50 seconds and one tenth per annum would give 4050.[67]

James Legge's translation of the *Book of History* was first published in 1865. But throughout these long years Medhurst's findings appear to have been totally neglected, buried, as it were, among Legge's voluminous notes. Only very recently has this matter been brought to the notice of modern astronomy. Dr. H. K. C. Yee, an American-trained astrophysicist, using modern precession formulae, has not only reviewed Medhurst's findings about vernal equinox, but has also extended his investigations into Yao's three other instructions regarding the determination of summer solstice, autumnal equinox, and winter solstice. Except for the last one about winter solstice, the translation of which from Chinese into English has caused uncertainty, Dr. Yee, in summing up his analysis, has concluded that "the period described in *yaodian* is indeed around the years 2200 B.C" [68]

As can be readily seen, this point is of exceeding importance to the study of China's ancient history. For *yaodian, Canon of Yao,* is the very first document in the *Book of History,* and as such it has been a primary target of modern skepticism. However, in presenting his analysis, Dr. Yee is not without reservations. He thinks that there are still a few questions left unanswered; and final and conclusive answers for them may be found only through future discoveries or by those who can identify ancient Chinese star names to a certainty, and who also know more about the nature and capability of astronomical instruments used at Yao's time and about the precise locations of the four observation posts Yao had established. It is hoped that after the publication of this book new interest may be kindled on the subject, and such answers as Dr. Yee is looking for may be forthcoming soon. Nevertheless, speaking objectively, as a result of these studies, we now seem to have much more solid reason than ever before to believe in the authenticity of *yaodian* as an ancient document as well as in the historicity of both the men and the events it purports to describe.

To return, just as Yao endeavored to make better measurements in the skies, so he also tried to give a more satisfactory government on the earth. As shown above, in the time of Shaohao, and very likely even earlier than that, the empire had already been divided into nine regions. In order to superintend the divers houses and tribes settling or roaming in those regions, the Yellow Emperor had established two supervisors; and following him, Zhuanxu had installed a Southern Rectifier and a Northern Rectifier. Now, having stationed four ministers at the four limits of the country to observe the heavens, Yao established another office called *siyue,* "Four Mountains," to oversee the mundane affairs of the empire. The canon, however, has not given us a description of its functions; nor do we know for certain whether the office consisted of one man or four men. But judging from the entire text of the canon, especially from the conversations that are reported to have passed between Yao and the Four Mountains, it seems that there were four of them, not only serving as their sovereign's closest advisers but also keeping themselves well informed about all important happenings in different places inside the vast dominion. So it may be reasonable to assume, as their title obviously appears to imply, that besides maintaining regular personal presence at the court, they were usually posted each at a commanding site in one of the four directions to observe and supervise the activities of various houses, tribes, or nations. Thus the policy of greater centralized control seems to have taken one more step forward under Yao's direction.

Indeed, this policy must be said to have started with the Yellow Emperor. When the founder of the house granted fourteen of his twenty-five sons surnames, it was not only out of recognition of the sheer reality that these sons had grown strong enough to head a separate house, or to lead an independent band and to settle or roam wherever they would like to. But politically, the astute monarch must have appreciated too the wisdom of that innovation. By having fourteen of his sons building up strong posts in different parts of the country, and going in directions that nobody could have knowledge of in advance, he himself would have far more effective control over the empire than the myriad nations were in the habit of yielding to him. But whatever the designs of the Yellow Emperor and of his successors, the main obstacle that this policy of greater centralized control had to encounter was the nomadic state of the people at large. As long as a majority of them remained without some kind of permanent residence, the way to exert steady and constant supervision over them would be tenuous, fragile, depending much on chance.

Toward the close of the reign of Di Ku, however, there was a perceptible change. It appears that before Yao was elevated to the throne, he had already been invested as Prince of Tang.[69] Hence, after his accession, he was generally known as Tang Yao. Now, Tang was not a surname, but the name of an area of land in the present-day Shanxi province.[70] Of course, before him, there might have been others assigned to particular pieces of land and made the lords thereof. But strictly according to the sources available to us, the record of Yao's having been named Prince of Tang seems to be the very first of such instances. And the significance is unmistakable. For this is the first time we meet with a lord identified not only by his own name, but also by the name of a territory with which he was associated. On the one hand, this appears to show that agriculture had already developed to such an extent that the people were becoming more drawn to the idea of ownership of land. On the other, by having lords each allotted a definite division of territory, two meanings of importance distinctly emerged. First, within the allocated land the lord so named was recognized as the master, and none other. And second, the one who granted the lord this recognition must have been an authority even higher, who had the power not only to make such a grant but also to enforce its recognition by all concerned, to make similar grants to others, and to protect all such lords from mutual encroachment or from outside aggression. In short, the basic ideas of fief, enfeoffment, and feudalism had been germinated. Thus, etymologically speaking, Tang Yao, or Yao of Tang, can be said to be just the same as William of Normandy, Henry of Navarre, or Frederick von Hohenzollern.

· 4 ·
THE GREAT FLOOD AND SHUN

Yao's reign so far only symbolized the continual progress the people were making. Historically, it would not have received much more notice than those of Zhuanxu and Di Ku had not two unprecedented events taken place during his lifetime—one an act of God, and the other entirely of his own making. For sometime during Yao's reign the Great Flood occurred. Whether this is the same legendary flood that swept over the earth, as attested by the Bible and other records, we need not discuss here. But the extent of the inundation was so vast that it covered all of Yao's domain, the valleys of both the Yellow River and the Yangtze. And Yao himself was said in the canon to have described it thus: "Like endless boiling water, the flood is pouring forth destruction. Boundless and overwhelming, it overtops hills and mountains. Rising and ever rising, it threatens the very heavens. How the people must be groaning and suffering!" Both Yao and the empire were in dire straits. A man was sorely needed to control the flood, and Yao sought advice from the Four Mountains. Unanimously they recommended Gun, Prince of Chong [71] and a descendant of Zhuanxu. At first Yao hesitated. He said that Gun was "prone to disobeying orders and also not averse to causing injuries to his peers." But when the Four Mountains persisted, Gun was given charge of the undertaking.

While Gun strove against the flood, Yao was deeply worried too about another problem. The frail prototype of government that his house had been building up for generations was rapidly falling apart, not through his misrule but through uncontrollable circumstances. The nine regions which the empire had been divided into were now cut by the spreading waters into unrecognizable shapes, with all communication lines either twisted asunder or indistinguishably submerged. The lords or princes to whom definite territories had been allocated were no longer able to abide by the demarcations sanctioned by the imperial house. Out of sheer necessity, every surname, every tribe, every band of men, were struggling the best they could to gain some place of safety; and there existed no power that could stop them.

Not that Yao feared the possibilities of rebellion. In the face of the dire prospect that one and all might be eventually drowned, even the most ambitious and unscrupulous of his subjects could be trusted not to feel much of an appetite for usurpation. What Yao dreaded, however, was something much harder to cope with—a simple and inevitable disintegration of the empire. Against this gloomy probability Yao felt himself powerless and helpless. He wanted dearly to give up his throne to someone who could deal with the situation better than he could, or at least to share the burden and the anxieties with him. He again sought the advice of the Four Mountains, along with some others. One of the latter recommended Yao's own eldest son, Zhu by name.[72] Yao's reply shows that he had given long thought to the problem. He said, "Alas! Zhu is abusive and disputatious. How can he do?" For in his thorough and collected consideration, if the empire could be saved, it would not be through the use of force, for no human force could be a match against this ever-rising flood; it could be only through harmony, or rather by one who could bring all the people together to ward off the common danger in unison. He knew his own son well, of course. The very fact that Zhu was "abusive and disputatious" put him out of the question. Then someone recommended another.[73] And Yao's estimation of that man revealed again what he was looking for. Referring to the nominee, he said, "Alas! When he is not given an assignment, he can talk; but after he has been given the assignment, his actions turn out differently." Now that the flood was raging on, what the empire needed was one whose actions and whose words invariably proved to be the same, so that the people could place implicit confidence in him.

By this time Gun had been fighting the flood nearly nine years, and the inundation still went on rampant and unchecked. Yao was growing desperate. He offered the throne to the Four Mountains. But being aware of the enormous responsibilities of that dignity, not one of them would accept it. At last, when Yao insisted that they nominate someone, even though he be from the most humble and obscure station, they recommended Shun. The *Canon of Yao* in this connection, though couched in the briefest wording possible, gives us nonetheless a key to Yao's thinking. Upon the recommendation, "Yao said, 'Yes, I have heard of him. What kind of man is he?' The Mountains answered, 'Son of Gu. His father is stupid and contumelious; his stepmother, arrogant and abusive; his half brother Xiang, conceited and contemptuous. But through his own filial conduct he has succeeded in making the whole family live together in harmony, leading each of them to better self-discipline so that not one of them has proceeded to open wickedness.' Yao said, 'I will try him.' "

Apparently Yao had conducted a private investigation of Shun even before he asked the Four Mountains about him. Shun was not a lord of a house or a chief of a tribe. In fact, he was not even head of his family; his father was, instead. And that family was a very small one indeed, consisting of only a father, a stepmother, himself, and his younger half brother.

This is an interesting fact, for it seems to show that the old large patriarchal family system which had developed prior to this time was perhaps beginning to break up. Earlier, especially in the purely nomadic days, when safety could be sought only through numbers, it was natural that people should attach themselves to large-sized houses or clans. But now that agricultural settlers had become more and more common, that a better degree of peace and order had been kept since the time of the Yellow Emperor, and that definite areas of land had been assigned to certain lords or princes so that they would be made responsible for the safety of persons living within their domains, many individuals, either out of disagreement with their elders or chiefs or just out of a desire to be independent and venturesome, must have no longer wanted to tie themselves to the strings of their old houses and decided to strike out for themselves.

Gu, also known as Gusou, must have been one of these. Perhaps this trend toward smaller families had started even earlier. Here we have no definite proof, but only a conjecture. In the *Historical Records,* it is expressly mentioned that Shun was the sixth-generation descendant of Zhuanxu, but "from Qiongchan to Shun, all the six generations had fallen low and were commoners." [74] Had Qiongchan committed some grievous offense for which he had been degraded and banished by his imperial father? Or had the trend to strike out independently in small families started that early? At any rate, when Yao made his investigations about Shun and secretly considered the possibility of raising him to the highest dignity of the empire, there is no question but that the latter was of the humblest rank and position.

How did Shun then manage to draw the notice of Yao, and of the Four Mountains? Several documents relating to Shun, which Confucius had originally compiled in the *Book of History,* are now irretrievably lost; but from authoritative sources such as the works of Mencius and others, who had probably read the original documents before their loss, we can still gather some information. Perhaps the fact that Shun was directly descended from Emperor Zhuanxu and yet had fallen into such misfortunes might have marked him out at the very outset as an object of curiosity and attention.

Perhaps the singular perversity of his father, of his stepmother, and of his half brother, and also their concerted atrocious behavior toward him, had helped too to excite sympathy for him. But chiefly it is his own attitude toward those adversities and his reactions toward his kinsfolk's unseemly and unreasonable conduct that had aroused people's admiration. His father was called Gusou, "Blind Oldster," probably because he was half blind, as the definition of the word *gu* seems to indicate;[75] and probably also because he was, in the opinion of his contemporaries, unable to distinguish right and wrong.[76] In any event, if there ever existed a father who would use his physical deficiency as a means to incite a son's pity and thus work his will upon him, and who, when assured of the son's unfailing loyalty and devotion, would proceed to exploit that advantage to the utmost limit without scruple and contrition, Gusou seems to have been that kind of man. Shun's mother having died early, Gusou had married again. The second wife bore him another son, Xiang. If Shun had been treated like a slave by his father before, he was now treated worse than a slave by the three of them. All the responsibilities for providing the family with sustenance, with all other chores to boot, were piled upon his young shoulders. Perhaps, in those days when ample supplies could be procured from hunting and fishing, and when, if time permitted, any fallow land could be cultivated for the use of its yield without bothering to ask leave from anyone, such tasks as were given to Shun might be said to be not too difficult, provided one was never afraid, or sparing, of ceaseless toil. But then came the flood. The incessant threat of the rising inundation drove the shiftless family from one location to another, and that alone must have increased Shun's hardship a hundredfold. According to the records, early in his life Shun was forced to acquire many and varied experiences. He had farmed, fished, engaged in pottery, made utensils and implements, and also dealt in trade. And all these occupations he had pursued each in a different place, west as far as the southern mountains of the modern Shanxi province and east as far as the central portion of present-day Shandong, with hundreds of miles lying in between.[77]

Had Shun been of average intelligence, his peculiar miserable lot might not have aroused much curiosity. But as he was an exceptionally gifted man, his actions under those circumstances could not have gone long unnoticed. To begin with, he impressed all he happened to meet with his humility and eagerness to learn. In taking up a new occupation, he was always anxious to get instructions from people more experienced and knowledgeable, "taking delight in what was good, ever ready to give up his own way to follow that of others." [78] And then he struck these same people not only with his capacity to learn quickly, but also with his talent to improve upon what he had learned, and especially with his willingness to share his improvement with others.[79] Moreover, in face of the rising flood, Shun seemed to be endowed with a special instinct of knowing what kinds of places were comparatively safe to live. And as his reputation in this respect grew and spread, more and more people began to follow after him. It was said about the last place he moved into: "In one year it became a village; in two years, a hamlet; in three years, a town of considerable size." [80]

Notwithstanding his growing fame, notwithstanding his no longer being a teenager but a full-grown man, notwithstanding his proved changeless and unswerving devotion, Shun's father, stepmother, and half brother all treated him the same as before. Whenever Gusou, "Blind Oldster," felt a liking for it, with or without the stepmother's instigation or the half brother's incitement, he would subject Shun to a thrashing, and Shun would submit to it as well as he could. In time, he even developed a sort of system to cope with his father's irrational, violent tempers.[81] If Gusou had a chore for him to do, he would always be there to attend to it. If the father had got himself into such a rage as to threaten to do him serious bodily harm, then search as the purblind man might, he would not be able to find him. In any event, when the thrashing was bearable, Shun would bear it without protest; but if it exceeded bearable limits, Shun would just run away and wait until Gusou's mood changed. Thus, while never failing in his duties toward his father, Shun never allowed himself to be maimed permanently in any manner, lest, as he feared, Gusou should suffer remorse afterward. Thus even at the age of twenty Shun became known for his singular filial piety.[82] And because of such sacrifices he thought it was his duty to make, it never entered into his mind to take a wife for himself. And so by the time he was thirty, he was still continuing making those sacrifices and remained unwed.

It was then that Yao decided to consider Shun as a likely candidate for succession to the throne. And now, looking at the matter from Yao's standpoint, the choice does not appear at all unreasonable. Shun was a commoner, but was also a descendant of Zhuanxu. Even though the nine branches of Yao's blood relations might not welcome Shun as warmly as they would one of their own, yet because of Shun's lineage, they could not very well oppose him. Also, Shun's being a commoner, not a head of a house or a chief of a tribe, had its obvious advantages. It would make the "hundred surnames" less suspicious that Shun would be principally interested in the well-being of his own house, or his own tribe, to the exclusion of that of others. As to Shun's other qualifications, Yao seemed to be quite satisfied with his own investigations. Since Shun had moved from place to place and engaged in all sorts of occupations, if anybody could be said to be conversant with the general conditions of the people caught in this crisis of inundation, Shun must be counted as such. And as his experiences would amply bear out, he was decidedly a man of parts. But even more important to Yao, it was evident that every action and every nature of Shun seemed to be so clearly motivated by, and oriented toward, harmony. And harmony is what Yao thought the empire needed most at that critical moment.

Yet the decision was too crucial for Yao to make lightly. He wanted personally to put Shun to more tests. At this time, Shun and his family had moved to Yu,[83] at the bend of the River Gui in the southwestern corner of the modern Shanxi province, not far from Yao's own Tang. As to Yao's initial approach to Shun, the narrative in the canon is simple: "The emperor said, 'I will try him. I will wive him with my two daughters and see his behavior with them.' On this he gave orders and sent his two daughters to the bend of the Gui to be wives of the Yu family." [84]

Gusou, his wife, and his younger son Xiang were not exactly thrilled by the honor that had so unexpectedly fallen from the blue on Shun. But neither were they displeased with the flocks of sheep and cattle, and the loads of grain and cereals, that had accompanied the brides as dowry. But not knowing Yao's ultimate designs for Shun, they secretly plotted to seize the goods for their sole possession. Now that they had so much wealth in hand, they felt they had no more need of Shun. So, while building a granary, Gusou called to Shun to help him on the roof. As soon as Shun climbed up, however, the father got down, took away the ladder, and set the structure on fire.[85] But fortunatley for the son, Gusou had left behind on the roof his large bamboo hat, which the people then were wont to wear against both sun and rain. Having another hat himself, Shun used the two hats like wings and half flew and half wobbled down to the ground, unharmed.

Disappointed with the result, the three plotted again. They asked Shun to dig a well. But no sooner had Shun gone down deep than they proceeded to cover up the well with the earth that had been dug up. They had no idea that Shun had previously dug a tunnel connecting it with outside. And now using this as an exit, he slowly crawled out. But before he reappeared, his half brother Xiang was jubilant, crying out aloud, "How well has this scheme succeeded! The merit is all mine. Let my father and mother have his cattle and sheep. Let them have his granaries and storehouses. His shield and spear shall be mine. His lute shall be mine. His bow shall be mine. His two wives I shall make attend to me in my bed." [86] At this Xiang rushed to his brother's quarters. But as he entered the latter's room, what was not his astonishment when he saw Shun himself playing with the lute on the bed! Agitating and blushing awkwardly, Xiang muttered, "I am come because I was much concerned about you." And Shun replied, "There are many chores I have left unfinished. Please do them for me." Thus the harmony of the whole family was saved without a trace of visible stress and tension. And well we may imagine how Yao's two daughters could have this incident reported to their imperial father with so much deserved confidence and pride about their husband's conduct.

Now Yao summoned Shun to his seat of government and began putting him to test in various fields of administration. According to the canon, Shun was first put in charge of "the instruction of the five codes," that is, the codes governing proper behavior with respect to the five human relationships, namely: between sovereign and subject, between parent and offspring, between husband and wife, between elder and younger, and between friend and friend. His position therefore may be somewhat compared to the principal of a modern educational academy; but the functions involved were much more demanding than those of the counterpart. For he had to see to it that his students not only understood his instructions but also acted fully in accord with them. This was a duty very difficult to fulfill. But knowing of Shun's past, it is perhaps safe to suggest that none could have taught better than he did. And so the canon duly recorded that after his having served in that office, the five codes "came to be unanimously observed."

In our present view, this is all credible if we only know what the canon meant by that statement. Since such teachings necessarily involved much personal contact, and since in those days there could not have been any large educational institution or school system to speak of, very likely the objects of Shun's instructions were centered around, or limited to, the nine branches of Yao's blood relations. And this is of course the aim of Yao's first test. It is to find out whether Shun could make himself accepted, respected, and obeyed by the first line of supporters of the imperial regime. And Shun passed the test with unanimous satisfaction.

Then, according to the canon, Shun was "put in charge of regulating the hundred affairs, and the hundred affairs were all regulated in order and in time." This means that after Shun had won over the nine branches of blood relations of the imperial house, Yao wanted to test him with directing the affairs of "the hundred surnames"; and Shun again acquitted himself well in this function, thus gaining the goodwill and confidence of all the houses and clans of the empire. So as a third test, Yao appointed him to be the "Host of the Four Entrances," whose duty was to receive the chiefs or princes of the divers tribes and nations that came from the four quarters of the domain, and to deal with their varied businesses. And it is recorded that as a result of his management, "all the Four Entrances were reverent, contented, and harmonious."

Thus Shun had proved himself completely capable of following in the footsteps of Yao in the prosecution and continuance of his policy of harmony. Yet Yao still did not consider the tests sufficient. Had the circumstances been normal, like the time when Yao himself ascended the throne, these qualities of Shun's, which had already been weighed and found not wanting, would have been enough. But the times were abnormal. The flood was still rising. Gun was obviously at his wits' end to check it. And the empire was getting into a worse and worse state of disintegration. Yao, with his policy of harmony, could only manage to slow somewhat the speed of decay; and he himself would have been the first to admit that the final collapse of his government might come at any moment. To save it, the man at the helm had to be one more gifted than himself; indeed, he had to be endowed with a superior genius to be able to cope with, and overcome, any kind of emergency. Could Shun be such a man? And Yao put him to a final test.

The canon says, "He was sent to the great plains at the foot of the mountain. He suffered violent winds and terrible thunderstorms. And he was never confused." Was Shun sent out to the wilderness alone, or with a small retinue? How long was he sent out? What provisions were given him? The canon does not go into any detail. But since this is explicitly mentioned as the final test, we may well assume how much importance Yao had attached to it. It was to test Shun's resourcefulness, clear-headedness, stamina, and perseverance. And whatever the test was, we can also assume that it must have been an exceedingly difficult one, and Shun passed it too with flying colors.

By this time Yao was well advanced in age.[87] So, as recorded in the canon, he "said, 'Come, you Shun! I have investigated into your deeds and compared them with your words. Three years have passed, and you have proved that you can in truth put your words into deeds. You do now ascend the imperial throne.' Shun, however, wished to decline in favor of someone more virtuous. At any rate, he would not consent to be successor." So finally an arrangement was made, which, though not stated explicitly in the canon, may be fully ascertained by studying the text as a whole.[88] There were to be two emperors at the same time, one reigning, one ruling. Yao was the reigning emperor, in whose name every order would be decreed and everything executed. But Shun would be the co-emperor to decree and to execute. In other words, except in name, Shun was to bear the responsibility of the empire alone. It was he and he only who would have to see that the flood was checked, the people given safety and prosperity, and the empire restored to its effectiveness and glory.

· 5 ·

SHUN AS YAO'S CO-EMPEROR

Yao had already prepared for the occasion. Shun's accession would be solemnized by the most dignified ceremonies that time up to then had devised. All of the Four Mountains, all of "the hundred surnames," and all of the lords, princes, and chiefs of myriad tribes and nations—all, that is, who could come or who cared to come—were invited to take part in this august scene. In Yao's opinion, this was essential. He wanted to dramatize the occasion. He wanted to revive the empire with a fresh feeling of hope. And in order to demonstrate a new beginning, he chose the first day of the first month of the new year for the ceremonies.

On the appointed day, Shun went first to Yao's ancestral temple—which happened to be Shun's too, since he himself was directly descended from Zhuanxu—"to receive the final sanction" of his coming into power. Thereafter, he examined the jade astronomical instruments which were used to calculate the movements of the seven celestial bodies—the sun, the moon, and the five planets Mercury, Venus, Mars, Jupiter, and Saturn. Even though his mind must then have been chiefly preoccupied with the problems arising from the Great Flood, he did not forget that making an accurate calendar was still one of the principal duties entrusted to the sovereign. This done, he went out of the capital to the open country in the south and sacrificed, as according to the formal procedure, to the Lord Above, then to the Six Venerables, to the spirits of the mountains and rivers, and to all other deities.[89]

And immediately after these ceremonies were over, he began to take his own measures. Daily he met with the Four Mountains and received the various heads of houses, lords of surnames, and chiefs of tribes or nations—which, for brevity's sake, we shall hereafter simply cover with one term, "princes." He divided these princes into five grades;[90] and to each of them he issued an insignia of authority—a token of jade varying in size and shape for different grades, which every prince was required to carry on his person. And these tokens were so constructed that they fitted into a sort of frame which was in the custody of the emperor or co-emperor so that their genuineness might be tested and impostors might be detected.[91] Perhaps this was a device created by Shun's ingenious mind. Or perhaps this device had been used before and Shun was only issuing new insignia. Nor do we know about the number of the princes present on this occasion. It could be that a large majority of them had gathered in the imperial seat partly out of curiosity and partly out of sheer desperation in face of the general inundation. It could be also that the number of those who came was very limited either because of the difficulties of communication or because most of them had lost faith in the ability of the imperial authority to do anything to relieve the situation. But as many princes as had come, Shun was able to persuade one and all to accept those insignia and acknowledge his authority. And this was very important for Shun. For in order to set about his undertaking, he must first of all have at least some idea of the number of people he could possibly count upon for their cooperation. And he devoted one entire month to acquainting himself with these princes and their problems.

But no sooner was this accomplished than he started off on an inspection tour. Thus the canon recorded: "In the second month of the year he made the tour of inspection eastward. He arrived at Taizong (i.e., Taishan),[92] where he offered a bonfire to heaven, and sacrificed in order to the mountains and rivers. Thereafter he gave audience to the princes of the eastern regions. He put in accord their seasons and months and rectified the days. He standardized their musical instruments, scales, weights, and measures. Then he practiced with them the five ceremonies, in which the five grades of jade, three kinds of silk, two living animals, and one dead animal were all duly presented. After these ceremonies were finished, he had them practice them once again." The above narrative is too succinct, too factual, and seemingly dwells too much on nonessentials. Nevertheless, Shun's purposes in making the tour are thereby vividly revealed.

Having lived as a commoner all his life except for three years, having also been taken into full confidence by Yao, and having watched and studied how Gun as well as the people at large had been fighting against the flood, Shun must have come to these conclusions: The battle against the flood had not fared well because the people had not been able to work together. Not that they did not want to work together; but they did not know how to work together. In face of such an unprecedented threat, to be able to do something effective at all it is absolutely necessary for the people to bind themselves together, working with one plan, coordinated under one direction, and subject to one discipline. The word "mobilization," of course, had not been invented then. But what Shun wanted was no less than total mobilization.

That is why he had taken the tour so quickly after his accession to authority. It was not merely a fact-finding trip; it was to bring to the people his message of mobilization, to make them accept the idea, to organize them to practice it even before he left them. He chose Taishan as the meeting place for the princes of the eastern regions not so much because it was considered to be a sacred mountain as because it provided high ground and therefore a safe place for the meeting. He had no idea for *fengchan*.[93] That was for better times, not for this occasion. His worship of heaven and the other deities was therefore in the simplest manner possible; yet all the while we cannot but think that his heart must have been immersed in the deepest prayers for the success of his mission. And when he received the princes either individually or collectively, how he must have endeavored to bare his innermost thoughts to them! And here it is that latter-day historians must share the profound regret which Confucius expressed so long ago—we know only what people said about Shun; we have no documents directly attributable to Shun himself to make us appreciate him the better.

Notwithstanding, the actions he took are self-evident. First, in any scheme of mobilization, there are some purely mechanical matters that must be taken care of at the very outset. To begin with, there must be synchronization: If the concerted plan for fighting the flood called for the completion of some preparatory works before a certain date, that date must be the same for all parties concerned. Hence the rectification of the day. This is probably the easiest part of Shun's mission. Since calendar-making had been long recognized as a principal function of the imperial house, the people naturally were prepared to accept whatever Shun might ordain in this connection. The next thing to do, however, is not so simple. In those days, communication was not an easy matter. Though the written word had been invented and developed to a rather high degree, the people who could read or write were still very few in number. Moreover, in dealing with emergencies, especially before the age of telegraph and radio, for the matter of transmitting messages to numerous persons and all at once, written communication probably was far less convenient than the primitive methods of using drums, cymbals, and pipes. But to be reliable, these instruments had first to be standardized so that whenever messages were given through them, their meanings would be clearly understood. As to the scales, weights, and measures, the importance of making them uniform for huge engineering projects should be obvious. Yet to persuade the people to give up the implements they were accustomed to and to accept a new scheme of things must have been difficult and toilsome.

But the hardest part of Shun's mission was, from the standpoint of this historian, to win over the princes as well as the common people, one and all, and to adopt and enforce a new order of discipline. For discipline cannot be built except on a basis of dependable respect for authority; and authority cannot be exercised except through a recognizable chain of command. Unless Shun's orders were implicitly obeyed by the princes, and those of the princes by their lieutenants, and those of their lieutenants by the common people, even if Shun had a workable master plan to fight the flood there would be no way to carry it through. Furthermore, extensive as the Great Flood was, in fighting it, it was impracticable to rely upon physical force to maintain discipline. The inundation was not like an ordinary enemy: It did not pose danger on any particular spot or on any specific front; it posed danger everywhere. And frightened by the hopeless prospects, the natural inclination of anyone confronting it was to run away from it as fast as he could. Under such circumstances, even the strictest discipline imposed by the sternest martinet would not be of much avail. So in order to fight the flood effectually, a discipline of a much higher order was needed. It could not be imposed from without, backed by arrows and swords as it were; it had to arise from within the men themselves.

Whether Shun had convinced the princes of the soundness of his reasoning or not, they agreed to go along with his plan to hold the five kinds of ceremonies which the co-emperor had formulated. Of course they had known of the five kinds of ceremonies before: These were (1) the Propitious Ceremonies, pertaining to the worship of Heaven and the other deities as well as the veneration of ancestral spirits; (2) the Somber Ceremonies, pertaining to death and funeral; (3) the Martial Ceremonies, pertaining to the preparation and prosecution of war; (4) the Amicable Ceremonies, pertaining to receptions both public and private; and (5) the Joyous Ceremonies, pertaining to betrothal and marriage. But if these ceremonies had existed before, they had been in very crude forms, nothing like the elaborate schemes which Shun now had carefully drawn up. Moreover, when these ceremonies had been held formerly, the number of people who took part was more or less restricted. But now in Shun's ceremonies, there was no limitation to the people joining them; in fact, the larger the number, the more welcome to Shun. Not only all the princes and their retinues were asked to join, but the common people in the adjacent countryside were invited as well. And the new ceremonies were markedly different from the old ones in another aspect. In the old ceremonies, only a very limited few were assigned definite functions to carry out, while the rest acted more or less as mere observers. But in the new ceremonies, not only was everyone given a part to play, but each had to play his part properly and well. For unless he did, his mistake would be immediately noticed by all to his own humiliation and corrected by his nearest superior in the presence of the whole assembly.

Take, for instance, the matter of offering. In all these ceremonies, whenever a participant came to the scene, he was supposed to bring an offering as a token of courtesy, or tribute, to whoever happened to be in charge of the ceremony. This was probably a traditional custom derived from time immemorial. But Shun now converted the custom into a prerequisite, and he regulated in detail what kind of offering each of the participants should bring. For example, in the ceremonies where the co-emperor himself presided, the princes would first come forth in order of their ranks, each offering his own jade insignia as a tribute. This seems to have a double significance. On the one hand, it was to demonstrate the genuineness of their insignia by willingly submitting them to be tested. On the other, it was also a tacit acknowledgment that since they had acquired their authority from the emperor, it was also for him to take away if he wanted to. As the princes were divided into five grades, and the jade insignias were accordingly of five kinds, this is the reason why the canon mentioned specifically, "the five grades of jade."

After the princes, in the ceremonial procession, would come their heirs apparent. Each of these would be required to bring a piece of silk as offering.[94] For reasons we cannot be sure of, instead of five grades, the heirs apparent were divided into three, with the first grade offering silk in purplish color, the second in black, and the third in yellow. Then, after the heirs apparent, would follow the officers of the princes. The officers of the first rank would each bring a live lamb; those of the second rank, each a live goose; and those of the third rank, each a dead fowl.[95] Hence the canon: "He practiced with them the five ceremonies, in which the five grades of jade, three kinds of silk, two living animals, and one dead animal, were all duly presented." [96]

Thus it was through these ceremonies that Shun attempted to instruct the people in the technique of organization as well as in the sense of discipline. He tried to inculcate them with the necessary deference and obedience to authority, with the clear recognition of the various links in the chain of command, and above all with the keen realization of the duties and responsibilities each of them had to play. As they had to practice the five kinds of ceremonies in succession, it was Shun's hope that they would learn to know how to conduct themselves in various changes of situation. And when they had performed them all, lest they should forget, Shun made them repeat the ceremonies once again. Had we had no inkling of what was in Shun's mind, we would probably have thought how trivial and inconsequent these doings were, bordering almost upon the ludicrous. We might have wondered, also, how the people, primitive and unaccustomed to restraint as they must have been, could have subjected themselves to the constraint of such rigmarole. But if we look at the situation with the same insight as Shun did, then we can see how well and how persuasively he could have exhorted the people to bend to his way of thinking. The danger that faced them all was the flood. He, as co-emperor, would do his best to check and control it with a central plan. But in order to make the plan work, he had to have the help of everyone; and in order to make everyone do his share, they had to have a close-knit organization. The ceremonies were therefore devised to train them in two things: first, to know that individual action, however good and however vigorous, is never so effective as concerted action—or, in other words, the value of pulling together in harmony, and second, to understand that each one, high and low, has a definite role to act in every situation. The failing of one would automatically affect the others, and therefore the well-being of the whole; and what is more, each one, through his own reasoning, had to find out for himself what was being expected of him, or what was the proper thing for him to do—in short, a sense of propriety.

How well Shun succeeded in his mission the brief account of his life will presently tell. It is, however, this historian's opinion that Shun gave the Chinese a heritage perhaps even more enduring than what he himself had at first thought possible. From his time on down to this day, these ideals—harmony and propriety—have been deeply embedded in the minds of the Chinese people. Harmony is prized above everything, in the family, in government, in society. And propriety is a word that is almost daily used by every Chinese, certainly more frequently used by them than by any other people. The Chinese character is *li*. Before Shun's time its meaning had probably been confined to rites and ceremonies, or rituals and ceremonials. But after Shun it began to assume another significance—what is fitting and proper, or what is as it should be in reason. And many modern Chinese, in using the word *li*, often do not bother to make a distinction between the two meanings.

To return, after Shun had accomplished his mission in the east, the canon continues in its narration: "In the fifth month, he took his tour of inspection southward. He arrived at the Southern Mountain, and observed the same ceremonies as at Tai. In the eighth month, he took his tour of inspection westward. He arrived at the Western Mountain, and he acted likewise as before. In the eleventh month, he took his tour of inspection northward. He arrived at the Northern mountain, and he observed the same ceremonies as he had in the West.[97] He then returned. Thereupon he went to the ancestral temple and offered a single bullock."

Having familiarized himself with the actual conditions of the empire as much as he could, Shun was now prepared, with Yao's approval, to put all the plans he had formulated into execution:

1. A decree was issued that hereafter the co-emperor would take a tour of inspection every five years. And within the interval between two inspection tours, the princes of the four directions would be required to appear at least once in the imperial court by turns. They would submit their reports of government in words, which would be examined against their deeds. As a result of these examinations, they would be awarded chariots and robes in accordance with their services.

2. Inasmuch as the flood had disrupted direct communications between many places, the old administrative system of dividing the empire into nine regions had become unrealistic. So now it was determined that until the flood was brought into control, for the sake of expediency the empire was to be divided into twelve administrative regions. And each of these regional governments was to render sacrifices to the highest mountain within its limits, and to make it the temporary regional seat for its operations. And each of them would thenceforth concentrate its work on deepening the streams within its jurisdiction, beginning with those that originated from those mountains.

3. While the ordinary administrations of all localities were left in the hands of the princes, for the purpose of assisting as well as overseeing their activities, Shun created sixteen additional offices besides the Four Mountains, one half of them to be concerned with the regulation and improvement of land use, and the other half with the training and organization of the people. And to fill these posts, upon Shun's recommendation, Yao appointed eight

men descended from Zhuanxu and eight men descended from Di Ku, who were all well known for their abilities and virtues.[98]

4. Although Shun strongly believed in the principle of building up self-discipline from within, he was too practical a ruler to depend on this alone. Whether China had had a penal code before him, we are not certain. But the canon certainly made it clear that he did issue a code of his own. However, the language it used in describing the code is exceedingly obscure: "Images are to be employed to signify the punishments; and the five punishments themselves may be commuted to banishment or alleviated by pardon. In addition, the whip is to be used as punishment for administrative offenses; and the stick, for educational ones. Where the offense is redeemable, money will be accepted for redemption.[99] Where the offense is inadvertent or caused by misfortune, it will be granted pardon. But where it is deliberate or recurrent, it will suffer the prescribed penalty." And this laconic description ends with Shun giving a solemn advice to all the princes or officers entrusted with administration of justice: "Be reverent! Be reverent! Be ever sparing of punishment!"

Traditionally, Ciyou, the barbarian intruder from the south who had fought against the Yellow Emperor, was supposed to have devised "the five punishments" to deal with his enemies.[100] These punishments were de-capitation, castration, amputation of a limb, cutting off the nose, and brand-ing the forehead. After Ciyou's overthrow, these were continued first by the Jiuli, and then in Yao and Shun's time by the Sanmiao tribes, which had succeeded the Jiuli in populating the south. It appears that the people of the north had at first viewed these atrocities with abhorrence; but as time passed, some of the princes had also begun to adopt them as a means to boost their own powers. And now as Shun had demanded of them a renewed effort to fight the inundation, it is possible, too, that not a few of them had resorted to such punishments in an endeavor to attain the objective. But Shun, while appreciating the necessity of using punishment in effective government, was inclined to think that indulgence in such cruelties might be more conducive to discord than harmony. He issued, therefore, the penal code to clarify the confusion. The five punishments were allowed to remain in law, and the culprits would be sentenced each according to his deserts; but the sentences would be carried out not physically but in other forms. Those to be branded on the forehead would be required to wear a black band on the head; those to have their noses cut off would have their clothes covered with reddish mud; those to have their limbs amputated would have those particular limbs circled with dark ink; those to be castrated would have their feet shod with un-matched shoes; and those to be decapitated would wear a coarse jacket with-out a collar.[101] It was Shun's hope that making the culprits appear so conspicuous and so ignominious in the midst of their own community might bring forth the salutary effects of genuine remorse. And if such signs did occur, then in the case of lighter offenses, the penitent would be pardoned forthwith, and in the case of heavier offenses, would be simply banished.

5. Much attention as Shun paid to the self-discipline of the people, he also realized that the key to the success of his plan of concerted action was the implicit willingness of the princes of the empire to follow his leadership. After his tour of inspection, he was assured that he had the confidence of a large majority of them. Still, he had found a few uncooperative. And among these there were four who were especially intransigent. He knew that unless he took decisive actions against them, his entire plan might be corroded and jeopardized. Two of them happened to be former ministers of Yao.[102] So now, with Yao's sanction, he had them exiled, one to an island in the north and the other to a mountain in the south.

6. The third of these intransigents, however, was much more difficult to handle. It was the Sanmiao tribes. As successors to the Jiuli, they now had the possession of a vast extent of land south of the Yangtze River, that lies between the modern Dongting Lake of Hunan and Poyang Lake of Jiangxi.[103] All along, since the time of Ciyou, these comparatively less civilized southerners had been a source of nagging pain to the imperial authority. They would waver openly in their allegiance anytime the central regime showed signs of stumbling. And this trait had become especially noticeable of late, as the flood had made havoc of the communications between the north and the south. As a matter of fact, it was because of this unsettled condition of these Sanmiao tribes that Shun, in his first inspection tour to the south, had summoned the regional princes to meet him at Huoshan, a mountain north of the Yangtze, and not at Hengshan, right in the heartland of the Sanmiao country.[104] However, to control the flood in central China, it was absolutely necessary to clear up all the areas along the Yangtze and its tributaries. Yet squatting astraddle the middle portion of that mighty river, the Sanmiao tribes would neither defer to Shun's instructions nor cooperate with him in any joint enterprises. Shun was therefore placed in a dire dilemma. Leave them alone? That would mean the Yangtze Valley could never be cleared up, and the entire battle against the inundation might thereby be hopelessly lost. Subjugate them by force, as Zhuanxu had subjugated the Jiuli before? Not to speak of Shun's innate aversions toward violence, that would necessitate a substantial diversion of usable manpower from the central plan of flood control, which he could hardly afford. But Shun did get out of the dilemma successfully, for the canon states clearly, "He had the Sanmiao tribes moved to Sanwei."

Sanwei is at the extreme northwestern corner of China proper, near the modern Dunhuang of Gansu province, more than two thousand kilometers away from the original abode of the Sanmiao. How did Shun manage to move them that far? Unfortunately we are left with no recourse other than conjecture. History has furnished us many proofs that the Sanmiao tribes, or more correctly a large part of them, did actually migrate to that area. But as to how they were persuaded to migrate there, the only thing we are reasonably sure of is that Shun must have relied more on diplomacy than on force. As the inundation raged on and food became really scanty for the Sanmiao, it would not be unlike Shun to seize an opportune moment, send them free provisions, and couple the generosity with an offer: For those who wanted to stay behind, he would continue furnishing them with supplies provided that they pledge him full obedience; and for those who would not agree to such terms, he would still supply them with what they might need, all the way if necessary, provided that they migrate to a place far above the Yellow River and the Yangtze valleys, where he must forthwith proceed with his flood-control projects. And under such circumstances, it may not be inconceivable that as many Sanmiao chose to migrate as to stay behind. And whether this was the way Shun persuaded them or not, for such successes as this, and especially for this success, the co-emperor was acclaimed throughout the length and breadth of the empire.[105]

7. But there remained one more decision for Shun to make, which was perhaps the most difficult one he had made in his entire life. This was in relation to Gun, the man who had been entrusted by Yao against his better judgment with the overall direction of flood control, and who was now numbered by the canon as the fourth intransigent. Before Shun came to be known to Yao, Gun had already fought the flood without success for some nine years. Now another four years had passed, and Gun's failure had become even more obvious. During that last year when Shun made his empire-wide tour of inspection, the co-emperor had been motivated not only by the conviction that the entire people must be mobilized, but also by the realization that a more effective method than Gun's must be found in order to bring this gigantic task to a successful conclusion.

He had, of course, studied Gun's performance, observed his engineering projects, and discussed with him all the important aspects of the problem. Gun held that the best way to check the flood was to build dikes. He had built as many dikes as possible. He even advocated that for cities quite distant from the threat of immediate inundation dikes should be also built as a precautionary measure.[106] But the dikes appeared to hold only when the water ceased to rise. As the flood kept on rising, however, his dikes failed almost one and all. Yet he insisted that there was nothing wrong with his policy; the trouble was that the dikes had not been built high enough. So he kept on demanding that the people build more dikes, higher dikes. Shun did not think this practicable, and inquired wherever he could of a better method to control the flood. And nowhere did he find a view more basically different from Gun's than that of Gun's own son, Yu. To Yu, his father's method would have no doubt worked, had this been but an ordinary rise of the rivers, which would subside as soon as the crest of the overflow had been reached. But inasmuch as this was a general flood which mankind had not experienced before, and no one could be sure what would be the highest point of the crest and when that would arrive, the only way to do something about it would be to direct the waters to flow into the oceans as fast as they could—to deepen or widen the channels wherever possible, to open up or remove whatever obstacles might stand in their way.[107]

Shun liked the idea and passed it on to Gun. But before the former returned to the capital from his tour, the latter's reaction had already become widely known. Instead of answering the criticisms of his method, Gun expressed his opposition to Shun's being elevated to the position of co-emperor, alleging that Shun was unfit to serve in that capacity, having been only a commoner all his life and never having been a prince before. Shun's hand was forced. He could do nothing but report to Yao. As a result, Gun was banished to the Feather Mountain on the coast of the China Sea in present-day Haizhou, Jiangsu,[108] where he died three years later.[109] And Yu, the son, was named to take over his father's responsibilities.

· 6 ·

CONTROL OF THE FLOOD BY YU

Now Shun felt that he had the empire organized well enough both to prevent further disintegration of governmental authority and to provide a firmer foundation for more effectual flood control. The empire was realistically divided into twelve regions, and communications between them and the imperial seat, though necessarily still uncertain and hazardous under the circumstances, were more or less regularly maintained and kept open. In addition, besides the Four Mountains, Shun had sixteen overseers, all capable and trustworthy men, either residing in these regions or going from place to place, to superintend the doings of the diverse princes, to transmit to them the orders of the central government, and to help them in local flood-control projects as well as in the training and organization of the populace. And as these twelve regional governments, all safely based on mountainous highland, were each engaged in dredging their own local streams, the task for Yu was simplified. Thenceforth he could concentrate on dealing with the four principal rivers of the empire—the Yellow River, the Yangtze, the Huai, and the Ji [110]—and their larger tributaries. And from the reports of the overseers, Shun felt confident that whatever materials Yu might need for his projects, he would have the willing cooperation of all the princes; and whatever manpower Yu might require in any locality, he would have as much as a spontaneous self-disciplined populace could supply him with.

Moreover, Shun had a team organized to work with Yu, or under Yu. Two of its members were of special importance because their names were originally joined together to form the title of an independent document, *yiji*.[111] Yi was an expert on animals as well as on the use of fire.[112] His duty was to help Yu to clear up the dense growths in the hills and mountains, in the marshlands, and alongside the waters, and also to provide the workers and the people with as much meat as he could obtain. The second man, Ji, was one who should be by now familiar to the reader. For he was no other than Qi,[113] "the Abandoned One," Yao's half brother. This young man had schooled himself in agriculture, and was now recognized as a specialist on cereals and vegetables. So he was given the responsibility to teach the people to utilize whatever land they could get and to vegetate it with whatever was most suited to its soil.[114] And he seems from the very beginning to have performed so well that people no longer addressed him by his own name but simply by the title of his office, Ji, officer or minister of agriculture. Yu, of course, was entrusted with the overall command; and Shun could not have found a leader more conscientious or more energetic.

Yu received his appointment just after he had married at Tushan, in the north-central part of modern Anhui province.[115] Four days after the nuptials, he left his bride to take up his duties.[116] Thereafter he remained abroad for some thirteen years,[117] fastened to his task. In due time after his departure, a son was born to him, who was destined to become his heir and the founder of the Xia dynasty; but he never saw him as an infant. And during those thirteen years, although he had occasion to pass near his home three times, he was so much pressed with work that he did not cross his threshold even once.[118] He traversed the empire, back and forth, again and again. He ascended the mountains in order to determine the courses of the streams. He made markings alongside all the waters in order to show the varying levels of the rising or receding flood. He used carts for dry land, boats for waters, sledges for miry places, and spikes for mountains. Wherever no conveyances could be found, he just walked, a measuring rope in one hand, and a pair of compasses and a T square in the other.[119] He surveyed. He charted. He superintended. And finally, as he summed up himself, he was able "to open up passages for the streams throughout the nine regions and conduct them to the four seas." [120] But before he could do so, he had toiled so hard that his arms, calves, and shanks were all so parched that they turned hairless;[121] and his feet were maimed in such a way that they had to be dragged forth one after the other in a sort of shambling and leaping manner.[122] And down to this day the Chinese people, when they see someone walk with this kind of gait, call it the "Yu step."

In the *Book of History,* despite its having suffered so many losses, we still have a document called *yugong,* *"Yu's Levies."* Except for its extremely brief introductory remark [123] and its not much longer postscript eulogizing Yu's achievements, it could have been the very report submitted by the great flood controller himself to Shun after the completion of his Herculean labors. And traditionally, it has been regarded always as such by Chinese scholars, acknowledging that the introduction and postscript were probably added to it later by the official historian *(shi)* of the Xia dynasty founded by his son. It is also likely because of this that Confucius did not list Yu among the Five Premier Emperors *(wudi),* by which term he included only the Yellow Emperor, Zhuanxu, Di Ku, Di Yao, and Di Shun. For, as the Master explained, in the case of the Five Premier Emperors, he could only rely on what had been told about them; but in the case of *sanwang* (the founders of the Three Dynasties), he had their own works to rely upon.

According to this document, Yu began his labors at a place called Hukou, or "Pot's Mouth," a hill on the western borders of present-day Shanxi province. Even now, the Yellow River, as it passes the hill in its southward flow, still seethes like a boiling pot. And south of the Pot's Mouth we have another lofty canyon, Longmen, or "Dragon's Gate," where the great historian Sima Qian was to be born some two thousand years after Yu's time. At present, it is through these narrow passes that the Yellow River sweeps down impetuously to make a dividing line between Shanxi and Shaanxi provinces. We have no idea whether or not the same conditions obtained before the Great Flood. But, as mentioned before, Yao's seat of government was situated near the center of modern Shanxi. Surrounded with hills and mountains on almost all sides, it was perhaps the safest place in the empire during that time of unprecedented deluge. However, just when Yu received his appointment, the capital was threatened by a danger which had not been anticipated. Pot's Mouth and Dragon's Gate are close to its western borders. It may have been that the rapid rise of waters caused some incalculable movement of earth, and a spur of the mountain encroached upon the stream. And the Yellow River, unable to find a free course through these passes, began to overflow the adjacent areas. It was on account of this urgency that Yu had left his wedding bed so precipitately. So, in order to ward off the imminent threat to the imperial seat, he started his work at Pot's Mouth, even though this emergency undertaking involved a temporary departure from his own main plan for the control of the flood.

He cleared up whatever obstructed these passes so that the Yellow River could again flow freely downward. But to make the capital doubly safe, he had to perform additional preventive labors. He crossed the mighty stream and entered the neighboring country of the modern Shaanxi province. After having made sure that no more excessive volumes of water could issue forth

to give trouble from that direction, he returned and took similar precautionary measures regarding the streams and mountains in Shanxi, to the south of
the capital. Now he followed the main flow of the Yellow River and went
downstream, and finally he reached the extensive plains of the east, where he
could put his own theory of controlling the flood into execution.

To him, as we have already intimated before, the causes for the rising of
the waters might be many, but the main reason for their continually increasing to higher and higher levels and overflowing larger and larger land areas
was only one: They could not be emptied into the seas as fast as they
accumulated. So the only feasible remedy for the situation was to help the
waters empty themselves. Inasmuch as the Yellow River Valley formed the
most populous section of the empire, his most important problem was to
apply his theory to the vast body of water enclosed there. He not only dug
and deepened one main channel leading to the sea; he dug and deepened
altogether nine channels so that the country could be drained many times
faster than it had been before.[124]

This done, Yu turned southward and used the same plan to deal first with
the Ji and then with the Huai—the two large streams that then flowed between the Yellow River and the Yangtze. He dredged the main channels;
and where there were tributaries, he also dredged them. He made use of
lakes, swamps, and marshlands; he left many of them as they were even after
the inundation had subsided, so that they could remain to receive the overflow in case of another rise of the waters. Now he turned his attention to the
Yangtze. Fortunately for him, this vast valley at his time was not as populous
as the valleys in the north, and he found the scheme that had worked well for
the other rivers even more workable for this one. He fashioned three outlets
to lead the Yangtze to the ocean, and preserved several large lakes as emergency basins. Then he traced westward the sources of this mighty river, first
along one of its principal tributaries, the Han, that led him back to the
heartland of modern China proper, just below the then imperial seat, and
then returning again to the main stream of the Yangtze and going from there
upward to the present-day Sichuan. And from Sichuan he made his way far
up to the northwest, to the very site where the Sanmiao who had been
persuaded by Shun to move had migrated. And everywhere he went, he saw
to it that the streams were all confined in their proper channels.

All this, however, constituted but a part of his program—a major part, to
be sure, but still only a part. For he still had to ascertain as precisely as he
could what effects these works of his had produced and to think out what
further measures of improvement could be introduced and how these could
be carried out. Lacking modern conveniences such as airplanes and helicop-
ters, he planned the only thing humanly possible. He would ascend every
hill or mountain that came into his purview; and while offering sacrifices to

the spirits of these elevations, he would survey the adjacent countries from every vantage point. He would find out how much, if any, the flood had subsided; whether or not the streams were flowing properly; and if there were still some excessive volumes of water, in which direction and to what recipient basins these could be directed. And he did this survey systematically. He divided the mountains of the empire, which he knew so well, into three ranges, all aligning from the west toward the east: the north, the middle, and the south. All in all, these three ranges undulate over all of China proper except for the extreme southerly provinces. Yu went over them all, range by range, mountaintop by mountaintop. And it can be assumed that after each visit, he would either be satisfied with the results of his labors, or find still some more work to do. It was only in the end of his report that he stated with some satisfaction that "throughout the nine regions a similar order was effected:—the grounds along the waters were everywhere made habitable; the hills and mountains were cleared of their superfluous wood and sacrificed to; the sources of the streams were cleared; the marshes were well banked; and access to the capital was secured for all within the four seas."

Indeed, with the help of the team Shun had organized for him, Yu had achieved even more. And these achievements may now be divided into two categories. The first consists of works carried out in connection with flood control; and the second, of those with additional aims. Of the former, one has already been mentioned in Yu's own concluding passage as quoted above— the cleaning of the hills and mountains of their superfluous wood. Originally, with the rising of the flood, not only were the people continually driven to higher and higher ground, but so also were wild animals and water reptiles, which must have made human survival even more precarious. Thus, as was stated by Mencius, "Shun charged Yi with the use of fire, and Yi set to flame the excessive growths in the mountains as well as in the marshlands so that the birds and beasts fled away to hide themselves." [125] And since, as is noted before, Shun had also entrusted Yi with the duty of providing meat for the people and workers,[126] it may be safely presumed that before the birds and beasts were allowed to escape, a large porportion of them must have been captured or slaughtered for provision. Thus the clearing of the woods seems to be the very first step that must have been taken before any effective flood-control measures could be introduced; and Yi, by virtue of his office, became Yu's most constant companion during those thirteen years. As a result of this association, it is said that the two men had together produced a sort of log, or a record, of what they saw and encountered in their travels across the empire, which was called *Shan Hai Jing, Book on Mountains and Seas.* In our present time, there is a book bearing that title. But it seems doubtful that Yu, or Yi, or both, ever wrote such a log; and even if they did, that this present version, so replete with obscure and fanciful accounts, could have been the original. At any rate, Confucius made no reference to the book, nor did Sima Qian see fit to quote from it. But perhaps in writing a history of Yu and his accomplishments, it may not be too amiss to make a brief mention of it.

The second achievement in the first category was mostly the work of "the Abandoned One." Summing this up, Yu was recorded to have said, "While I deepened the channels and canals, and conducted them to the larger streams, Ji taught the multitude to sow grain and showed them how to procure food through toil (in the fields) in addition to flesh meat." [127] Since Ji's teachings involved sowing, culturing, and harvesting, which must be done in different seasons, his duties must have caused him to travel more or less independently of Yu, though under his general direction. This may be the reason why, after Yu had become emperor and the time came for him to name a successor, he preferred Yi to Ji; he knew him better.[128]

The third achievement was also mentioned by Yu himself: "The people were taught to exchange what they had for what they had not, and also to move their abode to more suitable places." [129] Notwithstanding the brevity of the language, one can easily imagine the enormous proportions of this undertaking. In order to bring such an immense program to a passably satisfactory conclusion, a very large organization was needed—larger than Yu's immediate engineering corps, larger even than the combined personnel of both his corps and the team Shun had organized for his assistance. The cooperation of all the princes, of all the surnames, of all the tribes and nations must be enlisted. And here we can see how helpful and how vital the services of Shun's sixteen overseers must have been, and also how the seeds Shun had earlier planted in the people about harmony and about organization must have been at last brought to happy fruition.

Presumably it was with the same unstinted assistance and cooperation from all sides that Yu was able also to achieve success in matters clearly beyond the objective and jurisdiction of flood control, and which Yu could have put into execution only under the express instructions of Shun. The first of these was a relatively uncomplicated task. In the document *Yu's Levies,* in reporting the progress of his work, Yu had followed the old system of dividing the empire into nine regions, instead of twelve as Shun had decreed. This seems to indicate that Shun had only adopted the twelve-region division as a temporary measure with the intention to revert to the original nine after the abatement of the inundation. And for this purpose, he had probably given, as Yu had certainly executed, the order that the boundaries of the nine regions be clearly defined by the mountains and seas that were already in existence as well as by the channels of streams which might be newly constructed through Yu's labors. We do not know for certain exactly when the nine-region system was restored; it might have happened either during Shun's own reign or shortly after his death. Nevertheless, speaking from the standpoint of history, we must be thankful to these two emperors for giving us for the first time a clear picture of how ancient China was administratively divided. (See Map II.)

The second task was much more complicated. As soon as a region was cleared of superfluous waters and its land became cultivable, a study of the soil of the fields and an estimate of their yield was made to form the basis of revenue collection. The standard rate for revenue was understood to be a tithe.[130] However, both the cultivable fields and the revenues were divided into three classes, and under each class there were three grades. Thus the value of the ground ranged from the first to the ninth degree, and the taxable amount of revenue ranged the same. On the surface, this scheme appears to be simple enough, for theoretically at least the taxable amount of revenue can be quite easily regulated according to the character of the ground. But the actual practice Yu and his associates had adopted was more complex and more flexible. They seemed to have also taken into consideration such factors as the density of population, the adequacy or inadequacy of irrigation, and, especially, how long and how much that particular region in question had been inundated. Take, for instance, the imperial seat. It was a large region, but it had apparently suffered the least from the flood. So although the character of its fields was rated only the average of the middle class, i.e., the fifth degree, its contribution of revenue was rated the first of the highest class, with some proportion of the second. Again, take the region where Yu had constructed nine channels to lead the Yellow River out to the sea, and which had obviously suffered the most from the flood, being receptacle for all downward-flowing waters for a very long time. It was ruled that while its fields should be graded as the lowest of the middle class, i.e., the sixth degree, its revenue should be the lowest of the lowest class. The reassessment of this region would come only after the land had been cultivated for thirteen years; and then, not until then, would its fields be reevaluated according to the same standards that had been applied to those of the other regions.

The above revenue was, of course, collected from agricultural settlers. We are inclined to think that the flood, and Yu's subsequent control of it, must have accelerated the expansion of this class of people. Whatever wild animals remained must have been driven, first by the inundation and then by Yi's flames, into higher mountains or denser forests, and were no longer so easily accessible as a meat supply. And as the waters kept on receding before they reached the final level of settlement, the fish supply was also likely to have become more elusive. Thus just as Ji was eager to teach, so there must have been a number of people as anxious to learn the new art of producing "food through toil" in the fields. But much as the imperial government wanted to encourage the development of agriculture, there was no ignoring

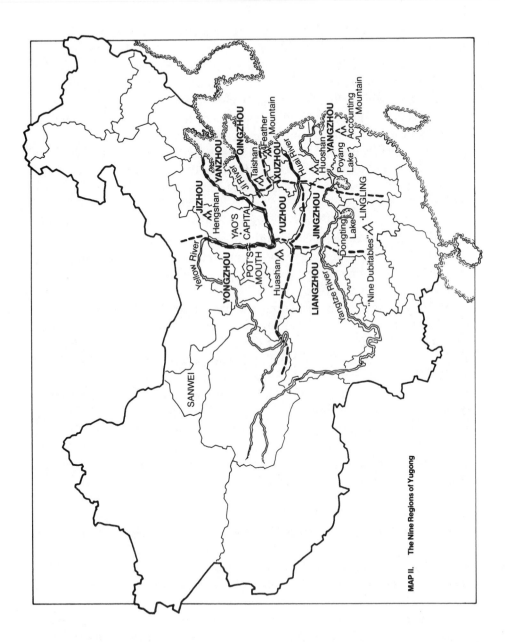

MAP II.   The Nine Regions of Yugong

the fact that there were still numerous people who were bound by the old tradition, or who lived in areas untouched by the flood and wanted to continue in their primitive nomadic way of life. Since the unification of the empire by the Yellow Emperor, these tribes or nations had been made to pay tributes of one kind or another to the imperial house. So now, as land revenue was to be collected from agricultural settlers, it was deemed also high time to clarify and redesignate the tributes that each of them was obligated to pay. And Yu in his report listed them all, some of which may be given here as examples, namely: furs from island tribes in the northeast (the present-day Manchuria); lacquer, silk, marine products, five-colored earth, sounding stones, and oyster pearls from the eastern regions; precious metals, grass garments, ivory, wood for bows, grindstones, and great tortoises from the southern regions; stones for arrowheads, skins of bears and foxes, iron, and jade from the western regions—each item being a famous product of its place of origin.

And in order to make the conveyance of these revenues and tributes as light a burden as possible, Yu also outlined in the report the various routes by which the people residing in each of the nine regions could bring them to the imperial capital, taking care to use water portage to the maximum with only a minimum of land transportation.

And finally we have the crowning achievement of all, which Yu described thus: "The fields were all classified, and all revenues were established with reference to the three characters of the soil. The Central Nation then conferred lands and surnames so that all professed a foremost love of virtue and would not act in any manner contradictory to imperial action." This is indeed an achievement of vision, and also of the utmost difficulty. Even the Yellow Emperor, in the heyday of his power as the first conqueror of China, could not have hoped to achieve such a state of things. As mentioned before, the Yellow Emperor awarded surnames to fourteen of his sons; but he did not confer on them lands. Since all led a more or less nomadic way of life, neither the father nor the sons would relish restrictions being imposed upon their freedom of movement. Nor did the Yellow Emperor confer surnames on other nations or tribes. For as long as the population was more nomadic than agricultural, even if he should choose to confer surnames on those tribes or nations, there would be no way to ensure their continued observance. As soon as the receivers of surnames moved out of his sight, they could abandon them or change them at will without his being the wiser. But meanwhile, so long as the majority of people were without surnames and without fixed or known domicile locations, the maintenance of peace and order in the empire must have been an all but impossible task, especially in view of the fact that nomadism encourages predatory habits. Thus through the reigns of Zhuanxu and Di Ku, even though these capable successors of the Yellow Emperor did their utmost to strengthen control over the myriad tribes and nations, at best their rule can be said to have been only limitedly effective, spotty and sporadic. Where the imperial power could be made to be physically felt, it was of course submitted to; but speaking in general, it must have been honored more by infraction than by obedience. Yao tried to reinforce the control by posting the so-called Four Mountains in the four directions of the empire. But the endeavor was soon aborted by the Great Flood. And as the inundation continued, it made such a havoc of imperial prestige and authority as to almost cause a total disintegration of the country. However, with Yao's installation of Shun as co-emperor, and with the introduction of those flood-control measures which Shun so dramatically popularized on his tours, hope was instilled anew in the entire population where there had been only despair, harmony where there had been only discord, and above all discipline where there had been only chaos. And what is more, Shun's central and concerted plan for subjugating the flood worked. Thus after the abatement of the inundation, the prestige of the Central Nation as represented by Yao, Shun, and Yu stood at its highest peak, never before reached by any government of man.

At such a juncture, Shun, after consulting with Yao and Yu and others, must have felt that it was an opportunity in their lifetime to realize the fondest dream they all had cherished. So he gave the order "to confer lands and surnames," and Yu carried it out. And all the houses, tribes, and nations, nomads and husbandmen alike, one and all, willingly submitted, pledging that they each would stay within their allotments and not go outside those confines "contrary to imperial action." It may be said, therefore, that this is the time that a sort of overall framework for the ancient Chinese feudal system was first laid out, with the lands so conferred becoming fiefs, the heads of the people with the same surnames becoming enfeoffed princes, and the emperor becoming the acknowledged and undisputed sovereign. But, more important, this must be said to be the very first time that China achieved an effective united government for all the population within its vast domain, that is, within the then known world. And, incidentally, it is also from this time, more especially from the document *yugong,* that the Chinese people have derived the name for their country—*zhongguo,* "Central Nation." [131]

· 7 ·

THE GOVERNMENT OF SHUN

At the fourteenth year after Yao had elevated Shun to the position of co-emperor, the former was able to see the successful control of the flood and the complete vindication of his choice. And Yao lived some more years to enjoy watching the empire flourish in unprecedented peace and prosperity made possible by the harmonious and benevolent rule of Shun as well as by a further expansion of agricultural development hitherto thought not possible. He was perhaps both delighted and amused at a song which seems to have obtained some currency among the people:

> At sunrise I rise to work,
> At sunset I return to rest.
> I drink from the well I dug,
> I eat from the yield of the field I tilled,
> The power of the Emperor—
> What has that got to do with me? [132]

But at his passing, "All the people mourned for him as for a parent. And for three years the eight instruments of music were spontaneously stopped and hushed." [133]

At the end of the three years' mourning, Shun left the capital and withdrew to a retreat "south of the South River in order to yield the imperial seat to Yao's son Zhu" [134] so that the people might have a choice as to who should succeed the deceased sovereign. If they preferred Zhu, Shun would be happy to abide by their wishes. But "the princes under heaven, repairing to the court to renew their allegiance, did not go to the son of Yao, but to Shun. The people who had disputes to settle did not go to the son of Yao, but to Shun. And the minstrels and songsters did not sing of the son of Yao, but of Shun. . . . It was after these things that Shun went back to the Central Nation and occupied the seat of the Son of Heaven."

However, for reasons not clear to us, or perhaps just to signify a change of authority, Shun established his own capital some two hundred kilometers southwest of Yao's former seat.[135] And there Shun was to reign many years,[136] which, along with the last years of Yao's reign, perhaps constituted a period of idyllic tranquillity and happiness for the entire people of China that was to stir such admiration in Confucius some seventeen hundred years later.

And certainly Shun did much to contribute to the splendor of that idyllic picture. To begin with, he reorganized the administration of the empire, giving us a structure which for the first time bears a clear resemblance to our own modern ideas of government. He divided his court into departments, and selected the best personnel to head them. He created a new office that was to have the overall supervision of all "the hundred affairs"—a precursor to the latter-day office of prime minister. And for that post he named Yu. Next came the department of agriculture, and naturally he chose "the Abandoned One" to be its minister. Next he had an office which appears to combine the functions of two modern departments—interior and education; and which may be translated as the department of commonalty. For, as Shun indicated, the duties of this minister were to harmonize the people and to instruct them in the proper conduct to be pursued with regard to the five relationships among men—relationships between sovereign and subject, between parents and children, between husband and wife, between brother and brother, and between friend and friend. In other words, this office was given the responsibility for the organizing and training of the populace so that they would all be oriented toward the social objectives Shun had in mind: harmony and propriety. And for this important task Shun appointed Xie, Di Ku's son by his second wife, half brother to both Yao and "the Abandoned One," who had shown special capacity for that line of work during the flood as one of the sixteen overseers.[137]

The fourth department was justice. In those early days there appeared no fine distinction between the functions of the prosecutor and the judge, or between those of the police and the jailer. These seem to have all been the charge of that single office. In addition, it was laden with the responsibility of seeing to it that nomads did not make encroachments or incursions on agricultural settlers. The latter were protected only by their respective princes, whose authority was restricted to the limits of their allocated territories; and as it was common for the roving raiders, after having inflicted injuries on their victims, to flee to other princedoms, so it was incumbent on the imperial minister of justice to track them down and bring them to retribution. For this post Shun appointed one Gaoyao, who was famed for his own merits. In the *Book of History,* we still have a document called *gaoyaomo,* or the *Counsels of Gaoyao,* which purports to be a record of sagacious advice he had given to Shun and Yu. Later, it was Yu's intention, after he himself had succeeded Shun as emperor, to pass on the throne eventually to Gaoyao; but unfortunately Gaoyao died before the end of Yu's reign.

There was also a department of works in charge of craftsmen who worked on earth, stone, metal, leather, etc. An artificer renowned for his inventive genius was named to take the post.[138] Then there was the department of animal husbandry; the selection of the minister naturally fell on Yi, the fire expert and meat supplier, and Yu's constant companion in his travels in subjugating the flood. Now we come to the department of the sacrifices and ceremonies, which was understandably of great importance in these ancient times. Regarding the appointment of these ministers so far, only in the case of the prime minister were the Four Mountains consulted first; all the rest were Shun's own choices. However, in the case of the minister of sacrifices and ceremonies, since the post involved the matter of worship of deities and veneration of ancestors, with which all houses, tribes, and nations were concerned, Shun specially asked for the opinion of the Four Mountains. As a result, he appointed a man whom they recommended and who apparently enjoyed the spiritual confidence of all.[139]

Then there was a department whose functions need some explanation.

Here we recite the *Canon of Yao* verbatim and give it as literal a translation as possible.:

> The emperor said, "Kui, I appoint you to be minister of music to teach the heirs apparent to be straightforward and yet mild, gentle and yet dignified, strong and yet not oppressive, ingenuous and yet not arrogant. As men's wishes may be expressed through words, and words may be made to endure by putting them into songs, so let notes be attached to whatever may endure, and let these be harmonized into melodies. (In this way) the eight different kinds of musical instruments can all be coordinated so that no one shall take from, or interfere with, another. Thus both spirits and men will be brought together in harmony."
>
> Kui replied, "Yes, Sire. Even when I used stones (as instruments) to beat upon, the hundred wild beasts had danced in unison."

This passage has often puzzled scholars in the past. But to this historian, the meaning appears to be this: Shun was thinking about the future of the empire. He had succeeded in uniting it under the guiding principle of harmony, thanks to the pressure of the Great Flood. But could this harmony last? He recollected that he had employed the five ceremonies to inculcate the people with the sense of propriety which is so necessary to any kind of human organization. Could he now use music to teach people harmony? The future of the empire, no doubt, depended upon the leadership of the next generation; and surely none could represent that leadership more appositely than the heirs apparent of the princes who were then in power. So he created this new department and chose the most versatile musician of his day to head it in order to give instructions to the future leaders of the empire. But lest his own purpose should not be clearly understood, he carefully worded his directive, laying repeated emphasis on the idea of harmony. And the minister understood Shun's intentions well. Hence he gave the emperor a quick and unequivocal assurance: He himself in his own experience had been able to impress even wild beasts with a sense of harmony; he would certainly do his best with these heirs apparent.

Only one last office remains. Today we would call it "chief secretary" or "chief assistant." Its duty was "to give forth the emperor's orders and report back to him day and night truthfully and accurately." Thus all in all there were nine departments. Although one or two of these may be said to have been colored by antiquity, the structure as a whole bears a surprisingly modern complexion.

So much for the internal reorganization of the imperial court. Externally the administrations of the numerous princedoms or tribes needed supervision. This, of course, could be best done by having men representing the central authority on the spot. Shun's system clearly follows this line of thinking. To begin with, he retained the Four Mountains. This was, as we know, an old institution; and the men who held these offices were all senior or prestigious statesmen whose counsels Shun had always sought on important matters. But even while the flood was raging on, Shun knew that the multitudinous duties were much more than the four men alone could shoulder, and he had sixteen overseers installed to help them. And inasmuch as he had redivided the empire into twelve regions, perhaps even before the abatement of the flood, out of the sixteen he had appointed twelve to be Regional Pastors, each residing in a designated region. Thus the responsibilities which had been concentrated in four men were now distributed among twelve, with the original Four Mountains still serving possibly on a higher level of supervision. This system was continued for some time after Shun's accession to the throne at Yao's death. But as we know, the twelve regions were soon to be reduced again to nine, either by Shun himself or by Yu. It seems likely that he was experimenting with the system and watching its actual practice in order to arrive at a final decision.

And in this experiment he was probably helped by another administrative device which he initiated. Previously we have mentioned the tours of inspection which he used to take every five years in order to check up on the divers local administrations. We have also noted that the princes were required to appear at court by turns and submit their reports so that their words could be examined against their deeds. Now Shun added to these a new regulation: "Every three years there was an examination of merits; and after these examinations the undeserving were degraded, and the deserving promoted." How the deserving were promoted, we have no definite idea. The canon only states that they "received chariots and robes." And during the later part of his reign, it was also recorded that Shun himself had specifically designed formal robes with many colors, each suited to a different rank of prince or a different grade of officer to wear. As to the degrading of the undeserving, there was a suggestion that the insignia which was the token of authority received by a prince from the emperor was employed as a means to show the sovereign's disapprobation. When a prince deserved to be degraded after the first examination, the insignia would be taken away from him and placed in the temporary custody of the imperial court. If he showed improvement on the next examination held three years later, the insignia would be returned to him. But if he continued to be undeserving, not only would the insignia not be returned, but he would be demoted. In the event that he still made no effort to better himself, then three years after the third examination, his fief would be substantially reduced.[140] There is no way to ascertain whether this practice was actually carried out, but the spirit of the scheme certainly appears to be in harmony with Shun's general philosophy. He always preferred to prod the wrongdoer to transform himself through persuasion, admonition, or warning rather than by inflicting actual punishment on him.

Indeed, Shun seemed to be so conversant with the modern ideas of division of labor and delegation of authority that the entire empire was well governed without his appearing to make any effort.[141] The continuity of his long reign gave the people unprecedented happiness. And pursuant to his own ideals of harmony, and probably with the help of his minister of music, he himself composed a piece of music and set it to dancing, which he called *shao,* or the *Harmonizer.*[142] Unfortunately, this is now lost. But in the time of Confucius it still existed. When Confucius heard it for the first time in the princedom of Qi (the present-day north Shandong), he was so struck with it that "for three months he did not know the taste of flesh. He said, 'I never thought that music could have been made so sublime as that!' "[143]

Shun had a son. We do not know much about this offspring; all the sources contented themselves with saying that he was "not like" his father, the same as Yao's son Zhu was not like Yao.[144] At any rate, it was apparent that Shun had never harbored any desire to leave the throne to his son. Toward the end of his reign,[145] he named Yu co-emperor, and caused the latter to go through all the ceremonies which he himself had gone through under Yao. And thereafter he left practically all government in the hands of Yu, just as Yao had done with him before.

A few years later, however, a sultry cloud rose from the south and darkened the halcyon skies of Shun's dominion. The remnants of the Sanmiao tribes, who had elected to stay in their native land instead of migrating to the northwest, had, for the duration of the flood, cooperated quite submissively with Shun's government as well as with Yu's engineering labors. But after the abatement of the inundation, they had prospered and grown more numerous along with the rest of the empire. And with the increase of their numbers they reverted to a degree to their former intransigence. Even while Yu was still serving as prime minister, he had reminded Shun of this jarring note.[146] But Shun had counseled patience.[147] Now, as Yu began to apply a more vigorous policy after becoming co-emperor, the Sanmiao's resistance became more obstinate; and at Yu's insistence, Shun finally agreed to the use of force. Thereupon Yu himself led an expedition against the Sanmiao in their own territory. For thirty days he fought hard, but to no avail. At last, listening to the remonstrances of Yi, who had accompanied him in this campaign, Yu returned and reported to Shun acknowledging that the emperor's policy was the better. Shun was pleased. And what with the renewal of his old gentle practices, the prestige of his proven harmonious intentions, and the possibility of Yu's resorting to force anew, if necessary, some seventy days after Yu's withdrawal the Sanmiao themselves declared their final submission.[148]

It was after this that despite his exceedingly advanced years Shun took one more tour to the south—not so much an official tour of inspection as a personal tour of goodwill. He penetrated deep into the Sanmiao country, farther south than Hengshan, the generally recognized Southern Mountain of the empire, where on his first accession to authority he would have liked to have met with the princes of the southern regions, had not the hostility of the Sanmiao tribes at that time forced him to change his plans. It must have been a source of profound satisfaction to him that the Sanmiao were finally united with the Central Nation and he could freely preach to them his doctrine of harmony and propriety. But as he reached the very southerly limits of the Sanmiao territory, a range of mountains called Jiuyi, or the Nine Dubitables, the infirmities of old age at last caught up with him. He died and was buried there.[149]

NOTES

1. *Historical Records, taishigong zixu.*

2. See above, pp. 36–37.

3. *Historical Records, qinshihuangdi benji.* Some editions have *renhuang* (Human Emperor) instead of *taihuang* (Primal Emperor). On close examination of the context, the latter seems preferable. It may also be of interest to note that the First Emperor decided to combine the *huang* of *sanhuang* with the *di* of *wudi* to form the title *huangdi* for himself. Since then, Chinese emperors have always used that title.

4. Examples of such works are those by Huangfu Mi, Sima Zhen, and Zheng Qiao.

5. Such names can be found in *Guanzi, Zhuangzi, Liezi, Lushi Chunqiu, Huainanzi,* etc.

6. See above, p. 4. We really do not know if Nuwa is a she, though *nu* means "woman" or "lady."

7. *Hanfeizi, wudu.*

8. *Book of Changes, xici,* II, chap. 2.

9. *Historical Records, taishigong zixu.*

10. Ban Gu, *Qian Han Shu, yiwenzhi.*

11. Kong Anguo, *Shangshuxu.*

12. *Book of Changes, xici,* I, chap. 20.

13. This is according to the chronology of Dong Zuobin, *Zhongguo Nianli Jianpu.*

14. *Book of History, guming.* Some scholars, however, maintain that the River Scheme displayed is but a scheme of the Eight Trigrams.

15. *Huainanzi, xiuwu xun.*

16. *Book of Changes, xici,* II, chap. 2.

17. Ibid.

18. *Lushi Chunqiu, lisulan,* 4, *yongmin.* Of Shusha, however, we know nothing.

19. Ibid., *shenfenlan,* 6, *shenshi.*

20. See above, p. 38.

21. Obviously a man of some repute, of whom, however, we know nothing.

22. Traditionally, the Yellow Emperor is said to have actually reigned a hundred years. See *Bamboo Chronicles* and Huangfu Mi, *Diwang Shiji.* But neither of these two books is too reliable, and Confucius's meaning here is by no means definitive.

23. The Three Dynasties are Xia, Shang (or Yin), and Zhou. In the discourse Confucius mentioned the founders of the Three Dynasties as *sanwang.*

24. Zai Wo was also known as Zai Yu. *Wo* and *yu* both mean "I" or "me." So they seem to have been interchangeable.

25. See above, p. 54. This estimate is based on a calculation of seventeen generations.

26. See Xu Shen's preface to his own dictionary; also see above, p. 26.

27. The original course of the lower stream of the Yellow River is much more northerly than the present one. It joined the sea close by the present-day port of Tientsin. Some studies, however, have alleged that the house of Shennong had thrived originally in the west of China proper. See Fan Wenlan, *Zhongguo Tongshi,* I, p. 16, and Guo Moruo, *Zhongguo Shigao,* I, p. 108.

28. *Dadai Liji*, chap. 75, *yongbing*. Confucius is quoted as describing Ciyou as "a man from among the common people, greedy for power."

29. Ibid. Also see *Guanzi, dishu*.

30. He was prince of Shaodian, present-day Xinzheng.

31. The plains were called Banquan.

32. The place was called Zhuolu. Now Zhoulu is the name of a city in Nei Mongol Zizhiqu.

33. The Chinese character *huang* here is different from the *huang* of *sanhuang*. It means "yellow."

34. See commentaries on *Historical Records* by Sima Zhen, a scholar in the 7th century A.D.

35. The quotation following is a condensed version.

36. In modern Gansu.

37. The Bear Mountain is in Henan, and the Xiang in Hunan.

38. The Hunzhou were nomadic tribes based in present-day Mongolia.

39. In Nei Mongol Zizhiqu.

40. The *Historical Records* mentions Fenghou ("Wind Prince"), Limu ("Mighty Shepherd"), Changxian ("Always Before"), and Dahong ("Great Swan"). *Liezi, huangdi* (on the Yellow Emperor) mentions also Tianlao ("Heaven Old") and Taishanji ("Lingering at Taishan"). Together with Danao, the reputed inventor of the *ganzhi* system, these are probably the Seven Sages of the Yellow Emperor referred to in *Zhuangzi, xuwugui*.

41. As can be seen from Zai Wo's question to Confucius, even at that early date there appeared already to be a distinct popular tendency to immortalize the Yellow Emperor. Confucius's attitude to the contrary notwithstanding, this tendency continued. By the time of the Warring States, as can be gathered from *Zhuangzi* and *Liezi*, the Yellow Emperor, if he was not already regarded as an immortal, was portrayed as one deeply steeped in the study of the secrets of immortality. Then by the 1st century B.C. the popular legend became complete. The Yellow Emperor was said not to have died. What was buried in the Bridge Mountain was only his cap and garments. After he had completed a certain process necessary for immortalization, a dragon had descended from heaven and had borne him aloft.

42. See Liu Xiang, *Lienuzhuan*.

43. *Sunzi*, chap. 5, commentaries by Du Mu.

44. Zai Wo never bothered to ask about Shaohao, and so Confucius made no comments on him as emperor. This example was followed by the *Historical Records*.

45. *Zuozhuan*, Duke Zhao, 17th year.

46. The Chinese character for "opening" here is *qi*, and that for "closing" is *bi*. They were often used in ancient times with reference to opening and closing doors. So these may well imply that the two Birds were in charge of sunrises and sunsets. However, Du Yu, a 3rd century A.D. statesman-scholar, who is famed for his annotations and commentaries on *Zuozhuan*, thinks that "opening" means to establish when spring and summer begin, and "closing" when autumn and winter begin.

47. *Guo Yu, chuyu*; also see above, p. 13.

48. The character *jiu* means "nine," so *jiuli* may also be translated as "nine tribes of Li."

49. All underlined names are those of the Yellow Emperor's imperial successors, and the dates are the dates of their reigns traditionally assigned to them. It will be noticed that there are two three-year interregnums, one between Yao and Shun, and the other between Shun and Yu. These are supposed to be years of mourning devoted to the two deceased emperors.

50. Ban Gu in his *Qian Han Shu, lulizhi*, alleges that there were five generations between Zhuanxu and Gun.

51. *Guo Yu, chuyu*; also see above, p. 13.

52. See *Historical Records, taishigong zixu* and *lishu*. Probably because in the colder climes of the north the use of fire was more in demand and also more in need of regulation, the Northern Rectifier was also called Fire Rectifier.

53. Ban Gu, *Qian Han Shu, yiwenzhi*.

54. Zheng Qiao, *Tongzhi, wudiji*.

55. This is the *taichu* calendar issued by the Martial Emperor of Han.

56. *Virtues of the Five Premier Emperors (wudide)*.

57. *Genealogy of the Premier Emperors (dixixing)*.

58. *Shangshu Dazhuan*. Sixteen is according to the Chinese method of counting age; according to the Western method, it would be fifteen.

59. See above, p. 25.

60. There are three important names in this history, all of which, according to modern pronunciation, should be transcribed as Qi, though each is represented by a different Chinese character. In order to avoid confusion, we transcribe only the name of the primal ancestor of the house of Zhou as Qi. In the case of the primal ancestor of the house of Shang, we use the ancient pronunciation of his name—Xie. The third Qi is the founder of the Xia dynasty and son of Yu, the flood controller. He has another name, though little known—Kai. So we shall in the following chapter transcribe his name as Qi(Kai).

61. See Chap. IV, Sec. 4.

62. The *Bamboo Chronicles* has it that Di Zhi was dethroned after having reigned nine years. Of course, his death could have occurred about the same time as his dethronement.

63. This is so translated by James Legge in *The Chinese Classics*.

64. Many Chinese scholars, notably Duan Yucai, thought that the canon was written by the *shi* of the Xia dynasty.

65. In the once popular but now antiquated version of the *Book of History*, *yaodian* was the first document and *shundian* the second. But in the opinion of many scholars, these were just two parts of the original one document, *yaodian* (the *Canon of Yao*). Duan Yucai, 1734–1815, was the first man to put them back together again in his *Guwen Shangshu Zhuanyi*. Then Sun Xinyan, 1752–1818, did the same in his *Shangshu Jinguwen Zhushu*. Their example is now followed by most modern editions; one instance is Qu Wanli, *Shangshu Shiyi*.

In this book, in referring to the first-batch documents of the *Book of History*, Duan Yucai's text is strictly followed.

66. Ban Gu in *Baihu Tongyi* defines the nine branches of blood relations as follows: (1) those who bear the paternal surname, (2) males born of one's father's married sisters, (3) males born of one's own married sisters, (4) males born of one's married daughters, (5) one's mother's parents, (6) one's mother's brothers and sisters, (7) males born of one's mother's brothers and sisters, (8) one's wife's family, and (9) one's wife's mother's family before marriage.

67. James Legge, *The Chinese Classics*, III, *The Shoo King*, p. 19. The reader will note that Medhurst spelled Yao's name "Yaou" and that there is also a slight disparity between his chronology and what has been given here, a difference of four years.

68. For details of Dr. Yee's analysis, see Appendix, note 29.

69. *Bamboo Chronicles*, 45th year of Di Ku: "The emperor issued to the Prince of Tang his order of investiture."

70. Tang is also known as Tao Tang. Now the Chinese character *tao* usually signifies "pottery." Could this mean that Tang was known for its pottery? Lacking other substantiation, we venture no conjecture here. See *Zuozhuan*, Duke Xiang, 29th year, and Duke Ai, 6th year.

71. See *Bamboo Chronicles*. Some authorities place Chong at the vicinity of modern Huxian of Shaanxi, southwest of Xian.

72. According to the *Canon of Yao*, the man who recommended Zhu was one Fangqi.

73. According to the canon, the nominee was Gonggong, and the man who nominated him was Huandou.

74. *Historical Records, wudi benji*. Also see genealogical chart, above, p. 61.

75. See Xu Shen's dictionary.

76. See *Book of History, yaodian (Canon of Yao)*, commentaries by Kong Anguo.

77. *Historical Records, wudi benji*; also, *Shangshu Dazhuan*. Shun is said to have farmed in Lishan, fished in Leize, engaged in pottery by the side of the river, made utensils and implements in Shouqiu, and dealt in trade at Fuxia.

78. *Mencius, gongsunchou*, I.

79. *Huainanzi, yuandao xun*; also, *Hanfeizi*, vol. XV, chap. 36, *nanyi*. For instance, it is said that as Shun learned to make pottery, he discovered new ways of making it less susceptible to disfiguration; and soon all the potters turned around to learn from him.

80. *Historical Records, wudi benji*. This is a literal translation. Perhaps the ancients' understanding of the sizes of village, hamlet, and town is different from ours.

81. *Kongzi Jiayu, liuben*.

82. *Historical Records, wudi benji*.

83. Yu was later designated as Shun's fief. Hence Shun was known as Yu Shun, or Shun of Yu.

84. The two daughters' names are E'huang and Nuying. See Liu Xiang, *Lienuzhuan*.

85. *Mencius, wanzhang*, I. Much of this passage is literal translation.

86. It seems that there may have been a custom at that time that after the death of an older brother, his younger brother inherited everything, including the deceased's wife or wives. This custom continued to be observed by some Mongolian tribes in later centuries, but not in China.

87. At the time Yao offered the throne to the Four Mountains, according to the canon, Yao said expressly, "I have reigned seventy years." Yao was known to have ascended the throne at the age of sixteen. So he was then already eighty-six. Add to this the three years he had put Shun through the tests, and we have eighty-nine. But as we are not too sure of ancient chronology, we must make the dates as well as the age of people less definite than we should like to.

88. See also *Mencius, wanzhang*, I.

89. See above, p. 7.

90. The five grades were known in the Zhou dynasty as *gong, hou, bo, zi*, and *nan*, which are translated by some as duke, marquis, count, viscount, and baron.

91. See *Zhou Li, chunguanzongbo*, I: *dianrui*.

92. *Taizong* means "Tai the Elder," or "Tai the Venerable."

93. See above, pp. 9–10.

94. It is interesting to note that this custom of offering silk from inferior to superior was still preserved in Tibet until the Communist occupation of 1951.

95. The Chinese character for "goose" here is *yan*, which is usually translated as "wild goose"; and that for "fowl" is *zhi*, which is usually translated as "pheasant." It seems therefore that in those days both wild geese and pheasants abounded, and the latter even more than the former.

96. In regular ceremonies held in later dynasties, after the princes presented their insignia to the sovereign, these were as a rule returned after their formal verification. It is presumed that Shun did the same with all the offerings at this time so that they could be used again for practice in the other ceremonies that followed. See Kong Anguo's commentaries on this point in the *Canon of Yao (Yaodian)*.

97. In this first inspection tour of Shun, the four mountains which he visited are Taishan in the east, Huoshan in the south (Anhui province), Huashan in the west (Shaanxi province), Hengshan in the north (Shanxi province). See *Shangshu Dazhuan*. The reader will note that the Southern Mountain is not the one in the modern Hunan province, for that region was at that time inhabited by the intransigent Sanmiao tribes.

98. See *Zuozhuan*, Duke Wen, 18th year. Except for this one measure, all the other measures taken by Shun were described in the canon itself. It should also be of interest to note that for those overseeing positions he chose only descendants from Zhuanxu and from Di Ku; and that, in equal numbers.

99. The Chinese character used here is *jin*, which, according to modern usage, means "gold" or "money." In those days, it may have been copper or whatever was used as currency.

100. *Book of History, luxing*.

101. See *Shangshu Dazhuan*; also, Ban Gu, *Baihu Tongyi, wuxing*, and *Qian Han Shu, wudiji, yuanguang*, 1st year.

102. The two were Gonggong and Huandou. See above, note 73. Perhaps it is because of that incident that they were resentful of Shun.

103. See *Zhangguoche*, Wu Qi's response to Wei Wuhou.

104. The Chinese character *heng* for this Hengshan is different from the *heng* of the Hengshan in Shanxi (note 97).

105. The exact wording in the canon is *tianxia xianfu* ("all under heaven willingly obeyed").

106. *Lushi Chunqiu, shenfen lan, junshou*; *Huainanzi, yuandao xun*. Incidentally, some Chinese believe it was Gun's idea that started the practice of building walls around cities.

107. *Mencius, tengwengong*, II.

108. See *Hanfeizi, waichu shuo*, 34; and *Lushi Chunqiu, shijun lan, xinglun*. Also see *Chu Ci, lisao*, by Qu Yuan.

109. *Chu Ci, tianwen.* There is a widespread but erroneous belief that Gun was executed at the Feather Mountain. This is due to some modern scholars' failure to understand the correct ancient meaning of the Chinese character *ji.* See Duan Yucai, *Guwen Shangshu Zhuanyi.*

110. In Yu's time, all these four rivers flowed independently to the ocean. But now the Ji is lost because of its having been absorbed by the Yellow River.

111. This document is lost. However, in the antiquated version of the *Book of History,* there is still a document titled *yiji.* But its text was bodily taken out of the document *gaoyaomo.* In Duan Yucai's version, which this book follows, there is only the document *gaoyaomo,* no *yiji.*

112. *Book of History, gaoyaomo.* Also see *Mencius, tengwengong,* I.

113. Genealogical chart, p. 64, and also note 60.

114. *Book of History, gaoyaomo.*

115. See Du Yu's comments on Tushan in *Zuozhuan,* Duke Ai, 7th year.

116. *Book of History, gaoyaomo.*

117. *Historical Records, xia benji.* For a different estimate of time, see *Mencius, tengwengong,* I.

118. *Mencius, tengwengong,* I.

119. *Historical Records, xia benji.*

120. *Book of History, gaoyaomo.*

121. *Zhuangzi, tianxia.*

122. *Xunzi, feixiang.*

123. The reader must separate this introductory remark from the introductory note attributed to Confucius. This remark is incorporated in the document as part of its text.

124. Unfortunately the traces of these channels disappeared after the Yellow River shifted its course, for the first time but not the last time, in 601 B.C., some sixteen centuries after the time of Yu.

125. *Mencius, tengwengong,* I.

126. *Book of History, gaoyaomo.* See also above, p. 87.

127. Ibid.

128. Another possible reason may be that Ji was considerably younger than Yi.

129. *Book of History, gaoyaomo.*

130. *Mencius, tengwengong,* I.

131. Actually the document in the *Book of History* used the term *zhongbang.* But the *Historical Records,* while incorporating most of this document, word for word, in *xia benji,* changed *zhongbang* into *zhongguo.* This is likely because the founder of the Han dynasty, of which Sima Qian was subject, was named Liu Bang, and the Chinese way of paying respect to a sovereign is not to use his name wherever avoidable. The two characters *bang* and *guo* both mean the same—"nation" or "country." So Sima Qian substituted *guo* for *bang.*

132. Huangfu Mi, *Diwang Shiji.*

133. Literal translation from a passage in *Book of History, yaodian (Canon of Yao).*

134. This quotation and the one immediately following in the same paragraph are from *Mencius, wangzhang,* I.

135. Yao's capital was Pingyang, in the present-day Linfen district, Shanxi. Shun's capital was Puban, in the present-day Yongji district, Shanxi. Perhaps because Puban was located at the bend of the Yellow River, where the stream turns eastward, Shun thought that it could facilitate communication with the divers regions of the empire.

136. Thirty-nine years according to *Historical Records, wudi benji.*

137. Ibid., commentaries by Sima Zhen.

138. His name was Chui. A bamboo arrow fashioned by Chui was considered an imperial treasure as late as the Zhou dynasty. See *Book of History, guming.*

139. The minister's name was Baiyi.

140. *Shangshu Dazhuan.*

141. *Confucian Analects, weilinggong.* "The Master said, 'To have governed well without seeming to do anything—may not this be said of Shun? What did he do? He did nothing but reverently and humbly occupy his imperial seat.' "

142. This definition of the character *shao* is given in *Gujinyunhui.*

143. *Confucian Analects, shu'er.*

144. We know, however, that the name of Shun's son was Shangjun.

145. According to *Historical Records, wudi benji,* it was the thirty-third year of Shun's reign.

146. *Book of History, gaoyaomo.*

147. See *Hanfeizi, wudu;* and Liu Xiang, *Shuoyuan,* chap. 1.

148. *Book of History, dayumo* (second-batch document). Also see *Mozi, jianai.*

149. *Historical Records, wudi benji:* "In the thirty-ninth year after he ascended the throne, Shun took a tour of inspection to the south. He died in the wilds of Cangwu. He was buried at Jiuyi. This is now called Lingling." The names of Jiuyi and Lingling are still used for the same places today.

The age of Shun when he died, however, is not a settled matter. The canon records: "In the thirtieth year of his life, Shun was called to government. Thirty years he was on the throne (with Yo). Fifty years he went on high in a tour and died." The confusion arises from "fifty years." If "fifty years" include the "thirty years" before, then Shun died at eighty. But if "fifty years" came after the "thirty years," then Shun's age would have been a hundred and ten.

Sima Qian wrote in the *Historical Records, wudi benji:* "At the age of twenty, Shun was known for his filial piety. At thirty, he was chosen by Yao. At fifty, he served as acting emperor (that is, he acted and decreed in his own name, no longer in Yao's name as he had done as co-emperor before). At fifty-eight, Yao died. At sixty-one (after three years' mourning), he acceded to the throne as Yao's successor. In the thirty-ninth year . . . he died . . . [see the first paragraph of this note]." This would have made Shun's age exactly a hundred.

CHAPTER III

THE XIA DYNASTY

(23rd–18th Century B.C.*)*

· 1 ·

THE XIA PEOPLE

At Shun's death, all the people mourned for him three years, the same as they had mourned for Yao before. At the end of the period of mourning, Yu withdrew to his fief [1] in order to yield the imperial seat to Shun's son. "But the people of the world followed him, just as after the death of Yao, instead of following Yao's son, they had followed Shun."[2] So Yu ascended the throne; and, for reasons again not clear to us, he moved his capital to a new site, some eighty kilometers to the east of Shun's former seat.[3]

While still in the service of Yao and Shun, Yu was enfeoffed as Prince of Xia. So as emperor, like Tang Yao and Yu Shun before him, the place name was appended to his name, and he was known as Xia Yu. And it is also from Xia that the Chinese, as a people, first acquired a name for themselves—the Xia people. Prior to this time, there is no record indicating that the Chinese had called themselves by any particular appellation. Indeed, as they appear to have laid so much emphasis upon their houses, or clans, it is the surnames of these that have come down to us clearly and traceably. But speaking from the enthnological point of view, there should have been an overall nomenclature for all the houses that were apparently of one racial origin. But this is simply and conspicuously lacking.

However, once the name Xia came into use, it was adopted by all who considered themselves belonging to it. Its usage continued even after the termination of the Xia dynasty, through the Shang and Zhou dynasties, until the time of the First Emperor of Qin (246–210 B.C.), when the nomadic tribes of Mongolia, awed by his conquest and power, began to call the Chinese the Qin people.[4] And it is from the word Qin (pronounced like "chin") that the name China is derived for the West. But as to the Chinese themselves, they have always had little respect for the First Emperor. And when Qin was displaced shortly afterward by the Han dynasty, which is in many ways one of the most glorious dynasties in Chinese history, the Chinese gladly began calling themselves the Han people. And this has remained so to the present day.[5]

But what is the meaning of the word "Xia"? Xu Shen's dictionary defines it simply as "people of the Central Nation." Now, when Yu first used the term "Central Nation" in the document *Yugong, Yu's Levies,* he meant only the central authority, or, at most, the people residing inside the imperial domain, which was then confined to a small portion of the modern Shanxi province. By the time of Xu Shen (2nd century A.D.), however, the term "Central Nation" had already come to mean the whole of China, forty or fifty times larger in area than what Yu had in mind. So Xu Shen's definition is after the fact, and gives no indication whatever about the original meaning of the word. Now, however, if we look up the word in a modern Chinese dictionary, we usually find this notation: "Xia's meaning in the ancient times is great. The Central Nation is possessed of greatness in culture, in glory, and in standards of propriety and justice." [6] Even if we had not known that this notation is based on a comment made in the 7th century A.D. , later than Xu Shen by some five hundred years, we would not be misled by what seems an obvious rationalization. The notation may satisfy the vanity of the latter-day Chinese, but affords no assurance that the ancients really subscribed to the significance thus attributed to them.

In order to find the true meaning of the word, it is therefore necessary to research in a different direction. As opposed to the Xia, it behooves us to find out by what names the ancients called the other peoples. In a document composed in the middle of the 2nd century B.C.,[7] it is stated, "(The people) to the east are called *Yi* . . . to the south are called *Man* . . . to the west are called *Rong* . . . to the north are called *Di."* By that time the Han people have already become so conceited that derogatory tones implying the inferiority of these tribes or nations are manifest in the document. It is clear that the Chinese by then considered themselves the only civilized people and the others as barbarians or savages. But how did the ancients themselves regard the Yi, the Man, the Rong, and the Di? Did they actually from the very outset consider these as their inferiors? Since the definitions given in latter-day dictionaries are manifestly colored by bias, the only way that can possibly lead to unadulterated truth seems to be to go back directly to the beginning when these words themselves were first coined. And here the Chinese written language is of immeasurable help and value. By studying the peculiar features the ancients used in constructing the characters for these appellations, we may acquire some understanding of what original opinions they may have entertained toward those tribes or nations.[8]

Take *yi.* This character is formed by combining two others—those for "big" and "bow." And "big" is in turn a composite of another two—"one" and "man." So the implication of *yi* is a big man carrying a bow—a person clearly to be respected and feared, not to be despised. The character *man,* however, presents a different picture. This character, too, consists of two parts, the upper of which indicates what the pronunciation should be like, and the lower shows a serpent in coil. Does this mean that the ancients considered these people nothing better than serpents? It could be. But the real significance may not be so subtle. What the ancients want to demonstrate may be just that these are the people who live in a land infested with reptiles—an affirmation of a fact rather than an expression of an opinion. As regards *rong,* it is a combination of characters meaning "spear" and "armor." Surely, any person armed with both spear and armor is not to be treated with disesteem. As to *di,* it is also a combination of two characters—"dog" and "fire." It conjures up an image of a campfire with dogs on guard. It definitely suggests a style of living peculiar to the Di people; but it does not necessarily convey any idea of denigration.

In contrast, how is the character *xia* constructed? It is a picture of a man working with two bare hands and two bare feet. How is such a person to be compared with a big man carrying a bow? Or with one armed with both spear and armor? Or with one assisted by dogs? Or even with one who knows how to live with serpents? If there is a sense of inferiority anywhere, should it not be more aptly attached to the man who can depend upon only his own bare hands and feet to fend for himself? Yet *xia* is the character which the ancients chose to call themselves by. Why? The reason appears to be indeed simple and clear. The ancients formed these characters with only one purpose in mind—to describe the different ways of living each of these peoples pursued. The Yi used archery to hunt game; the Man inhabited a land where reptiles abounded; the Rong were armed with spears and armor; and the Di were associated with dogs and campfire; while they themselves—the Xia—lived by cultivating "food through toil," [9] working with bare hands and feet in the fields. In other words the Yi, Man, Rong, and Di were all nomads, while the Xia were husbandmen or agricultural settlers.

Moreover, the character *xia* has another meaning,[10] which suits well with this explanation. It means the summer season. And summer is indeed the season that sharply shows the difference between the two ways of living. It is in summer that the crops the husbandman has labored so hard to cultivate will have grown to their full measure in the fields so that they can be unmistakably seen at a distance.

Thus by a close study of the compositions of these characters, it seems reasonable to assume that, in the beginning at least, the Xia people could not have harbored any sense of superiority over the other nomadic tribes or nations. Their becoming agricultural settlers is of recent date; either they themselves, or their immediate ancestors, were nomads not so long ago. As yet, they could not be sure of the success of their new adventure; so there was no reason for them to condemn the others who were still following the old way of living. Nor is there any racial bias hidden in the meaning of these characters. The Yi, the Man, the Rong, and the Di were all men, like the Xia. The difference between them was only in occupation or in custom, not in race or in origin. And anyone who was not satisfied with his own occupation could change it as he pleased. If a Xia, after a crop failure, wished to return to nomadic life again, he had his freedom to do so. And if a Yi, a Man, a Rong, or a Di found a piece of unoccupied land and wanted to settle down as a husbandman, it was his free choice too.

And as far as the imperial regime, or the "Central Nation," was concerned, all these were regarded as its subjects—to be required to pay tribute alike, and to be treated alike by it in return. The only situation in which the imperial regime might feel that it was its duty to intervene was when one of these peoples tried to interfere with the others in pursuit of their chosen separate living. And this, naturally, was bound to occur much oftener with the nomads raiding the husbandmen for food supplies than vice versa. It is therefore in this connection that the word *xia* made its first appearance in the Chinese written language—and for that matter, the words *man* and *yi* too. In the *Canon of Yao,* the very first document in the *Book of History,*[11] when Emperor Shun established the ministry of justice and named Gaoyao its minister, he charged him not only with the general duties of punishing the wrongdoers, but also with the specific responsibility to check "the Man and the Yi from disturbing the Xia." The Man and the Yi are very likely used here as a sort of generic term to cover all nomadic tribes. Or it may be that the eastern and southern parts of China being more conducive to agricultural development, there were more people converted to husbandry in those areas, and consequently more conflicts had arisen to warrant special attention. This policy, of course, worked to the advantage of the husbandmen. It afforded them greater security and provided agricultural expansion with more encouragement. But nonetheless it must be recognized as a product of circumstances, born of necessity, so to speak. And aside from this, there does not seem to have existed any other political action or social practice that tended to derogate or discriminate against the nomads.

As time lengthened, however, the gulf between the two ways of living became wider and wider. As agricultural settlements are formed more or less on the basis of the principle of permanence in domicile, they make a far more fertile ground for the development of culture than the unstable conditions of continual vagrancy. And the more these communities made advances in the crafts, in the arts, or in the written language, the more they tended to look down upon the nomadic tribes who had remained in a state of stagnancy. Although the history of the up-and-down relationship between these two divergent and contentious ways of living runs into millennia, and also in zigzags, as we shall presently see, it is nonetheless natural that the Xia people should have been imbued early with a sense of superiority that kept gathering momentum with the march of time. Thus about a thousand years after Yu, when the founder of the Zhou dynasty spoke of the Xia, he qualified it with an epithet *hua* and introduced a new term, *huaxia,* that is, "the glorious Xia people," or "the glorious Xia land." [12] And *hua* became so popular that another six hundred years later it was no longer used as a qualifying word but as a synonym, or a substitute, and then a replacement for *xia.*[13] And since then the Chinese have called themselves the Hua people too. As has been noted before, the name of Xia gave way to Qin, which in turn yielded to Han.[14] So, all in all, the Chinese today have three names for themselves: the Han people, the Central Nation people, and the Hua people. Thus, when Matthew Ricci first came from the West to China toward the end of the 16th century, he found to his surprise that the Chinese did not call their country Cathay but "Ciumquo or Ciumhoa," [15] that is, *zhongguo,* meaning Central Nation, or *zhonghua,* meaning Central Glorious Land.[16] And for the origination of both of these names the Chinese are indebted, either directly or indirectly, to Yu.

· 2 ·
YU

Many Western scholars are impressed with the fact that Yu is sometimes called Yu the Great by the Chinese; and, more remarkably, appears to be the only man throughout the history of China to have been dignified by such an epithet. This is true, but the reasons for it may be different from what many Westerners have thought. The appellation is derived from the third document in the *Book of History,* which bears the title *dayumo, Counsels of Yu the Great.*[17] Now, as we have noted before, most Chinese scholars agree that the early documents of the *Book of History* were composed by the official historians *(shi)* of the Xia dynasty; it is therefore no surprise that they should have endowed its primal founder with this special distinction. But then why have not the later dynasties honored their own meritorious sovereigns with like titles? (In Western histories many kings and emperors have been styled "the Great.") This is because after the Shang dynasty displaced the Xia, a system began to develop for conferring posthumous titles on deceased monarchs and princes. By the time of the Zhou, as we shall explain in a later chapter, a sophisticated and exhaustive code for the practice was even drafted so that simple words such as "the Great" were no longer needed. And, except for a brief interruption by the First Emperor of Qin, this code has been more or less religiously observed down to the last days of the Manchu dynasty.

Whatever measure of greatness we may attribute to Yu, there is no question but that he was as selfless and as dedicated to the well-being of the people of the empire as either of his two predecessors. Nevertheless, he has left with us an impression distinctly different from both Yao and Shun. For, manifestly, he was made of much sterner stuff. Besides what has been written about him in the preceding chapter, he may be said to be generally known to the Chinese in the street today for three proverbial characteristics. He was never sparing of himself, not only physically (as we have already learned in how he conducted himself during the Great Flood), but mentally and morally too. Every time he heard someone criticize him, he would make a low obeisance in deep appreciation.[18] He detested idling. Often when he saw the change of a shade in the sun, even though it was but by an inch, he would express regret that he had not accomplished anything during that brief passage of time.[19] He was as contemptuous as he was apprehensive of luxury and of pleasures. One bit of advice he used to give was later put into a song by his descendants:

> When the palace is a wild of lust,
> And the country is a wild for hunting;
> When wine is sweet, and music the delight;
> When there are lofty roofs and carved walls;—
> The existence of any one of these things
> Has never been but the prelude to ruin.[20]

As regards wine, it is said to have been brewed for the first time in Yu's reign. The brewer, elated with his own discovery, sought to ingratiate himself with the emperor by presenting it first to him. After tasting the wine, Yu liked it very much. Then he said, "In the future generations there will be princes who will lose their states because of their indulgence in this." Thereafter, he kept the brewer at a distance, and would never touch wine again.[21]

But, above all, Yu was an engineer and a mathematician. And as such, he is credited with some legendary accomplishments. As mentioned previously, whereas the mythical River Scheme is attributed to Paoxi, the equally mythical Luo Script is attributed to Yu.[22] And as the legend would have it, the script was supposedly borne out of the flowing stream and presented to him by a tortoise. Though the intervention of that mystic reptile may be regarded as pure fabrication, yet it must be acknowledged that it is perfectly within the realm of possibility for a man, gifted with a genius in mathematics as Yu undoubtedly was, to have arranged the numbers in a manner so that all additions of them—vertical, horizontal, or diagonal—should come out with the same aggregate of 15. And this design he could very well have contrived, while engaged in flood-control projects alongside the River Luo.

Besides the Luo Script, Yu was also said to have "collected metal from the nine regions (of the empire), made it into nine tripods, and engraved the images of the nine regions on them." [23] From a description given in the 7th century B.C., the "images" seem to have consisted of charts of these territories as well as pictures of men and beasts that inhabit them.[24] After the Xia was overthrown by the Shang, the latter considered the tripods symbols of imperial authority and caused them to be moved to its own capital. Later, as the Zhou displaced the Shang, it did the same.[25] At the end of the Zhou dynasty, the tripods were duly turned over to Qin.[26] But upon their being transported upriver, one of them was sunk in the stream.[27] As to the other eight, we have no record thereafter. Presumably, when the Qin palaces were all burned to the ground in a tumultuous revolution a few decades later, these tripods must have been consumed too in the huge conflagration.

Yu, however, has also given posterity something more useful and more popular than either the Luo Script or the "Nine Tripods." This is known as *xiazheng* in the Chinese lunar calendar. *Zheng* means "proper." But in the Chinese calendar, *zheng* month means the first month of the year. Now, since the time of the Yellow Emperor, the months of the year are said to have been named in accordance with the *ganzhi* system. Inasmuch as there are only twelve months to the year and there are also only twelve terrestrial-branch characters to match, no matter how the heavenly-trunk characters may vary in the rotation, the last character for the name of each month will always remain the same. For example, if this month in this year is *jiazi* (hard wood rat), in the next year the month will be *bingzi* (sun fire rat), and in the third year the month will be *wuzi* (mountain earth rat), and so on. Thus, whatever the rotation, there will be a month named *zi* in each year; and the twelve months will run through the whole series of terrestrial-branch characters from *zi* (rat) to *hai* (pig). However, there is the question of what month should be designated as the beginning of a new year. We have no idea what the practice was before Yu's time. But Yu appears to have designated the *yin* (tiger) as the *zheng* (first month),[28] which usually falls between January and February in the Gregorian calendar. When the Shang dynasty overthrew the Xia, it changed the *zheng* to the *chou* (ox) month, the one preceding the *yin* (tiger); and Shang's first months therefore fell as a rule between December and January in the Gregorian calendar. After the Zhou dynasty was established, it named for its *zheng* the *zi* (rat) month, which falls between November and December.[29] While there is no record giving any reason why the changes had to be made repeatedly, human vanity suggests that each of the two succeeding dynasties might have been motivated by no cause other than to show that it was one month ahead of its respective predecessors. At any rate, this seems to have been the spirit in which the First Emperor of Qin took the matter. When he conquered all of China, he moved the *zheng* still one month ahead of the Zhou to the *hai*, which falls between October and November.[30]

Fortunately for the people of these dynasties, the *zheng* which each of them set up had only to do with the conduct of government business. For instance, it was in the *zheng* month that the emperor had to sacrifice to heaven and venerate the ancestors at the temples; and, after these ceremonies, an audience would be held for the princes and high officers. Thus, so far as the people were concerned, except for matters in which the government was directly involved, they could just proceed with their own affairs without bothering to number the months from the *zheng*. However, to the agrarian population at large, the *xiazheng* is much more convenient. For, counting from the *yin* (tiger), the first three months, following the true course of nature as it was, actually form the spring season; the next three months, summer; the third three months, autumn; and the last three months, winter. So the people could make their plans for plowing, planting, cultivating the crops, and harvesting entirely according to this simple computation. Thus for some sixteen centuries, beginning from the end of the Xia dynasty, though the calendar was always issued by the government, yet in the matter of numbering the months from the first to the twelfth, there appear to have been two ways—one used by the officials, and the other by the agricultural populace. It was only in 104 B.C. that Hanwudi, the Martial Emperor of the Han dynasty, abolished the difference by restoring the *xiazheng*, that is, by again making the *yin* month officially the first month of the year. And this has lasted to date. Hence, whenever the lunar calendar is used by the Chinese, often they refer to it still as the Xia calendar.

Besides the Luo Script. the Nine Tripods, and the *xiazheng*, Yu also left posterity a grand scheme for the reorganization of the empire. Whether he actually tried to put it into execution there is no record to tell. But the plan can be found in its entirety in the last part of the *Book of History* document *Yugong, Yu's Levies*. Before we present a translation of it here, a word of explanation is necessary.

Yu, as a matter of historical fact, had no knowledge that there existed other worlds outside the then China. And what is more, he himself had traversed almost the entire length and breadth of that one world. Moreover, he saw for himself how the Great Flood had driven the multitudes to move from one end to another, and also how, after he had brought the flood under control, the people were again wandering about, each seeking a desirable place in which to live. All this could not but have made deep impressions upon him, and prompted him to think that if ever there was an opportunity to reshape the empire, this must be the time and no other. And his mind being of mathematical bent, he drafted therefore a perfectly symmetrical scheme for the redistribution of the land of the empire.

He envisaged that the "Central Nation" should be really central. Accordingly, in his scheme, he would place the imperial seat at the very center of the empire, from the standpoint of both geography and of population. If his present capital did not conform to the requirement, that would not matter. He could have the capital as well as the necessary population moved later, when he was ready to carry out the scheme. He recognized also that agriculture was the way of life in the future, and at any rate an agricultural population would offer the central authority a stabler support and more material prosperity than the nomads; so he visualized that he must populate the immediate surrounding areas of the imperial seat with only the Xia people—that is, the husbandmen—and put them directly under the control of the imperial court. But how large should this imperial domain be? And where should he place the various princedoms and other tribes or nations? As the Chinese unit of distance is called *li* (which is a little more than half a kilometer), Yu's mathematical mind instantly came up with an answer: The imperial domain should be one thousand *li* square, while the largest princedoms should be allowed only one hundred *li* square each. As to where he should put these various princedoms and other tribes or nations, he would have zones drawn up to show where they all should be, and also what relationships the central authority would want to have with them. Thus the following from *Yu's Levies:*

> Five hundred *li* (in each direction from the capital) constitute *dianfu*, "the Adjacent Zone." From within the first hundred *li*, the people will bring as revenue the whole plant of grain; from within the second, they will bring the ears; from within the third, they will bring the grain with husks; from within the fourth, they will bring the grain unhusked; from within the fifth, they will bring the refined grain.[31]
>
> Five hundred *li* (outside the Adjacent Zone) constitute *houfu*, "the Enfeoffed Zone." The land within the first hundred *li* is to be fiefs for the ministers and high officers of the Imperial Court; the land within the second hundred *li*, fiefs for the *nan*;[32] and the land within the remaining three hundred *li*, fiefs for the various *hou*.[33]
>
> Five hundred *li* (beyond) constitute *suifu*, "the Pacified Zone." Within the first three hundred *li*, (the people) are to be inculcated in arts and learning; within the next two hundred *li*, they are to be exhorted to devote their energies to armed defense.
>
> Five hundred *li* (remoter still) constitute *yaofu*, "the Sworn Zone."[34] The first three hundred *li* are to be occupied by the Yi tribes; the next two hundred by criminals undergoing the lesser banishment.
>
> Five hundred *li* (the most remote) constitute *huanfu*, "the Wild Zone." The first three hundred *li* are to be occupied by the Man tribes; the next two hundred by criminals undergoing the greater banishment.

From the above passage we can draw the following diagram as an illustration:

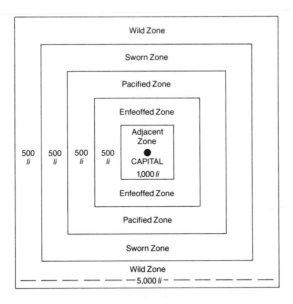

Did Yu really think that he could put the scheme into practice? It is difficult to appraise the mind of a man who can be said to have had experiences in moving mountains and changing the courses of rivers. There is, however, an indication that even while he was engaged in "conferring lands and surnames" on behalf of the Central Nation after the subjugation of the flood, he seemed to have already developed the idea, either by himself or with the concurrence of Shun, that the empire should consist of five zones.[35] In any event, toward the close of his reign Yu assembled all the princes of the empire at a mountain in modern Zhejiang province, the far southeastern corner of his extensive dominion.[36] To this meeting there "came some ten thousand nations, each prince holding his jade insignia or his piece of silk." [37] The purpose of the convocation was to examine the accounts of these nations; and so the mountain was thereafter given the name Kuaiji, meaning "Accounting," which it still bears today.[38] The Prince of Fangfeng came later than the appointed time, and Yu had him executed.[39] Why was the meeting held at such a remote corner of his vast domain? Was it to acquaint the princes with the extent as well as the terrain of the empire so that they might become the more receptive to the idea of relocation? Why must the accounting of the ten thousand nations be done at one time and in one place? Was it to serve as a sort of statistical basis for a later redistribution of land? Why must such a severe penalty be inflicted upon the one prince who came late? Was it to make an example of him and strike awe into the others so that when the plan for reorganization was proclaimed, implicit obedience would be ensured? But these questions cannot be answered. For Yu died almost immediately after, and was buried inside a cave of the very mountain at which the meeting had been held.[40]

Yu had originally named Gaoyao as his successor, shortly after his accession to the throne. But Gaoyao died early. So Yu designated Yi, his former constant travel companion, to succeed him instead. But upon his death, the throne eventually passed on not to Yi, but to his own son Qi(Kai),[41] the one who was born not long after he had taken over the duties of flood control. As to how this event came to pass, there are two versions, one of which is found in *Mencius*:

> Wan Zhang asked, "People say, 'By the time of Yu, Virtue has declined. Yu transmitted (the Empire) not to the worthiest, but to his son.' Was it so?"
>
> Mencius replied, "No, it was not so. . . . Seven years after Yu presented Yi to Heaven, he died. At the end of the three years' mourning, Yi withdrew from the son of Yu to the north of Mount Ji. But the princes as well as the people who had disputes to settle did not go to Yi but to Qi(Kai), all saying, 'He is the son of our sovereign.' And the minstrels and songsters did not sing of Yi but of Qi(Kai), all saying, 'He is the son of our sovereign.' Now, Zhu (Yao's son) was unlike his father; and the son of Shun was unlike his, too. Moreover, Shun had assisted Yao, and Yu had assisted Shun for many years; they each had conferred benefits on the people for a long time.
>
> "But Qi(Kai) was very worthy. He was capable of following reverentially in Yu's footsteps. Besides, the years Yi assisted Yu were few; he had not conferred benefits on the people long.
>
> "The periods of service of the three—Shun, Yu, and Yi—were so different. As to why the son of one man is worthy and that of another not, that is an act of Heaven. Men have nothing to do with it.[42]

There is, however, a second version of almost equal antiquity, which tells a quite different story:

> Yu loved Yi well and intended to leave him the empire. Notwithstanding, he employed all Qi(Kai)'s men as officers. When he reached old age, he declared that he considered Qi(Kai) not worthy enough, and transmitted the throne to Yi. But all authority that carried weight was on the side of Qi(Kai). So Qi(Kai), with the help of his friends and allies, struggled with Yi for the possession of the empire; and Qi(Kai) won.
>
> Thus on the surface Yu did transmit the empire to Yi. But in reality Yu had allowed Qi(Kai) to wrest the empire for himself. From this it is plain that Yu was not up to the standards of Yao and Shun.[43]

But however we may speculate the way this event may have happened, it is a historical fact that after Qi(Kai) succeeded his father, he did not hesitate to see to it that he himself was succeeded by his own son, thus establishing the first definitive dynasty in China—the Xia dynasty. And thenceforth hereditary succession became the rule; and the ideal concept of Yao and Shun to transmit the ultimate authority of the nation to the worthiest of its subjects, though never forgotten by the people, and sometimes crudely distorted and shamelessly exploited by unscrupulous politicians for their own advantage, has never again been put into practice. Philosophers may speculate whether the concept, idealistic as it is, could have ever been institutionalized, even if Yu had successfully transmitted the empire to Yi; but historians can only concentrate on facts as they were and proceed with the narrative as it is.

· 3 ·

QI(KAI)

Perhaps with a view to consolidating his position, Qi(Kai) called for a meeting of the princes of the empire almost immediately following his accession.[44] And perhaps in order to accentuate the fact that he was Yu's son, he had the meeting held not at the imperial seat, nor at a remote extremity of the dominion, but in the very fief he had inherited from his father.[45] The assemblage apparently ended to his satisfaction, for it served well to confirm his authority. Nevertheless, shortly after, a strong voice of dissent arose from the people of Hu,[46] who dwelt some forty kilometers to the southwest of modern Xi'an in the Shaanxi province, or about 250 kilometers distant from the Xia capital Anyi. These, however, were not Yi's associates or allies but Qi(Kai)'s own close kinsmen, their prince being the emperor's half brother.[47] Unmindful of their relationship, they declared that Qi(Kai) had usurped power in open violation of both the express will of Yu and the sanctified tradition of Yao and Shun. But while they seem to have limited their criticisms to protestations, Qi(Kai) took immediate action. Mustering up a strong force, he led an expedition against them in person. Evidently he took them by surprise; for before they knew it he had already arrived and encamped at Gan, on the very outskirts of Hu. The *Book of History* still retains a document titled the *Gan Address (ganshi),* which for the purpose of studying Qi(Kai) and his times it is worthwhile to quote in full:

A great battle was to be fought at Gan. Thus the six ministers (and their hosts) were summoned. The *wang* (emperor) said:
"Ah! All you who are engaged in my six armies, I have a solemn announcement to make to you.
"The Prince of Hu has cruelly abused the five elements and negligently abandoned the ways of Heaven, Earth, and Man. On this account Heaven has deter-

mined to destroy him; and I am now reverently executing the punishment ordered by Heaven.

"If you, men on the left side, do not attack on the left, you will have disregarded my orders. If you, men on the right side, do not attack on the right, you will have disregarded my orders. If you, charioteers, do not drive the horses as hard as they can be properly driven, you will have disregarded my orders.

"You who obey my orders will be rewarded in the ancestral temple. And you who disobey my orders will be punished at the *she* altar.[48] And I will also punish your children with you!"

There are several observations that may be made on the above document. To take the minor points first, this is the very first time in Chinese history that the emperor was called *wang*. Prior to this, from the Yellow Emperor to Yao and Shun, the title had been *di*.[49] But here in this document, which was undoubtedly written by an official historian of the Xia, if not right on the scene, certainly not long after, the title given to Qi(Kai) is *wang*. This is of course what Qi(Kai) had chosen to call himself—to signify perhaps a decisive break with the old established traditions. According to Xu Shen's dictionary, "*Wang* is where all the world goes to." And from the oracle-bone inscriptions, we know that the character *wang* is represented by the picture of a big man standing alone over the land.[50] Both of these probably are as accurate a reflection of Qi(Kai)'s ideas as can be. He was the man, not Yi, that the whole world went to; and as such, he should be the only man ruling over the land. And he was, conceivably, also responsible for introducing a new practice: While an emperor was alive, he was called *wang;* but after he died, he could be called *di* too, just to show that there was no difference between the two titles. This practice lasted through the Xia and the Shang dynasties. But by the time of the Zhou, the title *di* was dropped altogether; their emperors were called *wang*, both dead and alive.[51]

The second point of interest is Qi(Kai)'s military organization. His six armies were commanded by six men who evidently served in time of peace as his ministers. So in those days no distinction was drawn between civilian and military functions; the same officers were given charge of both. It should be also of interest to note that chariots driven by horses were already in use. And this of course can be interpreted as one more step taken by men in warfare.

The third point deserving notice is that Qi(Kai)'s denunciation of the people of Hu is, to say the least, based on exceedingly vague and ambiguous grounds. The Prince of Hu was said to have cruelly abused the five elements, i.e., mètal, wood, water, fire, and earth. Was this an accusation against him for fashioning weapons out of these elements in order to fight Qi(Kai)? But Qi(Kai) was doing that very thing himself. Again, the Prince of Hu was charged with having negligently abandoned the ways of Heaven, Earth, and Man. Presumably, it was Qi(Kai)'s claim that he, being *wang*, was the only man who could understand the three ways and link them together. But that is exactly what the dispute was about. It was the people of Hu's contention that Qi(Kai) did not qualify for the position of *wang* because of the simple fact that he was not Yu's choice. Thus so far as arguments are concerned, right seems to be on the other side.

So we come to the last and major point. Qi(Kai) was manifestly relying on the sheer might of his armed force to overwhelm the enemy as much as he was relying on the naked brutality of his discipline to ensure that that armed force would do the work for him. Anyone who would not fight to the utmost of his capacity would be regarded as disobedient to his orders; and as such, not only would he himself be punished after the battle, but his children would be punished with him. Nor is that all. For the word "punish" used in the translation does not give full signification to the character *lu* used by Qi(Kai) in his address. The latter carries a far more ominous and frightening meaning. It is to punish; but it is also, if need be, to punish to the extreme; in short, to kill. So if Qi(Kai) so wished, he could have not only the disobedient men themselves killed at the *she* altar, but also their children! [52]

What a contrast this *Gan Address* affords to the *Canon of Yao (Yaodian)*, which is pervaded with so much humaneness and so much selflessness!

But Qi(Kai) won the day. And the incident left only some writers to lament centuries later: "The people of Hu fought for what was right, and they were destroyed." [53]

· 4 ·

REGRESSION AND CHAOS

Qi(Kai) did not survive his triumph long.[54] He was succeeded by his son Taikang. This was the first time the throne came so easily to a man. Prior to Yao, even though the transmission of authority was limited to the descendants of the Yellow Emperor and his principal wife, the choice of a successor seems to have required the prior consent of at least the nine branches of blood relations if not the hundred surnames. Yao and Shun, of course, set a different example. Not only were their successors handpicked on the basis of merit long before their own deaths, but these heirs apparent were also given actual direction of the government for many years on a trial basis. But Taikang's accession was a total departure both from the old tradition and from Yao and Shun's practice. With him, to have been born the eldest son to Qi(Kai) was enough to inherit the empire. Nor did he appear to have any adequate experience in government. Even if Qi(Kai) had had any inclination to apprentice the son in administration, his reign was too short to give the latter sufficient time for proper training.

THE XIA EMPERORS

(1) Yu, 2205–2198 B.C.	(2) Qi (Kai), 2197–2189 B.C. . .	(3)	Taikang, 2188–2159 B.C.
		. . (4)	Zhongkang, 2158–2147 B.C.

(5) Xiang, 2146–2119 B.C. . . . . (6) Shaokang, 2079–2058 B.C.
     (Murdered by Hanzhuo, who ruled 2118–2080 B.C.)

(7) Zhu, 2057–2041 B.C. . . . . (8) Huai, 2040–2015 B.C. . . . (9) Mang, 2014–1997 B.C.

(10) Xie, 1996–1981 B.C. . . . . (11) Bujiang 1980–1922 B.C.
     . . . . (12) Juan, 1921–1901 B.C. . . . (13) Jin, 1900–1880 B.C.

(14) Kongjia, 1879–1849 B.C. . . (15) Gao, 1848–1838 B.C. . . . . (16) Fa, 1837–1819 B.C.

(17) Jie, 1818–1767 B.C.

Note: The Xia dynasty consists of fourteen generations with seventeen emperors. These are all given in the *Historical Records*. But as explained before, Sima Qian did not give any dates to any of these emperors. (See above, p. 41.) The dates here, derived from traditional chronology, are given only for rough reference.

    Yu was given the surname Si, so the house of Xia had Si as its surname. However, though this fact was noted in all ancient records, in the narration of events only the given names of individuals concerned were mentioned, seldom accompanied by their surnames.

    Thus Taikang came to power without a good understanding of how to exercise it and with only one model to emulate—his own deceased father. Conscious of the glory that Qi(Kai) had acquired by breaking established rules, Taikang himself was not averse to following the example. He was inordinately fond of hunting, and he enjoyed the nomadic way of living. His most trusted friend was Houyi, prince of Qiong,[55] descended from a long line of famed archers, and himself also renowned for his extraordinary skill in archery. To this man Taikang delegated all authority of government. And one of their first actions was to take a decisive step against the further promotion of agriculture. As has been noted before, from the time of Shaohao, the practice of the imperial government, wittingly or unwittingly, may be said to have been weighted on the side of encouraging the people to adopt the new agricultural way of life. Under Shun, this culminated in the establishment of the ministry of agriculture *(ji)* as one of the foremost ministries with the famed "Abandoned One" as the minister. And in order to prevent the nomads from encroaching upon the husbandmen, Shun explicitly enjoined his minister of justice to pay special attention to the matter. This policy was continued under both Yu and Qi(Kai); and after "the

Abaondoned One's" death, Qi(Kai) also saw fit to name his son minister of agriculture. But now Taikang felt that there was no longer any necessity for maintaining the ministry. Agriculture had already been developed enough; to expand it further would be to reduce the more the land area needed by the nomads. So he summarily abolished the office of *ji;* and "the Abandoned One's" son, his remonstrances perhaps too vigorous for the emperor's liking, was forced to flee to the northern parts of modern Shaanxi seeking refuge between the western and the northern nomadic tribes.[56]

Perhaps it was for the same reasons that Taikang disliked the imperial seat used by both his grandfather and father. This region had become too densely agricultural for hunting game. So he crossed the Yellow River and settled at Zhenxun in the southwest of modern Gong district, Henan.[57] But even this new site, with all the necessary imperial entourage that followed, was not satisfactory to him. Leaving Houyi behind to take complete charge, he roamed farther west along the southern bank of the Luo River in an endeavor to slake his insatiable appetite for the chase. For some one hundred days he lingered and loitered in the area. Then Houyi seized the opportunity and made himself master of the imperial government. In vain Taikang's mother and his five brothers went up the Luo River to look for him, seeking some way to restore him to the throne. But they were on the northern bank, and he was on the southern. They could not locate him; and in desperation the five brothers poured forth their plaints in several songs which now form a document in the *Book of History—Songs of Five Sons.*[58]

Houyi, however, dared not rule in his own name. He persuaded one of the brothers, Zhongkang, to return to Zhenxun and ascend the throne. But he was as fond of the chase as the emperor he had dethroned, and he himself ruled with the same kind of negligence.[59] He was particularly negligent about the traditional imperial duties of calendar-making, which to his way of thinking must have worked more to the benefit of the husbandmen than to that of the nomads. As has been related before, Yao had posted four officers to the limits of the four directions of the empire to observe the movements of the sun. This practice was continued thereafter, with four brothers from two families—Xi and He—given the charge hereditarily. Again, as has been noted previously, it was the duty of the imperial court, if not the emperor himself, to coordinate these astronomical observations and see to it that an accurate calendar be issued to the populace each year in advance. Now, in the very first year of Zhongkang's reign, an eclipse occurred without its being foretold.[60] A strong murmur of dissatisfaction diffused throughout the empire. In face of this widespread discontent, Houyi did not blame himself for having failed in exercising necessary coordination, but made scapegoats of Princes Xi and He, alleging that they had "allowed the days to go into confusion" because they were "sunk in the excess of wine." [61] In the name of Emperor

Zhongkang, he directed a minister, Yin, to lead the six armies into an expedition against them; and in the *Book of History* there is a document bearing the title, *Punitive Expedition of Yin (yinzheng)*, which purports to be the proclamation issued by the commander of his forces, laying the entire blame at the door of the two families for their dereliction of duty.[62]

How the expedition concluded, there is no record to tell us. Since these princes were by virtue of their office posted in the four extremities of the empire, one wonders how a single expedition could have sufficed. Conceivably, after the threat was made, the four officers made a liberal admission of their errors, and the matter was adjudged to have come to an end. However, while this might have satisfied Houyi, it probably did not satisfy the people at large. As general disapproval persisted, Houyi took another measure. He considered his own skill in archery invincible, and he aimed to silence the murmuring opposition by a display of stark force. One of his loudest critics was the son of Shun's minister of music,[63] who happened to be also known for excessive greediness. So seizing some pretext, Houyi personally led an expedition against him, and had his entire house annihilated.

Such an action could have precipitated the empire into civil war. But after the event, Houyi reverted to his practice of government by negligence. While the princes were intimidated by his prowess, they were also relaxed by his lack of active interference. Thus on the surface at least, some tranquillity was again restored to the empire. Then Zhongkang passed away, and Houyi put the deceased's heir, Xiang, on the throne. If the tyrant had shown little respect for the father before, he showed even less for the son. He now maintained his own headquarters at his fief Qiong, south of modern Luoyang, Henan. Not wanting Xiang to be too near him, in which case he must of necessity yield to the nominal sovereign some dignity or precedence, he had the emperor moved, or rather banished, to a place some three hundred kilometers to the east, called Zhenguan.[64] Then he spent most of his time in hunting; and disregarding his own experience with Taikang, he in turn delegated all authority to Hanzhuo, his most trusted lieutenant.[65] He thought he had nothing to fear from this younger man. Whereas Taikang was his inferior, he was far superior to Hanzhuo in physical prowess. But what Hanzhuo lacked in brawn, he made up in cunning. "Outside the palace, he bought people with bribes; and inside, he seduced Houyi's young wife with charms." [66] Thus Houyi was kept ignorant of everything that was going on. At last, when he returned from a chase, he was ambushed and killed.

Hanzhuo now took over everything Houyi had possessed—his domain, his palace, his wife. He even took over the name Prince of Qiong without alteration and without compunction. He did not bother himself with the nominal sovereign Xiang, who at the death of Houyi seemed to have gained some independence in the site of his banishment. Nor did Hanzhuo make any pretensions as to the control of the empire. He appeared to be quite aware of his inability to impose his will upon others. In fact, there is no record extant from which we can garner any information except for the fact that during this period Hanzhuo had produced two sons by Houyi's wife. Presently, however, these two grew up to be doughty warriors; and with their help Hanzhuo proceeded to execute a scheme which he had probably long formulated in his mind. He launched a surprise attack against Xiang. Xiang was slain, but the attacker would not rest. He wanted to exterminate the entire imperial house. He did not leave anyone alive in the palace, and he thought he had succeeded. But Hanzhuo was mistaken. He had no knowledge that Xiang's empress was pregnant, and she had made her escape "through a hole." [67] She fled to her own clan, some 150 kilometers to the northeast.[68] And in due time a son was born, whom she named Shaokang, or Kang Junior, in commemoration of both his grandfather Zhongkang and his granduncle Taikang so that the child would never forget from what lofty status he had sprung.[69] And Shaokang is destined to be remembered ever afterward by the Chinese as the man who, through sheer tenacity of purpose and indomitable spirit, fought against overwhelming odds and finally succeeded in wreaking his vengeance upon his enemy and restoring the fallen Xia dynasty.

· 5 ·

RESURGENCE AND DECLINE

When Shaokang came of age, he served his mother's clan as chief shepherd. But somehow one of Hanzhuo's sons heard of his existence, and sent a spy to search for him.[70] Ever alert and cautious, Shaokang quickly discovered his danger. And sensing that his kinsmen were too weak to resist the enemy, he fled in disguise to a more powerful and populous princedom, Youyu,[71] that lay halfway between his mother's clan and Hanzhuo's dominion. His purpose was twofold: On the one hand, Hanzhuo and his sons would never suspect that he had dared to come so near to them; and on the other, he could watch their activities more closely. Gradually he earned the trust of the prince of Youyu and became his chief cook. And finding that the lord was secretly as sympathetic to the lost cause of Xia as he was resentful of the usurpation of Hanzhuo, Shaokang revealed his own identity in confidence. Thereupon, the prince, following the example of Yao toward Shun, married him to his two daughters, and gave him for a dowry the village of Lun.[72] At last he had a sort of base to speak of—a territory of ten *li* square, and a population of five hundred. With this he started to plan his revenge on Hanzhuo.

But he soon found out to his exasperation that all his plots were of no avail. All the strength he could muster or count upon was inadequate to meet that of Hanzhuo. Moreover, because of his proximity to the enemy, he could act only in utter secrecy; any untimely disclosure would be an invitation to disaster. He saw years and years slip by, yet he got nowhere. A son was born to him shortly after his marriage, and the child grew to manhood. But his dreams of wreaking his vengeance were still as elusive as ever.

Then, at long last, a chance came. For some time Shaokang had had an ally in a former minister of his father's, Mi by name, who was one of the very few who had escaped alive from Hanzhuo's attack on the late emperor. But up to now Mi could not do much except offer advice. However, a recent change of fortune altered everything. Mi had come into the inheritance of Youli, a princedom of considerable size, about three hundred kilometers to the north of Shaokang's village.[73] They put their heads together and worked out a plan. As Mi's territory was at a considerable distance from Hanzhuo's domain, Mi could openly collect a large force under some pretense and secretly prepare to march against Hanzhuo without causing the latter undue alarm. As for Shaokang, though he must still lie low because of Hanzhuo's proximity, he could intensify his guerrilla operations.

Before long, the plans bore fruit. Shaokang's agents found out that Hanzhuo's younger son was having an incestuous affair with his sister-in-law. One night the couple were surprised in their assignation. In the darkness the woman was killed, but the man slipped away. However, he did not escape far. He was caught up by Shaokang's hounds, and was put to death on the spot.[74]

The rest of the narrative is simple to tell. Mi, using the restoration of the Xia rule as a slogan, was able to rally a large number of supporters. While he marched in the open against Hanzhuo, Shaokang organized a diversionary force, commanded by his son Zhu, to attack the enemy in the rear. Both expeditions were successful. Mi killed Hanzhuo in battle,[75] and Zhu slew the usurper's remaining son in his fortress.[76] Then Shaokang betook himself to Yu's old imperial seat, Anyi, north of the Yellow River, and was acknowledged by all the princes of the empire as their lawful sovereign.[77]

The history of Shaokang has ever since been regarded by the Chinese people as an inexhaustible source of inspiration whenever they find themselves in dire distress. Every time they suffered national calamity at the hands of foreign invaders, when a few of them retreated or were driven to a remote corner, without help and without hope, they would always quote to themselves the passage from the *Zuozhuan* that Shaokang once had had "only a territory of ten *li* square, and a population of five hundred." And this quotation, though no salutary effects might be expected from it in the long run, would seldom fail to revive flagging spirit for the moment.

Shaokang was succeeded by his son Zhu. In both their reigns, the empire seemingly entered another period of union and tranquillity. But the truth may be that their actual rule extended only to the former dominion of Hanzhuo with a few minor additions such as the princedom of Shaokang's father-in-law, his mother's clan, and Mi's Youli. Beyond these, they were probably quite content, if the multitudinous princes only paid them lip service by addressing them as *wang,* and refrained from doing anything to challenge their imperial claims. Although there is no definitive record attesting to such a state of things, there are other indications that bear mute witness. For instance, shortly after Shaokang assumed the imperial title, he ordered the restoration of the ministry of agriculture and named a descendant of "the Abandoned One," Gongliu, to be its minister.[78] But it seems that the minister did not come to the imperial court, as he should have, but continued to manage his own affairs in his chosen locale of residence, no less than three hundred kilometers distant.[79] The acquisition of a ministerial title would no doubt enhance the prestige of a subject; but the continued absence of an important minister from his office could not add to the dignity of the sovereign. If the absence was tolerated, as it apparently was, this could be for only one reason: The title was used as an inducement to submission, and nothing more was expected from the recipient.

Perhaps, too, Shaokang had never truly intended to return to the old policy of Shun and Yu that encouraged agricultural development at the expense of the nomads. He himself had been more accustomed to the latter's way of living. He had served as chief shepherd in his mother's clan; and in conducting guerrilla operations against Hanzhuo's sons, he must have also adapted himself to the mobile, nomadic life. At the end of his reign, it is recorded that he invested his younger son by a concubine, Wuyu, with a fief around the Kuaiji (Accounting) Mountain (where Yu had held his last meeting of the princes of the empire, had died, and was buried) so that annual sacrifices could be rendered to him as the primal founder of the Xia dynasty.[80] The fief was given the name Yue, which some natives later corrupted into Viet. Eventually all the people inhabiting South China in the 1st and 2nd centuries B.C., from modern Zhejiang, through Fujian, Guangdong, and Guangxi provinces, as far as Vietnam, came to call themselves one Yue or another, such as Eastern Yue and Southern Yue, etc., with the appellation "the Hundred Yue" serving as a sort of overall nomenclature; and many of them even pretended that they were descended from the Great Flood Controller through Shaokang's son Wuyu.[81]

Some scholars, however, have been skeptical of this enfeoffment because they do not think that Shaokang's authority could have extended that far. But if we recognize the fact that the empire was still largely nomadic, or had reverted more or less to nomadism, then the investment is as credible as it was feasible. Wuyu, being a younger son by a concubine, might not have relished the idea of living under the perpetual domination of the heir apparent, Zhu. The smoldering resentment between the two might have grown into open bickering that could be resolved only by this settlement. To have Wuyu sent to a place as remote as Yue would be welcome not only to Wuyu, who probably saw it as an opportunity to establish an independent kingdom, but also to Zhu, who could very well have taken secret delight in the removal of a potential rival. And to these people who, one and all, were used to nomadic ways, there did not seem to exist any difficulty in the proposition other than that Wuyu be supplied with ample followers and provisions. And since the ostensible or declared purpose of the enfeoffment was for proper annual veneration of their foremost ancestor, Shaokang would certainly have seen to it that the younger son was given more than enough of both.

In any event, after the passing of Shaokang and Zhu, the empire apparently declined even further. By the time of Xie, about eighty years after the so-called Restoration, two of the princes of the house of Shang, which was to displace the Xia eventually, began to call themselves *wang*.[82] And a number of the princes of the empire also appeared to be acting independently, without fear of restraint from the imperial authority. The stories of these two *wang* of the Shang may well illustrate the point. The first of them, Hai, was credited with having trained a herd of "servant-oxen." It is said that before him only horses were used to draw chariots; but he taught bovines to pull carts. Since the term "servant-oxen" seems to imply much more than simply drawing carts, it is quite possible that this Hai might also have made the discovery that water buffaloes could be used to till the fields. At any rate, he and his herd became the envy of the neighboring Prince of Yi. He was enticed to make a visit there with his "servant-oxen," whereupon his herd was seized and he himself was murdered. Back in his own state, his brother Heng and his son Shangjia took over. Borrowing an army from another neighboring princedom to augment their own, they destroyed Yi and recovered the "servant-oxen." All these turbulent events occurred, and both Hai and Heng presumed to call themselves *wang*, without the imperial regime's taking any action to bring forth a semblance of order and discipline in the empire. This is certainly different from the times when Yu assembled the princes at the Kuaiji Mountain and executed the one who came late, or when Qi(Kai) gathered his six armies and crushed the Prince of Hu without mercy at the first sign of defiance.

There is another story that geographically demonstrates the increasingly limited control the later Xia emperors had over the empire. When Kongjia ascended the throne some two hundred years after Shaokang, two live dragons were found,[83] which to our modern thinking could have been the last remnants of a vanishing breed of reptiles. Not knowing how to feed these animals, the emperor sought for someone who could. In response came one Liu Lei, who claimed to have learned the art or skill from a family which had bred dragons for Yao. So he was given the charge. Presently one of the dragons died, and Liu Lei presented its meat to the emperor, who ate it and liked it, and asked for more. Realizing that the meat would be soon exhausted and that his inability to breed dragons would be discovered, Liu Lei fled with his family to Lu,[84] in modern Shandong—only some sixty kilometers from where Shaokang's mother's clan used to be. And there Liu Lei was able to find perfect safety, and his family thrived and prospered thereafter.[85] So apparently the Xia's sway had become so reduced that it did not even cover the extent of Shaokang's former dominion.

While the Xia declined politically, it is also plain that the country as a whole retrogressed. Except for certain areas such as the territories adjacent to the old capitals of emperors Yao, Shun, and Yu, the people by and large seem to have reverted more or less to the old nomadic way of life. Or it may be perhaps more accurate to say they had adopted a bilateral sort of living—half agricultural and half nomadic. This is evidenced by the ceaseless migrations of the House of Shang. According to the *Historical Records* as well as one of the introductory notes in the *Book of History* attributed to Confucius, from the time when Xie, Yao's half brother and Shun's minister of commonalty was enfeoffed to the time when his thirteenth-generation descendant Tang began to build up a power base to challenge the Xia dynasty, the house of Shang had migrated no less than eight times. Although there is no detailed information about all of the eight places they occupied, we know definitely about three of them.[86] Xie was given Shangqiu, in modern Henan, as his fief, from which the house of Shang derived its name. But by the time of Houyi, the appellation of the place was changed to Zhenguan; and it was to this locality that the usurper had Emperor Xiang banished. Where then were the Shang? They had obviously migrated elsewhere. When we encounter them again, six generations after Xie,[87] it is when their chieftain Hai chose to call himself *wang* and had become famed for having trained a herd of "servant-oxen." We do not know exactly where the site of their habitation was; but we do know it was in the neighborhood of Yi, where Hai was murdered. And Yi is a district still bearing the same name in modern Hebei, about five hundred kilometers north of Shangqiu, Xie's original fief. Then when we finally come to Tang, the man who was to overthrow the Xia dynasty, he had moved back to Bo, quite adjacent to Shangqiu.[88] How far afield, back and forth, have the Shang roamed!

Perhaps it was these incessant migrations of multitudinous houses or tribes that added to the confusion of the times. But chaotic as the state of the empire undoubtedly was, the Xia was yet able to maintain its imperial pretensions until the emergence of Tang. Besides "Wang" Hai and "Wang" Heng of the Shang, there seemed to have been no other princes presumptuous enough openly to assume the title *wang*. And even with the Shang, after the death of those two, their immediate successors appear also to have voluntarily dropped the title, thus tacitly acknowledging their submission again to the imperial house. How was this possible in view of the increasing and obvious deterioration of the Xia dynasty? The explanation may be found in the rise of a so-called "hegemon." We shall read much more about the divers hegemons later, especially in the mid-Zhou dynasty. But it is during the declining years of the Xia that the first hegemon made its appearance.[89] The term "hegemon" means a princedom, which either through the good fortune of capable leadership or because of a combination of favorable circumstances had grown so much in strength that it could dominate a large part of the empire, but instead of using its power to subvert or displace the existing dynasty chose to uphold or bolster up the declining dignity of the reigning imperial house, if not in reality, at least in name. The reasons for its choosing such a policy might be varied; but as the ways of men generally are, the basic motivation was no other than self-interest. Though the circumstances facing each hegemon may have been different, in their calculations they all seem to have come to the same conclusion: If they sought to overthrow the existing dynasty, they might have to meet with an opposition too strong to overcome; but if they essayed to help maintain the traditional order, they might use the name of the reigning imperial house to impose their own will upon the other princes and thus make the objective of self-aggrandizement so much the easier to obtain.

In the latter part of the Xia dynasty, the princedom that achieved the status of hegemon was Kunwu.[90] Originally its fief was located in modern Puyang, Hebei. But in its nomadic migrations, it was also known for a time that it used the present-day Xuchang, Henan, as a base of operations.[91] From these facts it may be assumed that it dominated a central belt of the empire, an area of great strategic importance, about two hundred kilometers in length. But of what it did to achieve that position, or of how it helped to sustain the tottering Xia dynasty, we have no precise record. We only know for certain that it was finally destroyed on a day of "soft wood hare," *yimao,* in the very last year of the Xia rule,[92] the narrative of which we shall presently recount.

As a matter of fact, when one studies the history of the Xia from Taikang to its fall, after the age of Yao, Shun, and Yu, one cannot help feeling somewhat as we may feel in studying Western history, when it descends so abruptly and unexpectedly from the heights of Greece and Rome to the dismal void of the Dark Ages. Perhaps the conditions that obtained in Europe then are not unlike those that prevailed in China during this period. For some three or four hundred years, or more, human progress appears to have just stood still. Agricultural developments gave way to nomadic reversions; and knowledge and arts, if not falling into disuse, were simply not pursued. Yu might have fashioned the famous Nine Tripods out of metal; but if one should look for more production of such artifacts, one would have to wait until the rise of the Shang, whose bronzes are now renowned for their unequaled skill and unsurpassed technique throughout the world.[93] Official historians *(shi)* were probably still kept by the imperial house; but what they could record was only bare, skeletal genealogical charts or sacrificial tablets which came to be known later as *pudie* or *dieji,* and no more. Indeed, when Confucius compiled the *Book of History,* as we have noted before, he selected altogether one hundred documents, the names of which are all given in his own introductory notes *(shuxu),* along with a brief account of how each of them came to be composed. Yet throughout the Xia dynasty, outside of *Yu's Levies (yugong),* he collected only three documents, namely: the *Gan Address (ganshi),* the *Songs of the Five Sons (wuzizhige),* and the *Punitive Expedition of Yin (yinzheng).* As we know, it has been alleged that Confucius made the compilation to show by the old documents how the beliefs as well as the practices of the ancient sages were in agreement with his own ideals. Now, among the three Xia documents, except for the second one, which may be said to have some negative value in support of Confucius's ethical principles, the first serves only to illustrate the ruthless exploitation of brutal force, and the third the criminal negligence of some ministers on the one hand and the unscrupulous manipulation of a usurper on the other— examples totally contradictory to his own teachings. Perhaps Confucius included them in the book simply because the Xia had never composed any other documents for him to choose from. Perhaps this is also his way to show that between the *Punitive Expedition of Yin* and the next document composed by Tang, the founder of the Shang dynasty, for some three or four centuries, the Chinese culture had just retrogressed, not progressed at all.

· 6 ·

THE RULE OF JIE AND THE RISE OF TANG

When the Chinese speak of evil monarchs in the past, they usually mention Jie and Zou.[94] Jie was the last emperor of the Xia dynasty, and Zou the last of the Shang. As many traditional sources would have it, the two emperors are both ascribed with all the wickedness and all the vices that can accumulate in a man. But from the objective viewpoint of history, they may have been more maligned than they deserved, more victimized by their victors' propaganda than by their own conduct or misconduct. And of the two, the allegations against Jie were probably the less justified.

Undoubtedly Jie was a cruel, oppressive man. Undoubtedly too he was fond of women and wine and loved ease and indolence.[95] But one wonders whether such attributes could not be applied to most ancient despots, especially to those whose mind was accustomed to the crude and capricious aberrations of primitive nomadism. It is therefore refreshing to note that the great historian Sima Qian never used any excessive language in his descriptions of Jie in the *Historical Records*. He only related succinctly: "Since the time of Kongjia, most of the princes had turned away from the Xia. Jie, instead of pursuing ways of virtue, vaunted his military might and used it to injure the hundred surnames until they could bear it no more." [96] Herein is the cause of Jie's downfall in a nutshell.

Jie was a man with the strength of a giant. With his bare hands he could "break an animal's horn, straighten a crooked hook, wind up metal in coil, push a large ox backward, kill huge tortoises in the water, and capture grizzly bears on land." [97] With such a man, it is conceivable that he became easily adept in the nomadic arts of hunting and making war. And events prove that he did. He soon taught the hegemon Kunwu to know its place, and reduced it from the position of a domineering ally to that of a subservient supporter. He was also the one and only emperor of the Xia who, after Qi(Kai), ever called a meeting of the princes of the empire.[98] It was duly held at Reng, the former locale of Shaokang's mother's clan. When one of the princes left the meeting against his wishes, he went after the truant and had his whole house destroyed.[99] Later, when another lord rebelled, he led an expedition against him; and he was placated only after the latter had surrendered not only himself but also his sister, famed for her beauty, for the monarch's ravishment.[100] Indeed, surveying the world thereafter, Jie found many reasons to be satisfied with his own triumphs. In order to show that he was above all other humans, he was said to have invented the first sedan chair, using men to carry him aloft.[101]

In fact, Jie was a true follower of his redoubtable ancestor Qi(Kai), who was such an outspoken advocate of ruthless force and who had so mercilessly crushed his enemy, the people of Hu. He might even have gone down in history as another Shaokang, who had once again restored glory to the declining Xia, had it not been his bad fortune to run into a man born with a far clearer vision about how the empire should be governed. For not long after the meeting of the princes convoked by Jie, the house of Shang, led by its young prince Tang,[102] moved back to Bo, in an area adjacent to the meeting place, Reng. Although the Shang people had not resided in this particular locality before, they were quite familiar with its background. It was not far from Shangqiu, the original fief of their primal ancestor Xie. And, what is more, it had at one time served as the imperial seat of Di Ku, father to Xie himself. In fact, it seems that Tang had deliberately chosen to migrate back to this spot in order "to follow in the footsteps of the ancestral emperor." [103] For, after settling there, his first act was to compose an *An-*

nouncement to the Emperor (digao), a sort of ritualistic document offered to Di Ku in a veneration ceremony. The composition was originally included by Confucius in the *Book of History*. But unfortunately it is now lost. Had it been extant, we might have learned much more about Tang's intentions. But the very fact that he had led his house back to the former imperial seat of their most elevated progenitor and had immediately composed a document addressed to him demonstrates clearly what lofty aspirations he must have had.

As mentioned before, Xie, the founder of the house of Shang, was not only half brother to Yao, but had also served under Shun as minister of commonalty.[104] If any man was familiar with Yao's ideal that government of the empire is for the benefit of the people and not for the advantage of any individual, or with Shun's doctrine that human relationships should be guided and controlled mainly by the principles of harmony and propriety, that man should have been Xie. Though the Shang, as Xie's descendants, might not have placed their faith implicitly in these beliefs, yet since to train and inculcate the people in such beliefs had been the primary duty of Shun's minister of commonalty, they could not but have passed on these ideas from generation to generation, even though they might have done so only very perfunctorily and desultorily. But if none of the Shang had taken these ideas seriously over the years, when the time came, Tang did.

As young Tang surveyed the China of his time, he must have seen a very sorry picture indeed. To him it must have looked like circles and circles, all dominated by atrocious despots. Jie was only the most eminent and formidable one; the others were no less barbaric and ferocious. The nomadic tribes— the Yi, the Man, the Rong, the Di—did not fare badly even when they dwelt in the midst of agricultural settlements, as many of them did. Their life was still the same as before. Whenever they were strong enough to attack others, they would attack; and whenever they were too weak to resist their own attackers, they would just scamper off to other lands. But the people who suffered most were the husbandmen. For they had to fear and suffer raids not only from the nomadic tribes, but also incursions of neighboring princes who, since the time of Taikang, had also more or less taken up the nomadic ways of living. And what is worse, even without those outside raids or incursions, they would constantly have to fear and suffer oppression from their own lords. A few, very few, of these latter might have treated their agricultural populace relatively well.[105] But these were rare exceptions. By and large, even though there is no documentary evidence that China had ever developed a system of serfdom, these princes regarded the husbandmen within their dominions, if not as serfs, only as human resources from which supplies and services could be extorted. As such, they would give them whatever protection they could; but if they could not, they themselves would just run away with their own kinsmen as any nomadic tribes would do, and leave the people who were tied to the land to their own fate. As for the husbandmen, once a change of masters was effected, they would find no alteration in their miserable situation. Both the old and the new lords would extract tributes from them, both would molest their womenfolk, both would use their own kinsmen as officers to lord over them. There might be some slight difference in the degree of cruelty and oppressiveness, but all were cruel and oppressive. Perhaps many husbandmen would have liked to return to nomadism, and some probably did; but the bulk of them, having engaged in farming for generations, simply did not know how to change. Moreover, as it was in the interest of their masters not to let them change, these princes would most certainly see to it that such changes did not occur too often. And contemplating the sufferings of these people, how a man with so much compassion as Tang was endowed must have grieved for them!

And the Shang, as a princely house, had been preying upon others like this for so many hundreds of years, and had also been a prey to others in return. As has been noted before, the Shang had migrated eight times from the time of Xie till Tang's own settlement at Bo. Either they must have moved into territories where the land was richer and the defense weaker, or they might have been driven from one location to another by foes too strong for them. They were in Bo now. How long could they remain here? The duty of an emperor was to keep peace and order throughout the empire. But Jie knew only how to extort tributes from the princes for his own pleasure and indulgence, and he showed no concern for the well-being of the people. Besides, Jie's authority seemed to extend only to areas accessible to his forces; as for those areas lying beyond that perimeter of his influence, he just let their princes go on being raided or raiding others. Surely there should be a remedy to such an unbearable state of things. But what could the remedy be?

Tang was a very resourceful man. But as he thought the matter over, the problem appeared too tremendous for him to put entire trust in his own resourcefulness. He remembered that Yao had been confronted with a situation not dissimilar to this. When faced with the Great Flood and the imminent collapse of his empire, Yao, sensitive to his own limitations, had searched far and wide for a man more gifted than himself to help him, and found Shun in the end. So Tang decided to do the same. He looked for such a man everywhere. We do not know how many times he was disappointed, as he must have been, in this quest. But eventually he met with Yi Yin,[106] and between the two there formed a relationship as ideal and as perfect as could have ever been found between a minister and a sovereign.

Yi Yin was originally a husbandman in a princedom about a hundred kilometers to the northwest of Tang's Bo.[107] Being a husbandman, he knew all about the sufferings of the agricultural population, the oppressions and the irresponsibilities of the so-called princes of the empire as well as the lawlessness and savagery of the nomadic tribes. But unlike other husbandmen, Yi Yin was not resigned to his own fate. He had heard how the entire people under heaven had benefited and prospered under the rule of Yao and Shun. And he tried to learn as much as he could, wherever he could, and from whomever he could, how that condition had been brought about by those two monarchs. In those days learning was rare among the people, high or low. So Yi Yin, though young, soon became renowned for the knowledge and wisdom he had accumulated. And he delighted in talking to others about Yao and Shun and the principles these famed sovereigns had stood for. He often said with pride that as far as he was concerned, "in any matters contrary to the righteousness which Yao and Shun prescribed, or contrary to their principles, though he had been offered the throne, he would not have regarded it; though there had been yoked for him a thousand teams of horses, he would not have looked at them. Indeed, in any matters contrary to the righteousness which they prescribed, or contrary to their principles, he would neither have given nor taken a single straw." [108]

His reputation now reached the ears of Tang, who immediately dispatched envoys, bearing gifts, to invite him to enter his service. But Yi Yin declined, saying, "What use have I for such gifts?" Thrice Tang repeated his invitation, each time with more gifts; and thrice Yi Yin turned it down. Then, after Tang's last messenger had departed, Yi Yin, convinced of Tang's sincerity, had second thoughts about the youthful prince. He said to himself, "Instead of abiding in these plowed fields and regaling myself with the principles of Yao and Shun, would it not be better for me to make this prince a prince like Yao and Shun? Would it not be better for me to give the people a chance to live like the people who lived under Yao and Shun? Would it not be better for me to see these things happen in my own lifetime? Heaven having created these men, it is His will that the ones who are enlightened earlier instruct those who are late in getting enlightenment; the ones who become awakened to the high principles sooner make the others awaken too. I am one of Heaven's people who have awakened sooner. It is for me to awaken the rest of the people. If I do not awaken them, who will?" [109] "And he thought that if there should be a single man or woman under heaven who could not live a life such as the people had enjoyed under the benefits conferred by Yao and Shun, it would be as if he himself pushed him into a ditch." [110] Thus thinking, Yi Yin went straight to see Tang himself.[111]

Tang received Yi Yin as a teacher.[112] And between the two, a plan was soon developed to put into practice the principles of Yao and Shun, as they understood them. They recognized that the agricultural way of life was the

wave of the future; and it is only through the development and expansion of
agriculture that the empire could obtain a larger degree of peace and stability. Shun clearly foresaw that prospect when he ordered his minister of
justice to give agricultural settlements all protection against nomadic raids or
incursions. But with Shun gone, and with Jie on the throne, no such policy
could now be expected from the imperial court. What could a prince like
Tang do to improve the situation? He chose to refrain from attacking or
encroaching upon others weaker than himself, which was easy; and also to
make his own princedom so strong that it could stand up against any forces
bent upon rapine and destruction, which was much more difficult.

There is no extant record telling us precisely what Tang and Yi Yin did.
But from sundry sources we may gather some inkling about the direction of
their endeavors. During this period, Tang was known to have authored
another document in addition to the *Announcement to the Emperor (digao)*.
This was called *liwo, Regulations Governing Fertile Soil.*[113] The title itself
appears to make clear that the document was an embodiment of Tang's land
laws. If the document had not been lost, it might rank with *Yu's Levies
(yugong)* in value, and might furnish us with an unequivocal answer to the
question whether the ancients had ever practiced the so-called "well-field
system." As things stand, lacking firm evidence in the affirmative, this point
has long remained a matter of disagreement among Chinese scholars. But
according to no less an authority than Mencius, the ancients did practice the
system, which he described thus:

> A square *li* forms a "well" (*jing* 井). A "well" consists of nine hundred
> *mu*[114] (divided into nine equal squares, resembling the character *jing,* like
> 田). The central square is the public land, while the other eight squares are
> assigned to eight families as their private fields, each a hundred *mu*. All the eight
> families are required to cultivate the public field in common. Not until the public
> work is finished may they presume to attend to their private business.[115]

From the same authority we have a discussion of the land-tax systems used
by the three successive dynasties of Xia, Shang (or Yin), and Zhou:

> Under the Xia emperors, the allocation is fifty *mu* (for each husbandman),
> from which a levy *(gong)* is exacted. With the people of Yin, the allocation is
> seventy *mu* each, and the system (of taxation) is called "aid" *zhu*). With the
> people of Zhou, the allocation is a hundred *mu* each, and the system is called
> "common" *(che)*. In reality, what was collected in all these was a tithe. By
> "common" it is meant to share in common. By "aid" it is meant to work through
> aid.
>
> Longzi[116] said, "For regulating the land, there is no system better than aid;
> and no system not better than levy. For by the levy system, the regular amount
> (of taxation) was fixed by taking the average of several years. In good years,

when the grain lies about in abundance, much more may be taken without being oppressive; but the actual taking (being the average) is less than what can be taken. But in bad years, even after manuring the fields, the produce is still deficient, and yet the full amount is required. Now, (to be a sovereign) is to be father and mother to the people. If the sovereign causes great distress to the people—toiling for a whole year and yet unable to feed their parents; driven to borrowing till their old and young lie dying in ditches or water-channels—how can he justify his claim to be father and mother to the people?" [117]

From the above, one may visualize how the Xia people had probably viewed the levy system in the reign of Jie. The imperial government was both unwilling and unable to furnish the husbandmen proper protection against raids and incursions; and yet when the latter managed to scrape through after a year's hard toil, they would still be encumbered with the tithe, no matter what kind of crop they might have gathered, not to mention the other abuses they might suffer at the hands of their so-called superiors. Under these circumstances it is conceivable that Tang and Yi Yin introduced, or rather reintroduced, the well-field system in their own small territory to mitigate the situation. All fertile land was divided into wells, to each of which was assigned eight husbandmen with their families. These were required to cultivate the central field first for the government before they could work on their private fields. And at the end of the year, no matter whether it was good or bad, the government would take only whatever was produced in the central field and would not impose any other levy on them.

Was this system invented by Tang or Yi Yin? Nowhere in any of the extant Shang documents, or in any of the other ancient records, can we find a basis for such an assertion. It seems therefore more likely that if the system was practiced by the ancients at all, it must have been prior to Tang's time. Perhaps after the subjugation of the Great Flood, when Yu first promulgated a uniform system of levies throughout the empire, the rate of the levy was fixed to be the tithe, but the procedure of collection was left to the various princedoms or nations. As a result, both systems—the simple levy as well as the well-field—might have been used. But by the time of Qi(Kai), who had more regard for discipline and efficiency than for anything else, or still later, in the times of Houyi and Hanzhuo, who had regard only for their own comfort and convenience and no regard at all for the well-being of the husbandmen, the simple levy system was preferred and consequently adopted as the uniform rule for collecting the tithe, because it could be depended upon to produce the same amount of revenue in bad years. And so the well-field system was abolished until it was revived by Tang and Yi Yin.

In this connection it is interesting to note that there are quite a few findings in the recent oracle-bone discoveries that tend to give substantial support, though not conclusive proof, to the assumption that the ancients, especially the Shang people, had practiced the well-field system.[118] In the divination inscriptions there are often found the characters *tu tian,* meaning "to exert toil in the fields." Here one emperor ordered a prince to lead "a multitude to exert toil in the fields" in one place; and there another emperor commanded a general to do the same to another. And the way the character "field" *(tian)* was inscribed especially invites our attention. Ordinarily, it was inscribed as ⊞ . But when the term *tu tian,* "exerting toil in the fields," was used, the character often took the forms ⊞, ⊞ and even ⊞. Surely one may not be accused of indulging in pure fancy if one supposes that these were orders given by those emperors to clear the grounds of certain areas which were formerly wilderness, so that the land might be apportioned among husbandmen for cultivation according to the well-field system. And, also, it may not be too rash to infer that if the later Shang emperors continued to undertake such agrarian ventures with so much zeal, they might very well have taken the lesson from Tang and Yi Yin, who had founded their dynasty.

To return, after having put their land program into execution, the two founders of Shang endeavored to arm and train the husbandmen in Bo for self-defense. In those days, weapons made of metal, mainly bronze, were not easy to come by; and understandably the ruling house in each princedom was wont to keep them for use solely by themselves or their kinsmen. Sticks and staffs, darts and slings, even bows with stone-headed arrows, of course, could be fashioned by common people; but the princes, as a rule, did not encourage the production of such weapons on a large scale, especially if they were not for their own use. While these lords might continuously and vociferously profess their determination to provide all necessary protection to their agricultural population, and while they might even sincerely desire the latter's prosperity, if only for the hope they might milk the more from them, manifestly it was not in their own interest to allow their subjects to become strong enough to defy them. Moreover, they could always find some means to keep the lowly husbandman in his place. During cultivation seasons, the toilers in the field are of course too hard-worked to have any spare time. But after the crops are gathered, it is also easy for the princes to devise many services to require of their subjects. Thus, all in all, the agrarian population in the Xia dynasty must have been kept most of the time unarmed and defenseless.

But Tang and Yi Yin changed that in their tiny princedom of Shang. Breaking with the general, customary practice, they sought not only to arm their husbandmen but also to train them to use military weapons with the greatest dexterity. Since all understood that this was for the defense, or in the interest, of the entire populace, a conscription system seems to have been introduced without fanfare from the rulers and with complete acceptance by the ruled. We have no clear record for these. But from Tang's own lips we know that when Jie finally launched an expedition against him, it was in the midst of a busy cultivation season; and that Tang's principal charge against the tyrant was that he had deliberately taken advantage of the time to force Tang's men to leave their fields unattended.[119] Again, from the oracle-bone inscriptions we learn that in the reign of Wuding, 1324–1266 B.C., when the Shang empire was threatened by an invasion from the northwestern nomadic tribes, this tenth-generation descendant of Tang repeatedly ordered conscription of forces: Here three thousand were conscripted; there, five thousand. The largest number conscripted on one particular date was ten thousand.[120] Admittedly this occurred some three hundred years later, and the conscription system could have been developed in the interval. But during these centuries, except for the war between Jie and Tang, no large armed conflict had taken place. So it seems more probable than not that whatever conscription system the Shang had, though it might have been improved by later emperors, was first introduced by the founders of the dynasty. Moreover, it appears that Wuding remembered the men who were responsible for the success of the earlier war. For at the moment of the national crisis he had to face himself, he sacrificed not only to Tang and his other ancestors for their intervention with heaven, but also to Yi Yin especially for the latter's guidance.[121]

Meanwhile, with Yi Yin's assistance, Tang determined to conduct a model administration for his people. Later, after having extended the same kind of government throughout the empire, he was eulogized as follows: "Our sovereign keeps aloof from dissolute music and women. He does not seek to accumulate goods and riches. If anyone is virtuous, he elevates him to high office; if anyone is meritorious of service, he grants him rewards. He follows others' advice as faithfully as if they were derived from his own mind; he never spares himself in correcting his errors. Always leaning towards leniency, always compassionate and benevolent, he makes his integrity shine on millions of people." [122]

One wonders how many monarchs in the history of the world deserve such a description. But perhaps nothing impressed the people of Bo so strongly and so strikingly as Tang's employment of officers. In all other princedoms, and in Jie's imperial court itself, the established rule was that the kinsmen of the ruling house monopolized the high offices. But, true to his eulogy, Tang broke with the rule sharply. Yi Yin served him both as teacher and as prime minister; and until Yi Yin came to Bo, he had no prior connection with the house of Shang. And after Yi Yin, Tang appears to have selected all the officers of the little princedom purely on the basis of merit, many of them probably from the ranks of the husbandmen themselves. If nothing else secured for Tang the loyalty of his people, this act by itself probably would.

· 7 ·

THE FALL OF XIA

At that time the territory under Tang's control was very small, no larger than seventy *li* square (about forty kilometers square).[123] But with such capable men as Tang and Yi Yin to administer it, it soon attained an unprecedented degree of prosperity. It could have been a prey to predatory nomadic tribes or envious adjacent princes; but as the strength of its armed husbandmen grew, Tang felt sure that this would serve as an effective deterrent. However, he had some reservations about a neighbor to the west, the Prince of Ge, a man known for excessive arrogance and rapaciousness. If the people of Ge had been poor before, they were now plunged into even more insufferable depths of deprivation by his oppressive extortions. And finally, squeeze them as hard as the tyrant would, he could not squeeze anything out of them anymore. Now that Bo had prospered so much in contrast, with its granaries all filled, Tang rightly feared that his ravenous neighbor might be secretly plotting a surprise attack. To ward off this potential danger, Tang tried first to convert this petty despot to a path of righteousness. In the *Book of History,* there was originally a document called the *Tang Expedition (tangzheng)* pertaining to this event. Though it is no longer extant, Mencius, who was apparently conversant with it before the loss, gave us the following account.

> When Tang dwelt in Bo, he bordered upon the state of Ge. The prince of Ge abandoned himself to wickedness, neglecting all sacrifices. Tang sent a messenger to inquire why he did not sacrifice. He replied, "I have no proper sacrificial animals to offer." Thereupon Tang sent him a number of oxen and sheep. But the prince of Ge ate them, not using them for sacrifice. Tang sent a messenger again to ask why he did not sacrifice. He replied, "I have no necessary cereals to offer." Tang ordered the people [of Bo] to go and till the fields for him, with the old and feeble carrying provisions for the workers in advance. But when the latter were on the way, the prince of Ge set upon them with his men. He robbed them of the wine, the food, the millet, the rice; and killed those who refused to give them up. There was a small boy who brought some meat and millet for the workers; he was robbed and killed too.
>
> Thus with reference to this incident it is written in the *Book* [*of History*], "The prince of Ge wreaked his enmity on the provision carriers." Because of the murder of the boy, Tang led an expedition against him. And all within the four seas said of Tang, "He did this not out of a desire to enrich himself with the land, but to avenge a common man and woman." [124]

The expedition, of course, ended in Tang's triumph. Tang's fame soared even higher as a result of his treatment of the conquered state. Only the tyrant was destroyed, but the rest of the people were given a new life. They were incorporated into the community of Shang, sharing with them his enlightened and benevolent rule. The consequences of this Ge expedition were so far-reaching that we read again from Mencius:

> Tang's first expedition began with Ge. After that, all under heaven put their faith and hope in him. Later, when he took his expedition eastward, the rude tribes in the west complained; when he took his expedition southward, the uncultured nations in the north complained. Their cry was, "Why must he come to us later?" Everywhere the people longed for him as they would be longing for rain in a great drought. (And when his expedition did come, so calm and assured would be the people) that market-goers would not stop going to the market and the plowers in the fields would not alter their work schedule. While he punished the rulers, he consoled the people. His arrival was like a timely rainfall. The people were overjoyed. Thus it is recorded in the *Book [of History]* that the people all said, "We have waited for the Lord. Now that our Lord has come, we shall be able to breathe again!" [125]

All in all, in his lifetime Tang "undertook eleven expeditions, and thereafter he had no more enemy under heaven." [126] However, after this first expedition to Ge, both he and Yi Yin were more perturbed than elated with their own success. Jie was still the acknowledged sovereign of the empire, and no state could legitimately invade or incorporate another without his express sanction. Moreover, speaking strictly from the standpoint of force, whatever Tang could muster up was nothing to compare with that of Jie. Even if the emperor should think it beneath his dignity to use armed force against Tang himself, he could order the hegemon Kunwu to do so, whose base was then located between the Yellow River and the Ji River, only some 150 kilometers north of Bo. Thus from every consideration, legal or practical, Tang's situation was very precarious. So rather than wait for Jie's displeasure, Tang, after consultation with Yi Yin, decided to send the latter to seek an audience with Jie at the imperial capital. The envoy was not only to explain the necessity for the Ge expedition and renew Tang's allegiance to the Xia, but also to recommend dutifully to Jie to adopt the principles of Yao and Shun in the government of the empire. It was even agreed between Tang and Yi Yin that if Jie was willing to accept the recommendation, Yi Yin could remain in the capital to assist the sovereign in the implementation of the policy.[127] What they both wished to see was not their own personal aggrandizement but the betterment of the empire such as Yao and Shun would have desired. Altogether, under Tang's orders, Yi Yin was to undertake similar missions to Jie four more times.[128] And in all of them he failed to attain the main objective of persuading the emperor to follow their advice. But in the first few instances he did seem to have succeeded in placating Jie so that the monarch did nothing to punish Tang or interfere with his freedom of action.

However, with the return of Yi Yin from the first mission, Tang's fame spread much faster than probably either of them had at first thought possible. All the people of the empire began to turn their attention to them. While the whole country was going aimlessly adrift, Tang's position became singularly clear. He stood for harmony for the whole; proper conduct for every individual, high and low alike; and full protection for all, both nomads and husbandmen. And Tang, both by nature and by design, did everything possible to live up to his own beliefs. One day in a wilderness he saw a trapper who, after putting up nets on all four sides, uttered this prayer: "Whether you descend from the sky, or ascend from the earth, or come from any of the directions, may you all be entrapped by my nets." Tang lamented, "Alas! This is depriving the animals of every possible chance." He asked the man to take down the nets on three sides, leaving only one side intact. Then he taught him to pray thus: "If you want to go left, go left; if you want to go right, go right; if you want to go up, go up; if you want to go down, go down. I will take only those who go wrong." [129] Although this advice might not have profited the trapper much, it certainly benefited the giver no end. The story was told and retold, from princedom to princedom, and all the people who heard it were saying, "So much compassion has Tang! It is even extended to animals." And so what with the wide dissemination of the popular acclaim, what with the continuing growth of his military strength, what with the unfailing success of his several subsequent expeditions, in a few years no less than forty states, some to the west and the others to the south of Bo, acknowledged their submission to Tang.[130]

At length Jie became awake to the realities of the situation. More and more states were deserting him to follow Tang. Notwithstanding, as a final act of allegiance, Tang sent Yi Yin once more to Jie for the fifth and last time. If only the emperor would revise his ways of government, there was nothing that Tang would not do for the sovereign. But Jie pretended not to mind the remonstrance, while secretly determined to exterminate Tang for good.[131] On the one hand, he gave instructions to the hegemon Kunwu to prepare for an attack upon Shang; on the other, he treated Yi Yin with the same courtesy and indulgence as before. When Yi Yin found that even the people in the imperial capital were becoming increasingly discontented with Jie's rule, he came to the emperor and reported the situation, saying: "If your majesty persists in not heeding me, you will lose your destiny and be destroyed in no time." Jie clapped his hands and replied with laughter, "There, you are talking nonsense again. I am possessed of the people as the sun is possessed of the sky. Can the sun be destroyed? I shall perish only when the sun perishes." [132] Thereupon Yi Yin considered his mission at an end and proceeded to return to Bo; and Jie let him go unharmed, lest Tang should be forewarned of his real intentions.

Jie had planned to launch the joint assault with Kunwu against Shang at the busiest season of cultivation. Knowing that Tang's forces were composed mainly of husbandmen, he had calculated that that would be the time when his enemy could least effectively organize for defense. But the preparations of Kunwu just across the River Ji were noticed by the people of Bo; and upon Yi Yin's return, Tang realized that much as he would like to avoid it, there was no longer any way possible for him to escape from the use of force. And once this all-important point was decided upon, they took immediate actions. A meeting of all Tang's allies and subordinate princes was called;[133] and a united army was speedily raised, with Tang assuming full command and Yi Yin serving as his chief lieutenant. And before Kunwu got wind of what they were doing, they had already crossed the Ji River and destroyed two of its allies in quick succession.[134] The hegemon's forces, taken by surprise, were forced to beat a precipitate retreat westward in the direction of the imperial seat, hoping to join with Jie. And Tang followed closely on their heels.

So disorganized were Kunwu's forces that though they could have stopped Tang's advance at the left bank of the Yellow River, they let the enemy cross the mighty stream almost unopposed. Again, they could have held them in check at Zhongtiao, "the Middle Branch Mountain," [135] with little effort, but they let them climb over without resistance. Now Tang entered into the plateau of Mingtiao, "the Singing Branch," and he saw the Xia capital stretched below. But between him and the city, he found also that Jie had assembled a huge force which was now being further augmented by Kunwu's remnants. It was an army far greater than Tang's own troops had apparently expected; and Tang himself could feel his own men waver in the advance. Before giving battle, he assembled them together and exhorted them thus:[136]

Come, you multitudinous people, listen all to my words. It is not I, this humble person, who dare to start a rebellion. But the Xia emperor has perpetrated many crimes. It is Heaven's will that he be punished.

(Only a while ago) you multitudes were saying, "The emperor has no pity for us. He is forcing us to leave our works in the fields. He is bent on cutting us up." I have heard these words from you multitudinous people. The Xia emperor has in fact committed this crime. As I fear the Lord Above, I dare not but seek to punish him.

But now you seem to be saying, "What can we do about this Xia crime?"

The Xia emperor has put forth all the strength he can muster up. He has extorted all the manpower he can from the Xia capital by sheer oppression. He has a numerous force. But these men are all spiritless and in discord with him. They are saying this (of their emperor), "May the sun perish this instant! I'd sooner perish with you together." This is the condition of the Xia. I am determined to go forward.

Assist me, I pray you. Assist me, you princes, to carry out the punishment ordered by Heaven. (When this is done), I will greatly reward you. On no account disbelieve me—I will not eat my words. If you do not obey what I have spoken here, I will punish you; and I will also punish your children with you. There will be no forgiveness.[137]

The battle was joined. It was the day of "soft wood hare," *yimao*,[138] in the late summer of the thirty-first year of Jie's reign.[139] There was a tumultuous cloudburst with terrific thunders, but the battle raged on. Before the day was over, the hegemon Kunwu was slain and the Xia army was routed. Under darkness they fled in utter confusion. A smaller band, led by Jie's son Chunwei, made their escape northward, ended up in the deserts of modern Mongolia, and eventually became assimilated with the indigent indigenous tribes.[140] Jie also got away with his closest entourage; and before they decamped, he managed to take all the treasures and jades he had collected in his palace with him. He knew he could not go west; the flight would have been soon halted by the turbulent waters of the Yellow River. And for the same reason he could not go south, for the Xia capital was close to the bend of the mighty stream. As to the north, better informed than his son, he was far more aware of the scarcity of supplies in those sandy plains. The only possible escape seemed therefore to lie eastward. Though this was the very direction from which Tang had come, yet the territory had been long controlled by his subordinate and ally Kunwu, where he could hope to find some people willing to give him succor and refuge. Besides, he and his men had always indulged in hunting game, and they were used to the nomadic way of living. So skirting around Tang's advancing forces, he stole across the mountains and made a dash to the east. Many a time he stopped on the way to ask for help. But again and again he was disappointed. The people, both disaffected with his past rule and fearful of his present demands, just ran away at the sight of him and his men.[141] It was not until he reached Sanzhong, a state located in modern Dingtao in eastern Shandong, some 450 kilometers from his former capital as the crow flies, that its prince was willing to give him shelter at the price of all the jades and treasures he could deliver. But he was not destined to enjoy the repose long. Tang's pursuing troops soon arrived. Sanzhong was taken, along with the same jades and treasures; and Jie had to flee for his life again.[142]

In his desperation Jie now could see only one last possible place of safe refuge—Yue, where Shaokang's younger son Wuyu had gone to. From records, or from family tales told to him, he knew that this branch of his house had been enfeoffed in the southwestern extremity of the empire; or rather it had succeeded in establishing a sort of independent kingdom outside his former dominion. But contact between the two branches had been long disrupted. Jie probably had little knowledge of how Yue had actually fared these centuries. Nor had he any definite idea as to what terrain or what wild tribes or nations were interposed between Yue and his present position. But this was his last possible resort; and recklessly he darted southward. Before he could get halfway there, however, he was caught by Tang's pursuing troops, made a prisoner, and held as an exile under surveillance at Nanchao in modern Anhui province, until he died of natural causes.[143] And thus came to an end the first of the so-called "Three Dynasties" in the early Chinese history—the Xia dynasty.

NOTES

1. His fief was called Xia. It is south of the Yellow River in modern Henan. It still contains a district bearing the name Yu. The particular place where Yu withdrew himself was called Yangcheng, in the present-day Dengfeng district.

2. *Mencius, wanzhang,* 1.

3. Yu's capital was Anyi, in the district of the same name in modern Shanxi. See Ban Gu, *Qian Han Shu, dilizhi,* and Fa Ye, *Hou Han Shu, junguozhi.* Some scholars, however, believe that Yu made Yangcheng his capital.

4. See Ban Gu, *Qian Han Shu, xiongnu liezhuan,* 1.

5. Some Chinese, mostly in southern China, also call themselves the Tang people after the Tang dynasty, another glorious dynasty of China.

6. See *Ci Hai.*

7. *Li Ji, wangzhi.*

8. The compositions of these characters can all be found in Xu Shen's dictionary.

9. *Book of History, gaoyaomo.* Also see above, p. 91.

10. See any Chinese dictionary.

11. See Chap. II, note 65.

12. *Book of History, wucheng.*

13. *Zuozhuan,* Duke Ding, 10th year.

14. See above, pp. 106–7.

15. *China in the 16th Century, The Journals of Matthew Ricci 1583–1610,* p. 7.

16. Some Chinese scholars have maintained that *huaxia* is derived from Huashan, a mountain range in Shaanxi, and from Xiashui, another name for the Han River which flows from Shaanxi to join the Yangtze in Hubei. They allege that this is the region in which the Chinese were originally based. But this could not be. For the capitals of Yao, Shun, and Yu were all situated to the north of the region, separated from it by the mighty Yellow River.

17. In the antiquated version of the *Book of History,* the entire text of *dayumo* may be found. But many Chinese scholars have expressed skepticisms about the authenticity of the text, though not about the title.

18. *Book of History, gaoyaomo;* also *Mencius, gongsunchou,* 1.

19. *Jin Shu, taokan liezhuan.*

20. *Book of History, wuzizhige,* as translated by James Legge.

21. *Zhangguoche, weiche.* The brewer's name is Yidi. Also, see *Mencius, lilou,* 1.

22. See above, p. 52.

23. Ban Gu, *Qian Han Shu, jiaosizhi.*

24. *Zuozhuan,* Duke Xuan, 3rd year.

25. Ibid. See also *Historical Records, zhou benji.*

26. *Historical Records, zhou benji* and *qin benji.*

27. Ban Gu, *Qian Han Shu, jiaosizhi.* Also see *Historical Records, qinshihuangdi benji,* 28th year.

28. *Bamboo Chronicles.*

29. *Historical Records, lishu.*

30. Ban Gu, *Qian Han Shu, lulizhi.*

31. This is to alleviate the burden of transportation; the greater the distance, the lighter the burden. See Duan Yucai, *Guwen Shangshu Zhuanyi;* also Sun Xingyan, *Shangshu Jinguwen Zhushu.*

32. The lowest grade of feudal princes. A *nan*'s fief is supposed to be fifty *li* square.

33. The higher grade of feudal princes. Their fiefs vary from seventy *li* square to one hundred *li* square.

34. Sworn as in "sworn allegiance."

35. See *Book of History, gaoyaomo*. Yu was recorded therein to have said, "I have assisted in completing the five zones, extending over five thousand *li*."

36. The tenth year of Yu's reign according to the *Historical Records*; the eighth year according to the *Bamboo Chronicles*.

37. *Zuozhuan*, Duke Ai, 7th year.

38. *Historical Records, xia benji*.

39. *Guo Yu, luyu; Bamboo Chronicles; Hanfeizi, shixie*.

40. *Historical Records, taishigong zixu*; Huangfu Mi, *Diwang Shiji*.

41. For transcribing the name Qi(Kai), see Chap. II, note 60. For Qi's having another name, Kai, see *Mozi, gengzhu*.

42. *Mencius, wanzhang*, I.

43. *Hanfeizi, waichu shuo*, right II.

44. *Bamboo Chronicles*; also *Zuozhuan*, Duke Zhao, 4th year.

45. Ibid. See Du Yu's comments.

46. *Historical Records, xia benji*; see commentaries by Sima Zhen and Zhang Shoujie.

47. *Huainanzi, qisu xun*, commentaries by Gao You. Also see *Historical Records, xia benji, taishigong*'s remarks.

48. See above, p. 8. *She* may be translated as "Spirit of the Land."

49. While Yao and Shun were called Di Yao and Di Shun in both the two discourses of Confucius—*Virtues of the Five Premier Emperors* and *Genealogy of Premier Emperors*—and in the *Historical Records, wudi benji*; Yu was mentioned only once as Di Yu in the *Historical Records*.

50. See Guo Moruo, *Jiagu Wenzi Yanjiu*, pp. 45–46.

51. Some Chinese scholars who like to harp upon the "good ancient days" maintain that the three dynasties had called their emperors *wang* because they did not think they were worthy of being called *di*, whose virtues are far superior. This is ascribing too much modesty to those who themselves did not seem to lay too much claim on that particular virtue.

52. In modern Chinese dictionaries, *lu* is usually defined as "to kill." But in ancient times, its meanings, besides "to kill," include "to disgrace," "to humiliate," or "to punish." See *Zuozhuan*, Duke Wen, 6th year.

53. *Huainanzi, qisu xun*.

54. Except for the *Bamboo Chronicles*, all ancient sources place Qi(Kai)'s reign between nine and ten years.

55. Houyi was given Qionggu as his fief, about twenty-five kilometers south of modern Luoyang.

56. *Guo Yu, zhouyu; Historical Records, zhou benji*.

57. *Bamboo Chronicles*.

58. *Book of History, wuzizhige*. For using second-batch documents as sources, see Appendix, especially its Item Five.

Some scholars maintain that *wuzi* does not mean "five sons," but is one Wu Guan, a brother of Taikang, who staged an abortive revolt. But this is in disagreement with *Book of History, shuxu*, which explicitly says, "Taikang lost his state. His five brothers, while looking for him at the bend of the Luo, composed *wuzizhige, Songs of Five Sons*."

59. *Zuozhuan*, Duke Xiang, 4th year.

60. This has been computed to be October 22, 2137 B.C. See Dong Zuobin, *Yin Lipu*, part II, chap. 3, p. 4.

61. *Book of History, shuxu*.

62. Although the expedition is acknowledged to be a historical fact, and the proclamation a certainty, yet it is generally agreed that the original document has been lost and the present version is a forgery.

63. His name was Bofeng. See *Zuozhuan*, Duke Zhao, 28th year.

64. Some scholars think that Zhenguan was the fief of a prince related to the Xia, and Xiang fled to his kinsman there for protection. See Qian Mu, *Guoshi Dagang*, I.

65. *Zuozhuan*, Duke Xiang, 4th year.

66. Ibid.

67. *Zuozhuan*, Duke Ai, 1st year.

68. The place was called Youreng, in modern Jining district, Shandong.

69. Brothers in ancient times were often given descriptive names to mark the order of birth, such as *bo* or *tai* for the firstborn, *zhong* for the second, *shu* for the third, and *ji* for the fourth. *Shao* means "young" or "younger."

70. *Zuozhuan*, Duke Ai, 1st year.

71. Modern Yucheng, Henan.

72. Southeast of Yucheng.

73. Modern Dezhou, Shandong, about three hundred kilometers north of Yucheng.

74. *Chu Ci, tianwen*.

75. *Zuozhuan*, Duke Xiang, 4th year.

76. Ibid.; also, Duke Ai, 1st year.

77. *Bamboo Chronicles*.

78. Ibid.

79. *Historical Records, zhou benji*.

80. *Historical Records, yuewanggoujian shijia*. See also *Wuyue Chunqiu*.

81. *Historical Records, dongyue liezhuan*; also, Ban Gu, *Qian Han Shu, nanyuewang liezhuan* and *minyuewang liezhuan*.

82. See *Bamboo Chronicles; Chu Ci, tianwen*; and Wang Guowei, *Yin Bucizhong Suojian Xiangong-xianwang Kao*.

83. *Historical Records, xia benji*.

84. Ibid.; see the commentaries. Also see *Shangshu Dazhuan*.

85. The Han dynasty was founded in the 2nd century B.C. by Liu Bang, who traced his genealogical descent back to Liu Lei. See *Historical Records, hangaozu benji*.

86. See Wang Guowei, *Yin Bucizhong Suojian Xiangongxianwang Kao*.

87. *Historical Records, yin benji*; also, Dong Zuobin, *Jiaguxue Liushinian*, p. 72.

88. Wang Guowei, *Yin Bucizhong Suojian Xiangongxianwang Kao*.

89. Ban Gu, *Baihu Tongyi*, I, *hao*. The Chinese character for "hegemon" is *ba*. Sometimes *bo* is also used.

90. *Guo Yu, zhengyu*. Also see Ying Shao, *Fengsu Tongyi*.

91. *Zuozhuan*, Duke Zhao, 12th year.

92. *Zuozhuan*, Duke Zhao, 19th year.

93. This is acknowledged by all Western scholars. See, for example, Kenneth Scott Latourette, *The Chinese: Their History and Culture*, p. 31.

94. The name should be transliterated as Zhou, according to the Pinyin system. But since he was the last Shang emperor, who was to be overthrown by the Zhou dynasty, in order to avoid confusion we have given it as Zou.

95. See *Hanshi Waizhuan*, chap. 4; Liu Xiang, *Liennuzhuan*; and Huangfu Mi, *Diwang Shiji*.

96. *Historical Records, xia benji.*

97. *Huainanzi, zhushu xun.*

98. *Zuozhuan*, Duke Zhao, 4th year.

99. *Bamboo Chronicles.*

100. *Guo Yu, jinyu.*

101. *Bamboo Chronicles.*

102. Tang had several names. For instance, he was born on a *yi* (soft wood) day, so he was called Dayi, as is shown in the oracle-bone inscriptions. When he spoke of himself, he gave the name Lu.

103. This is from *Book of History, shuxu*, attributed to Confucius. The literal translation should be "to follow the ancestral Emperor in habitation."

104. See above, p. 97.

105. One may find a good example in Gugong Danfu (*Historical Records, zhou benji*), though his times are later than those of Tang.

106. In the oracle-bone inscriptions, Yi Yin is sometimes called Huang Yin. Also see Wang Guowei, *Gushi Xinzheng*, chap. IV, sec. 1.

107. *Mencius, wanzhang*, I. The princedom was Youshen, modern Chenliu, Henan.

108. Ibid.

109. Ibid.

110. Ibid.

111. Ibid. There are, however, two other versions of how Yi Yin came to Tang: (1) Having heard of Yi Yin, Tang invited him to enter his service. Yi Yin was willing, but the prince of Youshen would not allow him to leave his princedom. So Tang asked for the hand of the prince's daughter in marriage. The prince of Youshen was pleased, and he allowed Yi Yin to accompany the bride as a cook. See *Lushi Chunqiu, xiaoxinglan; benwei.* (2) Yi Yin himself sought to enter into Tang's service. He got into the latter's good graces through his cooking. See *Hanfeizi, nanyan.*

112. *Mencius, gongsunchou*, II.

113. *Book of History, shuxu.*

114. 6.6 *mu* make an acre.

115. *Mencius, tengwengong*, I.

116. A contemporary of Mencius and an agricultural expert.

117. *Mencius, tengwengong*, I.

118. Dong Zuobin, *Yin Lipu*, part II, chap. 4, sec. 4.

119. *Book of History, tangshi.*

120. Dong Zuobin, *Yin Lipu*, part II, chap. 9, sec. 1.

121. Ibid. One of the dates Wuding sacrificed to Yi Yin is the day of *renzi* (sea water rat) in the fifth moon of the thirty-ninth year of his reign.

122. *Book of History, zhonghuizhigao.*

123. *Mencius, lianghuiwang*, II. One may wonder how a tiny princedom like Shang could have conquered a vast empire such as ancient China. But as late as 19th century A.D., such a phenomenon happened in Africa. In 1816 a minor clan chief named Cheka, with 1,500 followers occupying perhaps one hundred square miles, began to build the Zulu empire, which by 1826 ruled over two million people and hundreds of thousands of square miles.

124. *Mencius, tengwengong*, II.

125. Ibid., *lianghuiwang*, II.

126. Ibid., *tengwengong*, II.

127. See *Book of History, shuxu*, and *Historical Records, yin benji.*

128. *Mencius, gaozi*, II.

129. *Lushi Chunqiu, mengdongji, yiyong.*

130. *Shangshu Dazhuan* says that the forty states are south of the River Han. The *Bamboo Chronicles* mentions that in the 17th year of Jie's reign, Tang sent Yi Yin to Jie, probably for the first time; in the 21st year, Tang sent an expedition to Youluo and conquered it; and in the 22nd year, Jing (modern Hubei) submitted to Tang.

131. There is a story that Jie summoned Tang to his court and had him imprisoned for a while and then released. We have not seen fit to use it, for it bears too much similarity to the imprisonment of Wen Wang of Zhou by the last emperor of Shang.

132. *Shangshu Dazhuan* and *Hanshi Waizhuan*, chap. II.

133. *Zuozhuan*, Duke Zhao, 4th year.

134. *Book of Poetry, shangsong: changfa.* The ode says, "After punishing Wei and Gu, the turn came to Kunwu and Xia Jie."

135. The mountain was called Er at that time. See *Book of History, shuxu.*

136. The following is a literal translation of *Book of History, tangshi*, the *Address of Tang*. The original text used here is from Duan Yucai, *Guwen Shangshu Zhuanyi.*

137. The reader may wonder if this last remark is in accord with Tang's known compassion. But the severe punishment was probably the practice of the times, which, originating with Qi(Kai), had already obtained for centuries. See above, p. 118.

138. *Zuozhuan*, Duke Zhao, 18th year.

139. *Bamboo Chronicles.*

140. *Historical Records, xiongnu liezhuan.*

141. See some instances mentioned in *Shangshu Dazhuan.*

142. *Book of History, shuxu.*

143. *Book of History, zhonghuizhigao*; also see *Bamboo Chronicles.*

CHAPTER IV

THE SHANG DYNASTY

(18th–14th Century B.C.)

· 1 ·
DELIMITATIONS OF THE SHANG EMPIRE

In their ancient records the Chinese always maintained that they were possessed of one vast empire embracing the then known world in its entirety. But as to the limits of that dominion, no precise demarcations were ever given. As has been noted before, the *Historical Records* describes the rule of the Yellow Emperor in this manner: "Wherever under heaven there were people who disobeyed him, he would go after them; but as soon as they were pacified, he would leave them. He crossed mountains and opened roads, never stopping anywhere to rest for long. On the east he went as far as the ocean and ascended the venerable Taishan. On the west he went as far as the Kongtong mountains and ascended the Rooster Head Peak. On the south he went as far as the Yangtze and ascended the Bear and the Xiang ranges. On the north he chased away the Hunzhou barbarians and convoked a meeting of the lords and princes at Mount Fu." [1] Indeed, these notations are more like the entries of a travel log than the delimitations of an empire. And perhaps their true meaning is just that, and no more—except for one difference. Wherever the Yellow Emperor went, he asserted his authority and no one remained there to challenge it long. (See Map I.)

The extent of territory, as envisioned by this desultory description, is roughly some 1,000 kilometers in width and 1,600 kilometers in length. One may well raise the question: Could a primitive conqueror of remote antiquity, devoid of sophistication in the intricacies of organization and discipline, have achieved a durable conquest of such stupendous proportions? Yet historical facts have shown that, with nomadic nations, exploits even more gargantuan and incredible are not only possible but real. Some forty centuries after the passing of the Yellow Emperor, while mankind in general had advanced appreciably in civilization and government, while written lan-

146

guage had already developed in many quarters capable of recording events in detailed accuracy, Genghis Khan, who began his career with only some twoscore followers, all like himself unschooled in these civilized arts, was able in his lifetime to sweep across the immense hinterland of two continents, from the Gobi in Asia to the Black Forest in Europe. And consequently his grandson Batu, who trampled all Russia under his iron hoof, became the first of the khans of the Golden Horde who ruled over that extensive Eurasian region for some two centuries. While Batu was holding court in his pitched tent on the banks of the Volga to receive embassies from the pope, if he had been asked what was the extent of his domain, he probably could have given an answer no more precise than just naming the few most important mountains and rivers he and his horsemen had climbed over or ferried across.

Modern China has endeavored through archaeological excavations to find confirmation for her ancient records. But except for the so-called oracle bones, the findings so far pertain mostly to neolithic or prehistorical times. Still, an observation of interest deserves mention here. Painted pottery, typified by large, bulbous red pots painted with bold geometric designs, usually in black, was first found in Yangshao, Henan.[2] Then similar articles were excavated in many sites, separated by great distances, from Manchuria [3] to Gansu.[4] If one examines the map that gives a rough sketch of the Yellow Emperor's conquering perambulations, one may well imagine that there exists some relationship between them and those sites. This is not to say that the spread of what is known as the "Yangshao culture" has anything to do directly with the military activities of the Yellow Emperor. But if the spread of this culture had occurred before the time of the first known conqueror of China, the fact of itself might have in part inspired the conquest. If, on the other hand, the spread had occurred after his time, then his conquest might have been a primal factor responsible for the dissemination of the art of making painted pottery.

The Yellow Emperor was not known to have divided his dominion regionally for administrative purpose. The first intimation of a division of the empire into nine regions is attributed to Shaohao, his son and successor.[5] Although this is nothing more than an unsubstantiated allusion, yet it has analogues in history. After the death of Genghis, the Mongol Empire, though all acknowledgedly under the overlordship of one khakhan (great khan), was divided into four khanates—the personal domain of the khakhan, the Jagatai Khanate, the Chinchar Khanate (which is known to the West as the Golden Horde), and the Ilkhanate, each of the latter three khanates under a different khan. But inasmuch as the early generations of the Mongol conquerors were still largely nomadic, they saw no need to draw territorial demarcations between the western possessions of the khakhan and the Jagatai Khanate, or between the Jagatai Khanate and the Golden Horde, or between the Golden Horde and the Ilkhanate, as a result of which armed conflicts for the use of waters or grasslands were not uncommon among themselves. Shaohao's divisions were likely even more chaotic. While most of the nations conquered by the Mongols were agricultural, with fixed dwellings and cities, Shaohao's dominion was peopled largely by nomads. It is no wonder that Shaohao, being incessantly beset with the necessity of having to track down his own acknowledged subjects, tried to send out officers to those nine regions to encourage the tribes or houses to engage more in agriculture.[6] Zhuanxu was said to be a more capable ruler. He was credited with the subjugation of the Jiuli tribes and the extension of imperial authority to the area between the two lakes, Dongting and Poyang, south of the Yangtze.[7] Yet in the matter of delimiting his vast domain, there is no record to indicate that he had made any headway.

It is in this light that Di Ku's enfeoffment of his son Yao as Prince of Tang may be viewed as a sort of political effort to guide the country toward further agrarian development, the better for the administration of the empire.[8] But the process was painfully slow. There are indications that besides Yao there were others who were enfeoffed; but the number does not appear to be large.[9] Moreover, whatever enfeoffments might have been, these were often nullified almost as soon as they had been made. For one reason or another, the enfeoffed tribes or houses themselves might not keep to the confines of their so-called fiefs. Or other tribes or houses, stronger or more numerous, would simply move into the supposed forbidden territories without any leave. It is in this light too that Yao's posting the so-called Four Mountains in the four quarters may be considered as another forward step taken in the interest of effective administration.[10]

But it remained for Shun to put the regional divisions into actual administrative use. Because of the flood, many communication lines were disrupted and Shun was compelled to divide the empire temporarily into twelve regions instead of nine.[11] Yet, again because of the flood, not only was he able to cause them to establish their headquarters each on the site of a high mountain, but he was successful in assigning them specific functions such as the training and organization of people and the deepening of the channels of streams within their own jurisdictions, which they apparently performed willingly to his satisfaction. At the same time, in order to prepare for an eventual return to the old system of division, he instructed Yu that in the course of his subjugating the flood, he should also see to it that the boundaries of the nine regions be clearly defined.[12] Indeed, it was only after this task was accomplished that the Central Nation was in a position "to confer lands and surnames" in consequence of which all the houses, tribes, and nations pledged not to encroach upon each other's allocated territories.

As can be seen from Map II, the dominion of Yao and Shun embraced all of the middle and lower parts of the Yellow River and the Yangtze valleys. However, as far as the delimitation of the frontiers is concerned, it leaves much to be desired. In fact, there are no frontiers to speak of. Apparently, the ancients believed that theirs was a universal dominion that automatically embraced the entire world. The nine regions were its principal and most important parts, and Yu had traversed the length and breadth of them all. Beyond them, except for the east, which was circumscribed by the ocean as it is now, there were only barren wastes to the north, sandy plateaus to the west, underdeveloped wildernesses to the south. These fringe areas were the very ends of the earth, so to speak, and they were all so thinly populated that they could be simply regarded as unimportant extensions of several border regions in contact with them. To the ancients, therefore, it was unnecessary to mark out the exact frontiers of the empire as it was right and proper for Yu to make this report to Shun: "O emperor! All under the bright heaven, from the shores of the ocean to the corners of green growths, all the black-haired people of the myriad nations, high and low, willingly acknowledge themselves to be your subjects." [13]

But this state of things did not last long. With the removal of the common danger of the flood, the old spirit of nomadic independence started reasserting itself. Though all the tribes and nations had pledged to restrict their movements within the confines of their allocated portions of land, as time went on they felt increasingly resentful of the constraint imposed on their freedom. The Sanmiao tribes were probably just the first to express such discontent in action.[14] And as their rebellion broke out in the open, all the princes of the empire must have been watching closely to see what would happen. It was because of the fear that a show of weakness might doom the empire to irreversible breakup that Yu insisted on, and Shun grudgingly agreed to, the use of force. However, thanks to Shun's milder policy and personal influence, the Sanmiao returned to the fold before long, and the empire was preserved intact for the moment.

But this incident must have made a deep impression on Yu. He realized more than ever that the empire they had striven so hard to erect was simply built on sand. In order to make it endure, he must think up a new system. Hence his grand scheme of reorganization.[15] As he visualized it, he would have his Imperial Domain, a thousand *li* square, entirely peopled with husbandmen. In the next zone, which is five hundred *li* in each direction from the Imperial Domain, he would have princes enfeoffed whose inclinations should be decidedly more agricultural than nomadic. And in the next zone, the Pacified Zone, he would settle the tribes or nations which were both friendly and receptive of cultural dissemination. But as to the rest of the empire, he would just leave it to the nomads. If any of these should acknowledge his sovereignty and swear allegiance to him, he would call their territories the Sworn Zone. As for those who did not or would not, he would keep them as far as possible and let them roam wherever they would in their own Wild Zone.

But Yu died before he could put any part of his scheme into practice. And shortly after came the reign of Taikang and the subsequent usurpation by Houyi and Hanzhuo, which ushered in an era of the ascendancy of nomadism. Not to speak of the central authorities who abandoned themselves to the pleasures of the chase, nor of those nations or tribes who had always been nomads, even with the "hundred surnames" whom Yao and Shun had formerly depended upon for the building of a better empire, reversion to the nomadic way of life seems to have become the fashion. Of this there can be no better illustration than the incessant migrations of the house of Shang.[16] If such was the way the descendants of Shun's minister of commonalty had been conducting themselves, what else could be expected from other surnames? Thus, in a manner of speaking, except for the segment of agrarian population which was by circumstances tied to the soil, the country as a whole had again become nomadic. As nomads are by nature no respecters of boundaries, so the system of fiefs which Di Ku, Yao, Shun, and Yu had successively sought so much to build up for the sake of a more effective administration of the empire crumbled without a sound. If a few of their enfeoffments were remembered still, it was only as adornments to family lineage and nothing more. Yet, even for the nomads, they must needs know something about their own whereabouts, or a little about the general geography lying in the four directions. Thus a vague knowledge of the nine regions was retained by the general public, and in time the term "nine regions" itself came to be used and accepted as an expression meaning "the known world" as a whole.

In this situation, the worst sufferers were the agrarian population. If the rise of Tang must be attributed to a single factor, perhaps it may be said to be his vision and readiness to teach and train the husbandmen to organize and arm themselves for self-defense.[17] But once he did that, he altered the structural pattern of the empire. In making war, nomads seldom worry over logistics; more often than not they roam far and wide in entire tribes, including women and children, and settle in newly invaded lands without wasting any concern about what is to happen to their original base. But with the husbandmen, everything is different. In launching an expedition against a distant enemy, not the whole populace but only a limited number of men can be employed for the adventure. Moreover, while logistics for conveying necessary supplies to the front is a matter of first importance, anxiety about the safety of the home base is all the more a matter of perpetual preoccupation. Under such conditions it is difficult to expect an army of husbandmen to effect as extensive conquests as organized nomadic forces can, especially in ancient times when communications were so crude and primitive. Consequently the Shang Empire, as founded by Tang, is much more restricted in scope than either the nine regions Yu had charted or the rough limits the Yellow Emperor had traversed.

Understandably, detailed records or definitive descriptions about either the divisions or the boundaries of the Shang Empire are lacking. But from indirect sources, especially from the recently discovered oracle-bone inscriptions, a bare sketch may be attempted. It is not certain that Tang had charted his domain on the model of Yu's grand scheme of reorganization.[18] Yet a casual survey of the accompanying map (Map III) may perhaps convince a skeptical reader of some similarities between them. In the center there is the imperial domain, which the Shang called *zhongshang*, or Central Shang.[19] On the outside of this, the regions in the four directions are named respectively *dongtu, nantu, xitu,* and *beitu,* or East Land, South Land, West Land, and North Land.[20] Beyond the boundaries of these four "lands" we have the various nations that are obviously nomadic tribes and whose names, starting from the southeast in the map and winding through the south and the west to the north, are *yu, ren, qiang, gui,* and *tu,* which are likely what they each called themselves. But the Shang chose to add to every one of these appellations another word—*fang. Fang* means "direction" or "territory." Originally, the addition was probably meant only to indicate the direction or the territory where a particular nomadic tribe was accustomed to roam, and therefore could be located. Thus *guifang* signified the "Gui direction" or the "Gui territory." But before long this signification seems to have been lost in constant usage, and *guifang* emerged as a complete proper name for that particular nation. Thus, for example, when Wuding, the twenty-second emperor of the dynasty, made war upon them, both the oracle-bone inscriptions and the *Book of Changes* [21] had it that he made war upon Guifang, not upon Gui.

So much for the general outline of the Shang Empire. Yet there are many gaps to fill up. Take, for instance, Central Shang. How should its boundaries be drawn? Indeed, we do not know. However, as a poor substitute, we do have some information about what cities it is supposed to have incorporated or included. When Tang started his conquering career, it was at Bo or Shangqiu that he built up a power base. But after the overthrow of the Xia, for reasons that will be discussed later, he had his administrative capital established in a different locality, some 280 kilometers to the west. Then after him, several of his successors caused the capital to be moved again and again. Until the fifth and last time, all the cities were on the south side of the Yellow River. But when Pangeng (nineteenth emperor) moved to Yin, he crossed over to the north side. Yin served thereafter as the imperial seat for

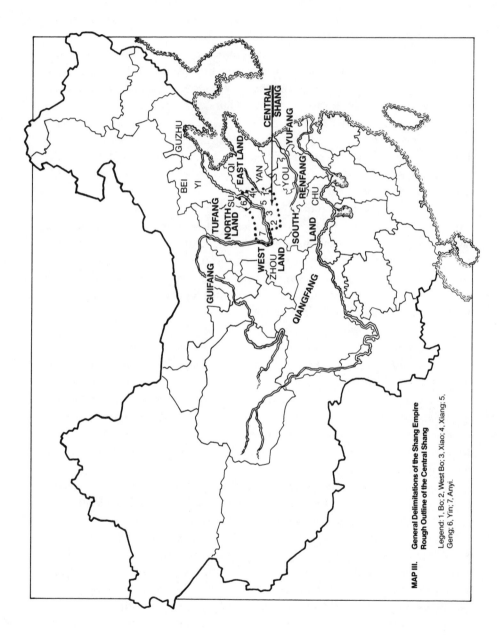

MAP III.   General Delimitations of the Shang Empire
Rough Outline of the Central Shang

Legend: 1, Bo; 2, West Bo; 3, Xiao; 4, Xiang; 5,
Geng; 6, Yin; 7, Anyi.

some two and a half centuries, and no further transference was made. It is for this reason that the Shang dynasty is also known as the Yin dynasty. But as is seen from the oracle-bone inscriptions, the Shang themselves never called their dynasty Yin, but always Shang. As a matter of fact, no matter where they moved their administrative capital, they continued to call Bo the "Great City Shang" or the "Heavenly City Shang." And here it is that throughout the entire duration of the dynasty they maintained their principal ancestral temples; and every time a major crisis occurred, the reigning emperor seldom failed to return to offer sacrifices and ask for protection.[22] In addition, there are also indications that the old Xia capital, Anyi, had also been annexed and placed directly under imperial rule.[23] So, all in all, it seems reasonable to assume that these seven cities, plus their adjacent lands, should be considered as integral parts of what the Shang called the "Central Shang."

If we know little about the exact extent of the "Central Shang," we know even less about that of the "Four Lands," that is, *dongtu, nantu, xitu,* and *beitu.* Perhaps the Shang themselves used these terms very loosely and never had precise delimitations for them. What was implied was that all the nations or tribes inhabiting these lands definitely acknowledged allegiance to the imperial house, paying whatever tribute was required of them, and pledging to live within their own allocated or traditional areas and not to encroach upon one another. As to the epithets "east, "west," "south," and "north," these were just added to give a sort of general indication of where these states happened to lie. And whatever materials we have found in the records seem all to bear out this interpretation.

Take *dongtu,* "the East Land." We are certain of only two places: one, which was later to become the birthplace of Confucius; and the other, the capital of a powerful state in the Zhou dynasty. But the rest appears to be entirely shrouded in obscurity. From Mencius we learn that at the time the Zhou displaced the Shang, no less than fifty states were overturned around this region,[24] let alone those who submitted peacefully to the new regime. But none of these, whether overturned or not, can be identified. In fact, one cannot even be sure that the fifty overturned states were all in the East Land. For Mencius mentioned that a Shang lord was driven to a corner of the sea and slain there; and from the *Historical Records* we know that this was the same lord dispatched by the last Shang emperor on an errand to the north.[25] So the Zhou army, in their victorious march across the Shang Empire, may very well have overturned states both in the East Land and in the North Land.

Turning to the south, we find that the oracle bones have yielded some place names. As a matter of fact, from their inscriptions, a Chinese scholar has traced in detail the routes which the last Shang emperor took when leading an expedition against Renfang, from his imperial seat Yin and back again, including every stop he made in between.[26] The only trouble we find here is that the names were inscribed in archaic characters and few of them can be identified with modern places. Thus though we are pretty certain that the Shang Empire extended to south of the Huai River, we are unable to delineate the frontiers clearly.

Strictly speaking, the region described immediately above is in the southeasterly direction from the Central Shang. The real *nantu* or South Land, therefore, should be more to its west. Here, however, we know of only one state—Chu. This undoubtedly was a precursor to the state bearing the same name, which became one of the most powerful or important states in the Zhou dynasty. Even at the time of the Shang, it appeared to be of considerable size, and the imperial house treated it with special attentiveness. Wuding had a consort who was a princess of Chu. And when a prince of Chu visited the last Shang emperor at the capital, Yin, he was feasted by the latter, and the event was singularly recorded in the oracle-bone inscriptions.[27] Yet as to the precise confines of Chu, we have nothing to follow except the traditional understanding that its territories conformed somewhat with those formerly occupied by the Sanmiao tribes, with some portions in modern Hubei and Jiangxi and the remaining areas in Hunan.

The same sort of story may be told about *xitu* or the West Land, with a slight difference. Because of the three years' war Wuding was obliged to wage against Guifang, the oracle bones have produced a large number of appellations belonging to generals, princes, or places. However, this abundant yield has not profited us correspondingly. Because of the antiquity of the writing, we hardly know how to pronounce most of the characters; and so far as place names are concerned, the inability to do so makes it all but impossible to identify them with modern localities. Notwithstanding, all in all, they create an indelible impression that the Shang were in firm control of at least a half of the modern Shaanxi province. But it seems equally certain that their sway could not have gone much farther beyond Zhou, the state that was to overthrow the Shang some one and a half centuries later. For at the peak of the fighting, Wuding deemed it necessary to take a singular precaution: He asked the lord of a neighboring state of Zhou to keep a sharp eye on that princedom lest it should choose to side with Guifang.[28]

The oracle bones, however, are not productive at all in shedding light on the North Land, *beitu*. But a few bronze utensils and weaponry that date back to Shang yield some valuable information. From the inscriptions of a tripod and some other sacrificial vessels, we learn of a *beibo*. While *bei* means "north," *bo* may be translated as either "count" or "hegemon." It may very well be that the Shang had charged this lord and his successors, who were probably their kinsmen, with the special duty of supervising the North Land. This hypothesis is further strengthened by the very name of his state, which is represented by a character *bei* that is distinctly composed of two parts, one meaning "north" and the other "city" or "country." [29] And the seat of this state appears to have been situated not far from modern Peking. Moreover, several pieces of bronze weaponry have been discovered in modern Yixian, where Wang Hai, the Shang ancestor of the "servant-oxen" fame, had met with his foul death.[30] These weapons did not go back to the times of Wang Hai, but they can be traced to mid-Shang. And the inscriptions engraved on them clearly reveal that they were made for lords who followed the Shang practice of naming their males after the cyclic characters of their birthdays.[31] Furthermore, these bronze artifacts are supplemented by three historical facts. Throughout the Shang dynasty no nomadic tribes are known to have ever harassed this northeastern region in any manner. Then, toward the end of the dynasty, there existed two remarkable brothers, widely reputed for their resolute and unyielding pacifism, who were sons of a prince of a state in modern west Manchuria.[32] And lastly, after the Zhou had vanquished the Shang, the conqueror, out of sheer respect for one of the Shang kinsmen who was famed for his virtue and wisdom, permitted him, and even helped him, to migrate to northern Korea with enough following to form a minor nation so that he would not have to suffer the humiliation of acknowledging a new, alien sovereign.[33] Based on all these grounds, some Chinese scholars have concluded that the Shang influence could have reached across south Manchuria to the borders of Korea.[34]

From the above it is apparent that the map of the Shang bears a certain resemblance to Yu's grand scheme of reorganization. It is by no means mathematically symmetrical; it is far more geographically realistic. But in essence it seems to be rooted in Yu's concept about how a universal world empire should be organized. The Central Shang is just another name for Yu's idea of an Adjacent Zone.[35] The Four Lands may be said to be a combination of Yu's Enfeoffed Zone and Pacified Zone. The states closer to the Central Shang are those of whom more rigid obedience is likely exacted; the farther the distance, the more relaxed the requirements. But upon one and all of those states, the obligation is imposed to acknowledge the sovereignty of the Shang. In return, they are given the assurances of imperial protection both against encroachments of each other from within and against nomadic incursions from without. The Central Shang and the Four Lands therefore may be said to constitute the bulk of the Shang Empire. And the wax and wane of Shang power may be measured by the vigor or laxity with which its authority was asserted or enforced in the Four Lands. When a strong ruler was at the helm, his commands were seldom ignored by the farthest state with impunity; but when a weak ruler was on the throne, his wishes might be little respected outside of the immediate environs of the Central Shang. The Central Shang, as according to our map, is roughly 300 kilometers long and 200 kilometers wide—about the size of West Virginia in the United States, or of Belgium and the Netherlands combined in Europe. And the whole empire is some 1,000 kilometers from east to west, and 1,500 kilometers from north to south: It comprises a territory almost as large as France, West Germany, Italy, and Spain combined; or a little larger than the United States of America at the time Louisiana was admitted to the Union in 1812.

As to the several *fang,* these may be likened to Yu's Sworn Zone and Wild Zone. For all practical purposes, the Shang did not regard them as component parts of their dominion. In fact, they were quite ready and willing to let the several nomadic tribes who inhabited them roam wherever they would, or fight among themselves as much as they desired, provided that they made no incursions into the Four Lands. So far as we know, throughout the six and a half centuries of Shang rule, they never entered into serious conflict with these tribes except in two cases. The first was against Guifang and Tufang (1311–1308 B.C?) by Wuding; and the second, against Renfang and Yufang (1165 B.C.? and 1135 B.C?) by Zou, the last Shang emperor. In the former event, as we shall see, Wuding's success was outstanding. After three years' strenuous war, he was able to compel those fierce northwestern tribes to recognize his overlordship and to impose on them a sort of Pax Sinica that apparently lasted until the end of the dynasty.

Yet from the panoramic view of history, it is nothing more than an episode in the long and seemingly ceaseless struggle between men following two opposing ways of life. For these tribes, along with their neighbors, the Qiangs, continued to inhabit and dominate the northern deserts and the western plateaus of China; and as time rolled on, their heirs and successors, under various names such as Xiongnu, from which the West derived the word "Huns," or the "Mongol," a nomenclature that Genghis Khan was to hurl like thunder on the whole world, would continue repeatedly and periodically to bring havoc and distress on the Chinese people for many, many centuries to come. As for Zou's expeditions against the Renfang and Yufang in the southwest, while his military achievements are of doubtful value, his efforts may be viewed as another phase in the continual process of attrition and absorption of nomads by husbandmen, in the lands where both the climate and the soil favor that kind of solution. For only some five hundred years afterward, by the time Chinese history entered the so-called Spring and Autumn period, the names of Renfang and Yufang were already completely forgotten, and what had been formerly regarded as barbarian tribes were obviously wholly and inseparably assimilated by the "Xia people."[36]

· 2 ·

TANG

Having captured and banished Jie, Tang returned to Bo. While his followers were elated with his triumphant success and began addressing him as Tang the Successful, the conqueror himself was seized with a sense of shame.[37] He had fought Jie for a just cause. Nevertheless he had resorted to the use of force against his lawful sovereign, which he knew Yao and Shun would never have countenanced. When his aides remonstrated with him, he said, "What I fear is that future generations will be using me as material to fill their mouths with." He was so afraid that his actions might be misunderstood by posterity that Zhonghui, one of his chief assistants, next to Yi Yin in importance, wrote a declaration and issued it abroad more to reassure the dejected prince than to explain his position to the public.

The minister began with this postulation:

As Heaven has endowed the people with desires and passions, without a ruler, there will be chaos. So Heaven sees to it men of intelligence are born in order that the people may be well governed. The Xia emperor has befouled his own nature; and the people were as if they had fallen into mire or burning charcoal. It is then that Heaven has graciously given you, our Wang, courage and wisdom to set up a bright example and a correct standard for the myriad nations and to continue the old ways of Yu. You are now only following the natural course, honoring and obeying the Mandate of Heaven. The Xia emperor was but an offender who falsely used Heaven as a pretense to spread about his own commands. On this account the Lord Above has viewed him with disapprobation, caused the Shang to receive His mandate, and employed you to bring light to the multitude.

Then the minister extolled Tang's virtues,[38] and recounted how the use of force had been thrust upon him in spite of himself, first by the criminal atrocities of the tyrant of Ge; then by the hopes and prayers of divers peoples who, suffering under the unbearable misrule of their princes, had looked to Tang for their only possible salvation; and finally by the inordinate jealousy of Jie, who had regarded the Shang as something that must be totally exterminated, "even as the weeds would have regarded the springing corn." And he intimated that under the present circumstances Tang should not rely only on his own perceptions but listen to the advice of others. Thus the minister declared: "So I have heard, he who finds teachers for himself will end up becoming *wang;* he who says that others are not equal to himself will come to ruin. He who likes to ask becomes enlarged, and he who uses only himself is small." And he concluded, suggesting that since Tang had already set the task for himself, he had better finish it: "Alas! If one wants to be wary at the end, one should have been careful in the beginning. If one is determined to promote virtue, one cannot help overthrowing the wicked and vicious. Revere and honor the way of Heaven! This is the only course ever to preserve heaven's mandate."

Whether or not Tang's self-dissatisfaction was alleviated by his minister or ministers' advice, the state of the empire urgently demanded his attention. So on his own initiative he invited the princes in all the four directions to attend a meeting at Bo. Altogether there came some three thousand of them,[39] most of them probably from the regions which were to be called, later, the Four Lands. At the meeting, an empty throne was placed where the sovereign should have sat. "As the princes all congregated, Tang took the imperial seal which he had captured from Jie, stepped forward, and placed it to the left of the throne. He then bowed low twice and returned to the ranks of the princes. Indicating the throne, he said to them, 'This is the seat of the Son of Heaven. It should be occupied only by men of virtue. The world is not to be possessed by one house alone. Only men of virtue deserve its possession.' And he asked all the princes present to take the seat if they please, and he asked time and again. But all the princes wanted none but Tang to occupy it. Thus Tang acceded to the seat of the Son of Heaven." [40]

After his enthronement, Tang named Yi Yin the prime minister and Zhonghui the deputy. Then the new emperor issued a proclamation, setting forth the guiding policies of his rule:[41]

> You princes, I wish to declare this to you: May you all without exception work for the well-being of the people, and direct your effort toward that end! If you fail to do so, I shall have to inflict drastic punishment on you, and you shall have no reason to resent me.
>
> I have heard that in the ancient times Yu and Gaoyao toiled untiringly outside for the well-being of the people so that all could live in safety and security. Within the four directions, the four streams—the Yangtze, the Ji, the Yellow River, and the Huai—were well regulated that the multitudes could each enjoy their habitations. And so did Prince Ji, who gave instructions about the spreading of agriculture and the cultivation of numerous grains. These three venerables all worked for the well-being of the people, and their services have been recognized by posterity. (On the other hand), in the past Ciyou and his associates created havoc for the hundred surnames; and the Lord Above saw to it that they did not come to a good end. These facts are all confirmed by the words of former emperors. It behooves us to be persuaded by them.
>
> Thus I declare: Unless you are ready and willing to abide by this guidance, you are not to return to your own state, and you shall not for this resent me.

The language of this proclamation may be terse, but its message is unmistakable. Tang's policy is to promote agriculture and discourage irresponsible nomadism. The four examples are well and carefully chosen. Not to reiterate Ji's services, Yu is remembered not only for the subjugation of the flood but also for his having conferred lands and surnames afterward, which had especially contributed to the fact that all people then could live in safety and security and the multitudes could each enjoy their habitations. If the meaning of this is still obscure, then the inclusion of Gaoyao in the list of the "three venerables" should make it manifest. It was Gaoyao who had vigorously and faithfully carried out the duty entrusted to him by Shun to prevent and punish any nomads making raids on agricultural settlements. And the naming of Ciyou as the contrary example must have struck the princes in attendance even with more conscious awe. If Ciyou was by common understanding considered to be the most formidable of ancient nomadic chieftains, whose life had centered on rapine and destruction, his sorry ending was also known to all. He and his hordes were all slaughtered by the Yellow Emperor.

But Tang did not rely only on past examples to guide the thoughts of the princes; he had a more practical means contrived to control their actions. Unless they agreed to abide by his policy—to pledge at least not to encroach upon one another's land, as the nomadic tribes were wont to do—they would not be allowed to return to their respective states. But the territories of their states were not clearly demarcated, the princes might well argue. This, however, was a matter not difficult to settle. As all the princes were gathered there in Bo, they each could delineate their boundaries with their neighbors by direct negotiations; and if any of them should be unable to reach an agreement in this manner, Tang himself could always be called upon to render an impartial judgment. Thus before the meeting was over, Tang had already secured not only the allegiance of all the princes but also their pledge to abide by his declared policies.

Yet Tang was too realistic a man to put his trust only in words and promises. So at the close of the meeting, probably after an appropriate parade of Shang's armed might, he said to the princes half seriously and half jokingly, "I take special delight in martial qualities. Let me be known as *wudi,* 'the Martial Emperor.' " [42] Though, as is known in history, he never found any other occasion in his reign to use force again, yet it is perhaps this precautionary demonstration that he was not shy of using it that made the actual usage unnecessary.

It is also in line with this thinking that he decided upon another action. While continuing to recognize Bo as his capital, he planned to move his administrative headquarters, or imperial seat, to another site better located for the supervision of the newly won empire. He honored Bo with the title "Great City Shang," or "Heavenly City Shang." He kept there the principal ancestral temples so that he and his successors could periodically return to render veneration. In addition, he designed to maintain Bo as a power base of the Shang, as it had always been. To the south and east of the city he had a vast tract of land declared the imperial preserve, reserved especially for the chase,[43] "in order to provide fresh or preserved meat for the veneration ceremonies in the temples and also to train officers and soldiers in archery and chariot warfare to prepare for emergency."[44]

The place he chose as his administrative seat is some 280 kilometers to the west of Bo, and he promptly and aptly named it West Bo.[45] It commands several advantages. Firstly, even though Jie had been captured and the Xia domain around Anyi had been incorporated with the Central Shang, there was no telling but that the remnants of the house of Xia might yet turn restive and intransigent. Whereas it would be difficult to keep an eye on their activities from the great distance of the "Heavenly City Shang," the close proximity of West Bo would make the surveillance easier. Secondly, the terrain of the new site is well suited for defense. On the north it faces the Luo, a tributary of the mighty Yellow River; and on the three other sides it is surrounded by tall hills with three difficult passes.[46] Thirdly, Tang's virtues and capabilities as well as the prestige of the house of Shang were respected the most in the so-called East Land and North Land, both through the conqueror's own recent victories and through the past migrations and exploits of his many ancestors. In the South Land, there were also some states that had submitted to him quite early in his rising career.[47] But in the West Land he was comparatively less known. So it was to this region that he felt he must address more attention as the new sovereign, and West Bo could serve him the better for the purpose. How well he eventually succeeded in the endeavor is testified by an ode that his descendants later composed in his honor:

> In the days of Tang the Successful,
> Starting with the Di [48] and with the Qiang,
> There was none that durst not come to pay him tribute;
> There was none that durst not acknowledge him as *wang*.[49]

And ever since the time of Tang, throughout the more than six centuries of the Shang rule, the so-called Qiangfang was never known to have caused the imperial house any disturbance.

Over and above these, there seems to have been yet another objective for his establishing the administrative capital at West Bo. One of his avowed policies being the promotion of agriculture, nowhere could Tang have found a better location to demonstrate his intentions in that direction than the areas adjacent to the new capital. For here was the land which Taikang and Houyi had so fondly used as their hunting grounds. And here it had also been not so long ago that the hegemon Kunwu and his horde had so aimlessly roamed. The population was still very sparse; but the soil was fertile, the water plentiful, and the climate as good as that in Bo for the cultivation of the grains. And so here it was, conceivably, that Tang led his people again "to exert toil in the fields" *(tu tian)*, and thus set an example for many of his successors to follow.[50] And perhaps this also accounts for the several transferences of the administrative capital after Tang, for which the extant ancient records have afforded little explanation, and which otherwise would have seemed so inexplicable. In moving the capital from one place to another, Tang's successors could have been just following the founder's example. They saw that the land around the old site was already fully developed; and they found an incentive in "exerting toil in the fields" around the new.

And in this matter Tang himself could very well have derived the idea from Yu's grand scheme of reorganization. For Yu had made it plain that he wanted to people his imperial domain with only husbandmen;[51] and Tang had also from the very beginning of his career subscribed to the principle that a country could be made secure and prosperous only through the promotion of agriculture. The moving of the administrative capital from one corner of the Central Shang to another appears therefore to be a policy deliberately formulated by Tang and tirelessly pursued by his successors in order that every part of the territory directly under the imperial control be as highly developed in agriculture as possible. And manifestly the policy bore splendid fruit. In time, the Central Shang became not only a citadel of power but also a center of wealth. For inevitably the development of a settled agricultural way of life was conducive to advancement in the arts and crafts, which in turn produced not only improved tools, implements, and utensils for ordinary consumption, but also articles of beauty and refinement for enjoyment, for luxury, or for special ceremonies, such as those molten in bronze or carved out of jade. And the Shang people were the first to take advantage of the progress, to "use oxen carts to carry merchandise to trade them far" [52] in the so-called Four Lands and possibly even in the nomadic regions *(fang)*. Thus the term *shangren,* which had originally and literally meant only "man from Shang" or "men from Shang," gradually took on a new meaning—"merchant" or "merchants." It is so used by the Chinese to this day.

Tang was so determined to show that his policies as well as the way of life he wanted the people to adopt were altogether different from those of the preceding dynasty that he sought to dramatize the change by all sorts of means. The Xia emperors had used black as the formal color: Their formal wear was black; on military occasions they rode black horses; in offering sacrifices they chose black animals; and for solemn events such as laying the dead into the coffin, they held the ceremonies in the evening. Tang altered all these: His formal wear was now white; on military occasions he rode white horses; in offering sacrifices he chose white animals; and for solemn events such as laying the dead into the coffin, he held the ceremonies at noontime.[53] Again, as the veneration of the *she* had long become a tradition,[54] the Xia emperors had made it a rule that the *she* altar should be built with an earth foundation and surrounded by pine trees. Tang decreed that it should be built differently—laid on a stone foundation and surrounded by cypress.[55] Furthermore, since the issuance of a calendar was one of the principal duties of a sovereign, and it cannot stand radical changes by instant command, Tang made no changes in the calendar but formally designated the *chou* (ox) month to replace the *yin* (tiger) month as the *zheng,* or the official beginning of the year.[56] However, being the most earnest promoter of agriculture of his time, he realized of course that the so-called *xiazheng* was better suited to the farming population; so he saw to it that his alteration was concerned only with the conduct of government functions, and did not at all interfere with the customary cultivation seasons used by the husbandmen.

Indeed, his energetic and ceaseless exertions toward the increase of agricultural production in the Central Shang appear to have paid off even during his lifetime. Not long after his assumption of the imperial reins, the entire empire was afflicted with a long drought that lasted nearly seven years.[57] But because of his foresight, in the first several years he managed to cope with the situation passably well, partly by using the surplus grain he had previously stored and partly by striving to maintain the yields in the fields through a greater use of irrigation. However, at the end of the fifth year, still with no relief in sight, Tang found both the empire and the Central Shang in dire straits. The Luo River, on which West Bo depended for water supply, was parched into cracks, and other streams were in about the same condition. All these years both he and the people everywhere had sacrificed to the Lord Above, to the lesser gods, and also to their numerous ancestors, to pray for rain or for intercession. But the drought had continued unrelentingly. So now it was suggested to Tang that as all ordinary sacrifices had proved of no avail, what heaven must have wanted was a human sacrifice. Tang listened and asked the *taishi* to consult with the tortoise. Then, after having done so, the *taishi* reported the same. At this, Tang appointed a day to offer the required human sacrifice at the Mulberry Woods close by the city of West Bo. And when the day came, as a multitude gathered to see the sight, whom did they see but Tang himself coming on a white cart drawn by a white horse. He had already fasted and washed himself clean, his naked body now covered with white rushes. Presently he alighted. Holding a three-legged tripod aloft, he fell low and prayed:

> May I, your humble son, presume to make this announcement to you, O most great and sovereign Lord Above! I have offended. I dare not ask for your pardon. Whatever I have done, I do not seek to hide; the examination of it is by your

mind, O Lord. I myself have offended; the people in the myriad regions have no part in my offenses. If, however, the people in the myriad regions have offended in your eyes, the offenses must also rest upon my person. So, pray, my Lord Above, and pray, you spirits who serve Him, do not let the fact that I am no good, that only one man is no good, be a cause for the destruction of so many men's lives!" [58]

And after he had uttered this prayer, he cut off his own hair, tied up his own hands, and offered himself as the sacrifice. Presently, as according to some ancient accounts, a cloudburst descended and rain fell on a very wide area. The drought was at last relieved. Whether or not this last part of the narration was fabricated or exaggerated, the very fact that Tang had at first saved so many states from starvation by supplying them with grains from the Central Shang and had later offered his own person to Heaven as sacrifice in order to seek deliverance from the impending calamity, needless to say, served the more to heighten his prestige and consolidate his empire.

Tang, however, did not live long after the end of the drought. He died at the thirteenth year of his reign. Besides what has been related of him above, Tang was said to have composed an imperial anthem that combined music with dancing and that was called *dahuo*, "Great Salvation." It was still played and admired some ten centuries later in the period of Spring and Autumn;[59] but it was irretrievably lost afterward, probably in the period of the Warring States. Again, there is also a record indicating that Tang wanted to lighten the burden of many distant states in the matter of tribute. He was quoted to have told Yi Yin, "When these princes come to pay tribute, some are from places where there is a lack of horses and oxen, and some are required to pay tribute with things which are not produced in their own states. All these must have worked hardship upon them. Now, I would like to have from them only such tributes as are produced in their own states, easy to procure and not costly. Please, make an order to that effect and list the tributes that should be required from the four directions." [60] Yi Yin did so accordingly. But unfortunately, the original list is lost to us.

Perhaps Tang was especially remembered by Chinese scholars, when Confucian classics were still widely read, for the motto he had caused to be engraved on his washbasin.[61] Confucius had it singled out as an instance of man's inflexible aspiration to better himself, and urged it on his disciples as well as on all men to emulate. It reads, "Make yourself new today! Make yourself newer every day. Make yourself yet newer the next day."

The Shang of course venerated Tang especially as the founder of their dynasty. It is generally assumed by Chinese historians that the practice of conferring posthumous titles on deceased sovereigns began with the Shang's so honoring Tang. But whether there was any actual ceremony held for such an event as the later dynasties developed, we are not at all certain. There are, however, definitive records showing that through the Shang history, in their official compositions, whenever there was need to mention Tang, he was much less often referred to by his name than by the titles *gaozu*,[62] "the High Progenitor"; *liezu*,[63] "the Glorious Progenitor"; or *gaohou*,[64] "the High Sovereign." And this has apparently established a precedent which later dynasties, beginning with the Han, have unfailingly followed.[65]

In all events, Tang will always be remembered by the Chinese people as the very first revolutionary in their history, and a most successful one. In fact, the term for "revolution," which they use today, may be said to have derived from Tang. It consists of two characters, *geming,* which may be literally translated as "overturn the mandate." It was first used by the *Book of Changes,* one of the most ancient books in China. Speaking of Tang, the book made this brief comment: He "overturned the mandate in accord with Heaven and in response to the people." [66]

THE HOUSE OF SHANG

I. BEFORE TANG

Di Ku ... Xie (founder) ... Zhaoming ... Xiangtu ... Canruo ... Caoyu ... Ming ... Hai*ᵃ* ... Shangjia (Wei) *ᵇ* ... Baoyi ... Baobing ... Baoding*ᶜ* ... Zhuren ... Zhugui ... Tang (Dayi) *ᵈ*

> Notes: *a.* Hai is the one who was supposed to have trained a herd of "servant-oxen." In the *Historical Records,* his name was erroneously transcribed as Zheng.
> *b.* Shangjia was the first to be named after the "celestial trunk character" of his birthday according to the *ganzhi* system. Thereafter, as can be seen from the chart, all his descendants followed the practice.
> *c. Historical Records* had Baoding placed between Shangjia and Baoyi.
> *d.* Tang's given name was Dayi. *Historical Records* had it as Tianyi (Heavenly Yi).

II. AFTER TANG

(1)   Tang 1766–1754 ... Taiding ... (4)   Taijia 1753–1721 ... (5)   Woding 1720–1692
... (2)   Waibing   ... (6)   Taigeng 1691–1667 ...
... (3)   Zhongren

(Taigeng) ... (7)   Xiaojia 1666–1650
... (8)   Yongji 1649–1638
... (9)   Taiwu 1637–1563 ... (10)   Zhongding 1562–1550 ... (13)   Zuyi 1525–1507 ...
... (11)   Wairen 1549–1535
... (12)   Hetanjia 1534–1526

(Zuyi) ... (14)   Zuxin 1506–1491 ... (16)   Zuding 1465–1435 ... (18)   Yangjia 1408–1402
... (15)   Wojia 1490–1466 ... (17)   Nangeng 1433–1409 ... (19)   Pangeng 1401–1374
... (20)   Xiaoxin 1373–1353
... (21)   Xiaoyi 1352–1325 ...

(Xiaoyi) ... (22)   Wuding 1324–1266 ... (23)   Zugeng 1265–1259
... (24)   Zujia 1258–1226 ... (25)   Linxin 1225–1220
... (26)   Kangding 1219–1199 ...

(Kangding) ... (27)   Wuyi 1198–1195 ... (28)   Wenwuding 1194–1192 ... (29)   Diyi 1191–1155 ...
(Diyi) ... (30)   Dixin, otherwise known as Zou.

> *Note:* The numerals represent the sequence of succession; .... represents direct lineal descent; and names paralleling each other are brothers. The dates, except for the last of the line, Zou, are based on traditional chronology, given here just for rough reference.
> Xie, the founder, was given the surname Zi; so the house of Shang had Zi as its surname.

· 3 ·

YI YIN AND TAIJIA

Tang had three sons. The eldest died early. At Tang's death, he was succeeded by the second son.[67] But before Tang died, he gave Yi Yin a new position with the title *baoheng*, which may be translated as "lord protector and weigher"; or simply *aheng*, "the weigher." [68] In the whole history of China, except possibly in one other case which was to occur in the period of the Three Kingdoms some two thousand years later,[69] there has never been an association between two men, notwithstanding the different roles each of them had to play in life, that was so close, so harmonious, so perfect, so free of friction, of envy, of jealousy, or of suspicion, as between these two. Tang treated Yi Yin always more like a teacher than a minister. Even while he was alive, once in a proclamation, he openly referred to his prime minister not by his name, nor by his office, but by an unheard-of laudatory nomenclature—"the foremost sage of our time." [70] So by giving Yi Yin the new position on his deathbed, Tang meant that his lifelong friend and mentor should have the final authority thereafter in weighing all matters of state, even though his own son and successor would enjoy the trappings and dignities of the sovereign.

Tang's second son, however, died almost immediately after his accession. According to the tradition of the house of Shang, he was succeeded by his younger brother, Tang's third and remaining son. But this prince also died shortly after. So Yi Yin enthroned the only son of Tang's eldest son, Taijia, as the emperor.

Taijai was, as the Romans would have said later, "born in the purple." When he opened his eyes to the world for the first time, Tang had probably already acquired dominion over the empire. His own father having died young, Taijia never benefited from firm paternal guidance in childhood. When his turn came to occupy the throne, he was just old enough to think that he knew everything, but too young in fact to know anything, and he behaved or misbehaved accordingly. Yi Yin therefore deemed it necessary to give him instructions on how to be a ruler; and in order to impress his young mind with their full significance, the lord protector and weigher also thought it best to deliver the message in a most solemn ceremony. On the first day of the month of *yichou* (soft wood ox) in the first year of Taijia's reign,[71] he assembled at the ancestral temple all the dignitaries of the empire, all the princes of the Four Lands, and all the high officers of the Central Shang. After offering proper sacrifices to the Shang forebears, he formally presented to them their heir and successor, the present sovereign. For a moment he paused; and all in attendance watched intently to see what he was going to do.

Then in the presence of the whole assembly, Yi Yin addressed himself to the youthful ruler.[72] He spoke first of how the last Xia emperor had offended Heaven by failing to follow the examples of his own ancestors, and how Taijia's grandfather Tang had through his virtuous actions replaced the Xia's cruel tyranny with a humane rule that won the hearts of the entire population. Then he besought the young monarch to take special care about how he commenced his reign. For unless a ruler could conduct himself well in the sight of his own family as well as in the sight of the people of the imperial domain, he could not be expected to extend his influence over the whole empire. And he continued:

Oh! The late emperor began with careful attention to the bonds that hold men together. He listened to expostulations, never seeking to resist them. He always tried to conform to the standards set up by former sages. When in high position, he showed he could view all things with objective clarity; when in inferior position, he never failed in loyalty. From others he never demanded perfection; but from himself he always asked if he could not do better. It was thus that he arrived at the possession of the myriad regions. How arduous and painstaking that task had been!

(And he did even more for you.) He searched far and wide for wise men who should be helpful to you, his offspring and heir.

Moreover, he laid down the punishments for officers, and gave strong warning to people who are in positions of authority, as follows:

"If you dare to indulge in constant dancing in your palaces, or in drunken singing in your chambers—this is called the rage of witchery.

"If you dare to abandon yourselves to women or riches, or to roaming and hunting—this is called the rage of debauchery.

"If you dare to despise the words of the sages, to resist the counsels of the loyal and upright, to put far from you the elderly and virtuous, and to associate yourselves with obstreperous youths—this is called the rage of derangement.

"These are the three rages and ten vices. If a high officer is afflicted with any one of these, his house will surely come to grief; if a prince is so afflicted, his state will surely come to ruin. The ministers who do not try to correct these vices in their prince shall be punished with branding."

Now, these rules are minutely enjoined upon all, who were trained to become officers.

Oh, you who now succeed to the throne, do revere these instructions in your person! Do remember them! These are sacred counsels of vast importance, memorable words whose truths are self-evident. The ways of the Lord Above are not invariable. To those who do good, He sends down all blessings. To those who do evil, He sends down all calamities. Be virtuous: If you be so even in small things, the myriad regions will have cause for congratulation. If you be not virtuous even in things that may not be great, it may bring downfall to you and your house.

Of what misdeeds Taijia had done to deserve such a lecture, there are no records to inform us. Conceivably he committed quite a few that could be included among the three rages and ten vices. And the young monarch was certainly not given any reason to regard the admonition lightly, for Yi Yin took pains to advise him that if he, as his minister, did not try to correct the sovereign in these errors, he himself would have to suffer branding according to Tang's punishment.

The sternness of the lecture and the solemnity of its delivery notwithstanding, as soon as the ceremony was over, Taijia went back to his old ways as if he had not heard it at all. After a while, Yi Yin was compelled to mull over his dilemma once again. He felt he must now make the double nature of his own position perfectly clear to the refractory youth. He was not only a minister to a reigning sovereign but also a friend and partner to his grandfather, the founder of the dynasty. As the former, the young man might well choose to ignore him; but as the latter, he should be forewarned that he could not defy him with impunity. And lest the warning, if given verbally, might only go in one ear and out the other, the lord protector and weigher sent Taijia a written communication:

> Our late sovereign kept his eye continually on the clear commands from Heaven. In this manner he served all the spirits above and below, the spirit of the land (she), the spirit of the grains (ji), and the spirits of the ancestral temple—he served them all with reverence and with solicitude. Thus Heaven took notice of his virtues and conferred on him the Great Mandate to soothe and tranquilize the myriad regions. And I, Yin, was personally on his left side or on his right side to help him settle the people. It is thus that you, heir sovereign, have come to be charged with succession.
>
> Now, I, Yin, personally saw all that happened to Xia, which has at present become our West City. In the old days, the Xia emperors were ever seeking to improve themselves, even to the end of their lives. So their ministers followed them toward the same end. But afterward, some of their successors would not attempt to move toward such an end; and neither did their ministers.[73]
>
> Take warning, O heir-sovereign! Reverently conduct yourself as a sovereign. If you, the sovereign, do not conduct yourself as a sovereign should, you will make your own grandfather ashamed of you.

But Taijia paid no attention to the communication. Yi Yin's mind was now almost made up. Yet he still hesitated. He wanted to give one more chance to the youthful monarch before taking the drastic action he had been contemplating. He went to see Taijia and spoke to him in a tone more persuasive than comminatory:

> Our late sovereign would always stir himself before there was even light; he would seek to clarify his own thoughts while waiting for the morning. Also, he sought on every side for men of ability and virtue to guide and instruct his offspring. (I am one of those charged with this duty.) Pray, do not frustrate this charge and bring on yourself your overthrow.
>
> Be careful to strive after the virtue of self-restraint. Think only on plans that may endure.

Be like a forester. After he has set the spring, he goes and examines it to see if the arrow is pointed in the right direction. Then he lets it go. If you will only reverentially determine your own objective and follow your grandfather's ways, I shall be delighted to be able to show to all ages that I have discharged my trust.

Yet Taijia would not mend his ways. So Yi Yin said to himself: "This is unrighteousness grown out of nature compounded with practice. I cannot permit him to be further associated with men who are not oriented toward righteousness." Thereupon he built a palace at Tong, close by Tang's burial grounds, and caused Taijia to be moved and confined there. He thought pensively, "Now he is near the remains of our late sovereign. May he learn his lessons from the proximity so that he will not go astray in later life!"

There Taijia lived almost two years—first in anxiety, then in sorrow, and later in deep and serious meditation. In the end, he was seen to have become sincerely virtuous.[74]

On the first day of the twelfth month in the third year of Taijia's reign, Yi Yin came to see the young prince, bringing with him the imperial cap and robes.[75] He requested Taijia to put them on, and then escorted him back to the imperial seat. In a written document he addressed the returned monarch thus:

Without the sovereign, the people cannot have the guidance which provides them proper livelihood; without the people, the sovereign will have no cause to rule over the four quarters. Great Heaven has graciously favored the house of Shang, making it possible that the heir sovereign has at last attained to virtue. This is indeed a blessing that will extend to ten thousand generations without end.

Taijia's contrition was heartfelt. Doing obeisance with his hands to the face and his head to the ground, he replied:

I, a little child, did not understand what virtue is, and was making myself quite unworthy. I let my desires run wild without restraint, and my self-indulgence violate all rules of propriety. I was inviting ruin to my own person.

Now, calamities sent by Heaven may be avoided; but from calamities brought on by oneself there can be no escape. In the past I have turned my back on your instructions, my teacher and my guardian. Indeed, I have made a very sorry beginning.

But, thanks to you, I am now corrected and saved. May I continue to depend on you hereafter in my efforts to obtain a good end.

In return, Yi Yin did obeisance with his hands to the face and his head to the ground, saying: "To cultivate his person, to make himself truly virtuous, and thus to bring together all below him to a harmonious concord—this is the work of the intelligent sovereign. O my sovereign, do cultivate your virtue with zeal. Do model after your glorious progenitor.[76] And do not allow yourself to be complacent or negligent at any time. And I shall respond to your goodness with unreserved devotion." [77]

After watching Taijia rule the empire for a while and finding nothing exceptionable, Yi Yin decided to retire from active participation in the government. On his departure, he submitted one last memorandum, setting forth his views on the virtues that a sovereign should possess.[78] He was fearful that though the young emperor's character appeared to have completely reformed, yet the reformation might not endure through lack of perseverance. So he again pointed out how difficult it is to rely on Heaven, the Mandate of Heaven being so inconstant. The reason why the Xia had lost, and the Shang had won, the Mandate was that while the Xia emperor had degenerated into oppressive misrule, both Tang and Yi Yin himself were single-heartedly devoted to virtue. "Virtue has no constant teacher; it is to pursue whatever is good. And the pursuance of good may involve changes of course at times; this, again, must be always harmonized by single-heartedness." In the case of a sovereign, the single-hearted aim should be "to secure forever the happy life of the multitudes of people. . . . If one ordinary man or one ordinary woman does not find an opportunity to give full development to himself, the people's lord cannot be said to have achieved unqualified success."

After Yi Yin's retirement, Taijia did not belie his trust. He ruled on alone very wisely and effectively. When he died, the people thought so well of him that they conferred on him the posthumous title *taizong*, "Grand Ancestor." [79] He was one of only three emperors in the entire dynasty, besides Tang, who were given such honors.

Yi Yin, however, lived even longer than Taijia. He died in the reign of Woding, Taijia's son and successor. Woding buried him with all the honors due to an emperor. In the *Book of History*, Confucius had originally included a document titled *woding*, which was composed in commemoration of the event. But this is lost. In the recently discovered oracle bones, definitive inscriptions are found to testify that throughout the Shang dynasty Yi Yin was venerated by the Shang descendants side by side with their ancestors.[80]

· 4 ·

GAPS IN SHANG HISTORY

After Taijia, there is a long and apparent gap in the Shang history. In the course of some three hundred years following the burial of Yi Yin by Woding and preceding the last transference of the imperial seat by Pangeng (the nineteenth emperor), Confucius had originally collected eight documents, each relating to some incident that had occurred. Although we may

still perceive a faint glimmering of the contents of these compositions from
their titles and, also, from the exceedingly brief introductory notes that give
a sort of narration about the origin or background of each of them, the
documents themselves are totally lost to us. Sima Qian in his *Historical
Records* has given us a complete list of the emperors of the Shang dynasty in
the order of succession, with an explanation of the lineal relationship of each
to his predecessor. But so far as a consistent historical narrative is concerned,
he had little to add to what we can gather from the titles and introductory
notes of the eight lost documents. In fact, sometimes the great historian
himself seemed to have foundered in confusion, and his account of the Shang
dynasty falls far short of his other accounts in clarity and cogency. This
conspicuous lack of substance has led many scholars at one time or another to
question the authenticity of ancient Chinese history. Some have even suspected the dependability of the list of the Shang emperors which Sima Qian
claimed to have derived from *pudie* and *dieji* "stored in metal cabinets inside
stone chambers" of the Han imperial palace.

With the recent discovery of the oracle bones, however, these doubts have
been dispelled. The *Historical Records* enumerated twenty-nine emperors
following Tang.[81] From the divination inscriptions we now find confirmation not only of the accuracy of these names but also of their chronological
sequence. There is only one error found in Sima Qian's descriptions of the
respective lineal relationships of these emperors. In one instance, the successor (the thirteenth emperor, Zuyi) was given as the predecessor's son; but
actually he was his nephew.[82] But except for this one isolated mistake, the
authenticity of the *Historical Records* becomes manifestly self-evident.

Indeed, the oracle bones have done even more. In addition to the list of the
Shang emperors, the *Historical Records* had traced the genealogical descent of
Tang backward generation by generation up to Di Ku, fourteen generations
in all. The divination inscriptions have again confirmed all these except for
two minor discrepancies.[83] One discrepancy is an error in sequence. The
other is that the seventh-generation descendant of Di Ku was named by the
Historical Records as *Zhen;* but according to the inscriptions it should have
been *Hai*. However, as one eminent researcher has pointed out, this may not
have been a mistake on the part of the *Historical Records,* but just a ty-
pographical error introduced through clerical copying, for the ancient characters *zhen* and *hai* were not too dissimilar in writing.[84]

But to this historian, the oracle bones seem to have rendered an even
greater service. They have furnished a passable and probable explanation for
the apparent gaps in Shang history. As is evidenced by the inscriptions, the
Shang emperors were verily a superstitious lot. For everything under heaven, they would want to know in advance what was going to happen; and
they would not hesitate to ask for a prediction through their traditional

formula of divination. And a pragmatic breed they were too. For they required their scribes not only to inscribe the diviners' answers but also the actual events as they occurred later, on the same bones or shells. Thus from these inscriptions we have a kaleidoscopic view of the true and variegated facets of life the Shang emperors had been leading almost from day to day.

The oracle bones so far discovered, however, do not cover the Shang dynasty in its entirety. As they were all excavated from modern Anyang, Henan, which is the site of the last Shang capital, Yin, they pertain only to the latter part of the dynasty, beginning with Pangeng (the nineteenth emperor), who had transferred the imperial seat there, and ending with Di Xin, otherwise known as Zou, the last of the line, covering a period of about two and a half centuries. According to the most knowledgeable estimate, the total number of these bones amounts to more than 109,000.[85] A large quantity of them, of course, have been found to bear only scanty or worthless inscriptions. But supposing that the average bone contains only three characters, the total wordage exceeds 300,000, which should have yielded sufficient material for any historian to write a continuous and consistent history about the latter part of the Shang. Yet strange and disappointing as it may seem, the truth is quite to the contrary. While the divination inscriptions have proved immeasurably valuable in confirming or correcting the ancient records which China has always had, to use them, and to use them only, as materials to write a new history of this period is all but impossible. The reason for this disappointment is not far to seek. It can be seen only too clearly in the very nature of the inscriptions themselves.

Without going into a detailed classification of these oracle bones, a cursory study instantly reveals that the largest number of them are related to inquiries and answers about the reigning emperor's personal well-being. This is, of course, expected from a monarchy, whose institutions are centered on one person. But the Shang emperors appear to have carried the practice much further than is usually imagined. Every night an inquiry would be asked if any ill would befall the sovereign. And as if that were not enough, every ten days, on the day before, the same question would be asked for the decade that was to follow. Since most of the answers were in the negative, as they were bound to be, it can be readily observed that a large number of these bones carry no historical significance whatever.

The next-largest category is concerned with sacrifices. Chinese ancient books have commonly characterized the Shang as singularly "devoted to spirits." [86] But not until the oracle bones were discovered could any modern scholar realize to what excess such devotion extended. It is interesting to note that except for *shangdi* or Heaven, whom the Shang seemed not to have dared profane by offering sacrifice more than once annually (and this at the beginning of the year),[87] there were no spirits whom they would not like to honor as often as possible. This especially applies to their own ancestors, starting with Di Ku, through Tang, to the immediate predecessor of the reigning monarch. As we know, it was Shang tradition to name their male members by the celestial-trunk cyclic names of their birthdays; so the practice was to venerate every one of them on the days bearing the same appellation. For example, take Tang. Being born on a *yi* day, his given name was Dayi, and therefore he received his sacrifices on the *yi* days. Or take Taijia; he was born on a *jia* day, so he was entitled to be sacrificed to on the *jia* days. Now, remember that in every ten days in the cyclic calendar there is a *jia* and a *yi;* one can imagine how many sacrifices there could be in a year. Moreover, not only these male ancestors were venerated, but also their principal wives. However, as the wives' birthdays were not always precisely known, they came to be sacrificed to on the cyclic days of their deaths. Nor is this all. There were so many different veneration ceremonies. Even after a sort of simplification by Zujia (the twenty-fourth emperor), there remained five principal ceremonies—one using drum music, the second accompanied by feather dance, the third stressing wine and meat, the fourth offering fresh millet, and the fifth a veneration of all the ancestors in unison. But besides the five principal ceremonies, there were still twelve other minor ones, whose significance is beyond our present understanding.[88] But whether understood or not, these ceremonies were frequently held all the same. Then consider the fact that the longer the dynasty lasted, the more ancestors the Shang acquired, and the more sacrifices they had to render to them. Thus in the end they were compelled to make one accommodation. They discontinued the individual veneration of some less important ancestors, relegating them to a position to be venerated only in the ceremonies where all were honored in unison. And as for those whom they considered they must venerate individually, they tried to conduct all of the ceremonies within thirty-six ten-day series—that is, all within a year's time.[89] This matter was of course one of tremendous importance to the Shang people. But from a historian's point of view, aside from taking notice of this practice and setting it forth as an illustration of their singular devotion to the spirits such as we have done here, there does not seem to be any need to expatiate upon them further.

The third category of inscriptions is answers to inquiries about hunting and fishing by the sovereign. As mentioned before, when Tang moved his administrative capital to West Bo, he had specially reserved a vast tract of land to the southeast of the Heavenly City Shang and created an imperial preserve for the chase.[90] But, as was noted by a scholar later in the first century B.C., "When Tang first established an imperial preserve, it was in order to provide fresh or preserved meat for the veneration ceremonies in the temples, and also in order to train officers and soldiers in archery and chariot warfare to prepare for emergency. But as the dynasty declined, (his descendants) indulged in riding and hunting only to rob the people of their time and use up their strength to exhaustion." [91] Indeed, that seems to have been the case. We have an inscription relating a chase by Wuding, the twenty-second emperor. In that one incident alone, he and his hunters were mentioned to have captured or slaughtered "1 tiger, 40 deer, 164 foxes, and 159 fawns." [92] This may well illustrate both the abundance of wildlife and the magnitude of an imperial hunt at the time. Yet Wuding should by no means be characterized as a prince who engaged in the chase for the chase's sake. He was a man who could perhaps be said to have adhered quite faithfully to Tang's legacy. But not so with the twenty-seventh emperor, Wuyi, or with the thirtieth and last emperor, Zou. The former, in his three years' short reign, hunted thirty-nine times and at eighteen different places. As to the last emperor, though he reigned longer, he is known to have hunted at least 310 times and at eighty-seven different places.[93] These facts are of course of some interest to a historian, for they serve to show an aspect of the life of the times as well as to furnish one of the possible causes for the decline of the house of Shang. But even if the author of the *Historical Records* had had access to these oracle bones, it is doubtful whether he would have given them more attention than we have given here.

Another large category of inscriptions consists of inquiries and answers regarding weather. In numbers, they are about the same as divinations concerning the chase. Since the inquiries regarding weather were all made more or less independently, it may be inferred that while many of the Shang emperors were eager to gratify their personal indulgence, there were also those who were quite solicitous of the well-being of their agrarian population. In fact, there are many inscriptions where the sovereign was shown to have prayed to the Lord Above for rain. And from the bones used in the period of the twenty-eighth emperor, Wenwuding, a modern scholar was even able to reconstruct a sort of weather report month by month, beginning from the late winter of a certain year to the early summer of the next, with all the rains, snow flurries, snows, and winds fully accounted.[94] And from these studies he drew a conclusion that the climate of the Yin area (modern Anyang, Henan) some thirty-three centuries ago was not substantially different from what it is today. This is, of course, very valuable information. Yet while its importance in any research work concerning the development of meteorology and climatology may be inestimable, its significance in the writing of a general history of the Shang must be considered to be rather restricted.

A fifth category comprises miscellaneous requests or entreaties. An imperial consort was with child; would it be a boy? She was about to give birth; would both the mother and the infant fare well? A son was taken ill; would he die? And of course there are many requests that must appear at once both amusing and absurd to the modern mind. An emperor dreamed of a dead tiger; could this portend evil? He was suffering from a toothache; would his deceased father intercede with the spirits to cure him of the terrible pain?

Thus so far as the above categories are concerned, though all of their inscriptions make worthwhile studies, each from a particular angle of interest, yet from the standpoint of a historian, none of them can be said to have possessed engrossing significance. As a matter of fact, out of the more than 100,000 oracle bones, covering some two and a half centuries, besides those connected with "exerting toil in the fields" (*tu tian*) which we discussed previously,[95] the inscriptions that are truly of historical value are very limited in number. And they all relate to two wars—the first fought by Wuding against the nomads in the northwest, and the second by the last emperor Zou against the tribes in the southeast.[96] Yet the first war occupied only three years; and the second war, though it involved three separate expeditions, seems to have lasted no more than twenty months in total. Now, had these two wars been unknown to historians in the past, these discoveries would have been nothing less than sensational. But as it is, both of these armed conflicts have been recorded in ancient books. The *Book of Changes* has specifically noted that Wuding "had fought against Guifang, and taken three years to overcome them." [97] In the *Zuozhuan*, the most famous contemporary commentaries on Confucius's *Spring and Autumn Annals* (*Chunqiu*), references to the last Shang emperor's exploits are found in two places: "After Zou of Shang engaged in a hunt in Li,[98] the eastern barbarians revolted." [99] Again, "Zou conquered the eastern barbarians but lost his own life afterward." [100]

This is, of course, not to belittle the contributions of the oracle-bone findings. It is only to make clear two points. Firstly, with all the divination inscriptions available to us, within the space of some 250 years we have found only two separate events that occurred within a total duration of less than five years that are worthy of being treated as historical material. And secondly, these two events, even without the knowledge of the oracle-bone findings, have already been duly taken notice of by ancient Chinese books. So it may not be too rash to assume that if there are apparent gaps in the ancient accounts of the Shang dynasty, the gaps may be only apparent and not real. It is not that these ancient accounts missed recording any important events; it is rather that other than those events they did record, there was scarcely anything worthy of being recorded.

If this is the case with the later part of the Shang dynasty, it could have also been the case with the earlier part. Although no oracle bones have been discovered for the period preceding Pangeng, as the lives of all Shang emperors must have followed more or less the same sort of pattern, their reigns may have been similarly and equally uneventful. Indeed, as this matter is

examined from a historian's perspective, all this continued routine uneventfulness may be said to have resulted from design by the founder of the
dynasty. For, knowingly or unknowingly, Tang had left to his descendants
not only an empire, but also an imperial system which enabled them to enjoy
maximum power and privilege with minimum care and concern, the like of
which the world may have never seen.

The emperor's power base was the Central Shang. Situated in the heartland of China, it was his personal domain. In comparison with other states, it
was overwhelming by its sheer size. It was, if not actually at least nominally,
a hundred times larger than any of the large states within the Four Lands.[101]
Moreover, it was by far the most highly developed region in agriculture;
therefore, also the richest and most populous. Thus, from every consideration of strength and wealth, the Shang emperor need not feel any apprehension regarding the possible emergence of rivalry or rebellion among the
enfeoffed states. The utmost trouble they could give was to delay or refuse
the payment of tributes. But as the Tang system went, the tributes collected
from them were intended to be only tokens of submission, neither an unbearable burden to the payer nor a *sine qua non* means of subsistence for the
payee. So if a few of the states or even a number of them should take
advantage of some internal dissension within the Central Shang, or of a weak
sovereign on the throne, and decline to live up to their obligations, it would
do the imperial house no more serious harm than injury to its pride. But as
soon as a strong monarch came again to the fore, without his resorting to the
use of force, the stray princes would all know which way the wind was
blowing and hasten to return to the fold to save their own skins. Thus there
occurred several periods in the Shang history when its authority over the
Four Lands waned, which have been noted in the ancient books. Yet, until a
new situation arose that made Tang's design no longer realistic, not a single
enfeoffed state was known to have dared to rear its head to challenge the
might of the Shang.

If the Shang emperors could find little within the limits of the Four Lands
that might cause them any uneasiness, they probably saw even less when
they surveyed the nomadic tribes beyond. Not to speak of the prepon-
derance of the Shang population, the system Tang had devised seemed to be
almost foolproof against their irruptions. Within the Four Lands, there were
aligned rows upon rows of enfeoffed states, the closer to the Central Shang,
the more susceptible to its influence, therefore the more loyal to the imperial
cause. Once a border state was invaded, it would automatically ask for aid
and succor from the imperial house; alarm would be sounded, and the whole
empire would be placed on the alert. If a few of the border states, with their
forces now united under the emperor's instructions, could drive away the
invaders, well and good; if not, then the few outlying states might suffer, but

it would be all but impossible for the invaders to penetrate deep enough to approach the Central Shang. In the meantime, the emperor could take full advantage of the conscription system that Tang had formulated, mobilize as large a force as he deemed fit, and chase away or punish the offenders as drastically as he thought necessary. This is how Wuding was able to subjugate Guifang, the most formidable nomads that had ever threatened Shang. This is also why throughout the Shang dynasty there were only two armed conflicts with these tribes serious enough to be chronicled.

As we see, therefore, the Shang emperors were free from most of the chronic worries that would beset ruling monarchs. But there was still one kind of worry from which Tang in all his wisdom could not have contrived a scheme to release them entirely—factious infighting and internal intrigues. But these are by nature clandestine activities; unless they break into the open, their contours are seldom revealed in history. At any rate, even though we are pretty certain that the Shang rulers must have suffered such afflictions from time to time as have all other crowned heads, yet not one single oracle bone out of all those so far discovered has yielded any inscription to support this generalization. Perhaps the diviners and the scribes, as a class of men, were not influential enough to be involved in conspiracies or machinations. Perhaps the Shang people as a whole just believed too firmly in the incorruptible righteousness of the spirits to dare to inquire of them on matters of doubtful rectitude.

Such are the facts as well as some possible explanations for them. As the oracle bones seem to bear out, and as the above analysis of Tang's system appears to indicate, outside of the few major events which have already found their way into the ancient books, there simply did not occur any others worthy of being written into history. If one should insist on a more detailed narrative, one would have to go into repetition upon repetition of a monotonous routine, characterized by numberless veneration ceremonies, indulgences in the chase, or engagements in "exerting toil in the fields." If one should choose to ignore these, then all that would be left to write about would be the deaths and accessions of the emperors. And this is precisely what the great historian Sima Qian recorded in his *Historical Records*.

· 5 ·

TRANSFERENCES OF THE CAPITAL
AND
CHANGES IN THE MODE OF SUCCESSION

As for the few major events that occurred in the Shang dynasty, especially in its earlier part before the removal of the capital to Yin, we shall have to return to the accounts given in the *Book of History* or in the *Historical Records* as our main sources of information. But here again it almost seems as if we have departed from the vacuity of a gap only to enter into the bewilderment of a jigsaw puzzle. For nearly all the documents related to these events which Confucius originally collected in the *Book of History* are lost, and we have with us today only the titles and the very brief and sometimes abstruse and almost incomprehensible introductory notes.

Perhaps, considering the routine uneventfulness of the Shang dynasty, it is not unnatural that the first event to be recorded is one truly of an extraordinary nature. In the time of Taiwu (the ninth emperor), on the grounds of the imperial court there suddenly sprouted forth a mulberry tree and a stalk of grain together like one plant.[102] In one night it grew so large that it could scarcely be encircled by a man's two arms. Taiwu was terrified. He asked his prime minister, Yi Zhi,[103] what this phenomenon could portend. The prime minister replied, "Could it be because there were shortcomings in your majesty's government? It would behoove your majesty to make virtuous amends." Taiwu followed this admonition, and the ominous growth soon withered and crumbled to dust. Thereafter he entrusted the government wholly to Yi Zhi; and the latter, ably assisted by another minister named Wu Xian,[104] made shine again the glory of the Shang Empire. So grateful was the emperor that he presented the prime minister to the ancestral temple, declaring that thenceforth he would no longer treat him as a subject, but as a friend. Yi Zhi humbly declined the honor and begged his sovereign to forgive him for this one and only act of disobedience. The several incidents of this event were all celebrated in separate compositions, but as noted before, none of them is extant.

If the loss of the above documents is deplorable, the deprivation of the next three is even more grievous to a historian. For they are related to the three transferences of the capital, of which there is no other record. In order to show the depths of our puzzlement, it may be best to give here in full all the information that can be obtained from the two sources on this matter.

From the introductory notes (*shuxu*) to the *Book of History,* we have these notations which may be translated literally as follows:

> Zhongding moved to Xiao. Thus (the document) *zhongding* was composed.
> Hetanjia resided at Xiang. Thus (the document) *hetanjia* was composed.
> Zuyi (was) ruined by water at Geng. Thus (the document) *zuyi* was composed.[105]

These notations are immediately followed by another about one more transference. Fortunately this document is preserved in its entirety, and we shall discuss it later at length. Its introductory note reads:

> Pangeng moved for the fifth time.[106] (As he) was about to set up the capital at Yin, the people murmured in resentment. Thus (the document) *pangeng* was composed.

The *Historical Records* has nothing to add to these transferences. In fact, it recounts them almost in the same style and wording as the introductory notes without any amplification.[107] But in the case of Zuyi, it does not mention that his capital was ruined by water. Moreover, it describes the reign of this thirteenth emperor thus:

> In the time of Hetanjia, Yin declined. Hetanjia died and was succeeded by his son Zuyi. After the accession of Zuyi, Yin entered into a period of resurgence. Wu Xianr was then charged with the government.

Again, in another paragraph, it attempts to give a summary description of the general conditions that obtained prior to Pangeng's moving of the capital to Yin:

> Since the time of Zhongding, the throne was transmitted not to the eldest sons but to the sons of brothers. Sometimes the sons of brothers struggled for succession among themselves. The disturbance lasted nearly nine reigns. Because of this, the princes of enfeoffed states failed to come to the court to pay tribute.

Now this last passage, to say the least, is confusing, if not contradictory to the one about Zuyi quoted just above. For Zuyi's reign is right in the middle of this period, and it has already been recorded to have brought a resurgence to the empire. Perhaps it is because of the awareness of this contradiction that the *Historical Records* also mentions specifically in another paragraph: "In the time of Emperor Yangjia, Yin declined." And Yangjia was the eighteenth emperor, his reign exactly the ninth counting from that of Zhongding.

The above are all the records obtainable. Not to speak of the points where they are confusing or contradictory, their inadequacy to form the basis for a coherent narrative is only too self-evident. Indeed, they have raised more questions than they have answered. Firstly, what were the compulsory reasons that drove the Shang to make three changes of imperial seat within such a short duration of some thirty years, or within the consecutive reigns of four emperors? Secondly, if there was continuous disturbance for nine reigns because of the adoption of a new mode of succession, had this anything to do with the three transferences of the capital? If so, how? Thirdly, did Zuyi actually bring about a resurgence of the empire within this period of general disturbance? If so, how does this reconcile with the record that he "was ruined by water at Geng"? Fourthly, if Geng was ruined by water, where did the Shang set up its capital afterward for more than a century before Pangeng ascended the throne? And if the capital was set up elsewhere, how can it be said that when Pangeng transferred it to Yin, he "moved for the fifth time"? And finally, if Zuyi had succeeded in restoring order to the empire, how could the disturbance over the struggle for succession have persisted even unto Yangjia's reign? Unable to answer these questions, most Chinese historians have chosen either to brush aside this part of Shang history as unreliable or to content themselves with merely quoting from the *Historical Records* or the introductory notes of the *Book of History*. But now with the discovery of the oracle bones, an unexpected new light has been thrown upon some of those puzzling points; and it is hoped therefore that our attempt here to reconstruct the history of this period on that basis in the following pages may not be adjudged too precipitate or too presumptuous.

What was then the motivation that caused the Shang repeatedly to change their capital? As noted before, when Pangeng planned to move to Yin, which was to be the fifth and the last transference for the dynasty, he was met with bitter opposition. But after the removal, Yin proved so satisfactory that after his death the people remembered what difficulties he had gone through in persuading them to make the move, and composed a document in his commemoration, which consists of three parts and purports to be a record of what he had spoken to them before, during, and after the event.[108] In the document, the forceful ruler was recorded to have said:

> Of old, our former emperors, with a view to obtaining achievements to exceed previous records, had departed from the hills[109] and caused us to descend to lower (plains). (This has resulted in) our capitals being variously afflicted with misfortune or attended with success.

From this it may be assumed that the three transferences before Pangeng were all inspired by a desire of each of the three emperors to establish a good record for his own reign so that it should compare favorably with their ancestors'.

But in what field of endeavors could they hope to achieve so much as to be able "to exceed previous records"? Certainly not in the military. For not only was the glorious example of Tang hard to emulate, but also there was no cause at all for making war. All the states within the Four Lands had already acknowledged allegiance to Shang; and beyond them, in the various *fang*, there were only divers nomadic tribes. As yet, these tribes were just an unorganized lot; to try to bring them under control would be as pointless as to sieve water. To endeavor then to excell in administrative or judicial fields? But human civilization was still on a level when administration was simple and justice crude. What a conscientious sovereign needed to do was to set his heart in the right place; beyond that, he would have neither the sophistication nor the audacity to presume that he could surpass his forebears. Unable to find an adequate explanation, some scholars have also suggested that the Shang people were perhaps after all not as highly developed agriculturally as has been taken for granted; and the repeated moving of the capital might have derived from their being still nomadic-oriented or from their

reverting to nomadism. But between the death of Tang and the first transference of imperial seat by Zhongding, there was an interposition of eight
emperors and a lapse of some two centuries. If there had been such an
atavistic tendency, why had it not revealed itself before the time of the tenth
emperor? Moreover, if many of the monarchs were addicted to the chase, as
they truly were, they had both opportunities and hunting grounds in abundance to gratify their inclinations without the need of resorting to the cumbersome inconvenience of moving a capital. The examples of Wuding,
Wuyi, and Zou have been cited before.[110] Not one of the three had ever
contemplated a transference of the capital again; and yet they probably had
indulged themselves in the chase with more vigor or with more abandon
than the others.

There appears to be, therefore, only one field of endeavor in which the
Shang monarchs might apply their zeal and energy and hope to obtain results
that could be measurably reckoned "to exceed previous records." And this is
in the further expansion of agriculture, which may be accurately computed
both in increased acreage and in increased production. When Tang first
moved his administrative seat from the Great City Shang to West Bo, one of
his reasons for choosing the new site was that it was circumscribed by the
Luo River on the north and by tall hills on the three other sides.[111] While
this configuration of surface makes excellent terrain for defense, it also limits
the extent of cultivable land available within the area. This, however, was
not much of a problem either for Tang or for Tang's immediate successors,
for they had a sort of "virgin land" to begin with. But by the time of the
ninth emperor, Taiwu, the situation must have changed considerably. The
Historical Records has recorded that after the incident of the mulberry tree
and the stalk of grain, he was frightened into making "virtuous amends" that
restored the glory of the dynasty.[112] We have no precise information regarding those amends, but one thing we may be sure of is that he would have
undoubtedly followed the program that Tang had pursued in the Great City
Shang and later again in West Bo, a principal part of which was *tu tian,*
"exerting toil in the fields." Thus conceivably by the end of Taiwu's reign
all the arable land within the hills of West Bo had been fully cultivated, and
there was no space left for further expansion. In the meantime, the population must have grown manifold after such a long period of peace and prosperity. How to provide work for the growing number of unemployed men—
that is, how to find more land for them to till—therefore became a problem of
ever mounting urgency.

Confronted with this situation, Taiwu's son and successor Zhongding was
forced to make a decision. He was likely a well-intentioned prince, overly
eager "to exceed previous records." But his ambition was not matched by his
foresight. His choice of a new site must have been a sorry one, for Pangeng

lamented openly that after the transference, the capital had been first "afflicted with misfortune." In any event, less than a score of years after his decease, the twelfth emperor, Hetanjia, had again to remove the imperial seat to a new location. Yet this change was not "attended with success" either, and misfortune continued to dog the footsteps of the imperial house. Hetanjia was said to have reigned only nine years.[113] And no sooner had he passed away than the thirteenth emperor, Zuyi, decided on another transference.

Thus in less than forty years the Shang had transferred its administrative capital three times. The repeated changes must have occasioned a sharp decline of confidence among the people at large; and the confusion and turmoil that was bound to follow such removals could not but have served as easy excuses for many states to waver in their allegiance and to defer payment of tributes. Moreover, these continual frustrations and disappointments must have given rise to serious dissensions within the imperial house itself. It seems to be therefore no coincidence that at this juncture, and at no other, there occurred an abrupt and drastic alteration in the traditional mode of succession to the throne.

If one takes a look at the genealogical chart of the Shang emperors which we have prepared with the benefit of the findings of the oracle bones, one will readily observe that the relationship by which the thirteenth, the sixteenth, the seventeenth, and the eighteenth emperors came to the throne is quite different from that of the rest. It was the Shang tradition, which must have originated from early nomadic times, that after the death of an elder brother, he was to be succeeded not by his son, but by a younger brother, next in age and born also of the deceased father's principal wife. But after the death of the youngest brother, the succession would not revert to the eldest or elder brother's son, but instead go to his own eldest son, born of a principal wife.[114] Now, as according to the chart, because Tang's eldest son died young, he was succeeded by the second son, who in turn, after an early demise, was succeeded by the third son. And it was because neither of these two had issue that Yi Yin finally placed the eldest son's only son on the throne. From there on, however, the succession always followed the traditional mode as outlined above. And so the sixth and the ninth emperors both were succeeded by their own sons, not by their elder brothers'. But when it came to the twelfth emperor, Hetanjia, he was succeeded not by his own son, as the practice should have been, but by Zuyi, son of his eldest brother, Zhongding, the tenth emperor. And this altered, irregular mode of succession continued for some time until the death of the twenty-first emperor, the youngest of four brothers, who was succeeded by his own son, Wuding. Thereafter the old tradition prevailed again.

Now, as noted before, there is no difference between this genealogical chart and that of the *Historical Records*, except for one error in the latter. The *Historical Records* named Zuyi as Hetanjia's son. Had this been so, the succession would have been in perfect accord with the customary practice. But as we have learned from the oracle bones, Zuyi was not Hetanjia's son but Zhongding's; and once we realize that, the alteration of the mode of succession becomes instantly obvious. Zuyi was therefore the very first who broke the tradition. And consequently he must be said to be also responsible for the "disturbance" that was to last through several reigns that followed, as the *Historical Records* has related. Moreover, as we remember from the introductory notes (*shuxu*) in the *Book of History*, "Zuyi (was) ruined by water at Geng." So, all in all, the image of this thirteenth emperor of Shang cannot be said to be a happy or commendable one.

Yet, all this notwithstanding, the *Historical Records* has also recorded: "After the accession of Zuyi, Yin entered into a period of resurgence. Wu Xianr was then charged with the government." And to add to these complications (if we feel our faith in the *Historical Records* somewhat shaken), the fact that Zuyi was a good emperor and that in his government he was ably assisted by Wu Xianr is confirmed by another document in the *Book of History*, the authenticity and reliability of which has never been in question.[115] Furthermore, that Wu Xianr was the son of the famous minister Wu Xian who had served so well under Taiwu, the one of the mysterious mulberry-and-grain fame, is materially supported too by a bronze tripod which the former had especially made in remembrance of his father.[116] So, indeed, the threads of history are all tangled here, and there did not seem at first to be any prospect of unraveling them.

Once again, however, the oracle bones come to our rescue, baring a secret long buried in the past. From some of the inscriptions we learn definitely that Zuyi was venerated after his demise by the Shang people as *zhongzong*, "the Middle Ancestor," [117] of equal rank with Taijia, who had been honored before as *taizong*, "the Grand Ancestor." [118] As has been explained previously, these posthumous honors were very hard to come by. Out of the long line of thirty emperors, except for Tang, who as the founder of the dynasty deservedly occupied a position of his own, only three were singled out for such distinctions. Besides Taijia and Zuyi, only Wuding, the twenty-second emperor, under whom the Shang attained to the zenith of power, was to receive the title *gaozong*, "the High Ancestor." From this one can easily see in what high esteem Zuyi was held by his descendants.

This finding of the oracle bones is of crucial importance to the reconstruction of the history of this period. For prior to this, Chinese historians, following another mistaken notation made by the *Historical Records*, have always taken for granted that the Shang had venerated Taiwu as the Middle Ancestor, and not Zuyi.[119] In the ancient records there is one significant passage which refers distinctly to *zhongzong;* but until the oracle bones revealed the true identity, all the scholars in the past had ascribed it to the wrong emperor. The passage reads:

> In the old times there was the Yin emperor *zhongzong.* Grave, humble, reverential, and cautious, he always sought to measure his own actions in accordance with the Mandate of Heaven. In ruling over the people, he was ever fearful (of doing anything contrary). He never dared indulge in indolent ease. It is thus that *zhongzong* enjoyed the possession of the empire for seventy-five years.[120]

The man who delivered the above utterance is none else than the famed *zhougong,* "Duke of Zhou," one of the three principal founders of the Zhou dynasty that displaced the Shang in the twelfth century B.C. He did so on the occasion of giving advice to his young orphaned nephew who had just succeeded to the throne as the second emperor of the new dynasty. The sagacious uncle was warning the youthful monarch against indulgence in idleness and complacency, having begun his speech by emphasizing the importance of agriculture in the life of a ruling prince:

> If you know about the toil of sowing and reaping in the first place, then in your comfort and ease you will understand what the little people depend upon for their livelihood. I have observed among the little people. There are cases where the parents have diligently labored in sowing and reaping; but the sons have failed to appreciate the painful toil involved. The sons become idle and complacent; they abandon themselves to vulgarism in speech, then to disorderliness in conduct. And (if they are remonstrated with), they will throw contempt upon their parents, saying, "These old people have heard nothing and know nothing."

And it was immediately after offering this advice that the duke mentioned *zhongzong* as a good example for his nephew to model himself after. Thus it may be safely inferred that the former Shang (or Yin) emperor had personally known "the painful toil" endured by his agrarian population, and had devoted his seventy-five-year reign to the betterment of their livelihood.

The above jibes well with Pangeng's pronouncement that when his predecessors made their transferences of the capital, among whom Zuyi was included, their motivation was to obtain achievements "to exceed previous records." Also, the very fact that Zuyi was venerated as the Middle Ancestor leaves no more room for doubt about the truthfulness of the account of the *Historical Records* that "after the accession of Zuyi, Yin entered a period of resurgence." Yet there is still the matter of his being "ruined by water at Geng" to thrash out. Formerly, some Chinese scholars, while the oracle bones remained buried, suggested as a way out that after suffering the calamity at Geng, Zuyi might have moved the capital elsewhere and contrived to accomplish the resurgence afterward.[121] But this is in sharp contradiction with the document *pangeng*. Not only does its introductory note explicitly stipulate that when Pangeng moved to Yin it was the fifth transference for the dynasty, but in the document itself, that monarch was reported to have said clearly that up to his time the Shang had had altogether only five capitals.[122] Though Pangeng did not name the five capitals one by one, from the authentic records we can only find these five and no other, to wit, Bo, West Bo, Xiao, Xiang, and Geng. So it seems almost certain that Zuyi could not have set up any other capital outside of Geng during his long reign.

Thus the question remained long unsolved and seemingly unsolvable. But with the revelation found in the oracle bones, we begin to see light at the end of the tunnel. Had Zuyi indeed made such an inept choice of a capital that it was destoryed by water shortly after the removal, he would more likely have been remembered for his incompetence than venerated as the Middle Ancestor. If any misconception had been formed here, therefore, it could have been very well due to a misunderstanding of the introductory note because of its archaic wording. It says that "Zuyi (was) ruined by water at Geng"; it may have actually meant that "Zuyi (moved to) Geng, (which was later) ruined by water." While this explanation is plausible, there is yet another one even more probable. The ancient Chinese character *pi* 圮 ("ruined by water") is much like another character in form, in shape, and even in the number of strokes. This second one is *yi* 圯 , meaning "bridge." The only difference between the two is that the last stroke of the latter, ㄴ , is longer than that of the former.[123] So there is great likelihood that the character *pi* might have resulted from a mistaken transcription by a scribe or a copyist. The one used in the original should have been *yi;* and consequently the introductory note should have been translated as "Zuyi built bridges at Geng. Thus (the document) Zuyi was composed." If this is the case, as we believe it is, it may very well mean that Geng, being right on the bank of the Yellow River, also abounded in streams. Both before and after it was made the capital, Zuyi had to build many bridges there to facilitate the settlement.

But whether *pi* or *yi* is the correct character, we can feel reasonably sure that Geng had proved to be a very satisfactory capital for the Shang people throughout the long reign of the Middle Ancestor, and had continued as the imperial seat for the next five emperors that followed him until the time of Pangeng. But with the lapse of about a century and a half, the course and the formation of the Yellow River must have undergone many changes. What had been an unquestionable fountainhead of beneficence was now turning into an ominous source of incalculable potential danger. Pangeng saw the handwriting on the wall and decided to transfer the capital again. And it was only after his removal to Yin that Geng was finally ruined by water.

Based on the above, we can now reconstruct the history of this period roughly as follows:

At the end of the reign of Taiwu, all the arable lands within the tall hills of West Bo had been fully utilized. In order "to exceed the previous records" of former emperors as well as to find more land for the surplus population to cultivate, Zhongding, the tenth emperor, decided to "depart from the hills," "descend to lower plains," and build up a new capital at Xiao. This site, however, did not turn out to be a happy choice from the agricultural point of view. For a variety of reasons, which could have been poor soil, inclement weather, or even a series of natural calamities, after some twenty years and two reigns, the Shang finally acknowledged failure. And when Hetanjia ascended the throne, he had the imperial seat transferred at once to Xiang. But if the last site had not done well, this new one fared even worse. From the very outset, it seems to have been "afflicted with misfortune"; and judging from the reasons which later made Zuyi establish his capital at Geng right on the bank of the Yellow River, shortage of water supply must have been the principal cause of Xiang's woes. The dearth of that precious substance, so necessary to the husbandmen, must have been discovered very early upon settlement; and even while Hetanjia was still in power, demands must have been made for another change. As the emperor, either out of stubbornness or out of indecision, refused or hesitated to take action, the persistent dissatisfaction burst out in open disturbance at his death. Zuyi, son of the tenth emperor, was apparently not slow to lend his weight and name. A struggle for power ensued. Whether it was accompanied by violence or not, out of the "disturbance," the sons of Hetanjia, who had a better claim to the throne, were pushed aside, and Zuyi emerged as the thirteenth emperor, the first to break away from the traditional mode of succession.

This new ruler was an exceptionally capable man. Since his rule was to last over seventy-five years, the longest reign ever known in Chinese history, he must have ascended the throne not much older than twenty. Though young and inexperienced, he was by nature "grave, humble, reverent, and cautious," and in all actions he took, to use the language of the ancient times, "he always sought to measure (them) in accordance with the Mandate of Heaven" or in the words we use today, he always tried to consult with the desire and the opinion of the people. First, he moved the capital to Geng. Because of its proximity to the Yellow River, no matter how much water was needed for irrigation or other consumption, there was no fear of shortage. The people were immensely pleased, and in a few years they openly hailed the city as being "attended with success" in contrast with the two previous failures. Then, side by side with the removal of the capital, Zuyi picked out Wu Xianr and placed him in charge of the government. This was done not casually but after careful deliberation. He had overcome his adversaries, the sons of his uncle Hetanjia; but these were his close kinsmen, and of necessity most of the officers who now served under him were as much related to them as they were to him. There was no telling how many of them still entertained loyal or sympathetic feelings for the lost cause; and bitterness, he knew only too well, lingers much longer in the vanquished than in the victor. Now, Wu Xianr was the scion of Wu Xian, who had been such an exemplary minister to his own grandfather Taiwu. Not only was he known as a very effective administrator, but he was also trusted by one and all in the court. If anyone could contrive to bind the wounds of factionalism, there could be no better man than Wu Xianr. So Zuyi made him prime minister, and throughout their lives, neither of them had any cause to regret the selection.

And what is more, Zuyi accomplished something during his long reign, which the Shang people were to remember ever afterward with affection and with admiration. The fact was, ever since Zhongding moved the capital from West Bo to Xiao, the Shang had been on the decline. For some forty years the trend had continued and worsened. Aggravated at first by the poor performances of two capitals, and then accelerated by the "disturbance" that culminated in an unheard-of alteration of the traditional mode of succession, the downward descent probably hit bottom during the last years of Hetan-jia's reign and the early years of Zuyi's own, when all "the princes of enfeoffed states failed to come to the court to pay tribute." But Zuyi was not a man to forget the Mandate of Heaven which his ancestors had received and preserved, and which he had now put in the care of his own person. He worked hard and patiently. "He never dared indulge in indolent ease." And slowly and steadily, with the help of Wu Xianr, he built up once more an effective government and an even richer and more powerful Central Shang. As the trend grew clearer and clearer during his long reign, it may be assumed that all the states that had gone astray returned either voluntarily or under pressure to the fold again. This is the real resurgence for the Shang people after their departure from West Bo. This is why at his death he was honored with the title *zhongzong*, the first time for some two centuries after Taijia had been venerated as *taizong*.

But if Zuyi did everything he could to restore the glory of Shang, he did nothing to solve the problem of succession which he himself had generated. Hereafter, in cases like his own, was the throne to go to the youngest brother's son or to the eldest or elder brother's? Perhaps in his position, he being the originator of the problem, there was nothing that he could do. In any event, when he died, there was no cause for trouble. Having reigned seventy-five years, if he had had brothers, he left none to survive him. Without any commotion, therefore, he was succeeded by the elder of his two sons, Zuxin, as the fourteenth emperor. After the death of this monarch, there was still no problem. For the rule that brother should succeed brother had never come into dispute, and the second son, Wojia, ascended the throne as a matter of course. But after the death of the fifteenth emperor, though facts are lacking on this point, a serious crisis seems to have presented itself.[124] While the sons of the second brother, Wojia, might have desired to return to the traditional mode, the sons of the elder brother, Zuxin, must have insisted on following the example of their grandfather Zuyi himself. It is very likely, as the *Historical Records* indicates, that the succession was not settled without another "disturbance." But disturbance or no disturbance, in the end a curious arrangement, to which the genealogical chart bears mute witness, appears to have been worked out as a sort of temporary solution. Zuxin's son Zuding was enthroned as the sixteenth emperor; but upon his decease, it was not his brother or his son but Wojia's son Nangeng that succeeded to him as the seventeenth emperor. However, the arrangement was apparently a patchwork that gave no one full satisfaction but allowed everybody to jockey for advantage. Thus, even while the seventeenth emperor was alive, the atmosphere of the court must have been charged with ceaseless tension; and by the time of his demise, the feuding could very well have gone past the point of no return. It is therefore more probable than not that only after a violent contest of strength, the faction led by the sons of Zuding succeeded in overcoming the opposition of the sons of Nangeng; and Yangjia, being the eldest of the former, was able to accede as the eighteenth emperor. The struggle must have drained the imperial house of all vigor and morale. Even after the succession of Yanjia was made secure, resentment must have remained deep in many who, having sided or sympathized with the defeated faction, were now compelled to serve under the other. A house divided cannot be expected to rule effectively over the empire. Thus the *Historical Records* records quite truthfully, "At the time of Yangjia, Yin declined."

The above seems to be the only coherent narrative that can be pieced together from the confusing ancient records. Until more discoveries like the oracle bones are made, we may not be able to recount the actual facts for certain. But in the meantime there is no question whatever about the authenticity of the document *pangeng*. And, as we shall presently see, both the speeches by Pangeng before, during, and after the transference of the capital to Yin, as recorded in the document, and the circumstances surrounding that event, as indicated by those very speeches, are all fully consistent with our narrative.

NOTES

1. See above, p. 58.

2. A village in Minchi district, south of the Yellow River in northwest Henan.

For a good survey of Yangshao culture, see Chang Kwang-chih, *The Archaeology of Ancient China*, pp. 91–142. Modern estimates place the spread of the culture between 6,000 and 3,000 B.C.

3. Jingxi district, Liaoning province.

4. Ningding district.

5. See above, p. 60.

6. Ibid.

7. See above, p. 62.

8. See above, pp. 68–69.

9. See above, p. 69. Gun was said to have been enfeoffed as Prince of Chong, for instance.

10. See above, p. 68.

11. See above, p. 82.

12. See above, pp. 91–92.

13. *Book of History, gaoyaomo.*

14. See above, p. 100.

15. See above, pp. 113–16.

16. See above, p. 127.

17. See above, pp. 136–37.

18. See above, pp. 113–16.

19. Dong Zuobin, *Yin Lipu,* part II, chap. 9.

20. Ibid.

21. *Book of Changes, jiji* hexagram.

22. Dong Zuobin, *Yin Lipu,* part II, chap. 5, sec. 5.

23. There are four indications: (1) According to *Book of History, shuxu,* Tang destroyed the *she* altar of Xia, the symbol of independence. (2) There is no intimation in any record that the land of Xia was ever given to any other as a fief by the Shang. (3) As the sacrificial odes of Shang sang of Tang, "After punishing Wei and Gu, the turn came to Kunwu and Xia Jie" *(above, Chap. III, n. 134)*, and as three of the imperial seat sites (4, 5, and 6 on the map) appear to be within the former territories of Wei, Gu, and Kunwu, it seems safe to assume that Tang had also incorporated the Xia domain into his "Central Shang." And (4) in *Li Ji, ziyi,* and in the document *taijia* of the *Book of History,* Anyi was called the "West City Xia."

24. *Mencius, tengwengong,* II.

25. *Historical Records, yin benji.* The lord's name was Feilian.

26. Dong Zuobin, *Yin Lipu,* part II, chap. 9, sec. 3.

27. Ibid., chap. 8, sec. 7.

28. Ibid., chap. 9, *wuding ripu.*

29. Wang Guowei, *Beiboding Ba.*

30. See above, p. 126.

31. Wang Guowei, *Shang Sangoubing Ba.*

32. *Historical Records, boyi liezhuan.*

33. *Historical Records, zhou benji* and *songweizi shijia.*

34. Wang Guowei, *Shang Sangoubing Ba.*

35. See diagram, p. 115.

36. The exclusion of the various *fang* from the Shang dominion, realistic as it was, brought about a restrictive effect on information concerning those areas. For centuries, before the southeast was fully assimilated, the "Xia people" did not have much knowledge about what was happening south of the Huai River. Thus when Taibo of Zhou fled to Wu, a place north of modern Shanghai, no one at his time was sure where he had gone. And until the middle of the 5th century B.C., the ancient records did not have any definitive information about the descendants of Wuyu, the younger son of Shao-kang, one of whom was presently to make Yue the strongest state in the Zhou Empire. So much for the southeast; the northwest fared even worse. Writing in the 3rd century B.C., the poet Qu Yuan did not know where Sanwei was, the place to which Shun had induced some of the Sanmiao tribes to migrate during the flood.

This phenomenon, however, did not occur uniquely in China. We read the following from Gibbon's *Decline and Fall of the Roman Empire* (Modern Library Edition), vol. II, chap. XXXI, pp 434–35:

By the revolution of Britain the limits of science as well as of empire were contracted. The dark cloud which had been cleared by the Phoenician discoveries, and finally dispelled by the arms of Caesar, again settled on the shores of the Atlantic, and a Roman province was again lost among the fabulous islands of the ocean. One hundred and fifty years after the reign of Honorius the gravest historian of the times (Procopius) describes the wonders of a remote isle, whose eastern and western parts are divided by an antique wall, the boundary of life and death, or, more properly, of truth and fiction. The east is a fair country, inhabited by a civilized people; the air is healthy, the waters are pure and plentiful, and the earth yields her regular and fruitful increase. In the west, beyond the wall, the air is infectious and mortal, the ground is covered with serpents; and this dreary solitude is the region of departed spirits, who are transported from the opposite shores in substantial boats and by living rowers. Some families of fishermen, the subjects of the Franks, are excused from tribute, in consideration of the mysterious office which is performed by these Charons of the ocean. Each in his turn is summoned at the hour of midnight, to hear the voices, and even the names, of the ghosts: he is sensible of their weight, and he feels himself impelled by an unknown, but irresistible power. After this dream of fancy, we read with astonishment that the name of this island is *Brittia;* that it lies in the ocean, against the mouth of the Rhine, and less than thirty miles from the continent. . . .

37. *Book of History, zhonghuizhigao.* Also see *Zuozhuan,* Duke Xiang, 29th year.

38. See above, p. 137.

39. *Shangshu Dazhuan.*

40. Ibid. The passage in quotation marks is a paraphrase.

41. According to *Book of History, shuxu,* this is known as *tanggao,* the *Declaration of Tang.* But the original composition, included by Confucius in the *Book of History,* is now lost. The present version is not considered authentic. Sima Qian, however, has preserved another version in the *Historical Records,* which forms the basis of our translation here.

42. *Historical Records, yin benji.* Also see *Book of Poetry, shangsong: changfa.*

43. Dong Zuobin, *Yin Lipu,* part II, chap. 8, sec. 7.

44. *Huainanzi, taizu xun.*

45. See Map III.

46. The passes are called Chengao, Jianggu, and Huanyuan.

47. See above, p. 140 and note 130.

48. Di (a different character than the one used for the northern nomadic tribes) was the name of a minority group of Qiang.

49. *Book of Poetry, shangsong: yinwu.*

50. See above, pp. 135–36.

51. See above, p. 114.

52. *Book of History, jiugao.*

53. *Li Ji, tangong,* II.

54. See above, p. 8.

55. *Confucian Analects, bayi;* and *Huainanzi, qisu xun.*

56. See above, pp. 112–13.

57. Liu Xiang, *Shuoyuan,* chap. I; Huangfu Mi, *Diwang Shiji;* and also see the following note.

58. This version of the prayer is a combination of the texts found in *Confucian Analects, yaoyue,* and in *Lushi Chunqiu, jiqiuji: shunmin.*

59. *Zuozhuan,* Duke Xiang, 29th year.

60. *Yi Zhou Shu, wanghui.*

61. *Da Xue (Great Learning).*

62. *Book of History, pangeng,* III.

63. Ibid., *taijia,* II. Also *Book of Poetry, shangsong: liezu.*

64. *Book of History, pangeng,* II.

65. For instance, the founder of the Han dynasty was given the posthumous title *gaozu;* and the founder of the Qing (Manchu) dynasty, *taizu* ("Grand Progenitor").

66. *Book of Changes, ge* hexagram. The passage is actually a comment on both Tang and Wu Wang, founder of the Zhou dynasty.

67. *Mencius, wanzhang,* I; *Historical Records, yin benji.* Also, see the genealogical chart of the house of Shang.

68. *Book of History, yixun.*

69. The one other case is the association between Liu Bei and Zhuge Liang.

70. *Book of History, tangshi.* Also *Mozi, shangxian.*

71. The date is found both in *Book of History, yixun,* and in Ban Gu, *Qian Han Shu, lulizhi.* Please note that the month of ox (*chou*) is the *zheng* month of Shang. Through astronomical calculations Dong Zuobin reached a conclusion that the year was 1738 B.C. See his *Yin Lipu,* part I, chap. 6.

72. *Book of History, yixun.* For using second-batch documents as sources, see Appendix, particularly its Item Five.

73. An obvious reference to Houyi and Hanzhuo. See above, pp. 120–22.

74. *Book of History, taijia,* I.

75. Ibid., II.

76. An obvious reference to Tang. See above, p. 164.

77. This last passage is a condensed paraphrase from *Book of History, taijia,* II.

78. Ibid., *xianyouyide.*

79. The characters *zu* and *zong* are usually used together in colloquial Chinese as one term, *zuzong,* which means "ancestor" or "ancestors." But in conferring posthumous titles on deceased sovereigns, since the time of the Shang, a practice has developed to use the two separately. While *zu* was generally reserved for the founder of a dynasty, *zong* was applied to other emperors considered to be worthy of such titles. Thus we translate *zu* as "progenitor" and *zong* as "ancestor." As to the two other emperors who were similarly honored, they will be discussed in later pages.

80. See *Book of History, shuxu; Historical Records, yin benji;* and *Bamboo Chronicles.* In *Bamboo Chronicles,* however, there is a passage to this effect: "In the seventh year, *wang* (Taijia) stole out of Tong and killed Yi Yin. Heaven sent down a great fog three days. Wang established Yi Yin's two sons, Yi Zhi and Yi Fen, as his heirs; restored to them his land, and divided it between them." Both the wording and the style of the passage are quite different from the rest of the book. It has been long suspected as an interpolation by someone in the period of the Warring States, or later, who was skeptical of such ingenuous self-disinterestedness as Yi Yin had demonstrated. After the discovery of the oracle bones, we know that the story of Yi Yin as told in *shuxu* and the *Historical Records* is authentic. For oracle-bone inscriptions showing the veneration of Yi Yin by Shang emperors, see Wang Guowei, *Gushi Xinzheng,* chap. IV, sec. 1.

81. *Historical Records, yin benji* and *sandai shibiao.* Also, see the genealogical table of the House of Shang, II, After Tang.

82. Wang Guowei, *Yin Bucizhong Suojian Xiangongxianwang Kao, zhongzongzuyi.* Zuyi was not Hetanjia's son but Zhongding's.

83. See the genealogical table of the House of Shang, I, Before Tang. For the wrong sequence, see note *c* in the table.

84. Wang Guowei, *Yin Bucizhong Suojian Xiangongxianwang Kao.*

85. Dong Zuobin, *Jiaguxue Liushinian,* p. 13.

86. See *Li Ji, biaoji;* and Ban Gu, *Baihu Tongyi, sanjiao.*

87. *Li Ji, jiaotesheng.*

88. Dong Zuobin, *Jiaguxue Liushinian,* p. 113. Also see *Yin Lipu, sipu,* by the same author.

89. Ibid.

90. See above, pp. 159–60.

91. *Huainanzi, taizu xun.*

92. Dong Zuobin, *Jiaguxue Liushinian,* p. 93.

93. Ibid., p. 92.

94. Dong Zuobin, *Yin Lipu,* part II, chap. 9, sec. 2.

95. See above, pp. 135–36.

96. Dong Zuobin, *Yin Lipu,* part II, chap. 8, sec. 7; and chap. 9, secs. 1 and 3.

97. *Book of Changes, jiji* hexagram.

98. The exact location unknown, somewhere in modern Anhui.

99. *Zuozhuan,* Duke Zhao, 4th year.

100. Ibid., 11th year.

101. According to Yu's grand scheme, the imperial domain is supposed to be one thousand *li* square, and the largest feudal state only one hundred *li* square. This arrangement was accepted as accomplished fact in the Zhou dynasty.

102. This story is recorded in both *Book of History, shuxu,* and *Historical Records, yin benji.*

103. Some scholars have maintained that Yi Zhi was Yi Yin's son. But the distance in time makes this unlikely, though it may be probable that Yi Zhi was related to Yi Yin in some manner.

104. Wu Xian had a son who was to be prime minister to Zuyi (the thirteenth emperor), and whose name, though different in Chinese character, happens to be pronounced the same as the father's. In order to distinguish them, we shall romanize the son's name as Wu Xianr, with an *r* added to Xian, a somewhat colloquial way of pronunciation in Peking.

105. All words in parentheses are added to make the meanings clear. For the locations of these capitals, see Map III.

106. The first time, Tang moved from Bo to West Bo; the second time, Zhongding moved from West Bo to Xiao; the third time, Hetanjia moved from Xiao to Xiang; the fourth time, Zuyi moved from Xiang to Geng; and the fifth time, Pangeng moved from Geng to Yin.

107. The *Historical Records,* however, gives different characters to the names of two capitals—*ao* for *xiao* and *xing* for *geng.* But most scholars think that though the characters are different, the places are the same.

108. See *Book of History, pangeng,* comments by Kong Anguo.

109. An obvious reference to West Bo, Tang's hilly capital.

110. See above, p. 173.

111. See above, p. 160.

112. *Historical Records, yin benji;* also above, p. 177.

113. *Bamboo Chronicles.*

114. See Wang Guowei, *Yin Bucizhong Suojian Xiangongxianwang Kao.*

115. *Book of History, junshi.* The author of this document is the famed Duke of Zhou. In it he enumerated the good emperors of the Shang as well as the praiseworthy ministers who helped each of them. Among others, he said, "In the time of Zuyi, there was such a one as Wu Xianr."

116. Ruan Yuan, *Jiguzai Zhongdingyiqi Kuanshi.*

117. Wang Guowei, *Yin Bucizhong Suojian Xiangongxianwang Kao.*

118. See above, p. 169.

119. *Historical Records, yin benji.*

120. *Book of History, wuyi.* The Duke of Zhou mentioned *zhongzong* only by the posthumous title,

as the Chinese were wont to do, and not by his given name. So until the discovery of the oracle bones, Chinese scholars had always ascribed all the duke's praises of *zhongzong* to Taiwu and not to Zuyi, including the seventy-five-year-long reign.

121. See *Bamboo Chronicles*. It mentions two other places to which the Shang had moved after Geng.

This usually has been suspected as a spurious interpolation.

122. *Book of History, pangeng*, 1.

123. See Xu Shen's dictionary, or any comprehensive modern Chinese dictionary.

124. See *Historical Records, yin benji* and *sandai shibiao*.

CHAPTER V

THE SHANG, NOW ALSO CALLED THE YIN, DYNASTY

(14th–12th Century B.C.)

· 1 ·

PANGENG AND THE TRANSFER OF THE CAPITAL TO YIN

While Yangjia was still emperor, the dangers posed by the Yellow River were already becoming manifest. This mighty river was, as it still is today, a tortuous, treacherous stream. It carries silt from the loess land hundreds of miles upriver and deposits it on the lower plains it traverses. To the lower land on either bank, it provides an abundant supply of water. And as the years go by, because of continued accumulation of sediment, the bed rises higher and higher. In ordinary times the river would just simply spill out and absorb whatever land it needed. But in case of excessive rainfall, or of a sudden and abnormal thawing of the glaciers in the Pamirs, of which the Chinese in the times of the Shang had little knowledge, the flowing waters which usually look so tame and placid would turn into a ferocious torrent of monstrous proportions that would sweep aside any dike or barrier that might stand in its way, swamp fields and cities alike, and overwhelm everything in sight, men, animals, and all, except for the few who happened to have the luck or the foresight to escape to higher places. This is why the Yellow River, though it has yielded the Chinese innumerable benefits, is also known as "China's Sorrow."

As the Yellow River behaves in this manner even today, the situation must have been no better in the times of Yangjia and Pangeng, when much less was known about flood control. What they did to protect Geng was probably confined to the building of dikes—more dikes, higher dikes, outer dikes, inner dikes. But dikes, as history has demonstrated again and again, provide protection against the Yellow River only under normal conditions and for a limited period of time. In the last year of Yangjia, the water had overflowed some outer dikes, and many of the homes in the outskirts were ruined.[1] By then, over a hundred years since Zuyi had moved the capital to Geng, the accumulation of silt must have raised the stream in the springtime to a level almost as high as the highest dikes, and certainly higher than the city itself. An open discussion of the crisis followed. Pangeng, as second brother to Yangjia and the next in the line of succession, strongly advocated that the capital be moved to a place of safety, preferably somewhere on the other side of the river with a higher terrain relatively free of inundation.

There should have been no opposition to such a proposal. The danger was obvious enough. Yet, as Pangeng sensed, the people were not in a state to calmly evaluate the facts. Although no frank disputation surfaced in the open, rumors of all kinds were being whispered among the populace tending to sabotage his proposal. The arguments murmured in those whispers were all unsound, but they were nonetheless effective. As Pangeng examined them, they ran, in the main, along these lines: There was no real need for the transfer of the capital; all talk about the river possibly rising to un- heard-of heights were just groundless speculations fabricated to frighten the people. The advocates for the move had in fact another sinister purpose in mind. Most of the officers now serving in the court were still the old func- tionaries who had served for many years and who had descended from families long in the service of the dynasty. While a few of them might have sympathized with the vanquished faction in the recent struggle for the throne, nearly all of them were now suspect in the eyes of those in power. Because these officers had all rendered meritorious services in the past, and because they were real friends to the people, the men in control had so far not dared replace them with their own men. So the transfer of the capital was now proposed not actually out of necessity, but simply as a device to remove these officers from their positions of trust and responsibility. Once the capital was in the process of transfer, or once after the transfer was completed, the old officers would be declared in fault or incompetent in the execution of orders, and their positions would be given to men who would no longer mind the interests of the people but only try to accumulate wealth and treasure for those in power.

Pangeng now found himself in a very difficult situation. Had these charges been made out in the open, he could have easily disproved them. But they were disseminated in secret. Moreover, he knew exactly who were responsible for the insidious agitation, yet he dared not expose them. The dynasty had suffered decline enough as a result of the recent struggle for succession; to expose these agitators would be to prolong the internecine feud further, which might lead to a bloodier conflict, plunging the house of Shang into irreversible ruin.

And now, Yangjia having died, Pangeng himself was occupying the throne. Before his brother's death, he had already helped select a new site for capital—Yin, which had so many desirable qualities that even the opponents could not find any fault with the choice. Notwithstanding, the hidden saboteurs intensified their malicious campaign. Ignoring the obvious advantages of Yin, they concentrated their attacks on the motivations they claimed for the proposed transference. In the meantime, because of the inaction of the year before, the river had risen visibly higher. There was no time left for procrastination; any more delay could mean inescapable destruction. How Pangeng dealt with this explosive situation can be found in the document that bears his name. As literal a translation as possible follows:

Part I

Pangeng resolved to move to Yin. The people did not want to depart from their present habitations. He summoned the divers relations (of the imperial house) [2] and made to them this declaration:

"When our late emperor (zuyi) came and fixed the settlement in this place, he did so out of weighty concern for the people. It was not his purpose to kill all of them by not helping them to preserve their lives.

"On this matter I have consulted with the tortoise, and obtained the reply, 'This is no more the place for us.'

"In the time of our former emperors, even though they carefully observed established laws and practices, even though in everything they did they faithfully obeyed the commands of Heaven, yet they did not indulge in constant repose, they did not abide ever in the same city. Up to now we have already had five capitals. [3]

"If we fail to follow these past precedents, we shall be refusing to acknowledge that Heaven is about to issue a command to end our lives here. How can we say then that (by staying here) we may the better pursue the glorious course of our former emperors?

"As from the stump of a felled tree there are sprouts and shoots, Heaven will prolong our lives and perpetuate Its Mandate to us in the new city so that we may continue and recover our former emperors' great possessions and secure tranquillity for the four quarters of the empire."

Pangeng sought to make the people aware of his views. (He knew) he must begin with those who were in high places. He directed them to adhere strictly to time-proved standards of integrity in the enforcement of laws and regulations, declaring, "Let no one dare suppress the complaints or remonstrances of the little people."

Then the emperor ordered the numerous officers to come to the court and addressed them to this effect:

"Come, all of you! I will tell you how you should conduct yourselves. Make humble your mind. Do not be arrogant. Do not let yourselves be led by personal comforts and complacency.

"In the early times, our former emperors, also on purpose, shared the government with men who had served long in their offices. When an emperor had a decision to make public, these officers always endeavored to disseminate its significance to the widest extent possible, never concealing his intent in any manner. Thus the emperor respected these officers for their not speaking out of bounds; and thus the people became transformed (according as the emperor had desired).

"Now, however, all you make is disturbing noises, shaking the confidence of the people by slanted, shallow mumbles. I do not know what you have to complain about.

"In this matter, I am not myself abandoning my proper virtue; it is you who have concealed the goodness of my intentions, not standing in awe of me, your sovereign! I see through you as clearly as one sees through a fire. If you have been permitted to go on in this erratic manner, it is because I have purposely refrained from exercising my power.[4]

"When the net has its line, there is order and not confusion. When the husbandman labors upon the fields and devotes his strength to reaping, there is then the autumn harvest. If you can humble your mind and work for the real good of the people as well as for your relatives and friends, then you may boast of the merits you have accumulated.

"But you do not seem to be afraid of evil far and near. You are like the lazy husbandman given to indolence. You do not toil till twilight; you do not labor upon the fields. How can you expect to have rice or millet?

"You do not speak to the people with words of harmony and good cheer. You are generating venom within yourselves. Trying to create failure and calamity, pursuing the course of villainy and treason, you are surely bringing disaster on your own persons. You have sown evil among the people; you shall reap nothing but pain. When that comes, will it avail you to repent?

"Take a good look at the poor little people. Even when they have (real) complaints to make, they will yet be careful and not speak out of bounds. How much more you should mind your own conduct, since I have the power to control the length or the shortness of your lives!

"Why do you not report to me, and must go about exciting people with groundless talk and sinking them into deep fright? This is like setting fire to the grass plain. Once it blazes to such an extent as to be unapproachable, it will be impossible to beat it out. (If this happens), it will be you who have caused the disturbance; and I will not be the one to blame.

"Now, however, Chi Ren[5] has said, 'In the employment of men, it behooves us to seek those who have been long and experienced in service. It is different from choosing utensils, in which case we do not seek old ones, but new.'

"Our former emperors and your forefathers and fathers shared together the comforts and the toils of the state. How should I dare to inflict undeserved punishments on you? For generations you have been chosen for service; I will not cover up your merits. Now, I am offering the great sacrifice to our former emperors; your forefathers are also invited to follow and share in the same. Whether this will result in blessings or calamities afterward, I on my part will not dare take any action that may not be proper and righteous.

"However, I will tell you how you should deal with this difficult situation. Like an archer, when you shoot, you must have a target. Do not show disrespect to persons advanced in years. Do not trifle with the weak, the orphaned, and the young. Be a true leader in your various posts. Exert your utmost; and listen to and carry out whatever I, your sovereign, may plan and decide.

"Far and near, if any one of you commits a crime that deserves death, he shall die for that crime. If any one of you does a good deed, his merit for that deed shall be displayed. If the nation prospers, it will be because you all have done your duty. If it does not, it will be because I have failed to punish properly.

"All of you, be sure to keep in mind what I have told you. From this day onward, attend respectfully to your respective business; observe strictly the chain of command in relation to your official positions; and bring your mouths within measurements—lest punishment come upon your person, when repentance will be of no avail."

Part II

Having built the means of transport, Pangeng was ready to move the people across the river. (As he was fearful that) they might still be dissatisfied with the transfer, he wished to address them and persuade them with great earnestness. At his orders all the multitude came respectfully to the court. He called to them and said:

"Listen clearly to my words, and do not disregard my commands.

"Oh! Of old, my imperial ancestors cherished nothing in their minds but to nourish and protect the people. They, the former emperors and the people, shared their worries and sorrows so closely that they could always with joint efforts overcome misfortunes caused by unseasonable nature.

"But when enormous calamities descended upon them, our former emperors would not fondly dwell upon what they themselves had built (in the old places). They would think only of the people's well-being, and on that account determine to move elsewhere. Why do you not reflect that I am doing the very same thing that I have heard the former emperors did? My only purpose is to nourish you, to protect you, so that together we may rejoice in future prosperity. It is not as though I am punishing you because you have done something wrong.

"If I have asked you to entertain a better opinion of the new city, it is also for your sake, in an effort to see to it that your aspirations for a better life may be fulfilled.

"Now I am ready to move you across to settle comfortably in the new capital. But you do not appear to have sympathy for the anxieties in my mind; you keep a great reserve in opening up your own minds. (If you have genuine complaints), why don't you speak up with sincerity and try to move me, your sovereign?

"What you are doing will only be causing you yourselves distress and pain. It is like sailing a boat; if you do not cross the stream in time, your cargo will be spoiled. And if you do not concentrate your mind on the sailing, your boat may capsize and sink. Should these things happen, you would have no one to blame for the delay and the loss. You could then only be angry with yourselves. But would that cure you of your distress?

"You have no long plans. Nor do you think about the calamity that is bound to fall (if we stay here). You may have today, but you shall have nothing afterward. What deliverance from above can you be looking for?

"Now I charge you to have but one mind. Do not let filth arise and besoil your own persons with the stench. I am afraid that men may have been leaning against your bodies and perverted your minds.

"The measures I have taken are forecast to prolong your lease of life from Heaven. Do I force you by my majesty? What I want is only for the purpose of supporting and feeding you all.

"I keep on thinking how my late Divine Sovereign (Tang) had toiled together with your forebears. Because of this, I dearly wish that I would be able to nourish you as much as I do cherish you.

"Were I to err in my government and tarry long here, the High Sovereign (Tang) would send down on me great punishment for my criminal dereliction, and say, 'Why do you treat my people so atrociously?' But if you, you myriads of people, are bent on not prolonging your own lives by not joining me in one mind to carry out my plans—me, your sovereign—then the late emperor will send down on you great punishment for your criminal dereliction, saying, 'Why do you not unite yourselves with my young offspring but commit this act of deviation from virtue?' When this punishment comes from above, you will have no escape.

"Our former emperors had toiled together with your forefathers and fathers. You ought to labor with me for the nourishment of the people. If you intend to do this purpose injury, it will be on your own conscience. But (the spirits of) our former emperors will be casting questioning glances at (the spirits of) your forefathers and fathers; and (the spirits of) your forefathers and fathers will surely cut you off, abandon you, and see you die without succor.

"(On the other hand), if I have some ministers who participate in my government, but who are preoccupied with the acquisition of wealth and treasures [6] (for themselves or for me), surely your forefathers and fathers will report to my High Sovereign (Tang) and he will say, 'Let punishment be executed on my descendant!' And then the High Sovereign will hurl down great disasters (on me and my ministers).

"Now, I have announced to you my inalterable determination. Do you constantly respect my great concern. Let us not get alienated, or distant, from one another. Share in my plans and thoughts, and follow me. Let every one of you set up this target in the very center of your heart.

"If there be men, bad or unprincipled, presumptuous or irreverent, who commit acts of villainy or treason by design or by chance, (for lesser offenses) I will have their noses cut off; (but for greater offenses) I will have them utterly exterminated, I will leave none of their children, I will not let them have any seed grow in the new city.

"Go! Live and prosper! I will now transfer you (to the new capital), that you may forever establish your families there."

Part III

Pangeng had now completed the transfer. Having fixed the residences for the people and laid out the foundations for the public buildings, he made various adjustments in the matter of official positions.[7] Then, to comfort and soothe the multitude, he declared:

"Do not play or be idle. Exert yourselves to build up a great destiny.

"Now, I have disclosed to you all my heart, my belly, my kidney, my bowels; I have made plain to you, my people, everything in my mind. I will not incriminate any of you (for anything that has happened). Nor do I expect you to instigate one another to form factions to defame me, your sovereign.

"Of old, our former emperors, with a view to obtaining achievements to exceed previous records, had departed from the hills and caused us to descend to lower (plains). (This has resulted in) our capitals being variously afflicted with misfortune or attended with success.

"But in the recent days (many of) our people were forced by water to leave

their dwellings, unable to find a permanent settlement. And yet you asked me
why I must trouble and stir you all—you myriads of people—to remove here.

"(The answer must be clear to you now.) It is because the Lord Above intends
to restore to us the virtues of our High Progenitor, and also to our house good
government, that we, I and those who are diligent and reverential, while humbly
cherishing the lives of the people in our care, have been successful in moving to
this new city where we can abide permanently.

"It is thus that I, inexperienced as I am, presumed to discard the plans of some
of you. I had to choose what was best. And you, too, have not taken on yourselves
to oppose the reply of the tortoise. So we all have contributed to this great
success.

"Ah, you chiefs of districts, you heads of departments, and all you, the hundreds of officers. You each may still have some cause for dissatisfaction hidden in
you; would that you continue to exercise restraint over your feelings!

"I will exert myself in the selection and direction of you (officers). Do you
think reverently always of my multitudes of people. I will not lend my shoulder
to anyone who is desirous of riches. I will use and respect those who humbly
dedicate themselves to the betterment and increase of the people, nourishing
them and planning to make their settlement secure.

"I have now made plain to you my mind—about whom I approve and whom I
disapprove. Let none of you dare to disregard my will!

"Do not seek to accumulate riches and treasures. Seek to establish your merit
in promoting the life and prosperity of people.

"Display your virtue on behalf of the people. Forever bear this, and this only,
in your hearts."

The above is the document *pangeng* in its entirety. Formerly, this has
been always considered by Chinese scholars to be an archaic composition
exceedingly difficult to comprehend.[8] But now, as the oracle bones have
enabled us to understand better the violent course of factionalism that had
resulted from repeated struggles over succession, every passage, every sentence of the document assumes a clear significance that bares both the in-
ward intents and the outward policies of that astute, noble, and forceful
monarch. While his determination to move to Yin was inflexible, being
solidly based on a conviction that the ruin of Geng was close at hand, he was
as patient as he could be with those who had been insidiously conspiring to
block the transference. He seems to have had precise knowledge about the
subversive arguments these conspirators were using to stir up the people, and
in his speeches he countered and refuted them point by point. He was
apparently even aware of the identities of those responsible; but he refrained
from taking any summary actions against them. On the contrary, he sought
by every means he could think of to convince both the people and the
conspirators of his own good faith as well as the wisdom of his decision. He
explained, he expostulated. He coaxed, he coerced. He threatened, he reas-
sured. He appealed to their superstition, and at the same time he called upon
the very spirits they believed in to send down disasters on himself if he

should do wrong. Instead of using the transfer as a device to rid himself of suspected intransigents, as his opponents had charged that he would, he promised that if they carried out their duties and his orders properly, they would not only be continued in their offices, but even be promoted later according to their deserts. And after the completion of the transfer, he did just that, nothing less. In short, his purpose shone out bright and clear through the pages of this document. It was not to add fuel to the fires of dissension; it was to bind up the wounds of factionalism. And the entire history of the dynasty afterward bears testimony that he succeeded eminently in the task that he had set for himself.

As a matter of fact, his policy was fully vindicated even during his own lifetime. Geng was completely ruined by water shortly after its abandonment, and Yin turned out to be a capital as satisfactory as any could desire. The recent excavations that have produced the oracle bones have also uncovered the ruins of some palaces and burial grounds of the Shang emperors; from a study of these, there can be no doubt that modern Anyang, Henan, is the very site of ancient Yin.[9] It is not situated directly on the banks of the Yellow River, but at the bend of one of its tributaries called by the Shang people the Huan,[10] a name still being used by the Chinese today. The Yellow River, however, was flowing at that time in its original course, as described in *Yu's Levies* (*yugong*), so Yin was on the northwest of that mighty stream. But except for that, the passing of centuries, or millennia, seems to have wrought little change in the topography. Looking westward, a traveler today will see a long chain of tall peaks rising at a distance to form a branch range of the Taihang Mountains. To the north and to the south there are also some remote undulations. But toward the east, as far as the eye can see, there is a vast, uninterrupted, and seemingly endless plain. And because of the gradual sloping nature of the terrain, as the excavators have found out from the ruins, this region, or at least the area adjacent to the old capital, Yin, does not seem to have borne any trace of ever being flooded during the last three thousand years.[11] As has been noted before, from a study of meteorological inscriptions found in the oracle bones, a conclusion has been reached that the climate of the region in the Shang dynasty was not different from what it is today.[12] Some three hundred kilometers south of Peking, the weather conditions are typically temperate, cold in winter and hot in summer, with plenty of days in the year favorable to vegetation. And judging from what the native inhabitants are now cultivating in the fields, the Shang people might very well have cultivated the same things in their time—wheat in winter and millet in spring.[13] Thus at the close of springtime, the fields around Yin must have been a very pleasant sight to see: It is truly as one of the worthy sons of the Shang had sung, "How luxuriantly the stalks of wheat have grown; how smooth and oily the millet sprouts look." [14]

It is therefore no wonder that the Shang dynasty revived its glory again after the removal to Yin. As a matter of fact, it grew so prosperous in time that though the Shang people continued to call themselves Shang, the other peoples outside the Central Shang took to calling them Yin Shang,[15] or simply Yin. And this usage was adopted by the Zhou, who as successors to the Shang always referred to them as the Yin. And inasmuch as we have to rely on many Zhou documents as our primary sources for writing this history from now on, it is perhaps best that we too follow the same practice.

· 2 ·

THE ACCESSION OF WUDING

Pangeng was the second of four brothers. So after his death, he was succeeded by the third brother; and after the death of the latter, the throne passed on to the fourth brother. Now at the death of this last emperor, if history had repeated itself, there would have been another struggle for succession accompanied by another "disturbance." But so far as can be ascertained from all ancient records as well as from the oracle bones, no such thing ever occurred. After the passing of the fourth brother, his son Wuding acceded without any semblance of a crisis.

So the old traditional mode of succession had returned to take hold again. And what is more, it appears to have continued to prevail to the very end of the dynasty, apparently without further ado and with unanimous support from all parties concerned at all times. What had happened to bring this about? Lacking either records or oracle bones to substantiate our conjecture, we can only base it upon reasoned assumptions. Conceivably, memory of the difficulties experienced by Pangeng in the removal of the capital was deeply embedded in the minds of the Shang people—memories of the bitterness of the struggle over succession as well as the severity of the "disturbance" that ensued, let alone the loss of prestige and authority over the enfeoffed states. And recalling these, they must have felt a terrible shock at how easily the matter of transferring the capital—such a reasonable and inevitable thing to do, from hindsight—could have caused a catastrophe; and then an immense relief at how narrowly and how luckily they had managed to escape unscathed, thanks to the restraint, moderation, earnestness, and wisdom of Pangeng. Had that noble and capable monarch acted a little hastily, or a little highhandedly, a disastrous civil war could have been precipitated. Or had he acted slowly or irresolutely, the whole population might have become overwhelmed by water, as Geng actually was shortly after. The more they pondered over this matter, the more they became grateful to Pangeng, and the more they felt sensitive to the conditions that had brought them so close to the brink of disaster, and the more they were conscious that the altered mode of succession was the very root of all the troubles. Perhaps, more than anyone else, Pangeng himself realized that unless the mode was changed back to the traditional practice (that is, at the end of the youngest brother's reign, the succession would go to his own eldest son, and no other's), it would continue to be a source of "disturbance" for future generations. And he was also aware that no one was in a more advantageous position than he was to propose such a return. Since he was the second of four brothers, his own sons were barred from any claims to succession. And since there were two more brothers to follow him to the throne, the youngest one was probably not in any position of strength as yet; so Pangeng's coming out openly for a return to the old mode of succession could not be taken amiss as an act of partiality or favoritism. And farsighted and selfless as Pangeng truly was, he made the proposal and secured its endorsement by all parties concerned even before his death. Thus the mode of succession was changed back again by common consent. And for this, just as much as for his transferring the capital from Geng to Yin, the people composed the document *pangeng* after his demise, not only to remember him but also to remind and warn later generations of the fearful evils of factionalism.

Pangeng's youngest brother, Xiaoyi, was not a particularly noteworthy emperor. But he did one thing rather unprecedented in Shang history. In the middle years of his reign he ordered his son Wuding, the heir apparent, to take leave from the imperial court, to go forth and live among the common people, and to acquire learning and knowledge from men renowned for their wisdom and virtue.[16] Thus Wuding departed and remained away from the court for a number of years. He was recorded to have studied specially under one famed teacher, Gan Pan. Then he traveled extensively in the Yellow River Valley, starting at the bend of the stream where the three modern provinces of Shaanxi, Shanxi, and Henan converge, and pushing eastward as far as Bo, the original power base of Tang.[17] Roughly, he covered the entire length of what was then known as the Central Shang. And everywhere he went, he tried to familiarize himself with the conditions of the "little people."[18] Also, with a view to either deepening his own experience through solitude or enlarging his knowledge about the hardship of life, he even spent some time in a wilderness.[19]

Then, after his ascension to the throne, Wuding himself also did one thing which is almost unbelievable. We would have hardly lent it credence in this history had it not been fully substantiated by many ancient records, one of which is no less than a statement by the Duke of Zhou, the most knowledgeable and reliable authority on Shang, or Yin, history, who lived only some two hundred years after Wuding. Said the duke:

> When we came to the time of *gaozong*, before he acceded to the throne, he toiled away from the court and among the little people. After his accession, while

he was in mourning, he did not speak at all for three years. Because he did not speak at first, when he spoke, his words were all conducive to harmony. He dared not indulge in useless and easy ways, but dedicated himself to meliorate and tranquilize the Yin Empire, until all the people, great or small, (became so contented that) not a murmur was heard. It was thus that *gaozong* enjoyed the possession of the empire for fifty-nine years.[20]

If this account about Wuding's three-year-long silence is remarkable enough, the rest of the story, as told in other records, is even more curious. In those days, there was indeed a custom for a son to mourn his deceased father for three years. And in case of an emperor, while he was in mourning, the practice was for all officers to attend to their respective duties, taking instructions only from the prime minister.[21] This was intended on the one hand not to disturb the mourner in his grief, and on the other to encourage him in the pursuance of his filial piety. But the strictest observance of this rule was never construed to imply that the emperor successor could not give commands if he chose to; nor was there any known tradition or superstition that forbade him to speak at will. Wuding's conduct in this connection is therefore, to say the least, extraordinary; and if we had not learned of his unusually tenacious nature afterward, we would have thought it almost humanly impossible. But this Wuding did.

But after the three years were over, he still would not break his silence. It was then that all officers of the court became sorely troubled. They addressed him: "The sovereign speaks in order to issue commands. If your majesty does not speak, from where are we to get commands to observe and obey?" Instead of speaking, Wuding wrote down this reply: "To make myself a standard to rectify the four quarters, I fear that my virtues are not enough to qualify me. Because of this, I do not wish to speak." [22] But as the officers insisted, he spoke eventually. He did not speak, however, about any business of the court or of the empire; he spoke only of a dream he had dreamt. In the dream he saw a man whom Heaven had sent down to be an adviser to him. When he awoke, he remembered the man's features well. He had been looking for him among the ministers, among the officers, and among the numerous attendants in the court, but he had met with disappointment after disappointment; no one looked like him. So perhaps it would be necessary for him to search far and wide for this man. As he could describe this adviser of his dream in full detail, the ministers had a picture made of him. This was copied and issued abroad to help in the search. Finally, at a narrow pass in modern Shaanzhou, Henan, about 150 kilometers west of West Bo, a man was found by the name of Fu Yue bearing a resemblance. According to some, he was a common laborer engaged in beating earth within a wooden framework for the purpose of building a wall at the pass.[23] According to others, he was a prisoner in a chain gang sentenced to do hard labor.[24] In any event, he was brought to the presence of Wuding, who recognized him instantly as the man in the dream. And the emperor forthwith appointed him high councilor *(gong)*, and charged him with the duty of giving advice day and night.[25]

Wuding said to his adviser: "Suppose me to be a metal weapon; I will use you for a whetstone. Suppose me to be crossing a great stream; I will use you for a boat. Suppose this is a year of drought; I will use you for a copious rain. Open up your mind to enrich my mind. You will be like medicine to me. If the medicine does not make me feel its bitter, dizzying effects, it will not cure me of my sickness. Think of me as if I am walking barefoot with my eyes not on the ground; (if you do not guide me), my feet will be surely wounded." [26] Then he charged again, "Do teach me as to what my aims should be. If I am to brew spirits, you are to be the yeast and malt. If I am to make soup, you are to be the salt and spice. Strain and stretch yourself to cultivate me. Do not abandon me. I may thus succeed in carrying out your instructions." [27] And like a fairy tale, now that he was joined with Fu Yue, Wuding ruled happily ever after.

This narrative, even as it is, is unusual enough for a history. But when we consider it in the light of the man's character, it becomes truly remarkable. For by all evidence he was one of the most active rulers of the Yin dynasty, distinguished for his robust health and restless energy. As noted before, he was said to have reigned fifty-nine years, and lived up to one hundred.[28] And the oracle bones bear abundant testimony to his vigor and virility. He seems to have thrown himself with equal zeal and gusto to the chase [29] and to the "exertion of toil in the fields" *(tu tian)*.[30] And during his long life, so far as we can gather from the inscriptions that have been found, he took no less than sixty-four women for wives, and fathered no less than fifty-three male offspring.[31] It is difficult, therefore, to think of such a man keeping continued and uninterrupted silence for three years, or indulging and believing in fanciful dreams. Yet, as the oracle bones bear irrefutable witness, there can be no doubt about the truth of the narrative. For among the inscriptions there are found several mentions of "Teacher Pan," and also of "Dream Father." Though the bones are too fragmented to provide a meaningful text, yet there is no question that by "Teacher Pan" was meant Gan Pan, and by "Dream Father" Fu Yue.[32]

Formerly, Chinese historians could only accept these events as historical facts without being able to explain them. But now since we have discovered through the oracle bones that factionalism was the main issue dominating Yin politics since the alteration of the traditional mode of succession by the Middle Ancestor, Zuyi, we feel that all these events can be reasonably explained. As mentioned before, after Pangeng encountered so much difficulty in transferring the capital to Yin, the Yin people, especially the imperial house itself, became aware of the source of the evil and decided to remove it by returning to the original mode of succession, as a result of which Wuding, being the youngest brother's eldest son, eventually benefited. Though this was a resolution by unanimous consent, yet before it was put into effect, none could be sure what the outcome would be. As a matter of fact, as soon as Wuding's father, Xiaoyi, succeeded his third brother as emperor, apprehensions intensified. As there were four brothers in Xiaoyi's generation, so there must have been at least as many factions. While all of them probably paid lip service to Wuding as their commonly acknowledged heir apparent, each of them could not have been slow to jockey for position, pressing for special favors directly or indirectly as conditions for support. Faced with this situation, Wuding, ever alert and deep-thinking man that he was, must have soon found out that not only were there not enough favors to distribute, but the granting of some to one might be the surest way to incur the enmity of others. And should he continue to stay in the center of this entanglement, he might end up becoming ensnared unawares in an insoluble web of divisiveness, jeopardizing his own chances of a peaceful and harmonious succession. So, probably at his own suggestion, he had his father order him to depart from the court for an extended leave of absence. His outward pretext was to study under famous teachers such as Gan Pan and to learn about the ways of the common people by living among them, which he actually did. But his inner purpose was to get away from these factions as far as possible lest he become involved prematurely in their bickering, discordant politics.

He returned, of course, to the court when his father became critically ill. And after the latter's decease, he ascended the throne without any opposition and without any incident. This was as all had pledged, and also as he himself had seen to it that it would be. Yet even after the enthronement, he was still not sure of his own situation. The bickering, the feuding, the jockeying for advantage among the factions were as intense as they had always been; and he was afraid that taking any position on any matter would incur the open resistance or silent hostility of one or another. He thought the whole matter over. It was best to utilize the ancient practice and let all the officers attend to their respective duties, taking instructions from the incumbent prime minister. While these administrators would go about their business without interruption, he could study them on the sidelines objectively and impartially, appraising their abilities, observing their affiliations, and watching, above all, the machinations and manipulations of the various factions. Thus he deliberately adopted the tactics of total silence, knowing well that only in this manner could any of his thoughts be protected from exposure and distortion.

But, over and above, he had one supreme purpose in mind. He had been chosen to head the empire; he must do everything he could to bring harmony to all, starting, especially, with the factions of the imperial house itself. So far, by refraining from speaking, he had avoided taking sides. But sooner or later, at the latest at the end of the three years' mourning, he must speak out and make decisions. Even though he himself was resolved to be just and fair on all matters and to all factions, would all of them agree with his policies and obey his commands implicitly? He knew by his own long and silent observations that this would be too much to expect. So he hit on the idea of having an adviser sent down from Heaven, who would be imparting to him directions inspired by divine wisdom. Thus the "Dream Father" Fu Yue was conjured into being. Fu was probably a man Wuding had known and trusted while he was living incognito among the "little people." And with Fu accepted and acknowledged by all as the man in his dream, from then on whatever Wuding decided to do after consulting with him, the people, one and all, would feel they had threefold reasons to comply: Not only was he the sovereign, not only were his decisions fair and just, but all the guidance had derived from Heaven. Thus cooperation and tranquillity was secured from all the factions voluntarily; and it is truly as the Duke of Zhou said of him, "Because he did not speak at first, when he spoke, his words were all conducive to harmony."

But whether this is what really happened or not, the story of Wuding's dream and the sudden elevation of Fu Yue from a common workman to the highest honors of the empire is one of the most celebrated historical events and forms a cherished part of the Chinese heritage. From that time on down to this day, many a Chinese, while living in poverty and want, has often sought comfort and encouragement in the story, hoping and dreaming that if only he should persevere in the accumulation of wisdom and virtue in his own person, someday he too might have a chance to meet with a Wuding who would reward his talents and merits with immediate and unstinted recognition.[33]

· 3 ·

THE PEAK OF YIN POWER

Wuding's reign thereafter, like most of his predecessors', was for a long time uneventful. But with his boundless energy, with his fertile resourcefulness, and with his inimitable patience, the Yin reached a level of efficiency never experienced before, and the Yin authority again fully extended to all the enfeoffed states within the Four Lands. And this assumption is amply borne out by the events that occurred on and after the twenty-eighth year of his reign.

At that year, Wuding was seventy.[34] If the oracle bones had not yielded a plethora of inscriptions, we would never have been able to imagine what he was doing. For at that advanced age, such was the lusty manhood of that intrepid emperor that he went a-hunting in the imperial preserve to the southeast of the Great City Shang. Apparently he was so deeply engrossed with the chase that he would not give up this pleasure even when winter arrived. Instead, he went farther and farther to the east following the tracks of wild beasts until he reached somewhere in the southeast of modern Shandong. Then, on a "hard wood horse" day (jiawu), the twelfth of the first moon in the twenty-ninth year of his reign, he personally went after a rhinoceros, in a chariot accompanied only by a driver and one of his sons. The chariot ran into a rock at the foot of a hill. It overturned, and both the aged monarch and the young prince were thrown out. However, he was saved from serious injury, perhaps by the heavy winter clothes he wore; and he went on conducting business as usual. In the next month he sacrificed to the Yellow River close by and prayed for a good year, as if he had nothing else to worry about.

As a matter of fact, all this appearance was for outside consumption. He was actually deliberating with himself all the time on one of the most important decisions he had to make in his entire lifetime. Though the oracle bones are too fragmented and the inscriptions too laconic to provide a solid basis for an incontrovertible narrative, yet from a systematic study of them a rough outline of the events that actually took place can be clearly drawn.[35] At the very time Wuding strayed so far into the East Land away from the capital Yin, away even from the limits of the Central Shang, his mind was preoccupied with problems that were arising in the opposite direction, in the northwest of his far-flung empire. For while he had succeeded in consolidating his control over all the enfeoffed states with such vigor as no emperor before him had displayed, he had also observed with apprehension that the nomadic tribes in the northwest had grown considerably in numbers over the centuries, and that recently they had become far more audacious and far more aggressive than in the time of any of his predecessors. These now consisted of three tribes. The two large ones were Guifang [36] and Tufang, with Guifang lying more to the west than to the north and Tufang more to the north than to the west, and with the former stronger than the latter. And between the two there was a third and less numerous tribe, known as Xiazhi.[37] All three had been making frequent incursions into the nearby enfeoffed states. Before Wuding took this eastward hunting trip, he had already come to a realization that unless some measures were devised to resolve the issue, these tribes would be a perpetual source of continual and increasing disturbance to the empire. Although to chastise them temporarily would not be too difficult to do, yet it would be only a makeshift measure.

To seek a sort of permanent settlement that could stop them from further irruptions, if not forever at least for a long time to come, was the crux of the problem. Even while he was in the capital, he had considered various options and almost come to a conclusion. But lest his intended enemies get wind of his intentions, he had purposely undertaken the journey eastward in the opposite direction, ostensibly to gratify his passion for the chase. But before his departure, he had taken care to enjoin the princes of the enfeoffed states adjacent to those tribes to keep a close watch on their activities and to keep himself constantly posted on them.[38] In addition, he had ordered several of these princes whom he considered most capable and trustworthy to come later to join him, outwardly to participate in the hunt but actually to be consulted on his final decisions.

Now his mind was made up. His military plans were simple and bold, seizing the initiative, taking full advantage of the element of surprise, and using his troops as carefully as a miser would use his coins. What he wanted to avoid most was giving the three tribes a chance to form a union, or an alliance, that would enable them to take joint actions. (See Map IV.) So in order to forestall that possibility, he planned to launch a surprise expedition against Xiazhi and subdue and occupy it quickly before the other two tribes became aware of what was happening. And once Xiazhi was taken, a serious physical barrier would have been erected between the hordes of Guifang and Tufang. Though the two could still communicate with each other by way of the north side of the Yellow River and arrange some kind of scheme for mutual defense, their contact would be more difficult and less effective, and they could be the more easily defeated singly, one after the other. And in that event, it was Wuding's intention to overwhelm Tufang first and then to turn the whole weight of his military might on Guifang, the strongest of the three tribes.

Thus in the second moon of the twenty-ninth year of his reign, almost immediately after his sacrificing to the Yellow River, he issued an order to levy an armed force in preparation for an expedition against Xiazhi. And in the following month, i.e., the third moon, he named General Wang Cheng as commander of the proposed expedition. Although the inscriptions do not make clear that these were secret orders, from an examination of the subsequent events every evidence seems to indicate that they were. It appears that with respect to such important decisions involving peace or war, it was the Yin practice in every instance to issue two orders to the same effect, the second repeating the first. Upon the issuance of the first, all preparations for the decreed project would begin; but it is only upon the issuance of the second that final actions were expected to be put into execution. Thus the second order for launching the expedition against Xiazhi was not issued till the eleventh moon of the twenty-ninth year, and the second order reaffirm-

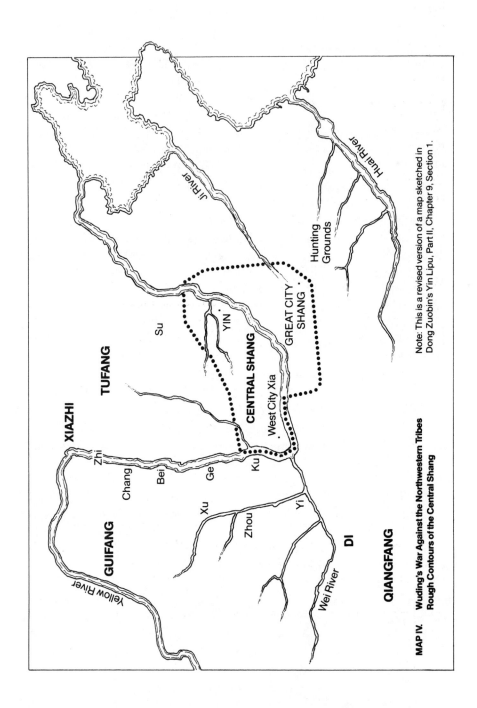

MAP IV. **Wuding's War Against the Northwestern Tribes**
Rough Contours of the Central Shang

Note: This is a revised version of a map sketched in
Dong Zuobin's Yin Lipu, Part II, Chapter 9, Section 1.

ing Wang Cheng as commander not issued till the twelfth moon, each about nine months after the first order. And it was not until Wang Cheng received his second order that actual hostilities against Xiazhi commenced.

Now to us, the interval between the first and the second order may seem perhaps rather too protracted. But looking at the matter from the perspective of the ancients, this was probably as speedy and as prompt as Wuding could have made it. Between Yin and the grounds where he was hunting, there was a distance of some 250 kilometers; and between Yin and the nearest regions frequented by any one of the three tribes, another 400 kilometers intervened. Assuming that all the preparations were made in the vicinities of Yin, and all men were levied from localities as close to the target area as possible, still, every soldier and every weapon would have to be assembled in place before the second order could be issued. And judging from the character of Wuding, all these must have been mulled over and checked over again and again in his calculations.

And in accord with his calculations, shortly after his naming General Wang Cheng to lead the Xiazhi expeditionary force for the first time, his most trusted lieutenant in the northwest arrived on the fourteenth day of the third moon. This was Zhijin,[39] prince of the strategic state of Zhi, which jutted out at the very northwestern corner of the empire, straddling the Yellow River, possessing lands on both of its banks, and abutting Guifang to the west and Tufang to the east. If a war was to be fought against either of these nomads, Zhijin's princedom would be the very first to bear the brunt. So after consultations with him, on the fourth day after his arrival, the emperor commanded that five thousand men be levied and held ready for the subjugation of Tufang.

It seemed therefore that everything was proceeding according to plan. Yet there was one thing that Wuding had failed to include in his considerations, which appeared to have brought on some distracting consequences—his own tumble from the chariot in the chase after the rhinoceros. When Zhijin came, he reported the activities of Tufang and Guifang. Both of these tribes were making encroachments upon his princedom: Tufang had infringed on the eastern borders, damaging two villages, and Guifang had set their cattle loose on the farmlands in the west. But these did not seem to alarm the emperor, as apparently they had not alarmed the prince. Had these incursions been serious, the latter would not have dared leave his princedom; and even if he had left, the former would likely have asked him to return at once. But Zhijin was to remain together with Wuding for some more months, which they must have used for making all the necessary preparations for the forthcoming war.

Notwithstanding, Wuding could not help being continually disturbed by reports that poured in from the border states during these months. Here a messenger came from the Prince of Chang,[40] a southerly neighbor of Zhijin, with the news that some seventy-five Guifang nomads were grazing their cattle and sheep in one of its villages. There, two envoys arrived in succession from Su,[41] just to the south of Tufang, carrying dispatches that the latter were raiding into its territory with greater frequency and in larger numbers, and in one of the recent encounters it captured no less than thirty-one invaders. The emperor did not like the look of things. Was it possible that these tribes had heard of his accident, mistaken his tumble for his death, and were thus emboldened to take advantage of the resultant weakened situation of the empire? And if this misinformation should be allowed to continue uncorrected, they might well be tempted to undertake joint massive irruptions with the consequence that all initiative would be wrested out of his own hands, and all the plans he had made would be laid to naught.

Of course, he must not let this happen. He must catch them all unprepared when launching his attack on Xiazhi. Thus on the twenty-first day of the eighth moon, he conducted a big hunt near the Great City Shang, in which not only did he show his imperial presence in person, but one of his aides conspicuously suffered a tumble from a chariot and another got seriously injured. This was probably staged on purpose—to demonstrate to all who wanted to know that he was alive and well; to suggest that if there was any rumor about his death, it was likely due to a mistaken identity; and also to make the multitudes, especially the three tribes, believe that he was so fond of the chase that he might yet linger awhile to indulge himself in the gratification of this passion before returning to the capital. But no sooner had this last hunt been held than the oracle bones mentioned no more about the whereabouts of the monarch. Apparently Wuding had returned to Yin as expeditiously as he could.

Back in Yin, there occurred an incident that is as revealing of the superstitious nature of the Yin people as it is of the true character of Wuding. At the end of the tenth moon, he sacrificed to Yi Yin. On the first day of the eleventh moon, he sought for divination on the matter of launching the expedition. The answer the tortoise gave was ominous, to say the least. It read distinctly, "The army will meet with disaster!" And deeply shaken the emperor must have felt. For although the inscriptions that follow these portentous words are far from clear, the characters that can be recognized show unmistakably that the monarch was lamenting the loss of "old ministers" who could have helped him make wise decisions in this hour of need. Was he thinking of "Teacher Pan" or "Dream Father"? Either of them might have been dead or retired from service for some time. But however he regretted the loss, Wuding was too intrepid a man to be deterred by an unfavorable divination. Six days later, on the sixth day of the same eleventh moon, he issued not only the second order for the expedition against Xiazhi, but also the first order for the expedition against Tufang. Twenty days after that, he enjoined another general to put himself and his troops under the command of Wang Cheng to enlarge the expeditionary force, or, perhaps, to insure it against possible disaster. Then on the twelfth day of the twelfth moon in this twenty-ninth year of his reign, Wuding issued the second and therefore the final order to Wang Cheng, naming him again the commander against Xiazhi, which meant that the general must carry out the command immediately. The die was cast. There was no turning back.

The success of the expedition against Xiazhi was instantaneous. Both Wuding's preparations and Wang Cheng's tactical deployments must have been so well concealed that these nomads were completely taken by surprise. Their territories were occupied almost without resistance; and throughout the remaining three years of war we encounter no more mention of the name Xiazhi in the inscriptions, presumably because no further disturbance arose from the tribe or from the region they formerly occupied.

This was a matter of primary importance to Wuding. For now a wall had been built, so to speak, to separate Guifang and Tufang. If they wanted to maintain communication with each other, they would have to go farther beyond the bend of the Yellow River. And this was the time that Wuding thought most opportune to begin, and concentrate, his assault on Tufang, while keeping the entire line facing Guifang in a holding and defensive position. But if his seizure of Xiazhi had shocked Tufang into momentary stupor and inaction, the reactions of Guifang were far different from what he had expected. They were as swift and as violent as he himself would have directed. We have no record of who was the chieftain of Guifang at this moment; but from the rapid unfolding of events, we may well salute him as a leader of uncommon energy and audacity, a worthy match for Wuding. In the month during or immediately after Wang Cheng's conquest of Xiazhi,[42] Guifang dispatched their hordes far and wide into the border states on the west side of the Yellow River that acknowledged allegiance to Yin.[43] They made inroads into the very suburbs of the capital city of Bei, ravaging four villages on the way. They cut a swath of fire and sword as far south as Yi and beyond. Yet in spite of these furious rampagings, Wuding would not let himself be diverted from his original plans. When these border states clamored for relief, he only sent one general, Xue, to go to the state of Ge as a coordinator of local forces to resist Guifang's irruptions.

In the early months of the thirtieth year the emperor himself inspected all the troops poised for the invasion of Tufang. But Guifang was also not slow to size up the situation. Their chieftain dashed to Tufang and took an oath of alliance with the latter. But before they could form an effective plan for joint defense, Wuding had already completed his inspections. On the fourth day of the fifth moon, he formally named Zhijin commander against Tufang.

And lest any mishap should befall the army, he boosted its strength not only by ordering another general to put his troops under Zhijin's command, but also by dispatching three imperial clans to assist in the campaign. Then in the middle of the sixth moon, Zhijin received his final order, and his forces began entering Tufang. However, while Wuding was hoping for an easy and complete victory over Tufang, Guifang burst out again against the bordering states—this time in considerably larger numbers and in a seemingly far better organized manner. Their main force laid siege to Bei, and their vanguards penetrated so deep into West Land as to come to the very edge of the Yellow River on the opposite shores of the Central Shang. The entire imperial domain took alarm. Was the answer of the tortoise to come true? Wuding issued his first order for war against Guifang.

On the scoreboard of the conflict, it was now fifty for the emperor and fifty for Guifang. By a quick and vigorous assault on Tufang, Wuding was apparently able to occupy all their land; but because Guifang had made a timely alliance with their fellow nomads, most of the latter seemed to have eluded capture or destruction, escaped with their lives and weapons through the northern route, and cast in their lot more firmly with their allies. This was decidedly what Wuding had not wanted, but had been unable to prevent. Nevertheless, from here on the oracle bones carry no more records about Tufang. Conceivably they had become subordinated to Guifang. It is only at the end of the war when Guifang submitted to the emperor that inscriptions appeared again to record that Tufang submitted too.

But not knowing how the matter would turn out as we do from hindsight, the actions taken by Wuding illustrate well his caution and determination as well as his anxiety and desperation. No sooner had he given the first order for war against Guifang than he announced that he himself would take over the supreme command and lead the forces to march against the enemy. In the three months between the seventh moon and the ninth moon, he commanded repeated levies of men as follows:

Seventh moon	
28th day	Levied 3,000 men
Eighth moon	
8th day	Levied 3,000 men
20th day	Levied 3,000 men
23rd day	Levied 5,000 men
27th day	Levied 3,000 men
30th day	Levied 3,000 men
Ninth moon	
6th day	Levied 3,000 men

Altogether the men levied for the war against Guifang totaled 23,000. And while he was busily engaging in these military activities, he also did not forget to offer sacrifices to his various ancestors as well as to the spirits of rivers and mountains and others, asking for their intercession.

It is unfortunate that from the oracle bones we cannot learn about, and describe, the progress of the war. Perhaps the emperor was too much preoccupied to have time to spare for divination. Perhaps, too, remembering that the tortoise had at first predicted that the army would meet with disaster, he was fearful of going through another experience that might both distract his own mind and dispirit his men. At any rate, in the tenth moon of the thirtieth year he himself went to the front and took over direct command. And judging from the few known events that ensued, Guifang proved as formidable and as obstinate an adversary as the monarch had long suspected. The contest at first must have been very fierce and indecisive. For, in the eleventh moon, he called upon all the princes in the border areas to join in the fight. Then he directed Ku, a princedom not exactly on the border line, to enter into the war. And as a sort of forerunner of things to come, Zhou, a state right in the front, situated between Guifang and Ku, which should have heeded the emperor's bidding at his first call, seemed rather reluctant to make up its mind; and Wuding had to tell the Prince of Ku to keep a sharp eye on Zhou lest it should choose to side with the hostile tribes. But as no further development of this matter can be traced among the inscriptions, it may be assumed that Zhou at the last moment chose to espouse the cause of loyalty, when the imperial army began to show signs of gaining the upper hand. But before this state of the war was reached, Wuding was even driven to call upon the Di, a branch of the Qiang nomads, who inhabited a region farther south, to give support to his forces.

The war continued throughout the thirty-first year of Wuding's reign. But by the beginning of the thirty-second year, Guifang's resistance at last melted. On the twenty-second day of the first moon, numerous enemies were captured, and high officers had to journey back and forth to put the prisoners in safe confinement. And on the same day, Zhijin asked for instructions about what should be done with Guifang. Should an effort be made to capture or exterminate all of them? Though there is a hiatus in the inscriptions after this, it seems likely that the wise sovereign had already decided on a policy of clemency. Calls were sent out directing Guifang to surrender. But as their gallant but feckless chieftain stubbornly refused, on the thirtieth day of the seventh moon Wuding commanded the prince of Yue to conduct mopping-up operations inside the former land of Guifang. In the ninth moon he himself venerated Yi Yin for a third time in the course of the war, probably thanking him for the foundation of military preparedness he had laid for the empire. And toward the end of the month the monarch arrived in person inside the former territory of Guifang and announced that he would grant pardon to all the nomads.

Yet even after this pronouncement, negotiations for the surrender of Guifang and Tufang took another fifty days. But the nomads had suffered so much that even their spirited leaders could no longer incite them to continue the hopeless fight. Moreover, the terms Wuding imposed were much more generous than they expected. What was required of them was only that they acknowledge allegiance to the imperial house and refrain from making further incursions outside the territories demarcated by the emperor as their fiefs. Perhaps it was their inherent pride that resisted the recognition of a superior, or perhaps it was the adjustment of the territorial demarcations, which the tribes wanted to enlarge and the victors wanted to reduce, that caused the delay in the negotiations. In the end, both Guifang and Tufang had to accept what the sovereign was willing to grant. On the twelfth day of the eleventh moon Guifang yielded. And on the 29th day Tufang followed suit. Then on the twenty-sixth day of the twelfth moon Zhijin was ordered by the emperor to proceed with formal decrees of investiture to Tufang and Guifang respectively, to invest their chieftains as subordinate princes of the empire. And thus the war concluded. From the issuance of the second order to Wang Cheng to begin his attack on Xiazhi, which was in the twelfth moon of the twenty-ninth year, to the time of the final enfeoffment of Guifang and Tufang, which was in the twelfth moon of the thirty-second year, had been exactly three years.[44]

Wuding was now seventy-three years old, yet he was to rule over the empire some twenty-six years more. Grateful for his magnanimity and fearful of his wrath, the nomadic tribes, throughout the remainder of his reign and, in fact, until the very end of the dynasty, never caused trouble to Yin again. And as far as the enfeoffed princes in the Four Lands were concerned, they were all as submissive to the emperor as they could ever be. Still, before his life was over, Wuding did one more thing so that the empire might become even more secure.

Among the enfeoffed states he had found two with a record not to his liking. One of them was called Shiwei, and the other Dapeng. They both were derived from the same ancestry, and they both were enfeoffed in the north of the modern Jiangsu province in neighboring areas.[45] At the time when the imperial house sank into decline, probably at the beginning of the reign of the eighteenth emperor, Yangjia, both took advantage of the situation and began to call themselves *bo,* or hegemons. Outwardly they pretended that they were protecting the interests of the dynasty where it could not protect them itself; but actually they were enlarging their own influence at its expense. As the imperial house was then too much preoccupied with its own factional discord to do anything about them, it did the only thing realistic under the circumstances. It formally invested them as *bo,* but gave the title a different meaning. According to the imperial doubletalk, *bo* did not signify "hegemon" but something like "field marshal," or one who was outside the imperial court but given the power by the emperor to send punitive expeditions against other states, if necessary, on his majesty's behalf.

This arrangement seems to have been mutually satisfactory. On the one hand, it legitimized all the *bo*'s actions without curbing their freedom; on the other, it preserved in appearance, at least, the unity of the empire as well as the dignity of the imperial court. Later, as Yin gradually resurged from its decline, the two states were of course compelled to make readjustments in their behavior. Though they retained the title, they became more tractable in their actions. And by the time Wuding exerted his vigorous control, the two submitted meekly, like all the rest of the enfeoffed states. However, Wuding remembered their past. He felt that intransigence should not be allowed to stand unpunished even on record. So toward the close of his long reign, he had the two states summarily destroyed.[46] And his rule over the empire was truly like what Mencius said of him ten centuries later: "Wuding had all the princes coming to the court to pay him homage. He possessed all under Heaven. He ruled over them as if they were things he could move around in his palm." [47]

· 4 ·

APPROACHING THE END

After Wuding, the reigns of his successors were again as uneventful as most of those before him. As Tang had laid the foundation of a political system that could enable his descendants to enjoy maximum power and prestige with minimum care and concern, so Wuding had wrought it almost to perfection. Benefited by the system, and convinced that it was all but unbeatable, the Yin emperors who followed Wuding went on blithely in their old routine ways, some more conscious of their duties to Heaven and to the people, others more eager to gratify their own appetites and whims. But so far as Chinese history is concerned, despite the discovery of the oracle bones, it had apparently entered again into a period of renewed vacuity, interspersed by some isolated incidents that pop out from the ancient records like oases in a desert, few and far between. If we are to give a full account of all of them here, as we intend to do, it is not to entertain the reader with the mirage-like qualities of those events but more to demonstrate the solid reality of that extensive uneventfulness.

Wuding was succeeded by his son Zugeng. There is reason, however, to believe that there was another son who, rather than Zugeng, should have inherited the imperial patrimony, and who was known to posterity as Xiaoji, or Ji the Filially Pious.[48] Now by this appellation we know that he was born on a *ji* day. But we are not sure at all if the character *xiao* was not added later by his admirers or sympathizers in recognition of that virtue by which he had so ill-fatedly distinguished himself. As a matter of fact, every evidence seems to indicate that he, like his brothers, had been given the name Zuji.[49] His mother was Wuding's principal wife in the early years of that doughty emperor's long reign; and he, being their only son, was the acknowledged heir apparent. But then his mother died, and Wuding took another principal wife who later gave birth to two sons—Zugeng and Zujia. From then on the father's attitude toward the eldest son underwent a dour change. Howsoever Zuji might conduct himself in accord with the most demanding standards of filial piety, there seemed to be nothing he could do that would please the parent. In the end the harsh monarch deprived the innocent heir apparent of all his honors and banished him from the court, and Zuji suffered the injustice without a murmur and with all filial submissiveness. According to some accounts, he was said to have died in exile.[50] But according to a recent study made by one of the most recondite scholars of China at the turn of the 20th century and based on a careful examination of relevant oracle bones in company with a document in the *Book of History*, it appears definitely established that Zuji actually survived his long-lived father; and after his half brother Zugeng became emperor, he was invited back to the court and restored all the honors due to an imperial prince.[51]

The document mentioned above is titled *gaozong tongri*, which may be literally translated as *High Ancestor Tong-Veneration Day*. As has been explained previously, there are five principal veneration ceremonies practiced by the Yin, one of which, using drum music, was called *tong*.[52] Formerly, because of the obscure wording of the title, many Chinese scholars mistakenly thought that the occasion was the veneration of Tang by Wuding. But now we understand that it was Zugeng conducting the ceremony in veneration of Wuding. The father having lived such a long and glorious life, the son was devoutly wishing that he could have one like it. He prayed therefore to the High Ancestor to intercede on his behalf, and he spared no expenses for the ceremony, using more sacrifices and more ornaments than ever before. Then there occurred a strange incident which constituted the basis for the document. As it is revealing at once of the two-sided nature of the superstitious beliefs of the Yin people, it is perhaps to our interest to consider it in full:

> On the day of the *tong* veneration for the High Ancestor, there appeared a crowing pheasant.[53]
> Zuji said (to himself), "It is necessary first to rectify the emperor and make him understand the matter properly."

Accordingly, he lectured to the emperor thus: "In Its inspection of men below, Heaven's first consideration is of their righteousness. The lives Heaven bestows on men are long for some and short for others. (If some of the lives do not appear to have lived to their full lengths), it is not that Heaven cuts them short; it is that men themselves bring an end to their lives in the middle of them. Some of the men may not have complied with the standards of virtue; others may have not acknowledged their own misdeeds. As Heaven has bestowed upon them their lives, so Heaven has to make rectifications in accordance with their respective virtue (or lack of virtue). Yet they will still say, 'Why is this happening to us?'

"Oh! The sovereign's duty is to care reverently for the people. (As to the length or shortness of life), everything is as Heaven wills. And as for the ceremonies and sacrifices, it is proper not to exceed what has been practiced in recent years."

Whether Zugeng had heeded this advice or not, his reign was not long.[54] Upon his death, he was succeeded by his brother Zujia, of whom the Duke of Zhou—in the document from which we have already quoted twice before, the first time about the Middle Ancestor, *zhongzong,* and the second time about the High Ancestor, *gaozong*—had this to say:

In the case of Zujia, he would not unrighteously become emperor, and had at first lived the life of the little people. Thus when he came to the throne, he came with the knowledge of what the little people depended upon for livelihood. He was able to protect and benefit the masses. He durst not treat with contempt even the widower or the widow. Thus it was that Zujia enjoyed the possession of the empire for thirty-three years.[55]

From this it may be inferred that when Wuding disowned Zuji as the heir apparent, Zujia, even though knowing that he himself, being Zugeng's younger brother, would eventually profit from it, did not think well of this turn of events, but rather sympathized with his victimized half brother. After the latter's banishment, he must have also voluntarily imposed on himself a sort of exile, and lived more or less incognito for a period of time among the common people. And judging from the language used by the Duke of Zhou, placing him on the same level with the Middle Ancestor and the High Ancestor, we may well realize in what high esteem both the Yin people and the duke himself must have held this monarch.

But however well regarded Zujia was, we cannot find many events in his reign that need to be narrated in this history. Not that materials are lacking, for the oracle bones have yielded a profusion of inscriptions ascribed to his reign, which has caused one of the principal archaeologists who made a systematic study of them to become Zujia's sincere admirer.[56] Yet all this admiration notwithstanding, Zujia's achievements can be summed up in two items. The first is that he made a significant improvement in the calendar. Up to his time, whenever a leap month had to be inserted, the practice was simply to let the year have thirteen moons and designate them in the serial order, that is, from the first to the thirteenth, without the people knowing which month was the leap month. But Zujia introduced a new idea. The leap month was to be inserted where it should be; that is, if it happened after the third moon, there would be a second third moon; and at the end of the year, there would be still only the twelfth moon, not a thirteenth.

While this achievement may be said to be of importance to the development of the lunar calendar in general, the second is a matter purely of interest to the Yin people. For Zujia was the emperor who, realizing that the veneration ceremonies had become too numerous and too cumbersome, had the courage to risk both the displeasure of the spirits and the disapproval of their believers, who probably constituted the bulk of the population at the time, and to try to simplify the system by reducing the ceremonies into five major ones.[57] Though he was able to carry out the reform, he ran into bitter opposition. A controversy followed that lasted throughout the remaining century and a half of the dynasty, and even continued for some time beyond. For several hundred years later, in the time of Zhou, there were still those who believed that if Zujia had not given offense to the spirits, the Yin would not have come to an early end as it did.[58]

However the controversy persisted, Zujia's two sons, who mounted the throne successively as the twenty-fifth and the twenty-sixth emperors, followed the reform faithfully. But by the time of his grandson Wuyi, a reversion took place. The reigning monarch's ears were won over by the old school, and the veneration ceremonies went back to the ancient chaotic tracks again.[59]

The man who had acted so independently of his grandfather's legacy was also known for his excessive indulgence in the chase. He was the one who had in his three years' short reign hunted thirty-nine times and at eighteen different places.[60] He was undoubtedly a doughty and dexterous archer, for the oracle bones bore many an inscription about his shooting at a deer, at a rhinoceros, at a boar, etc.[61] The *Historical Records* also had this short account about him:

> Emperor Wuyi was a man without virtue. He made an effigy and called it the God of Heaven. He played dice with it, and had other men act as referees. When the God of Heaven lost, he would humiliate it no end. He would place it inside a leather bag filled with blood; then he would hang it up in the air, and he would bend himself over to shoot at it with arrow. He called this the shooting of Heaven.
>
> Wuyi hunted in between the Yellow River and the Wei River.[62] On a sudden, thunder exploded. Wuyi was struck dead.[63]

Wuyi's son and successor, Wenwuding, was a man without any significant distinction. But if his reign is as uneventful as many others, it is again not because of any want of oracle bones. For, out of the inscriptions pertaining to a very limited period of his reign, just a few months in his sixth and seventh years, a modern scholar is able to reconstruct a sort of weather report for Yin, with all the rains, snowfalls, and winds fully accounted for.[64] But out of the whole lot of the other inscriptions accumulated during his twelve years' reign, no event of historical significance can be found to deserve mention here.

Wenwuding was succeeded by his son Di Yi, under whom the veneration reforms of Zuyi were reintroduced, and to a degree improved and strengthened. He carefully regulated that all the ancestors should be venerated in the five major ceremonies by turns, and that the entire round of these ceremonies should be 360 days in total—in other words, not exceeding one year's time. Thus the Yin people came to equate a year with a whole round of venerations, and they took to calling a year simply a veneration (si). For instance, if a divination was inscribed in the third year of Di Yi, it would begin with the characters wei wang san si, that is, "In the third veneration of Wang," Wang meaning the reigning emperor.[65] This practice was continued by his son Di Xin,[66] otherwise known as Zou, who was fated to be the one to bring an end to the dynasty.

However, in the early years of Zou's reign no one could have seen or even imagined the end approaching. The Central Shang remained the largest, the strongest, the richest unit of the empire, as ever; and the system so carefully built up by Tang and so vigorously fortified by Wuding and others seemed all but invulnerable and indestructible. Yet Zou lost the possession of the empire in the end and got himself slain in the bargain. For Zou was considered the most wicked monarch that ever lived in Chinese history, and every abominable crime and every execrable atrocity has been ascribed to his name. While many scholars nowadays are prone to think that Zou was perhaps more sinned against than sinning, a victim of his victors' propaganda, still, from a historian's impartial observation, one of Confucius's principal disciples may have rendered a judgment more appropriate for the circumstances. Said he, "For all his wickedness, Zou could not have been so evil as he was reported to be." But he went on and drew a moral lesson: "Therefore an educated man should detest dwelling in a sunken place such as a low basin, where all the filth of the world is continuously pouring in." [67] And, indeed, Zou may be said to be but a product, or a prisoner, of his environment, which is not unlike that description. The problem with Zou was that he realized the strength of his position, but not its weakness; he wanted to exploit the imperial system for his own enjoyment, and he never thought it possible that there could have existed a chink in the dynastic armor, a deadly vulnerable point like Achilles' heel. There was no restraining force whatever against his doing evil; and there was every incentive for him to indulge in self-gratification. While all his wickedness might yet have been insufficient to cause the collapse of the Yin imperial system by itself, it certainly helped to weaken it so that when a rival system came into existence to compete for power, it was no longer strong enough to survive the challenge.

· 5 ·

THE LAST YIN EMPEROR AND THE SIGNS OF HIS TIME

Ironically, the last Yin emperor, Zou, probably did not know that his name was Zou. He was born on a *xin* day, so his given name was Xin. After he became emperor, he was acclaimed as Di Xin. Then, according to the *Historical Records,* after his loss of the empire, or shortly before the loss, probably without his being aware of it, "All under heaven called him Zou." [68] And Zou was one of the most despicable appellations that could be applied to a man, either posthumously or while still alive. It meant "One who maims the righteous and injures the good." [69]

Perhaps his early childhood had something to do with his later turn of mind. He was not his father's eldest son. He had an older half brother, who was known as Qi, Prince of Wei. But the prince was born of a concubine, and Zou of the principal wife.[70] So there was no question that he should be the heir apparent. But before his position was formalized, the matter hung in unexpected suspense for a critical period of time that must have sorely tried the souls of both mother and child. The Prince of Wei, from very early days, was reputed far and wide for exceeding worthiness; and the father was said to have seriously contemplated ignoring the tradition and naming him successor. In the end, however, tradition won.[71] But it did not do so without exacting a heavy toll on the dynasty. For the newly confirmed crown prince, his tender age notwithstanding, was endowed by nature with more than a common measure of envy, spite, and malice; and this traumatic experience, along with its many tribulations, left an indelible scar in his young mind which exercised a poisonous influence on the rest of his life. He knew that he had almost been discarded in favor of another; yet he felt that man for man, he was way above all the others in inborn qualities, outclassing both the worthy and unworthy indiscriminately. And how he longed to prove that to the world! Thus the *Historical Records* sums up his character when he grew up as follows:

> Emperor Zou was equipped with an incisive mind, quick to argue and quick to retort. His senses of hearing and seeing were very sharp and keen. His dexterity and his strength were more than those of ordinary men. He could fight off or kill ferocious beasts with bare hands. His intelligence was enough to refute re-

monstrance, and he could use speech well to cover up wrongdoing. He flaunted his talents and capabilities ostentatiously before his ministers. He wanted to shout down the whole world with a loud voice. He thought that there existed no man but was inferior to him.[72]

Perhaps, too, such presumption and arrogance did not develop fully until later in his life. For all we know, at the time he mounted the throne, he might have been not yet in his teens. At any rate, the first signal act he took after coming of age was one that, even though it was undoubtedly of a vainglorious nature, might have called for cautious approval from the Yin people rather than unthinking disapprobation. Apparently he had surveyed the empire with the statecraft that must have been passed on by his forebears from generation to generation, especially from such capable men as Wuding. And examining his patrimony in the light of the lessons he had learned from their experiences, he could not but feel that the imperial position had been always one of utmost security and self-confidence. No enfeoffed state within the Four Lands had offered, or could ever offer, serious rivalry to the dynasty, the largest of them being so much smaller than the Central Shang in size, in population, and in wealth. Even if any one of them should grow intransigent and aggressive at a time the imperial house happened to be weak and disorganized, the only thing that needed be done was to exercise tact and patience. The wayward states could very well find themselves embroiled with other princedoms in their self-aggrandizement. Or, if they did not, the next thing to do would be to bestow on them such a title as *bo*, which, though outwardly empowering them to act in the name of the emperor, would at once cater to their vanity and yet prevent them from running berserk, thus enabling the imperial house to buy time. And limited in strength as these enfeoffed states were basically, and ever jealous of one another as they had always been, these "field marshals"—or "hegemons" as they liked to call themselves—would sooner or later come to a halt in the course of their expansion. And then as soon as the imperial house could revive its vigor and renew its power, it could seize an opportune moment of its own choosing and make a short shrift of them, as Wuding had done with Shiwei and Dapeng.[73] All in all, this kind of statecraft must have been particularly appealing to a mind like Zou's. And survey the enfeoffed states within the Four Lands as he doubtless did in the early years of his reign, he must have found with mixed feelings that he could not espy even the shadow of a potential hegemon on the horizon. While this showed that all was tranquillity and submission within his entire domain, to his regret it seemed to be also depriving him of a chance "to exceed previous records" of his predecessors.

He was then about twenty, in the tenth year of his reign, eager for glory, ready to flex his young muscles. He looked beyond the Four Lands, and what he saw again disappointed him. The northwestern tribes, Guifang and Tufang, whom his fourth-time great-grandfather Wuding had subdued, were now almost as docile and obedient as the states within the Four Lands. In the west, the Qiangfang, along with the Di, who dated their submission to the early days of Tang, had never wavered in their allegiance since.[74] In the south, beyond the enfeoffed state of Chu, what was known to man at that time was only wild mountains and inhospitable jungles. So there were only the southeastern tribes left that could occupy some of Zou's attention. But the so-called Renfang and Yufang were but loose conglomerations of ill-organized and ill-disciplined tribes, who, unlike their northwestern counterparts in the time of Wuding, had never been a real threat to any of the enfeoffed states within the East Land or the South Land. True, the Renfang, the more numerous of the two, had occasionally indulged in the hit-and-run tactics of the nomads. But these had happened many times before, and Zou's predecessors had not treated them as anything of importance. However, Zou's mind was made up. He wanted to win glory to match that of the High Ancestor. So on the sixteenth day of the ninth moon in his tenth year he ordered an expedition against Renfang.[75] And following the example of Wuding, who used the Prince of Zhi, the state nearest to the enemy, as a sort of field commander, Zou named Prince Xi of You, whose fief was adjacent to Renfang, in a similar position.

Shortly after the issuance of the order, the emperor set out for You to take personal command. And in order to show how important he considered the expedition, he went first to the Great City Shang to report the undertaking to his ancestors in an appropriate ceremony. From Yin to Shang the distance is less than 250 kilometers, but according to the oracle bones he seems to have taken more than thirty-five days to cover it. This of course may be explained by the possibility of his having had other businesses to attend to along the route; but it does not appear to speak for any urgency in the situation at the front. From the Great City Shang to You there are some 300 kilometers, which Zou covered in twenty-seven days, a more reasonable pace than before, but still quite leisurely. He stayed in You for about ten days. Then he left for a sort of inspection tour, apparently along the front line. From the second day of the twelfth moon in the tenth year to the ninth day of the first moon in the eleventh year—in about thirty-seven days—he visited fourteen places before returning to You. It was plain that he went beyond the boundaries of You and traversed much that must have been the territories of Renfang. But what surprises us is that throughout the trip, not an engagement with nor even a sight of the enemy was recorded in the oracle bones. There is only one occasion when on the twenty-third day of the twelfth moon the emperor stopped at a place which many modern scholars believe is modern Huoshan, Anhui, it was inscribed that precautionary defensive measures were taken against Linfang, obviously a tribe that had recently been assimilated by the Yin culture, but whose loyalty was still in doubt. However, nothing happened in spite of the apprehensiveness, and the next day his majesty proceeded with his trip without further ado.

After his return to You, he stayed there for about a month, presumably to see to it that all was pacified in the southeast. Manifestly everything went well, and he entertained both himself and his men with a day of hunting. On the eleventh day of the second moon, he left You, but not to return to Yin. He went instead in a contrary direction, northeastward for fourteen days until he arrived at Qi, in the heart of modern Shandong, about six hundred kilometers from You. He could have returned from there to the Great City Shang, which is about four hundred kilometers to the west. But he did not; he turned southward for ten days along the seacoast till he came to two places where he had visited before on his recent inspection tour to the front. Then he started for home. Bypassing You, he reached the Great City Shang some seventy-three days after his departure from Qi. He spent only one day there reporting the success of his expedition to the ancestors; but he did not return to Yin until another fifty-five days later. From the inscriptions we know that he spent two days in between on the chase. But as to how he used the rest of his time, we have no information.

Although this so-called expedition looks more like a pleasure excursion than a military enterprise, it seems safe to assume that Zou returned to his imperial seat with an ego even more inflated than before, and with a confidence in his own capability and destiny more than any of his predecessors had ever entertained. In his own estimation, he probably overexaggerated the strength of the southeastern tribes, and therefore correspondingly enhanced the power of his own intellect and the glory of his own triumph. In his eyes Guifang and Tufang could not have been more stubborn enemies than Renfang and Yufang, and the High Ancestor not more capable than himself. In fact, had he and Wuding changed places, he might have subjugated those unruly tribes much sooner than in three years. And when a reigning monarch was disposed to think in this manner, courtiers would not be lacking to voice their hearty agreement and enthusiastic acclamation.

Had Zou lived in the early days of the Shang when ministers like Yi Yin could sternly correct their sovereign's mistakes, or in the later period of the Yin when emperors like Wuding and Zujia had lived incognito among the "little people," he might have conducted himself more sensibly and not come to so tragic an end. But the dynasty had already lasted some six centuries, and the social modes were all altered; and in his thinking and in his behavior Zou was probably as much a victim of the trends of the times as the people were the victims of his oppressions.

The main trend the Yin exhibited at the time was a perceptible and accelerated drift toward unrestrained gratification of the senses. In a manner of speaking, this was a natural and inescapable development for men who, having finally and completely left the crude, casual, nomadic ways behind, were entering into a richer, more florid life which was being created by a progressive agrarian society. Counting from Pangeng, by now Yin had been the imperial seat of the empire for over two centuries, longer already than West Bo. Unlike the latter city, which was enclosed on three sides by tall hills and on the remaining side by a wide river, the fertile plains of Yin, both to the south and to the east, set no visible limits to cultivation by husband-men. And thanks to Wuding's firm and effectual rule, unprecedented peace and order prevailed throughout the empire, which encouraged the Yin traders to push their merchandise to the farthest corners of the frontiers. On the heels of this rapid expansion both in agriculture and in commerce, a new society emerged with much more affluence than any man had ever experienced. And side by side with the increasing accumulation of riches rode men's insatiable desire to gratify their wants and fancies.

This determined orientation toward a more luxurious way of living by the Yin people is best seen in the bronzes they have left to posterity. The perfection and complexity of casting these alloys of copper and lead testifies to the highly advanced technological level they had attained. At first, because most of the bronzes were unearthed from the Yin region, all of such incredible artistic excellence, and because they seem to have sprung up of a sudden, with no known origins, many occidental scholars thought that this cultural achievement must have been introduced from the West. But this supposition is unsubstantiated. While the Near East used the lost-wax process, Chinese casters developed a system of complicated piece molds prepared from refined whitish-buff clay.[76] As far as the Chinese are concerned, they have always believed that this is an indigenous technology that began very early, at least earlier than the Xia dynasty. According to one ancient source,[77] before fashioning the Nine Tripods, Yu the Great had weapons made of bronze. And although the Nine Tripods were unfortunately lost, the very fact that an eyewitness had described them even as late as the 7th century B.C. attests that the tripods were real and that technological development must have advanced enough by Yu's time to make their manufacture possible.[78] More-over, there are extant several bronze weapons and at least one bronze tripod that predate the Yin period.[79] In any event, this question has been resolved recently by Chinese archaeological discoveries [80] which have yielded a num-ber of bronzes, less varied in shape, simpler in design, and coarser in work-manship than the Yin products. So there is now a general agreement among scholars, both West and East, that the bronze culture was developed entirely independently by the Chinese, but brought to its magnificent heights only in the later Yin period.[81]

The bronzes the Yin artisans produced may be divided into five categories: (1) musical instruments, (2) military weapons, (3) food receptacles, (4) drinking vessels, and (5) miscellaneous utensils. Among the musical instruments, there are bells, gongs, drums, cymbals, and clappers. It was the Yin custom to have sixteen bells for a set, ranging from the largest to the smallest. When they were rung one after another in harmony, conceivably their performance may be likened to that of modern chimes. Sometimes very large bells were made to commemorate special occasions, which, like tripods of enormous proportions, were considered treasures rather than musical instruments.[82] The drums and gongs were also used for nonmusical purposes. In battle, the beating of drums signified an order to advance, and that of gongs to retreat.

Among military weapons, axes, spears, lances, halberds, helmets, and arrowheads have been found. But it is in the food receptacles and drinking vessels that we have met with the largest variety, differing in shape, in size, and in appearance, many of them being modeled after birds or animals. In fact, there are so many that we have no precise idea how each of them should be properly used. However, we do know that in general the food receptacles are of two kinds—simple containers and cooking utensils. Most of the tripods belong to the latter. The three legs allow firewood or charcoal to be placed to heat up what is contained above. And with some of these tripods, the legs were purposely made hollow so that the heat could be distributed more readily. As to the drinking vessels, they exceed even the food receptacles in variety and number. They too may be subdivided in two kinds—containers that were used to hold large amounts of spirits or water, and vessels that served the purpose of drinking by individuals. Many of the containers, however, seem also to be wine warmers. By keeping fire burning beneath them, the wine may be kept quite warm. From this it seems likely that the Chinese, who prefer to have their wines warmed rather than chilled, derive their habit from times of great antiquity.

As for the miscellaneous utensils, the most common ones found are washbasins, vases, and bowls, etc. In addition, there are bronze plates polished to a mirror surface on one side. These were used by the ancients as mirrors.

Many of the bronzes are described in the West as ritual vessels used for religious rites or veneration ceremonies. This is, of course, possible, and in some cases very probable. But the plain truth may be that except for a very limited number they were simply houseware or tableware for the rich and high-positioned in Yin society. In the *Book of Changes*, one of the most ancient books of China, under the hexagram *ding*, "Tripod," it is stated:

The tripod is derived from the image (the upper trigram representing fire, and the lower trigram representing wood). Using wood to build up fire, it is for the purpose of cooking. The sages cooked food in order to offer it to the Lord Above, and also cooked at large in order to provide sustenance for worthy people.

The ever growing tendency toward the gratification of the senses may be further observed in the elaborate decorations that were engraved on the bronzes. These are mainly combinations of geometric patterns and highly formalized animal forms. To the Chinese, the patterns are just aesthetic designs; and the animal forms, including the dragon or the serpent, are just those with which the ancients were familiar either by experience or through folklore. There is, however, one typical motif which frequently mystifies an observer—the so-called *t'ao t'ieh*.[83] It consists of zoomorphic facial elements—eyes, horns, ears, eyebrows, and jaws—disposed across the principal surfaces of the sides of the vessel as though an animal had been split lengthwise and the two halves laid out about a medial nasal ridge.[84] The presence of this motif is explained in ancient books. In regard to the bronzes of the Zhou dynasty, which in the main follow the pattern of the Yin, one of these books states explicitly:

> On the tripods of Zhou, the *t'ao t'ieh* is engraved. It has a head but no body; it may devour, but cannot swallow. It will hurt itself. This is to say it gets what it deserves.[85]

In another book, even older and more authoritative, it is said of a man—"greedy of drinking and eating, covetous of money and riches, ever ready to seize what he wants by improper means and exalt and display his prodigality through ostentatious conduct, insatiable and rapacious in his extortions, ac-cumulating wealth without end, making no exception of orphans or widows, and feeling no compassion for the poor and the destitute"—that such a one was numbered by the world among its most wicked and nicknamed *t'ao t'ieh*, after the fabulous voracious beast of remote antiquity.[86] So, perhaps, this motif was engraved on the bronzes less for any mythical belief than for a moral purpose. It was to caution the users who were rich enough to have acquired such costly utensils not to overindulge themselves in senseless wastefulness.

But whatever the interpretations of these decorations may be, admiration for the workmanship of the bronzes is universal. As described by one West-ern connoisseur, "Within a limited repertoire, the variety is unlimited. A supreme confidence inspires every line." [87] And as adjudged by another, "These are technically unequaled in the ancient world, which, together with their strength of artistic conception, places the Chinese artisan on a footing with those of ancient Egypt and Mesopotamia." [88] But from a historian's standpoint, another observation may be added. Not only are these bronzes technologically advanced and artistically admirable, but they appear to have been so abundant that hardly a Western museum of repute is without a collection of them. This can but lead to one conclusion: A much higher standard of living now obtained in Yin society than ever before. At the beginning of the bronze industry, only the reigning sovereign and a few high-positioned men could have afforded its products; by the time of the later Yin, the community at large had become increasingly affluent and the artisans in the field had grown considerably in numbers, and more and more Yin people indulged themselves in the luxury of having bronzes, in addition to potteries, for table service and house ware.

Side by side with the expanding use of the bronzes, the later Yin also saw the popularization of jade. The working of "true" jade (which is nephrite) and its hard stone substitutes has been pursued in China more seriously than in any other part of the world, indeed, from nearly the beginning of Chinese civilization.[89] Perhaps this pursuit began even with the Stone Age. Working on stones, the Chinese soon found nephrite to be one of the hardest and, also, one endowed with the largest range of colors. And they learned to mold it for use or for ornament by grinding it with diverse tools at first made of bamboo, wood, or bone. The earliest mention of jade occurs in the *Book of History*, when Shun, after his appointment as co-emperor, began his imperial duties with the examination of the jade astronomical instruments employed for the observation of the celestial bodies.[90] And Shun undoubtedly was the man who first put jade to practical use on a large scale. Because both the hardness and the texture of nephrite make anything made of it difficult to duplicate, Shun had the insignia of the five grades of princes all manufactured from this kind of stone.[91] These tokens of authority were called *gui*. According to China's first lexicographer, a *gui* is "round at the top, square at the bottom; for the prince of the first rank, it is nine inches long; for the second and for the third, seven inches; and for the fourth and for the fifth, five inches." [92] The *gui*, therefore, may be likened to a scepter or a baton in the West. In China, it was sometimes also given a high officer entrusted with a temporary mission of great importance with the understanding that when the mission was accomplished, it would be returned. Thus after Yu had finished controlling the flood, classifying the fields and taxes, and conferring lands and surnames, it was recorded at the end of the document *Yu's Levies* that he "surrendered the dark-colored *gui* and reported the completion of his task." [93] So all in all the *gui* was a symbol of authority, a mark of distinction, which the owner usually carried about his person. And as time went on, by way of imitation, a custom developed that if one had a piece of jade, one wanted to make it into an ornament to be worn constantly.

Besides the *gui*, there is another form for which the ancients showed a predilection in fashioning jade. This is called *bi*—a round disk, either with or without a hole in the center. The largest *bi* was said to be about a foot in diameter.[94] These precious jades were often used as presents, or as rewards from a prince to his loyal subjects, or as a tribute from a lord to his sovereign. Because they were exceedingly valuable, sometimes even half a *bi* was used for similar purposes. In any event, by the time of the last emperor of the Xia dynasty, the value of jade must have been recognized by all. No matter whether it was artistically designed or not, no matter whether it was large or small, no matter whether its texture was fine or coarse, every piece could probably find a ready purchaser in exchange for commodities. Thus Jie, after his disastrous defeat at the hands of Tang, took all the precious jades along in his flight.[95] This value placed on jade apparently continued to grow so that in the reign of Pangeng jades were equated with cowries as the currency of the empire.[96] And in this jade had an undoubted advantage over the cowrie, for the former can be made into all sorts of ornaments to adorn palaces and homes as well as persons, while the latter cannot. So in the later Yin period there was a plenitude of jade ornaments such as men had not seen before; and Zou was said to have even included in his wardrobe a suit completely made of precious jades.[97]

The third channel through which the Yin people sought to express enjoyment of their new affluence was building. For reasons that are still not fully understood by us, the Chinese ancients seldom used stone as material for construction; they relied instead on wood. Consequently, after so many wars and revolutions, there exist nowadays in China not many buildings that can boast of being over a thousand years old; and anything from Yin, had it survived, would have to have lasted at least some three thousand years. However, even as it is, in the excavations around modern Anyang, archaeologists have found ruins indicating that the Yin people had already gained considerable sophistication in architecture.[98] While some dwellings were little better than hovels or cells, the imperial palace seems to have been built in accordance with a preconceived plan, which evidently set a pattern for its counterparts of later dynasties, including the existing one in Peking. In the middle of the palace's spacious premises, an imaginary line can be drawn parallel to the magnetic line between the North and South Poles, and all the halls, suites, rooms, corridors, and passageways are arranged symmetrically on both sides, with the gates and doors of the main chambers for the most part facing south. At a section in the front, traces of three grand portals, horizontally arrayed, have been found. In one inner section, there are vestiges of nine halls standing side by side, each about a hundred square meters in size. But these are only a part of one palace which modern archaeologists have found. From another source, much closer to Yin in time, we learn, "At the time of Zou, the city was enlarged considerably. To the south as far as Chaoge, to the north as far as Handan and Shaqiu, there were scattered many resort palaces and hideaway mansions."[99] Of course, Zou could not have built them all for his own use; many of these must have been owned by those who had the means to construct or to acquire them.

The development of bronzes, jades, and better dwellings constitutes a natural step in the movement toward a higher level of culture. However, with the increase of affluence, the Yin people seemed to have unfolded another aspect of their society which cannot be viewed as progressive. Toward the end of the dynasty there appeared a popular fad of addiction to drink. After the overthrow of Zou, this unfortunate emperor was, of course, denounced among other things for having led the nation into a state of dissolute intemperance. But actually the people themselves should have shared much of the blame. In the *Book of History,* there is a document that attests to the true conditions of that time. Several years after Zou was slain, when the second emperor of the new dynasty had finally pacified the area around Yin[100] and made it a fief for one of his kinsmen, he still found it necessary to issue a special announcement warning against the unrestrained use of intoxicating spirits.[101]

Besides this "drinking problem," the Yin people suffered an even worse affliction that not only blackens their own name but tarnishes the heritage they left for posterity. Ancient Chinese records are replete with descriptions of the various cruelties Zou committed during his lifetime (which we shall narrate in due course), but none of them carries any account of the atrocities his predecessors had perpetrated before him. Thus, when modern archaeologists, in search for oracle bones, made some gruesome discoveries, it came as a total shock to many Chinese scholars well versed in their ancient history. For besides the ruins of the imperial palace, they also found ten or eleven burial grounds for the Yin emperors after the transference of the capital to Yin.[102] And in several of these, to the amazement of the excavators, in addition to bronzes, jades, potteries, chariots, and other valuable artifacts, along with the interment of the dead sovereign at the center, not only were guards and attendants buried around him, but scores and even hundreds of men and women, mostly in their twenties or thirties, were immolated on the outside in rows upon rows. It has been conjectured that these latter might have been captives or hostages that were killed at the passing of an emperor in order to throw fright into the divers nations or tribes from which they had been originally taken. Moreover, the practice seems to have been pursued for at least several generations. Had it started earlier, even before the removal of the capital to Yin? Or was it introduced only later, say, after the reign of Wuding, when at the demise of that august and mighty conqueror it was feared that the news might have caused unruly nations or tribes to break forth into disturbance, unless accompanied by a show of brutal force and awesome determination? Or was it just a matter of absolute power corrupting absolutely, or too much concern for one's own security breeding too much unconcern or insensitivity for others? It is impossible to tell. Nor can we reason out why these atrocities were never written about in any of the ancient books. Were the authors simply ignorant of this abominable practice? Or were they so ashamed of the inhumanity that they chose to disregard it entirely? In view of their lack of squeamishness in describing all the horrible acts committed by Zou, we are inclined to think that it is the former, not the latter, that was the cause of the omission. In any event, there is no question but that such acts of barbarism had been repeatedly perpetrated before Zou's time. So if Zou committed crimes of similar nature, he did so not without a series of precedents or examples.

Thus in the love of luxury, in the addiction to drink, and in the proneness to inhumanity, Zou was but following the drift of the Yin mainstream. He may be said to have been at the very head of this foul and revolting current, both because of his position and because of his egocentricity; but to single him out as an isolated, abnormal monstrosity would be less than fair to him and more than fair to the Yin society at large.

Still, with all his faults and with all his evildoing, Zou might yet have preserved his empire had it not been his ill luck to have his historical path run across that of a man who had humanity enough to aspire to save the world from all tyranny and oppression, wisdom enough to discern a weakness in the seemingly indestructible Yin imperial system, and perseverance enough to work incessantly to bring about a successful revolution—the celebrated "Cultural Emperor of Zhou" (Zhou Wen Wang).[103]

NOTES

1. *Book of History*, pangeng, comments by Zheng Kangcheng.

2. The character *qi* means both "relations" and "sorrow" or "sorrowful." In the past many scholars, because they were confused about the circumstances surrounding the event, thought this meant that the people were sorrowful or discontented. See Sun Xingyan, *Shangshu Jinguwen Zhushu*.

3. See *Book of History*, pangeng, comments by Ma Rong and Zheng Kangcheng. The five capitals are Bo, West Bo, Xiao, Xiang, and Geng.

4. For this translation here, see Sun Xingyan, *Shangshu Jinguwen Zhushu*.

5. Obviously a man of renown, widely known for

his wisdom in a time probably prior to Pangeng. But of him we know nothing.

6. The Chinese characters here are *bei* and *yu*. Bei means "cowries," which the Shang people used for money; and *yu* means "jades" or "precious stones."

7. This is the only sentence in the entire document which is not exactly clear. (See comments by Zheng Kangcheng and others.) The literal translation of the Chinese characters should be "thereupon made proper its (or their) positions." The author is of the opinion that Pangeng, having evaluated the performances of the various officers in the process of transfer, made some changes in the makeup of his government. These changes were slight and just. Nonetheless he thought it necessary to reassure the people of his good faith.

8. The fact that *pangeng* was considered a most difficult document to comprehend was openly acknowledged by one of the most renowned scholars of the early 9th century A.D., Han Yu. (See his essay on "advanced education," *Jinxuejie.*) Before the discovery of the oracle bones, the Chinese were confused about the circumstances surrounding the emperor's removal of the capital to Yin. Some of the scholars, following a misleading notation in the *Historical Records,* even thought that Yin was no other than West Bo, and that when Pangeng moved to Yin, he was returning to Tang's old administrative capital. Moreover, because they could not understand the basis for the factionalism, they attributed the opposition to the rich and powerful families who were accustomed to easy living and therefore adverse to the removal of the capital. This obviously does not make much sense, since the danger of inundation would have threatened the rich and the poor alike. For an example of this kind of explanation, see James Legge's translation of the document.

9. Dong Zuobin, *Jiaguxue Liushinian,* p. 15.

10. The Huan, flowing further down, merges with the Wei. This was mentioned by Yu in *Book of History, yugong.*

11. Dong Zuobin, *Jiaguxue Liushinian,* p. 15.

12. See above, p. 173.

13. Dong Zuobin, *Yin Lipu,* part II, chap. 9, sec. 3.

14. The song of Jizi, as quoted in *Historical Records, songweizi shijia.*

15. In later days, Chinese have used the term *yinshang* to mean "rich merchants." See above, p. 161.

16. See *Book of History, yueming* and *wuyi;* also, *Guo Yu, chuyu.*

17. *Book of History, yueming,* III; *Guo Yu, chuyu,* I.

18. *Book of History, wuyi.*

19. Ibid., *yueming,* III.

20. Ibid., *wuyi. Gaozong* is of course "High Ancestor," Wuding's posthumous title. Also see *Confucian Analects, xianwen.*

21. *Confucian Analects, xianwen.*

22. *Guo Yu, chuyu,* I.

23. His occupation is not specified in *Guo Yu, chuyu;* nor in *Book of History, shuxu. Mozi (shangxian)* says only, "Wearing rough cloth and using a chain for belt, he worked as a laborer at the city wall of Fu Cliff."

24. *Historical Records, yin benji.*

25. *Gong* may be translated as "duke." And if he is charged with the duties of the principal administrative officer, he may indeed be called prime minister. Both the *Historical Records* and the document *yueming* (the authenticity of which has been questioned) in the *Book of History* stated that Wuding had appointed Fu Yue prime minister. But *Guo Yu, chuyu,* only mentioned that he made him a *gong.* According to ancient practice an emperor might have three *gong,* whose duties were "to sit down and discuss the policies and principles *(dao)* of government with the sovereign." This seems to be more likely the office Wuding had charged Fu Yue with. Hence, the translation of *gong* here as "high councilor."

26. This passage appears both in *Guo Yu, chuyu,* I, and in *Book of History, yueming.* Though the authenticity of the latter is in doubt, this passage is above suspicion.

27. This is partly from *chuyu* and partly from *yueming.*

28. Huangfu Mi, *Diwang Shiji.*

29. See above, p. 173.

30. See above, pp. 135–36.

31. Dong Zuobin, *Jiaguxue Liushinian,* p. 92. In 1976, an undisturbed royal tomb was discovered intact at Anyang. It has been thought to be that of one of Wuding's wives. But this still has to be confirmed. See *Kaogu* (1979), no. 2, pp. 165–70.

32. Ibid., p. 91.

33. It is, however, a curious fact that the Duke of Zhou, in the *Book of History* document *junshi* (see above, p. 182, note 115), where he enumerated all the good emperors of Yin as well as the praiseworthy ministers who served each of them, mentioned only Gan Pan, and not Fu Yue, alongside Wuding. Perhaps the duke, who had a far better knowledge of Yin history and a far deeper insight into Yin politics, considered Fu Yue but a front man dreamed up by Wuding for his own purpose.

34. Dong Zuobin, *Yin Lipu,* part II, chap. 9, sec. 1.

35. All the inscriptions related to the events narrated here may be found in Dong Zuobin's *Yin Lipu,* part II, chap. 9, sec. 1. The interpretation of these events is the author's.

36. Ibid., pp. 39–40. In the inscriptions, the tribe's name consists of two characters somewhat like *lufang.* But there is no questioin that it is the Guifang mentioned in the *Book of Changes.*

37. The character for the *zhi* in Xiazhi has no equal in modern Chinese. So we do not know how it should be pronounced; but because it resembles a modern character *zhi,* we are using it here for convenience's sake.

38. Before Wuding's chariot accident, there is an inscription to this effect: "Yue sent a messenger to report," Yue being one of the states adjacent to Guifang. Then shortly after the accident, several princes or messengers came to report on the incursions of Tufang and Guifang.

39. The character *jin* is not modern, and therefore not pronounceable. Here the pronunciation of a modern character that bears some resemblance to it is used for convenience's sake.

40. The same as *zhi* and *jin.* See notes 37 and 39.

41. See notes 37 and 40.

42. This was the thirteenth moon in the twenty-ninth year of Wuding's reign. At that time, whenever the Yin had a leap month, they would have thirteen moons for the year.

43. See Map IV.

44. This is in full accord with the statements found in the *Book of Changes.* In the *jiji* hexagram, we have: "Gaozong fought Guifang and took three years to overcome them." Again, in the *weiji* hexagram: "Exert the utmost to fight Guifang. After three years, the effort will be rewarded by the Great Nation."

45. See *Guo Yu, zhengyu,* comments by Wei Zhao. Also see above, p. 128.

46. *Guo Yu, zhengyu.* The *Bamboo Chronicles* had it that Dapeng was destroyed in Wuding's forty-third year, and Shiwei in his fiftieth year.

47. *Mencius, gongsunchou,* I.

48. See *Zhuangzi, waiwu; Xunzi, xing'e* and *dalue;* Huangfu Mi, *Diwang Shiji;* and also Wang Guowei, *Gaozong Tongri Shuo.*

49. For instance, one of the oracle-bone inscriptions ascribed to Emperor Zujia refers to "Brother Ji" and "Brother Geng." Also see Yang Rongguo, *Zhongguo Gudai Sixianshi,* pp. 11–13.

50. *Bamboo Chronicles;* Huangfu Mi, *Diwang Shiji.*

51. Wang Guowei, *Gaozong Tongri Shuo.*

52. See above, p. 172.

53. According to the *Historical Records, yin benji,* the pheasant was said to have lighted on the ear of the veneration tripod and crowed.

54. The *Bamboo Chronicles* had eleven years for his reign; all other accounts, only six years.

55. *Book of History, wuyi.*

56. Dong Zuobin, *Jiaguxue Liushinian,* pp. 107–18; and also *Yin Lipu, zujia sipu.*

57. See above, p. 172.

58. *Guo Yu, zhouyu,* III.

59. Dong Zuobin, *Jiaguxue Liushinian,* p. 104.

60. See above, p. 173.

61. Dong Zuobin, *Jiaguxue Liushinian,* p. 93.

62. See Map IV.

63. *Historical Records, yin benji.*

64. Dong Zuobin, *Yin Lipu,* part II, chap. 9, sec. 2; also see above, p. 173.

65. Dong Zuobin, *Yin Lipu,* part I, chap. 3. Also see *Shangshu Dazhuan.*

66. Dong Zuobin, *Jiaguxue Liushinian,* p. 102.

67. *Confucian Analects, zizhang.* The disciple who made the remark was Zigong.

68. *Historical Records, yin benji.*

69. Ibid. See comments by Pei Yin.

70. Ibid.

71. *Lushi Chunqiu, zhongdongji, dangwu.*

72. *Historical Records, yin benji.*

73. See above, pp. 214–15.

74. See above, p. 160.

75. The facts in this narration are all based on the divination inscriptions pertaining to this episode given in full in Dong Zuobin's *Yin Lipu,* part II, chap. 9, sec. 3.

76. Nelson Gallery of Art and Atkins Museum, *Art of the Orient,* p. 7.

77. *Yue Jue Shu.*

78. See above, p. 112. Also see *Mozi, gengzhu.*

79. See above, pp. 155 and 182.

80. Excavations have been done in other Shang sites beside Anyang such as Yangshi, Zhengzhou, and some areas in Shaanxi and Shanxi. See Chang, Kwang-chih, *The Archaeology of Ancient China,* pp. 218–40 and 258–59.

81. This opinion seems to be fully shared by Western scholars. See, for instance, Peter C. Swann, *Chinese Monumental Art,* p. 36.

82. Ruan Yuan, *Jiguzai Zhongdingyiqi Kuanshi.*

83. This romantization is according to the Wade-Giles system. Since the West is accustomed to this term, it is used here to avoid confusion.

84. Nelson Gallery of Art and Atkins Museum, *Art of the Orient,* p. 7.

85. *Lushi Chunqiu, xianshilan, xianshi.*

86. *Zuozhuan,* Duke Wen, 18th year.

87. Peter C. Swann, *Chinese Monumental Art,* p. 37.

88. Nelson Gallery of Art and Atkins Museum, *Art of the Orient,* p. 7.

89. Ibid., p. 20.

90. See above, p. 77.

91. Ibid.

92. Xu Shen's dictionary.

93. *Book of History, yugong.*

94. *Huainanzi, yuandao xun.*

95. See above, p. 142.

96. See above, p. 197, note 6. See also Wang Guowei, *Shuo Juepeng.*

97. *Historical Records, yin benji.*

98. Dong Zuobin, *Jiaguxue Liushinian,* pp. 16–17 and 30–31.

99. See *Historical Records, yin benji,* comments by Zhang Shoujie; and *Bamboo Chronicles.* The distance from Chaoge in the south to Handan or Shaqiu in the north is roughly seventy-five kilometers.

100. Actually the man who pacified the area was the Duke of Zhou, the second emperor's uncle. The emperor being still a boy, the uncle acted in his name.

101. *Book of History, jiugao.*

102. Dong Zuobin, *Jiaguxue Liushinian,* pp. 32–37.

103. This is the posthumous title given to the first founder of the Zhou dynasty. The character *wen,* when used as a simple adjective, is usually translated as "literary," "refined," or "versed in literature," etc. But according to the first code of posthumous titles, supposedly devised by the Duke of Zhou, the founder's son, *wen* means one "who charts the heaven and maps the earth," "who knows the way, is possessed of virtue, and widely informed," "who is industrious in studies and eager to learn," and "who is compassionate, benevolent, and loves the people," etc. So it is translated here, rather tentatively, as "cultural."

CHAPTER VI

THE PERIOD OF TRANSITION BETWEEN YIN AND ZHOU

· 1 ·
THE ORIGINS OF ZHOU
(25th–12th Century B.C.)

The Zhou traced their origins back to the famed "Abandoned One," Di Ku's son, Yao's half brother, and Shun's minister of agriculture, who was venerated by later generations as Ji, or Houji, "Deity of Agriculture." He was borne by Di Ku's principal wife, Jiangyuan.[1] Either before or, more likely, after the Zhou had acquired the possession of the empire, his descendants composed an ode in commemoration of the unusual circumstances that surrounded his birth:

As regards the beginning of our people,
It goes back to Jiangyuan.
How were our people begun?
At the ceremony of bonfire sacrifice to Heaven,
Prayers were offered that she be not without issue.
Then following the footprints sent down by the Lord Above
    and feeling the hallowed air,
She tried to put her foot inside the prints, but it hardly covered the space of a toe.
She felt disturbed and became pregnant.
Thus conceived and thus born was Houji.

He was placed in a narrow lane,
The oxen and sheep would not hurt him.

233

He was placed in the wood,
It chanced that woodsmen came and gave him nourishment.
He was placed on the cold ice,
And birds sheltered him with their wings.
When the birds flew away,
Houji began to wail.[2]

And that was the moment when the mother, marveling at these occurrences, finally came and took home the infant whose conception had so disturbed her at first. The child was therefore given the name Qi, "the Abandoned One." [3] When he grew up and became famous, he was also awarded the surname Ji.[4] So his full name was, in the Chinese fashion, Ji Qi. But he was better known to posterity as Houji, "Prince (or Deity, or Spirit) of Agriculture."

What Houji did during the Great Flood has already been related. After Shun's demise, he continued to serve Yu as minister of agriculture. When he himself died, it seems more because his son Buku had also acquired special expertise in husbandry than because the office was hereditary that the junior Ji was named minister to succeed him. But after the atavistic emperor Tai-kang acceded to the throne, the ministry was abolished. And Buku, who had strongly opposed the action, apparently incurred the monarch's deep displeasure and was forced to seek refuge in the northern parts of modern Gansu and Shaanxi provinces, between the then western and northern nomadic tribes. But even there, in the midst of peoples who followed an entirely different, if not hostile, way of living, "he dared not neglect his own profession, but pursued his own particular virtue whenever possible . . . so that his descendants would follow the example of their forebears and not feel ashamed of them." [5]

But because of this flight into uncultured areas, the lineage of the Zhou from there on is less than clear. Altogether the *Historical Records* lists fifteen names supposedly representing fifteen generations from "the Abandoned One" to Wen Wang (see chart of Wen Wang's antecedents). Assuming that all the names are correct, of which we are by no means certain, there are obviously many gaps unfilled. This is made evident by comparing it with the genealogical charts of the Shang, or Yin. The founders of the two houses were half brothers. And at the end of the Yin dynasty—the period of time with which we are now concerned—we have Di Xin, or Zou, as the last living representative of the Shang on the one hand, and Wen Wang, or Ji Chang, as his contemporary and counterpart of the Zhou on the other. Now, counting from the Shang's primal ancestor to Di Xin, there are thirty generations, which contrast sharply with the fifteen generations of the Zhou. The disparity is conspicuous. So, conceivably, in the need of adjusting themselves to their new environment, not a few of Buku's descendants made more concessions to the nomadic way of life than the inflexible minister of agriculture would have tolerated. As it is not in the nature of nomads to crowd their memories with genealogical nonessentials in their harsh struggle for survival, probably as many names of the Zhou ancestors were forgotten as were remembered.

LINEAL DESCENT OF THE HOUSE OF ZHOU BEFORE WEN WANG

Di Ku . . . Qi (Houji) . . . Buku . . . Ju . . . Gongliu . . . Qingjie . . . Huangpu . . . Chafu . . . Huiyu . . . Gongfei . . . Gaoyu . . . Yayu . . . Gongshu Zulei . . . Gugong Danfu . . . Jili . . . Chang (Wen Wang)

Note: The above is based on the *Historical Records.* Apparently there are many gaps unfilled. See page 234.

In any event, all this time the Zhou did not seem to be possessed of any definitive area of land which they might claim as their own—at least not until Gongliu, or Duke Liu, appeared on the scene. And Duke Liu was the second of the ancestors for whom the Zhou had an ode composed, in honor both of him and of his settlement at a place called Bin:

Deeply devoted to the people was Duke Liu.
Unable to rest in comfort and ease,
He went to every field and every corner to round up the population.
He put up the accumulated produce in storage,
He stowed the dried meat and preserved foods
In small bags and large sacks.
He thought only of the safety of the people and the glory of the nation.
Then with bows and arrows all ready to shoot,
With shields, spears, and axes held aloft,
He ordered the march to begin.

Deeply devoted to the people was Duke Liu.
He himself had surveyed the place (where he was planning to settle)
The numerous and thriving multitude.
It was only after they had signified their agreement that he made the proclamation,
So that there could be no sighs or murmurs afterward.
He had ascended to the hilltops,
He had descended again to the plains.
What should be given him to wear (for so much trouble he had taken for the
    people)?
There could be only jade and jadelike gems,
And an ornamented scabbard for his sword.

Deeply devoted to the people was Duke Liu.
He went to the place of a hundred springs,
And scanned the wide plain around.
He climbed atop the ridge on the south,
And sighted the location where he wanted the capital to be.

Its wildness had space enough for the multitudes;
Here and there such and such buildings and dwellings could be constructed,
And thither and yonder accommodations for strangers.
Now he told out what he had in mind;
Then he talked to this one and to that one.

Deeply devoted to the people was Duke Liu.
Now that the capital had been built, all could depend on it.
In dignified order all his officers came,
And he caused the mats and hand-stools to be spread,
And they took their places on the mats and leaned on the stools.
He had sent to the herds,
And taken pigs from the pen,
And poured out the spirits from calabashes.
So he gave them to eat and to drink;
And so they honored him as their ruler, and obeyed him as their elder.

Deeply devoted to the people was Duke Liu.
The territories were broad and long.
He used the hilltop to determine the points of time by means of the shadows of the
    sun.
Then he surveyed the light and the shade of the land,
And viewed the courses of the streams and springs.
He built up an army of three troops.
He measured the marshes and the plains,
And fixed the revenues on the system of common cultivation of the fields.[6]
He also surveyed the land west of the hills, the land of the setting sun.
And the settlement of Bin became truly large and great.

Deeply devoted to the people was Duke Liu.
Having settled in temporary lodgings in Bin,
He crossed the Wei with boats to gather materials,
Even such materials as whetstones and iron.
And after the settlement was built and the boundaries defined,
The people became numerous and prosperous,
Occupying both sides of the Huang Brook,
And pushing on up that of Guo;
And as more and more people came to settle,
They went on to the country beyond the stream Rui.[7]

In the annals of men, there are few extant compositions that describe the migration of an ancient tribe as graphically as this ode. The original area occupied by the Zhou, very likely adjacent to modern Ordos, must have been either too unproductive for husbandry or too near to the savage tribes for comfort or safety. So Duke Liu had selected a new site, farther south, gone there for personal inspection, and returned to consult with the people. Having secured their agreement to migrate there, he proclaimed his decision to that effect. Then he went about rounding up his people, seeing to it that all possessions they could not carry with them be stored in safe places to await future transportation, and that on their present journey they be adequately provided with victuals. And fearful that they might be waylaid, their march began with a full display of military might and readiness.

And the new settlement proved very successful. As noted in the *Historical Records*, "Although Gongliu was still living between barbarian tribes, he renewed the enterprises formerly undertaken by Houji. He made husbandry his principal business, utilizing every piece of land according to its fitness. . . . As for the people who wanted to come, or wished to pass through, he would assist them with aid; as for those who wanted to remain, he would enable them to enjoy the accumulation of possessions; one and all dependent on him for their prosperity and well-being. And the people loved him; and large numbers moved into the area and attached themselves to him. Thus the destiny of Zhou started on its way." [8]

Both the ode and the *Historical Records* are explicit. There are only three points that need to be cleared up. The first is the location of Bin. Although some of the names given in the poem can no longer be identified, there is no question that the place is north of the Wei River, where in our modern times we still have a district bearing the name Bin. The second point is about the time of this occurrence. Even though definitive information is lacking, from one ancient source we have the intimation that Gongliu probably thrived at the time of Shaokang (2079–2058 B.C.). After Shaokang had succeeded in ridding the empire of the usurper Hanzhuo and restoring the dynastic rule of Xia, he was said to have reestablished the ministry of agriculture; and Gongliu was thought to have been the man named by him as its minister.[9] But no matter whether this account is authentic or not, there is no evidence that Gongliu had ever taken up the duties of that office in the distant Xia capital. Apparently he spent his whole life thereafter in Bin and in nowhere else. The third point is related to the character *gong*, which we have translated as "duke." Was *gong* just part of the name Gongliu? Or was it really a title? In view of the fact that his next two best-known descendants were both called *gong*—Gugong Danfu and Gongji—we are inclined to think *gong* was used as a title.

Now, *gong* is a title the ancients used either for a duke or for the "three high councilors" of the emperor.[10] In either case, it was supposed to be one of the highest honors that the imperial court could award. Did the Zhou princes receive the title from the Xia, or the Yin (Shang) sovereign? We doubt it. It was probably self-proclaimed. In the time of the Xia, because of the laxity of imperial control after Taikang, it is likely that every prince within the empire, if he was bold and powerful enough, could call himself by any title he chose to—the only title to shy from being *wang*, the use of which was recognized as an imperial prerogative. With the advent of Yin, control became tighter. However, as the land the Zhou were occupying was surrounded by nomadic tribes and situated on the outside of the generally accepted limits of the West Land, in spite of their cultural affinities, the Yin court could not but treat the Zhou differently from the regularly enfeoffed states of the empire. Perhaps because Zhou was living in constant apprehension of savage inroads, it might have early extended overtures to Yin, offering allegiance in exchange for imperial protection. But probably for the very reason Zhou was eager to have the protection, Yin was reluctant to make a total commitment. So a sort of vague understanding might have been reached, but there did not seem to have been anything formal and concrete to the complete satisfaction of Zhou. And Yin continued to regard Zhou as nothing more than a buffer state between its West Land and the nomadic barbarians, whose protection was difficult to ensure and whose loyalty was therefore not wholly dependable. This is very likely the reason why Wuding, while waging a fierce war against Guifang, took the special caution to instruct the Prince of Ku to keep a sharp eye on the movements of Zhou lest it should choose to side with the enemy.[11]

But how was the name Zhou derived? Again we are left in the dark. There is a surmise by scholars of the first century A.D. that the progeny of Houji had taken this name for their nation because *zhou* means "providing for all needs." [12] But this sounds more like a rationalization than a historical truth. Also, we are ignorant of when the name was first adopted. Before the discovery of the oracle bones, Chinese history traditionally alleged that it was first used by Gugong Danfu.[13] But now it is known for certain that Zhou as a state existed even in the time of Wuding, more than a century earlier.

From Gongliu to Gugong Danfu the *Historical Records* lists ten generations. Although we cannot be sure of this, we may roughly date Gugong Danfu as a younger contemporary of the twenty-sixth emperor of Yin, Kanding, a grandson of Wuding. According to the *Historical Records,* "Gugong Danfu again reestablished the enterprise of Houji and Gongliu." It seems therefore that for quite a few generations before him the Zhou had reverted to being nomads, and it was not until this new ruler appeared that agriculture was revived as the principal occupation. And what happened to him in consequence of his adopting this policy may furnish an explanation of why Gongliu's undertaking in the past had not survived him long. For once an agricultural settlement became prosperous, it was a constant temptation for the surrounding nomads to prey upon. While resistance would involve endless vigilance and ceaseless attrition, an easy escape could be secured by a return to nomadism. The way Gugong Danfu dealt with the situation, however, is what distinguished him, and may have been the reason for the people's honoring him later with the title Gugong, "Ancient Duke."

As is narrated in the *Historical Records*,[14] "No sooner had the Zhou prospered than the Xunyu [15] tribes coveted their possessions and kept on attacking them. The Zhou tried appeasement at first by giving them what goods they had demanded. But scarcely after these peace offerings had been delivered, attacks were renewed. At last, the savages made no secret of what they desired. They must have the possession of all the land and all the people within it. The entire population was aroused. They wanted to fight. However, the Ancient Duke said, 'The reason why the people wish to have a ruler is that they hope to be benefited by him. The purpose for which the savage tribes attack us is that they want our land and our people. For the people, there should not be much difference between being ruled by me and being ruled by them. Now, for me, the people want to fight. To have their fathers and sons slaughtered for my sake, and yet for me to rule over them—this is something I have no heart to do.' So, with only his kith and kin, he departed from Bin, crossed over the Qi and Ju rivers, climbed past the Liang Mountains, and settled at the foot of Mount Qishan.[16] But the entire population of Bin, supporting the old and carrying the young, followed him to the very place. And so also came many people from neighboring areas, who had heard of his benevolent rule, to join him." [17]

Now, this plateau which the Ancient Duke had chosen for his new habitation happens to be the upper portion of a very extensive fertile valley—the valley of the Wei River. With a numerous populace willingly putting themselves under his care, he realized he must provide them with better protection than he had done before at Bin. Deliberately, therefore, he suppressed the nomadic way of living among the people. He divided the land into districts, appointed officers to take charge, and built forts and strong walls for defense.[18] And to the end of his life, whether it was due to distance or to his preparedness, no nomadic tribes ever troubled him again.

The relationship between Zhou and Yin, however, remained distant. As Zhou grew perceptibly stronger and more prosperous, though the Qishan territory was apparently farther outside the limits of the West Land than Bin, the imperial court now wanted to have the newly established state numbered among its enfeoffed princedoms. Credence, therefore, may be given to an account that during the reign of the twenty-seventh emperor, Wuyi, a decree was issued formally investing Danfu, Prince of Zhou, with the land around Qishan as his fief.[19] But as to his having been given the rank of duke, that still seems unbelievable. Nevertheless, so far as the prince himself was concerned, he probably had had himself called by that title all along. Moreover, considering the investiture but a recognition of an accomplished fact, he might even have viewed this act of the Yin as an unwelcome intrusion into his own hard-won authority. Furthermore, he could have conceivably also harbored resentment against the ruling dynasty for a long time. In his thinking, had the imperial court really been eager to do its duty by him, it would have protected him adequately in the first place at Bin and rendered the subsequent forced migration unnecessary. While it would have been impolitic not to accept the investiture as an honor, he might already have begun to think it expedient to augment the power of Zhou. Thus we have the cryptic lines of a stanza which his progeny sang of him after they had already overthrown the Yin and exalted him posthumously with the title Tai Wang, "Grand Emperor":[20]

> A descendant of Houji,
> Verily was Tai Wang.
> He dwelt on the south of Mount Qi
> And began the clipping of Shang.

What the Ancient Duke actually did for "the clipping of Shang" was not recorded. But his secret aspirations were revealed by events related to the selection of his successor. He was very happily married. As a matter of fact, the house of Zhou was said to have enjoyed exceptional connubial bliss for three consecutive generations, from him to his grandson Wen Wang. Beautiful and wise, the Ancient Duke's consort Taijiang was not only his constant companion but also his closest adviser.[21] He did nothing without consulting with her first, an instance of which was recorded in the choosing of the Qishan territory as the new site for habitation.[22] She bore him three sons, all taught by her to grow up to be models of men, each in his own way. Their names were Taibo, Zhongyong, and Jili, with *tai* meaning the firstborn; *zhong,* the second, and *ji,* the youngest. It chanced that the youngest married early, and his wife, Tairen, was a paragon of virtue. "When she was with child, her eyes would not look at sordid sights; her ears would not hear obscene sounds; her mouth would not utter uncouth words. She sought to instruct her child even during the pregnancy." [23] And thus a grandson was born to the Ancient Duke, who named it forthwith Chang, a more propitious word than which he could not ever have found. For *chang* means "good," "bright," and "to prosper"—all three at once.

From the very birth of this grandchild, the Ancient Duke was drawn to him. While the infant impressed the grandfather with its remarkable precocity, the old man poured forth into its innocent ears all the innermost thoughts that he had seldom dared to confide to others. And he kept on saying to himself, "If our house is destined to rise to greater heights, it must be through Chang." As he said this so often, both Taibo and Zhongyong could not help overhearing it at times; and both of them felt that if they had not been in the way, their father would surely have liked to transmit the ducal throne to Chang. However, in the matter of succession, the house of Zhou, unlike the Yin, had long adopted the rule of primogeniture. So by this time-honored practice Taibo, as the firstborn, should succeed to the throne after the Ancient Duke's death; and in case anything happened to him, Zhongyong as the second son should take his place; and there would be no chance whatever for Jili, the youngest son, let alone his offspring. Thus Taibo and Zhongyong put their heads together and decided on the only course that they thought was filially advisable. They waited until the Ancient Duke was seriously ill; and pretending that they had heard of a rare herb that could cure the illness, they went together in search of it with only a few of their closest associates.[24] And lest their whereabouts should be discovered, they left Qishan, which was then at the very northwestern end of the Yin Empire, and headed in an exactly southeasterly direction. They did not stop until they reached Wu, the modern Wu Xian of Jiangsu province, a wild spot on the seacoast, peopled sparsely by some Man savages, at that time far beyond the known limits of the East Land and South Land, probably even farther beyond the land of Renfang and Yufang. There, at last, they felt safe from search and discovery. In time, they gathered about a thousand Man families and set up a princedom. While Zhongyong married, Taibo would not, in order to show that he loved his second brother as much as he loved the youngest one. He chose to remain single to the end of his life so that after his death the princedom would pass on to Zhongyong and his issue, as it eventually did. The existence of Wu was discovered only after the Zhou finally succeeded in overthrowing the Yin, when relations between the two branches of the same house were resumed.[25] And the Chinese people, beginning with Confucius, have since applauded Taibo and Zhongyong for their selfless action as representing the best in men, preferring of their own choice the abdication of a position of great advantage to the possessing of it.[26]

To return to Zhou, at the death of the Ancient Duke, because neither of his elder sons could be found, the ducal throne passed on to the third son, Jili, who was then known as Gongji, or Duke Ji. Although the chronology of this period is not certain, Duke Ji's rule was said to have lasted about twenty-five years.[27] But in comparison with his predecessor, the Ancient Duke, or with his successor, his own son Chang, who each enjoyed a long life, his reign is usually treated in Chinese histories as a sort of interregnum. And interregnum it may be said to have been indeed, for he lived between the one who began to dream about the seemingly impossible dream of overthrowing the Yin, and the other who thought out all practical plans to realize that dream and yet chose to stop short of the final act. But even as it was, Duke Ji did much to further the fortunes of Zhou. For he expanded its territories to the greatest extent possible under the circumstances, and thereby built up a powerful army that his successors could put to greater use.

From meager records, it is noted that during his reign Duke Ji fought no less than seven wars.[28] Only three years after he acceded to the ducal throne, he waged a war against Cheng, a princedom on the banks of the River Wei, about eighty kilometers to the east of Zhou. This proved an easy conquest and a very beneficial one; it opened up the wealth of the fertile middle Wei Valley to him. But at the same time it seemed also to have produced some repercussions in the Yin court, which sounded a warning. Cheng, like Zhou, was outside the formal limits of the West Land of the Yin Empire; so the absorption of the one by the other was, in appearance at least, below the notice of the imperial court. But had Duke Ji gone farther eastward, he would have encroached upon certain enfeoffed states within the West Land, which would have reported his action to Yin, and the whole might and wrath of the imperial house would no doubt have been brought about to bear upon him. Duke Ji took the warning seriously. Throughout his remaining years, he never turned eastward again; and all the six wars he fought thereafter were against the nomadic tribes either to the west or to the north of Zhou.[29] Although we can no longer trace the beginnings, or the courses, of these conflicts, it seems reasonably certain that all of them were started by Duke Ji himself, one after another, as if pursuing a preconceived plan. And in all of these expeditions he was successful—except for one, in which he suffered a terrible defeat, probably because he had ventured too far away from his home base, attacking a tribe that by its name seemed to have derived its origins from so distant a place as modern Peking.[30] But in all the other five campaigns he won great victories. And in one of them alone, against the so-called Western Tribes of Guirong, who were apparently scattered descendants of Guifang, he was said to have taken prisoner twenty of their kings.[31] Undoubtedly as a result of these aggressive hostilities the territory of Zhou was considerably augmented, just as the prestige of its military prowess was enhanced.

In proportion with the growth of Zhou developed the sensitivity of Yin. When the Ancient Duke first established himself at the foot of Qishan, the imperial court hardly paid it any attention, thinking that it might not survive for long. As Zhou gradually consolidated itself, the court deemed it simply routine and expedient to issue a decree formally investing its prince with the land he had already acquired as his fief. If he was presumptuous enough to address himself as a duke, so long as he did not flaunt the title outside of his own state, the emperor could well close his eyes to the vain conceit. But the conquest of Cheng gave the court a minor surprise. Still, as Cheng itself was outside the West Land, the only thing that need be done was to let Zhou know of the sovereign's displeasure. And Zhou's subsequent actions had pleased Yin indeed. Not only did it refrain from encroaching farther eastward, it turned its energies against the nomadic tribes to the west and to the north. Moreover, after its prince, the self-styled Duke Ji, had won a first victory over the Yiju tribe, he had personally come to the court to pay tribute. And in return the emperor had rewarded him with jades and horses. But as Zhou continued to win victories, it clamored—importunately to the court—for additional honors. The court suspected that Zhou wanted an official recognition of its prince as a duke, but that was an honor the dynasty did not wish lightly to give. In the end, the twenty-eighth emperor, Wenwuding, issued an order naming Jili *mushi,* or "pastor general," having charge of raising horses, cattle, and sheep along the borders.[32] However the court's envoy might have embellished the appointment with florid persuasions, the title itself did not appear to carry with it great honor. Whether Duke Ji felt gratified or insulted by this singular distinction it is not possible to say for certain. But there is a story, probably spurious, that a few years later, after the duke had won two more signal victories over the nomads, the emperor commended him officially, gave him many jades as presents, and honored him with the title *bo,* "field marshal." So it seemed that in modern parlance the Zhou had arrived at last. But just to show how almighty the imperial Yin was, and also how unpredictable a sovereign's pleasure could be, shortly afterward, when the newly invested field marshal made his appearance at a border fort, he was seized, detained, and disgraced.[33] Although this story may not be credited, nonetheless it shows the relationship between Yin and Zhou in its true light. The latter, however powerful it might have grown, was still powerless against the awesome might of the imperial majesty built up by Tang and fortified by Wuding. Yet at the same time, even though the former was superciliously confident that the latter could never do it any mortal harm, it was also paying it more and more attention as a sort of growing nuisance.

Then Duke Ji died and was succeeded by his son Chang.

· 2 ·

THE RISE OF ZHOU UNDER JI CHANG
(1165–1115 B.C.)

Ji Chang succeeded to his princedom probably only a very short time—two years, according to one chronologist[34]—after Di Xin, who was later to be known as Zou, acceded to the imperial throne at Yin. While Di Xin was not yet in his teens, Ji Chang was already in the prime of his life.[35] He was a tall man,[36] so powerfully built that his chest was said to have been endowed with four breasts.[37] Both his grandfather and his father had seen to it that he had had the best education available in the then barren west. And eager to learn by nature, he soon taught himself to become thoroughly familiar with every branch of knowledge of his day, from studies of government and ethics to the practical arts of agriculture and animal husbandry, and even to the occult mysteries of the craft of divination. Widely known for his filial piety while a crown prince,[38] he was naturally bitter about the frustrations and humiliations his father had suffered at the hands of the imperial court.[39] And remembering what his grandfather had confided in him during early childhood about the seemingly impossible dream of "clipping Shang," his ingenious mind could not but have felt at times both the temptation and the challenge of the very idea. Yet, if there ever lived a clear- and cool-headed man, it was this Ji Chang of Zhou. And if there ever lived a man who was also deeply conscientious of his duties as a subject toward his sovereign, it was he too. Thus out of this strange combination of conflicting aspects of a very strong character, a tortuous course of history was forged.

Ji Chang must have calmly and objectively assessed the situation many a time. All his grandfather's wild schemes notwithstanding there was no way, so far as he could perceive, to "clip Shang." Just as the Yin emperors were convinced that their imperial system was invulnerable, so the Prince of Zhou realized too that it was virtually unbeatable. The Central Shang was, if not a hundred times larger than Zhou in size, at least that many times richer in wealth, and that many times more numerous in population. And to try to catch up with Yin in these respects was simply physically impossible. Yet if to catch up with Yin was impossible, to reduce the degree of disparity was not only desirable but imperative. For as long as Zhou remained at such a disadvantage, it would be always hopelessly at the mercy of the Yin; and to the extent it could enlarge, strengthen, or enrich itself, it would be to that extent less subject to the affliction of mistreatment or injustice from the imperial power.

But how could this be done? As Ji Chang saw it, the key to the whole problem lay in two factors—population and husbandry. Just as the strength of a nation in those days depended upon the size of its population, so the state of its wealth depended upon the one main industry—agriculture. This was how Yin had prospered; and this was what Zhou should emulate. As a rule, population can be increased only slowly through birth; but in a state like Zhou, it could be multiplied, and that very rapidly, through immigration. As it was, not many people had found reason to migrate to Zhou. So the crux was to provide enough inducements to make the people in other states willing to migrate to Zhou, and publicize these inducements ahead so that they would not only be willing, but more than eager to do so. And indeed Zhou was happily located for the purpose. Thanks to his grandfather the Ancient Duke, the Qishan plateau offered wide virgin fields for newcomers to till. And thanks to his father, Duke Ji, not only was the Zhou territory made secure from molestations by nomadic tribes, but the middle portion of the fertile Wei Valley, also sparsely populated, was put under his control. Moreover, Ji Chang found advantage too in the fact that the imperial court did not exactly number Zhou as one of the enfeoffed states inside the West Land. Had it been otherwise, his activities would have been watched and scrutinized by Yin more closely. But as the situation stood, he could always allege the propinquity of the savage tribes as pretext for his actions. If he wanted to induce more people to migrate to Zhou, and if he did enact many measures to that effect, it was only to strengthen his princedom against the barbarian hordes so that Zhou would make a better buffer state between them and the Yin Empire.

Perhaps one of the greatest losses in Chinese history is that of the decrees, proclamations, laws, and regulations issued by Ji Chang with a view to attaining that objective. Originally, these had all been well preserved in the imperial archives of Zhou. Even as late as the 5th century B.C., Confucius was able to say, "The government of Wen Wang and Wu Wang are published in the tablets of wood and bamboo." [40] And when the sage's grandson paid tribute to his grandfather a century later, he also could state with assurance that the Master, in handing down his doctrines, "had traced their origins back to Yao and Shun and had taken their models from the laws and regulations of Wen Wang and Wu Wang," [41] speaking of the latter with manifest confidence that confirmation could be obtained by simply reading them. But unfortunately the tablets that bore these laws and regulations were lost, presumably in the last turbulent years of the Warring States. Nevertheless, glimpses of some of the measures taken by Ji Chang in the period we are presently concerned with may be gathered from Mencius, himself a disciple of Confucius's grandson. A passage of his book reads:

> Formerly, Wen Wang's government of Qi was as follows: The husbandmen each cultivated a hundred *mu* out of nine hundred; the officers could transmit their emoluments as patrimony to their descendants; the passes and markets served only as checkpoints or inspection posts, not to levy taxes; there were no prohibitions respecting streams or marshes, or hills or ridges; when a man was punished for a crime, his wife and children would not be involved in the guilt.[42]

The above is of course only too laconic a summary of several measures taken by Ji Chang; but from in between the lines the basic motivation of that astute prince may be clearly seen. Like the Yin, the system for land use Zhou adopted was the well-field system.[43] But while the Yin allocated to each husbandman only seventy *mu* in a "well," Ji Chang now allocated a hundred *mu*. This was possible because most of the land of Zhou was still virgin soil, with fields more available than men. Moreover, inasmuch as farming implements must have greatly improved since the early days of Shang, whereas formerly seventy *mu* would have taxed the strength of a husbandman to till, now they left him with energy to spare. Thus with a clear proclamation that Zhou was to provide a hundred *mu* for each newly arrived husbandman, it must have sounded like a clarion call to move westward for all those who yearned to have a better living for their families.

Next to the husbandmen, the kind of men Ji Chang wanted most was qualified administrators. If Zhou's population was to increase as he hoped, the more it increased, the more need there would be for good and capable administrators to help minister to the people's wants and build up a government to their satisfaction. But such administrators were hard to come by. In Ji Chang's opinion, they must be men of learning in the first place; and learning was a rare article in those days indeed. He knew only too well about the uncultured condition of the West; and he had probably also a good idea of what it was like in the rest of the empire. The entire environment was not conducive to learning and culture. Each enfeoffed state had only a few administrative positions, which, as a rule, were filled by the ruling prince's kinsmen. So even if there should be men of learning among the common people, they were well aware that they had little prospect for employment or advancement in life. Now, if they felt this way about their own state, they must have thought the same of Zhou. So to encourage such men to come to help him, he had to provide them with inducements no less persuasive than what he had offered to the husbandmen. Thus the second provision in the book *Mencius,* which may be paraphrased to this effect: "Men employed as officers were to be paid with emoluments that would be inherited by their descendants for generations." This regulation made plain two points. Firstly, Zhou would employ men who were qualified as officers, regardless of their background or lineage. In other words, all positions were open to talents, whatever their origins. And secondly, once a man was employed as officer and did well in his position, he would be treated like a kinsman of Zhou, with emolument not only paid to himself while alive but also paid to his descendants as long as Zhou lasted.

If Ji Chang was hopeful that eventually immigrants would come in droves, he was also realistic enough to know that he would be lucky, if only a trickle arrived at first; and what he must do was to make these arrivals feel welcome and comfortable so that word would be passed on to those who had stayed behind. We have no information as to the positive actions he might have taken in this respect, but from the above passage in *Mencius* it is clear that he did everything possible to prevent any unnecessary inconveniences or apprehensions. In those days most of the princedoms were interested only in increasing their revenue; and passes and markets were established much too often to extort money in the name of taxes from strangers or travelers. For this reason Ji Chang made it clear that no taxes of any kind would be imposed on any person or any goods going through Zhou; and that if checks and inspections were conducted in passes and markets at all, it was only to ensure peace and order for the safety and convenience of the people. Again, he was afraid that the immigrants, upon their first arrival in Zhou, might find it difficult to scrape up a living. So he abolished all restrictions respecting streams, waters, marshes, hills, ridges, and wooded areas. If the newcomers had nothing to eat, they could catch as many fish or any other game as they needed; and if they had nothing for fuel, they could gather as much firewood as they wanted. Moreover, as the practice of the time was that when a man committed a crime and suffered a penalty, his wife and children would be involved in the punishment, Ji Chang feared that this might become a deterrent to people leaving their homeland for a strange country. At home, even if the wife and children were involved, a man could still rely on his kinfolk or friends to take some care of them. But from inside an alien country where he had none of these, such relief or assistance could not be expected. So Ji Chang introduced a new regulation. In Zhou, if one was punished for a crime, neither one's wife nor one's children would be involved in the punishment. Thus in the case of an immigrant, if such a misfortune should befall him, one solace he could still have was that his family would still be free and secure, with as much chance to make a living for themselves as others.

Had the aims of Ji Chang's government been confined to the furtherance of the above policies, he would undoubtedly have been treated by later historians as an astute statesman of his time who had made his nation more populous, richer, and stronger. However, Confucius rated him much more highly, even though the great sage himself was a descendant of the house of Shang, which the Zhou overthrew. Said Confucius:

> In the *Book of Poetry*, it is written, "Profound was Wen Wang. Clearly and unceasingly, with reverence he conducted himself toward the goal." [44] For a ruler of men, the goal is humanity.[45]

Indeed, all Ji Chang's actions seemed to have been oriented toward that goal, and all his motivations to have sprung from genuine and spontaneous sentiments of compassion—compassion for men in general and compassion for the weak and destitute in particular. There is a story about him which, though trivial, illustrates well this aspect of his nature.[46] "Under his orders a pond was being dug, in the process of which a skeleton was found. Upon being reported the matter by an officer, he instructed, 'Bury the dead fittingly at another place.' But the officer said, 'The dead has no one responsible for him.' Answered the prince, 'He who claims the possession of the world must be responsible for everyone in the world. He who claims the possession of a princedom must be responsible for everyone in his princedom. Should I not be responsible for this dead man?' So the skeleton was buried with clothes and coffin and all in a manner fitting and proper."

And Mencius reports further in his book:

There were those old and wifeless, the widowers; or old and husbandless, the widows; or old and childless, the lonely ones; or young and fatherless, the or- phans—these four classes are the most destitute of the people, having no one to whom they can tell their wants. And Wen Wang, with his government aimed at the pursuit of humanity, always made these four classes the first objects of his regard.[47]

And according to the same authority, Ji Chang seems to have developed a social-security system to take care of the old, which, though primitive in our eyes, was evidently quite practical in his time.

Boyi,[48] avoiding Zou, was dwelling on the coast of the northern sea when he heard of the rise of Wen Wang. He roused himself and said, "Let me go and follow him. I have heard that *xibo* [49] knows how to take good care of the old."

Taigong,[50] avoiding Zou, was dwelling on the coast of the eastern sea when he heard of the rise of Wen Wang. He roused himself and said, "Let me go and follow him. I have heard that *xibo* knows how to take good care of the old."

(But how did Wen Wang take care of the old?)

To every homestead five *mu* were allocated (for private use). Around the walls were planted mulberry trees, with which the women fed the silkworms; and thus the old were able to have silk to wear. (Each family was provided with) five brood hens and two brood sows, which were kept to their breeding seasons; and thus the old were able to have meat to eat. Each husbandman cultivating his field of one hundred *mu*, his family—say, of eight mouths—would be secure against hunger.

This is how it was said that *xibo* knew how to take good care of the old. He regulated the fields and dwellings for the people; he taught them to plant the mulberry trees and to feed and breed those animals; he directed their wives and children as to how they should nourish their aged. At fifty, a man cannot keep himself warm without silk. At seventy, his appetite cannot be satisfied without meat. When not kept warm, a person suffers cold; when not supplied with enough nourishing food, a man suffers starvation. Among Wen Wang's subjects, there were no aged people who suffered cold or starvation. This is how it was done.[51]

The above, of course, represents only fragmentary aspects of Ji Chang's innovations; it by no means gives a full picture of his entire program. Never- theless, the essential spirit that motivated Ji Chang in his doings can be palpably felt through them. In fact, this was made very plain by a sort of rhymed summation, which in our modern times would have been called a jingle or a slogan, and which was very likely composed by Ji Chang himself in order to show his true intent to the people:

> Zhou may have its kith and kin,
> But none is rated worthier than a virtuous man.
> And whatever wrongs any one of the people may have done,
> The blame shall be laid on me, your prince, the one man.[52]

The success of Ji Chang's program has subsequent history as its testimony. No doubt the number of migrants attracted to Zhou could not have been many at first. But as Ji Chang persevered over the years, it may be said that both his intentions and his actions were constantly put to test; and as they were never found wanting, his fame was bound to rise and the immigration to increase. Then, after some twenty or thirty years, unexpected assistance came from a quarter he least expected. While word of his benevolent rule spread, Di Xin's misrule became more and more manifest in the empire. The contrast grew so sharp and conspicuous that many who were driven to flee the oppressions and atrocities of Yin automatically and unhesitatingly sought refuge in the far borderland of Zhou.[53]

And Ji Chang devoted much of his time to seek out the virtuous and capable men from among the immigrants and place them in positions of responsibility and trust. And talking with them, he would even forgo his noonday meal, when there was not enough time.[54] And true to his word, he treated them as equals to his own kith and kin. When his fourth son, the celebrated Duke of Zhou, later spoke of the ministers who had helped him effectively during his reign, out of the five names mentioned, only one was his kinsman, and the other four were apparently outsiders.[55] As a matter of fact, two of them, before their elevation, had employed themselves as mere trappers.[56] However, of all those who came to Zhou, none are better known to the latter-day Chinese than Boyi and Taigong, mentioned by Mencius in the passage we have quoted above. But strange as it is, Boyi represents not one man, but two; and Taigong is not a real name at all.

When Mencius spoke of Boyi, he actually meant two brothers—Boyi and Shuqi. Describing these two, an ancient authority said, "Their eyes would not look at discordant colors; their ears would not hear discordant sounds. If a ruler was not what they thought a ruler ought to be, they would not serve him. If a people were not what they thought a people ought to be, they would not be ruler to them. They would not live in any place where violent government obtained, or where violent people resided." [57] In short, they were pure and singleminded idealists, believing in pacifism and detesting anything that savored of violence or contention. By birth, they were sons of the Prince of Guzhu, a state situated on the western borders of modern

Manchuria. After their father's death, Boyi, being the eldest son, should have inherited the patrimony; but declaring that the deceased parent would have preferred Shuqi as successor, he fled the country to pursue a hermit's life. But Shuqi, instead of taking over the throne, left it to the charge of a third brother, and went to live with Boyi. However, finding the world, especially Yin under Di Xin, quite repulsive, and hearing about the exemplary rule of Ji Chang, they finally made their way to Zhou. But as they did not seek to be known, they lived a quiet, retired life of their own, and took no part in Zhou government. It was only after Ji Chang's death that through an act not of their making, nor to their liking, they cut a unique and distinctive place for themselves in ancient Chinese history.

Taigong is an entirely different historical figure. While Boyi and Shuqi are personalities known only to a limited number of sophisticated people in China, Taigong has been celebrated as a popular hero in folklore over the centuries.[58] To the students of military science, Taigong is generally recognized as the foremost master of the early times, even though the book attributed to him is not regarded as all authentic.[59] As a matter of fact, from the 8th century A.D. down to the later part of the 14th, he was venerated as the deity of war; and temples were built by the dynasties in those some six hundred years in every corner of China in his honor.[60] Moreover, for those who believe that human affairs are inalterably controlled by Fate, Taigong is always cited as the classical example of a man who, despite his learning and ability, was predestined not to prosper till very late in life, not a moment sooner. For he did not meet Ji Chang until he was seventy-two years old,[61] whereupon he was raised from total obscurity to the highest position of honor. And some twenty years afterward, serving as the chief of staff of Zhou's armed forces, he led them to final triumph over Yin. For this feat of arms he was invested with one of the largest fiefs of the empire, which he transmitted to his descendants for many generations. He did not die until he was well over a hundred years old.[62]

Although Taigong's origin was traced back to the so-called Four Mountains of Emperor Yao,[63] we know very little about his life before his arrival in Zhou. He was said to be a native of the eastern seacoast, and his given name was Shang.[64] But inasmuch as the descendants of the Four Mountains happened to possess two different surnames, Jiang and Lu, he was alternately known as Jiang Shang and Lu Shang, with the former adopted in the folklore and the latter in the authoritative *Historical Records*. According to some ancient sources, he had also a courtesy name, Ziya, or simply Ya.[65] This seems indeed to be one of the very first times in Chinese history when a man was recorded to have a courtesy name in addition to his given name. And this instance may very well have been the occasion by virtue of which the usage began to come into fashion. For after his meeting with Ji Chang, the latter respected him so much that he never called him by name but addressed him invariably with deference and affection as *shishangfu*—"Teacher, Uncle Shang." [66] If the prince chose to be so reverential, how could the others be less than respectful? Hence the necessity for Taigong's associates to give him a courtesy name by which they could call him.

There is no question but that he was one of the best informed and most learned men of his time. Of Ji Chang's four outsider-ministers mentioned by the Duke of Zhou, three were said to have studied previously under him.[67] There is also no question that he was endowed with an exceedingly ingenious and resourceful mind. For in the contest with Yin, history ascribes most of the crafty machinations of Zhou to his invention. Yet for all this, when he came to Zhou, he was described as "poor, destitute, and very advanced in years." [68] Some accounts had it that he had sought employment in divers princedoms before, and had actually served Di Xin at Yin at one time. But for one reason or another he had been rejected or dismissed by them; none of them had found any use for his talents.[69] Others told that he was driven to employ himself as a butcher at the resort town of Chaoge,[70] and then as a rice dealer at Mengjin, an important crossing point on the Yellow River.[71] But in both cases, because of fortuitous circumstances, his business adventures had ended in abysmal failure.[72] There is also a tale that he was married to an old spinster with some inheritance who had financed these transactions; but as a result of the reverses, she had him summarily divorced and chased out of her house.[73]

But no matter how different the accounts of his early life are, all sources agree on the circumstances of his first meeting with the Prince of Zhou.[74] It was a day Ji Chang had chosen for hunting. But interested in the art of divination as he was, before he set off, he sought a prediction. The answer he got was far from what he had anticipated. It said, "What is to be captured is neither a dragon nor a serpent, neither a tiger nor a bear, but something far more helpful to a ruler of men." And Ji Chang went wondering. Now he came to the north bank of the Wei River. And beside a spring on the Sandy Rock Creek (Panxi)[75] he saw an old man fishing with a hook, the curved prong of which had been straightened.[76] He knew that the mind of the angler was not on fishing, and he fell into talking with him. And once the talk started, he became so impressed that in the end he said, "You are precisely the kind of man my grandfather looked for." So he took him home in his own chariot, and installed him as his teacher. While thenceforth he never called him by any name other than "Teacher, Uncle Shang," others began to refer to him as *taigongwang,* "the man Grand Duke had looked for." And in time this was simply shortened into Taigong.

From there on there was no major decision taken by Ji Chang without first consulting with Taigong. What they conferred about was not recorded;

but it may be safely assumed that all their discussions were centered on the ways and means of further strengthening the state of Zhou. And from an examination of subsequent events and a study of such books as *Zhou Li,* reputedly written by Ji Chang's son the Duke of Zhou himself, a conclusion may be reached that the plans they first drew together were connected with the civil and military reorganization of Ji Chang's princedom. They continued the use of the well-field system for the allocation of land,[77] but organized their civil administration more or less in accordance with the following table:[78]

CIVIL ORGANIZATION	
UNITS	*NUMBER OF FAMILIES*
bi, "neighborhood"	5
lu, "village" (5 *bi*)	25
zu, "clan" (4 *lu*)	100
dang, "ward" (5 *zu*)	500
zhou, "district" (5 *dang*)	2,500
xiang, "department" (5 *zhou*)	12,500

And side by side with the civil administration, their military organization may be listed as follows:[79]

MILITARY ORGANIZATION	
UNITS	*NUMBER OF MEN*
wu, "squad"	5
liang, "platoon" (5 *wu*)	25
zu,[80] "company" (4 *liang*)	100
lu, "battalion" (5 *zu*)	500
shi, "division" (5 *lu*)	2,500
jun, "army" (5 *shi*)	12,500

From an examination of the two tables, it may be readily seen that the scheme of civil administration furnished the very basis for that of military organization. Roughly speaking, from each family of the nation an able-bodied man was drafted for the service. The Zhou, however, appears to have developed a rather sophisticated system of conscription that aimed at greater equity. Though for our purpose it is too complex to describe in detail because it was interlinked with the allocation of land which was divided into three grades—superior, medium, and inferior land—a bare outline may be sketched here. For a family of seven persons, on the average three males between fifteen and sixty-five years old were considered usable;[81] for two families each of six, five males were considered usable; and for a family of five, two were considered usable. But when mobilization was ordered for a major undertaking away from home, the rule was that from each family no more than one man was to be conscripted. The rest were to be held as reserves, or required to attend to the duties or works left unattended by those who had departed.[82]

A distinctive feature of the system is that the officers of both the civil administration and the military organization were the same body of men. For each unit of civil administration, from "neighborhood" and "village" on to "district" and "department," there was of course an administrator, each with a different title to suit his station. When an order for military mobilization took place, it was these same administrators who served as officers in command of their respective units. Thus, automatically, the neighborhood leader became the sergeant of his squad of five, and the chief administrator of the department the commanding general of his army of 12,500 men. We have no information of how large the population of Zhou was in the last years of Ji Chang's reign, or of how many departments his princedom was divided into. But we know that when his son Wu Wang finally embarked on the conquest of Yin, his invading troops numbered 45,000.[83] As an army was composed of 12,500 men, this would amount to 3.6 armies. According to many authoritative sources, when the Zhou first established their empire, they decreed that only the emperor could have an armed force of six armies.[84] Of course, this could have been a later regulation; but it could also have been the actual practice of Ji Chang and his son. And presumably, when the latter invaded Yin, he must have left sufficient troops behind to guard the rear and maintain peace and order in Zhou. So to have kept 2.4 armies for that use would not have been unreasonable. If so, then supposing that Zhou had divided the entire population into six departments, and that the average family was one of six persons, it may be computed that at that time Zhou had altogether a population of some 450,000.

Perhaps we should have given the "military organization" a different name. For its functions were not entirely military. According to the book *Zhou Li*, it was "to form the basis of the armed force, to work on labor projects in the fields, to suppress and pursue robbers and thieves, to enforce the collection of taxes and levies." [85] In the reign of Ji Chang, that is, before his imprisonment by Di Xin, this organization was probably used for the three latter, and not at all for military, purposes. Nonetheless, military training and military exercises were held regularly in every season of the year in the form of hunting, and the strictest discipline was inculcated and maintained.[86]

The advantage of this system is self-evident. The officers are accustomed to the men; and the men are accustomed to one another. As has been noted by a famed commentator,[87] the organization is so structured in order that "the men's feelings for one another will incline them toward mutual concern; their loyalties for one another will urge them toward reciprocal assistance; they can recognize one another by apparels and appearance in the daytime, and by voices and sounds in the dark." In an agrarian society, where the population is largely tied to the land, perhaps no political system is more conducive to effective government than this one. It needs no constabulary or police to maintain peace and order; the people themselves constitute one permanent and ubiquitous vigilance committee. Hardly any expenditure is needed for public works projects; except for articles not locally obtainable, all materials and all manpower may be supplied by the communities involved. Nor is there a large staff required for any level of local administration; other than a few necessary full-time scribes or custodians, most of the positions can be taken by part-time "usable" men drafted for the work. And incidentally, no organization can produce a more accurate and complete census at any moment's notice. For all units of the administration will see to it that no misrepresentation will occur, since each of the families is obligated to fulfill its quota of conscription on the basis of the census. It is indeed as is described by many Chinese scholars, "The system is as efficient as the mind directing the arm, the arm the wrist, and the wrist the fingers." And inasmuch as it is also the least expensive way to train and maintain the largest possible standing army, it has also been postulated by numerous Chinese statesmen as the policy "that houses the soldier within the habitation of the husbandman." And ever since the time of Zhou, most Chinese dynasties have modeled their local administration, with various degrees of modification, after this structure devised by Ji Chang and Taigong. It is even so with the so-called system of "people's communes" which the Chinese Communists have adopted today.

In addition, there is some reason to believe that Taigong might have revolutionized the Chinese art of making war at this juncture, especially in the use of chariots. As we know, this was an era in which cavalry had not yet come into use. Until the stirrup was invented, which was still about some eight centuries away, no horse rider could shoot his arrow straight or lunge his spear firmly. At this time, the horse was therefore used either to carry a messenger or to draw a chariot. As noted before, chariots had been used in battle as early as the time of Qi(Kai), son of Yu the Great, when he fought against the people of Hu.[88] But down to the time of Taigong, these had been used, either singly or severally, more as a means of conveyance for princes or generals than as a principal weapon of war. Thus, as we have read before, though Emperor Wuding suffered an accident while riding on a chariot in a hunt, throughout his three years' war against the northwestern tribes, among all the oracle-bone inscriptions related to his military preparations and campaigns, the word "chariot" was not mentioned a single time. But when Zhou and Yin fought their final battle, it was specifically recorded that Zhou had on its side "three hundred war chariots." [89] Each war chariot in those days was drawn by four horses, and carried three armored warriors standing inside its coverless coach box, with the one at the center serving as the driver, and the two others at the right and left wielding weapons, flanked and followed by seventy-two foot soldiers.[90] It seems that under Taigong's guidance the Zhou began to train and deploy the chariots in groups of five, ten, fifty, and even one hundred. In the book attributed to him, he was said to have expounded to this effect: "Chariots are to be used to assault the enemy's strong positions, to crush his obduracy, and to bar his retreat. . . . With a hundred chariots, ten thousand foot soldiers can be routed." He also outlined ten situations in which chariots should not be employed, and eight opportunities when they could be used with advantage.[91] Clearly when the Zhou and Yin fought that fateful and decisive battle at Shepherds' Wild (*muye*),[92] the Zhou chariots were precisely deployed as Taigong had directed. And the terrifying effect it produced then is conceivably not unlike that created by the very first massive use of armored tanks in modern warfare.

To return to Zhou, while Taigong bent his energies on improving its armed force, Ji Chang laid more emphasis on instructing the people in the higher ideals of ethics and human relationships. He sought "to inculcate the principle of reverence toward life through ceremonies of various venerations so that the people would not become reckless and abandoned to passions; to inculcate the principles of dignity for oneself and consideration for others through ceremonies of competitive archery and goodfellowship festivals held in each community so that the people would not become contentious and bellicose; to inculcate the principles of proper attachment between the sexes through ceremonies of betrothal and marriage so that the people would not be led astray by unruly emotions; to inculcate the principles of harmony through music so that the people would not become discordant . . . and to inculcate the principle of good living through hard work by building up sound customs and traditions so that the people would not become idle and indolent." [93] And in his political organization, Ji Chang sought that "within a neighborhood the 5 families should labor for mutual protection; within a village the 25 families should shelter one another in need; within a clan the 100 families should share one another's grief and bury their dead together; within a ward the 500 families should rescue one another in emergency; within a district the 2,500 families should give aid and succor to one another whenever necessary, and within a department the 12,500 families should visit with and learn from one another." [94]

Moreover, just as there are reasons to believe that Taigong revolutionized ancient Chinese warfare by introducing the use of chariots en masse, so there are grounds to affirm that Ji Chang was the man who founded the first educational system in China. As a rule, Chinese historians used to ascribe this particular distinction to Emperor Shun for his having established a ministry of music to instruct the heirs apparent of subordinate princedoms in the importance of harmony and proper conduct. And traditionally it has been maintained that both the Xia and the Shang dynasties had continued the practice, each using a different name for the institution.[95] But with the discovery of the oracle bones, no confirmation for such allegations has been found. In the case of Zhou, however, there are ample proofs that Ji Chang did establish an academy for advanced students in his capital—a hall circled with water called *biyong*.[96] In the countryside, primary schools were also established for the enrollment of boys starting with the age of eight. After they reached fifteen, if they qualified, they could enter the academy to be educated along with the sons of officers and nobles.[97] In the academy there were "three elderly men of virtue" and "five men with varied experiences" serving as instructors.[98]

From a study of all available records about Ji Chang, therefore, one cannot help being convinced that in the first two-thirds of his rule of Zhou, even though he had probably begun it with his grandfather's idea of "clipping Shang" in his mind, and with the injustices his father had suffered at the hands of the imperial court in his memory, he had soon grown out of the narrow confines of such vainglorious ambitions and petty vengefulness. His became truly a mind concerned only with the raising of cultural standards for men. And he seems to have found personal satisfaction in nothing else than giving his people a government that could lead them in the right direction. Indeed, if we may say so, he appears to have identified himself with the cause of the advancement of Culture, with a capital C. And Confucius especially deeply appreciated this trait of Ji Chang's character, and inwardly considered him as his own spiritual predecessor. When, some six centuries later, the sage's life was threatened by the people of Kuang, who had mistaken him for a man they abominated, as his disciples all feared grievously for his safety, in desperation he consoled them with these words:

> After the death of Wen Wang, is not the cause of Culture lodged here in me? If Heaven had wished to let the cause of Culture perish, it should not have given me a chance to know of the cause and take part in it; if Heaven does not wish to let the cause of Culture perish, what can the people of Kuang do to me?[99]

This profession, while revealing Confucius's own innermost aspirations, perhaps even more loudly proclaims his admiration for Ji Chang.

And throughout this period Ji Chang seems to have entertained no designs on the authority of Yin. If he had encouraged Taigong to strengthen Zhou's military forces, it was more for self-protection than for aggression. In *Mencius* there is an allusion to an event, which on the one hand shows that much of the history of this period has been lost, and on the other reveals Ji Chang as a man unfailingly oriented toward the ends of harmony, nonviolence, and peaceful coexistence among men. The passage reads:

> It requires a perfectly virtuous prince to be able, with a great country, to serve a small one—as, for instance, Tang served Ge,[100] and Wen Wang served Kunyi.[101]

We know little about Kunyi. But the character *yi* signifies big men brandishing bows, or, in other words, a tribe of fierce nomads. So conceivably Kunyi were remnants of Guifang whom Emperor Wuding had suppressed before.[102] As noted above, most of the nomads who had coveted the land of Zhou had been chased away by Duke Ji, Ji Chang's father. But it is not unlikely that after several decades they returned to haunt and harass their old prey. To their surprise they found Zhou quite different from other border states—not only more prosperous, but far more numerous and far better organized and armed. Indeed, had Ji Chang so wished, he could easily have chastened Kunyi, or even subjugated and enslaved them. But Ji Chang did nothing like that. Even though we have no knowledge of what exactly took place, it may be assumed, as the event was likened to Tang and Ge, that instead of fighting or even frightening off the savage nomads, Ji Chang simply gave them sufficient presents to satisfy their wants. And realizing how strong and well prepared the Zhou were, Kunyi just accepted and enjoyed these peace offerings regularly and acquiesced in the arrangement for quite a length of time.

Since this was how Ji Chang had conducted himself toward Kunyi, his behavior toward Yin must have been even more respectful and submissive. Indeed, had not the Yin emperor, Di Xin, decided just then to take an action which was unprecedented in relations between Yin and Zhou, the course of history might have been entirely different. But, as it was, he summoned Ji Chang to the capital to serve in the imperial court as one of his three high councilors *(gong)*.

· 3 ·

DI XIN'S MISRULE AND JI CHANG'S IMPRISONMENT
(1131–1124 B.C.)

Di Xin returned from his expedition against the southeastern tribes probably at the time Ji Chang was beginning to see some results from the measures he had so assiduously introduced to encourage migration to Zhou. If Di Xin had any knowledge of it, he probably disregarded it as nothing of importance. He had just traversed much of the southeastern frontier of the empire; the population there was very sparse. The northwest must have been similar in this respect; therefore, it was no wonder, and certainly no offense, that an upstart like Zhou should want a larger population.

At any rate, elated with success in his recent expedition, the youthful monarch was bent on proving to the world that "there existed no man but was inferior to him." [103] He dabbled at first in government, and it must be said that the early results were good. The men he chose to occupy high positions were all known to be virtuous men. In the councils of the imperial house itself, he paid due deference to his elder brother, Prince of Wei, whose worthiness had long been recognized by all.[104] Then there were two positions of great honor, though devoid of actual power—senior tutor and junior tutor. Whether or not it was Di Xin himself who had created these offices to gain the goodwill of his kinsmen, we cannot be sure; but for the first post he named Jizi, one of his uncles, widely acclaimed for learning and wisdom; and for the second, he selected a cousin, Bigan, reputed for integrity. And these three—Prince of Wei, Jizi, and Bigan—were called the "three good men of Yin" later by Confucius.[105] As to the actual administration of his government, Di Xin also found a few honest men to put in charge; one was Shang Rong, a man whom even the Zhou came later to respect. Moreover, from an extensive study of the oracle bones, a modern scholar maintains that under Di Xin, the veneration ceremonies were more systematically simplified, and the divination inscriptions were recorded with greater care and accuracy, than in any of his predecessors' reigns; and that if such things could be taken as a sort of criterion to evaluate the efficacy of Yin government, Di Xin should be adjudged a very capable and efficient administrator.[106]

However, from the same oracle bones, we also learn that Di Xin hunted 310 times in eighty-seven different places.[107] And it should be noted that this count does not cover his entire reign, only those years that produced the inscriptions. Because it is impossible to tell what years these were, we can only venture an estimate of the span. If he hunted on the average ten times a year, it should be thirty-one years; if twenty times, then fifteen and a half years. As we know for certain that his expedition to the southeast fell in the tenth and eleventh years of his reign,[108] so it may be conjectured that his love for the chase was displayed for some fifteen to thirty years, in other words, in the very prime of his life, when he was between twenty and fifty years old. This point is raised here not to dispute his ability and efficacy as an administrator, but rather to demonstrate that he shortly became bored with details of administration.

There is also a story that illustrates his growing appetite for luxury. Chopsticks had then begun to come into use; but instead of having them made of bamboo or wood as was the practice, he had them manufactured of ivory especially for himself. Upon hearing of this, Jizi, the senior tutor, was said to have mused:

> Now he has made ivory chopsticks. It is not likely that he will continue to have food contained in earthenware; to be sure, he will have bowls made of jade. With ivory chopsticks and jade bowls, he will certainly not be content with coarse fare, rough clothing, or thatched dwellings. He will have garments of many layers of silk, high pavilions and spacious halls. And he will demand everything in similar measure; and the whole wide world may not be enough to gratify his wants. How much do I dread the end![109]

Had not events proved Jizi right, his lamentations over chopsticks might be laughed off as the unnecessary rant of an overly conservative mind. But the sagacious senior tutor had been observing the restless sovereign for years; his judgment, though prompted by the making of ivory chopsticks, was based on much more. At any rate, like many of the events pertaining to this period, we have no definitive ideas about their proper chronology.[110] Conceivably this incident happened after Di Xin became bored not only with government but also possibly with the chase, when his shifty and capricious mind started wandering off in search of new thrills and unexplored pleasures.

Di Xin was now approaching fifty. He had been lord and master of the Yin Empire over forty years. If formerly he had wanted to prove to the world that "there existed no man but was inferior to him," now he believed he had proved it. He made it a point to keep his elder brother, Prince of Wei, at a distance; and he seldom gave audience to the senior tutor, Jizi, or to the junior tutor, Bigan. He sought advice from none, and he brooked not the slightest show of disobedience or even difference. Just beyond the north of the imperial domain, not far from Yin, there was a state called Su, which for some reason or for no reason at all incurred his displeasure; and making a mountain out of a molehill, he led a force in person to punish it. But the people of Su knew the best way to soothe his anger; they presented him with their fairest maiden, Daji by name. And once Di Xin took her, he doted upon her no end. There was nothing that he would not do to please the new concubine.[111] He had heard many pieces of music and seen many kinds of dance before; but now he ordered the best musicians of the empire to compose new music so that Daji and her maids could dance to it for him. The old music and dance, composed for veneration purposes, had been solemn and somber rather than entertaining; now he wanted compositions to be pleasing, provocative, totally free from inhibition.[112] Although he had built many pleasure palaces before, he now started building a far better one for his favorite, south of Yin near Chaoge, which he called Deer Terrace. The halls and chambers were constructed of precious stones, and the gates of marble.[113] The palace was about two kilometers square; and from the ground up to the top of the building overlooking a hill, the height was over a thousand feet. It took seven years to complete. Because of the expense, Di Xin levied new tributes and increased the collection of grains throughout the empire. In addition, he searched far and wide for dogs, horses, and beautiful and curious objects to fill the palace and to amuse Daji.[114]

While Di Xin's oppressive misrule was becoming daily more transparent, the reputation of Ji Chang's benevolent government was growing. The emperor was perhaps too busy entertaining, or being entertained by, his concubine to be aware of the contrast until it was brought to his notice by Prince Hu of Chong, a neighbor of Zhou. Chong was situated inside the West Land, but on the south of the Wei River; and watching Zhou's constant and continuing growth on the opposite shores, Prince Hu took alarm. He reported Ji Chang's activities to Di Xin, insinuating that Ji Chang had been deliberately pursuing a course of action to show the emperor to disadvantage.[115] If Prince Hu had expected an instant outburst of imperial wrath, he was disappointed. For in line with his egomaniacal mind, the emperor prided himself on his devious shrewdness. Instead of denouncing Ji Chang or ordering an expedition against Zhou, he summoned the calumniated prince to come to Yin to serve as one of the "three high councilors" in the court.[116]

The institution of *sangong* or "three high councilors" was a very ancient one. It was not a regular estabishment, but according to tradition, if the emperor saw fit, he could name three men whom he considered the worthiest in his empire to the post, whose duties were "to sit down and discuss the policies and principles of government" with him.[117] Thus on this occasion, besides Ji Chang, Di Xin appointed two other men—the Prince of Jiu [118] and the Prince of E.[119] These were princes of two states adjacent to the Central Shang, who were apparently well regarded by the people and who were also suspected of being critical of him. So the ancient institution was revived and the appointments were made, outwardly to honor the three men but actually to put all of them under close surveillance at the imperial seat.

Of the three, Ji Chang was the only one in a position to defy the command. His princedom, strictly speaking, was not an enfeoffed state. What territories Zhou had acquired it had won by itself. Although its population was as yet far smaller than that of the Central Shang, its armed force, with all the improvements introduced by Taigong, could be counted upon to acquit itself well against any outside invasion. Moreover, the emperor's capriciousness was well known; while there was no apparent cause for his granting the Prince of Zhou such a singular honor, there was every reason to fear a harmful design. These thoughts must have crossed Ji Chang's mind, and many of his advisers must have argued against his acceptance of the appointment. But in the end Ji Chang himself decided to obey the emperor's summons. He had taught his people to value culture above violence; could he espouse the cause of violence at the very appearance of a first test? He had sought to inculcate loyalty in his own men; could he afford to be disloyal to his own acknowleged superior? He said, "If a father is not virtuous, should the son therefore refuse to serve him? If a sovereign is not well intentioned, should a subject refuse to minister to him on that score? I, who have acknowledged allegiance to the emperor, will never rebel against him." [120] And he came to Yin.

The three high councilors assumed office, however, only to regret it. They were not allowed to discuss any policies or principles of government, but instead they were made to feel the perpetual presence of dire tension and imminent peril. Of the three, the Prince of Jiu was the first to break. In desperation he tried to ingratiate himself with the despot by following the example of the people of Su and presenting him with a beautiful maiden. But unfortunately for him, when the damsel was brought to the monarch's embrace, she found his majesty's person repugnant and revolting. This was a mortification Di Xin had never experienced before. He flew into uncontrollable rage. And such was the fury of a man spurned that, not satisfied with putting the girl to death on the spot, he ordered her sponsor to be also killed and his body ground into minced meat. Thereupon the Prince of E denounced the atrocity to the tyrant's face, and got himself similarly treated for his pains.[121]

Ji Chang heard of this and sighed. But he did not know that he was being watched by Prince Hu of Chong, who had come to Yin especially for the purpose, and who now hastened to report to Di Xin, adding: "Ji Chang has been piling up good and virtuous deeds. He appears to be very good-natured, but is truly crafty. His crown prince, Ji Fa, is an audacious and determined man. And he has another son, Ji Dan, who is humble, thrifty, and well versed in all the knowledge of our day. If we must compete with them in the conduct of government, we shall suffer in the comparison. If we let Ji Chang go free, we shall come to disaster in the end. The right place for a cap, however old, is on the top of the head; and the right place for the shoes, however new, is to be trod by the feet. The one thing certain is that Ji Chang is planning to subvert your majesty. It is best that he be done away with before his plans come to fruition." [122] But once again Prince Hu overshot the mark. For by this time Di Xin had cooled his rage sufficiently. Returning to his crafty self, he thought that if he should put Ji Chang to death, he would still have his sons to deal with. He ordered imprisonment instead.

Thus Ji Chang was imprisoned at a place called Youli,[123] not far from Deer Terrace, for some seven years.[124] Had Ji Chang been an ordinary man, he might have found it hard to maintain his sanity, hearing almost daily about new and gruesome cruelties that the tyrant had devised or perpetrated, and not knowing when his own turn for suffering a horrible death would come. But he concentrated his attention on the study of a subject which had long interested him—the art of divination. Formerly, while in Zhou, even though he was fascinated as much by the intellectual as by the supernatural aspects of the art, he had been too busy running a government to have sufficient time to engage in systematic speculations. But now he had all his time to himself. And out of the tireless study of seven years came the scheme of thought both in symbols and in writing that forms the core of a unique book—*Zhou Yi*, or *Yi Jing (I Ching)*, the *Book of Changes*.[125]

From time immemorial the Chinese had practiced two principal ways of divination. One was "to burn a tortoiseshell and examine its cracks," and the other "to let *shi* stalks fall through one's fingers to determine the numbers." [126] But the art of interpreting the cracks or the numbers has been long lost.[127] There is, however, reason to assume that the interpretations were all based on postulations that originated from the Eight Trigrams attributed to Paoxi.[128] By the time of Ji Chang, two schools appear to have developed. The first was called *linshan*, "linking the mountains," supposedly introduced or practiced in the Xia dynasty; and the second *guicang*, "returning to storage," devised or improved by the Yin, or Shang.[129] Presumably the two schools passed on their experiences, or teachings, more by mouth than by writing, more by symbols than by words. And Ji Chang, with his special interest in divination, must have been thoroughly versed in both of them. It is no wonder that he found neither of them up to his own standards. For these two systems were developed not consistently or methodically, but desultorily and sporadically from time to time by various diviners.

From the standpoint of history, perhaps too much credit has been given to Ji Chang's contribution to the *Book of Changes*. For one thing, the Chinese traditionally believed that it was this "Cultural Emperor of Zhou" who first put one trigram upon another and transposed the two into a hexagram; and by alternating the positions of the Eight Trigrams up and down, had formed altogether sixty-four hexagrams. For instance, when a ☰ is placed on another ☰, you have ䷀; and when it is placed upon ☷, you have ䷊; and when the positions are reversed, the hexagram becomes ䷋. But this practice seems to have existed long before Ji Chang.[130] What he found wanting was not in the number of hexagrams, but in the significance ascribed to each of them. Many hexagrams may have been transmitted without any meaning attached to them; others may have been given meanings, but meanings, from Ji Chang's point of view, that had been imperfectly construed. And, above all, since both systems, whether "linking the mountains" or "returning to storage," were random structures erected by many a hand from different eras and with varying degrees of intellect, neither possessed a unity of thought or a concord in design. So Ji Chang brushed them aside as materials useful only for reference, and worked entirely anew on a scheme of his own. As there are sixty-four hexagrams, so there are 384 lines, six broken or unbroken lines for each hexagram. Ji Chang gave meaning not only to every hexagram, but also to every line. It seems that wherever the explanations of either of the two schools were usable, he would use them. Wherever their wording was too crude, he would refine it. But throughout, his own meditations were his guide, so that the general philosophy which pervades every line and every hexagram is his. Later, his son Ji Dan, the famed Duke of Zhou, saw fit to add some comments to the work here and there; and when Confucius studied it some six centuries after, he also wrote further commentaries, which have come to be known as the *Ten Wings*. These three portions now appear together as one volume in the Chinese classics—the *Book of Changes*.

Instead of being considered a book of philosophy, the popular conception of the *Book of Changes*—one hesitates to say "misconception"—is that of a wonder book for forecasting the future: If one could only penetrate into the deep recesses of its treasured secrets, there would be nothing about one's destiny barred from precognition. How much truth there is in this, or whether such a book is at all possible, it is not for a historian to say. From the historical point of view, however, it can be seen that the philosophy of the work conforms to the circumstances Ji Chang was then in, and how he might well have viewed them. This is evident in the evaluation he gave to two hexagrams. The sixty-four hexagrams are headed by the hexagram ☰, called *qian*, which represents Heaven, or the essence of positive force in the universe or in human activities. The Duke of Zhou summed up his father's analyses of this foremost hexagram with this comment: "Heaven walks ever vigorously; taking example, a cultured man forever seeks to improve on himself and never ceases." Then, of all the sixty-four hexagrams, there is only one with its six lines each free of calamity, mishap, or regret. But the hexagram is not the one representing Heaven but another. For, with all its positive virtues, the topmost line of *qian*, becoming overvigorous and overconfident, is headed toward an inevitable fall. The hexagram that is entirely removed from such defects is ☷, called Humility. The obvious idea is that if one is humble by nature or by cultivation, and acts continually in that spirit, no matter in what distress he may find himself, he will always be able to come out unharmed. From these hexagrams one can visualize the philosophy with which Ji Chang must have inspired himself during his imprisonment. Even while his life was hanging on a thread for seven years, he did not neglect to improve himself and persevere in the task, just as the sun walks across the sky, day in and day out. Again, even though his own situation looked so desperate and hopeless, he continued unswervingly to let meekness be his guide. From this, therefore, one may also perceive the motivation for the entire structure of his work. The sixty-four hexagrams represent the large contours of sixty-four possible situations in human life; and the 384 lines represent the varying predicaments in which an individual may find himself within one of these general situations. And through a philosophy of self-improvement and perseverance, humility and patience, Ji Chang sought less to forecast the future than to furnish a guidebook for the 384 possible human conditions, so that, given a particular predicament within a particular situation, an individual might know what dangers or pitfalls he should beware of as well as how best to conduct himself.

To return to our narration, while the Prince of Zhou was thus cudgeling his brains over this scheme of thought in perpetual fear that his brains might at any moment be actually cudgeled out of him, the emperor was also feeling some stings of uneasiness. The monstrous slaughter of the two well-regarded princes so adjacent to the imperial domain did not contribute to the continuance of solid support from the people of the Central Shang. Nor did the imprisonment of the innocuous Ji Chang reinforce the fidelity of the enfeoffed princes in the Four Lands. As a matter of fact, many of the princes started wondering openly how they themselves would be treated should they come to the imperial seat and incur the displeasure of the sovereign. As recorded in the *Historical Records,* "The people were becoming resentful, and some of the enfeoffed states began to waver in their allegiance." [131] But Daji, the favorite, persuaded the emperor to think that the cause for this was in his having not displayed the full awesomeness of his majesty: His punishments were too light and the people were not afraid of them; he must make them much harsher. So together they devised a new form of punishment which they called *paoluo,* "scorch and burn." At first they fashioned a sort of large flatiron, subjected it to fire so that it became red-hot, and then forced whomever they condemned to grab it with his bare hands. But this did not work very well, for the condemned could still resist to the utmost of his strength. So in lieu of a flatiron they erected a bronze pillar, covered its surface with fat, and chained the condemned to it. Then they built a fire at the foot of the pillar. As the condemned desperately strove to escape from the scorching heat, he would try to climb up the pillar; but as the pillar was greased, he could not hold onto it for long; yet he would try climbing up again and again, until he was finally exhausted, fell limp into the fire, and was burned to death. The emperor and his favorite would watch the scene laughing.[132] If a moment in history should be chosen to date the time the people of Yin started calling their lord and master Zou,[133] it might well be then.

But though this horrible punishment seemed to have frightened the people into mute submissiveness, it appeared also to discourage more and more enfeoffed princes from coming to the capital to pay court to the emperor. This tendency was becoming annually more noticeable, and at last Di Xin was aroused to take some action. Perhaps the vassal states were already viewing him as debauched, no longer vigorous enough to lead an army or to pursue the chase. If so, he would prove them mistaken. He ordered a big hunt to be held at Li,[134] to the southeast of the Heavenly City Shang, and invited as many princes as would come to join with him in the game.[135] The place was chosen manifestly for two purposes—to remind one and all first of their allegiance to him as the descendant of the great Tang, and second of his own early triumph in the subjugation of the southeastern tribe Renfang. In the chase he did his best to show that he was still his old self. But to many of the participants who watched him closely, he seemed to drink more, and more often than necessary, and not to be clear-headed at times. Rumors of his infirmity started to spread. Hardly after the hunt had ended, the second-largest of the southeastern tribes, Yufang, began to raise the banners of revolt.[136]

Di Xin had already returned to Yin when he received the intelligence. He was reluctant to leave the arms of Daji again. He ordered therefore that an expeditionary force be organized by the frontier states and supplemented by the Yin army to quash the rebellion.[137] The order was obeyed. But then many of the princes of the empire took advantage of the opportunity to express to him a pious wish which was not at all to his liking.

The wish was expressed side by side with a petition brought to him by the envoy of Zhou. During the last seven years, many a mission had been dispatched by that western state to the imperial court, bearing annual tribute or special gifts, and earnestly entreating the release of their prince. But to all these supplications Di Xin had turned a deaf ear. This time, however, the Zhou envoy, San Yisheng, had come with many unique gifts, such as striped horses from the north, white foxes from the west, and huge tortoises from the south; and he had presented them through the emperor's favorite minister, Feizhong.[138] Nor was this all. About the same time the envoy submitted his petition, the pious wish of a large number of enfeoffed princes was also made known to the monarch: If it should be his majesty's intention to continue the detention of the Prince of Zhou, it would be the desire of these princes to come to the capital to share the same punishment.[139] Di Xin was astounded. Was this a threat of concerted revolt?

Cunning man that he was, he immediately summoned the envoy of Zhou and asked him to produce the gifts. Viewing them one by one, he said with obvious glee: "Ah, how loyal your prince must have been to me! Any one of these gifts should have been enough to secure his release; and there are so many of them!" [140] So he thrust aside the pious wish of the princes as if he had never heard it. And forthwith he had Ji Chang brought to his presence. To the latter's surprise, he rewarded him with symbolic bows, arrows, axes, halberds, and appointed him there and then to be *xibo,* "Field Marshal of the West," with full authority to wage war and launch expeditions in the name of his majesty himself. And in making the appointment Di Xin was of course remembering the statecraft he had learned from the experiences of his ancestors—how Shiwei and Dapeng had been made field marshals, (or "hegemons" as they chose to style themselves), and how eventually Wuding had made short shrift of them.[141]

Ji Chang was taken aback by this singular and unexpected honor. However, sensitive to the monarch's suspicious mind, he wished to reassure him that whatever his suspicions, he, a subect, would never make war against his sovereign. But he realized too that such a reassurance, if worded indiscreetly, might be taken for presumption. So he said he would like to requite his majesty's graciousness by surrendering "ten thousand square *li* of territory on the west bank of the Luo River" to the emperor.[142] Now, the boundaries of the West Land of the Yin Empire stopped on the east banks of the Luo River; and all land to the west had always been more or less abandoned to the nomadic tribes. Thus indirectly Ji Chang was saying that since he had been given the authority to wage war, if he should have to use it, he would use it westward and not eastward; and if he should be able to conquer any land, he would be conquering it for the empire and not for himself. And hearing this, Di Xin was well pleased. Then, seizing the moment of the despot's pleasure, Ji Chang requested that the "scorch and burn" punishment be abolished.[143] And the tyrant, to show his magnanimity, consented.

But as Ji Chang was about to depart, cunning again took over Di Xin's considerations. It would be to his advantage to incite the newly appointed field marshal to fight some of the enfeoffed states and thus to weaken, if not to destroy, his popularity among his fellow princes. The emperor volunteered, "Xibo, the one who gave me calumnious information against you is Prince Hu of Chong." [144]

· 4 ·

THE EXPANSION OF ZHOU AFTER JI CHANG'S RELEASE
(1124–1115 B.C.)

Serene and clear-headed as Ji Chang was, when he returned to Zhou, his mind was divided and could not be reconciled with itself. The whole world now knew that he had ample cause to resent Di Xin; and if he should openly revolt at the moment, the whole world would no doubt blame the tyrant rather than him. Yet for all the bitterness he felt, he could not bring himself to do violence to his own pledge of fidelity to Yin. Out of these conflicting sentiments he was certain of only one thing: While he must do his best to avoid an open rift with Di Xin, he must also do everything possible to secure the safety and preservation of Zhou.

On leaving for Yin to take up the post of high councilor seven years before, Ji Chang had left the princedom in charge of his son, Crown Prince Ji Fa, and bidden him consult with the ministers he had chosen, and more especially with Taigong, on every important decision that had to be taken. Now, upon his return, he found that everything had been going as well as it could under the circumstances. And he learned particularly that it was Taigong who had conceived the scheme that finally succeeded in securing his freedom [145]—the selection of the special gifts for the tyrant's delectation, the submission of them through the venal favorite Feizhong, and, above all, the manifold secret manipulations that had resulted in persuading so many princes to express their pious wish at just the right moment. And gratefully Ji Chang confided his own dilemma to his "Teacher, Uncle Shang." While the latter, as a military strategist, always tended to give a freer exercise to power and policy, the former, as a philosopher, was inveterately inclined to lean back more on the side of duty and propriety. Thus, out of their discussions, a course of action was forged, often confusing and zigzagging, but forward-looking and inexorable all the same. For even if Ji Chang would not go as far as Taigong might have liked, he could not but agree that, theoretically at least, the best defense was offense, and that if he wanted to avoid an open break with Yin, the most practical way was to augment Zhou's strength imperceptibly and by degrees so that while it was growing, Yin might not notice it; and after it had fully grown, Yin might not want to break with Zhou anymore. As is recorded in the *Historical Records,* their discussions were "mostly related to military strategies and unusual expedients. It is because of this that when later generations study the arts of war or the clandestine maneuvers of Zhou, they ascribe the origins of these to Taigong." [146]

Since many of the actions taken were "unusual expedients" or "clandestine maneuvers," they are generally hidden from the view of the historian. Nevertheless a few events and their consequences may be noted. One of Ji Chang's first acts after consultation with Taigong and others, however, was an open and easy one. He had already been the Prince of Zhou for some forty years. But he declared this year of his return to be the first year of his new reign.[147] In ancient times, examples of such changes were not wanting: Whenever a prince felt that there was something to celebrate, he could initiate a new reign within his own princedom.[148] To Ji Chang, his return to freedom, or his appointment as *xibo,* was a suitable occasion to so commemorate. But even here, to men like Taigong, the interpretation seems to have been different. They laid more emphasis on the authority the prince had received from the emperor; he could from now on wage war or launch expeditions against other states without restraint. They considered this new power an abdication of the Mandate of Heaven by Yin to Zhou. And history is to testify that after Ji Chang's death, the latter interpretation, and not his own, was regarded by his immediate posterity as the authentic one.

Some actions, also taken at once, were clearly not to Ji Chang's liking; and probably he had acceded only to the advice of his "Teacher, Uncle Shang" after much soul-searching. For orders were issued in his name "to construct a marble gate for the palace, to erect a Marvel Terrace for pleasure, to surround himself with ladies in attendance at court, and to sound bells and beat drums for him while holding audience" [149]—things which the princes of those days, following Di Xin's example, had been accustomed to indulge in, but which Ji Chang had never done before. But if he had objected to these orders in the beginning, he could not have argued against the results these actions brought. For upon hearing of this, Di Xin was reported to have said, "Now *xibo* has mended his ways, and has shown that he is ready to conform. I need not be concerned about him anymore." [150]

Yet, in sober moments, Di Xin was as crafty as he was avaricious. He wanted to put Ji Chang to one more test. He learned that the Prince of Zhou had with him a jade block on which he could write down characters with a brush and then wipe them off, and which he valued more than anything else in his possession. So he asked one of his ministers to go to Zhou and demand the block as a tribute. Ji Chang was ready to surrender it instantly. But after consultation with Taigong, he refused. The Yin minister who came as the envoy was known for his ability as well as his fidelity to the imperial house; if he should return with the mission so easily accomplished, the emperor might place even greater trust in him, which would not redound to the advantage of Zhou. So alongside the refusal, a secret word was conveyed to Di Xin's favorite minister, the venal Feizhong, that if he should persuade his master to send himself to Zhou instead, the block would be there for his taking. The scheme worked. And shortly after Feizhong returned to Yin with the jade block, the favorite was given overall charge of the Yin governemnt by the tyrant.[151]

It was about this time that Di Xin took more and more to drink. The revolt of the southeastern tribe Yufang had been quashed. And Ji Chang, who had posed so much of a problem a while ago, was now behaving as dutifully as any vassal prince should. He had nothing more to worry about— except for one thing: He found, to his chagrin, he was losing his virility. He doted on Daji as much as ever. The more he doted, the more aid he sought from strong spirits. But gradually, even drink, however potent and however frequently consumed, seemed to wane in its effect. He had to think up other stimulants. "He made pools of wine. He hung up meats like a forest. And he ordered men and women to chase after each other naked in the midst of these, engaging in orgies day and night." [152]

While the emperor was thus desperately trying to regain his manhood, the Prince of Zhou was continuing to rule as he had before his imprisonment in spite of the new paraphernalia surrounding his court. He retained the marble gate, the drums and bells, and even the ladies in attendance in order to keep up the appearances he had assumed for his suspicious sovereign's consumption. But the Marvel Terrace he put to use other than his own enjoyment; he converted it into the premises of the academy, *biyong*, where the sons of nobles and officers, along with chosen scholars from the primary schools of the princedom, were to receive a higher education.[153] And indeed the people of Zhou seem to have had more faith in their prince's good intentions than Ji Chang himself thought they would. For when they were asked to build the Marvel Terrace, they built it with such zeal and alacrity that it was sung later in an ode:

> When he planned the commencement of the Marvel Terrace,
> He plotted it, and designed it;
> And the people in crowds took over the labor,
> And in no time they completed it.
> At the beginning he told them, "About this there is no hurry."
> But the people rushed over by themselves as if they were his children.[154]

Encouraged by such a display of unquestioned confidence in himself, the Prince of Zhou rededicated himself to the task of giving his people the best government possible, and also helping the people reach the highest state of society attainable. More than a year passed in this manner, and then there occurred a unique event in Chinese history. At the bend of the Yellow River, where the stream, originally flowing from north to south, makes a sharp turn toward the east, on its west bank before the turn there was a state called Rui,[155] and on its south bank immediately after the turn there was another state called Yu.[156] Their borders abutted, separated by a slice of land which had not been populated before, but which now, being populated, was claimed by both. Formerly in such cases the disputants would have gone to the imperial court for a decision. But now the princes of both states agreed that that would not do: The emperor was widely known to be more usually drunk than sober; and as for the ministers, Feizhong, who had the final say, was notoriously subject to subornation by bribery. There was only one person capable of rendering a judgment that would be respected by both—*xibo*. Not only was his personal integrity above question, but he was now fully empowered by his new position to make the adjudication. So the two princes decided to journey together to Zhou to seek Ji Chang's arbitration.

As told in the *Historical Records* and other ancient books,[157] "No sooner had they set foot on Zhou territory than they noticed a different atmosphere. An unusual sense of respect and consideration for other people pervaded the behavior of the multitude. When they walked on the road, the passersby yielded them the right of way with courtesy; when they went through paths in the fields, the husbandmen stopped their work politely in order to let them pass. When they entered the villages, men and women each attended to their businesses in separate orderly groups; and no white-haired people were seen carrying heavy loads. When they made way to a government office, they saw that an officer was being given a promotion, but he was protesting that another officer probably deserved it more. The two princes looked at each other and said, 'What we are contending about is what the Zhou people feel ashamed to do!' " So they settled their dispute right then between themselves, and went to see Ji Chang, reporting the agreement, and pledging that thereafter their two states would be always his to command. And hearing of this, some forty other states placed themselves voluntarily under the guidance of Zhou.[158]

The year after this "Yu-Rui Incident," an occasion arose when for the first time the Field Marshal of the West was given an opportunity, or rather the necessity, to use the army which Taigong had so diligently and efficiently built up for him. While his benevolent rule had helped to extend his influence eastward peacefully, the growing opulence of Zhou had served only to excite the cupidity and covetousness of the Kunyi tribes in the west. Apparently dissatisfied with the annual presents Ji Chang had so generously given them in the past, and mistaking his genuine love of peace for an inborn weakness of character, they now demanded more. But this time they misjudged. Even if the Prince of Zhou might have yielded to their extortions, the Field Marshal of the West could not. For to do so would have brought disgrace not only on himself but on the whole empire. The refusal led to a confrontation in arms. And needless to say, the Kunyi were so effectively defeated and dispersed[159] that they did not return to disturb the Zhou until a century and a half later.[160]

Ever since the return of Ji Chang, Prince Hu of Chong had been watching the developments in Zhou with intense uneasiness. He expected the field marshal to march against him at any moment, and was at first surprised, and then lulled, when *xibo* took no action against him. However, the peaceful penetration of Zhou into his neighboring states after the Yu-Rui Incident heightened his vigilance anew, and the rapid dispersal of the savage tribes by his rival's military might alarmed him even more. He found himself now at his wit's end. Measuring strength against strength, he was fully aware that Zhou had become too strong for him. And after his experiences with Di Xin, he knew too he could no longer rely on the emperor for protection. Moreover, his rival's appointment as *xibo* had placed him in an impossible position. While it would be perfectly legitimate for the field marshal to launch an expedition against him, for him to take the offensive would have been a criminal action. Under the circumstances, to form an open alliance against Ji Chang was out of the question. The only feasible thing was to seek a sort of clandestine understanding with as many princes as possible who for one reason or another would wish to obstruct the further expansion of Zhou. But try as he would, he could find only a very few princes who shared his fears or hatred of Ji Chang.

One of these was the Prince of Mi, which was also known as Mixu, situated on the northern shores of the Wei River.[161] This prince was a petty tyrant in his own princedom, a minor Di Xin as it were. He had always regarded Ji Chang with malice, blaming the latter for the intransigence of his own people, who were often outspoken in their praises of the enlightened rule of Zhou. And what annoyed him even more was that of late two small states adjacent to his own princedom—Ruan and Gong—had, following the example of others, openly acknowledged the protection of the Field Marshal of the West. In anger, he sent forces to occupy the two princedoms. He almost succeeded in his surprise attack, when the Zhou army rushed to their rescue. Thus we read from an ode which was composed later to commemorate the event:

> The Lord Above told Wen Wang:
> "Do not encourage people to rebel with promises of help;
> "Do not give in to desires of envy or greed;
> "Do not be the first to encroach upon another's land."
> But the men of Mi were disrespectful;
> They dared to obstruct the course of the great nation,
> They invaded Ruan and even as far as Gong.
>
> At this, our Wang rose majestic in his wrath.
> He marshaled his troops,
> To stop the invading foes,
> To consolidate the prosperity of Zhou,
> And to meet the expectations of all under Heaven.[162]

It was clear from this ode that Ji Chang, ever looking to the Lord Above for guidance for his actions, had never intended to invade Mi in the first place. But provoked by the latter's aggressions, he was constrained to act in response. However, their armies never actually joined in battle. For before his troops approached the "invading foes," the disaffected people of Mi had already "tied up their tyrant and announced their surrender to Zhou." [163]

The next conflict, however, was a real one, and took the Zhou armies far afield, beyond the limits of the West Land, across the Yellow River, and deep into the opposite shore as far as the northeastern confines of the imperial domain, or the Central Shang. For the principal adversary in this expedition was the princedom of Li, also known as Qi,[164] which was located toward the southeast of modern Shanxi province, separated from Yin only by the tall range of the Taihang Mountains. How the Zhou influence could have penetrated so far in so short a time is something at which to wonder. Nor is the cause of the conflict recorded in any of the ancient books. Presumably, after the Yu-Rui Incident, and after the surrender of the Mi people against their own lawful prince, the prestige of Ji Chang rose so high that while the weaker states eagerly sought his protection, even the stronger ones were not reluctant to welcome him in the adjudication of their disputes. And thus before long not only the enfeoffed states on the west bank of the Yellow River but also those on the east bank accepted his overall direction. Presumably too, as the experience of former Yin emperors could bear witness, a state which had hitherto been regarded as an equal by others, if it should choose to embark on a course of expansion, would sooner or later run head-on into collision with other states which simply did not wish it to expand any further. This is how the former Yin hegemons Shiwei and Dapeng had been checked in their careers of self-aggrandizement in the past; and this, too, is very likely what Di Xin had fondly wished for Zhou, when he appointed Ji Chang to be the Field Marshal of the West. However, the rise of Zhou was different from that of the other hegemons. First, up to that time, Zhou had not subjugated any other state by the use of force, but had rather persuaded them, or their peoples, to place themselves voluntarily under its protection or guidance through its own benevolent rule and astute maneuvers. Thus when a conflict arose with an outsider, these states elected of themselves to remain faithful to Zhou and give it unstinting support. And second, perhaps even more importantly, unlike the other former hegemons, Zhou had worked hard to build up a solid and prosperous base before it started to expand. By this time, though we lack statistics or records to document this point, it would seem that Zhou was now possessed of a very large population according to the standards of those days—to be sure still much smaller than that of the Central Shang, but by far larger than that of any of the other enfeoffed states. And coupled with this, there is the fact that Zhou's standing army was perhaps the largest in the empire, next only to that of the imperial house; and that, furthermore, it was trained and commanded by Taigong, the foremost military genius of the time. So the conflict between Zhou and Li was swiftly resolved in the utter defeat of the latter.

As this took place right on the borders of the imperial domain, so near to the court, it rudely shook the people of Yin. In the *Book of History*, there is extant a document pertaining to the event and titled *Xibo Inflicted a Disastrous Defeat on Li*, which reads:

> Xibo having inflicted a disastrous defeat on Li, Zu Yi [165] took fright and hastened to report to the emperor.
> He said, "O Son of Heaven! Heaven is about to bring an end to the Mandate It has granted on Yin. Neither men of wisdom nor the great tortoise can see anything good in the future. It is not that the spirits of our former emperors do not try to aid us, their own descendants. But by your own dissoluteness and revelries,

you yourself are bringing on the end!

"On this account, Heaven has abandoned us, and we can no longer eat our food in ease and peace. You do not act in accord with the good nature that Heaven has bestowed on you. You do not give obedience to the laws and traditions of the dynasty.

"Now, all the people are wishing the dynasty to perish, saying, 'Would that Heaven send down its wrath right away! Our present sovereign is doing nothing to hold fast to the Great Mandate; what use have we for him?' "

But the emperor said, "Ah! Am I not born with a fate decreed by Heaven Itself?"

Zu Yi returned and said, "Your crimes are many, and they are all displayed above. How can you speak as if Heaven should be still responsible for your fate? Surely Yin will perish soon. And it will be all your doing. And you will die a death that your country will mete out as your punishment."

All the military actions taken by the Prince of Zhou so far—against Kunyi, against Mi, and against Li—may be said to have been thrust upon him despite his peaceful inclinations. But the next and last use of force was undertaken on his own initiative. He would not have been human had he completely forgotten or forgiven Prince Hu of Chong for the injuries done to him. But the fact that he waited so long—six or seven years after his return to Zhou—bespeaks his patience rather than his lack of decision. Had the calumnious prince mended his ways and entreated Zhou to hold its revengeful hand, perhaps the developments might have been different. But as it was, Prince Hu built the walls of his city, Chong, ever thicker and higher so that they looked impregnable; and he continued without cease to instigate one fellow state after another against Zhou in the hope of checking its further expansion. Thus we read from the ode *huangyi* in the *Book of Poetry*:

The Lord Above told Wen Wang:
"Take measure against the country of your enemy;
"Gather together your brethren,
"And get ready your scaling ladders,
"And your engines of assault,
"To attack the walls of Chong."

At the commencement of the expedition, however, the field marshal issued these orders: "Do not kill the innocent. Do not destroy dwellings. Do not fill up wells. Do not cut down trees. Do not sequester domestic animals." [166] Perhaps it was because of these nonmilitaristic restrictions he imposed on his own troops that the fighting lasted more than three months.[167] Eventually Zhou triumphed, and the ode sang further:

Slow and sure were the engines of assault,
Against the walls of Chong high and strong.
Captives were brought in for questioning one after another;
And after their left ears were cut off, the dead enemies were peacefully buried.[168]

He sacrificed to the Lord Above and to the deities of war:
His aim was to induce submission by all,
That none might give him affront in the four directions.

Steady and strong were the engines of assault,
Against the walls of Chong solid and firm.
He attacked it, and let loose all his forces;
He made an end of its existence;
And throughout the four directions none dared oppose him further.[169]

After the capture of Chong, Ji Chang was deeply impressed with the strategic importance of the site. He built a new city a little to its east, named it Feng, and made it the seat of his newly enlarged domain.[170] The place was well chosen. Later, his son Wu Wang was to build another city to its east.[171] And the entire adjacent countryside, which may be called the metropolitan area of the modern Xian, has since established itself in history as one of China's most important political centers. It is situated in the heart of the fertile Wei Valley, which yields more grains than can be consumed by the local populace; and being surrounded by tall mountains on three sides and by the Yellow River on the east, the valley is easily defended. Moreover, because the whole terrain of China is like an inclining ladder, with its lowest level on the eastern seacoast, this region, being almost at the western extremity of China proper, holds a commanding position over all the plains that lie to its east or southeast. It has therefore been called "the seat of emperors or kings," and served, off and on, as China's imperial capital for no less than seven centuries.

After the conquest of Chong, Ji Chang's fame and power stood at its height. Had he wished, he could have turned his banners eastward in the direction of the Central Shang, and his troops, led by the doughty Taigong, would have followed to a man. But he did not do so. Instead, as Confucius said of him later, "Having possessed two of the three parts of the empire, he used them to serve the dynasty of Yin. Indeed, the virtue of the house of Zhou may be said to have reached the point of perfection." [172] That his influence extended to two-thirds of the Yin Empire there does not seem to be much doubt. Invested as Field Marshal of the West, the entire West Land should be construed as his designated jurisdiction; and with the capture of Chong, the last resistance to his authority appears to have died out. Since the settlement of the Yu-Rui Incident, Yu, located in between the West Land and the South Land, could well have spread the Zhou influence southward. In the *Book of Poetry*, there are two collections of poems signifying the early conversion to Zhou culture of distant lands as far south as the Yangtze River.[173] And in many ancient books, a Prince of Chu, allegedly even more advanced in years than Taigong, was recorded as having come to Zhou and offered his service to the field marshal.[174] We are not sure if he was the same one who had been specially feasted by Di Xin during the early years of the emperor's reign.[175] But no matter whether or not it was the same person, the very fact indicates that the entire South Land had been rather receptive to Zhou's supervision. As to the North Land, the kinsfolk of Yin, the so-called *beibo*,[176] may, or may not, have managed to keep part of it loyal to the imperial house. But after the summary defeat inflicted on Li, since no record shows the continuance of hostilities toward Zhou, it may also be assumed that not a small portion of the North Land had willingly placed itself within the sphere of influence of the Field Marshal of the West.

Was Di Xin aware of the situation? Even if he had been given intelligence reports, it is doubtful whether he or his immediate coterie was capable of grasping its full significance. By this time the emperor had become an inveterate alcoholic; and following his example, most of the courtiers were also given to drink. There is a story which, like others in this era, is without a definite date, but which could very well have happened at this critical juncture. "Zou (for by then an increasing number of people had started calling Di Xin by this ignominious name), having drunk day and night, suddenly awoke with the fear that he had lost count of time and did not know what day it was. He inquired to his left and to his right, and all did not know. So he sent a man to ask of Jizi, the senior tutor. Said Jizi to his own people, 'Being lord and master of the world, yet he and his court have all lost count of time; what a peril it is for the world! With the entire court not knowing what the day is, yet I alone know; what a peril it is for myself.' He told the messenger that he did not know what the day was either." [177]

Moreover, notwithstanding Zhou's expansion of influence, Ji Chang's behavior toward Di Xin was above reproach. He had not only fulfilled his own duties as a vassal prince to his sovereign, but had also used his influence to induce the other princes in the two-thirds of the empire under his sway to do the same. In those days, an enfeoffed state was bound to the ruling dynasty by three obligations: (1) to use the imperial calendar issued by the reigning emperor; (2) to pay an annual or periodical tribute; and (3) to place its military forces at the disposal of the imperial court, or to allow its manpower to be conscripted, in times of emergency. In return, the enfeoffed states were to receive two benefits from the sovereign: In case of disputes between states, the dynasty would adjudicate with fairness and equity; and in case of encroachment by other states or of incursion by savage tribes, it would provide them with protection. Now, Ji Chang's appointment as *xibo* had enabled him to act on behalf of the emperor in ensuring these benefits for the states that had placed themselves under his care. Of course, it may be argued that he had arrogated too much power to himself by expanding his influence far beyond the limits of the West Land. But then the limits of the so-called Four Lands had never been precisely delineated in the first place. Nor had the authority of the Field Marshal of the West been clearly defined at the time of his appointment. Moreover, if so many states had submitted to his direction, most of them had done so of their own volition. And perhaps what made the arrangement acceptable to the court of Yin is this: Wherever Xibo had extended his sway, he had seen to it that the enfeoffed states observed their duties toward the imperial house even more rigidly. Since there was no emergency to speak of, there was no occasion for the deployment of their troops or for the conscription of their manpower. But as to the use of the imperial calendar, and more especially, as to the payment of the tribute, there was no question but that the field marshal had taken care that none of the states under his leadership took advantage of the weakness of the Yin or failed to live up to its obligations.

Furthermore, from the standpoint of humanity, Ji Chang may have rendered even a greater service. With the government of Yin on the verge of disintegration, there was no telling what chaos might have ensued had not the Field Marshal of the West filled the power vacuum. There could have been numberless feuds and encroachments by one state on another, and countless conflicts and measureless bloodshed in consequence. But with the appearance of the Prince of Zhou, so thoroughly trusted by everyone for his integrity, for his compassion, and for his sense of justice and propriety, and so visibly and so vigorously supported by a military might that was feared by all, not only was peace and order firmly maintained within two-thirds of the empire, but a steadying influence could not but have been felt in the remaining third as well. Thus in a manner of speaking, it may be said that whatever ill will Di Xin might have felt toward Ji Chang, it was the latter's support of the imperial throne that prevented it from toppling.

But could such a relationship last? We only know that as long as Ji Chang lived, this seems to have been his objective. But shortly after he founded the city Feng, he died.

NOTES

1. See above, p. 8, and the genealogical chart "The Four Sons of Di Ku" on p. 64.

2. *Book of Poetry, daya: shengmin.*

3. For the romanization of the name Qi, see above, p. 64, note 60.

4. A different character than the one for agriculture.

5. *Guo Yu, zhouyu.* Also see *Historical Records, zhou benji.*

6. The Chinese character used here is *che.* See above, p. 134. This is considered by some scholars as a proof that the well-field system was practiced at that time.

7. *Book of Poetry, daya: gongliu.*

8. *Historical Records, zhou benji.*

9. *Bamboo Chronicles,* comments by Lin Chunpu. Also see above, p. 125.

10. See Chap. V, note 25.

11. See above, p. 213.

12. Ban Gu, *Baihu Tongyi, hao.* This is, however, not a literal translation, but a condensation of all the meanings attached to the character *zhou.*

13. This was first alleged by Huangfu Mi in his *Diwang Shiji.*

14. The following is a paraphrase of related passages in the *Historical Records, zhou benji.*

15. According to Wang Guowei, *Guifang Kunyi Yanyun Kao,* Xunyu was a name for a tribe of Guifang.

16. The Qi and Ju rivers, the Liang Mountains, and Mount Qishan are all still there in modern Shaanxi province.

17. Also see *Book of Poetry, daya: mian;* and *Mencius, lianghuiwang,* II.

18. *Historical Records, zhou benji.*

19. *Bamboo Chronicles.*

20. *Book of Poetry, Lusong: bigong.*

21. Liu Xiang, *Lienuzhuan.*

22. *Book of Poetry, daya: mian.*

23. Liu Xiang, *Lienuzhuan.*

24. *Historical Records, wutaibo shijia,* comments by Zhang Shoujie.

25. Ibid.

26. *Confucian Analects, taibo.*

27. *Bamboo Chronicles.*

28. All the seven wars may be found in the *Bamboo Chronicles.*

29. These tribes are Yiju, Western Tribes of Guirong, Yanjing, Yuwu, Shihu, and Yitu.

30. The Rong of Yanjing.

31. Fan Ye, *Hou Han Shu, xiqiang liezhuan.*

32. *Bamboo Chronicles.*

33. Ibid.

34. Dong Zuobin, *Yin Lipu,* part I, chap. 4.

35. According to the *Historical Records, zhou benji,* Wen Wang reigned fifty years. According to *Li Ji, wenwangshizi,* Wen Wang lived to ninety-seven. Although the latter account is to be disputed, it seems safe to assume that Ji Chang succeeded to his princedom at around thirty.

36. *Mencius, gaozi,* II.

37. *Huainanzi, xiuwu xun.*

38. *Li Ji, wenwangshizi.*

39. *Lushi Chunqiu, xiaoxinglan: shoushi.*

40. *Zhong Yong (Doctrine of the Mean).* In those days, before the invention of paper, writings were generally inscribed on wood or bamboo tablets.

41. Ibid.

42. *Mencius, lianghuiwang,* II.

43. See above, p. 134.

44. *Book of Poetry, daya: wenwang.*

45. *Da Xue (Great Learning).*

46. The version here follows *Lushi Chunqiu, mengdongji: yiyong.* The story also appears in *Huainanzi* and *Jiayi Xinshu.*

47. *Mencius, lianghuiwang,* II.

48. The story of Boyi will be told in later pages.

49. *Xibo* is a title given later to Ji Chang by Di Xin, or Zou.

50. The story of Taigong will be told in later pages.

51. *Mencius, jinxin,* I.

52. *Confucian Analects, yaoyue;* and *Mozi, jianai.*

53. See *Mencius, lilou,* I: "As the otter aids the deep waters, driving fish into them . . . so Zou aids Zhou, driving the people to it."

54. *Historical Records, zhou benji.*

55. *Book of History, junshi.* Only Guoshu was Ji Chang's younger brother. The other four—Hong Yao, San Yisheng, Taidian, and Nangong Kuo—were outsiders. See also *Shangshu Dazhuan.*

56. *Mozi, shangxian.* The two were Hong Yao and Taidian.

57. *Hanshi Waizhuan,* chap. III. Also see *Mencius, gongsunchou,* I.

58. The popular novel titled *Fengshen Bang* was written with Taigong as the central figure.

59. According to *Sui Shu, jingji zhi,* a book about military science titled *Liutao* is attributed to Taigong. There is another book called *Yinfu,* which is said to have been written by him. But it has nothing to do with military science.

60. The first time he was venerated as such was in 791 A.D. The practice continued until about 1380. See Du You, *Tongdian,* chap. 53; and *Xutongdian,* chap. 54.

61. *Hanshi Waizhuan,* chap. IV.

62. *Historical Records, qitaigong shijia.*

63. See above, p. 68.

64. *Historical Records, qitaigong shijia.* See commentaries by Sima Zhen.

65. Ibid.

66. Ibid.

67. *Shangshu Dazhuan.* The three are said to be Hong Yao, San Yisheng, and Nangong Kuo.

68. Literal translation of the wording of *Historical Records, qitaigong shijia.*

69. Ibid.

70. For Chaoge, see above, p. 228.

71. *Kuodizhi.*

72. *Historical Records, qitaigong shijia,* commentaries by Pei Yin.

73. Liu Xiang, *Shuoyuan,* chap. VIII.

74. The story is told in many ancient books, each only with some slight difference. The version given here in the main follows the *Historical Records, qitaigong shijia.*

75. Panxi is in the modern Baoji district, Shaanxi province.

76. *Zhuangzi, tianzifang.* As is usual with *Zhuangzi,* the story is related, but it is given a twist.

77. *Li Ji, wangzhi.*

78. See *Zhou Li, diguansitu.*

79. Ibid., *xiaositu.* The organizations as outlined in these charts relate to the urban areas. As to the rural areas, the organizations are largely the same, but the names of the units in the civil administration are different.

80. *Zu* for "clan" and *zu* for "company" are different characters. So are the two *lu.*

81. *Zhou Li, xiaositu.*

82. *Zhou Li, diguansitu.* Also see Wang Mingsheng, *Zhou Li Junfu Shuo.*

83. *Historical Records, zhou benji.*

84. *Zhou Li, xiaguansima;* and Ban Gu, *Qian Han Shu, xingfa zhi.*

85. *Zhou Li, xiaositu.*

86. Ibid., *xiaguansima.*

87. Zheng Xuan.

88. See above, pp. 117–19.

89. *Historical Records, zhou benji.*

90. Ma Duanlin, *Wenxian Tongkao, bingkao,* chap. 158. In case a prince or a general rode on the chariot, then his place was in the center, with the driver standing on the left.

91. *Liutao,* as quoted by ibid.

92. Muye was south of Chaoge. See Chap. VII, below.

93. *Zhou Li, diguansitu.* The quotation is a paraphrase. All the ceremonies will be discussed in the concluding chapters.

94. Ibid.

95. *Li Ji, wangzhi.*

96. *Book of Poetry, daya: lingtai.*

97. *Dadai Liji, baofu;* Ban Gu, *Baihu Tongyi. Shangshu Dazhuan,* however, maintains that the qualifying age for the primary schools was thirteen and for the academy twenty.

98. These are translations of the Chinese terms *sanlao* and *wugeng.*

99. *Confucian Analects, zihan.*

100. See above, p. 138.

101. *Mencius, lianghuiwang,* II.

102. See Wang Guowei, *Guifang Kunyi Yanyun Kao.*

103. See above, p. 221.

104. See above, p. 220.

105. *Confucian Analects, weizi.*

106. Dong Zuobin, *Jiaguxue Liushinian,* p. 98.

107. Ibid., p. 92.

108. See above, pp. 222–23.

109. *Hanfeizi, yulao* and *shuolin*.

110. The chronology of this period is very confused. Altogether there are sixteen versions. See Dong Zuobin, *Yin Lipu*, part 1, chap. 4.

111. *Guo Yu, jinyu*; and *Historical Records, yin benji*. The popular pronunciation of the character *da* in Daji is "dan." But according to both Xu Shen's dictionary and *Xiandai Hanyu Cidian* it should be pronounced as "da."

112. *Huainanzi, yuandao xun*; *Historical Records, yin benji*.

113. Perhaps it is because Zou had built such palaces that later monarchs shied away from using marble and stones for construction.

114. *Historical Records, yin benji*; and *Bamboo Chronicles*.

115. *Historical Records, zhou benji*.

116. Ibid., *yin benji*.

117. The quotation is a paraphrase of an excerpt from Ban Gu, *Qian Han Shu, baiguan gongqing biao*, 1.

118. Jiu was near modern Anyang, Henan.

119. E was near modern Qinyang, Henan, about 150 kilometers southwest of Yin.

120. *Lushi Chunqiu, shijun lan, xinglun*. We use the statement of Ji Chang, as cited in the book, but do not follow its chronology.

121. *Historical Records, yin benji*. See also the commentaries.

122. *Huainanzi, daoying xun*; *Historical Records, zhou benji*.

123. Youli was a village about five kilometers from modern Tangyin, Henan.

124. *Zuozhuan*, Duke Xiang, 31st year.

125. *Historical Records, taishigong zixu*. The work, or the system, was originally known as *Zhou Yi, yi* meaning "change" or "changes." After it was incorporated into the Confucian Classics, it was called *Yi Jing, jing* meaning "book" or "classic." *I Ching* is the popular Western transliteration of *Yi Jing*.

126. Ibid., *guice liezhuan*. James Legge translated *shi* stalks as milfoil stalks. The Chinese dictionary *Ci Hai* says *shi* is *Achillea sibirica*. The ancient Chinese believed that this particular plant could live several hundred years; and so, like the tortoise, which also has a long life, it could tell the future. See Ban Gu, *Baihu Tongyi*.

127. Ban Gu, *Qian Han Shu, yiwen zhi*, records that there were several books still extant in the Han dynasty. But these now are lost.

128. See above, p. 53.

129. See *Zhou Li, chunguanzongbo, taibu*, and the commentaries.

130. See Gu Yanwu, *Rizhilu*, 1.

131. *Historical Records, yin benji*.

132. See *Historical Records, yin benji*; also, Huangfu Mi, *Diwang Shiji*.

133. See above, p. 220.

134. The exact location of Li is not known. Probably in modern Anhui.

135. *Zuozhuan*, Duke Zhao, 4th year.

136. Ibid.

137. According to Dong Zuobin, *Yin Lipu*, part 1, chap. 3, the expedition against Yufang lasted from the tenth moon in the fortieth year to the sixth moon in the forty-first year of Di Xin's reign.

138. *Shangshu Dazhuan*; and *Historical Records, qitaigong shijia*.

139. *Zuozhuan*, Duke Xiang, 31st year.

140. *Shangshu Dazhuan*; *Historical Records, qitaigong shijia*.

141. See above, pp. 214–15.

142. *Historical Records, zhou benji*; *Hanfeizi, naner*. The Luo River still bears the same name; it is in modern Shaanxi.

143. Ibid.

144. *Historical Records, zhou benji*.

145. *Shangshu Dazhuan*; *Historical Records, qitaigong shijia*.

146. *Historical Records, qitaigong shijia*.

147. There is a great controversy about this point. See Dong Zuobin, *Yin Lipu*, part 1, chap. 4, sec. 2. Also see *Book of Poetry, daya: wenwangyousheng*; *Historical Records, yin benji*.

148. See Liu Shu's comments in *Zizhitongjian Waiji*.

149. *Huainanzi, daoyin xun*.

150. Ibid.

151. *Hanfeizi, yulao*.

152. *Historical Records, yin benji*.

153. *Book of Poetry, daya: lingtai (Marvel Terrace)*.

154. Ibid.

155. South of the modern Chaoyi district, Shaanxi.

156. West of the modern Shaanzhou, Henan.

157. The story is told in the *Historical Records, zhou benji*; *Shangshu Dazhuan*; and *Book of Poetry, daya: mian*. The quotation here is a paraphrase.

158. See comments on the *Book of Poetry, daya: mian*.

159. *Historical Records, zhou benji*; *Book of Poetry, daya: mian*.

160. This occurred in the reign of the fifth emperor of the Zhou dynasty, Mu Wang.

161. *Historical Records, zhou benji*; *Book of Poetry, daya: huangyi*.

162. *Book of Poetry, daya: huangyi*.

163. *Lushi Chunqiu, lisulan: yongmin*.

164. *Historical Records* and *Book of History, shuxu*, give the name Li; *Shangshu Dazhuan* and *Bamboo Chronicles* give the name Qi.

165. We know next to nothing about Zu Yi. Some scholars thought he was descended from Zuji (see above, pp. 216–17), taking the *zu* of his ancestor's name as surname.

166. Liu Xiang, *Shuoyuan*, chap. XV.

167. *Zuozhuan*, Duke Xi, 19th year.

168. In those times, the practice in war was to cut off the left ears of dead enemy soldiers in order to have an accurate count of the slain.

169. *Book of Poetry, daya: huangyi*.

170. About twenty kilometers east of modern Huxian, Shaanxi.

171. Named Hao, it was about twelve kilometers to the east of Feng.

172. *Confucian Analects, taibo*.

173. These two collections are called *zhounan* and *shaonan*.

174. *Historical Records, chu shijia*. Also see *Liezi, liming*; and Ban Gu, *Qian Han Shu, yiwenzhi*. The man's name is Yu Xiong.

175. See above, p. 154. According to Dong Zuobin, he was feasted in the fifteenth year of Di Xin's reign.

176. See above, pp. 154–55.

177. *Hanfeizi, shuolin*, 1.

CHAPTER VII

THE FOUNDING OF
THE ZHOU DYNASTY

· 1 ·

JI FA AND THE FALL OF YIN
(1115–1111 B.C.)

Ji Chang was very happily married with his principal wife, Taisi.[1] By her he had ten sons.[2] The eldest having died young,[3] the second son, Ji Fa, became the heir apparent. Among the ten sons, Ji Fa and his fourth brother, Ji Dan, were early noted for their virtue, their capacity, and their sense of filial piety. As soon as they grew into manhood, Ji Chang relied on them as he did his own two hands. And between the two brothers there also developed a bond and a trust that they did not share with the others.

Toward the close of Ji Chang's reign, a serious debate arose in the high councils of Zhou about the policy it should pursue toward Yin. Should Zhou continue to render dutiful submission to the imperial house, even though it had so corrupted and discredited itself? Or should they come forth to challenge its supremacy in the open? As long as Ji Chang lived, he stood adamantly for the former; and no one, not even Taigong, could persuade him to shift his position. But once Ji Chang was gone, the question was raised anew for Ji Fa. And indeed it was a hard decision to make—much harder than we may ever know, for so distant and so different are their times and their beliefs from our own. As a matter of fact, when Mencius analyzed the situation only some eight hundred years later, he wrote as follows of the rise of Zhou under Ji Chang, who, after the conquest of Yin by his son, was consecrated Wen Wang, or "Cultural Emperor":

How difficult it would be to match the achievements of Wen Wang! From Tang to Wuding, there appeared six or seven worthy and sage sovereigns. The world having attached itself to Yin for such a long time, this length of time itself made a

THE TEN SONS OF WEN WANG BY HIS PRINCIPAL WIFE

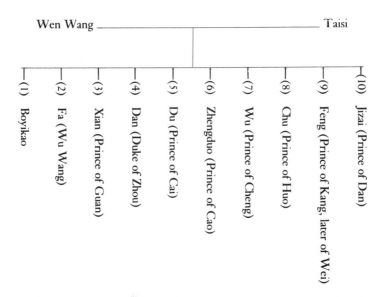

Wen Wang _____ Taisi

(1) Boyikao

(2) Fa (Wu Wang)

(3) Xian (Prince of Guan)

(4) Dan (Duke of Zhou)

(5) Du (Prince of Cai)

(6) Zhengduo (Prince of Cao)

(7) Wu (Prince of Cheng)

(8) Chu (Prince of Huo)

(9) Feng (Prince of Kang, later of Wei)

(10) Jizai (Prince of Dan)

change difficult. Wuding had all the princes coming to the court to pay him homage; he possessed all under Heaven; he ruled over them as if they were things he could move around in his palm. In time, Zou was not far removed from Wuding. There still remained the conventions of ancient heritage, and the influences of good government that had emanated from the earlier sovereigns. Moreover, there were such men as the Prince of Wei, Bigan, Jizi, and Jiaoli,[4] all men of ability and virtue, trying to assist him in government. For these reasons, it took a long time for him to lose the throne. There was not a foot of ground which he did not possess, nor a single individual who did not acknowledge himself to be his subject. Yet under such conditions Wen Wang was able to rise, with only a territory of a hundred _li_ square for a beginning. How difficult it must have been indeed![5]

If the difficulties which Wen Wang had to overcome in expanding the power of Zhou are primarily physical, those which his son had to face in making the crucial decision to revolt against Yin may be said to be less physical and more psychological. But this does not necessarily mean that Ji Fa had a much easier decision to make, or a much easier task to perform, than his father. As related before, Ji Fa was once described as "an audacious and determined man." [6] Audacious and determined he truly was; yet there were many incalculable factors in the situation that made him hesitate to embark at once upon a decisive course of action. Since his father's death, there were two men he trusted most. The first was Taigong, whom he now formally honored with the title "Teacher," and whose young daughter he had only recently taken in marriage as his principal wife. The second was, of course, his fourth brother, Ji Dan, who is better known to posterity as the Duke of Zhou *(zhougong)*, a title conferred on him later. From the questions Ji Fa is known to have addressed to these two in private, we may perceive what weighty considerations ceaselessly exercised his mind. He asked of Taigong, "I wish to know that victory could be won before a war is fought, or that the outcome would be good before the tortoise is consulted. Is there such a way?" Taigong answered, "If you have won over the hearts of multitudes in a war against one who has lost them, then before the war is fought, you will know that victory is yours. If you use virtue to combat evil, then before the tortoise is consulted, you will know that the outcome will be good. While the enemy keeps on doing people harm, let us keep on doing them good; even if they are not our people but his, we shall be able to use them better than he will." Again, Ji Fa asked the Duke of Zhou: "The whole world recognizes Yin as the Son of Heaven, and considers Zhou but a vassal state. For a vassal state to war against the Son of Heaven, is victory possible?" The duke replied, "He who does away with propriety is a thief. He who violates justice is an outlaw. He who loses the support of his people is but a lone individual. You will be attacking a thief, an outlaw, a lone individual. What has the Son of Heaven to do with the matter?" [7]

Even though Ji Fa was encouraged by these postulations, still he paused. He was, of course, aware of the principal inhibition that had precluded his father from ever taking up arms against Di Xin, however badly he had been treated by that despot. It was the late *xibo*'s rigid sense of moral propriety, more especially, of the fidelity of a subject to his sovereign: He had accepted investiture from the emperor; it was his duty to serve him, not to rebel against him. This, of course, was not a mistake on the field marshal's part; it was a circumstance that had been thrust upon him. And such a circumstance Ji Fa was now determined to avert. According to the practice of the age, when a son succeeded his father as prince of a vassal state, it was incumbent upon him to report the occasion to the imperial court and request a new investiture for himself. As Ji Fa had not yet decided whether or not to remain a vassal to Yin, he elected deliberately not to advise Yin of his succession. Again, according to the same practice, the son and successor should call the year after his father's death the first year of his reign within his own princedom. This also Ji Fa chose not to do. As he interpreted it, when his father introduced a new reign after his return to Zhou from imprisonment, the very fact that the emperor had granted him the power to wage war and launch expeditions of his own will was a surrender of the Mandate of Heaven by Yin to Zhou. So Ji Fa now considered the first year after his accession not the beginning of a new reign but a continuation of his father's reign. He gave it, however, a new appellation to signify the change; he called it the ninth year "after the acceptance of the Mandate." [8]

Being Ji Chang's son, Ji Fa understood well the importance of self-reliance. If he wanted to challenge the power of Yin, it would not be enough for him to depend on the prestige his father had enjoyed among the enfeoffed states and on the goodwill the people of all nations had entertained for him. He must, as Taigong had counseled, seek to win over the hearts of the multitudes for himself. And having been a faithful student of his father's policies and actions for so long, he knew there could bo no better way to obtain this objective than by surrounding himself with the most virtuous and capable men he could find. And in this respect he was particularly fortunate, for Ji Chang had seen to it that in his inheritance there would be not only those ministers who had served so ably and loyally, but also a host of younger clansmen of Zhou meticulously trained in schools for him to choose from. Altogether, at the top of his government, Ji Fa could number ten men in whom he placed special trust and of whom he used to say with pride, "I have ten ministers who can set chaos in order." [9] And below these topmost ten there were numerous others who were also willing to carry out his orders implicitly and efficiently. Thus, again, he was able to declare with confidence: "Zou may have myriads of officers, but they have myriads of minds. I have but three thousand officers, but they have only one mind." [10]

In those days the traditional period of mourning for a father's death was said to be three years, which in actual practice was completed in twenty-five months.[11] This time Ji Fa spent well in meditating about his father's greatness, in emulating the deceased in the continuance of a benevolent and vigorous government, and in thinking hard about the practical measures which he himself could take for the conquest of Yin. When the mourning period was over, in the eleventh year "after the acceptance of the Mandate," Ji Fa proclaimed that he would take a special excursion to the east for the purpose of holding a military review at Mengjin,[12] a place of great strategic importance on the Yellow River. Mengjin was about two hundred kilometers east of Feng, the then Zhou capital, and about the same distance southwest of Yin, the imperial seat. Almost exactly halfway between the two centers of power, it is one of the few points along the mighty turbulent stream where a crossing may be made relatively easily. As a city, Mengjin now lies on the south side of the river. And it appears to have had the same location at the time of Ji Fa, so his troops could have marched all the way from Zhou by land. Had there been a precise delimitation of the boundaries of the Central Shang, we would know for certain whether or not Mengjin was within its confines. As there was none, we are not sure on this point. But whether it was or was not, for the Zhou army to have come so far from the home base and so close to the imperial court was, to say the least, unprecedented in the known annals of the dynasty.

Ji Fa was of course fully aware of the seriousness of the challenge he had thus posed for Di Xin. Not that he feared an open confrontation; if Yin should choose to regard it this way, he was prepared for the consequences. However, it was not his intention to precipitate the issue just then. What he wanted from the excursion was to ascertain the exact extent of his own strength as against that of Yin—in other words, to know for certain how many of the numerous enfeoffed states which had submitted to Zhou leadership were really ready to follow him if he led them against Yin. So, instead of giving out that he himself had ordered the military review, he had "a special wooden tablet representing the spirit of his deceased father carried aloft on a war chariot amidst the forces; and proclaimed that he, as the crown prince, was acting under the instructions of the late *xibo.*" [13] This contrivance, while implying that Zhou had the legal authority to hold the review, was designed also to ease Yin's apprehensions.

Even though Ji Fa was thus endeavoring to give the excursion a nonbelligerent appearance, his hostile intentions toward Yin were clearly understood by many—especially by the two pacifists Boyi and Shuqi. At the commencement of the march, the two men came out of their seclusion, held fast to the reins of the horses that drew Ji Fa's chariot, and expostulated: "Your father has passed away only recently. You do not bury him but use his name to take up arms. Is this to be called filial piety? You are a subject to your sovereign, yet you purpose to slay him. Is this to be called humanity?" Outraged, the guards wanted to put the two brothers to the sword. But Taigong said, "These are men who believe in their own righteousness. Let them alone." [14]

And so the Zhou troops commenced their march without further interruption. But the two men of peace have long been remembered in Chinese history. For after Ji Fa conquered Yin, "even though the whole world acknowledged the sovereignty of Zhou, Boyi and Shuqi condemned it as a shameful act, and in their righteousness refused to eat any grain produced under Zhou rule. They went up Shouyang Mountain [15] and subsisted on wild plants. When they were about to perish from starvation, they sang this song:

> Climbing up the Western Mount,
> We have gathered some wild plants.[16]
> When violence is replaced by violence,
> Who knows which side is wrong?
> Gone were Divine Husbandmen, Shun, and
> Yu,[17]

> To whom are we to attach ourselves?
> Alack the day! Alack the day!
> Woe is our life! Woe is our fate!

And so they died of starvation on Shouyang Mountain"; [18] and the Chinese people ever since have grieved for them.

Before Ji Fa commenced the march, notices were given to the enfeoffed states that acknowledged Zhou's sway. Though they were not explicitly asked to take part in the military review, they knew that if they should join with their forces, they would be more than welcome. When Ji Fa arrived at Mengjin, he was pleased that some eight hundred princes, with their cohorts, had already gathered there waiting.[19] He issued to them this proclamation: "I am possessed of no wisdom. It is only because of the virtues previously accumulated by my forebears that I am here to share benefits with you. With this review, I shall seek to establish exhaustive standards of reward and punishment so that our benefits may be firmly continued." Then he ordered the crossing of the Yellow River. And "Teacher Uncle Shang, holding a yellow halberd in the left hand and waving a flag with white yaks' tails in the right, called out in a stentorian voice: 'Assemble together your hosts. Get ready your boats and rafts. Those who cross the river later than the appointed time shall be subject to the penalty of death!' " [20]

If the holding of a military review by Zhou at Mengjin could be excused on the ground that it could have fallen within the authority of a Field Marshal of the West, the crossing of the river certainly could not. For though there might be doubts about whether Mengjin was within the confines of the Central Shang, there could never be any question that the territory on the north bank of the Yellow River was part and parcel of the imperial domain. Ji Fa knew this, and so did all the enfeoffed princes who followed him that day. They knew also that once they had committed this act, which amounted to an outright invasion of the Yin, from then on their fortunes, come weal or woe, were bound inseparably with Zhou.

Even though Ji Fa, Ji Dan, and Taigong, remembering the teachings of Ji Chang, placed much less faith in superstition than in reality, they were not shy of using superstitions to bolster their action or their perception of reality. Thus as soon as Ji Fa boarded his boat on the southern bank, all eyes were agog looking for a sign from Heaven. It is recorded that when the boat reached midstream, a big white fish jumped on board, and Ji Fa took it and offered it forthwith as a sacrifice. Then, after he landed on the opposite shore and lodged himself in a dwelling temporarily, a column of fire descended on its roof and turned into a large red bird with a very soothing sound.[21] And soothsayers interpreted both signs as unmistakable omens that Zhou was to take over the Mandate of Heaven from Yin. As white was the color of Yin and red that of Zhou, Yin in the form of the white fish had offered itself as a sacrifice, and Zhou in the form of the red bird was to reach every rooftop to soothe the whole world.[22]

Now, "all the eight hundred enfeoffed princes came forward and said, 'It is time to launch our expedition against Zou.' But Wu Wang (the Martial Emperor, for this is the title by which Ji Fa was soon to be called) said, 'You are not acquainted with the decree of Heaven. The time has not arrived yet.'"[23] And he ordered all the hosts to go back to their former posts, and himself also returned to Zhou.

Why did Ji Fa make such a decision? Why did he not avail himself of this opportunity? As none of the ancient records provides an answer, we venture our own suggestions. History, of course, is not privy to the intelligence Ji Fa might have had about Yin at this juncture. However, from the events that happened afterward, we may make an educated conjecture. After Zhou had established its dynasty, it counted altogether 1,753 enfeoffed princes within the empire.[24] Granting that during this period of transition many old states might have been overthrown and many new states created, we may still take the number as a rough aggregate of the princedoms that existed at the time of the military review. If this hypothesis is accepted, then the eight hundred and some states that came at Zhou's call constituted less than half of the total. Even though Ji Fa might feel pleased that this could form the hard core of his own strength in challenging Yin, he must also have realized that in numbers at least the opposition was as strong as he himself. Under his father's direction, two-thirds of the empire seemed to have acknowledged Zhou's sway. So, apparently, a number of them had chosen to stay away from the review. Was this because of his own deficiency in leadership? Or was this because they were frightened off by the very idea of supplanting the ruling dynasty, an idea which since Tang's revolution six or seven centuries before none had dared entertain? In either case, measures had to be taken to remedy the situation.

But what concerned Ji Fa even more was the problem of the Central Shang. All the enfeoffed princes of the Four Lands notwithstanding, the source of Yin's main strength was concentrated in the imperial domain. So long as the house of Shang could command the steadfast support of its numerous populace, in a contest of sheer physical power it would be exceedingly difficult for any outside state to gain the upper hand. While, historically, the people of the Central Shang had always been staunchly loyal to the Yin court, it was nonetheless Ji Fa's hope that the misrule of the present sovereign had generated much alienation. But as it was, Ji Fa could not be at all sure of this. Even though not a few of them had started calling Di Xin by the derogatory name Zou, as yet there were no particularly noticeable signs of severe disaffection.

As a result of such considerations, Ji Fa must have concluded that it was far wiser to bide his time than to take immediate action. Thoroughly familiar with Di Xin's character and behavior, he was convinced that, given more time, that erratic, irresponsible sovereign would commit anew some shocking atrocities that would cause not only more enfeoffed states but also the vast population of the Central Shang to turn away from him. But supposing that Di Xin should die in the meantime, and a worthier successor accede to the imperial throne? Would not Ji Fa himself then be losing the chance of gaining the Mandate of Heaven? We have no idea how he might have viewed such a prospect. But he decided after the military review to continue to use the Yin calendar and pay the annual tribute to Yin, and also to ask the eight hundred princes to do the same.[25] Was this a guise to lull the imperial court into a state of greater complacency? Or was it an indication that he was quite willing to continue serving Yin, if Yin would only mend its ways? Writing some three thousand years later, it is impossible to say.

After the military review held by Ji Fa, however, Di Xin apparently went into a period of inert stupor. He did not seem to have awakened fully to the seriousness of the danger posed by Zhou. He neither made improvement in his administration nor reduced the burdens of the people. He placed his trust as before in the venal ministers he had put in office.[26] But he himself, though still doting upon Daji and indulging in drink, refrained for a time from committing such atrocities as had shocked the empire previously. Two years passed. All the while, Ji Fa did nothing further to cause undue anxieties; and tributes from all enfeoffed states were flowing smoothly and regularly into the coffers. Di Xin felt revived in spirits once more. But to his perplexity he also found himself running out of ways and means to please his favorite. It was one wintry day. The waters in Deer Terrace, half frozen, would chill to the bone. Looking out from inside their warm chambers, Di Xin and Daji spied an elderly man wading through a stream with bare shanks. How could he not be afraid of the cold, the favorite wondered. Forthwith Di Xin ordered that the man's shanks be cut off to see if he was not specially endowed with a different kind of marrow. Then they spotted a pregnant woman, and Daji expressed a wish to know whether the child she was carrying was a boy or a girl; and the monster of an emperor at once commanded that the woman's womb be ripped open to determine the sex of the unborn child.[27]

Disbelief and consternation struck the entire Yin people. But of all who were dumbfounded by the new atrocities, none were more wounded than the Prince of Wei, Senior Tutor Jizi, and Junior Tutor Bigan. They now felt that the overthrow of Yin by Zhou was becoming inevitable, and the calamity might descend at any moment. During the last two years they had used every occasion they were allowed a chance to approach the emperor to voice their fears and to press for reforms. Although they were disappointed that no salutary results whatsoever had issued from their remonstrances, yet in the inactivity of the emperor, or rather in the absence of acts of wild abandon, they had wishfully fancied a dim glimmer of hope. But now even this glimmer was gone. In vain they consulted each other on what to do, and they could not find any feasible plan. From a historian's hindsight, Yin could perhaps have been saved in one way—the replacement of Di Xin by another member of the imperial house, one worthier, or at least not an alcoholic. But this idea seems never to have entered the minds of the three men, any one of whom would have been a well-qualified candidate. Perhaps the history or the tradition of the dynasty itself rendered such a concept totally alien, or unthinkable, to the Yin people. By this time, Shang, or Yin, had already lasted over six hundred years. As we have formerly narrated, there were several times when the demise of an emperor had occasioned a struggle for succession; but a sovereign had never been replaced while yet alive either by fair means or by foul. Conceivably, this tradition was begun by Yi Yin.[28] For however worthless Taijia had at first demonstrated himself to be, Yi Yin never thought of doing away with him for one moment. The utmost he did was to place Taijia, as it were, in temporary protective custody; as soon as Taijia reformed himself, Yi Yin was eagerness itself to restore full sovereignty to the lawful sovereign. The examples of both Yi Yin and Taijia must have been planted so firmly in the minds of the Yin people that throughout those six centuries the inviolability of the person of the sovereign apparently prevailed as a sacred and unalterable doctrine.

The replacement of Zou being out of the question, the next thing remotely practicable was to rally the people inside the Central Shang for the defense of Yin against the imminent aggression of Zhou. But the success of such an undertaking was contingent on either the people's being so attached to the house of Shang that they were willing to die for it, or their being of such a spirited and vigorous temperament as not to tolerate the threat of outside domination. But neither condition was present. The Prince of Wei, apparently both of his own volition and at the urging of the senior tutor, did his utmost to explore the possibility in this direction; but before long he became completely disillusioned. In desperation, he consulted for one last time with the senior and junior tutors, and in the *Book of History,* a document is still preserved which records their conversation. It is to be noted that even in this hour of bitter frustration and abysmal despair they still held so much reverence for the position of the sovereign that they carefully refrained from mentioning Di Xin by name or accusing him directly of any of his crimes.

The Prince of Wei spoke to the following effect: "Senior tutor, junior tutor, the house of Yin, we may conclude, can no longer exercise rule over the four quarters of the empire. The great deeds of our forefathers were displayed in former ages; but by our being lost and maddened with wine,[29] we have destroyed the effects of their virtues in these times.

"The people of Yin, small or great, are given to thievery, to robbery, to all sorts of villainy and wickedness. The officers, high and low, imitate and vie with one another in violating the law. While so many crimes have been committed, there is no assurance at all that the culprits are apprehended and punished. Consequently the lesser people all rise up without restraint to do outrages upon each other. The dynasty of Yin is sinking into ruin. Its condition is like that of one crossing a turbulent stream, who can find neither ford nor bank. Verily, utter collapse may befall Yin at this moment."

He added, "Senior tutor, junior tutor, I am almost driven to insanity. The elderly people of our house are all withdrawn to the wilds (for safety). And yet you tell me nothing about how to avert the impending ruin. What am I to do?"

The senior tutor replied in this manner: "Oh, our late emperor's son. Heaven, in venomous wrath, has sent down calamities to waste the country of Yin. Hence this condition of being lost and maddened with wine. He has no fear where he ought to fear; and he does things to spite the aged elders and those who formerly held high positions.[30]

"And (taking example from him) the Yin people have become so wicked that they have stolen away the sacrificial animals designated for the veneration of the spirits. Yet the authorities looked at their conduct with connivance, and they were permitted to eat the sacrificial animals with impunity.

"Notwithstanding, when I turn my eyes to see how the people of Yin are governed, I see that they are being burdened and oppressed with taxes and extortions as if they were our hated foes. This is nothing short of asking them to return us relentless hate and enmity. The crimes, above and below, are alike. They are both derived from the one and same source, which causes us all to sicken without relief.

"Thus has calamity descended upon the house of Shang, and we are to suffer its dire consequences. But when ruin overtakes Shang, I am determined that I will not be a servant to another dynasty.

"As for you, our late sovereign's son, I say—Go away. What I said formerly may have been a hindrance to you.[31] But if you do not go away, our entire house may well perish with you.

"Let us do what is the best for each of us to serve our former emperors. To go into hiding is not for me." [32]

As was mentioned before, the Prince of Wei, Senior Tutor Jizi, and Junior Tutor Bigan were later called by Confucius "the three good men of Yin." [33] What Confucius meant is that had the Yin government been put in the charge of the three men, or in the charge of even one of them, Yin might yet have had a chance at this eleventh hour. But as the situation stood, all three saw no hope whatever. And the senior tutor, who probably at an earlier date had urged the Prince of Wei to do his utmost to rally the people to their cause, was now frankly fearful for the latter's safety. The prince, being the eldest son of the late emperor and also widely known for his worthiness, might well become a marked man for Zhou to harm. Thus Jizi urged him to go into hiding to await the outcome. But as yet the Prince of Wei was reluctant to follow the advice.[34]

During this triangular consultation, the junior tutor, Bigan, kept utter silence. He did not speak because he had already made up his mind. As he saw it, the key to the salvation of Yin still remained with Di Xin. If only the emperor could be persuaded to mend his ways, all yet would not be lost. So after the conference, Bigan went alone straight to Zou and poured out his heart in remonstrating with him. But no matter what language the junior tutor used, the torpid tyrant paid him no attention. Bigan said to himself, "To fear death and stop remonstrating—this is not courage. To go on remonstrating until, and only until, it is stopped by death—this is true loyalty." [35] Even though Zou disregarded him and went on indulging himself in his vicious pleasures as though the junior tutor were not present, Bigan kept on remonstrating for three days on end. Finally the drunken despot said, "I have heard that while an ordinary man's heart has five apertures, a sage's heart has seven. The way Bigan talks, he must be a sage. Let's see whether his heart has seven apertures or five." And he ordered Bigan to be killed on the spot to have his heart examined.[36]

Upon hearing of this, Jizi thought of following in the junior tutor's footsteps. Then he said, "To remonstrate, and yet to know at the same time that no remonstrance will be of avail—is that wisdom? To die remonstrating, that is loyalty; but to die as a result of the remonstrance will make the sovereign's wickedness the more conspicuous—is that not disloyalty too?" He picked up his lute and struck a sad note, which came to be known later as the *Song of Jizi*.[37] Then he let down his hair and pretended to be insane. He left the palace and lived among the slaves. Nevertheless, Zou had him arrested and put in prison. Thereupon, the Prince of Wei hesitated no longer. He went into hiding, as the senior tutor had advised him to do.[38]

When the news reached Zhou, Ji Fa decided that the time for punishing Zou had come.[39]

· 2 ·

THE BATTLE OF SHEPHERDS' WILD
—BEFORE AND AFTER (1111 B.C.)

It was the day of *guisi* (rain water serpent), the fourth day of the *chou* (ox) moon in the thirteenth year "after the acceptance of the mandate" [40] that Ji Fa left Zhou to launch the expedition against Yin.[41] For this enterprise he had especially mustered three hundred war chariots and, also, three thousand elite troops selected for outstanding bravery, speed, and prowess, called "bolting tigers." All in all, he had a force of 45,000 men bearing arms.[42]

Prior to the mobilization of his army—in fact, as soon as he had decided to break with Yin—he had announced that the Yin calendar would no longer be used in territories under his control, but replaced by a Zhou calendar which would begin the year a month ahead of Yin.[43] In other words, for all official functions thereafter, the year would begin with the *zi* (rat) moon as its first month *(zheng),* and not the *chou* (ox) moon.[44] To our modern thinking, this is trivial, almost bordering on the ridiculous. But to the ancients this was nothing short of a formal declaration of war, of independence and revolution.

Side by side with this announcement, Ji Fa sent envoys to all the enfeoffed princes of the empire to notify them that "Yin having committed enormous crimes, it behooved him to complete the punishment that was its due." [45] An appointment for a meeting at Mengjin was set for the end of the ox moon, and the princes were all invited to join him with their forces.[46] Not that he expected all of them to be there. Determined in purpose, audacious in making final decisions, Ji Fa was also careful in deliberation and meticulous in analysis. He never took any action until he had thought it through and through. He realized that other than the eight hundred and some princes who had taken part in the military review two years before, there would not be many ready and willing to jump on board his bandwagon before he had won a clear victory. Nevertheless, he decided that if Zou's despotic rule was to be stopped, he could not choose a better moment. Zhou's strength had always been derived from the west and the south of the empire; and he himself had used the last two years in extending the influence even farther, as far as the savage tribes on the western borders of modern Gansu, in the heartland of present-day Sichuan, and to the very distant edges of the confluence of the Yangtze and the Han. From those regions, all had presently sent forces to join in the expedition.[47] His weakness, however, was, as before, with the east and the north, more especially with the east. Because of their long historical associations with the house of Shang, and because of their physical remoteness from Zhou, the states in these two lands had invariably shown more loyalty toward the imperial court and viewed the rise of Zhou with alarm and uneasiness. Even though the latest developments in Yin might have caused them to waver in their accustomed allegiance, the utmost Ji Fa could hope for was that a number of them would elect to remain inactive or neutral in the forthcoming conflict, answering neither his own invitation nor Zou's summons to render their acknowledged sovereign succor and assistance. In the final analysis, therefore, Ji Fa could not but admit to himself that the contest was simply a contest between the men of Zhou and those of the Central Shang. Had it been any other time, he would have hesitated to make that fateful decision. And even now, despite the support of eight hundred states, Ji Fa still felt that in the matters of concentration of population and accumulation of resources, Yin had an indisputable advantage over Zhou. What he himself was relying on in this hazardous adventure was the simple fact that with the disembowelment of Bigan, the imprisonment of Jizi, and the disappearance of the Prince of Wei, the house of Shang had been dispossessed of capable and well-known men, trusted by its own people, to rally them around its banners. Yet even this, Ji Fa must have realized, was a factor so imponderable that unless it was put to actual test, its effects could not be told.

Ji Fa arrived at Mengjin just a little before the appointed date. The enfeoffed princes who had decided to join him were already there waiting. There is no record of the exact number. The *Historical Records* notes only that the princes had brought along with them 4,000 chariots.[48] If those chariots were all organized in the Zhou manner, there would have been three warriors and seventy-two foot soldiers to each, which would have swelled the numbers to some 300,000 men—a figure rather incredible for that age. However, most of the chariots, if not all, were probably not war chariots, but ordinary means of transportation used by the princes to carry themselves and their following to the meeting place. Supposing the number of princes was still eight hundred, and each of them brought along five chariots and a hundred men on the average, the hosts would have amounted to 4,000 chariots and 80,000 men, a figure that seems much more believable. Although this can be but a conjecture, it may not be too rash to assume that counting these forces together with Ji Fa's own 45,000 troops, a conservative estimate would come to a total of around 120,000.

On the opposite side, Zou claimed to have readied 700,000 men for the confrontation.[49] This was undoubtedly an exaggeration. But if it was deliberately propagated for the purpose of frightening the enemy, it did not produce the desired effect on Ji Fa. For, had Zou been able to gather such a large force under his command, the very first thing he could, and should, have done was to secure the defense of the north bank of the Yellow River opposite Mengjin and not to permit the invaders to cross over. But Ji Fa knew well that Zou had not even attempted to do this, for he and Taigong saw to it that all the key points both south and north of the strategic crossing were fully occupied and strongly guarded by their own troops. Moreover, he had also received intelligence that from Mengjin to Chaoge, south of Deer Terrace itself, there was almost no organized defense to speak of. Apparently, Zou and his ministers were still banking on the hope that what Ji Fa was doing was just holding another military review, and he would again withdraw as soon as he had crossed the river and shown off his prowess.

Now, Ji Fa gathered all the princes together and spoke to them about the great purpose of their undertaking.[50] Then he ordered the crossing of the river. This was completed on the day of *wuwu* (mountain earth horse), the twenty-ninth day of the ox moon, which was also the twenty-fifth day since his departure from Zhou.[51] Going about to inspect the troops, he spoke to them a second time. He commanded that the march to Yin commence the very next morning. And in the gray hours of that early dawn on the day of *jiwei* (sand earth sheep), the first day of the *yin* (tiger) moon, he spoke to the troops a third time. These three speeches were recorded by the accompanying Zhou historian and grouped together to form one document, which was titled the *Great Declaration* and was later included by Confucius in his *Book of History*. But the original versions of these speeches were lost later; and what we have today cannot be regarded as entirely genuine. Nevertheless, some passages, whose authenticity seems to be beyond doubt, have since been deeply embedded in the minds of the Chinese people as part and parcel of their cherished heritage. These are related to the relationship between the ruler and the ruled. In one place, Ji Fa declared:

> Heaven and Earth are parents to all creatures. Of all creatures men are the most intelligent. And of men, if anyone happens to be especially gifted, he may become the foremost ruler. To be the foremost ruler is to be father and mother to the people.

Again,

> Heaven, in order to protect the people below, has created for them rulers and teachers. And these rulers and teachers are so, only because they are able to give assistance to the Lord Above in securing prosperity and peace for the four quarters.

Again,

> Heaven sees as the people see. Heaven hears as the people hear.

And again,

> The ancients have said, "He who cherishes us is our sovereign. He who oppresses us is our enemy." Zou, the lone individual, having exercised ceaseless tyranny, is your perpetual enemy.

It is undoubtedly because Ji Fa was a sincere believer in these principles that posterity has compared his revolution with that of Tang and concluded that they both had "overturned the Mandate in accord with Heaven and in response to the people." [52]

Not long after the march had begun, on the banks of a small stream called Wei, the advance was stopped by an envoy from Zou,[53] who sought an audience with Ji Fa. The man had been posted there to keep the Zhou forces under surveillance, to see if they would be withdrawn after crossing the Yellow River, and to find out, if they were not withdrawn, where they would be heading. Ji Fa received him. And addressing the prince with the title he had presumably inherited from his father, the envoy asked, "Xibo, where are you heading?" Ji Fa answered straightforwardly, "I am heading for Yin." "When do you intend to reach there?" the envoy asked again. And Ji Fa answered once more without hesitation, "I intend to reach there the day of *jiazi* (hard wood rat)." And the envoy was permitted to dash back to report to Zou.[54]

Now from the crossing point to Yin the distance was some two hundred kilometers. And the day of hard wood rat was only six days away. With so large a number of troops, with so many lumbersome chariots, and with mountains to climb over and streams to bridge, Ji Fa intended to traverse the entire length in little more than five days. And he was not trying to mislead Zou's envoy either. He had studied the terrain carefully with Taigong, and they had concluded that this could be done. Moreover, he had told this to the envoy not without a purpose. When the intelligence was carried back to the despot, it would no doubt produce the effect of a shattering surprise; and hasten as he would, Zou could not have time to put up much of a defense. But shortly after the envoy's departure, it began to rain hard. Ji Fa ordered the march to push on. But the rain would not stop. Before long the troops became tired and weary, and the officers requested a rest. Ji Fa said, however, "I have already told the envoy to report back to Zou that we will arrive on the day of *jiazi*. If we should not arrive that day, it would discredit the envoy, which very likely might cause him to be put to death by Zou. We must hurry on to save the life of an innocent man." [55]

As a matter of fact, the Zhou troops reached Yin even sooner. On the very day before *jiazi*,[56] they arrived at Shepherds' Wild *(muye)* just outside Chaoge, the famed suburban town of Yin. In the gloam, the silhouette of Zou's pleasure palaces on the hills of Deer Terrace at not too far a distance could be descried. But Ji Fa ordered his men to encamp for the night. Here was the wild the townspeople of Yin reserved for grazing their cattle and sheep. Between the slight incline to the north and a stream called Pure Creek to the south, for several score of kilometers the land was as flat as a man's palm.[57] And here was a terrain adjudged by Taigong to be ideal ground for the deployment of war chariots.

At the crack of dawn, Ji Fa assembled all the officers of the invading force and delivered to them an address which has come down to us in its pristine form. Although from the standpoint of political philosophy this address offers no such high principles or lofty ideals as characterized the three speeches of the *Great Declaration*, yet from the standpoint of history it may be worth-while to quote it in full:

Carrying a golden battle-ax in the left hand and brandishing a white ensign with yaks' tails in the right, the sovereign spoke:

"Far you come, you men of the West Land!"

He continued:

"You princes of friendly states; you ministers and administrators;[58] you deputies, commanders of divisions and of brigades, captains of thousands and of hundreds; and you, men of Yong, of Shu, of Qiang, of Mao, of Wei, of Lu, of Peng, and of Pu.[59]

"Hold your halberds, lay down your shields, rest your lances.[60] I have a speech to make."

The sovereign said: "The ancients had a saying, 'The hen does not announce the morning. The crowing of a hen in the morning indicates the decadence of the family.' Now Zou, the sovereign of Shang, follows only the words of a woman. He is so befuddled that he has abandoned sacrificing to those whom he ought to requite with sacrifice. He is so befuddled that he has abandoned his own kith and kin, both on his father's side and on his mother's side, mistreating them all. It is only the riffraff of the four quarters, loaded with crimes, that he honors and exalts, that he employs and trusts, that he has made into ministers and great officers tyrannizing over the people and working their villainies in the country of Shang.

"Now, I, Fa, am only respectfully executing the punishment decreed by Heaven.

"In today's business, with the advance of every six or seven steps, you must stop and adjust your ranks. Exert yourselves accordingly, my brave sirs!

"You may strike four blows, five blows, six blows, or even seven blows. But do not forget that you must stop and adjust your ranks. Exert yourselves accordingly, my brave sirs!

"Be confident and fearless, like tigers, like panthers, like bears,[61] on this very countryside of Shang. But do not rush on those who fly to us to offer submission. Receive them, so that they may serve our West Land.

"Exert yourselves accordingly, my brave sirs! If you do not exert yourselves, you will be bringing destruction on your own persons." [62]

To most of our modern ears, this address must have sounded lackluster and uninspiring. But, upon reflection, one wonders if it was not a most appropriate one for the occasion. Ji Fa had no need to speak about the political philosophy of his revolution. That he had already pronounced again and again in his three previous speeches of the *Great Declaration*. Nor had he any need to expatiate much on the crimes of Zou. Not only had he mentioned them before, but they were all widely known. Nor did he feel it necessary to utter more words of encouragement or incitement to his troops. He was already as sure as he could be that victory would be won. His army had covered two hundred kilometers in the last five days, passed over mountains and forded streams without meeting any opposition, and were now encamped right at the foot of Zou's pleasure palace. If ever an enemy was found in utter unpreparedness and disarray, it was Zou at this moment. And now that the Yin tyrant was forced to give battle, Ji Fa had only a few worries in his mind. Either from intelligence or from simple reasoning, he probably had concluded that Zou, in this last hour of desperation, would conscript every able-bodied man in the metropolis and drive them forward to the front line for his defense. Although such a multitude would be a miserably undisciplined rabble that could be easily scattered in battle, in numbers they might at first have presented a formidable appearance that could have caused some dismay among Ji Fa's following. Thus the prince deemed it necessary to tell the assembled officers once again that the tyrant Zou had by his own doings alienated all the people of Shang—including the spirits, including even his own kith and kin. What supporters he might still have were only the riffraff of the empire that he had elevated to high positions to tyrannize over the people. So even if the entire population of Yin should pour forth into Shepherds' Wild, the Zhou army had in effect only a very limited number of self-serving scalawags to deal with.

But if Ji Fa felt that this was enough to reinforce the confidence of his own men, he had far more concern and compassion for the people of Yin who were to be thus thrown helter-skelter onto the battlefield. He foresaw the possibility that at the first collision of arms most of the rabble would take to their heels; and he dreaded to think of the prospect that in a maddening onrush to chase after them, his troops would engage in a general and indiscriminate massacre of innocent and harmless men. So, while doing his best not to dampen the fighting spirit of his forces on the one hand, he took pains, on the other, to caution the assembled officers about two things. First, in their advance against the enemy, they must see to it that their men stop after every five or six steps, or after striking at most six or seven blows. This was of course for the readjustment of the ranks, as they had been trained to do in actual hand-to-hand combat. But in the case of a general rout of the enemy, as Ji Fa was anticipating, if the rule was strictly enforced, a greater chance would be given to the fleeing multitude to make their escape. And second— and here one does not need any reflection to discern Ji Fa's intention—he commanded clearly that if there should be men coming out of the enemy lines and flying toward the Zhou side to offer submission, such men must not be rushed upon and harmed. Perhaps it is because of these considerations of his that Ji Fa's war against Zou was later characterized by Mencius as a war "by the most humane against the most inhumane." [63]

Now the day had broken, and the Yin hosts began to issue out of the city to meet the invaders. They were commanded by Zou himself. Upon receiving the intelligence a few days before that Ji Fa was heading for Yin, the surprised emperor had hastily issued urgent summons to as many enfeoffed princes as he thought were still loyal to him to come to his aid. In all, not much more than fifty states responded to the call and joined their forces with the imperial troops.[64] Thoroughly alarmed now, Zou realized that their united strength was insufficient for the defense. He ordered that the entire male population of the imperial seat be conscripted forthwith; and he pretended, as he had always claimed, that he had 700,000 men under arms. But actually the hastily assembled force totaled not more than 170,000.[65] Nevertheless, in appearance at least, they outnumbered Ji Fa's troops by far; and it was later described by an official Zhou historian that "Zou's hosts were as numerous as a forest." [66]

In the clear light of the morning, the two opposing armies slowly approached each other. As soon as Ji Fa judged that the distance between them was narrowed enough, he gave orders to Taigong to make the charge they had planned long in advance. At the command of the doughty warrior, suddenly 350 chariots burst forth in unison from the Zhou ranks in one thunderous assault.[67] It was a sight that no one on the Yin side, prince or subject, officer or soldier, had ever seen or experienced before. While seasoned warriors paled and trembled, the ill-disciplined multitude, frightened out of their wits, just turned on their heels and scrambled for their lives. It was each for himself and devil take the hindmost. The panic became contagious. Even the Yin imperial troops opened up a way for the invaders, pointing their weapons backward at the direction where Zou, safely stationed at a great distance in the rear, was watching the progress of the battle.

At this, Zou himself fled. He went straight back to Deer Terrace, "covered himself with garments of jade and pearls, set fire to the building, and burned himself to death." [68] Daji and another concubine also hanged themselves.[69]

Both the multitude and the main body of Yin's imperial army, however, fled toward the city, and Ji Fa and his troops followed them. Try to stop unnecessary slaughter as Ji Fa would, there was not much that he could do from the beginning. In the first place, the rout itself had generated a stampede, resulting in many being trodden to death by their own weight and numbers. Then, even if all Zhou's men obeyed their officers' injunctions and slowed down their pursuit at every five or six steps, there were still the cohorts of the eight hundred and some enfeoffed princes and also of the eight western and southern tribes who could hardly have been expected to exercise restraint at such an hour of easy triumph. In fact, as a historian described, at one place there had been so much carnage that a wooden pestle a soldier had carried for cooking purpose was found floating about in the blood that flowed.[70] Though this account was thought by Mencius[71] to be exaggerated, yet it seems only reasonable to assume that there was indeed much bloodshed in the battle of Shepherds' Wild. However, there is also another historical truth that we can be sure of: Had Ji Fa not been the man he was, there would have been far, far more. In any event, he finally managed to bring the killing to a stop by going himself to the very front line and placing his own person between the pursuers and the pursued. At this, all those of the latter who had fallen behind, being unacquainted with his intentions, fell prostrate in sheer terror. But Ji Fa shouted to them, "Have no fear! I come to bring you peace, not to treat you as enemy." Thereupon they all knocked their heads on the earth in gratitude, and "knocked them so hard, even like animals knocking off their horns." [72]

At the spread of this news, all the Yin troops laid down their arms. And Ji Fa waited so as to give more time to the conscripted people to flee to their homes at a less hurried pace. Then, when the situation was wholly under control, he waved to all the enfeoffed princes to follow him; and they proceeded to enter into Yin.

A number of Yin people, quite quietened by this time, gathered themselves by the side of the entrance of the city to watch the entry of the Zhou army. In the midst of the crowd there was Shang Rong, who had formerly served Zou as a minister, and was very much loved and respected by the people, but had been dismissed by the tyrant in the later part of his reign. [73] Presently the triumphant procession of the Zhou forces began, and shortly afterward a dignitary appeared riding in a chariot. The people, watching his approach, asked Shang Rong anxiously, "Is this our new sovereign?" And the former minister of Zou answered, "No. He looks too stern, too guarded, too impatient. He is probably the commander of the vanguard." And Shang Rong was right. It was the Duke of Bi. Then along came another chariot carrying another dignitary. The people asked again, "Is this our new sovereign?" And Shang Rong answered again, "No. He crouches forward like a tiger and glances about like an eagle. He exudes confidence and strength. It is probably the commanding general." And Shang Rong was right once more. It was Taigong. Then arrived another dignitary riding in a chariot. The people asked a third time, "Is this our new sovereign?" And Shang Rong answered, "He is pensive. He is tolerant. He is elated—but not for himself. No, he is not our new sovereign; he is probably his principal minister." And Shang Rong was right a third time, for it was the Duke of Zhou. Then came a chariot carrying a fourth dignitary. As soon as Shang Rong sighted him, he said, "He sees all. Yet from his countenance we do not know whether he is pleased or not pleased, or what he approves and what he disapproves. Yes, this is our new sovereign!" [74] And all the Yin people did obeisance with their faces to their hands and with their heads to the ground. And Ji Fa replied by putting his own hands to his face, with his heralds crying out: "May heaven bless us all!" [75]

That evening Ji Fa returned to the camp, looking as if victory had not yet been won. [76] He held counsel with his closest associates and said, "The Yin people are so numerous—too numerous. What should be done about them?" He asked this of Taigong, who answered, "I have heard of a saying: 'If you love a house, you love even the crow that perches on its roof. If you do not love a man, you do not even love the sight of the wall that encompasses his village.' If your majesty's inclination is bent toward extirpation, the decision is yours to make." Ji Fa shook his head. The Duke of Shao, a trusted kinsman whom he had personally selected to assist his principal minister, the Duke of Zhou, volunteered, "It is fitting and proper that the guilty should be punished and the innocent should go free. Let us sieve the good from the bad and uproot all that is evil."

Ji Fa hesitated, weighing the difficulties that the process was bound to run into. He asked the question of his brother Ji Dan, and the Duke of Zhou made this reply: "Let us proclaim peace for all. Let each and every man enjoy the safety of his hearth, and the fruits of his labor. There will be no scrutiny of his past conduct or of his relationship with the old regime. There is to be only an understanding that we shall be attached to none but those who will lead a life of virtue and humanity."

"Well and good," said Ji Fa, "this is what I intend to do." And the dark cloud on his countenance lifted. He looked, as indeed he should, like a man who had just come to the possession of the whole world.[77]

The next day, accompanied by his officers and the enfeoffed princes in ordered procession, Ji Fa went to the *she* altar of the Yin palace. There, in a simple ceremony, the senior diviner proclaimed: "The last descendant of the house of Yin, Zou, having violated and abandoned the bright virtues of former emperors, having given affront and offense to gods and spirits, having exercised tyranny and oppression over the people of Shang, the Lord Above, viewing all these evidences, has rendered His judgment." And Ji Fa did obeisance twice with his face to his hands and with his head to the ground, then said, "I have carried out the command to overturn Yin, and am now keeping the Mandate of Heaven in reverential custody." And again he did obeisance twice with his face to his hands and with his head to the ground.[78] When he rose, he was the acknowledged sovereign of the empire.

· 3 ·

THE GOVERNMENT OF WU WANG

Ji Fa now assumed the title Wu Wang, which may be translated as the Martial Emperor, or the Triumphant Emperor. At his time, it seems that the awarding of a posthumous title to a deceased personage had not yet come into full use. So Ji Fa was known as Wu Wang both while alive and later when dead.

With the realization of such a revolution, there were bound to be many changes and modifications in government. And it appears that all the measures that Ji Fa took fall under the following categories: (1) measures that were formalistic in nature but nonetheless essential for the demonstration of the "overturning of the Mandate"; (2) measures that aimed at winning over the people both of Yin and of the empire; (3) military measures that were necessary to make secure the results of the victory at Shepherds' Wild; and (4) political, or rather basic, measures that were devised to perpetuate the role of the house of Zhou as the custodian of the "Mandate of Heaven."

The measures of the first category were all taken almost immediately after Ji Fa's acclamation as the new sovereign Wu Wang. He sacrificed to Heaven in the traditional bonfire ceremony.[79] Then, out of respect for the preceding dynasty, he went to Tang's temple and paid homage to its great founder.[80] After that, he returned to his camp in Shepherds' Wild, where, with solemn rites in which the enfeoffed princes served as assistants or as attendants, he consecrated his great-grandfather the Ancient Duke as Tai Wang (Grand Emperor), his grandfather Duke Ji as Wang Ji (Emperor Ji), and his father Chang as Wen Wang (Cultural Emperor).[81] And in so honoring his forebears, he set a precedent that was to be followed by nearly every dynasty afterward.

And taking example from Tang, Wu Wang now proclaimed that the Zhou calendar, instead of the Yin calendar, should be adopted by the whole empire, with the zi (rat) moon replacing the chou (ox) moon as zheng, the official beginning month of the year. But unlike Tang, he also openly proclaimed that, in matters of cultivation, the husbandmen should follow the customary seasons as had been demarcated since the time of Xia.[82] The Xia having used black and the Yin having used white as the formal color,[83] Wu Wang now changed it to red. Thenceforth his formal wear was to be red; on military occasions, he would ride on red horses; in offering sacrifices, he would use animals with reddish hair; and for solemn rituals, such as laying the dead into the coffin, the ceremonies would be held at sunrise.[84] Again, as it was the practice of the Xia to plant pine and of the Yin to plant cypress around the she altar, so Wu Wang made it a rule that instead of the pine and the cypress, chestnut trees should be planted.[85] Orders to these effects were conveyed throughout the length and breadth of the dominion that came under his sway, and strict observance of them was expected. Although all this may appear trivial or unnecessary in our modern view, yet it was absolutely essential in the ancient days for a change of dynasty. For in every enfeoffed state, large or small, there was a she altar; and in every community there was many an occasion when formal wear was required. It was therefore in the observance of these rules, or in the failure to observe them, that the newly established imperial authority could find ready and unmistakable evidence as to whether or not any particular state or any particular community had sincerely submitted to its rule.

The second category of actions that Wu Wang took was directed toward winning the goodwill and inspiring the confidence and respect of the people of the empire in general and of Yin in particular. In a manner of speaking, after such an infamous reign as that of Zou, this was a comparatively easy task, which could be achieved simply by righting the wrongs the former tyrant had committed. This was precisely what Wu Wang did. He entered the palaces and saw a scandalous number of women. He asked, "Where are these women from?" "They were taken by Zou from many places," was the answer. And he ordered, "Let them be returned to where they were taken from." Also, he saw many precious jades, and asked, "Where are these from?" "They were extorted from many enfeoffed princes," was the answer. And he ordered again, "Let them be restored to their original owners." And the populace was at once impressed with the high order of his moral integrity and self-restraint.[86] Then, after inventories had been made of the treasures of Deer Terrace, and also of the grains Zou had accumulated in the granaries at a nearby suburb,[87] Wu Wang had them all distributed "to relieve the needy and the destitute." [88]

He had long known Shang Rong to be a very good minister of Yin. Now he sought him out and invited him to serve as his high councilor (gong).[89] But Shang Rong declined. Wu Wang knew that the former Yin minister was unwilling to serve a new dynasty. So he did not force him against his will, but instead erected a special column at the street where Shang Rong resided to mark the high esteem he held for him.[90] At the same time, he rebuilt the tomb of Bigan so that it would become a fitting monument for that worthy but ill-fated junior tutor.[91] Also, he released Jizi from prison.[92] Fully aware of the senior tutor's reputation as the most learned and sagacious man of Yin, Wu Wang wanted very much to learn from him. But having respected the feelings of Shang Rong not to serve the new dynasty, he felt he could hardly do otherwise to one of the most eminent members of the former imperial house. He therefore treated Jizi more or less like a guest, according him all sorts of honor but expecting no service from him in return.

When the Prince of Wei heard of all this, he emerged from hiding. He came directly to Wu Wang's camp, the upper portions of his body stripped of garments, his wrists bound together before his bare breast, with one hand holding a bunch of rushes and the other dragging forth a lamb, and accompanied by an attendant bearing sacrificial vessels—all this to show that he was regarding himself as no more than a captive, ready and willing to be used as a sacrifice like the lamb at the conqueror's will. As he approached, however, Wu Wang himself untied the prince's wrists and restored him to all the honors that he had enjoyed at the former Yin court.[93]

The third category of actions taken by Wu Wang were military measures. As a matter of fact, in a situation like this, they should have been of greater urgency than all others. But the battle of Shepherds' Wild had been so decisive that it left only few matters for Wu Wang to deal with. The first one was what should be done about the control of Yin. He could of course destroy it utterly, as hard and wiry Taigong had insinuated was not impossible; level the city to the ground, extirpate whatever population resisted, and force the remainder to migrate to wherever he chose. But that option he had rejected outright as not humane. He could also follow the precedent set by Tang, who, after defeating Jie, had incorporated the capital of Xia as part of the Central Shang and renamed it West City. But then in order to keep the restive populace of the Xia under closer surveillance, Tang himself had to move his own imperial seat from Bo to West Bo.[94] Could Wu Wang do the same? He probably saw insurmountable difficulties. Tang's age was much more nomadic than his own. It was relatively easy for the founder of the Shang dynasty to move his principal following from one area to another. But his own base in Zhou being entirely agricultural, it would be inconceivable to transfer it to some other place. Could he then make Yin his own imperial seat instead of Zhou? That thought too very likely never occurred to Wu Wang. For to do so would be not only unthinkably disappointing to his own people, but would be also placing his own safety in the hands of an alien and hostile nation. Could he leave Yin as it had always been under the administration of the house of Shang? That would be giving the vanquished foe a chance to renew his strength and wreak vengeance on himself at a later time. Could he entrust the government of Yin to one of his own kinsmen? That might work for a limited duration; but sooner or later, whether under a kinsman or not, with its numerous population and with its plentiful resources Yin was bound to become a rival power to Zhou, which could very well bring about serious discord or even political division within the empire.

So, after long and thorough deliberation, he came to a conclusion which he himself did not deem satisfactory, but which was the best he could do under the circumstances. To show his magnanimity to the fallen house of Shang, he invested Wugeng, Zou's son and heir, as Prince of Yin, who was allowed to continue the imperial ceremonies in veneration of their ancestors but also required to acknowledge allegiance to Zhou like all other enfeoffed princes.[95] As to the limits of Wugeng's fief, Wu Wang purposely left them undelineated, giving an impression to the Yin people that if they behaved well, they might hope to have the confines considerably enlarged later. For the time being, however, Wugeng's jurisdiction was restricted to the city limits of Yin, as they had been at the time when it was first founded by Pangeng. Of course, Yin had grown far beyond its original proportions since then. Not to speak of the normal, natural growth of a city within so long a period as three centuries, the imperial seat of Shang had expanded enormously, especially under Wuding, who in his long reign had made it the greatest political, military, and economic center the ancient world had ever seen; and again under Di Xin or Zou, who had tried to despoil the entire empire of its riches to serve his own cravings for luxury and grandeur at Yin. So now Wu Wang divided the extended parts of the metropolis into three portions, and put them respectively under the charge of three of his brothers—the Prince of Guan, the Prince of Cai, and the Prince of Huo—who were known as the "three supervisors."[96] Moreover, he ordered that the Prince of Guan and the Prince of Cai should also serve as advisers to Wugeng.[97] In brief, the authority exercised by Wugeng was minimal, and the entire populated area of Yin was placed under military occupation.

Alongside the formation of this military government for the control of Yin, the days immediately after the fall of Zou found Wu Wang also occupied with taking measures to mop up whatever pockets of resistance still remained and to extend his sway to the very frontiers of the Yin Empire. This was apparently not so difficult a problem as might have been imagined. Of all the ancient records pertaining to this period, only one took note of a few states that were overthrown in the process.[98] It appeared that Taigong and several other generals were entrusted with the task. And judging by the time they each spent receiving their orders and returning to report their successes, the longest being no more than five or six days, the distances they covered could not have been great. It may therefore be assumed that all these intransigent princedoms were located in the vicinity of Yin, and were probably among the fifty some states that had given aid to Zou in his final days. Moreover, they all clearly lay in an easterly direction from Yin. This was representative of the political situation of the times, for the influence of Zhou had been always dominant in the West Land, more felt in the South Land, less in the North Land, and hardly at all in the East Land. But be that what it might, after the battle of Shepherds' Wild, every contact must have been made to apply constant pressure on all enfeoffed states that had not yet openly acknowledged their allegiance to Zhou. And in order to hasten the hesitating ones to make up their minds, Wu Wang staged one of the greatest hunts in recorded ancient history.[99] Although the place he held it was not expressly mentioned in any of the ancient histories, by the number of animals killed and captured, it must have been no other than the vast imperial preserve to the southeast of the Great City Shang. As one record had it, there were taken "22 tigers, 2 mountain lions, 3,235 reindeer, 12 rhinoceroses, 721 yaks, 151 bears, 118 grizzly bears, 352 boars, 18 sleepy foxes,[100] 16 antelopes, 50 musk deer, 30 roebucks, and 3,508 deer."[101] The magnitude of the chase must have displayed the prowess of Zhou to the greatest advantage. For shortly afterward "652 states volunteered their submission."[102] And on the day of yiwei (soft wood sheep) in the mao (hare) moon—that is, the seventh day in the fourth month of the Zhou calendar, and exactly thirty-one days after the battle of Shepherds' Wild—Wu Wang was able to announce that he was now "sovereign of the four quarters, having accepted the homage of all the states that Yin had formerly possessed." [103]

And the last military measure Wu Wang took was demobilization, which he did quite dramatically. Assured now of dominion over the then known world, he set off for home with all the enfeoffed princes following in his train. Presently he arrived at his capital, Feng; he had left it some four months ago [104] and now returned the founder of a new dynasty. On the day of *dingwei* (kitchen fire sheep), with the princes from various domains serving as attendants and carrying sacrificial vessels, he sacrificed to his ancestors in the temple of the house of Zhou. Three days later, he venerated Heaven in a bonfire ceremony outside the city, solemnly announcing "the successful conclusion of the war." [105] And just prior to this, he ordered that "all the horses (used in the campaign) be set free to the south of Mount Hua, and all the oxen be let loose in the open country of Peach Forest *(taolin)* in order to demonstrate that he had no intention to use them again." [106]

Indeed, even as he was sincerely hoping that he would never have to use force in the empire anymore, his mind was being constantly exercised by the question of how to perpetuate the role of Zhou as the custodian of the Mandate of Heaven. There was even evidence that he had been spending many a sleepless night over the problem.[107] Assuredly he was the one person who knew all about the strength and weakness of the imperial system of Yin; and realistically he had long come to a conclusion that if he had succeeded in supplanting the house of Shang as "the sovereign of the four quarters," it was due much less to his capability than to his good fortune. Good fortune, first of all, in having had such an inventive genius as Wen Wang for his father, who was able to transform a strip of barren, desolate, and thinly inhabited land into a mighty and populous state to form his own power base. Good fortune again—perhaps even more crucial than the first—in having had Di Xin, the last sovereign of Yin, for both his father's and his own adversary. Had it been someone else on the imperial throne, less given to drink and debauchery, more sensitive to the responsibilities as well as the perils of sovereignty, it was doubtful that the state of Zhou, even with his father's resourcefulness, would ever have been allowed to grow into full strength while there was yet time to cut it down to size. Again, not to speak of other circumstances, even after Wu Wang himself had openly decided on revolution, had it not been for Di Xin's senseless atrocities which had alienated the people far and near, even at this last moment, with the superiority of the Central Shang both in numbers and in affluence, the sovereign of Yin could still have been more than a match for the Prince of Zhou, the latter's eight hundred allies notwithstanding. The more Wu Wang dwelt on the events, the more admiration he felt for Tang, who had founded the Yin imperial system. Could he copy it for the benefit of Zhou? He regretted that he could not. In the course of natural developments, Tang had established the Central

Shang in the heartland of the empire. It was not Tang's making; it happened to be his just for the taking. And being centered at Central Shang, his imperial house could issue commands to, and keep watch over, the Four Lands with such advantages as only a centrally located authority could possess. But Zhou was at the extreme western end of the empire; it could never rule the vast dominion in the same manner as Yin. If Yin, despite its central location, could not prevent Zhou from growing into such a position as to be able to displace it eventually, how could Zhou, being at the extreme western end, prevent other states from growing into similar positions at the other ends of the empire—at the south, at the north, and more especially at the east?

Then the solution came to him. If Zhou could not be moved to a central location, could not he move parts of Zhou, or rather portions of the Zhou forces, to the key points in the other regions to enforce his decrees and to keep watch over the enfeoffed states for him? In our modern thinking, this does not appear to be too difficult a thing to do; the matter may be easily solved by establishing garrison posts, or military bases, in areas of strategic importance, however remote they may be. But in ancient days, the problem was much more complicated. For with our modern means of transportation, we can shift garrison forces or transfer military personnel as often as we like and at any time we like. But in the age of Wu Wang, such an arrangement presented enormous and often unsurmountable difficulties. From Zhou to the eastern extreme of the empire the distance is no less than 1,200 kilometers; to make the men journey back and forth would have involved great hardships and unforeseeable hazards. Moreover, the people being yet partly nomadic, the geography and terrain of the empire being only primitively charted or not charted at all, and the languages spoken by the natives in various places being different from one another, unless the men entrusted with such missions were given a chance to stay in a locality long enough, they could scarcely be expected to effectively perform their function. Thus, though the reasoning of Wu Wang is not dissimilar to that of our modern times, his execution of the intent took a different form.

Historians, both Chinese and Western, are accustomed to describe ancient Chinese history as feudalistic in character. And Chinese historians, especially, are fond of citing the so-called "Three Dynasties"—Xia, Shang (or Yin), and Zhou—as the "Age of Feudalism." But strictly speaking, the political structures that obtained in the three dynasties are different from one another. The Xia was rather a confederation of states, and a very loose one at that. When Yu "conferred lands and surnames" on various peoples after the subjugation of the Great Flood,[108] the procedure was a recognition of the status quo, pure and simple. The multitude of nations were already there, each in its own locality. What they were induced or required to do was acknowledge the overlordship of the "Central Nation" as represented by emperors Yao and Shun. The chieftains of these nations were therefore considered to be enfeoffed princes; but actually they owed their fiefs only to the right of occupation and to themselves. Perhaps for a time in those years while the Great Flood was raging unchecked, and also immediately after it was brought under control, the entire country and people, being confronted with the common peril and inspired by a singular combination of rare leadership—the utterly selfless Yao, the infinitely resourceful Shun, and the tirelessly efficient Yu—were far more unified than they had ever been. But this could not have lasted long. The nomadic nature of the times soon made mockery of those "enfeoffments"; and Yu was compelled to seek a remedy by dreaming up a "grand scheme of reorganization," but dreamed in vain.[109] Throughout the Xia dynasty, though only the descendants of Yu were by universal consent given the prerogative of using the title *di* or *wang*, the actual authority of the imperial house extended only to where its military power could enforce obedience or extort tribute. The "enfeoffed states" were mostly as ancient as the house of Xia itself. Other than using the Xia calendar, which was more a matter of convenience than of obligation, they acknowledged the *di* or *wang* as *primus inter pares,* the first among equals, and nothing more.

But Tang succeeded in making a significant change. Under him, the loose confederation of states was transformed into a centrally controlled federation, verging toward true feudalism. By serving the last Xia emperor as loyally as he could under the most trying circumstances, he set an example for the enfeoffed princes about what loyalties he would be expecting from them.[110] By summoning these princes to a meeting and compelling them to agree to abide by his policies, he showed that should he so desire, he had in effect the power to destroy any one of them.[111] By enforcing a system of tribute from these princedoms, even though he purposely made it not burdensome, he established a practice that served constantly as a reminder to them of their allegiance to the imperial house.[112] And by putting Yu's "grand scheme of reorganization" into actual execution (though realistically modified), he founded an imperial system that appeared virtually indestructible. Under Wuding, the system was even further strengthened. That mighty potentate not only conscripted manpower from the enfeoffed states whenever necessary,[113] but also destroyed two powerful states, Shiwei and Dapeng, when he adjudged that they had gone out of bounds.[114]

However, it is only when Zhou displaced Shang as the ruling dynasty that feudalism attained its highest degree of development. Wuding might have destroyed two enfeoffed states, but he was not known to have created any. Even though at some time in the long dim past, some little number of the enfeoffed states might have owed their origins to some of the emperors, as far

as men's memory goes, until Wu Wang appeared on the scene, there is no
record that a sovereign had of his own will created a large number of states
within a very short period of time.

And Wu Wang did this clearly with a doublefold purpose: On the one
hand, he was using the enfeoffments to reward those of his following whose
services deserved such recognition; and on the other, he was availing himself
of the opportunity to establish a chain of permanent military bases in key,
strategic points of the empire. Perhaps this was possible for Wu Wang
because his age was yet a time when population everywhere was still very
sparse, when unoccupied lands were still available to men almost at any place
where they were determined to migrate and settle. Yet, for all that, Wu
Wang was wary of what repercussions might ensue if he put his plans into
effect all at once. So he proceeded with the enfeoffments very gingerly, and
chose to accomplish the whole scheme stage by stage.

While most of the enfeoffed princes were gathered in Zhou attending the
various ceremonies he was holding, he first made an exploratory move to feel
out their reaction. He had already sought out the direct lineal descendants of
Divine Husbandman, of the Yellow Emperor, of Yao, of Shun, and of Yu—
the famed ancient monarchs whom the Chinese people had always held in
the highest esteem. Though all of them, with the possible exception of the
descendant of Shun, were living in apparent obscurity, undistinguishable
from other common people, he now invested them as princes, each with a
small fief in the respective areas where they had been residing—the descendant of Divine Husbandman as Prince of Jiao in the west of modern Henan
province; that of the Yellow Emperor as Prince of Zhu in modern Shandong
province; that of Yao as Prince of Ji near present-day Peking; and that of Yu
as Prince of Qi on the border of Henan and Shandong.[115] The sites of these
fiefs suited Wu Wang's plan well, for they were widely scattered in different regions of the empire, so that if there should be resistance to the idea of
the creation of new princedoms by old vested interests, it was bound to
emerge out in the open somewhere. With the descendant of Shun, Wu
Wang took a bolder step. The man, Yu Yufu by name, was no stranger to
the conqueror. Although not an officer of high rank and important position,
he was serving the Zhou court in a very useful capacity as its chief potter.
Wu Wang now married his eldest daughter to Yu Yufu's son, and invested
the new son-in-law as Prince of Chen, a fief which over a thousand years
before Yu was said to have given to Shun's heir after his own succession to
the empire.[116] While, other than this single fact, neither Yu Yufu nor his
son was known to have had any direct personal connection with Chen, the
place Chen itself was generally recognized as one of great strategic importance, situated as it was not far from the confluence of the two principal
streams in the ancient world—the Yellow River and the Ji. In making this

investiture, Wu Wang was doubtless fully aware of the possibility that he might run into serious opposition, and was equally prepared to back up the decision with all his majesty and power. But his apprehensions turned out to be unwarranted. All the new enfeoffments, including that of Chen, were received by the princes assembled with acclamation, deeming it fitting and timely to do honor to those illustrious sovereigns of old. (See Map V.)

Once assured of the willingness of the enfeoffed princes to cooperate, or to acquiesce, Wu Wang created some two or three score new states.[117] A detailed description of these, however, is lacking. But from what we know about some of them, Wu Wang seemed to have handled the matter with extra care and caution. As a first step, a few enfeoffments were apparently carved out of the Zhou domain itself. For instance, the princedom of Bi was formed from the very vicinities of the city Feng and given to the captain of vanguards, the Duke of Bi.[118] This was intended, of course, to demonstrate that the imperial domain itself was treated not differently from other enfeoffed states. Then the Prince of Guan was awarded the fief of modern Zhengzhou, Henan; the Prince of Cai, modern Qinyang, Henan; and the Prince of Huo, modern Huoxian, Shanxi.[119] Guan and Cai were both parts of Central Shang, while Huo was probably conquered by Zhou even earlier.[120] Since they were conquered territories, Wu Wang was naturally expected to dispose of them at his will. However, these three places were all of great strategic importance, dominating, if not controlling, respectively the southern, western, and northern entrances to Yin. But by assigning these fiefs to the "three supervisors" of the former imperial seat, fresh hope was also given to the people still loyal to the fallen dynasty that if they behaved themselves well, these princes might soon repair to their own fiefs, and they themselves would be freed from alien supervision.

But Wu Wang's preoccupation was mainly with the east, and next to the east, the north. The south having acknowledged the sway of Zhou early, no special military base was required to ensure its fidelity. But the other two quarters, more especially the east, had always regarded the men of the West Land with condescension, if not with hostility. Thus not only new states must be created in their midst, but these states should be created in such a manner as not to provoke their open opposition. So Wu Wang first invested his sixth brother as Prince of Cao and his seventh brother as Prince of Cheng, with both of their fiefs on the eastern borders of modern Shandong province.[121] These enfeoffments had several advantages. Firstly, if we draw a line from Feng, the capital of Zhou, through Guan and Chen to these two fiefs, it is almost as straight as the flight of an arrow. Secondly, once these military bases were secured, they could keep the east more easily at bay. And thirdly—this is even more important—the two fiefs were at the east end of the vast hunting preserve of the Shang; thus Wu Wang could still claim

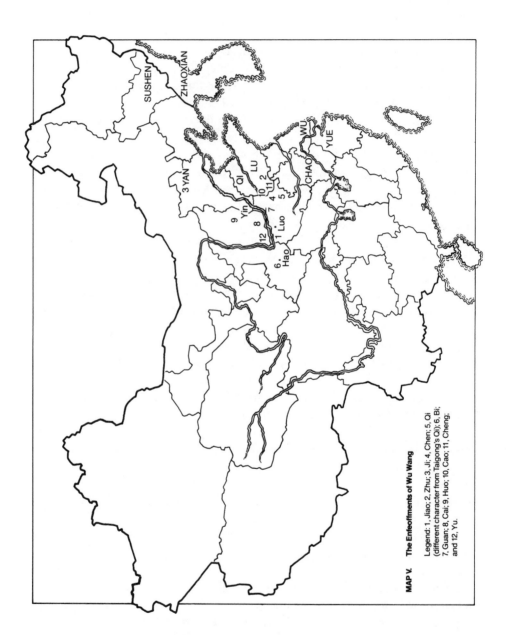

MAP V. The Enfeoffments of Wu Wang

Legend: 1, Jiao; 2, Zhu; 3, Ji; 4, Chen; 5, Qi (different character from Taigong's Qi); 6, Bi; 7, Guan; 8, Cai; 9, Huo; 10, Cao; 11, Cheng; and 12, Yu.

them as spoils of war, and no objections could be raised against his disposal of them.

Still, Wu Wang was not satisfied. What he wanted was one truly unified empire, no corner of which would be permitted to be outside his surveillance. So he climaxed his whole program by creating three additional fiefs—two in the farthest extremities of the East Land and one in the North Land. The two eastern fiefs were called Qi and Lu, with the former on the northern side and the latter on the southern side of the sacred mountain Taishan, and with both stretching eastward to the seacoast. The new fief in the North Land was called Yan, located almost at the exact site of modern Peking, whose strategic significance was self-evident, but at this time not yet so vital to Wu Wang as the two eastern fiefs. And from the selection of the princes for these fiefs we may see the enormous importance the founder of the new dynasty was attaching to them. For he named none else than Taigong for Qi, the Duke of Zhou for Lu, and the Duke of Shao for Yan.[122]

These were known by one and all as the three men most trusted by the new sovereign of the empire. Taigong was his teacher and father-in-law; the Duke of Zhou his brother and principal minister; and the Duke of Shao his kinsman and selected by himself to be the Duke of Zhou's chief assistant.[123] From this decision, we may also gather some insight into Wu Wang's reasoning. With the prestige of these men, it was difficult for any vested interests in those areas to voice any objection. Moreover, Wu Wang seemed to have made it clear to all concerned that the largest of the fiefs was to have no more than one hundred *li* square each (about fifty-two kilometers square)—a limited area, not too difficult for any sparsely populated country to make room for. Furthermore, lest some of the enfeoffed princes should fear the proximity of these powerful personages, he might have also explained that the three men were not to be stationed constantly in their fiefs; he had more need of them in the imperial court, and except for occasional visits, the three would have to run their princedoms mostly by proxy. At any rate, since the enfeoffed princes of Yin's former East Land and North Land were all assembled at Zhou at this juncture, if they still entertained any objections, real or imaginary, he could well trust to the three men themselves, the most capable men he could find in the whole empire, to ferret them out and smooth them away. And the result was what Wu Wang had wanted: These arrangements were universally accepted.

These enfeoffments, of course, constituted hereditary feudal states, most of which endured no less than three centuries until the system, as it was founded by Wu Wang and later reinforced by the Duke of Zhou, began to deteriorate. But while the system was effectually maintained, it was perhaps the most advanced form of feudalism ever established in China. However, it needs to be noted here that out of the fourteen investitures we have cited

above, except for the four small princedoms assigned to the descendants of
Divine Husbandman, the Yellow Emperor, Yao, and Yu, the remainders
were all given to Wu Wang's kith and kin—one to his son-in-law, one to his
father-in-law, two to his cousins,[124] and six to his brothers. As a matter of
fact, according to some ancient accounts, the number of princes invested by
Wu Wang and later by the Duke of Zhou and Wu Wang's successors
totaled seventy-one, among whom fifty-three were from the house of
Zhou.[125] In our modern view, this was arrant nepotism. But in that age, the
necessity, or the desirability, of such an arrangement seemed to have been
understood by all, both by the old enfeoffed princes and by the common
people at large. As it was openly confessed by the descendants of the imperial house sometime later, these princedoms were created simply "to form
fences and screens for Zhou." [126] And from the same source an explanation
was offered as basis for this thinking: "Even though brothers may engage in
fisticuffs inside the walls of the house, they will join together to fight invaders from outside." [127] At any rate, for good or for bad, if the Chinese up to
this time had been already more attached than other races to the belief that
blood is thicker than water, there is no doubt that their idiosyncrasy, or
obsession, in this respect was further, and perhaps decisively, strengthened
by Wu Wang's doings. Moreover, out of this system a concept also developed that the entire empire belonged bodily to the sovereign, who could
dispose of all its land and all its wealth at will—which would become a bane
to the whole Chinese nation for thousands of years to come. At his time,
however, Wu Wang was perhaps unaware of such pernicious ramifications.
His entire motivation was to establish dependable military bases in the key
areas of the empire in order to bolster his rule. For this, there can be no
better proof than the very name he first gave to the capital Taigong built for
the princedom of Qi. He called it simply "Barracks Mound." [128]

Besides the investitures mentioned above, there are two others uncon-
nected with Wu Wang's general feudal scheme, but also worthy of note.
After the conquest of Yin, Wu Wang discovered that the state of Wu at the
remote southeastern corner of the empire owed its origin to Taibo and
Zhongyong, who had selflessly abdicated their rights of succession so that his
own grandfather could inherit the dukedom of Zhou.[129] Contact was immediately resumed between the two branches of the same house. While the
reigning prince of Wu, a great-grandson of Zhongyong, voluntarily welcomed the suzereignty of the new dynasty, Wu Wang had his younger
brother brought from Wu to Zhou and invested as Prince of Yu, with a fief
in the former Central Shang, close to the ancient capital of Xia.[130]

The second extra enfeoffment was in connection with Jizi, the famed
senior tutor of Yin, whom Wu Wang had freed from imprisonment. The
emperor of Zhou, treating him neither as a captive nor as a subject but as a

guest, sought many a time to learn from his wisdom about the best way to govern the empire. But that was one topic which Jizi was reluctant to talk about. In the *Book of History* there is extant a document titled *hongfan,* the *Great Plan,* which purports to be the record of a conversation between Wu Wang and Jizi. While the monarch's earnest desire was humbly expressed in his opening remarks, Jizi's answers were lengthy, expansive, touching on all kinds of matters in the wide world, but bearing little on the subject of inquiry. For instance, the senior tutor harangued on an ancient version of what we moderns call ecology. The universe, according to him, consisted of five elements—water, fire, wood, metal, and earth. Unless a harmonious balance was maintained among them, there would be unseasonable calamities such as excessive rainfall, sunshine, heat, cold, or windstorms. Again, he talked about the ways to resolve great doubts that might occur to a ruler's mind, and he suggested that all the following must be consulted—the ruler's own heart, the ministers, the common people, divination by the tortoise, and divination by the *shi*-stalks. His own mind veering toward the inactive, Jizi seemed to attach special significance to the two methods of divination. Said he, "When the tortoise and the *shi*-stalks are both opposed to the views of men, it bodes well to lie still rather than to take action." He also attempted an analysis of what may be truly considered as blessings to men. And he reached a conclusion that there are only five things: "The first is long life; the second is riches; the third is good health; the fourth is habitual love of virtue; and the fifth is to die of ripe old age (without accident or illness)." There can be no question but that Wu Wang felt a sincere respect for the senior tutor's wit and learning, but he must also have been made fully conscious of the fact that for all his own humility and earnestness, Jizi would not want to serve the new dynasty in any capacity. In the end, the conqueror heeded the captive's wishes. He offered to help Jizi collect a following and migrate beyond the northeast frontiers of the empire, across the Yalu River, and settle in the north of modern Korea, at that time called Zhaoxian. The new land would be Jizi's fief, but the senior tutor of Yin would not be required to acknowledge allegiance and pay tribute to Zhou as a vassal nation. And Jizi agreed. On his way to Zhaoxian, he passed by the ruins of Zou's Deer Terrace, and his sorrow-laden heart burst out into a mournful song:

> How luxuriantly the stalks of wheat have grown,
> How smooth and oily the millet sprouts look!
> Alas, but for that imp of a brat,
> How well all this would have been!

And all the Yin people who heard were said to have shed tears.[131]

· 4 ·
THE PASSING OF WU WANG (1105 B.C.)

History is relatively well informed about the political and military measures Wu Wang took as founder of a new dynasty, but it is rather vague about the chronology of his personal activities during his short reign. There is evidence that he once went to the seat of his third brother, the Prince of Guan, assembled the "princes of the eastern corners" there, and lectured to them on the duties of enfeoffed rulers.[132] But we have no knowledge as to whether this was an isolated occurrence or one of many stops in a series of inspection tours. However, inasmuch as the empire had been won only very recently and Wu Wang was so energetic a monarch, it was probably the latter.

History also records that Wu Wang built a new capital city, called Hao, some twenty *li* to the east of Feng.[133] But again we have no precise information as to when he started building it and when he finished. Presumably, the construction was commenced before the overturning, and completed not long after the winning, of the Mandate of Heaven. But no sooner had Wu Wang moved into Hao than he became aware of its inherent shortcomings: Though the capital was fully designed to suit the needs of an imperial seat, its location was simply too far to the west of his far-flung empire to be truly advantageous.

In truth, his dominion, in respect of actual political control, was becoming much larger in size than that Yin had ever attained. Speaking of the west, Zhou itself had arisen out of a tract of land over which the previous dynasty had never seriously asserted its authority. In the south, the tribes inhabiting the Yangtze and the Han valleys had taken part in the battle of Shepherds' Wild under Wu Wang's banners. The greatest enlargement of Zhou's dominion, however, probably occurred in the southeast, after the conquest of Yin. As noted before, the Yin had contented itself with suzereignty only over what was called East Land and South Land. The regions farther beyond, whose delimitations were scarcely defined, were simply designated as Renfang and Yufang, and were more or less all abandoned to primitive or nomadic tribes answering to the names Ren or Yu. While politically the Yin had seldom essayed to exert control over this vast territory, the gradual conversion of those tribes to some sort of agrarian way of life must have been taking place for a considerable length of time. This ongoing process may be seen in the founding of the princedom of Wu by Taibo and Zhongyong in a remote corner of this ill-defined area about a century earlier. And now, with the reuniting of the two branches of the house of Zhou after the fall of Yin, the assimilation of those tribes, or nations, situated in between their lands must have gained fresh impetus from the new imperial court.

In the year after the battle of Shepherds' Wild, it was recorded that a prince of Chao came to Zhou to acknowledge allegiance to Wu Wang.[134] Chao, located about 150 kilometers south of the Huai River and about fifty kilometers north of the Yangtze, is the place where the last Xia emperor, Jie, in his extended flight from Tang's pursuing troops, was finally caught and made a prisoner.[135] Apparently, some time after that historical event, and perhaps more especially after the transference of the Shang capital to Yin, Chao seemed to have been left to its own fate, thriving or stagnating under the roaming feet of the Ren tribes. The voluntary appearance of a Prince of Chao at Zhou to proffer submission after such a long lapse of time was therefore more than welcome. Consequently, Wu Wang rewarded him with the title *bo*, "count," and commemorated the occasion with a special document, which was originally included by Confucius in the *Book of History* but was later lost.[136] This occurrence, of course, could have been a solitary incident, unrelated to the general development of the times. Yet as one of the obvious purposes for the composition of the special document was to encourage other nations or tribes in the area to follow suit, it may not be too rash to assume that the submission of Chao may well have been the forerunner of a number of others. At any rate, not long after the passing of Wu Wang, the names of Renfang and Yufang seem to have disappeared altogether from use, and in their place history takes note only of Huaiyi or Xurong.[137] Evidently these tribes, or rather the remnants of Ren and Yu, were effectively deprived of their freedom of movement in the former larger territories and now confined within the narrower limits of the Huai Valley or around modern Xuzhou in Jiangsu province.

Perhaps the remotest nation that paid homage to Wu Wang was Sushen. Living around the mountains of modern Jilin province, they are generally recognized as forefathers to the tribes later called the Manchu, who succeeded in conquering China in the 17th century A.D. and establishing a dynasty, the very last one in the pre-Republican history of China. As a tribute to Wu Wang, Sushen presented some arrows of their own making, with heads fashioned of stone and shafts of a special kind of wood about two feet long. Pleased with the gift from so distant a land, Wu Wang had inscriptions carved on the shafts to denote their origin. Some of the arrows he bestowed upon his son-in-law, the Prince of Chen. In the time of Confucius, these were found still well preserved in Chen's treasure coffers.[138]

Wu Wang was a typical example of the Western aphorism "Uneasy lies the head that wears a crown." And the larger his dominion, the more demanding of himself he became. Not only did he spend many a sleepless night worrying over the affairs of the empire, but he also encouraged others to speak out against him whenever they found a cause. In the *Book of History* there is a document titled *lu'ao*, *Hounds of lu*, which registers such an instance. Lu, a western tribe, sent in as their tribute some of their hounds. Formerly, when distant nations presented Wu Wang with gifts, he as a rule distributed them among various princes, as he had done with the arrows of Sushen. But these hounds Wu Wang seemed to have taken a particular liking to, and he kept them for himself. This was deemed improper by the Duke of Shao, who forthwith composed a document to voice his remonstrance.

> Oh! Because your majesty has been so clear-sighted as to pay careful attention to your virtues, the border nations on every side have willingly acknowledged their subjection. From near and from far they have come and paid tribute with their native products—clothes, food, and implements for use.
>
> Your majesty, making public the effect of the spreading of your virtues, has distributed these tributes to princes whose surnames are different from yours,[139] to encourage them not to neglect their duties. Also, you have distributed precious articles and jades to those of your own house to enhance their attachment. The recipients do not regard these things lightly, for they see in them the reflection of your virtue.
>
> When virtue prevails, it allows no contemptuous familiarity. When a prince treats superior men with familiarity, he cannot get them to give him all their heart. When he treats inferior men with familiarity, he cannot get them to put forth for him all their strength.
>
> It is only when one is not a thrall to one's own ears or eyes that one's conduct will be ruled by correctness.
>
> He who amuses himself with other men loses his own virtue. He who amuses himself with things loses his own will.
>
> One's will may find repose only in what is right. And one may listen only to words that are spoken in accordance with what is right.
>
> A prince must not do useless things to the injury of things useful. This is the way by which real merit may be achieved. He must not value strange things to the disparagement of things that supply our daily needs. This is the way to make sure that the people can enjoy self-sufficiency. Even dogs and horses, if they are not native to his country, he will not keep. Rare birds and wondrous animals which are foreign to his land, he will not nourish. He does not look on foreign things as precious and desirable; therefore, foreigners, fearing no encroachment from him, will come to him from afar. He treasures nothing but worthy men; therefore all the people near to him feel the effects of tranquillity and contentment.
>
> Oh! Day and night do exert yourself toward virtue. If you do not attend jealously to your small actions, your great virtue will be affected in the end by their accumulation. If you want to erect a mound nine fathoms high,[140] surely you will not let your work go unfinished for want of one last basketful of earth.
>
> If your majesty earnestly follows this course, your people will be able to preserve their possessions, and your throne descend from generation to generation.[141]

If a passing fancy for some hounds had called forth such a stern warning, one wonders what an austere life as a whole these early founders of the Zhou dynasty must have been leading. And indeed, as we have learned from other records, Wu Wang's mind was being constantly weighted down by much heavier worries:[142]

On his way returning to Zhou, for several stops, Wu Wang did not sleep in the nights. The attendants reported the matter to Younger Brother Dan, who came at once to him and inquired, "What is it that troubles and distresses you so much that you cannot sleep?"

He replied, "Sit down at ease. I will tell you."

(After a while) the emperor said, "O Dan! Heaven has been unwilling to accept sacrifices from Yin for the last sixty years, even since the time before I was born. I remember that in my childhood I could still see nomads shepherding their sheep in the fields and wild geese filling the wilds. (What an undeveloped country Zhou was then!) But because Heaven, though invisible, has not wished to accept sacrifices from Yin, we have attained to what we have today.

"While Heaven still favored Yin, It gave her numerous good men to serve her—I dare say, as many as 360, one for every day of the year.[143] Even though Zou neither used them nor heeded their advices, yet Yin still endured for sixty years. (This is of course due to the system that Tang had created, with the Central Shang lording over the empire, which made it all but indefeasible.)

"Alas! I have worried about this difficulty, for which I am unable to find a satisfactory solution. So long as I cannot build up an imperial domain (like that of Central Shang), I cannot feel secure about the favor of Heaven. Until then, what sleep do I care for?"

(Again the Emperor paused.) Presently he resumed, "Dan, now that I have received the clear Mandate of Heaven, I must aim to make the favor of Heaven secure, to build up a fitting seat for Heaven to repose in. I should hate to think that all the pains we had taken day and night in the past was only for the purpose of chasing after Zou, or of ensuring the safety of our West Land. I want to make virtue shine in every corner of the world like a brilliant daybreak."

The emperor continued, "Dan, you are the only brother who understands me fully. Whenever I asked you to do something, even while you were eating, you would push your food aside and carry out my orders. For me, you have all but given up your family life.

"Now, twice I have seen a messenger from Heaven, revealing to me that I have not long to live. I fear I am running out of time to build up the domain so close to my heart. I have confided this idea of the great domain only to you and to my son who is yet a child.

"From our early imperial ancestors, through generations, we have inherited the legacy that is now entrusted to my person. Like a famished husbandman looking forward to the harvest, I am looking forward to the fulfillment of my mission. Unless it is fulfilled, I shall be degrading our ancestors so much that they may not gain their rightful places in heaven from the Lord Above.

"You are a younger son to our father. Also, your mind is ever so resourceful. Indeed, you are fit to be successor to me to rule over this vast circle (that is, our empire). If I should entertain selfish thoughts, if I should think only of my wife and my son, I would be not only devoid of virtue in comparison with worthy men before me, but also a disappointment to the people below. I would not be able to face (the spirits of) our ancestors then.

"This is probably why Heaven has twice sent a messenger to forewarn me, so that I may make amends in time. It is indeed to give us a command that you as my brother should succeed me. I have no need to consult the tortoise or the *shi-*stalks on this matter. I shall even now decree that you shall succeed me."

Alarmed and fearful, Younger Brother Dan wept, put his hands together, (and did not know what to say).

(After a while,) the emperor said again, "O Dan! In planning to put Yin in her place, the only way is to place the imperial seat close by it so that whatever orders we may issue, we can see to it that they are easily enforced.

"As to where the location for the imperial seat should be, it will not be too difficult to find one, bearing this principle in mind.

"From where the Luo River joins the Yellow River to where the stream Yi joins the Luo, the land is flat with no natural defensible barriers. This is where the house of Xia had its original abode.[144]

"(But to its west I came across a site:) When I looked to the south, I sighted Mount Santu; when I looked to the north, I sighted the Taihang ranges; when I turned my head backward, I saw the Great River; and when I sat down and scanned eastward, the view extended as far as the plains of the Luo River and the stream Yi.[145] Here, within these confines, a place may be found where Heaven may want Its abode."

So ends the record of this conversation between these two brothers who had worked together almost like a single person for the founding of the Zhou dynasty. Nor has history any other account of actions Wu Wang might have taken afterward regarding the two matters which had been so conspicuously uppermost in his mind. What had happened then? Perhaps nothing at all. And there are strong reasons to believe that this must have been the case. For though Wu Wang had had a premonition of his early death, and impatient as he was to put his plans into execution while he yet had time, there were solid obstacles standing in the way of implementation, obstacles that may be said to be truly unsurmountable. Take the question of succession. The practice of the house of Zhou had invariably followed the principle of primogeniture. It was because of this rule that Taibo and Zhongyong, in order to abdicate their rights of succession in favor of their third brother, were compelled to make themselves disappear as though they had completely vanished from the earth. And as long as Wu Wang's own son, young Song, lived, there was no way for the monarch to transmit the throne to the Duke of Zhou, nor for the latter to accept it from the former. But then, it may be argued, the tradition of the house of Shang had been different, which was to have brother succeed brother. Could not Wu Wang now maintain that since the Zhou had conquered the empire, it was best to follow the Shang practice, making sure that the helm of the state would always be held by the capable hands of a mature man and not those of a feeble child? This could have made a feasible argument. But then another stumbling block would emerge. For the Shang tradition was to have brother succeed brother in the order of seniority. Had the Duke of Zhou been their father's third son and not the fourth, as he actually was, well could Wu Wang have adopted such a change. But as the matter stood, if such a change should be made, the succession would have to go first to the Prince of Guan—a choice Wu Wang himself did not seem to think appropriate or desirable.

If the obstacles standing in the way of the Duke of Zhou's succession were seemingly impassable, the difficulties confronting the establishment of a new imperial seat at the site Wu Wang had selected were equally insuperable. The strength of the Central Shang was recognized primarily in the great numbers of its population which were chiefly centered in the metropolis of Yin. If the Zhou were to build up a new imperial seat with the Central Shang as its model, where could Wu Wang get the population to fill it up with? Could he move the population of Zhou to the new site? That would not make much sense. Could he move the population of Yin? That would be not only reneging his own promise of generosity to the Yin people, it could also very well provoke them to instant unnecessary disturbance, if not open and violent revolt.

Doubtless, after the recorded conversation quoted above, there must have been other conferences held between the two brothers. While the Duke of Zhou would have persisted in declining the offer on the matter of succession and counseled more patience as regards the establishment of a new imperial seat, the elder brother, after he gained some restful sleep, must also have been persuaded to appreciate the practical aspects of either problem in a more serene and contemplative manner. In any event, shortly afterward, Wu Wang was taken seriously ill.[146] At one time, Taigong and the Duke of Shao so feared for his life that they said to the Duke of Zhou, "Let us consult the tortoise about his majesty's health." But the Duke of Zhou disagreed, saying, "We may not so distress (the spirits of) our former emperors."

Yet if there was anyone more fearful of Wu Wang's demise, it was the Duke of Zhou himself. He had known of his elder brother's premonition; so he thought there was no use to consult the tortoise in that respect. What he dreaded most was the consequences of Wu Wang's imminent death. The empire, conquered only too recently, was not yet in repose. If the throne was to be occupied by his nephew, a boy not yet in his teens, the entire responsibility of government would devolve upon the duke himself. To evade it would be to fail to live up to the obligations he owed the one brother whom he loved so dearly. To undertake it would be to run into countless perils, not only for himself but for the whole dynasty, which he was not at all sure he could overcome. In desperation, therefore, he built three altars of earth in private—one for his great-grandfather Tai Wang, one for his grandfather Wang Ji, one for his father, Wen Wang—and in a simple solemn ceremony addressed their spirits with an inscribed tablet, praying that they would intercede with the Lord Above to let his elder brother live and take his own life instead as a substitute. Then he consulted the tortoise three times, each time with respect to a particular forebear, to see if they would grant his prayer. And all three answers were favorable. Thus assured, he went at once to see Wu Wang and congratulate him, saying, "Your majesty will have no fear from this sickness. I have just received a message from our three former sovereigns, granting you time to plan for a lasting future." And the very next day Wu Wang began to recover.[147] The Duke of Zhou was infinitely thankful, but he never told anyone else of the matter, forbidding even those diviners who had taken part in the private ceremony to talk about it.

Perhaps, after his recovery, Wu Wang began to take his premonition of an early death not so seriously as before. Ruling the empire as vigorously as ever, he no longer felt an overriding urgency to find an instant solution for the two problems that had so harassed him previously.

But then, ironically, he was seized with another illness. He died only six years after the fall of Yin.[148]

NOTES

1. See *Book of Poetry, daya: daming.*

2. See chart of Wen Wang's ten sons, p. 280. Perhaps because Ji Chang made it his policy to encourage the increase of Zhou population, folklore since has alleged that he had a hundred sons, ten borne by the principal wife, eighty-nine by concubines, and one adopted. (See *Fengshen Bang,* the popular novel.) This is derived from a literal but obviously dubious interpretation of two lines of the ode *siqi* in the *Book of Poetry,* which may be roughly translated as: "Taisi inherited her brilliant fame, and from her came a hundred sons." This last expression seems to be but a figure of speech that includes her sons, grandsons, and even sons of later generations. At any rate, from authoritative records, besides the ten sons by Taisi, we know of only eight or nine others who were fathered by Ji Chang. (See *Zuozhuan,* Duke Yin, 11th year, and Duke Xi, 26th year. Also see *Historical Records, guancai shijia.*)

3. This is based on *Historical Records, guancai shijia.* According to folklore, as narrated in *Fengshen Bang,* at the time of Ji Chang's imprisonment, the eldest son, Boyikao, went to Yin to seek his father's release, but was cruelly put to death by Zou and Daji.

4. Jiaoli was the first envoy sent by Zou to Zhou to demand the jade block as tribute. See above, p. 268.

5. *Mencius, lianghuiwang,* II.

6. See above, p. 261.

7. See Liu Xiang, *Shuoyuan,* chap. XV.

8. *Historical Records, zhou benji;* also see Zhang Shoujie, *shiji zhengyi.*

9. *Confucian Analects, taibo.* Confucius said that there was a woman among the ten. Though the names of the ten were not given in any records, later scholars suggested that among them were Taigong, Hongyao, San Yisheng, Taidian, and Nangong Kuo. (These were formerly Ji Chang's ministers, Guo Shu having died before Ji Fa's accession.) Then there were the Duke of Zhou, Duke Shi of Shao, Duke Bi, and Duke Rong. (These were Ji Fa's kinsmen.) As Confucius had said that there was a woman among the ten, some scholars have maintained that it was Ji Fa's principal wife and Taigong's daughter, Yijiang.

10. *Book of History, taishi (Great Declaration),* I.

11. See *Yi Li, shisangli.*

12. *Historical Records, zhou benji.*

13. Ibid.

14. *Historical Records, boyi liezhuan.*

15. Shouyang Mountain is in modern Yongji, Shanxi province.

16. The Chinese character used here is *wei.* According to *Ci Hai,* it is *Osmunda regalis,* var. *japonica.*

17. These three were former emperors who had acquired the possession of the world without using force.

18. The passage in quotation marks is almost a literal translation of an excerpt from *Historical Records, boyi liezhuan.*

19. Ibid., *zhou benji.*

20. Ibid., and *qitaigong shijia.*

21. *Historical Records, zhou benji.* Also *Book of History, taishi.*

22. See commentaries of Ma Rong and Zheng Kangcheng as quoted by Pei Yin in *Historical Records, zhou benji.*

23. Almost a literal translation of the relevant passage in the *Historical Records, zhou benji.*

24. *Shangshu Dazhuan.*

25. In *Confucian Analects, taibo,* when Confucius mentioned that Zhou, while possessing two of the three parts of the empire, continued to serve Yin, he seemed to have included both Wen Wang and Wu Wang in the same statement. About the use of the Yin calendar, see Dong Zuobin, *Yin Lipu,* part I, chap. 4.

26. Besides Feizhong, *Historical Records, qin benji,* mentions Feilian and his son Elai.

27. *Book of History, taishi,* I and III; *Hanshi Waizhuan,* chap. X.

28. See Chap. III, Sec. 3.

29. An obvious reference to Di Xin.

30. Another reference to Di Xin.

31. This, according to some scholars, is a reference to the time when Di Xin's father wanted the Prince of Wei to be his heir and not Di Xin, and Jizi spoke against it. (See above, p. 220.) But if this were so, then by this time Jizi must have been some eighty or ninety years old, which, judging from later events, he apparently was not. From the wording of the Chinese passage, it may be more reasonable to assume that the senior tutor had previously urged the prince to stay and do his best to rally the people, but now realized that this was an impossible task and his former advice might have deterred the prince from leaving for safety.

32. *Book of History, weizi.*

33. *Confucian Analects, weizi.*

34. *Historical Records, songweizi shijia.*

35. Ibid.; *Dadai Liji, baofu;* and *Hanshi Waizhuan,* chap. III.

36. Ibid.

37. This song is lost.

38. *Historical Records, songweizi shijia.*

39. See *Lushi Chunqiu, xianshilan: xianshi.*

40. The day was given in the *Book of History, wucheng.* The year was given in the *Book of History, taishi.* However, there is a confusion about the exact year when the event took place. It arises from the fact that while the document *taishi* mentions the thirteenth year as the year, the introduction to the document (*shuxu*) mentions the eleventh year. It is thought that the latter may have been a clerical error.

41. Many traditional scholars compute this year to be 1122 B.C. Dong Zuobin, however, places it at 1111 B.C. (*Yin Lipu*, part I, chap. 4).

42. *Historical Records, zhou benji.*

43. See above, pp. 112–13.

44. See Dong Zuobin, *Yin Lipu*, part I, chap. 4.

45. *Historical Records, zhou benji.*

46. As the moon was ox moon, it was the first month of the year according to the Yin calendar, and the second month according to the Zhou calendar.

47. The Qiang, Lu, Peng, and Shu tribes were in Gansu and west Sichuan; the Mao and Wei tribes were around the modern Chunking area; and the Yong and Pu tribes were south of the Yangtze and the Han valleys. (See *Book of History, mushi.*)

48. *Historical Records, zhou benji.*

49. Ibid.

50. *Book of History, taishi,* I.

51. Ibid., II. See also *Historical Records, zhou benji.*

52. *Book of Changes, ge* hexagram. Also see above, p. 164.

53. The envoy was said to be Jiaoli (see above, p. 280).

54. *Lushi Chunqiu, shendalan: guiyin.*

55. Ibid. The quotation is a paraphrase.

56. *Book of History, wucheng.* The day was *guihai* (rain water pig).

57. *Historical Records, yin benji,* comments by Zhang Shoujie.

58. The actual wording in Chinese is *yushi, situ, sima, sikong,* which James Legge translated into "you managers of affairs, the ministers of instruction, of war, and of public works." This is literal translation, but may be confusing to Western readers who may wonder what a minister of instruction has to do in a battle. The thing we need to remember is that in ancient times peacetime cabinet ministers served as field commanders in wartime. (In this book, we have translated *situ* not as "minister of instruction" but as "minister of commonalty.")

59. See above, p. 290, note 47.

60. It seems that the officers in those days were armed either with a *ge* (halberd) and a *gan* (shield) or with a *mao* (lance) and a *gan*. The literal translation of this passage should be, "Weigh your halberds, match your shields, and stand erect your lances." I imagine that the officers were ordered to stand at ease. To weigh a halberd is to hold it as if to weigh it. To match a shield is to put it down side by side with the neighbors' shields. As the lance is too long, so the officer who was armed with one was asked to stand it upright on the ground.

61. The Chinese original uses two characters here—*xiong* and *pi*. The former is commonly translated as "bear"; and the latter, "grizzly bear" or "brown bear."

62. *Book of History, mushi.*

63. *Mencius, jinxin,* II.

64. Huangfu Mi, *Diwang Shiji.*

65. Ibid.

66. *Book of History, wucheng.*

67. *Historical Records, zhou benji;* also see comments by Zhang Shoujie. Wu Wang started from Zhou with 300 war chariots; but in the battle 350 chariots were deployed. Presumably 50 chariots, usable for war, were selected from among Zhou's allies.

68. *Historical Records, yin benji* and *zhou benji.*

69. Ibid., *zhou benji.*

70. *Book of History, wucheng.*

71. *Mencius, jinxin,* II.

72. Ibid.

73. *Historical Records, yin benji.*

74. Huangfu Mi, *Diwang Shiji,* as quoted in *Taiping Yulan.*

75. *Historical Records, zhou benji.*

76. *Shangshu Dazhuan.*

77. Ibid. The quotations are paraphrases.

78. *Historical Records, zhou benji.*

79. *Li Ji, dazhuan.*

80. *Huainanzi, zhushu xun.*

81. *Li Ji, dazhuan.*

82. *Yi Zhou Shu, zhouyue.*

83. See above, p. 161.

84. *Li Ji, tangong,* I.

85. *Confucian Analects, bayi; Huainanzi, qisu xun;* also see above, p. 162.

86. Liu Xiang, *Shuoyuan,* chap. XV.

87. The suburb was called Juqiao (Great Bridge).

88. *Historical Records, zhou benji; Yi Zhou Shu, keyin.*

89. See Liu Shu, *Zizhitongjian Waiji.*

90. *Historical Records, zhou benji.*

91. Ibid.

92. Ibid.

93. *Historical Records, songweizi shijia.* The rushes were used in ancient times to clean up the ground after the slaying of the sacrificial animal.

94. See above, p. 160.

95. *Historical Records, zhou benji.*

96. Ibid., and *yin benji, guancai shijia, songweizi shijia,* and *weikangshu shijia.* However, in all these accounts there are no precise delimitations of the various areas under the respective control of Wugeng and each of the three princes. But in *yin benji* it is explicitly mentioned that Wu Wang "invested Zou's son Wugeng so that the sacrifices to Yin's ancestors might continue. He commanded that he perform government (in Yin) as Pangeng had performed."

97. Ibid., *guancai shijia* and *songweizi shijia.*

98. *Yi Zhou Shu, shifu.* The states mentioned in the book, however, are not identifiable.

99. Ibid.; also *Historical Records, zhou benji.*

100. The Chinese character is pronounced "hao" or "he." The Chinese dictionaries define it as an animal looking like a fox but very fond of sleep. If a man keeps it as a pet and takes it out for a walk, it will fall into sleep every few steps.

101. *Yi Zhou Shu, shifu.*

102. Ibid.

103. Ibid.

104. Dong Zuobin (*Yin Lipu*, part I, chap. 4), basing his chronology on *Yi Zhou Shu,* computes the time to be three months. But the *Book of History, wucheng,* expressly gives the date of *dingwei* for his ancestral veneration. So we think it took him some four months to return to Feng.

105. *Book of History, wucheng.*

106. Mount Hua is to the east of Feng on the border of modern Shaanxi and Henan provinces. Peach Forest is to the east of Mount Hua.

107. *Yi Zhou Shu, duyi; Historical Records, zhou benji.*

108. See above, pp. 94–95.

109. See above, pp. 114–15.

110. See above, p. 139.

111. See above, pp. 158–59.

112. See above, p. 163.

113. See above, p. 212.

114. See above, p. 215.

115. *Historical Records, zhou benji.*

116. *Zuozhuan*, Duke Xiang, 25th year.

117. According to *Xunzi, jundao*, Zhou created altogether seventy-one new states. These may not have been all created by Wu Wang; some may have been created later by the Duke of Zhou or Wu Wang's son, Cheng Wang. Also see *Hanshi Waizhuan*, chap. IV.

118. *Historical Records, wei shijia.*

119. Ibid., *zhou benji.* Later, the Duke of Zhou transferred the fief of Cai to southeast Henan.

120. Probably in Wen Wang's campaign against Li. See above, pp. 271–72.

121. *Historical Records, guancai shijia.* Cao was in modern Dingtao, Shandong; Cheng was close by.

122. Ibid., *zhou benji.*

123. Some accounts had it that these three men also served Wu Wang as his *sangong.*

124. The Duke of Shao and the Duke of Bi. According to one account, the Duke of Bi was Wen Wang's son by a concubine. We base our accounts here on *Historical Records, yanshaogong shijia* and *wei shijia.*

125. *Xunzi, jundao*; also see *Hanshi Waizhuan*, chap. IV.

126. *Zuozhuan*, Duke Xi, 24th year.

127. Ibid.

128. *Historical Records, zhou benji* and *qitaigong shijia.*

129. See above, pp. 240–41.

130. *Historical Records, wutaibo shijia.*

131. *Historical Records, songweizi shijia.* "That imp of a brat" is an obvious reference to Zou.

132. *Yi Zhou Zhu, dakuang* and *wenzheng.*

133. *Book of Poetry, daya: wenwangyousheng.*

134. *Bamboo Chronicles.*

135. See above, p. 143.

136. See *Book of History, shuxu.*

137. See *Book of History, feishi.* Huaiyi means *yi* of the Huai, and Xurong means *rong* of Xu, that is, modern Xuzhou. For the meanings of *yi* and *rong*, see above, pp. 107–8.

138. *Guo Yu, luyu*, II; *Historical Records, kongzi shijia.*

139. This means those enfeoffed princes who did not belong to the house of Zhou, such as Qi, Chen, and Yin.

140. The Chinese character is *ren*, which is an ancient measure of varying lengths. James Legge translated it as "fathom."

141. The original document *lu'ao* is lost; the present version is considered a counterfeit. But it has formed the basis of so many remonstrances from ministers to their emperors in later dynasties that it deserves to be quoted in full here. For use of such second-batch documents, see Appendix.

142. The following is a paraphrase of a large section of *Yi Zhou Shu, duyi.* In some places we have followed the wording used in the *Historical Records, zhou benji.*

143. This is apparently an expression used by Wu Wang to emphasize the fact that heaven had given Yin enough good men to serve her.

144. Yu's original fief was Yangcheng. See above, p. 106, note 1.

145. This is a good description of the site of the modern city Luoyang, Henan.

146. The following account follows the *Book of History, jinteng.* The first time Wu Wang was taken seriously ill is said to be about two years after his conquest of Yin.

147. *Historical Records, luzhougong shijia.*

148. *Bamboo Chronicles*; Huangfu Mi, *Diwang Shiji.* The date is computed by Dong Zuobin to be 1105 B.C.

CHAPTER VIII

THE CONSOLIDATION
OF ZHOU

(1105–1097 B.C.)

· 1 ·
THE REGENCY OF THE DUKE OF ZHOU

The startling news of the demise of the only recently acknowledged sovereign of the world, coming so closely after his sudden overthrow of a dynasty that had lasted more than six centuries, resulted in another upheaval. Reviewing the records of this episode three thousand years later, we have a distinct perspective on the basic and violent human passions that were brought into play, the tortuous and traumatic developments that inevitably ensued, and the quick and dramatic conclusion that was reached as unexpectedly and yet inexorably as the intense climax in a Greek tragedy. Out of the entire panorama of tangled events, we perceive the giant figure of a man towering above all his contemporaries both in ability and in virtue, who despite the fact that he had been thrust into circumstances over which he had no control, blackened and tormented by calumnies he had every reason not to expect, and suspected and distrusted by the very ones he loved and was exerting his utmost to serve and protect, managed eventually to emerge out of this all but impossible situation completely vindicated and triumphant.

Nevertheless, even though this comprehensive view of the era stands out before our eyes unobstructed and clear, some of its scenes notably delineated in more than ordinary detail, there are a few conspicuous gaps. We cannot but think that these are entirely different from other gaps in ancient Chinese history. Those other gaps may have been occasioned by loss of relevant documents or materials, or by sheer uneventfulness. But these seem to have been caused by deliberate omission, at the will of none other than the very hero who had just successfully scraped through the dire crisis. One would think that it would be to his interest and advantage to have the whole story revealed to the public and to posterity, to have the villainies of his enemies fully exposed and his own merits thoroughly documented; not to say to paint his own side whiter and the other side blacker as many in similar circumstances would likely do. But from his sensitivity he elected instead to let mere facts speak for themselves; and it was undoubtedly in deference to his wishes that the official scribes of his day—the only historians that were in existence—recorded nothing but the barest essentials.

There is some evidence that five days after Wu Wang fell ill for the second and for the last time, he summoned the Duke of Zhou and told him that he must "make the throne safe for the small child, hold fast to that course, and regard all things else as unimportant."[1] However, this instruction was given in the midst of a random and rather obscure discussion on government. Though from the standpoint of historiography it may not be taken seriously as the deathbed testament of the dying monarch, yet to the Duke of Zhou, who was present, it is not to be denied that the words could have conveyed a profound and special significance.

Perhaps, after having conversed with his beloved and trusted brother at that time, Wu Wang was never lucid again. In any event, no sooner had the founder of the Zhou dynasty passed away than the Duke of Zhou led the imperial court and acclaimed Wu Wang's son and heir, Song, as Cheng Wang, "Emperor Successful."[2] The successor was then only thirteen years old,[3] and mindful of the wishes of his deceased father, he forthwith appointed his uncle Dan "prime minister in charge of all officers of the government."[4] The news of the boy's succession, however, overshadowed that of the duke's appointment. Almost instantly rumors abounded: There were many enfeoffed states still loyal to Yin or dissatisfied with Zhou that were just waiting for such a moment to wreak their vengeance. The frail hands of a thirteen-year-old sovereign were not to be feared; and the new prime minister, though noted for his talents in many ways, was apparently not in a position to steer the helm of the empire with vigor, hampered as he was by having to apply to a mere child for final approval on every matter of major importance. Unless this weakness was quickly remedied, widespread revolt could be expected. The Duke of Zhou consulted with Taigong and the Duke of Shao and decided on two immediate actions.

The first was to have Taigong at once proceed to his fief in the East Land and assume command at Barracks Mound.[5] At the same time, inasmuch as the Duke of Zhou himself could not go to his own fief, Lu, with the approval of the young sovereign the duke's eldest son, Boqin, was invested as Marquis of Lu and sent to take charge of that state in support of Taigong at Qi, which lay to its north.[6] These actions were taken in the fear that if a revolt should come, it would likely start first with the princes of the former East Land of Yin. And it was hoped that by reinforcing the two eastern military bases which Wu Wang had so carefully set up, and with the presence in the area of the person of Taigong, whose fame as the most formidable general was feared and respected by all, an open revolt might yet be averted at this critical hour. And lest any prince or state should misjudge the determination of the imperial court to stamp out intransigence at any cost, before Taigong departed for his post, the prime minister had the Duke of Shao issue to him an imperial tablet, proclaiming: "To the east as far as the sea, to the west as far as the Yellow River, to the south as far as the Ravine Mu on the Huai, and to the north as far as Wudi,[7] you (Taigong) are hereby authorized to launch punitive expeditions against any of the states within these limits, whatever grade of investiture they may be invested with."[8]

And the doughty warrior took the matter as seriously. In spite of his age he headed straight for his post with tireless speed. But finally the weight of his ninety-odd years caught up with him. When he came near to the borders of Qi, with Barracks Mound about half a day's distance away, he stopped at an inn before it was dark, and gave orders that he not be disturbed for the night. Then he overheard the innkeeper talk to himself: "I have heard that time is easy to lose and hard to keep. But our guest desires a sound and long sleep. It does not seem to be fitting for a man who is hurrying toward his fief!" At this, Taigong aroused himself and called to his following to get up too. They pushed on again through the dark of the night, and they arrived at Barracks Mound before the crack of dawn. They did not arrive an hour too soon. For the savage Lai tribes were already up in arms, just about ready to seize Barracks Mound by a surprise assault.[9]

The second action the Duke of Zhou took to combat the pernicious rumors was to proclaim himself regent, ruling over the empire during the minority of Cheng Wang. In order to show that he was possessed of all the prerogatives of a sovereign, he himself ascended the throne to receive all the enfeoffed princes who came to Zhou to pay homage.[10] But before taking the action, he had explained to both Taigong and the Duke of Shao, "It is because of the fear of revolt and disturbance in the empire that I have to risk my good name to take this step. Otherwise, I would not know how to face the spirits of our ancestors and of our late sovereigns."[11] His decision was apparently understood and endorsed by both of his colleagues. And for the days that immediately followed, it also appeared to have produced some salutary effects on the empire. While the states loyal to Zhou were eager to welcome the return of strong leadership, those that were averse to another period of uncertainty and turmoil were also not slow to reaffirm their allegiance. But at this very juncture there arose an ominous challenge from a quarter the regent had least feared.

From none of the ancient records can we gather a description about the individual characters of the "three supervisors"—princes of Guan, of Cai, and of Huo. Nor have we any information about the various and successive political or military measures they had taken in opposition to the regency of their own fourth brother, which finally culminated in their open rebellion against Zhou, with Wugeng of Yin, the vanquished foe, as their ally. From the bare facts that the ancient scribes have left us, however, the following scenario may be drawn. There can be no question that the Prince of Guan was the ringleader of the disturbance; but that he was so was evidently less due to his ability to lead than to his seniority of birth, he being the third son of Wen Wang, and the Prince of Cai the fifth and the Prince of Huo the eighth. Perhaps, his being born the third son had much to do with the shaping of his character. Squeezed in, as it were, between two exceptional personalities of the times, he was probably especially conscious of his own inferiority. Taught by their mutual father to be filial to their parents and respectful to their elders, the Prince of Guan, though lacking the brilliant qualities that had earmarked both Wu Wang and the Duke of Zhou from their early childhood, must have been on the whole not a bad son at all, behaving himself as tractably and as submissively as his training had made sure he would. Toward Wu Wang, who had been in succession the heir apparent, then the Prince of Zhou, and finally the sovereign of the empire, his conduct must have been equally exemplary, as blameless as befitted a younger brother and a dutiful subject. Apparently he was not a resourceful man, never boasting of any independent ideas; but whatever Wu Wang asked him to do, he could be trusted to carry it out to the utmost of his capacity. As to the Prince of Cai and the Prince of Huo, they were likely men of the same mold. Thus, after the fall of Yin, it was natural that Wu Wang should have appointed them to be the "three supervisors" to keep the former imperial metropolis under military control. What the conqueror needed there was men who could be depended upon in the execution of his orders, but who were neither required nor encouraged to make policies of their own.

While Wu Wang lived, there did not seem to have been any untoward problem. And had Wu Wang lived longer, or died with an adult heir and successor, the Prince of Guan and the two other supervisors might have gone on supervising Yin or repaired to their respective fiefs at imperial bidding without much ado. But as events occurred differently, there was at once brought into play a defective ingredient in the prince's makeup that had hitherto lain hidden from public view—his deep-rooted jealousy of his immediately younger brother, the Duke of Zhou. He probably was not unaware of the latter's virtues and talents; but, probably too, in the secret justification of his own resentment, he overemphasized the importance of seniority of birth. When Wu Wang became so close to the duke from early childhood and later made him his principal minister and confidant, Guan was not resentful of the former, because Wu Wang, being not only a monarch but also an elder brother, had the right to do whatever he wanted to do; but he was intensely resentful of the latter because he thought the younger brother had usurped the position that he himself was entitled to. Then came the accession of Cheng Wang and the appointment of the Duke of Zhou as prime minister. Much as Guan disliked the situation, he could not well complain of it in the open, for Cheng Wang was undoubtedly the lawful sovereign; and the appointment, also, could have been Wu Wang's dying wish. But now the duke had to declare himself the regent of the empire! If a regency had had to be established during his nephew's miniority, should not he, Guan himself, have been the regent and not the duke? Besides, in the making of this decision of such tremendous importance, why had he not been consulted? Indeed, the very fact that he had not been consulted was an unforgivable affront in itself!

Perhaps this was the one mistake for which the Duke of Zhou should take blame. Perhaps also the mistake was unavoidable. Circumstances might have been such that had not the duke proclaimed himself regent and assumed full sovereignty without delay, revolts could have mushroomed in many a place. Or the duke might have thoroughly considered the matter and decided after all that it was best not to consult with his only remaining elder brother beforehand. Indeed, judging from the actual events that happened afterward, the duke might well have thought that had he done so, Guan would have either objected to the institution of the regency or demanded to be the regent himself. And knowing the limits of Guan's capability and mindful of his own duties toward the deceased brother who had explicitly told him to hold fast to the singular course of making the throne safe for Cheng Wang and disregard all things else as matters of no consequence, the duke must have felt that that would only complicate, and not help, the situation at all. Had the duke then considered the possibility that Guan might break out in open intransigence? Very likely not. Guan had always shown so much devotion and conducted himself with so much willing obedience toward Wu Wang in the past; even though he might have viewed the idea of regency with disfavor, could not he be persuaded of its necessity for the sake of preserving the empire for their mutual nephew, Wu Wang's son? And here is where the duke misjudged. He had no conception of the intensity of the prince's jealousy.[12]

Upon the establishment of the regency, Guan began to voice his complaints to his two brother-supervisors and easily secured their agreement to oppose it. Perhaps Cai and Huo were too much influenced by their family training that younger brothers should always defer to their elder brothers. Perhaps, having now lived in Yin for some time, ambition might even have inclined them in favor of the Yin rule of succession, which was for brothers to succeed to brothers in the occupancy of the imperial throne in the order of seniority. If such a practice was to be adopted for Zhou, Guan should succeed to the empire, and not Cheng Wang. And once the regency was disestablished or overthrown and Guan became emperor in effect, surely the Duke of Zhou and those other brothers who had been siding with him would have been deprived of their claims. Under such circumstances, would not Cai and then Huo have their turns to become the sovereign of the world? In any event, Guan's objection to the regency was enthusiastically supported by Cai, he being so much nearer to the fulfilment of his ambition than Huo, so to speak, Thus this incident in history became known later as the "Guan-Cai Disturbance." [13] And together with Huo, the two began to spread word that they were opposed to the regency because they feared that the Duke of Zhou was entertaining sinister designs on the person of the boy emperor and intended to perpetuate his own rule by one foul means or another.

Against this calumnious attack the regent found himself in an impossible position. There was almost no way to clear his good name except to rescind the regency. Yet to do that, none knew better than he, would surely plunge the empire into instant disaster. Wugeng of Yin and quite a few eastern princes were already taking advantage of the discord and making clear that they were standing squarely behind the three supervisors. Although the latter might be thinking that they were using the former, actually it could be the former using the latter. At any rate, if the situation was not quickly resolved, the empire would undoubtedly be thrust into the very throes of an internecine conflict. Should he seek a fraternal settlement by holding a conference with the three refractory brothers? But where could the conference be held? With developments as they were, he himself could no longer go to Yin. Should he invite the three princes to come to Zhou instead? Suppose they should refuse to come; would not that make the rupture complete? The regent must have pondered over the matter long and hard before he finally decided on taking two measures for lacking something better. One was only a natural development in the course of human events, nothing of his own making; but the other was a deliberate undertaking on his own part that involved a drastic break from a long-standing tradition.

The first was the formal burial of Wu Wang. He announced that the funerary rites would be held in the sixth moon of this very first year of Cheng Wang's reign on the plateau of Bi, where Wen Wang had been buried before.[14] The announcement was conveyed throughout the length and breadth of the empire, summoning each and every enfeoffed prince to attend the ceremonies to pay their last homage to the founder of the dynasty. It was thought that the three supervisors, being Wu Wang's own brothers, would find it impossible to make up an excuse for all three of them to be absent, unless they were determined on an irreversible, total break. And should any one of the three only make an appearance, overtures would be proffered for a brotherly settlement. Yet lest this invitation or summons should fail of its purpose, the regent sought to add to it a second inducement. He wanted to indicate to his skeptics, especially to those three brothers of his, that his stand on the regency was by no means inflexible, if only a scheme could be worked out to ensure the safety of the empire. So he proclaimed that shortly after the interment of the deceased emperor, a second ceremony be conducted—the "capping ceremony" for the reigning sovereign.[15] Now the capping ceremony was a tradition that had begun as far back as the closing years of the Xia dynasty.[16] The custom was that when a young man reached twenty years old, a ceremony would be held in the presence of his relatives and friends to have him capped with three different caps worn by adults for various functions to show that he had attained full maturity.[17] Now Cheng Wang was only thirteen. But by having the capping ceremony held for him at this early age, the Duke of Zhou was deliberately breaking away from the time-honored tradition. He was seeking by this means not only to demonstrate to the world in general, through the enfeoffed princes who would be present, that the young sovereign was perfectly safe and sound, but also to intimate to his three brothers in particular that if only the empire could be made safe for Wu Wang's son, he himself would be willing at any moment to resign the regency and return all sovereignty to his newly "capped" nephew.

But if these had been the regent's intentions, he was sorely disappointed in the outcome. For not one of the three supervisors came to pay homage either to the dead or to the living emperor. Nor did Wugeng of Yin or any of the princes who had chosen to side with them. The Duke of Zhou had to content himself with the presence of those who had remained faithful to Zhou, even though they represented nearly all of the remaining states of the empire. Suppressing what mental anxiety he might have felt, he proceeded to conduct both of the ceremonies with such solemn simplicity and dignity as to earn Confucius's later commendation. He treated the young sovereign with every deference and respect that was his due; at the same time he deported himself with such proper majesty that none present could mistake who was the actual master of the empire. Surrounded by the attending princes, he presented the founder's son and heir to the ancestral temple; and under his instructions, while the imperial youth was being capped, the official scribe invoked this prayer:

May your majesty live long in years and close to the people!
May your majesty spend your time thriftily and use your riches generously!
May your majesty employ only men who are capable, and attach yourself only to those who are worthy!
On this auspicious day your majesty has been clothed with your first garments of maturity;

It behooves your majesty to leave behind your youthful thoughts and attend to
   your imperial duties;
It behooves your majesty reverentially to hold on to your Mandate of Heaven and
   serve as a model of men for the entire world,
So that you may follow in the footsteps of your forebears and the glory of the house
   will endure forever.[18]

But after the conclusion of the capping ceremony and after the departure
of the assembled princes, the Duke of Zhou could not conceal his despair any
longer. Under normal circumstances such flagrant intransigence as that of
Guan-Cai and Wugeng could not, and should not, have been tolerated by
any imperial court that was worthy of the name. As the regent, he should
have ordered a punitive expedition against them without further delay; but as
a son of Wen Wang, he simply had no heart to do so against his own
brothers. He was, of course, fully aware that the order could be issued by
Cheng Wang, as many of his own supporters were then advocating; but he
was also conscious that even if the young sovereign should be willing to issue
the order of his own will, he himself would have to take full responsibility for
the action. He would be blamed for having exercised undue influence upon
the youth; or, worse, he might even be accused of having extorted it from
him under duress. The only thing he thought he could do, therefore, was to
wait—wait hopefully until he could find some way to change his three brothers' minds. But time was not on his side, he knew that too. The three
supervisors might launch an invasion against Zhou any moment. And the
longer he waited the more his inability to cope with the situation would
become manifest, the more there might be disaffections among the enfeoffed
states, and the more perilous the crisis would become. So no matter whether
an invasion came forth imminently or not, his first and immediate concern
must be to see to it that the empire, or rather the remainder of it, be securely
defended.

He was inspecting the defenses along the Yellow River when he suffered
the severest shock he had ever known. A courier had just arrived from Hao,
the capital, advising him that Cheng Wang had of a sudden fallen terribly ill.
If the Duke of Zhou was ever stricken with panic, it must have been then.
Not only because he loved this nephew dearly, not only because he loved
him the more because the boy was the sovereign of Zhou and his most
beloved brother's son and heir; but should the young monarch have died at
the moment, all the fingers in the empire would have been pointed at him
with accusation; and all his devotion, his loyalty, and his integrity notwithstanding, he would be forever denied the chance to cleanse himself of the
unspeakable suspicion.

In desperation, he recalled the occasion when he had prayed to his three
ancestors for the life of Wu Wang on the verge of death for the first time.

His prayers had been granted then. Could he try to do the same again? But he was on the banks of the Yellow River, and his ancestors' spirits were reposing in the ancestral temple far away at Hao; it would not be feasible to build an altar here to beseech them to intercede with the Lord Above. Then suddenly an inspiration lighted on him. The deity of this great stream was one of the principal gods the people had always revered, who could surely be entreated to undertake for him the mission. He bid the official scribe who was accompanying him to write down a simple prayer there and then, imploring the river deity to convey it to Heaven above to take his own life as a substitute, so that his nephew could live in order to preserve the tranquillity of the empire. And following a superstitious practice of his day, he cut off all his fingernails and toenails as earnest of his pledge, wrapped them up carefully, and sank them into the stream.[19]

He rushed back to Hao. To his immense joy and relief, Cheng Wang was well again. But no sooner had the regent's mind been momentarily lightened than it was weighted down by a new distress. The Duke of Shao, who had been his chief assistant for so many years, who had always worked with him in closest harmony, and with whom he had shared every confidence and major decision, including those concerning the establishment of the regency as well as the complex problems arising out of the three supervisors' opposition, now suddenly declared his intention to go into retirement. Try as the regent would, he could not find out the reason for his resignation. He thought that Cheng Wang's recent illness must have something to do with the matter. One of the offices which the Duke of Shao had been holding concurrently was that of the grand guardian, whose responsibility was to protect and guard the person of the young monarch.[20] If the possibility of Cheng Wang's untimely demise could have so terrified the regent, could it not have produced the same effect on the grand guardian? Or could it be—and the regent could not help thinking further—that the latter was also beginning to entertain doubts about his own intentions? There was no question in his mind that the grand guardian was an honest and just man, as honest and just as he himself was; and he had trusted him as his right hand would trust his left hand; and he had also thought that he had been so trusted in return. Now, if he could not convince this most trusted friend and colleague of his sincere intentions, how could he persuade the outside world to believe in his good faith? The regent felt so much anguish in his heart that he poured it forth in a one-sided discourse with the grand guardian, the gist of which was preserved by a scribe in a document titled *junshi (Prince Shi)*,[21] *shi* being the Duke of Shao's given name:

> The Duke of Zhou spoke to the following effect: "Prince Shi, Heaven, unpitying, has sent down ruin on Yin. Yin has lost the Mandate, and we Zhou have

received it. I dare not say that our fortune would continue to prosper, even though I believe that Heaven favors those who are sincere in their intentions. I dare not say, either, that it would end in certain disaster.

"O prince, you have already told me, 'It all depends on ourselves!'

"As for me, I, too, have not dared rest in the favor of the Lord Above, never for a moment forgetting the terrors of Heaven. I have always sought, as much as a man can do, to lead the people not into disobeying Him. But there are some of us descendants who have succeeded to the good fortune, but who are vastly unable to reverence both Heaven above and the people below, and who are obstructing and abusing the glory of our forefathers. You are at home with these facts; you cannot be unaware of them.

"The Mandate of Heaven is not easy to gain. It will be lost when men fail to live up to the reverent and illustrious virtues of their forefathers.

"Now, I, Dan, being but a small person, have been unable to correct the situation. What I want is only to prolong the glory of our forefathers and make our youthful sovereign share in it."

(The duke) said again: "Heaven is not to be depended upon. Our only course is to extend the virtues of Wu Wang, so that Heaven will not find cause to remove the Mandate we have received since Wen Wang."

The duke said: "Prince Shi, I have heard that of ancient time, when Tang the Successful received the Mandate, he had Yi Yin who was able to make his virtues accord with Heaven. In the time of Taijia, he again had *baoheng*.[22] Taiwu had Yi Zhi and Chen Hu who helped him to accord with Heaven, and also Wu Xian who regulated the imperial household.[23] Zuyi had Wu Xianr.[24] Wuding had Gan Pan.[25]

"All these ministers had contributed so effectively to the government and preservation of Yin that the Yin ceremonies venerating their deceased emperors as companions of Heaven had endured for a long time."

. . . . . .

The duke said, "Prince Shi, formerly when the Lord Above had to take decisive action against Yin, he was persuaded by the virtues of Wen Wang,[26] and He targeted the Mandate on his person.

"But this was also because Wen Wang was able to harmonize and unite the portion of the great empire which he came to possess. And this was also because Wen Wang had such ministers as Guoshu, Hong Yao, San Yisheng, Taidian, and Nangong Kuo."[27]

(He) said again: "Had those capable men not come forth to assist him with advices and instructions, Wen Wang might not have been able to let the benefits of his virtue descend upon the people of our nation.

"But because those men could hold onto the virtues they each possessed, and assist him with single-minded devotion, acting in accord with the knowledge and dread of the majesty of Heaven, and never failing to give him enlightenment in time, they kept the fame of Wen Wang ever ascending until it was heard by the Lord Above. Thus it was that he finally received the Mandate which had belonged to Yin.

"It was the same four men [28] that Wu Wang depended upon when he inherited the possessions. Afterward, it was the same four men that helped Wu Wang carry out the majestic terror of Heaven and slay all his enemies. It was thus that

Wu Wang's fame ever ascended till his virtue was singularly acknowledged by the people of the empire in unison.

"Now with me, Dan, this small person, it is as if I were floating on a great stream. If I can go with you together, we may hope to cross it safely. Our young sovereign is in a condition as though he had not acceded to the throne. You must not lay the whole burden on me. It is for you to correct my errors and remedy my deficiencies. If you, with your age and experience, do not deign to help me, how can I ever hope to see the time of peace and prosperity when phoenixes will be singing,[29] let alone my being able to act in accord with Heaven!"

The duke said, "O Prince, please consider these things. We have received the Mandate which is unlimited and indefinite; but to it, also, there are attached enormous difficulties. What I have told you are counsels for a better future. I shall not let myself be led astray by what I fear posterity might think of me."

The duke said, "Our predecessor (Wu Wang), laying bare his heart, gave you charge of the government and asked you to be a guide to the people. He said, 'Do support your sovereign with intelligence, with energy, and with mutual trust, to carry aloft the Great Mandate. Do follow the example of Wen Wang, whose virtue was to worry himself ceaselessly (for the well-being of the people and of the state).'"

The duke said, "What I have told you, prince, is all true. O Shi, grand guardian, please think reverently, as I do, about the example of Yin—how Yin had fallen into such a terrible calamity, and how mindful we ourselves should be of the dread majesty of Heaven!

"If I were not truthful in my thoughts, I could not have spoken to you like this. Now, I simply say, 'The fulfilment of our destiny rests with us two.' Do you agree with me? If only you too will say, 'It rests with us two indeed,' then I am sure the favor of Heaven will come to us in abundance. However, if the burden proves too much for us to bear later, you, who are always able to hold onto your virtue reverently, may bring to light some men of ability from the younger generation and we may resign our places in their favor at that time.

"Alas! It is by the earnest assistance of us two that we have been able to keep the state as it is today. Let us not rest in idleness, but labor together to complete the work of Wen Wang so that his fame will climb even higher, so that as far as the corners of the sea where the sun rises there shall be no one disobedient to our rule."

The duke said, "I shall say no more. I am only distraught by anxieties about Heaven and about the people."

The duke said, "O Prince, you know well the ways of men. There is none but can begin a beginning. But it is the end that must needs be given thought to. Please dwell on this; and go and carry on your functions with your usual reverence."

Moved by this impassioned appeal, the grand guardian agreed to remain in office as before. But pondering the matter, the Duke of Zhou decided upon another action. He did not abrogate the regency, but he divided the actual administration of the empire in two, with Shaan (modern Shaanxian, Henan), which was halfway between Hao and Mengjin, serving as the dividing point. What territories lay to the west of Shaan were to be administered alone by the grand guardian; and what territories lay to the east, by himself.[30] On the map, the division appears to be unbalanced, the former much smaller in size than the latter. But as a matter of fact, the western portion was composed of the original domain of Zhou and all the other areas that had submitted to Zhou rule very early. It was the section of the empire that was wholly and unreservedly devoted to the cause of Wu Wang and his heir and successor. But the eastern portion was different. It consisted of nearly all the territories that had been only recently conquered by Wu Wang, and whose loyalties could not at all be taken for granted. Moreover, it included the princedoms of Guan, Cai, Huo, and Yin, as well as a number of others that had chosen openly to side with them. Even though these rebellious states, for their own reasons, had not yet taken definite offensive military actions against Zhou, there was no telling either how much the disaffection might spread or when actual hostilities would begin. In making the administrative division, therefore, the regent was assigning to the grand guardian a comparatively much easier and safer task, but reserving for himself a most difficult and hazardous one. And no sooner had he made the decision than he announced that he was betaking himself to the east without delay.

Apparently the duke's purpose for this action was threefold. Firstly, there was nothing that he wanted more than to refute the insidious aspersions cast on him. The grand guardian was a man known for his conscionable and incorruptible integrity even to his enemies. With such a man given undivided jurisdiction over the west, and with the person of the young sovereign in Hao thus entrusted clearly and solely to his care and protection, it must be evident to all that there could be no substance to the allegations that he, the regent, might be harboring sinister designs on Cheng Wang. Secondly, he was no doubt still hoping against hope that a reconciliation or even a compromise, could yet be effected with his estranged brothers. The division of the territories under his own control in two could well be interpreted as an invitation to the three supervisors that if only they should again uphold the sovereignty of Zhou, a scheme might be worked out dividing the empire into three or four parts with each of them taking charge of some part until Cheng Wang came of age. And thirdly, he was of course also preparing for the worst, as he must do under the circumstances. For the preservation of the empire, for the fulfilment of the mission left to him by his deceased and beloved brother, he must see to it that the Mandate of Heaven be kept safe and sound for his nephew the lawful sovereign. For this purpose, he himself had to go to the front, so to speak, of this undeclared contest, to rally the faithful, to prevent further disaffection, to strengthen all defenses, to make plans for every possible contingency. He was determined that he would not be the one to start a fratricidal war. Yet if war should come, all his efforts to the contrary notwithstanding, he must not be found negligent of his duties toward his imperial nephew.

But while he was betaking himself to the east, his heart was plummeting into even lower depths of hopeless despair. A rumor had just reached his ears. It was openly whispered by the three supervisors that he would never have divided the administration with the Duke of Shao had not they themselves stood adamant against his regency. Now that he was bound for the east, he was no doubt bent on a course aimed to crush his opposition at any cost. And once the opposition was crushed, who could prevent him from returning to Hao to pursue his sinister designs again?

History, as the Duke of Zhou would have his scribes record it, has told us little about his feelings at the time. But a latter-day popular poem has thus sung of him:

> While the Duke of Zhou was living in fear of floating
> calumnies,
>
> . . .
>
> Had he died then,
> Who could possibly know that his life had been true or false? [31]

· 2 ·
THE TRIALS OF THE DUKE OF ZHOU

The regent remained in the east more than two years.[32] We have no precise information as to where he went. All records mention only that he "lived in the east," using the same Chinese character, *ju*.[33] Presumably he had no fixed abode, but moved about from one place to another, the better to carry out his purposes. The two years were very trying years for him, and were also years of ominous stalemate and dreadful suspense for the empire. While the duke would not permit himself to start a civil—to him literally fratricidal—war, the rebels were incapable of launching one, for want of united and determined leadership. The men directly under control of the three supervisors were mostly from Zhou. While they were naturally partial to their own princes, they were acquainted, if not with the person of the duke, at least with his fame and record as Wu Wang's principal minister and most trusted brother. Though the rumors the unscrupulous princes had disseminated were malicious enough to arouse their suspicions against the regent, the allegations were not sufficiently substantiated to excite their anger so much as to make them ready and eager to take up arms against their homeland. Then the actions the duke had taken had dispersed much of the cloud of their suspicion. The capping ceremony had dispelled the doubts that some of them had entertained at first that the young sovereign could have already been done away with. And now, with the regent absenting himself from Hao, and with the grand guardian assuming sole protection of Cheng Wang, even though these men were encouraged to take undue pride in the part they had played in contributing to the safety of their lawful sovereign, they were the more disinclined to believe that there existed a *casus belli* between themselves and their kith and kin in the west.

Conscious of the lukewarm support of their own following, the three supervisors had from the very outset sought to form an alliance with Wugeng. Wugeng was, of course, more than willing; but his rule, being confined to the narrow limits of Pangeng's original city, had not much of a force to offer to strengthen their position. However, the name of the last representative of the house of Shang was still something to conjure with for those states which had formerly sworn allegiance to Yin. We do not know how many of them had become ultimately disaffected. But from Mencius we learn that the states that the Duke of Zhou had finally destroyed amounted to fifty.[34] This is almost the exact number of states other records have given as coming to the aid and succor of Zou on the eve of his fall.[35] Though, lacking definitive evidence, we are not at all sure that it was the same states that opposed Zhou in both wars, yet it does not seem unreasonable to assume that the princes who had been willing to cast in their lot with the sinking ship of Yin in its eleventh hour of distress might be the very ones eager to refloat it when given an unexpected chance. At any rate, their number is too paltry, when measured against the 1,700 and some states that were said to have acknowledged the supremacy of Zhou.[36] And none probably realized their weakness better than the three supervisors themselves. Having taken part in the battle of Shepherds' Wild, they must have known quite well that it would be foolhardy to launch an invasion against Zhou with such a meager force as they could muster up.

Their plan, if it could be called a plan, was to wait and work for more disaffection. And they pinned their hopes upon the states and tribes in the former Yin East Land, more especially upon a state called Yan and the savage tribes known as Huaiyi and Xurong. Perhaps had not the Duke of Zhou taken the precaution to send Taigong to Qi and his own son Boqin to Lu immediately after the death of Wu Wang, the disturbances the rebels could have created in the area might have been greater. But as it was, most of the states were too much awed by the presence of Taigong, renowned as the greatest general of the age. And the fact that no sooner had he arrived in Barracks Mound than he subdued the fierce Lai tribes added even more to credence in his invincibility. Thus whatever mischief the rebels had intended to instigate was to a large extent quietly deterred.

An exception, however, was the Prince of Yan. His state happened to abut Lu, the Duke of Zhou's own fief, now taken over by Boqin.[37] From many centuries back, even before the Shang moved their imperial seat to Yin, Yan seemed to have had close relations with the descendants of Tang.[38] Thus when the Prince of Yan submitted to the sovereignty of Zhou after the fall of Yin, it is likely that he had only made a virtue of necessity. The creation of the fief of Lu for the Duke of Zhou right within what he had always regarded as his own territory must have been gall and wormwood for him to swallow. Powerless to resist, he was as inwardly furious as he was outwardly acquiescent. While Zhou was strong and united, there was no way for him to vent his smoldering resentment. But now Zhou was divided and verging toward a fratricidal war, he saw his chance at last. Yet shrewd and wily man that he was, he had no desire to provoke the regent's son in the open, which might well bring the combined might of both Boqin and the redoubtable Taigong upon himself. He cast his eyes therefore to the south of his princedom and also to the south of Lu, where the tribes of Huaiyi and Xurong had been living quite disgruntled for the last few years. The founding of the new dynasty had led to the reopening of communications between the two branches of the house of Zhou, which in turn had accelerated the movement to convert nomadic territories into agrarian fields.[39] Heedless of the social causes that made this development inevitable, the Huaiyi and Xurong blamed it all on the house of Zhou. So now under the Prince of Yan's aiding and abetting, they embarked on a joint invasioin of Lu.[40] But they made the attack without the knowledge of the capability of Boqin. Thereupon, the son and heir of the regent assembled his men, harangued them on the necessity and the virtues of discipline, and then inflicted a decisive defeat on the invaders.[41]

Thus neither the plans of the three supervisors nor the machinations of Yin and Yan were of much avail, and the rebellious forces were forced to remain inactive for the most part of two years. Meanwhile, for reasons we have explained before, the regent was also marking time. The ancient records give no precise details about his doings; but here and there we may find some clues to form an educated conjecture. In the *Book of Poetry* there is an ode titled *qiyue, Seventh Moon*. It was noted by scholars in the 1st century B.C. that "this was composed by the Duke of Zhou, while going through the crisis. He wanted to outline how Houji and the other ancestors of Zhou had begun, and then spread, their culture; and how difficult and toilsome the enterprise had been that had finally led to the possession of the empire."[42] In several books of antiquity, there is also preserved, in texts that differ slightly one from another, what may be described as a sort of *Poor Richard's Almanac* that obtained in the early years of the Zhou dynasty.[43] Comparing the almanac with the ode, we may conclude that the latter is a very much abridged version of the former, in rhyme. The ode is of special interest to our history not only because it gives a clue to some of the activities the regent could have undertaken in those critical years, but also because it provides a vivid picture of the simple and strenuous life the people in general were leading in that period. The duke must have composed it in the seventh moon of the year, which roughly corresponds to the month of August in the

Gregorian calendar, when summer heat would have been at its hottest. It may be translated as follows:

> In the seventh moon the heat flows like fire;
> But in the ninth moon we put on our coats.
> In the days of the first moon, the winds start to blow;
> In the days of the second, our skins crack like chestnuts.
> Without clothes, fine or coarse, how can we get around the year?
> In the days of the third, we take our plows in hand;
> In the days of the fourth, we take our toes to the fields.
> I go with my wife and my children;
> We eat at the Southern Acre.
> There comes the land officer;[44]
> With us he is delighted.
>
> In the seventh moon the heat flows like fire;
> But in the ninth moon we put on our coats.
> In the spring the sun brings us warmth,
> And the oriole welcomes it with a song.
> A young lady, taking her deep basket,
> Picks her way through narrow paths
> In search of tender leaves of mulberry trees to feed the silkworms.
> Now the spring days have lengthened out,
> And she has gathered lots and lots of them;
> But the young lady's heart is afflicted with sadness—
> Is she wishing that she could have gone home with her betrothed, the son of the
>   prince?
>
> In the seventh moon the heat flows like fire;
> In the eighth moon the sedges and reeds grow luxuriant.
> These are silkworm months when the mulberry branches are stripped of their
>   leaves.
> We take yonder our axes and hatchets
> To lop off the branches that are distant and high,
> Pushing aside and sparing those that are low and female-like.
>
> In the seventh moon the shrike sings its song.
> In the eighth moon we start spinning.
> We make fabrics dark and yellow;
> And our red fabric is especially brilliant—
> It is to form the lower robe of the son of our prince.
>
> In the fourth moon the grass is in seed.
> In the fifth moon the cicada gives its note.
> In the eighth, we reap;
> In the tenth, the leaves fall.
> In the days of the first, we go after badgers,
> And also foxes and wildcats,
> To make furs for the son of our prince.

In the days of the second, we hold the chase together
And undertake to keep up the exercises of war.
When we capture boars of one year old, they are for ourselves;
When we capture boars of three years old, these we shall present to our prince.

In the fifth moon the locust moves its legs;
In the sixth moon the cicada makes sound with its wings;
In the eighth moon it is under the eaves;
In the ninth moon it is about the doors.
In the tenth moon the cricket enters under our beds.
We fill up the chinks and smoke out the rats;
We stop up the windows that face the north and we plaster the doors.
We call out to our wives and children:
"All these are for the changing of the year;
Now you may enter inside and dwell."

In the sixth moon we eat plums and berries;
In the seventh moon we cook sunflower seeds and beans;
In the eighth moon we knock down the dates;
In the tenth moon we reap the rice,
And make some of it into wine for the coming spring
For the benefit of bushy-browed elders.
In the seventh moon we eat melons;
In the eighth moon we cut down the bottlelike gourds.
In the ninth moon we gather hemp seed;
We collect sowthistle and also firewood
To use as fuel for feeding our fellow husbandmen.

In the ninth moon we build or repair vegetable gardens and storage sites.
In the tenth moon we deposit the sheaves in them—
The millets, both the early-sown and the late-sown,
And also other grains, the hemp, the beans, and the wheat.
"O my fellow husbandmen,
Our harvest is all collected.
Let us go back and work on our houses!
In the daytime collect the rushes,
At night rope them together into thatches.
Then get up quickly on the roofs!
For we must finish the work before we begin to sow the grains."

In the days of the second, we hew out ice blocks;
In the days of the third, we deposit them in the ice cellars.
In the days of the fourth, early one morning we offer in sacrifice a lamb with
    scallions.
In the ninth moon, it is cold with frost.
In the tenth moon we sweep and wash clean our fields and storage sites.
We prepare two bottles of wine for feasting
And say to one another, "Let us kill a young lamb
And go to the hall of our prince.

There we shall raise cups of rhinoceros horn
And drink a toast to him—May he live ten thousand years without end!"

From a study of the ode even three thousand years later we can glimpse some of the duke's motivations for its composition. His utmost wish was to preserve the empire for the house of Zhou. Divided though it was at the moment, he knew no better way of defending and strengthening it (or at least the part of it still under his control) than urging and encouraging the people to engage in agricural pursuits, as his ancestors had done before him. And while he was doing so, going from one place to another, he must have noticed that the almanac issued by the government was too long for the unlettered public to memorize. So the inspiration came to him that he should write a very condensed version and put it in rhyme. Besides, the purpose of the ode was manifold. Firstly, he wanted to make the people understand that if they wanted to protect themselves and their loved ones from cold and hunger, they not only had to work for it but also to plan the work well in advance. Secondly (and this of course has a special significance for our present discussion), he wanted to ensure that the people would not forget to hold the chase in their spare time "to keep up the exercises of war." Thirdly, he wanted to inculcate in the people a sort of spontaneous and affectionate devotion for their prince, and more especially, for the son of their prince. There can be no question that by "the son of the prince," the duke meant Cheng Wang, and it is more than likely that the people then knew it too. And fourthly, intentionally or not, he was also expressing a wistful wish of his own in the ode. For like the young lady that was afflicted with melancholy, he too was wishing that he could have gone home reunited with "the son of the prince."

Of course, if the regent was attempting to find a resolution for the dispute that was verging on armed conflict, he must have done more. And apparently he did. By all accounts he was a very humble man, always looking for men of ability and virtue to help or advise him. Once he was said to have told his son Boqin, the Marquis of Lu, that at that very moment there were about ten men he would like to have as teachers, about thirty he would like to have as friends, and about a hundred he would like to talk with at leisure and at random, besides some one thousand subordinates who would have to make reports to him now and then and whom he always intended to hear out.[45] And in order to scrape up time for meeting with so many men, he did not spare himself. He confessed to his son, "When I wash my hair, I often have to hold it up temporarily three times; when I take repast, I also have to let it be disrupted as frequently. Yet for all these efforts, I am in constant fear that I may have missed seeing some good men." [46] Again, it was said that during his regency it was his practice to dispatch inspectors to various enfeoffed states to find out if there were people suffering from cold or hunger, if there was injustice or dereliction of duty in the enforcement of law, or if there were good men not given employment. And when one of those princes came to the court, the regent would greet him courteously and tell him in confidence about his own findings in that state, saying: "Perhaps it is because my government and my instructions have been amiss that there are still people suffering from cold and hunger, that injustice and dereliction of duty still occur in the enforcement of law, that there are still good men not given employment." And invariably the prince, on return, would have those deficiencies remedied to the rejoicing of his princedom.[47] Since no precise dates are attached to these accounts, it may be assumed that that must have been the duke's habitual pattern of conduct. And if he had adopted such practices in ordinary times, it may be expected that in those two critical years he must have pursued them with even greater vigor and zeal. One can easily imagine that while in the east, the regent made his way continually from one place to another, from one state to another, talking tirelessly to the princes and to the people, to the old and to the young, or to whoever wanted to meet with him, seeking ways and means to improve their lot, looking for able and talented men to give them employment, and at the same time sounding out their views about the current political situation and trying to convince them of his own selfless intentions and the righteousness of the cause he believed in. There is nothing like it in all of Chinese history, both before and after. If we must compare it with something we are more familiar with, it may perhaps have resembled the best type of electioneering campaigns in some of our modern democracies—but utterly free of guile, free of vulgarity, free of artificiality. Thus it is that ever since then there has been a popular saying in China which is still oft-quoted today: "The Duke of Zhou let his repasts be disrupted, and won the heart of the whole world." [48]

Two years had elapsed since the regent's departure from Hao. From intelligence he now learned that the machinations of the insurgents, having so far proved fruitless, became the more intensified; and despite all his hints that he desired an amicable settlement with the three supervisors, war might be imminent. He felt confident that by this time he had restored the people's faith in him. But how dearly he wished that he could have said the same about his nephew. The imperial youth was approaching sixteen years old; he should be knowledgeable enough to discern right from wrong, to separate the true from the false. Had he kept his confidence in his uncle intact? Or had it been eroded or damaged by those invidious allegations? Anxious to convince Cheng Wang of his own earnest intent, yet reluctant to speak out openly against the three supervisors, he composed another poem and sent it to the young sovereign for his perusal. He called it *chixiao, Owl,* because the owl is a vicious bird that preys upon other birds' young.[49]

O Owl! O Owl!
You have deprived me of my young;
Do not destroy also my house!
Just to think with how much love and toil have I built it,
Even though you have shown no pity for my young I have taken so much pains in
    bringing up.

Before the skies are dark with rain,
I have gathered the roots of the mulberry tree
And bound round and round my window and door.
Now you people below,
Is there any one among you who dares to despise my house?

With my claws I scratch and scrape
Through the rushes I have gathered
And the other materials I have stored.
My mouth is all sore;
Still I say to myself, "I cannot call my house my own."

My wings are all injured,
My tail is all broken.
Yet my house is in a perilous condition:
It is being tossed about in the wind and rain,
And I can only cry out in anxiety and pain.[50]

Equipped with clear hindsight as we are, we can understand the subtle drift of the poem. The regent was employing the bird of nocturnal habits to represent the groundless allegations against him. Those rumors had already succeeded in driving him away from his nephew, yet they were threatening to do even more. They were aiming at the destruction of the empire which he had helped establish with so much care and toil. Out in the east he had been building up its defenses to the utmost of his capacity, and he could now point out with pride that so far as military preparedness was concerned, no one in the empire could dare view it with contempt. Nevertheless, despite all his endeavors, the empire was still as unsafe as is the perilous bird's nest being tossed about in a storm. And so long as the outside threat of the owl was not removed, or so long as his warning against it went unheeded, he himself could do nothing except to cry out in anxiety and in pain.

But to this poem there came no response. Perhaps its meaning was altogether too elusive for a boy in his teens to grasp. Perhaps the mind of the young emperor had already been much corroded by the slow poison of those rumors. Since the youth could not make up his mind whether the regent intended him ill or well, or which one of his uncles was to be believed and which one not, he just left the poem unanswered.[51] And the nightmare of doubt and suspense lengthened for the duke.

Then came autumn in the year. In the land around and adjacent to Hao, the imperial seat, "the grains looked ripe and abundant with every promise of a bumper crop. But before they could be reaped, Heaven sent down a great storm of thunder, lightning, and gust. The stalks of the grains were all beaten down and huge trees were torn up. The people were terrified. The emperor and the great officers, all in their caps of state," [52] hastened to the ancestral temple and prayed to the spirits of their forefathers for intercession with the Lord Above. Having completed their initial devotions, while the diviners were making preparations for divination by tortoise, the youthful emperor caught sight of the golden coffer which served as the repository for the records of past prayers in divination ceremonies. He opened it and examined the tablets. One of the very first he came across was the prayer that the Duke of Zhou had offered to the deity of the Yellow River some two years before, asking that Heaven take his life instead of that of Cheng Wang himself. It was very brief. It said simply, "If we have offended the Lord,[53] it is I who have given the offense, not our emperor, he being so young and unknowledgeable." [54] Cheng Wang dug farther into the coffer and discovered another tablet which bore the prayer the selfsame uncle had offered six years before to Tai Wang, Wang Ji, and Wen Wang. He read:

> Whereas your principal descendant Fa [55] is suffering from a severe and dangerous sickness, and whereas you three emperors in heaven have the responsibility of looking after him, I pray you to beseech the Lord Above to let me, Dan, substitute for his person.
>
> I was lovingly obedient to my father. I am also possessed of many parts and many talents that will fit me to serve spiritual beings. Your principal descendant, on the other hand, is not a man of so many parts and talents as I, Dan, am. He is not capable of serving spiritual beings.
>
> Moreover, he is the one who has received the Mandate derived from the hall of the Lord to extend protection and blessings to the four quarters of the empire. And he has succeeded in establishing your descendants in this lower world; and the people of the four quarters all stand in reverent awe of him. Oh, do not let the precious Heaven-conferred Mandate fall to the ground; and you, our former emperors, may perpetually attach yourselves to it and find repose.

Cheng Wang finished reading and asked the scribes and the other officers present about the matter. And they all verified it, saying, "It is only too true. Only the duke had charged us that we should never presume to talk about it." Holding the tablet in his hand, the young emperor wept. He said, "We need no longer ask for divination about the matter of the storm. The duke has toiled so hard for our house in the past; but I, being small, was unaware of it. Now Heaven has moved Its terrors in order to make shine the virtue of the Duke of Zhou before us. I must go and welcome him back in person. It is fitting and proper for our empire that I do so." [56]

· 3 ·

THE SUPPRESSION OF THE REBELLION (1101 B.C.)

The reconciliation between the nephew and the uncle was immediate and complete. And it came not a moment too soon, for the rebels had decided at last to launch an offensive against Zhou. This time, however, it was not the Prince of Guan or the Prince of Cai who had seized the initiative, but Wugeng of Yin. At the beginning of their joint intransigence, the forces under the command of the three supervisors were far superior to those of the last representative of the vanquished dynasty. But as the insurgency progressed, and as their strength could be increased only either by gaining new allies from states still loyal to the memory of the fallen imperial house or by recruiting from the population of the great metropolis of Yin, the proportional influence of Wugeng grew and grew. However, under such circumstances as theirs, there had been, and there could be, neither unison in interest nor unity in policy; so for almost three years they had remained in a state of indecision and inaction. But now the Prince of Yan, who had been frustrated in his machinations against Lu, and who saw that Wugeng had acquired a substantial ascendancy over his nominal supervisors, gave the last heir and claimant of the Yin Empire this counsel: "This is an opportunity that comes only once in a thousand years. You must undertake the great enterprise now!" [57] And Wugeng agreed. And willy-nilly the three Zhou princes were forced to follow suit to make war against their own house.

Their attacks came shortly after Cheng Wang had welcomed the Duke of Zhou back to Hao. While the regent was prepared to restore all authority to the lawful sovereign, the imperial youth, acknowledging his own immaturity and inexperience, insisted on the duke's continuing to act for him until he came of age. However, on the one and only matter of suppressing the rebels, the emperor was adamant. Apparently there were quite a few who advised against the use of force; and the Duke of Zhou appeared to be one of them, deeming that now that he himself was reunited with his nephew, there was a far better chance to reach a peaceful settlement with his three brothers. But infuriated by the latter's treachery, deception, and contumacy, the teenage monarch felt for them no forgiveness. He directed the regent forthwith to order a punitive expedition against the rebels,[58] and issued in his own name a *Great Proclamation, dagao,* calling upon all the loyal princes and peoples of the empire to join in the undertaking.[59]

This document is preserved for us in the *Book of History*. However, when we read it today, we cannot help wondering at the language it used. For it is clear that the Zhou people, Cheng Wang and the Duke of Zhou alike, were shy of speaking about the causes of the war, evidently embarrassed by its having been started by their own kin. The proclamation therefore ascribed the disturbance to a sort of supernatural origin, treating it as if it were an inescapable trial and tribulation that had been foreordained for Zhou to go through:

> Wen Wang has left us a great precious tortoise, which brings us intelligence from Heaven. We had consulted it upon our succession; and it had said even then, "There will be great trouble for West Land, and the people of West Land themselves will be involved in the commotion." Hence this turmoil.

But against Wugeng, the proclamation was quite explicit:

> Yin, of small worth, dares to attempt to mend his line which had already been broken by terrors sent down by Heaven. Learning of the defects existing within our empire and of the resultant uneasiness among our people, he says, "I will recover my patrimony and make the state of Zhou a border territory again."

And this passage was immediately followed by another reaffirming Zhou's own strength and confidence. Not only the people now were all united again against the rebels, but it was also a predestined conclusion that Zhou would win out in the end:

> One day the turmoil began. The very next day the people came forward, (each well) offering to send forth ten good men [60] to help me restore the tranquillity of the empire and perpetuate the plans of Wen Wang and Wu Wang. This great business I am engaging in shall have a successful conclusion. For it has been invariably confirmed by all the divinations I have taken.

But Cheng Wang wanted to make clear in the *Great Proclamation* that the decision to crush the rebellion was his own, no one else's. In fact, he made it a point for everyone to know that he had made the decision in spite of advice to the contrary.

> Now, you princes of various enfeoffed states, and you officers and administrators of my affairs, you all may say (as some of you have already said to me): "This is a matter of enormous difficulties. That there has been restlessness among the people, has its origins from within the imperial palace and the chambers of princes.[61] So we, your humble officers as well as the elders, do not think the expedition advisable. Will not your majesty act independently of the divination?" . . .
> But the sovereign says: "In the days past, I have pondered daily over the difficulties that we have talked about. When a deceased father has laid out his plans and started to build a house, if the son cannot raise up the wall, how much less can he complete the roof? Or if the father has broken up the ground, and the son cannot sow the seed, how much less can he reap the grain? In such a case, would the father who had been so dedicated to his purpose be able to say, 'I have an heir who will not abandon his patrimony'? How dare I, therefore, not uphold the Great Mandate that was entrusted to Wen Wang?"

And Cheng Wang addressed himself to the people and to the princes with this question:

> If a father has among his friends someone who attacks his child, will the elders of the people and his other friends encourage the attack and not come to the rescue?

And he ended the proclamation with a command and an appeal, bolstered up once more by a reaffirmation of faith that Heaven had predestined success for Zhou:

> Heaven is bent on destroying Yin. Like a husbandman, I dare not leave the business in my fields unfinished. Heaven has already showed Its favor to my forebears who brought about the pacification of the empire before. How could I have asked for divinations and then dared not to abide by them? Not only am I bound to follow in the footsteps of my forebears whose pacification purpose embraced all the limits of the land; but the divinations have been invariably favorable. I am therefore asking you to go forth in this expedition to the east. There is no mistake about the Mandate of Heaven. The predications of the divinations are all to the same effect.

The *Great Proclamation* notwithstanding, in the conflict that ensued, the young sovereign seems to have left the command of the Zhou forces entirely in the hands of the regent. If the nephew had been reticent about the causes, the uncle was even more so about the conduct and progress of the war. In fact, except for the manifest results of the conclusion, which could not be hidden from the knowledge of posterity, the ancient records have given us no information whatever. We know neither how many battles were fought nor how long the confrontation actually lasted. We have only a vague impression that real fighting was brief. And indeed it could well have been. While one side was obviously without concerted and effective leadership, the other was guided by one of the most energetic and accomplished men of his time. The victory of the latter was therefore, if not a foreordained event, a foregone conclusion. The great metropolis of Yin was overwhelmed for a second time. Wugeng was slain. The Prince of Guan hanged himself. The Prince of Cai and the Prince of Huo were taken alive.[62]

For all purposes the rebellion may be said to have come to an end. But the war was not completely over as yet. The paltry number of states that had given military support to the rebels and that were adjacent to Yin had been quickly subdued. But there still remained in the remote East Land Yan, the Huaiyi and Xurong tribes, and some of their allies. Militarily, this did not seem to present too much of a problem. With the forces of Taigong and Boqin closing in on them from one direction and the main Zhou army pressing on inexorably from the other, these could have been easily annihilated in this pincerlike operation. But the Duke of Zhou did not wish to finish the work himself. He had not been unwilling to take full responsibility for the assault of Yin, lest the good name of his imperial nephew should suffer from the taint of fighting and killing his uncles. But now that Yin had been won, he was eager to let the youthful monarch acquire the glory and renown of a conqueror. Thus while he remained planning and directing the main movements from behind the scenes, he had Cheng Wang take over personal command of all the Zhou forces in this last campaign. The operation was swiftly and successfully concluded. Yan was destroyed and its prince captured, and the Huaiyi and Xurong tribes were dispersed. In all, some seventeen nations were overturned.[63] For celebration of this feat of arms, two documents were specially composed to laud the gallantry or the mercifulness of the young sovereign.[64] If these had been preserved, we might have learned a little more about the war; but they were not.

· 4 ·

THE CLEARING OF THE AFTERMATH

The war left many problems as its aftermath. But the youthful emperor, having effected the conquest of Yan and the Huaiyi and Xurong tribes, appears to have returned to Hao and delegated all his authority once again to the regent, who remained in the east undertaking to resolve all of them. Both Wugeng and the Prince of Guan being dead, we hear no more about them from the ancient records. The Prince of Cai and the Prince of Huo were taken alive, but the Duke of Zhou punished them differently. It was recorded that the Prince of Cai "was imprisoned at a neighborhood outside the outer city wall, guarded by seven chariots." [65] Presumably, the city was the city of Hao, the imperial seat; and presumably too, he was kept a prisoner for the rest of his natural life. As to the Prince of Huo, "he was reduced to the status of common man, and for three years he was not to be included as one of imperial blood in all family and government functions." [66] It has been alleged by some scholars of relative antiquity that when the three years were over, he was reinvested as Marquis of Huo, with a smaller fief in modern Huoxian, Shanxi.[67] Though definitive confirmation for this is lacking, it seems to have accorded well with the general policy of the regent, who was as generous and humane toward all men as he was affectionate and forgiving to his own kith and kin.

The duke's fairmindedness was further demonstrated by his treatment of the Prince of Cai's son, named Hu, but better known as Caizhong, "Cai Junior." While the father was incarcerated, the duke was even then showing special regard for the son. Observing that the young man was bent on the pursuit of virtuous living, he appointed him a minister in his own fief, Lu, as an assistant to Boqin.[68] Caizhong having proved his worth in that capacity, the duke spoke to Cheng Wang and had him invested as Marquis of Cai, but given a different fief. The father's original enfeoffment was situated in the former Central Shang, north of the Yellow River and west of Yin, a much more populous and better-developed locality. The son's new fief was far south of the Yellow River, close by the Huai, which may be characterized as a sort of frontier region of the empire. Nevertheless, it was given the name Cai, or as the people came to call it, the new Cai. And on his being invested by Cheng Wang, the regent had a document composed specially to convey the significance of the occasion.[69]

The regent's liberal and clement policy seems not to have confined itself to the kinsmen of Zhou, but extended to others. Take the treatment of the Prince of Yan, for instance. As a principal instigator in the disturbance, he would have well deserved the severest penalty. However, he was only exiled to a place called Pugu.[70] Though we know nothing about what happened to him afterward, taking the Prince of Cai as a precedent, it may not be unreasonable to assume that since the Zhou had chosen only to exile him, the utmost punishment he suffered in Pugu was no more than life imprisonment. Toward the Huaiyi and Xurong tribes, the regent was even benevolent and helpful. After their submission, he learned that their land was pestered with elephants. Thereupon he employed his army in a systematic hunt and cleared the territory of those formidable beasts as far as the banks of the Yangtze. In commemoration of the event, instead of a document, the duke had a special piece of music composed, titled *Three Elephants,* to be appreciated the better by the unlettered tribes.[71]

The most difficult question to resolve was Yin, or rather what should be done about that all too populous metropolis. The regent remembered only too well how Wu Wang had been harassed by the same problem, and also that it was he himself who had recommended a generous and humane solution.[72] But that did not seem to have worked well for Zhou. There being such a disproportionate concentration of population in Yin, the preserving of it intact had tempted and enabled the three supervisors and Wugeng to exploit its numbers and its wealth to raise the standards of rebellion. And thinking of this, the regent could not help marveling at the foresight of his deceased beloved brother. Wu Wang had forewarned that so long as the Zhou could not build up an imperial domain to match that of the Central Shang, their Mandate of Heaven could not be said to be secure; and he had even envisaged the establishment of a new seat for the empire at Luo and confided his intentions to the duke himself.[73] As the duke saw it, therefore, there was only one course of action open to him—to reduce the population of Yin and to found a new capital for Zhou. He was, of course, aware of all the difficulties that had deterred Wu Wang from carrying out his intentions

during his short reign.[74] Nor was the duke insensitive to how much hardship
was involved for the people of Yin if he now decided to put the plans into
execution. But this he was resolved to do, come what might, that peace and
stability might be ensured for the dynasty. Yet as a man of inborn humaneness, judging from his subsequent actions, he must have been equally determined to temper his policy with leniency the best he could.

Now that Wugeng had revolted and had been slain, the regent could have
easily availed himself of the opportunity to terminate the role of the house of
Shang as leader of a nation, as Tang had terminated that of the house of Xia
before him. But this he did not elect to do. Instead, he had Cheng Wang
invest the Prince of Wei, Zou's brother, the Yin emperor Di Yi's eldest son,
and a man esteemed by all Yin people for his virtue, with new dignities as
the heir and representative of the house of Shang.[75] The Prince of Wei was
given the title *gong*, "duke," the highest rank of all investitures. He was also
permitted to use Yin rituals and Yin music to venerate his imperial ancestors.
In addition, on all ceremonial occasions of Zhou, he was to be formally
treated less like a vassal, more like a guest.[76] These were exceptional honors
never before granted to a subject. In the meantime, however, he was not to
be enfeoffed with Yin, but with a new site near to Tang's original capital,
Bo, now called Song.[77] And in the special document composed for his investiture as Duke of Song, it was also made explicit to him that he must carefully "observe all the laws and practices of the new dynasty and prove
himself a bulwark to the imperial house of Zhou." [78] In making this disposition, therefore, we can see that the regent was as magnanimous as he was
astute. While the total eradication of the house of Shang would undoubtedly
cause the Yin loyalists to harden their resentment against Zhou, the investment of the Prince of Wei in the former homeland of the Shang would serve
not only to mitigate their ill feelings, but also to remind them that whatever
misfortune they had suffered, they had only themselves to blame for not
having had a man like the esteemed prince as their last sovereign, but that
monster of a man Zou. Moreover, if the Prince of Wei was distinguished for
his virtue, he was also recognized by the discerning regent for his meekness,
which would make him the more amenable to Zhou sovereignty. Furthermore, the newly created fief of Song, like all the areas adjacent to Bo, was
situated in the center of a vast flat plain, fertile for cultivation, but lacking in
defensible natural barriers.[79] Only an exceptional political and military genius like Tang could have used that land to rise to preeminent power; and
the regent did not perceive much threat from that possibility in the near
future. And lastly, since Song as yet was very sparsely populated, and since
there was palpably a large segment of the Yin population who would rather
be ruled by a man of their own imperial house than an alien, presumably the
new Duke of Song was not only permitted but even encouraged to take with

him to his fief as many of those Yin people who had not taken active part in the rebellion as the regent himself deemed necessary or desirable. And, as later records are to bear testimony, this arrangement proved beneficial both to Zhou and to Shang. The Prince of Wei ruled well in Song, and all the people who followed him and settled there became quite contented with their changed circumstances.[80] Throughout the eight centuries that were to follow, Song never made trouble for Zhou.

As to the remainder of the population of Yin, except those who had been found to have actively associated with the rebels, they were placed under the jurisdiction of the regent's younger brother, Wen Wang's ninth son, Prince Feng.[81] That the people might forget the memories of the past dynasty, the sooner the better, the place was renamed Wei, and assigned to Prince Feng as his fief. In territory, Wei was made much smaller than the former metropolis of Yin, not larger than the usual size allotted to a first-grade enfeoffment, that is, about one hundred *li* square. But it seemed that the new Marquis of Wei was also entrusted with the authority to oversee the administrations of several states in the surrounding areas.[82] Moreover, he was concurrently named minister of justice of the imperial court, empowered to adjudicate cases involving the gravest offenses such as treason and conspiracy against the empire.[83] After such an experience as the Guan-Cai Disturbance, one may wonder why the regent had seemed to repeat the mistake of Wu Wang by concentrating so much power in the hands of a brother for a second time. But apparently he had given the matter careful thought. On the one hand, he knew that if his plans were all carried out as he fully intended them to be, the population of the former Yin would be substantially reduced. On the other, he had carefully studied the character of Prince Feng, and he was sure that in this brother he could place his trust. And the results of this disposition, as history bears witness, appear to have amply justified his judgment.

However, both on the occasion of the investiture of the marquis and after, the regent in the name of Cheng Wang issued no less than three proclamations,[84] which have all been preserved more or less intact in the *Book of History,* to serve as guidelines for the government of Wei. Conceivably these directions were purposely put forth in the form of proclamations for the benefit not only of the newly enfeoffed prince but for that of the populace of former Yin so that they might know precisely what they could expect from the new government and, also, what pattern of conduct they themselves should follow. And as such, these documents are of great interest to our history, for they reveal at once the duke's political beliefs as well as his practical skill in putting them into practice.

In the main, the course of action he was now determined to pursue is the same humanitarian policy he had recommended to Wu Wang after the victory at Shepherds' Wild.[85] But as a result of the recent disturbance and because of it, he was also putting teeth into this policy. In short, he aimed to make Zhou both loved and feared. Thus he commenced the very first document [86] by instructing the marquis to emulate their illustrious father Wen Wang:

> [He] was able to make shine his virtue. At the same time he was careful in the use of punishment. He did not dare slight the widow or the widower. He gave employment to men according to their merits. He showed respect to those who deserved respect. And he put fear into those who needed to have fear put into them. Thus he made his position perfectly clear to the people.

The duty of the ruler is therefore "to protect and regulate the people." And in pursuing this task, the marquis was exhorted that, besides taking lessons from Wen Wang, he must seek to learn "from wise Yin emperors," "from other wise monarchs of antiquity," and also "from old and experienced men of Yin, even those living in remote corners." As to protecting the people, the duke used two expressions describing what the proper attitude of government should be, which are still often quoted in China today. The marquis was told that "when the people suffered distress or affliction, he himself should feel as if he were suffering it in his own person"; and he should always protect them "as if he were protecting a newborn babe.'[87]

So much for inspiring love. But it was also the regent's intent to inspire fear. Thus in the first proclamation he dwelt in even greater length on the use of punishment. At the outset, he expressed a fear that the marquis might grow too callous and prone to cruelty. He warned:

> It is not you, Feng, who may inflict punishment or death on a person. Indeed, no one, of oneself, may inflict punishment or death on any person.

And he formulated for him these precepts:

> In cases outside of your immediate concern (that is, cases not involving treason or conspiracy against the empire), what you need to do is set forth the law and establish the facts, and let the judicial officers mete out penalties in accordance with the Yin penal code.
>
> As to cases involving important prisoners (those who have been accused of treason or conspiracy against the empire, or who otherwise deserve the death penalty), you must reflect upon each of them five or six days, yes, even up to ten days, or even up to three months in order to cover the grounds concerning their crime, to see if they truly deserve the punishment you may decide upon.
>
> In all cases, the punishments dispensed should be determined strictly in accordance with regular Yin laws. But you must see to it that the punishments, including the death penalties, be dispensed righteously. And you must not let them be warped by your own inclinations.

However, after having given the marquis the above restrictions that he might not indulge in excessive use of punishment, the regent was again afraid that the young prince might err on the side of softheartedness and leniency. He admonished:

Feng, though you are young in years, I know few have a heart as good as yours. As regards my own heart and virtue, you know them well too. When people commit crimes, they themselves are responsible for the punishments they will receive. They perpetrate villainy and treason; they kill or assault for plunder; they are irrational or contemptuous of death. Such criminals are abomination to all. If punishments are meted out to them, there is no one but will feel happy and relieved.

But over and above all, the regent's mind was exercised by considerations for the maintenance of tranquillity and stability in the empire. He bethought himself of the types of men who are by nature inclined toward intransigence and disturbance, and who therefore should be regarded as principal sources of threat to social and political harmony, and dealt with accordingly. He said,

O Feng, be reverent and understanding in inflicting punishment. When men commit small crimes which are not mischances, but done on purpose; when they intentionally and habitually engage in unlawful activities, though their crimes are small, yet you may not but put them to death. But in case of great crimes which are not done on purpose but from mischance, or misfortune, or accident, if the offenders make a full confession of their guilt, you may not put them to death.

And besides those inveterate criminals, the regent saw another serious menace to the good order of society, which he wished to check at the very source. He declared:

The foremost evil and greatest abomination are those who are sons not filial to their fathers, or who are brothers not affectionate to their brothers. . . . If we in charge of the government neglect to deal with these offenders, then the natural laws decreed by Heaven for the people will be thrown into great confusion and disorder. Therefore I say: You must with celerity bring such men to account in accordance with the laws of Wen Wang. Punish them forthwith and do not pardon them.

Besides the abovementioned points, the document reveals another aspect of the regent's policy. Not only had he directed the marquis to use strictly regular Yin laws in inflicting punishments (except in cases of sons and brothers who violated what he considered to be Heaven's natural laws), but apparently he had also made it his policy to retain as many old Yin officers in the new Wei administration as possible. For the goal he was striving after was to assimilate the Yin people as an integral part of the Zhou Empire, to make them feel that though their circumstances might have changed, their life was not much different, but indeed might even turn better, in that the Zhou rule was clearly more benevolent and more concerned with their welfare. Thus he told the marquis:

> It is your business to enlarge the imperial influence by protecting the people of Yin. It is this way that you may help the sovereign to consolidate the Mandate of Heaven and make the people a new people.

At the same time, however, the regent was anxious to let it be known that none of those officers so retained would be allowed to harbor sinister designs or adverse sentiments against Zhou. He warned sternly:

> If those who are disobedient to natural laws are to be severely dealt with, how much more so should be the officers employed in your state as instructors of youth, or as heads of departments, or even as petty officers charged with their several commissions, when they propagate and spread contrary teachings, seeking praises of people, forgetting the conditions of their employment, but intending to do harm to their rulers! This is sheer wickedness; such men are abomination to me. You must put an end to them at once. You must have them summarily executed. This is only doing what is right and just.

But the duke also feared that corruption of power might come from the Zhou officers assisting the marquis. So he admonished the newly enfeoffed prince:

> You are here prince and leader. If you cannot manage your own household, with your own petty officers, instructors, and heads of departments; if you use, or allow them to use, terror and oppression; then you yourself have deserted the imperial charge and you are governing your state without virtue.

And he ended his advice by emphasizing to the marquis that in government the exercise of virtue should be always preferred to the use of punishment:

> Feng, when I think of the people, clearly I see that they are to be led to happiness and tranquillity. I think of the virtues of former wise emperors of Yin who had so led them and achieved that objective. Now, the people are surely to follow us. If we do not lead them well, we cannot be said to have a government worthy of the name in this state.

Broad and comprehensive as the above instructions were, no sooner had the first proclamation been issued than the regent found one more serious threat to the peace and stability of Wei that he had neglected to take into consideration—the addiction of the Yin people to drink. He regarded the matter as one of such importance that he issued a special proclamation [88] to warn the populace against that intemperate habit. It was again put in the form of a written directive issued by Cheng Wang to the marquis. It began by saying that indulgence in drink usually "leads people to great confusion and loss of virtue." The Cultural Emperor having taught that spirits should be consumed only on occasions of sacrifice, this rule had invariably prevailed in West Land. As to former Yin emperors, from Tang to Di Yi, they had also "not dared to allow themselves in idleness or pleasure—how much less would they dare to indulge in drinking!" "But the last successor of these emperors gave his person to intoxication . . . abandoning himself to lewdness and dissipation, destroying all his majesty." "Thus Heaven sent down ruin on Yin, showed no love for Yin. . . . Not that Heaven is cruel and oppressive, but the people themselves have asked for Its punishment."

However, the Duke was too wise a statesman to think that drinking could be banned totally. He declared:

Now, you people in the land of Wei,[89] if you can employ your limbs, exerting them heartily for the cultivation of the grains and hastening about in the service of your fathers and elders; or if, with your carts and oxen, you go to great distances to trade in order that you may filially minister to the needs of your parents—then, when your parents are happy, you may wash yourselves clean and offer them the use of wine.

As to you multitudinous officers, heads of departments, and sons of princes, if you, following my instructions closely, have fulfilled your duties toward your ruler as faithfully as you have served your own elders . . . then you may minister the offerings of sacrifice and at the same time engage yourselves in festivity.

But other than these exceptions, the general rule was that everyone, including the marquis himself, "must keep a hard and unyielding control over drinking." And what the regent abhorred most was group drinking, which, as he had reasons to fear, could well lead to mass orgies ending in riot and disturbance. He commanded summarily, "If there are people who drink together in group, do not fail to apprehend them all. Send them to Zhou where I shall have them punished or killed." [90] Yet even in this matter the regent was not lacking in consideration for those Yin functionaries he had retained in office:

As to the officers and artificers of Yin who had been addicted to drink, it is not necessary to punish or kill them at once. Let them be taught for a time. If they learn their lesson, they shall be openly commended. If they disregard the lesson, showing no respect for me, the one man, then they are derelict in their duty and shall be classified with those who are to be either punished or killed.

So plainly the regent's intent was not to take pleasure in inflicting punishment upon the Yin people but to make them fear so much to be punished that they would reform their evil habits, incline their thoughts toward living in peace and harmony, forget the memories of Yin, and attach themselves to their new rulers.

In addition to the two above proclamations, the regent was said to have issued a third one, known as *zicai*, "Timber Material." [91] However, the version of this document we have today is too garbled to make lucid sense. But the author of the *Historical Records,* who had undoubtedly read the original, has written that "the Duke of Zhou repeatedly told the marquis to search for worthy men of Yin. . . . He composed the document *zicai* to demonstrate that such men should be listened to and modeled after." [92] And the great historian has related further: "Based upon these instructions the Marquis of Wei succeeded in harmonizing and assimilating his people, who were all overjoyed in his rule." [93]

· 5 ·

THE FOUNDING OF LUO AND THE RETURN OF SOVEREIGNTY TO CHENG WANG (1097 B.C.)

But besides those who were permitted to migrate to Song and those who were allowed to remain in Wei, there was still a third portion of Yin population for the regent to deal with. These were informally labeled by some of the Zhou scribes as "the obdurate people," [94] though they were never mentioned as such either by the regent or by Cheng Wang in their proclamations or announcements. In modern parlance, we would have called them the diehard Yin loyalists. And how to deal with them constituted a severe and crucial test for the duke's statesmanship. Perhaps a lesser man than he might have found the problem not difficult at all to resolve. The Gordian knot being ever susceptible to the clean cut of a sharp sword, it is only too frequent in history that conquerors of nations, or men of great power, have used massacre, or even genocide, as a means to provide easy escapes from worrisome situations. But not so with the Duke of Zhou, whose conception of his own responsibility in such a role we may clearly perceive from a conversation he had held with his imperial nephew. He was asked by Cheng Wang, "What kind of man was Emperor Shun?" And his answer was, "As a ruler, he loved to help men grow and multiply; and he hated killing." [95]

Just how many "obdurate people" there were we cannot be certain. But there must have been a considerable number, for when the duke addressed them in an announcement, he began with the words, "You numerous officers the Yin have left us." [96] And in another document the term "officers" was extended to include "employees, chiefs, heads of departments, small and great." [97] Again, as is attested by these two documents in the *Book of His-*

tory, although those men were all grouped together as officers of Yin, actually they were taken from four states—not only from Yin, but from Guan, Cai, and Huo as well.[98] Moreover, while there is evidence that many of the men were taken prisoner on the battlefield,[99] there is also proof that as many others were not.[100] Furthermore, these men were apparently permitted to bring their families—indeed, ordered to do so—to the place where they were to be held in captivity.[101] Thus, taking all these factors into consideration, the numbers of the obdurates could well run into thousands, or even tens of thousands.

It appears that even while the campaign against Yan was still going on, most of the obdurates had already been, or were being, transported, conceivably under their own power, to the hills of *jiubi,*[102] on the very site where Wu Wang had thought fit to build a new imperial seat.[103] The place was now given the name Luo, after the river that flows by. By the time the young sovereign had effected the conquest of Yan, the roundup of the obdurates and the conveyance of them to Luo were also completed. There, under guard and close supervision,[104] the captives were given land to cultivate and to put up dwellings for themselves to live in. We are tempted to present this as the first carefully planned concentration camp ever recorded in the history of man. But we decide against it because there seems to be a basic difference. While concentration camps of our modern times are generally organized as instruments of expediency, lasting no longer than the duration of the war which has brought them into being, the duke's disposition was intended for permanence, and actually endured accordingly. Again, we hesitate to liken it to labor camps or penal colonies. For by whatever motivations those recent or contemporary institutions may have been established, their main objective, by and large, is infliction of punishment. But not so with the Duke of Zhou's plans. Even though chastisement had undoubtedly played a major part in his considerations, yet the ends he strove to achieve were posited on a far loftier and more humane plane. He aimed not only to use the obdurates to help Zhou build a new imperial seat, but also to help those men build a new and free life for themselves that would enable them to share in the prosperity of the Zhou dynasty in a not too distant future.

The regent must have inspected the site many a time, thought out all the details beforehand, and talked the matter over again and again with his associates, especially with the grand guardian and with Cheng Wang. For himself, he must have reached the conclusion for some time that in looking for a place to build a new imperial seat, no better choice could be found than the very site Wu Wang had long discovered. "Luo being located in the very center of the empire, it is almost equidistant for people who come from the extremities of the four directions to pay homage." [105] Nevertheless, except for settling the obdurates for cultivation purposes as an initial measure, he had refrained from taking any definite action until peace and order were fully restored to the entire empire. Cheng Wang was now back in Hao from his successful campaign in the east. So the duke journeyed specially to the old capital to ask for the young sovereign's final approval. This obtained, he recommended that the grand guardian be sent to Luo before his own return to reexamine the site; and if the latter should find it satisfactory, to begin the construction process forthwith without waiting for him.[106] All this was done purposely by the regent in order to demonstrate to the world that the founding of the new imperial seat was not his own decision, but a joint one by the imperial court.

In the fifth year of Cheng Wang's reign, which was also the fifth year of the Duke of Zhou's regency,[107] on the day of *bingwu* (sun fire horse) in the third Zhou moon,[108] which was midwinter, when the husbandmen, having finished all seasonal activities, were at their greatest leisure, the grand guardian arrived at Luo. After surveying the site, he applied to divination on the day of *wushen* (mountain earth monkey), the third day after his arrival. The tortoise gave a propitious answer, and the grand guardian ordered the mobilization of the "Yin people" to start preparatory works on the site. The mobilization was completed five days later, and the regent arrived the very day after, early in the morning of the day of *yimao* (soft wood hare). Once again he applied to divination, this time inquiring about the respective sites of the twin cities he wanted to build.[109] Then he proceeded to inspect all the preparations that had been made. Satisfied with these, he sacrificed to Heaven three days later, using two oxen. The next day he conducted rites at the *she* altar of the new city, using one ox, one sheep, and one pig. And finally on the day of *jiazi* (hard wood rat), the first day of a new sixty-day cycle, he summoned all the chiefs of the Yin people, as well as the various princes and barons who had been placed in charge of them, and distributed the "work books." [110] These books are no longer extant, but from an account given in 509 B.C. we have a good description of them. They were drawn up by the regent's designated engineer, one Officer Mimou, who "had surveyed the length and breadth of the land, determined the different levels of the high and the low places, calculated the thickness or thinness of structures, measured the depths of ditches and moats, computed the quantities of materials and of earth needed for the construction, considered the distances from wherever these could be brought forth, estimated the time and the number of men required for each piece of work, deliberated on their expenses and the amounts of provisions necessary for their sustenance, and thus assessed the services expected from each of the working groups." [111] After the issuance of the work books, the regent "gave command to the Yin multitudes, who began to labor with great zeal." [112]

As has been intimated in the preceding paragraph, the new imperial seat the duke had planned actually consisted not of one city but of two cities, which were to be separated by a narrow stream, a tributary of the Luo River.[113] On the east side of the stream he intended to settle most of the Yin people; but on the west side he planned to build the ancestral temple of Zhou, the imperial palace, and other government edifices. Moreover, the proposed limits of the western city were large enough to provide accommodations for all those whose services were needed by the administration. For although the regent was earnestly hoping and tirelessly working for the assimilation of the two peoples of Zhou and Yin, yet prudence had enjoined him to make this division at least for the time being. The obdurates having proved themselves time and again stubbornly hostile,[114] aside from doing everything possible to induce and encourage them to put their trust in Zhou, it would have been sheer stupidity to construct a new imperial seat without paying due regard to the question of security. For this reason, he had planned too to give the western city, and not the eastern one, a strong long wall that would make it capable of sustaining a severe and protracted siege.

As travelers in China can tell, it is a common sight to find cities surrounded with walls. Many Chinese scholars have attributed the idea of building walls for cities first to Gun, Yu's father, who, in the time of the Great Flood, had advocated the erection of dikes, for their protection.[115] Others have credited this ingenuity to Prince Hu of Chong, Wen Wang's malicious rival, whose formidable walls were depicted by an ode of Zhou.[116] But Gun's walls, after all, might have been not much more than dikes, and Hu's not much more than ramparts of a fortress, resembling the castles of medieval Europe. If we are to look for the first authentic record of a long, continuous, unbroken wall built for the purpose of encompassing a city, not only with a number of buildings inside but with considerable tracts of used or unused land as well—and that in the very heart of a vast flat plain (as is customary with many Chinese cities)—then we can trace back only to the Duke of Zhou's construction at Luo. Though we are not certain about the height of the wall he had built,[117] from a study of modern archaeologists we learn that its length from east to west was 2,890 meters, and from north to south about 3,000 meters. "The city thus enclosed an area of no less than 2,000,000 square meters." [118]

Once the construction was completed, its significance became immediately obvious to all. On the one hand, it struck so much awe into the Yin obdurates that they were forced to abandon hope of wreaking easy vengeance on Zhou. On the other, it furnished an inspiring phenomenon for all the enfeoffed princes who came to Luo to admire and also to emulate. For an agrarian community, there did not seem to be any protection more practica-

ble and more effective. It was the best defense possible against surprise
attacks, whether from revengeful or rapacious neighbors or from marauding
bands or nomadic tribes. All harvested grains could be collected and stored
inside the walls, even if most of the arable land lay outside. In case of an
incursion, at the sound of the alarm all the populace dwelling without could
rush into the space within and help to man the battlements. Even if a siege
lasted long, besides the grains stored, there was still much cultivable land
inside to grow food to supplement the needs of the defenders. Thus the idea
initiated by the duke caught on, and many princes started building walls for
communities within their own fiefs. And foreseeing that this practice might
be exploited by ambitious princedoms to rival the power of Zhou, the regent
decreed that a large state could have its wall only a third as long as he built at
Luo; a medium state, a fifth as long; and a small state, a ninth.[119] Until Zhou
began to decline in the 8th century B.C., some three hundred years after the
duke had passed away, this rule seems to have held. But since then, the more
the authority of Zhou dwindled, the higher and the longer went the walls of
various states. According to the authoritative *Grand Compendium of Books,
Ancient and Modern (gujin tushu jicheng),* compiled under the auspices
of emperors Kangxi and Yongzheng, and published in the latter's reign
(A.D. 1723–1735),[120] there had been mentioned in the ancient books altogether 748 walled cities, which were mainly distributed in the Yellow River
Basin, the center of Zhou activities. Among these, 163 had their walls built
before 722 B.C., and 585 between 722 and 207 B.C., all within the duration of
the Zhou dynasty. But the idea did not die with Zhou. Chinese history is
replete with accounts of wall-building for cities from time to time. And the
greatest instance of all is, of course, the Great Wall, stretching over some
2,400 kilometers across the northern borders of China, built by the First
Emperor of Qin to protect his vast empire against inroads by barbarians
from the Gobi desert, and reinforced or renovated again and again by many
of his successors, the last time by the emperors of the Ming Dynasty,
A.D. 1368-1643.[121]

To return to the Duke of Zhou, the whole construction at Luo, including
the wall for one of the twin cities as well as public works for both, probably
took more than two years to finish.[122] With his imperial nephew's approval,
he named the newly constructed capital (which embraced both cities) Chengzhou, "Cheng Wang's Zhou," to distinguish it from the old capital, Hao,
which was often called Zongzhou, "Ancestral Zhou." To the walled city,
however, he gave an additional designation—*wangcheng,* "Imperial City." In
his time the Imperial City was always regarded as part of Chengzhou, the
separate appellation notwithstanding. But as time progressed, some generations later the Zhou people appeared to have become accustomed to treating
the two as disconnected entities, one Chengzhou and the other Wangcheng.
However, they would still lump them together sometimes under the name

Dongdu, "Eastern Capital."[123] And often too they would simply call it Luo. Hence the modern name Luoyang.

In the sixth year of the regency, the duke returned to Zongzhou. For the first time since Wu Wang's death, the entire empire seemed to be at last basking in the sunshine of prosperous tranquillity. All the vassal states and subject tribes that had formerly acknowledged allegiance to Zhou and survived the rebellion had again submitted obediently to its rule. As to the Yin people, the division of them into three parts had also worked well. Those who had followed the Prince of Wei to Song were showing every sign of pursuing a new peaceful life under their gentle leader; and those who had remained in the former Yin, now called the state of Wei, appeared to be quite contented too under the firm and fair-minded government of Marquis Feng. Even the obdurates at Luo seemed to have become calmly resigned to their changed fortunes. Though garrisons had still to be maintained to keep them under surveillance, they were observed to have been performing all the services required of them, especially in the construction of the imperial seat, with commendable diligence. Surveying the empire, the regent thus felt that it was time to demonstrate to the world that Zhou had consolidated its majesty and upheld the Mandate of Heaven. Consequently he called on all the enfeoffed princes and subject chieftains to meet at Zongzhou. Except for those who were excused by permission, such as Taigong of Qi, Marquis Feng of Wei, and Boqin of Lu, who had to see to the maintenance of peace and order not only in their own fiefs but in the surrounding areas, the attendance of all was required at the old capital.[124]

For this purpose, the duke had a special structure built in both of the imperial seats, Zongzhou and Chengzhou. Covered with a round roof, supported only by pillars, and open on all sides, it was called *mingtang*, the "Bright Hall."[125] It had been his intention to have the young sovereign preside at this meeting at Zongzhou. But when the day came, at the insistence of the imperial nephew, the uncle, as the regent, had to preside instead. All the princes and chieftains having assembled in their preassigned places, the duke took his own position in the hall. Standing on a raised altar, with his back toward a specially designed embroidered screen, a symbol of imperial authority, he made himself ready to receive homage.[126] Then the princes and chieftains stepped forth and advanced one after another to the altar, each according to his rank and seniority, to do obeisance and to offer his insignia of office for verification and confirmation.[127] And after having performed these duties, the dukes would withdraw and station themselves in front of the altar; the marquises, on the east of the eastern flight of steps; the counts, on the west of the western flight of steps; the viscounts, inside the pillars on the east; the barons, inside the pillars on the west; and finally the chieftains of Yi, Man, Rong, and Di outside the pillars.[128]

If the duke had yielded to his nephew's insistence to preside at this as-

semblage, it was perhaps because the circumstances of the moment might yet
have demanded the appearance of his firm and strong personality as the
custodian of majesty; but probably it was even more because he himself had
already formed another plan in his mind to show the young sovereign to
greater advantage. After the convocation of the assembly, he seems to have
remained in Zongzhou devoting much time to tutoring his imperial nephew
on the duties of a supreme ruler [129] as well as to engaging himself in what
later Chinese scholars have taken pride in referring to as *zhili zuoyue*.[130]
This term is nearly impossible to translate appropriately into English; but
lacking something better, we have tentatively sought to convey its meaning
by this cumbersome and rather obtuse phrasing: "the institutionalization of
proprieties and the composition of music." Also, it is a subject which historians, both Chinese and non-Chinese, almost never have discussed in length.
But as this book is intended to be a history of the Chinese heritage, we shall
make bold to expatiate on it as best we can in later chapters.

Then came the seventh year of the regency. As soon as the year was over,
according to the customary Chinese computation, Cheng Wang would be
adjudged of age, fully twenty years old. It was therefore the regent's intention to return full sovereignty to his nephew just before the end of the year.
For this purpose, he journeyed again to the new capital, and saw to it that all
the construction works, especially the Bright Hall and the imperial palace, be
completed in time, to the very last of the finishing touches. Then he set a
date at the close of the year for another assemblage of enfeoffed princes and
subject chieftains, and summoned all to them to attend, this time not excus-
ing anyone except for those who were under the young emperor's personal
direction. At the same time he also requested the presence of his imperial
nephew.

Thus Cheng Wang left the old imperial seat in charge of the grand
guardian, and came to the new capital that bore his name in the twelfth
moon of the year, on the day of *wuchen* (mountain earth dragon).[131] On
arrival, he first sacrificed to Wen Wang and Wu Wang, using a red-haired
ox for each.[132] Then he worshiped Heaven and other deities.[133] And finally,
at the appointed time, after all the princes and chieftains had assembled at
their predesignated places, he appeared at the Bright Hall. Standing at the
center of the raised altar under a red silk umbrella bordered with rare black
feathers, he faced to the south and started receiving homage. And whom did
the 1,800 and some princes and chieftains present behold leading the procession, doing obeisance to the sovereign, and offering to him their insignias for
verification and confirmation but the regent and Taigong! [134] While these
princes and chieftains, following the lead, were each going through the same
ceremonials, they could not help casting glances on the man who had just
relinquished the supreme power of the world he had held so resolutely and so
indomitably these last seven years, and who was now stationing himself

along with some others in front of the altar. And, in truth, as they watched to see how he was deporting himself, the duke was in every respect looking as attentive, as reverential, as fearful of the majesty of the young sovereign as the very humblest among themselves! [135]

The Zhou people never composed a special document to commemorate the occasion. The return of sovereignty to Cheng Wang could not have been more impressively demonstrated; nor could the continuation of the regent's policies have been more effectually assured. Neither of the two personages saw any need to explain or publicize the event by a proclamation or an announcement. Only a scribe thought fit to conclude the document that detailed some of Cheng Wang's movements on this visit to Luo with a very simple passage: "Thus the Duke of Zhou greatly protected the Mandate, as received by Wen Wang and Wu Wang, for seven years." [136]

NOTES

1. *Yi Zhou Shu, wuquan.*

2. *Historical Records, zhou benji.*

3. *Kongzi Jiayu, guansong.* Thirteen is according to the Chinese way of computing age. According to the Western way, Cheng Wang was only twelve.

4. *Bamboo Chronicles.*

5. *Historical Records, qitaigong shijia.*

6. Ibid., *luzhougong shijia.*

7. In modern Manchuria.

8. *Historical Records, qitaigong shijia.* From very ancient times there were known five grades of investiture—*gong, hou, bo, zi,* and *nan.* See above, Chap. II, note 93. The Chinese characters used in the tablet are *wuhoujiubo, shidezhengzhi,* which may be literally translated as: "Against any of the five marquises and nine counts (not to mention the lesser states), you may launch punitive expedition (at your discretion)." Also see *Zuozhuan,* Duke Xi, 4th year.

9. *Historical Records, qitaigong shijia.*

10. Ibid., *luzhougong shijia.*

11. Ibid.

12. For a discussion on this point, see *Mencius, gongsunchou,* II.

13. *Historical Records, zhou benji;* also *guancai shijia.*

14. *Historical Records, zhou benji.* For the date, see *Bamboo Chronicles.*

15. *Bamboo Chronicles; Kongzi Jiayu, guansong.*

16. *Kongzi Jiayu, guansong.* Also see *Li Ji, jiaotesheng.*

17. *Yi Li, shiguanli.* See commentaries by Zheng Kangcheng as quoted in Hu Peihui, *Yi Li Zhengyi.*

18. *Kongzi Jiayu, guansong.*

19. *Historical Records, luzhougong shijia.*

20. *Book of History, shuxu.*

21. *Book of History, junshi.* Also see *Historical Records, yanshaogong shijia.*

22. Another name for Yi Yin. See above, p. 165.

23. See above, p. 177. Of Chen Hu, however, we know nothing.

24. See above, pp. 178 and 186.

25. See above, p. 201.

26. The Chinese characters in the text are not *wen wang,* but *ning wang. Ning* means "pacifying"; so scholars in the past thought that Wen Wang was also called Ning Wang because he was the man who had pacified the empire. Modern scholarship, however, from a study of bronze inscriptions has reached a conclusion that *ning* is a clerical error and *wen* is the character that should have been used in the text. See Appendix, Item Four.

27. See above, p. 249, note 55. Taigong was not mentioned here, presumably because he was still alive.

28. At the time Wu Wang succeeded to Wen Wang, Guoshu having died, only four of the five men were left.

29. According to ancient fables, phoenixes would appear singing in times of peace and great prosperity.

30. *Historical Records, yanshaogong shijia.*

31. The original poem reads as follows:

> While the Duke of Zhou was living in fear of floating calumnies,
> Or while Wang Mang was pretending to be all humble and reverent toward men;
> Had each of them died then,
> Who could possibly know that his life had been true or false?

Wang Mang was a usurper in the 1st century B.C., who had first created a sort of regency modeled after the Duke of Zhou's, but then poisoned the young lawful sovereign to seize the throne for himself.

32. *Book of History, jinteng;* also *Historical Records, zhou benji.*

33. The Chinese character *ju* means "dwell," "reside," or "live."

34. *Mencius, tengwengong,* II. The narration is brief. Mencius may have meant that it was the result of the two wars, not just one, that fifty states were destroyed.

35. See above, p. 295.

36. See above, p. 285; and see *Shangshu Dazhuan.*

37. Both Yan and Lu were in modern Qufu, Shandong, Confucius's birthplace.

38. See *Bamboo Chronicles*. At one place it records that the seventeenth Shang emperor, Nangeng, resided at Yan. This has not been mentioned in this history because it has not been confirmed by other records.

39. See above, p. 312.

40. *Historical Records, luzhougong shijia.*

41. Ibid. Also *Book of History, feishi.*

42. Introductory note to the ode *qiyue*, as transmitted in *Mao Shi*.

43. See *Li Ji, yueling; Dadai Liji, xiaxiaozheng; Yi Zhou Shu, zhouyue* and *shixun*; and also scattered fragments in *Lushi Chunqiu*.

44. The Chinese character is *jun*. It means an ancient land officer, or agricultural officer, also called *tian* or *nong*, who taught the people husbandry and regulated the use of land. See *Li Ji, yueling* and *jiaotesheng*.

45. *Shangshu Dazhuan; Xunzi, yaowen.*

46. *Historical Records, luzhougong shijia.*

47. Liu Xiang, *Shuoyuan*, chap. I.

48. The saying in Chinese is *zhougong tubu, tianxia guixin.*

49. *Book of History, jinteng.*

50. *Book of Poetry, binfeng: chixiao.*

51. *Book of History, jinteng.*

52. Ibid.

53. The Chinese character used by the *Historical Records* is *shen*, which many Western missionaries have used for "God."

54. *Historical Records, luzhougong shijia.*

55. Fa is of course Wu Wang's given name. In *Book of History, jinteng*, instead of *fa*, the character used is *mou*, meaning "a certain person." This was because the scribe, out of respect for Wu Wang, did not dare mention him by his given name.

56. *Book of History, jinteng; Historical Records, luzhougong shijia.* Also see *Bamboo Chronicles* and *Shangshu Dazhuan.* It is in the *Historical Records* that the character *fa* was used in the prayer, not *mou* as in the *Book of History.*

57. *Shangshu Dazhuan.*

58. *Historical Records, luzhougong shijia;* also *zhou benji.*

59. *Book of History, dagao; Historical Records, luzhougong shijia.*
Dagao is the only other document beside *junshi*, Prince Shi, in which the term *ning wang* appears several times. (See note 26.) We are convinced that modern scholarship is correct to adjudge them to be clerical errors for *wen wang*. So here we have translated them as Wen Wang accordingly. But where the character *ning* appears independently, without *wang*, we feel we must rely more on the context. In some cases, the meaning "pacifying" or "pacification" certainly makes better sense.

60. In the Zhou conscription system each well usually contributed eight men for war, there being only eight families in a well. The people's volunteering to send forth ten men showed their enthusiasm for the expedition. For the Zhou conscription system, see above, p. 252. For the "Well-Field System," see above, p. 134.

61. An obvious reference to the three supervisors.

62. *Historical Records, zhou benji, luzhougong shijia,* and *guancai shijia.* Also *Book of History, caizhongzhiming;* and *Yi Zhou Shu, zuoluo.*

63. *Yi Zhou Shu, zuoluo.*

64. *Book of History, shuxu.* The two documents are *chengwangzheng* and *jiangpugu.*

65. Ibid., *caizhongzhiming.* Also see *Historical Records, guancai shijia.*

66. *Book of History, caizhongzhiming.*

67. Commentaries by Kong Anguo, who lived in the 1st century B.C.

68. *Historical Records, guancai shijia.*

69. *Book of History, caizhongzhiming.* The original document, however, is lost.

70. *Book of History, shuxu.*

71. *Lushi Chunqiu, zhongxiaji: guyue.*

72. See above, pp. 297–98.

73. See above, p. 316.

74. See above, p. 317.

75. *Historical Records, zhou benji; songweizi shijia.* Also *Book of History, weizizhiming.*

76. *Book of History, weizizhiming.* Also see *Book of Poetry, zhousong: youke, yougu,* and *zhenglu.*

77. *Historical Records, songweizi shijia.*

78. *Book of History, weizizhiming.*

79. Gu Donggao, *Chunqiu Dashibiao*, IV, *song-jiangyu lun.*

80. *Historical Records, songweizi shijia.*

81. Ibid., *weikangshu shijia.*

82. In *Book of History, kanggao,* the regent, is the name of Cheng Wang, called Feng.*menghou*, "senior marquis." The word *meng* ("senior") denotes that he was given such authority.

83. Ibid.

84. These are *kanggao, jiugao,* and *zicai* in the *Book of History*, although the text of the last one has been garbled. Also see *Historical Records, weikangshu shijia.*

85. See above, pp. 297–98.

86. *Book of History, kanggao.*

87. The expressions in Chinese are *tongguan naishen* and *ruobao chizi.*

88. *Book of History, jiugao.*

89. The Chinese word used in this instance is *mei*, not *wei*. But all commentators agree that *mei* was another name for a part of the former land of Yin. So in order to avoid confusion, we still use Wei.

90. In ancient usage the character *sha* means both "punish" and "kill."

91. *Book of History, shuxu; Historical Records, weikangshu shijia.*

92. *Historical Records, weikangshu shijia.*

93. Ibid.

94. *Book of History, shuxu.*

95. *Shangshu Dazhuan.*

96. *Book of History, duoshi.*

97. *Book of History, duofang.* The Chinese characters used here are *xubo xiaoda duozheng.*

98. Both in *duoshi* and in *duofang* in the *Book of History* the phrase "you people of the four states" was used. This also tends to confirm our narration that in the last days of the rebellion the three supervisors had to recruit their men mostly from Yin.

99. See *Book of History, duofang.*

100. In *Zuozhuan*, Duke Ding, 4th year, a passage reads: "When Wu Wang had subdued Shang, Cheng Wang completed the work of stabilization and chose and appointed princes of virtue to serve as bulworks and screens to Zhou. . . . Six clans of Yin—the Tiao, the Xu, the Xiao, the Suo, the Changshao, and the Weishao—were ordered to gather the members of their principal houses, collect those of the branches as well as their other kith and kin, to receive instructions and regulations from the Duke of Zhou and repair to Zhou. . . . To Kangshu (Marquis Feng of Wei) were given seven

clans of Yin. . . ." We have no information regarding the numbers of those thirteen clans. Otherwise we would have been tempted to say that the ratio between the people allowed to remain in Yin and those ordered "to repair to Zhou" was 7 to 6.

101. Ibid.

102. *Yi Zhou Shu, zuoluo.*

103. See above, p. 316.

104. See *Book of History, duofang.* The document mentions that the captives had already been under guard for five years. Some scholars think that the character for "five" may have been a clerical error; others believe that the plan to use them to build the new imperial seat might have been begun by Wu Wang in the last years of his reign. The author agrees with the former.

105. *Historical Records, zhou benji.*

106. Ibid. Also see *Book of History, shaogao.*

107. *Shangshu Dazhuan.*

108. *Book of History, shaogao.*

109. *Book of History, luogao.*

110. Ibid., *shaogao.*

111. *Zuozhuan,* Duke Zhao, 32nd year.

112. *Book of History, shaogao.*

113. The stream was called Chan. See Cai Chen's annotations on *Book of History, luogao.*

114. See *Book of History, duofang.* Also see comments by the 11th-century scholar Su Shi.

115. See above, p. 85, note 106.

116. *Book of Poetry, daya: huangyi.* See above, pp. 273–74.

117. In *Zuozhuan,* Duke Yin, 1st year. With reference to building city walls within an enfeoffed state, it is said that "any city wall exceeding one hundred *zhi* could become a threat to the state." In *Li Ji, fangji,* a *zhi* is defined in the commentaries as ten feet high and thirty feet long. But this rule obviously did not apply to the Duke of Zhou.

118. Cheng Te-k'un, *Archaeology in China,* III, p. 25.

119. *Zuozhuan,* Duke Yin, 1st year. Also see *Yi Zhou Shu, zuoluo.*

120. As cited by Li Chi in his *The Formation of the Chinese People* and quoted by Cheng Te-k'un, *Archaeology of China,* III, pp. 6–7.

121. The Great Wall of China was not built entirely by the First Emperor. Several large segments of it were built before him by other states in the period of the Warring States.

122. No explicit time for the construction is given in any of the ancient books. However, *Shangshu Dazhuan* expressly mentions that the Duke of Zhou "in the fifth year of his regency engaged in the construction of Chengzhou; in the sixth year undertook to institutionalize proprieties and compose music; and in the seventh year returned sovereignty to Cheng Wang." And in the *Book of History, kanggao* begins with these words: "In the third month, when the moon began to wane, the Duke of Zhou commenced foundations for the building of a new capital at Luo in the eastern part of the country." The date of "the third month" is confirmed by *shaogao* and *luogao.* Then in *luogao* it is stated that Cheng Wang was in the new capital "in the twelfth month" and asked the duke to remain there to take charge. And it concludes: "Thus the Duke of Zhou greatly protected the Mandate, as received by Wen Wang and Wu Wang, for seven years." We conclude therefore that the construction work was begun in the third month of the fifth year, and completed before the twelfth month of the seventh year, of the regency, when the Duke of Zhou returned full sovereignty to Cheng Wang.

123. See *Book of Poetry,* introductory note to *Xiaoya: jugong;* also *Zuozhuan,* Duke Zhao, 32nd year.

124. See *Yi Zhou Shu, mingtang; Li Ji, mingtangwei;* and Ma Duanlin, *Wenxian Tongkao,* chap. 106.

125. *Yi Zhou Shu, mingtang.*

126. Ibid. Also see *Li Ji, mingtangwei.*

127. See above, p. 77.

128. *Yi Zhou Shu, mingtang; Li Ji, mingtangwei.*

129. See *Li Ji, wenwangshizi; Yi Zhou Shu, chengkai;* and *Book of History, wuyi* and *lizheng.*

130. *Shangshu Dazhuan.*

131. *Book of History, luogao.*

132. Ibid. He did this before he worshiped Heaven presumably because the transfer of imperial authority from one member of the house to another was considered to be primarily a family affair.

133. Ibid.

134. *Yi Zhou Shu, wanghui.*

135. *Huainanzi, fanlun xun; Hanshi Waizhuan,* chap. 7. Also see *Historical Records, zhou benji* and *luzhougong shijia.*

136. *Book of History, luogao.* In *luogao,* there is a passage conveying an advice from the Duke of Zhou to Cheng Wang, which has had varied interpretations. One of these is to this effect: "To commemorate this accomplishment [the founding of Chengzhou], to add dignity to it, make this the first year." The idea is that Cheng Wang should use the occasion to announce the beginning of a new reign as Wen Wang did after his return from imprisonment. No one is certain whether or not this actually happened.

In 1963, from Baoji, Shaanxi, a bronze vessel called Hezun was excavated, bearing an inscription which may be roughly translated as follows:

> Wang, having first moved residence to Chengzhou, offered various sacrifices according to Wu Wang's rites, beginning from the heavenly chambers. On the day of *bingxu* in the fourth moon, Wang gave a lecture in the imperial palace to junior members of our house, saying, "In the past your fathers rendered service to Wen Wang. Then Wen Wang received the Great Mandate and Wu Wang conquered the Great City Shang. Thus (Wu Wang) prayed to Heaven, 'May I be permitted to reside in the central land from where I may lead the people to good government!' Alas! Many of you are too young, or not knowledgeable enough to understand. But you all must learn from the examples of your fathers, serving well Heaven, fulfilling all the missions assigned to you, so that, like them, you will be able to share in the sacrifices we offer."
>
> Wang is reverential and ever obedient to Heaven. His lecture has given enlightenment to this unworthy one.
>
> After the lecture, Wang awarded He thirty pairs of cowry shells.
>
> (The money) is used to make this *zun* in honor of (a word undecipherable). This is in Wang's fifth year.

From this, three points may be noted: (1) Since this *zun* was said to be made in Wang's fifth year, Cheng Wang must have adopted a new reign in accordance with the duke's advice. (2) Cheng Wang did know about Wu Wang's wish to remove his imperial seat to Chengzhou as related before in Chap. VII, Sec. 4. And (3) Cheng Wang had actually "moved residence" to Chengzhou, but for reasons to be discussed in the next chapter he went back to Hao and never returned. See *Wen Wu,* no. 1, 1976, pp. 60–66.

CHAPTER IX

ZHOUGONG AND THE ACCUMULATED HERITAGE

· 1 ·

THE LAST YEARS OF ZHOUGONG
(THE DUKE OF ZHOU)

The book of history has preserved for us a few exchanges of correspondence between the Duke of Zhou and Cheng Wang in this period. In one of these, the duke clearly indicated that as soon as sovereignty was returned to his imperial nephew, he himself would like to go into retirement and devote his time to the study of agriculture.[1] But that was not to be. For both the contingencies of the moment and the wishes of his sovereign would not permit him to indulge in that private inclination.

It was probably just after the meeting of the enfeoffed princes at the new capital that Cheng Wang invested his uncle with an additional personal fief inside the imperial domain and, also, a new title by which he is best known to posterity—Zhougong, "Duke of Zhou." [2] For, indeed, when the Chinese speak of their foremost sages before Confucius, they always mention seven names—Yao, Shun, Yu, Tang, Wen (for Wen Wang), Wu (for Wu Wang), and Zhougong. In calling him the Duke of Zhou throughout this narrative, we have certainly been committing an anachronism, but it is a deliberate error that may be excused because this is the way all Chinese histories wrote about him in the past and we have just followed their uniform example. We could have called him Prince Dan while he was serving as Wu Wang's chief minister, and the Marquis of Lu, after he was so enfeoffed following the overthrow of Yin, and the regent (a term we have used frequently anyway) through the seven years of his regency, reserving the name Zhougong, or Duke of Zhou, for the short period thereafter. But that, though strictly correct in chronology, may not be preferable from the standpoint of clarity and simplicity. Incidentally, this is also the way we have treated the Duke of Shao, Zhougong's most trusted lieutenant. His name was Shi, and the title of his investiture was Marquis of Yan. After Wu Wang's death, he was known to have concurrently held the office of grand guardian, and we have used this term too. But it was also only at this time, presumably after Cheng Wang's return from the meeting to the old capital, that he was, like Zhougong, invested with an additional personal fief and a new title—Shaogong, "Duke of Shao." [3]

The reason Cheng Wang made these two investitures is clear. He did not wish either Zhougong or Shaogong to proceed each to his own original fief and reside there, as other enfeoffed princes were enjoined to do; but he wanted them to remain, Zhougong in the new capital and Shaogong in the old, to help him rule over the vast empire as before, with Shaan as the dividing point between the two jurisdictions.[4] While reserving final authority for himself as a sovereign should, the young monarch knew that no arrangement could have served him better than to continue this scheme Zhougong had devised before. He was equally aware of Zhougong's indispensable value to the dynasty and of Shaogong's efficaciousness as an administrator. Next to Zhougong, Shaogong was perhaps the most respected and best loved man in the west. Once he was on an inspection tour in the countryside, and the people stopped him halfway to submit a very serious dispute. Lest he should cause them any inconvenience, he did not take them to an office at a distance, but stayed on the spot and gave a hearing under a birch-leaf pear tree. The judgment he rendered then and there was so true and so fair that it was remembered ever afterward. The people in the adjacent areas later composed a special song in his praise and also forbade anyone to do harm to the tree in order to preserve the memory of him.[5]

While the retention of Shaogong would have no doubt pleased the people in the west, Cheng Wang realized even more keenly that the continuation of Zhougong's presence in the east was a matter not only of vital importance but of critical urgency. For the young monarch had committed a political blunder which he himself knew only his uncle could resolve for him. It was only three years before that he had effected the subjugation of Yan and the Huaiyi tribes. If these victories had earned him a conqueror's fame and glory, they had also inadvertently caused him to perpetrate a mistake that was now to haunt him. At that time, he had left his uncle to take charge of the mopping-up operations and returned to the old capital himself, all flushed with his recent success. On arrival, in the exhilaration of the moment, he had issued a declaration titled *duofang, Numerous Regions,* to announce to all quarters of the empire his triumphant return. In the document, out of a buoyant impulse of magnanimity (for he was by nature a very generous man), he had unwittingly made a none too carefully worded promise to the "obdurate people" of Yin, apparently without the benefit of avuncular counsel. He had told them: "(If you only serve us well), Heaven Itself will take pity on you; and we, the sovereign of Zhou, will confer on you great rewards, even to the extent of selecting you to stand right in our own imperial court. Only attend dutifully to the businesses assigned to you, and you may rank among our great officers." [6] Certainly his intent was sincere, and the policy was one that Zhougong had previously discussed with him and jointly agreed upon. But what the regent had intended was that the appointment of obdurates to high positions would come after a long process of assimilation, a goal to aim after, to be reached eventually but not precipitately. The wording of the young sovereign's hastily drawn declaration seemed to imply that it would materialize at any moment, provided that they served Zhou well. And now that the obdurates had toiled hard for three years and had completed the construction of the new capital without fail, they made it clear that they had done their part and it was high time for them to collect the promised reward.

Perhaps Cheng Wang had distributed some minor rewards and lesser offices among them. But these seemed to have only whetted their appetite, and they clamored for more, asking explicitly for higher positions. Liberal and lenient though Cheng Wang was, he was three years older and so much better versed in statecraft. He realized what a dilemma he had placed himself in. The obdurates were diehards at heart: Given an inch, they would ask for an ell; and remembering their records in the past, there did not appear to be anything in the present that could give them complete satisfaction. Yet credit must be given to the youthful monarch that in face of this open intransigence, he never resorted to the use of sheer repression to impose his will, even though he had so much power in hand to command, even though impatience and impetuosity must have been coursing through his veins just as in those of any other young man his age. And perhaps the credit should all go to Zhougong, for it was he who had tutored his imperial nephew regarding the duties of a supreme ruler; and also it was Zhougong to whom the embarrassed sovereign finally applied for help.

So it was decided by Cheng Wang that he should still return to Zongzhou and rule from there for the moment, but in the meantime Zhougong would remain in Chengzhou and take charge as his surrogate for the whole east. Thus shortly after Cheng Wang's departure, Zhougong issued an announcement to the obdurates as follows: [7]

> In the third moon, at the new city of Luo, Zhougong desires to make this known to the officers of the former Shang emperor:
> The sovereign [8] has spoken to this effect: "You numerous officers the Yin has

left us. It is a matter for which none can console you that Heaven has sent down great ruin on Yin. We Zhou, having received the favoring Mandate, have borne the clear majesty of Heaven, inflicted punishment upon your monarch, and abolished the Mandate of Yin so as to complete the work of the Lord Above.

"Now, you numerous officers, it is not that our small nation dared to shoot at the Mandate of Yin. But Heaven was not with Yin. It would not strengthen Yin's misrule. Instead, It aided us. Otherwise, how could we have dared to seek after the imperial throne?

"Indeed, the Lord is not with Yin. For Heaven makes Its dreadfulness clear through the actions of the people.

"I have heard the saying, 'The Lord Above purposes to guide men to peace and prosperity.' Now, the last Xia emperor did not move toward peace and prosperity for his people. Thereupon the Lord sent down warnings, indicating the proper direction he should go. But the last Xia emperor did not heed the Lord, but proceeded to even greater dissoluteness with more blustering talk. Then Heaven no longer regarded him, nor listened to him, but disallowed his Mandate, and determined to inflict punishment on him. Thus It charged your early ancestor Tang the Successful to overturn Xia, and to rule the four quarters instead with good and competent men.

"From Tang the Successful to Di Yi, there was no emperor but sought to make shine his own virtue and to attend to sacrifices with care. On the one hand, Heaven, having erected the great establishment of Yin, saw to it that Yin be protected and well regulated. On the other, the Yin emperors themselves were also fearful of losing the favor of the Lord, doing everything in accord with His ways and for the benefit of the people.

"But now came the late successor emperor. So grossly inattentive was he to the clear wishes of Heaven! And how much less regard had he for your ancestor emperors who had labored so hard for your house! He abandoned himself utterly to dissipation, paying no heed whatever either to Heaven's manifest purpose or to the people's earnest entreaties. In consequence, the Lord Above withdrew His protection and sent down the great destruction on you.

"Heaven is never with those who do not implicitly observe Its virtue. Indeed, throughout the four quarters of the empire, there was no nation overthrown, whether small or great, but deserved its own punishment."

The sovereign again spoke to this effect: "You numerous officers of Yin. Our Zhou emperors [9] have always carried out the Lord's assignments with great diligence. They have received the Mandate with the command, 'Cut Yin off.' And they have done so, and reported so to the Lord.

"Our assignment does not allow us an alternative. Nor is it allowed your imperial house to follow any course but ours.

"Should I not say that you were exceedingly lawless? I did not want to remove you. But the cause for the removal originated from within your own city.

"I have also thought of this: Heaven has already inflicted many great calamities on you at Yin. Yin, as a place of residence, must be not right for you."

The sovereign spoke: "Therefore, I declare to you, you numerous officers. Because of these considerations, I have removed you to settle in the west.[10] Not that I, the one man, consider it my virtue to deprive you of your comfort and tranquillity. But this is Heaven's own decree. Do not disobey it. Even I dare not fall behind in obeying it. So do not bear me resentment.

"You know well, your own forefathers of Yin had their tablets and their records. It was Yin who superseded the Mandate of Xia.

"But presently you say, 'Xia officers were chosen and promoted to the imperial court of Yin; also, they had their places among the hundred ranks of officers.' Now, I, the one man, follow only one rule: Only the virtuous should be given employment. It is for this purpose that I sought you out from your former Heavenly City. I have so far taken pity on you. (If I have not distributed more offices among you), the fault is not mine. It is up to you to act in accord with the Mandate of Heaven."

The sovereign spoke: "You numerous officers. Formerly, when I came from Yan, I magnanimously spared the lives of you people of the four states.[11] Yet, if I wished, I could have inflicted on you the clear punishment of Heaven and removed you to exceedingly distant and barbarous places. Now, compare that against serving us in our capital here! Which is better, which is worse,[12] for you?"

The Sovereign spoke: "I declare to you, you numerous officers of Yin. I shall repeat the order I have given before. I shall not put you to death. Moreover, I have built my great city here on this Luo in order that people from the four directions may come to pay us respect, and you numerous officers may also serve us in various capacities. Is this better for you, or worse?

"Besides, you have already been given your land. Here you may well pursue your living and dwell in peace. If you are capable of conducting your life with reverential care, Heaven will display Its compassion on you. If you are not capable, it will be as if you did not want your land; and surely I will not hesitate to visit Heaven's punishment on your persons.

"Now, you may dwell here in this city and perpetuate your residence; you may pursue your occupations and enjoy the rest of your years in this Luo; and your children will also be able to prosper—all from your having removed here."

The sovereign also said: "I have spoken all this, that you may reside here long."

From a study of the above announcement, one can see how astutely Zhougong had handled this delicate yet explosive situation. The Yin obdurates were pressing the Zhou to yield to them a larger share in the government of the new capital, citing the example that after overthrowing the Xia, their ancestors had not only continued employing Xia officers in numerous lower positions, but had also chosen and promoted many of them to high offices in the imperial court itself. Whether this was factually true or not, we are not certain. It seems more likely to us that the obdurates had indulged either in fancy or in exaggeration. But whatever the case, Zhougong pointed out that since they knew their tablets and records so well, the only important thing they must remember was that Zhou had superseded Yin just as their ancestors had superseded Xia. Moreover, since the sovereign of Zhou had succeeded to the Mandate of Heaven, it was only out of his magnanimity that the lives of the people of the four rebellious states had been spared. He could still have them exiled and scattered to remote and wild regions, if he so desired. But instead he had removed them to Luo not only to build a new capital for Zhou but also to build a new and peaceful life for themselves. As to giving them a proper share in government, that certainly had been, and was still, his intention. But in employing men as officers, he followed only one rule. He did not care whether or not the man was from Yin; but he would give employment only to the virtuous. If they wished to be officers, even high officers, then let them first be virtuous and act in accord with the Mandate of Heaven. In the meantime, furthermore, they all had their allotted land to cultivate and their occupations to pursue; and they could raise their families here in peace and safety, with the sovereign's assurances that they would not be put to death as captives could have been. In short, it was a statement sincere yet firm, inflexible but not arrogant. On the one hand, it reminded the people what it was always in the power of a conqueror to do; and on the other, it also gave them hope that what they wanted to obtain was not unobtainable, provided they went about it properly and patiently. It was a policy of honest assimilation, to be persistently maintained and strenuously pursued as much against the perils and threats of continuing opposition as against the temptations to use violent means to suppress them.

Judging from Wu Wang's confidential testament to Zhougong,[13] and judging from the latter's own actions, it had undoubtedly been the intent of both men that once the new capital at Luo was built, Zhou should move its imperial seat from Hao to there, just as Tang had transferred his administrative headquarters from Bo to West Bo not long after his overthrow of the Xia.[14] This purpose was made the more evident by the fact that even before the construction of the new capital the regent had the Nine Tripods of Yu transported to Luo, not to Hao, as a formal symbol of the legitimate succession of dynastic sovereignty.[15] Perhaps it was again in the same spirit of Tang, who had honored Bo with the appellation Heavenly City Shang, that Zhougong designated Hao as Zongzhou, "Ancestral Zhou," nominally at least taking precedence ever Chengzhou, "Cheng Wang's Zhou," which was to be made the real center of imperial government. And the very fact that the new capital had been given such a name as Chengzhou indicates that Zhougong had earnestly intended that the second emperor of the new dynasty, as well as those who would come after him, would reside there permanently. And from the standpoint of geopolitics, this is indeed as it should have been for Zhou. Whereas Hao was situated almost at the western extremity of the far-flung empire, Luo was quite centrally located. As to its being largely populated by the Yin obdurates at the moment, that would not have to be much of a problem as soon as the imperial administration began to move in. With the concentration of political power and economic wealth in the area, which was bound to result from the transfer, it could be expected that the population, drawing recruitment from every source of the vast dominion, would be increased manifold in a short time. The momentary pre-ponderance of the Yin people would disappear, and their assimilation with the rest of the nation would become a certainty.

Well thought out as Zhougong's plan was, it did not proceed as he had hoped. The brief outburst of intransigence on the part of the Yin obdurates, though quickly and effectively quietened by his dexterous handling of the incident, seemed to have left a scar in Cheng Wang's mind far deeper than his uncle had anticipated. It probably wounded the youthful sovereign's pride more than it amplified his distrust of the Yin people. After the meeting of the enfeoffed princes, he returned to the old capital, never showing any desire to go back again to the city that was named after him. In the three years that ensued, he apparently left Zhougong in complete charge of Chengzhou; [16] even though the venerable duke appears to have journeyed to and fro several times between the two capitals, we have no record whatever indicating that the young monarch had taken a similar trip. Finally Zhou-gong asked for retirement; and perhaps on purpose, upon his departure from Chengzhou, he chose to reside not in Hao but in Feng, the city his father, Wen Wang, had built.[17] We cannot be sure why he did so; but it may well be construed as another form of pressure on his imperial nephew to urge him to move the imperial seat to Luo. But now Zhougong was dying, and on his deathbed he voiced his last wish: "Let me be buried at Chengzhou! For I want the whole world to know that I am a subject to my sovereign, Cheng Wang." But after his demise, Cheng Wang buried him instead at Bi,[18] declaring, "It is fitting that he lies near Wen Wang. I, the little son, desire to make known that I have never dared treat Zhougong as a subject." [19] And he honored him with the posthumous title *zhouwengong*, "Cultural Duke of Zhou," using the same word *wen* as his father Wu Wang had used to honor his grandfather Wen Wang.[20] Also, he issued a decree that the Marquis of Lu and his heirs, as descendants of Zhougong, could thereafter sacrifice to Heaven and to Wen Wang and use imperial music in the rituals—sovereign prerogatives that were never allowed to other enfeoffed princes—in order to commemorate the man who had saved the empire for the house of Zhou.[21]

However, though Cheng Wang was averse to going to Chengzhou even to comply with his uncle's dying wish, he was wise enough to continue the policy of assimilation that the duke had so painstakingly pursued. And in order to bolster the confidence of the Yin people in the Zhou government, he appointed Jun Chen, a younger son of Zhougong, to succeed to his father's post at Luo.[22] Thus Zhougong's policy of assimilating the Yin people in Chengzhou was prosecuted without interruption. Nevertheless, the pro-gress was slowed down by the apparent want of intention on the part of Cheng Wang to move his imperial seat to that city. Though this expected transfer did not happen, yet because Jun Chen was able to emulate his father

and carry out his mission with an equal combination of gentleness and firm-
ness, the Yin people showed no more signs of intransigence. Perhaps time
helped too. With each passing year, the obdurates became more resigned to
their fate. Moreover, the site of Luo itself contributed to the efficacy of the
process. Although its pretensions to the status of a co-capital were losing
credibility, the advantages of its central location soon converted it into a
convenient stopover for all routes of communication from north to south and
from west to east, in consequence of which population also increased. Thus
after the lapse of over a generation's time, in the twelfth year of Kang
Wang, Cheng Wang's son and successor, when a new administrator had to
be named to take charge of Luo at the death of Jun Chen, the Zhou appeared
to have felt assured at last that the assimilation of the Yin obdurates had
succeeded.[23]

Still, though the Nine Tripods were permitted to remain at Luo, the
imperial court showed no willingness to transfer its seat there. In fact, as
time lengthened, the successive emperors, growing more accustomed to the
luxuries of Hao which accumulated over the years, became even less disposed to change. The original designs of Wu Wang and Zhougong were, if
remembered at all, remembered only as a glorious anecdote, not as a binding
testament. Throughout the first three and a half centuries of Zhou rule, as far
as can be gleaned from ancient records, only one emperor, Xuan Wang
(827–782 B.C.), appears to have gone to the "Eastern Capital" and held a
meeting of the enfeoffed princes there.[24] As to the other monarchs, if they
ever visited the city at any time, it must be assumed that they did so only
momentarily either out of curiosity or for some inconsequential purposes.
Thus the palaces Zhougong had especially built for them in Wangcheng, the
"Imperial City," must have deteriorated through disuse and neglect. In contrast, the other half of the twin cities, because of the expansion of commerce
and increase of population, appeared to have prospered to such a degree as to
outshine its counterpart. Whereas the name Chengzhou was originally employed by Zhougong to denote the twin cities as a whole, it was now used by
the people at large to signify only the formerly nameless part to distinguish it
from Wangcheng on the other side of the stream. And when Hao, or
Zongzhou, was overrun in 771 B.C. by a surprise assault of Quanrong and
Xiyi, the fierce nomadic tribes of the north and of the west,[25] the Zhou were
at length forced to flee to the "Eastern Capital" and establish their imperial
court there out of sheer necessity. From all evidence we can gather, it
appears that they then settled mainly at the popularly called city of Chengzhou, and not at Wangcheng as Zhougong had originally planned.

Indeed, the Zhou ought to be grateful to Zhougong for his policy of
assimilation by which the Yin obdurates had been converted into loyal subjects. Otherwise, even after such a lapse of time, the imperial court would

have felt much more apprehensive about seeking refuge at Luo. Moreover, if there had been real diehard obdurates left, after such a devastating defeat, with the entire imperial domain staggering in disarray and dismay, no better moment could have been exploited to create disturbance and wreak vengeance. But nothing untoward happened, and the settlement of Zhou in the Eastern Capital was as peaceful as could have been expected under the circumstances. However, the prestige of Zhou suffered an irreparable decline. Yet, notwithstanding this inescapable consequence, the Zhou were to remain there with their nominal sovereignty retained for no less than five centuries, until their flickering candle was at last snuffed out by the rising power of Qin in 256 B.C.[26] And political theorists cannot help wondering what a different course history might have taken had the Zhou followed through early with Zhougong's plans and transferred their imperial seat from Hao to Chengzhou. The former being on the borders of the western frontier, its loss to the savage tribes, though grievously humiliating for the transient moment, would not have produced so disastrous an effect upon the dynasty. And Luo being situated at the heart of the empire, even if the wild tribes were audacious enough to plan a surprise assault, even if they were able to collect a few disgruntled princes as allies as was actually the case in that historic event,[27] while the distance alone might have discouraged them from making the attempt in the first place, their incursions could never have penetrated far into the heartland without providing ample time for the imperial court to organize effective resistance from the overwhelming remainder of loyal enfeoffed states. And the drastic decline of the Zhou might not have happened at all.

· 2 ·

ZHOUGONG THE MAN: HIS GENIUS AND HIS WRITINGS

If there is much about Zhougong's public life we do not know, about his private life we know almost nothing.

Undoubtedly he was one of the most gifted men in ancient China. Yet by all accounts, he was also one of her humblest. Ever eager to learn from others, he is said to have once confided to his son the Marquis of Lu that on any day in his life he could have found "ten men he would like to have as teachers." [28] Perhaps it is as a result of this compounding of an inborn versatile genius with a genuinely self-effacing spirit and a tirelessly inquiring mind that he was widely known in his own time as a man "of many parts and talents." [29] Yet such was his modesty that even though his accomplishments were many and varied, in all of his writings that are still extant we cannot find any reference or allusion made by him to them—except on one occasion. And that is when Wu Wang was seriously ill the first time and Zhougong prayed to his forebears to spare his beloved brother's life and take his own as a substitute. He had pleaded then: "I am also possessed of many parts and talents that will fit me to serve spiritual beings. Your principal descendant, on the other hand, is not a man of so many parts and talents as I, Dan, am; he is not capable of serving spiritual beings." [30]

There is a book extant titled *Zhou bi Suanjing,* which purports to comprise all the knowledge of astronomy and mathematics that had accumulated toward the close of the Shang, or the beginning of the Zhou, dynasty. It is the earliest book of its kind in China, and it is attributed to Zhougong.[31] The writing of such a book would have undoubtedly established him as the foremost astronomer and mathematician of his age; and this, indeed, may well have been an indubitable historical fact. But as Zhougong himself never made any assertions to that effect, we have no evidence other than the popular belief that has been transmitted to us from no one knows when to affirm this claim for him.

There is, of course, the building of the city Chengzhou, which may be said to have been an engineering feat of unqualified success for that era. As noted before, the engineer that attended to the details of the construction works was one Officer Mimou.[32] Yet there is also no denying that Zhougong was the one final authority responsible for all the basic designs of the new imperial seat. And for all we know, Mimou may have been an officer not only chosen by Zhougong, but also trained by him especially, or even personally, for that huge project.

Apart from these unsubstantiated assumptions, there is on record but a curious incident which seems to testify to Zhougong's scientific expertise. Sometime in the sixth year of his regency, there came a mission to Hao from a remote nation called Yuechang, which lay south of where the mainland of China joins the Indochina peninsula,[33] presumably precursors of the present-day Vietnamese. They came with a series of interpreters, for their language was so different that it had to be interpreted several times to be finally translated into Chinese. They presented a bevy of "white pheasants," saying, "The way is exceedingly distant. It is barred by mountains and rivers. We have not been able to communicate. So now we come with a series of interpreters to pay our homage." It happened that Zhougong was then not in Hao, but in Chengzhou, so Cheng Wang sent the envoy with his mission on to the Eastern Capital. Upon receiving them, Zhougong said, "A man of virtue will not accept gifts from anyone who has not benefited from his friendship. A ruler of virtue will not receive homage from those who are not subject to his government. Why are we honored with your presents?" The envoy replied, "I have been instructed by the gray-haired elders of our nation that it has been a considerable length of time since our land was afflicted by overpowering cloudbursts from the direction of the mainland. This must be because the Central Nation has been ruled by sages. It behooves us therefore to come and pay homage."

Though we doubt if Zhougong was susceptible to this kind of flattery, policy persuaded him to accept the white pheasants, which he submitted in turn to Cheng Wang. And attributing the homage as one evoked by the spirits of Wen Wang and Wu Wang, he asked the young sovereign to present them to the ancestral temple. However, on the point of departing for home, the envoy expressed fears that his mission might miss the way returning. Thereupon, Zhougong was said to have bestowed on him five chariots, each equipped with controls pointing to the south.[34] Many scholars since have been skeptical of this sequel because the use of lodestones was not definitely known in China until some seven hundred years later, in the period of the Warring States. Though we have no intention of crediting Zhougong with the invention of the compass, we believe there is yet another reasonable explanation for the occurrence. In the ruins of Luo, we have the remains of an ancient observatory built by Zhougong. One of the prominent structures that lies not much damaged is a large column the Zhou astronomers used to measure the hours of the day and ascertain the four directions by the shadow of the sun. So it seems not only possible, but quite probable, that when told by the envoy of his distress, Zhougong had given him those chariots each equipped with a set of miniature instruments modeled after those of the observatory, to help him on a sunny day to find out the time and the directions.

There is no question that Zhougong was a skilled and creative musician. After the conquest of Yin, under Wu Wang's orders he was said to have composed a piece of grand music called *dawu, Great Triumph,* to celebrate the victory.[35] And as related before, subsequent to the subjugation of the Huaiyi and Xurong, and to the clearing of the land between the Huai River and the Yangtze of pestiferous pachyderms for the benefit of those savage tribes, he composed another grand piece called *sanxiang, Three Elephants.*[36] A third major composition is recorded to have been produced by him, titled *shao, Following in the Footsteps of the Ancestors.*[37] In addition, for solemn veneration ceremonies, Zhougong wrote a number of songs, or odes, and set them to music. These melodies seemed to have been all preserved and practiced, at least in the state of Lu, Zhougong's original fief, until the end of the period of Spring and Autumn. But after Lu was overthrown by its powerful neighbors in the middle of the 3rd century B.C., all the musical scores were apparently lost.

Zhougong also demonstrated his versatility in writing. And here it is indeed that he has left the Chinese a rich and enduring heritage. For some two thousand years, from the middle of the 2nd century B.C. to the very end of the 19th century A.D., if not still later, every Chinese scholar worthy of the name was taught to recite by heart the so-called *wujing, Five Classics,* namely: (1) *Shi Jing,* the *Book of Poetry;* (2) *Shu Jing,* the *Book of History;* (3) *Yi Jing,* the *Book of Changes,* (4) *Li Jing,* the *Classic of Li,*[38] and (5) *Chunqiu, Spring and Autumn Annals* (which is a sort of annals of China from 722 B.C. to 481 B.C., written by Confucius not exactly as a chronicle of historical events but rather as an instrument to convey and illustrate his own political and social ideals). With the exception of the last, Zhougong was a principal contributor to the making of all the classics. As has been noted before, the main portion of the *Book of Changes* was originally written by Wen Wang, but subsequently enlarged by Zhougong.[39] The *Book of History,* excerpts from which have appeared many times in these pages, is, of course, a compilation of historical documents composed by different persons for different purposes and at different times, from as early as the 23rd century B.C. to as late as the 7th century B.C. Of the twenty-nine documents we have today,[40] ten are considered to have been produced, either partially in some instances or entirely in others, by the duke.[41] The *Book of Poetry* consists of some 305 poems. Although the authorship of those poems is generally uncertain, most Chinese scholars have found reason to believe that as many as forty-five of them were either written or edited by Zhougong. Besides the two poems we have already cited in the preceding chapter— *Seventh Moon (qiyue)* and *Owl (chixiao)*—there are attributed to him twelve "greater odes" that sing the praises of the Zhou ancestors and thirty-one "sacrificial odes" that the Zhou used in their veneration ceremonies.[42] As to the *Classic of Li,* a subject we shall presently discuss at length, it consists of four separate works—two principal books called *Zhou Li* and *Yi Li,* and two compilations of commentaries or discussions on the principles of Li.[43] While the commentaries or discussions are attributed to Confucius and his disciples severally, the two principal books are both ascribed to Zhougong.

Yet, imposing as the above list is, we shall not have completed the enumeration until we have added to the duke's credit another minor classic—*Er Ya,* the earliest Chinese attempt at lexicography. Even though many scholars have expressed reservations about the true authorship of this compilation, most of them have also affirmed their belief that at least the first part of it was by Zhougong.

In addition, Zhougong is known to have formulated, jointly with Taigong, a code for granting posthumous titles.

· 3 ·

ZHOU LI AND THE ZHOU SYSTEM OF GOVERNMENT

From the simple survey above, one can see how richly gifted was Zhougong by nature, and also how wide and varied was his own interest in human knowledge. In a manner of speaking, it may be truly said that his works are the embodiment of the most valuable heritage the Chinese people had accumulated from the earliest dawning hours of their civilization to the crystallization of such political and social institutions as obtained in his own day. And from the standpoint of this history, the two books *Zhou Li* and *Yi Li* are especially important. So before we proceed to discuss some of the major aspects of that heritage, a brief description of each of these works may be in order.

Li is perhaps one of the most difficult Chinese words to render into a Western language. In Chinese-English dictionaries, it is usually defined as "rites or rituals," or "forms and ceremonies." While this definition may be adequate in a large number of cases, it falls far short of conveying the true significance of the word. This deficiency can be well illustrated by the titles of the two books themselves. Just as the *li* in *Yi Li* may be aptly translated as "rituals or ceremonies," so the *li* in *Zhou Li* may not be. For whereas the former is in fact a book on ceremonies and rituals, the latter is conspicuously not. Instead, it deals mainly with the principles and organizations of the Zhou government. Except for some descriptions detailing the duties of sundry officials in ceremonial functions, the predominant portion of the work and also its principal purposes are not at all concerned with rites or rituals, or forms and ceremonies. The question that confronts the Western reader, then, is how can a book be called *li*, when all it is about is government organization? The answer is that the Chinese word *li* has a far broader and more sensitive meaning. Given a particular situation at a particular time, if a man's behavior is said to be in accord with *li*, it means that he has acted fittingly and properly for the good of all concerned. If it is said to be not in accord with *li*, then even if the man has disported himself with intelligence and with sensitivity, his conduct is still disapproved because it falls short of the ideal, recognized or recognizable to be fitting and proper for the common good. Rites or rituals, forms and ceremonies are called *li* not just because they are rites or rituals, forms and ceremonies, but because they are adjudged to be modes or manners that are fitting and proper for men to use to express their sentiments in certain human conditions. But if they lose that quality, then they are no longer in accord with *li* and must be reformed. The English word that comes closest to its meaning is "propriety" or "proprieties." Thus Zhougong's book on rites and ceremonies is given the title *Yi Li*, which may be translated as *Standard Proprieties* or *Model Proprieties*—in other words, rituals or ceremonies that men may use if need be as standards or models to express their various sentiments fittingly and properly. And for the same reason, the second book is called *Zhou Li, Zhou Proprieties.* For what is written in it is what Zhougong thought to be fitting and proper for the government organization of Zhou.

The titles *Zhou Li* and *Yi Li*, however, were not given to the books by Zhougong himself. *Yi Li* came into usage centuries later [44] and *Zhou Li* later still.[45]

Zhougong is recorded to have devoted much of his last years to *zhili zuoyue,* "the institutionalization of *li* and the composition of music." The two books are apparently part of the results of his labor in this endeavor. But as a book, *Zhou Li* is by its very nature more complex than *Yi Li;* and partly by design and partly by chance, as it were, it is further cloaked with a sort of mystery. For, strange as it may be, from all the evidence we can gather, neither Confucius nor his many disciples, including Mencius, appeared to have ever known about the existence of the book *Zhou Li.* What commentaries or discussions they made on the principles of *li* were all based on their studies of the book *Yi Li* and of the practices and mores of previous dynasties. And nowhere in their investigations was any reference made to *Zhou Li.* As to the book itself, it appeared only after the Fires of Qin, when the Han dynasty started an earnest search for lost books. It was known even then to be incomplete, with a sixth or the last part missing. Moreover, certain descriptions of the Zhou feudal system as outlined in the book are found at variance with an account given by no less an authority than Mencius. For these reasons, *Zhou Li* has been suspected by a few skeptics to be a forgery produced in the period of the Warring States.[46] But upon scrutiny of the text of the book itself, not only can the mystery and the discrepancy be explained, but little substance can be sifted to sustain the doubt that the book could have been written by anyone other than Zhougong.

What actually happened may be perhaps reconstructed as follows: Zhougong was recorded to have engaged in "the institutionalization of proprieties and the composition of music" in the sixth year of his regency.[47] By the term "institutionalization of proprieties," we may now understand that, along with a standardization of general "proprieties," he initiated a movement to reorganize the Zhou government. Having completed the initial plans, he submitted them to Cheng Wang. Thereupon the emperor issued a proclamation, which is preserved in the *Book of History* and reads in part:

> We establish the ministry of *zhongzai,* "prime minister," who presides over the government of the country, leads and supervises all officers, and ensures equality and uniformity throughout the land within the four seas;
> The ministry of *situ,* "minister of commonalty," [48] who presides over the instruction of the country, inculcates the duties pertaining to the five social relationships,[49] and trains the myriads of people to work together for common weal;
> The ministry of *zongbo,* "minister of the imperial household," who presides over the ceremonies of the country, manages the affairs between the spirits and men, and harmonizes the relations between high and low;
> The ministry of *sima,* "minister of war," who presides over the military administration of the country, commands the six hosts, and secures the tranquillity of all the states;

The ministry of *sikou,* "minister of justice," who presides over the prohibitions of the country, investigates the wicked and evil-disposed, and punishes those who commit acts of violence and disturb the peace; and

The ministry of *sikong,* "minister of works," who presides over the land of the country, sees to the establishment of people in the four directions,[50] and makes seasonable advantageous uses of the ground.

These six ministers, with their separate functions, are each to lead on their subordinates to set an example to the nine Regional Pastors and perfect the living conditions of the myriads of people.

In every six years the princes of the five domains [51] shall each attend the court once. At the end of the second six years, the sovereign shall use the four seasons to take inspection tours examining the implementations of the institutions at the sites of the Four Mountains.[52] The princes shall attend on him, each at the mountain of his quarter; and promotions and demotions shall be then made greatly clear.[53]

The above quotation carries all the major points of the proclamation, which in fact gives only the barest skeleton structure of the reorganized government. Perhaps it was Zhougong's intention to have it so. The process of reorganization needed time and, also, a measure of experimentation. It was best to have the general layout specified first, and then to fill in the details afterward. When he restored sovereignty to Cheng Wang at the end of the seventh year of his regency, that is, two years later, most likely much of the original reorganization program had already been carried out.

But Zhougong was not satisfied. As regent, he had been burdened with the multifarious responsibilities of the empire. In making those reorganization plans, he might have compromised too much with the exigencies of the moment. But now that he was retired, he had much more time to himself, and he devoted it to the writing of the two books that have come down to us as *Zhou Li* and *Yi Li.* And so far as *Zhou Li* is concerned, he was writing it not for the general public but strictly for Cheng Wang with a view to submitting it later to him for consideration and action. He was putting down what he thought to be intrinsically fitting and proper for the Zhou government, not at all concerned with whether any of the particulars might have already been put into effect or not. If they had been, well and good; if they had not, he was all the more ready to put them down so that Cheng Wang could later compare them with the existing dispositions and make his own adjustments.

The book, on the surface, treats entirely of the organization of the imperial court, or the government of Zhou inside the imperial domain, and hardly touches upon the feudal system of the enfeoffed princes outside. As the court was proclaimed to consist of six ministries, so it is plain that Zhougong originally intended to divide the book into six parts, a part for each ministry. However, when the book was rediscovered after the Fires of Qin, the part pertaining to the ministry of works *(sikong)* was found wanting.[54] Ever since then, many Chinese scholars have taken it for granted that it was lost. But it is equally possible, and to this historian more probable, that though Zhougong projected a sixth part, he died before he could begin it.

As can be seen from the five original parts, the principles of division of labor and delegation of authority are clearly drawn. Under each ministry, there are as many subordinate agencies as its functions may require; and under the agencies, there are again lower-level services. The number of agencies and services amount to some 275, with an average of fifty-five for each ministry. The staff of the five ministries total some 1,900 officers with ranks and 15,000 employees such as scribes, custodians, accountants, and other kinds of servitors, who are not recognized as officers.[55] The largest agency has a personnel of 224, and the smallest service only three. The official ranks are divided into six grades. Starting from the lowest grade upward, we have (1) *xiashi,* "lower-class officer," (2) *zhongshi,* "middle-class officer," (3) *shangshi,* "upper-class officer," (4) *xiadafu,* "lower-class administrator," (5) *zhongdafu,* "middle-class administrator," and (6) *shang-dafu,* "upper-class administrator." The ministers are ranked upper-class administrators; the deputy ministers and some heads of large agencies, middle-class administrators. The ratio of the distribution of ranks is roughly 1 upper-class administrator to 5 middle-class administrators to 20 lower-class administrators to 50 upper-class officers to 120 middle-class officers and to 200 lower-class officers.

For students of modern government, accustomed to the present-day bureaucracies with personnel running into millions, such an imperial court as described by Zhougong must appear primitive and insignificant. But in a time as early as the 11th century B.C., for one man to try to draw up, all by himself, a complete charter for a government with six ministries, to decide how many subordinate agencies and how many lower-level services these ministries should have, to determine for each agency or service how many officers with different ranks were required and how many scribes, custodians, accountants, and other kinds of servitors should be employed, and then to give every officer, high and low, a concise definition of his functions, and to adjudge what rank he was entitled to—to spell out all this in detail and to put it together as a systematic whole, that is indeed a project as ambitious as any individual statesman could ever have conceived. And the more one reads through the book, the more one is convinced that unless a man was equipped with such experiences as Zhougong himself, having administered the multitudinous affairs of an empire so many years and being so conversant with the detailed operations of every branch, agency, or service of the then existing government; and, yes, even more than that, unless he was also similarly endowed with a realistic, humanist, yet non-messianic vision to seek to make the entire political organization work for a common goal for mankind, he would not have been able to write such a book.

But from Zhougong's standpoint, the reorganization of the imperial court in accord with his highest sense of fittingness and propriety was not yet his whole concern. It was equally important for him to devise a system to perpetuate the Mandate of Heaven for the house of Zhou, just as Tang had done so before for the house of Shang. As changed circumstances had made Tang's system no longer adaptable, so it was imperative to think up other methods to secure effective control over those hundreds of enfeoffed prince-doms outside the imperial domain. But this was a very delicate matter. Before the plans could be implemented, it would be hazardous to leak such intentions to the outside. Hence the secrecy of the book, which, to use a modern parlance, was intended for Cheng Wang's eyes only. And prudent and cautious as he always was, he carried the circumspection even further. He did not spell out his whole program in one place; he scattered his ideas all about, here and there, concealed as it were among the diverse functions he assigned to various officers charged with specific responsibilities in dealing with the enfeoffed states. So if one glances at those items separately, one may not perceive anything remarkable. It is only when one pieces them together carefully that one sees a clear, consistent, and deeply thought-out scheme which, if skilfully executed step by step, would have substantially reduced the power and prestige of the enfeoffed princes and enormously enhanced those of the Zhou sovereign.

But Zhougong did not finish writing the book. Apparently he died before he could proceed with its projected sixth part. Whether the unfinished work was ever submitted to Cheng Wang or not, there is simply no information. But submitted or not, it was probably stowed away in one of the private storerooms of the Zhou palaces, unheeded and forgotten, to be left there suffering such various vicissitudes of fortune as only the course of a con-tinually declining dynasty could bring about over the centuries. Then came the time after the Fires of Qin, when extensive searches were made for lost books. And somehow the work managed to appear.[56] While all scholars took it for granted that it was one of the books that had been burned before under the orders of the First Emperor, this may very well have been the very first time that it actually surfaced from a long, unknown oblivion.

There was, of course, no need for Zhougong to describe the actual condi-tions of the then feudal system in his book. Cheng Wang knew them as well as he himself. What he wished to do was to outline the various ways or methods by which those conditions he considered unsatisfactory could be changed or reformed in the interest of Zhou. But what was the original system? For a brief account, we have to rely on Mencius, who lived some nine centuries after Zhougong. Says he in his book:

The particulars of the system cannot be learned. For the enfeoffed princes, disliking them as injurious to themselves, have all made away with the records of them. Still, I have learned about the general outline of the system.

The Son of Heaven constituted one level; the *gong* (duke) one; the *hou* (marquis) one; the *bo* (count) one; and the *zi* (viscount) and the *nan* (baron) each one of the same level. Altogether, there were five levels of dignity.

The Son of Heaven had personal jurisdiction over a territory of a thousand *li* square. A *gong* and a *hou* had each a hundred *li* square; a *bo* had seventy *li;* and a *zi* and a *nan* had each fifty *li*. Altogether, there were four grades of land allotment. Where a lord did not have a territory amounting to fifty *li* square, he could not have direct access to the Son of Heaven. He was attached to a nearby enfeoffed prince, and called a *fuyong,* "auxiliary dignitary." [57]

This is what Mencius learned about the Zhou fedual system. But he did not tell us about how it had begun and how it had been actually developing. So far as can be ascertained from ancient records, the classification of the princes into five grades *(gong, hou, bo, zi,* and *nan)* may be traced as far back as Yao and Shun.[58] But in the years of the Great Flood, the grading of those chieftains was conceivably conditioned by the numbers of men they each could muster up rather than by the sizes of the land they might lay claim to. After the subjugation of the flood, Yu was recorded to have "conferred land and surnames" in the name of the Central Nation,[59] which may be interpreted as an endeavor to allocate territories to the numberless clans or tribes, and thus to restrict their movements. But the undertaking failed because it was too much ahead of the time, and the country soon reverted largely to practices of nomadism.

However, as the progress of agriculture slowly forged ahead, at the time of Tang, the founder of the Shang dynasty was said to have begun his career with only a land of some seventy *li* square.[60] Perhaps this land should not have been rightly called his fief. As it was Tang's determined policy to promote agriculture, that much land was probably what the Shang people had more or less cultivated under his leadership. But beyond the confines of the seventy *li*, they were still free to roam. There is evidence, however, that after his accession to the imperial throne Tang had compelled all the princes of the empire to live within the boundaries of their own states, mutually agreed upon, and not to encroach upon others' territories.[61] And as time went on, with the agricultural way of life gradually and steadily replacing the nomadic, a tradition seems to have developed that outside of the imperial domain, which was acknowledgedly one thousand *li* square, the largest of the enfeoffed states should not claim the possession of land exceeding one hundred *li* square each; the lesser states, seventy *li* square each; and the small states, fifty *li* square each.[62] We have no information as to how the tradition had evolved. Perhaps, on the one hand, it was a sort of recognition of reality by the states themselves, none of them having a population numerous enough to cultivate a land larger than what they were supposed to be invested with. And, on the other, it was a kind of system which was clearly to the advantage of the ruling dynasty to promote: The largest state being limited to only a hundredth of the imperial domain in size, it would take a combination of one hundred such princedoms to match the strength of the Son of Heaven.

It is no wonder that when Wu Wang overthrew the Yin, he was quite ready and willing to continue the Yin system. What he wanted most then was to restore tranquillity to the empire. As long as the princes were satisfied with their own ranking of dignity and allotment of land, there was no reason for the new dynasty to stir up uneasiness and discontent. When he received their allegiance, therefore, he simply accepted all of them just as they were, or as they had always been—titles, enfeoffments, and all—without question. To be sure, he reaffirmed the standard, as Mencius has described, that the state of a duke or a marquis be limited to one hundred *li* square, that of a count to seventy *li* square, and that of a viscount or a baron to fifty *li* square. That was, of course, in the interest of the ruling house; and it also enabled Wu Wang to set up fiefs for Taigong, Zhougong, and Shaogong in the former Yin East Land and North Land without giving the old vested interests too much cause for alarm and opposition.[63] Meanwhile, most of the princes were also not unhappy with the reaffirmation of the old standard. Time still was when land was more plentiful than people; and in an arrangement that openly acknowledged the binding force of established tradition, the princes seemed to have found more assurances for the safety of their own positions, which the sudden rise of a new dynasty might at first have appeared to jeopardize.

But no actual measurement of any of the fiefs seems to have taken place at any time. Indeed, such an undertaking would have required more sophistication than those early ages could have provided. What size each fief was supposed to be was therefore based only upon estimates—and at that, estimates likely made by its own prince. Not only were these estimates unreliable, but they tended to be far smaller than the territory over which the prince could exert his control. For instance, Tang's fief was said to be seventy *li* square. But as we understand it, seventy *li* square was merely the rough area that the Shang people had developed agriculturally; outside of it, or adjacent to it, there was many times more land, settled by none, which they could lord over, or expand into, if they chose to. Undoubtedly it is out of such unoccupied areas that Tang eventually carved a portion and made it into a vast imperial preserve.[64] If this was so with Tang, there must have been many other cases like Tang's. Moreover, the passing of a millennium had no doubt wrought great changes on the political groupings of the country. When Yu convoked a meeting at Kuaiji, the "Accounting Mountain," some 10,000 nations were said to have attended.[65] But when Tang assembled all the princes at Bo after his overthrow of the Xia, only some 3,000 came at his summons.[66] Then, after Zhou had conquered Yin and counted all the enfeoffed states within the empire, the number was reduced to 1,753.[67] While the accuracy of these numbers is open to question, such a trend of development as a definite historical fact is certainly beyond doubt. Through the centuries, the process of absorption or assimilation among nations for one reason or another must have been proceeding apace, with or without imperial blessing. The very fact that the so-called *fuyong,* "auxiliary dignitaries," were recognized as entities attaching themselves to larger princedoms may be considered as a concession to reality by both the Yin and the Zhou dynasties. And if an enfeoffed prince should happen to have several *fuyong* attached to him, his state, though nominally not exceeding the standard land allotment, could be exercising actual control over a territory many times larger in size.[68]

As long as the empire was in a state of transition or of unrest such as during Wu Wang's short six-year reign or during Zhougong's seven-year regency, policy dictated that the matter be best kept in abeyance, and nothing should be done or even suggested to stir up this veritable hornet's nest. But now that Zhougong was retired and writing the book solely for Cheng Wang's personal guidance, he would have indeed been amiss if he had not given considerable thought to solving this problem of such importance to the security of the new dynasty. For, from a long-range point of view, the existence of those oversized states could not but be regarded as a grave menace to the imperial court. Where formerly a combination of a hundred large states was needed to match the strength of the ruling house, now an alliance of a few of them, say four or five, would suffice. Yet from the standpoint of real politics, this was a danger that could not be removed by quick, simple solution. To order the enfeoffed princes to abide strictly by the nominal standard was bound to provoke sabotage or resistance. To force them into observance might well plunge the empire into another dreadful disturbance. Remedy, therefore, could be sought only through method. And method is what Zhougong tried to supply in the book *Zhou Li.*

There are quite a few subtle and yet practicable ways devised by Zhougong to achieve his objective. But space permits us only to discuss the most important one of them, which is found in his discussions on the duties of the minister of commonalty, *situ.* Aside from describing the imperial domain as one thousand *li* square, he continues in a passage:

> In establishing enfeoffed states, measuring instruments shall be used to survey the land and delimit the territories. For each of the dukes, the enfeoffment shall be five hundred *li* square, one half of which is his due. For each of the marquises, the enfeoffment shall be four hundred *li* square, a third of which is his due. For each

of the counts, the enfeoffment shall be three hundred *li* square, a third of which is his due. For each of the viscounts, the enfeoffment shall be two hundred *li* square, a fourth of which is his due. For each of the barons, the enfeoffment shall be one hundred *li* square, a fourth of which is his due.[69]

This is the passage which skeptics point out is completely at variance with Mencius's account of the Zhou feudal system. But to those who are convinced of the book's authenticity, it is also the passage most revealing of Zhougong's designs. Despite its cryptic language, three salient points may be gleaned. On the surface, it grants outright recognition to the reality that existed at the time—that is, the larger states were in actual occupation of some five hundred *li* square each, and the smaller states some one hundred *li* square each. These states, one and all, must have been all along fearful of the ruling house's forcing them to return to the old standard and thus depriving them of much of their possessions. With such a regulation, if it was to be adopted by Cheng Wang, their fears would be substantially quietened.

However, Zhougong coupled this generosity with a condition. For instance, a duke was allowed a fief of five hundred *li* square, but only half of it was to be regarded as his due. Or a baron was allowed a fief of one hundred *li* square, but only one-fourth of it was to be regarded as his due. What is meant by this? It means that within what was his due, the duke or baron would be sole authority charged by the sovereign for its administration and for the management of its revenue. But outside what was his due, even though the area was still regarded as a part of his fief, his authority was to be restricted to that of supervision, leaving the administration and management of revenue in the hands of the local people. This arrangement was of course aimed at reducing the power of those oversized states. Yet it was carefully designed not to annoy them, especially the few powerful ones. Take a baron, for example. According to the traditional standard, his fief was to be only fifty *li* square. But now he claimed the possession of an area of one hundred *li* square. According to the scheme of *Zhou Li,* the one hundred *li* square would be legitimized as his fief, but in turn only one-fourth of it would be regarded as his due. Now, when an area of one hundred *li* square is divided into four parts, each part is exactly fifty *li* square. So the land that was actually allotted to the baron was not a whit less than he was supposed to have had originally; but in addition, he was legally given supervision over a land three times as large as his own. As for the duke, he profited even more. For by the old standard he would have only one hundred *li* square as his fief. But by the new scheme, one-half of five hundred *li* square would be placed under his direct control, and the other half under his overall supervision. To be sure, many a state might yet be likely to resent such a change as a diminution of their real authority. But as the scheme contrives to compensate their loss with a legitimate recognition of their unlawful enlargement, Zhougong seems to have thought, with reason, that there should be a good chance for its general acceptance by the enfeoffed princes.

And lastly, in order to avoid any possible disputation over the actual size of each fief, or over what was due to its prince, Zhougong made it a declared principle that "in establishing enfeoffed states, measuring instruments shall be used to survey the land and delimit the territories." For this purpose, he created in *Zhou Li* not one, but two official organs. The first one, a lower-level service under the ministry of commonalty, was charged with the easier duty of marking the boundaries of fiefs and building the *she* altars for enfeoffed princes.[70] But the second one was to be, in fact, the largest agency in the entire court. It was entrusted with the task of mapping out the whole empire and distinguishing the jurisdictions of enfeoffments.[71] From the very makeup of the agency, one can see how much importance Zhougong was attaching to it. Not only its personnel, as mentioned before, totaled 224; but while other large agencies were headed at most by two middle-class administrators, and small ones only by lower-class administrators, this one numbered among its staff four middle-class administrators and eight lower-class administrators. It was therefore clearly Zhougong's intention to advise Cheng Wang to have all the enfeoffed states surveyed and measured, and to push forward the program with vigor and determination. And lest any of the enfeoffed states should neglect to pay the matter proper attention at the time it was to be put into execution (though Zhougong made no attempt whatever to dramatize this fact in the book), the agency was placed not under the ministry of commonalty, but under the ministry of war!

This passage, as analyzed above, discloses plainly in what direction Zhougong's thoughts were bending. Besides this, there are a few more passages which, if studied closely, will reveal still other methods he had thought up for the purpose of reducing the power and prestige of the enfeoffed states and enhancing those of the sovereign.[72] But however important all of these were to Zhougong, for our study here they bear little significance. They are expediencies contrived by him to deal with peculiar Zhou exigencies of that period. They enable us to understand why Zhougong wanted to have his work kept secret before submitting it to Cheng Wang. But, as ideas or ideals, they have nothing to compare with those others which he incorporated in *Zhou Li* representing the crystallization of most valuable heritage transmitted from the earliest times. Notwithstanding, it behooves us in this connection to discuss an imaginary grand plan that, following an ancient vision, he had formulated for the empire, and that has since exercised a long and inestimable influence on latter-day China, especially on her external or foreign relations, and has brought on some final consequences far different from what Zhougong himself might have expected.

As may be seen from this history, ever since the Yellow Emperor, China never had a ruler but claimed dominion over the then entire known world. As centuries went by, and as there existed no other people or nation to gainsay or challenge the claim, the belief began to gain firm hold on the minds of the Chinese ancients that universal dominion was in the natural order of things, as natural as humanity itself. However, it remained for Yu to put the belief into a formal scheme. He conceived the idea of placing the seat of his government, or what was called the Central Nation, at the very center of the then known world, and dividing the rest of the land into five zones.[73] The scheme was never put into execution, but the idea caught the imagination of Tang some four centuries later. The founder of the Shang dynasty was of a more modest and practical turn of mind. Realizing that his own prestige could never approach that of Yu the great flood controller, he was satisfied with a humbler scheme for the perpetuation of his dynasty. He still claimed universal dominion, but divided the empire into three zones, not five.[74] His imperial domain, being geographically centrally located, was designated as the Central Shang; and outside the Central Shang there were the Four Lands in the four directions, enclosing all the states that had sworn allegiance to him; and outside the Four Lands there were the *fang,* or "directions," where uncultured, nomadic tribes roamed. If those tribes chose to acknowledge his sovereignty, they were of course welcome; if not, he was also happy to let them remain as they were, so long as they refrained from making incursions into the Four Lands. This arrangement had provided the Shang with so much advantage, making Central Shang overwhelmingly preponderant in population and in wealth, that it continually exercised the mind of the founders of Zhou, especially after they had first begun aspiring to wrest from Shang the Mandate of Heaven.

Now that the Zhou themselves had become masters of the world, it is no wonder that Zhougong himself should become attracted to the idea of utilizing a similar scheme to perpetuate their own dynastic rule. And when a mission arrived from Yuechang, a hitherto unheard-of nation in the extreme south, to pay homage, it could not but have rekindled his interest. On the one hand, it made him realize that the world was considerably larger than that Yu had traversed. On the other, he must have been pleased, too, with the confirmation Yuechang's mission had brought that even in such a remote country as theirs, the "glorious Xia land" [75] was still recognized as the Central Nation. Indeed, for this matter, he felt he had sufficient supporting evidence. In his campaigns he had traveled the whole length of the empire from the west to the east; and both as chief minister to Wu Wang and then as regent, he had collected and collated as much information as he could about all quarters of the known world. He knew from his own experience and knowledge that nowhere was to be found a greater concentration of population and a more advanced state of culture than that in Central Shang and Zhou. Now, with both of these areas under one unified control, what better, what more glorious "Central Nation" could there be? Moreover, he himself being a mathematician, he was very much impressed with the grandeur of exactitude and symmetry in Yu's scheme, which, he thought, needed only to be enlarged. Thus it is written in *Zhou Li:* [76]

> The national domain [77] is one thousand *li* square. Outside, the surrounding land in the four directions for five hundred *li* constitutes *houfu,* "Hou Zone." Farther beyond, five hundred *li* constitutes *dianfu,* "Dian Zone." Farther beyond, five hundred *li* constitutes *nanfu,* "Nan Zone." Farther beyond, five hundred *li* constitutes *caifu,* "Cai Zone." Farther beyond, five hundred *li* constitutes *weifu,* "Wei Zone." Farther beyond, five hundred *li* constitutes *manfu,* "Man Zone." Farther beyond, five hundred *li* constitutes *yifu,* "Yi Zone." Farther beyond, five hundred *li* constitutes *zhenfu,* "Zhen Zone." And farther beyond, five hundred *li* constitutes *fanfu,* "Fan Zone."

From the above the following diagram may be sketched:

DIAGRAM OF ZHOUGONG'S UNIVERSAL DOMINION

(The same for all the four directions, with five hundred *li* separating one parallel line from the other)

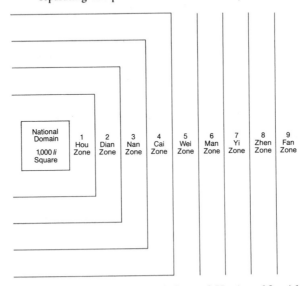

The difference between this scheme and that of Yu is self-evident. While Yu divided the empire into only five zones, including the national domain, which was called the "Adjacent Zone," Zhougong divided it into ten—the national domain plus nine zones. The extent of Yu's imaginary universal dominion, in each of the four directions, is thus computed to be 2,500 *li;* but that of Zhougong, 5,000 *li,* distant enough to have easily enclosed Yuechang within it.[78]

But Zhougong himself had told the envoy of Yuechang, "A ruler of virtue will not accept homage from those who are not subject to his government." [79] So even though he visualized that many possible advantages could accrue to the dynasty from pursuing such a geopolitical scheme, he appears to have had some second thoughts on the matter. Thus, in a later section of *Zhou Li,* while discussing the duties required of the states or tribes inhabiting the various zones, he gave another version of his scheme which does not tally entirely with the first: [80]

> The national domain is one thousand *li* square. Outside, the land for five hundred *li* in the four directions constitutes the Hou Zone, the princes of which shall come to the court to attend upon the sovereign once a year, paying tribute in articles usable for veneration. Beyond, five hundred *li* constitutes the Dian Zone, the princes of which shall come once every two years, paying tribute in goods usable to the imperial household. Farther beyond, five hundred *li* constitutes the Nan Zone, the princes of which shall come once every three years, paying tribute in utensils. Farther beyond, five hundred *li* constitutes the Cai Zone, the princes of which shall come once every four years, paying tribute in clothings. Farther beyond, five hundred *li* constitutes the Wei Zone, the princes of which shall come once every five years, paying tribute in native materials. Farther beyond, five hundred *li* constitutes the Yao Zone, the princes of which shall come once every six years, paying tribute in indigenous merchandise.
>
> Outside the nine regions, [81] the nations are called *fan.* They may come once in a generation, using as presents whatever they themselves consider to be valuable or precious.

From the above, two items of interest may be noted, the first easily understandable, the second needing some explanation. First, the tributes asked of the states or tribes are all of an inexpensive nature. This indicates that Zhougong was purposely following the traditional policy of Tang, who had not wanted tributes to be burdensome.[82] Moreover, the farther the distance of a prince, the less frequently he was required to present himself at the court, which again shows a deliberate avoidance of imposing hardship. What Zhougong wanted for Zhou, or the Central Nation, is therefore continual and unmistakable avowal of submission from those states, but not much more.

The second item, however, is not so simple. For there seems to have been an apparent incongruity between Zhougong's own two versions. In the first one, after the Wei Zone, which is the fifth in the diagram, there are four more zones—Man, Yi, Zhen, and Fan. But in the second version, after the

Wei Zone, only one more zone is mentioned; and it is designated not as Man, nor as Yi, nor as Zhen, but as Yao. Furthermore, the *fan* are described as nations "outside the nine regions"—in other words, outside the territories that were then definitely known to the ancients. These nations are not expressly specified as belonging to, or forming, a Fan Zone; and their princes, according to the wording of the text, seem to have been singularly exempted from all duties of coming to the court or paying tributes.

Chinese commentators have long worried about this apparent inconsistency.[83] But most of them have come to a conclusion that Zhougong gave the two different versions on purpose. The first is to convey how the universal dominion should be properly and fittingly divided, the second to convey how the ruling house of Zhou should conduct itself toward those zones or territories outside its own national domain. The first is concerned with theory, the second with reality. The fact is that while the extent of the universal dominion might be imagined to be some 5,000 *li* in each direction, Zhou's actual influence did not extend to much beyond 2,500 *li,* or five zones. Within these zones, the laws and orders of Zhou could be expected to be obeyed and enforced; but outside the fifth zone, a different situation prevailed. The land was peopled by various tribes or nations, some of whom had nominally sworn allegiance to Zhou and others had not at all. In fact, the farther off those tribes or nations were, the less likely they were to acknowledge Zhou's sovereignty.

Moreover, basically Zhougong was a man of peace. The book *Zhou Li* exudes a philosophy of harmony, of humanism, of prevailing with men through virtue and not through force. He had drawn up the scheme to serve as a sort of policy guideline for Cheng Wang and his successors to help perpetuate the Zhou dynasty. It was a plan aimed at strengthening the national domain by surrounding it with a sufficient number of protective zones of loyal and subordinate states—a sort of an enlargement of Tang's Four Lands, which the Shang had used with so much success. It was not aimed at adding zone after zone, expanding them just for expansion's sake. The plan, if rightly understood, Zhougong was sure would work well both for the security of the Central Nation and for the peace and prosperity of the whole empire; but he was afraid, too, that if misconstrued it might wrongfully lead to blind expansionism and ceaseless conflict, an ill wind which would blow no man to good. Thus when he came to discuss the duties required of the subordinate states, he wrote the second version and deliberately abandoned dividing the territories beyond the fifth zone into Man, Yi, and Zhen zones as he had done before, but lumped them together vaguely as one and called it Yao, which name Yu had previously employed. *Yao* means "sworn." Ever since Yu's time, it has been known to signify that people living in the Yao Zone were given a choice of whether or not they would like to swear allegiance to the Central Nation. If they wished to swear allegiance, their princes would be asked to come to the court once every six years and to pay tributes in indigenous merchandise. But if they did not wish to, Zhougong was quite willing to let them alone, living their own ways of life, not to be interfered with by the Central Nation.

Now, the Yao Zone was only some three thousand *li* distant from the center of the national domain, supposedly still within what the ancients vaguely called the nine regions. And Zhougong himself knew what little information the Zhou had about the nations or tribes inhabiting that area. But there had to be still other nations farther beyond, outside the nine regions— nations like Yuechang. Before the Yuechang mission came, the Zhou people had known nothing about that nation. Notwithstanding, since Yuechang itself had heard of the glorious Xia land and recognized it as the Central Nation, the Zhou people were conceited enough to fancy that if there were indeed such nations, these too would have the same feeling toward them- selves as Yuechang. Nevertheless, Zhougong thought that it would be not fitting and proper to regulate the duties of such nations. So he contented himself with his new wording in the second version, calling them the *fan* nations. As for the word *fan*, there are two Chinese characters which may be used interchangeably to represent it. The one bears a rough picture of foot- prints of wild animals, and the other symbolizes luxuriant growths of plant life.[84] Both appear to have suited well the descriptions that the Yuechang mission must have given of their native land. It is therefore natural that Zhougong should have chosen to call the farthest zone of his imaginary dominion in the first version the Fan Zone, and then to modify it later in the second version by stating simply, "Outside the nine regions, the nations are called *fan.*"

The above appears to have been the conclusion reached by many Chinese scholars on the subject. Whether they have interpreted Zhougong's mean- ings correctly or not, there is no question that the concept of Central Nation and universal dominion, which may be said to have been originated by Yu, revised by Tang, and then reinforced by Zhougong, has continuously exer- cised an immeasurable influence on the thinking of the Chinese people in general. While the full measure of its impact will be evaluated in a later chapter, two simple facts may be noted here. In the beginning, the term "Central Nation" was equated with the "imperial domain" of the sovereign, or the "national domain" of the ruling house. It was differentiated from the enfeoffed states because it was governed directly by the Son of Heaven, who was the one and only overlord of the universal dominion, while the states were governed each by their own prince. But after the First Emperor of Qin abolished feudalism, the whole territory of China was placed under his direct control; so from that time on the Chinese, when speaking of their own country vis-à-vis other nations outside, have called it Central Nation, *zhongguo.*

Again, until the advent of the West awakened the Chinese to the truth that theirs is not really the "Central Nation" of a universal dominion, the Chinese had for some thirty centuries actually believed that it was. Indeed, until that moment arrived, calling for an agonizing reappraisal, they had inveterately followed the guideline laid down by Zhougong, seeking always to make her peripheral nations acknowledge her supremacy, asking from them token tributes of submission, but otherwise seldom interfering in their internal affairs. In the meantime, true again to Zhougong's teachings, throughout her long history, except for some brief and isolated intervals, and except for the short years of the early Mongol or Yuan dynasty, when its rulers were not yet fully assimilated by Chinese culture, China never engaged in any systematic and relentless policy of conquest or expansion. Yet such was their own conceit that they seldom considered other states, known or unknown, as their equals. Theirs was the Central Nation. It did not matter whether any of the states acknowledged her as such or not. If they did not, they would sooner or later learn to do so, as Yuechang had done before, or as nearly all her peripheral neighbors did at one time or another. And nothing may attest to the enduring influence of the book *Zhou Li* more tangibly than this simple fact: When Westerners first appeared in China, even though the Chinese had neither encountered nor heard of them before, forthwith they called them at large Western *fan;* and when they learned later to distinguish them by their nationalities, they called them, to particularize, Portuguese *fan,* Dutch *fan,* French *fan,* or English *fan.*

· 4 ·

YI LI AND THE INSTITUTIONALIZATION OF GENERAL PROPRIETIES

If *Zhou Li* was written only for Cheng Wang and his successors, *Yi Li* was written for the general public. If there are some doubts about Zhougong's having written *Zhou Li,* there is no doubt at all about his having written *Yi Li.*

As related before, Confucius and his early disciples appear to have never known about *Zhou Li.* And what commentaries and discussions they made about the principles of *li* they based mostly on their studies of *Yi Li,* along with what they learned about the practices of previous dynasties. But there is such a concord, or a consistency, of thought that pervades both of the two books that while the contents of one often explains the contents of the other, not a single line is to be found in one that runs in contradiction to any line in the other.

What is *Yi Li?* Here is where the Chinese character *li* can be rightly translated into "ceremonies or rituals." So *Yi Li* may be rendered into English as *Forms of Ceremonies.* But for reasons given before, we prefer to translate it as *Standard Proprieties,* or *Model Proprieties.*[85] Why did Zhougong write the book? It is explained in the other book, *Zhou Li:* "Five kinds of ceremonies are to be used to guard against the deceptive nature of myriads of people and teach them about the Doctrine of the Mean. Six musical compositions are to be used to guard against rampant emotions of myriads of people and teach them about the Principle of Harmony."[86] In other words, Zhougong's purpose was to use those ceremonies and music to inculcate in the people, or to train them in developing, the sense of propriety, of knowing how to act in accordance with what is fitting and proper for every important human condition. The six musical compositions he spoke of, however, are lost.[87] As to the five kinds of ceremonies, these are not unknown to the readers of this history. For from the time of Shun the ancients have been accustomed to dividing their ceremonies into five kinds;[88] namely: (1) Propitious Ceremonies, i.e. those pertaining to the worship of Heaven and other deities as well as the veneration of ancestral spirits; (2) Somber Ceremonies, i.e. those pertaining to death, funerals, or natural calamity; (3) Martial Ceremonies, i.e. those pertaining to the preparation and prosecution of war; (4) Amicable Ceremonies, i.e. those pertaining to receptions of friends or visitors, both public and private; and (5) Joyous Ceremonies, i.e. those pertaining to happy occasions such as the "capping" of a youth, betrothal and marriage, and other entertainments and feastings.

The book *Yi Li,* as it is preserved today, comprises seventeen different ceremonies in the following order: (1) Capping, (2) Marriage, (3) Visit, (4) Communal Festivity, (5) Communal Archery, (6) Feast, as given by a prince to his ministers and administrators, (7) Grand Archery, as held by a prince with his officers, (8) Official Visit, as to a prince from the envoy of another, (9) Banquet, as given by a prince to the envoy, (10) Audience, as of a prince with the Sovereign, (11) Mourning Apparels, (12) Death, as of a parent, (13) Burial—days before and after, (14) Veneration After the Burial, (15) Seasonal Veneration of Ancestral Spirits, (16) Formal Veneration, as at the ancestral temple, and (17) Rites After the Formal Veneration. From a study of these contents, it should be pointed out that no Martial Ceremonies have been included. The two ceremonies that may be regarded to have some connection with military preparedness are (5) Communal Archery and (7) Grand Archery. But these were classified by the ancients as Joyous Ceremonies, archery being treated as a sport, the engagement in which was to be followed by much ceremonial conviviality.[89] Did Zhougong deliberately leave the Martial Ceremonies out? Or were there other ceremonies also not included by him? These are questions that cannot be answered.

But even with the seventeen ceremonies, one can see that the book covers such a variety of human conditions that they may be said to embrace the whole gamut of a man's adult life in those times—beginning at the age when one was formally acknowledged as mature, going through marriage, making friends, joining in communal festivities and sports, entering into a prince's service, accompanying the prince to attend an audience with the sovereign, suffering the loss of one's kith and kin, especially of one's own parents, and then trying to keep the memories of them alive through veneration ceremonies, hoping no doubt that one would oneself also be so remembered and venerated by one's own descendants. To a modern reader, the book must seem inconsequential and tedious; at best, it may hold a little interest as the world's oldest book on etiquette and protocol, but not much more. Yet if one examines it closely, one notices some distinctive features. While modern etiquette books as a rule place emphasis on individual conduct, such as how a person should behave under certain circumstances, *Yi Li* centers its discussions on the relationship between individuals and how that relationship should affect their behavior under the same circumstances. Then if one continues the study further, one finds that whereas modern etiquette books are simply collections of rules of good manners, isolated or disconnected from one another, each having its separate origin or *raison d' être,* it is not so with Zhougong's book, throughout which there runs an unmistakably consistent philosophy making all the ceremonies supplementary or complementary to one another. And one can readily perceive how a man who lived in those times would have been impressed by them. As a child, he would have on many occasions watched how his elders practiced those ceremonies; he might even have played practicing some of them himself as Confucius is known to have played, while he was a small boy.[90] And when he grew up, he would have become not only well versed in each ceremony he was expected to take part in, but also thoroughly imbued with the ideals or concepts that informed him how he should perform his part. It was not a matter of good manners to be learned by rote. It was a way of thinking that made him believe he was doing the only thing fitting and proper.

Of course, many of the ceremonies mentioned above must have been performed long before; many of them might have been innovated even at the dawn of civilization, starting with very crude forms and then developing into finer and still finer ones as time rolled on. Again, to use those ceremonies as a means to induce the people to act or live in a certain manner must also have been an idea not alien to many a leader of antiquity, virtuous or otherwise. So to credit Zhougong with singular originality would be far more than the duke would have done himself. In fact, if this applies to *Yi Li,* it applies to the other book, *Zhou Li,* equally well. For political institutions, like social institutions—or, for that matter, all contrivances by man—are invariably evolved by stages. Some men of genius may have made crucial innovations at times. But even those innovations may always be truthfully said to have owed their births to the existence or accumulation of previous conditions that have called for such changes or mutations. Thus the most we can say about Zhougong's contribution is that he had studied and observed all the political and social institutions the people of his own time had inherited from the past, mulled them over again and again in his mind, and then put them down in writing, preserving those practices he deemed worthy of endorsement, discarding others he deemed unworthy, and adding here and there some new features he thought necessary to further the cause which he himself believed in and believed all mankind should strive after—a society in which everybody knows how to conduct himself fittingly and properly toward others, a society in which all men endeavor to live and abide by the Doctrine of the Mean and the Principle of Harmony. How much in the two books is the product of his inventiveness and how much not it is impossible to tell. Confucius, who accepted this philosophy in its entirety, was to trace its origins as far back as to Yao and Shun.

However, one credit must be given to Zhougong. It is through the two books he wrote that the accumulated ancient political and social heritage has been transmitted to posterity. Confucius not only used the book *Yi Li* as a sort of textbook to instruct his disciples on the principles of *li*,[91] but he also admired the duke so much that he often dreamed of holding converse with him. When he was well advanced in years, he said, with palpable regret, "Alas, how my health must have declined! For some time now I have not dreamed of Zhougong." [92] Besides Zhougong, Confucius had great admiration for Yao, Shun, Yu, Tang, Wen Wang, and Wu Wang. Yet when we read of his praises of these latter personalities, his words, though earnest, factual, and carefully chosen, sound (to this historian at least) rather formal and impersonal. But when he spoke of Zhougong, he seems to have spoken with deep personal feeling. Said he, "If there existed a man who was possessed of all of Zhougong's admirable abilities, yet if he should be conceited of himself and niggardly in giving to others, then the rest of his qualities, however excellent, would not be worth looking at." [93] Perhaps this is the highest compliment one sage could have paid to another.

And the Chinese people were grateful to Zhougong. For more than a thousand years since the 1st century B.C., when the study of the Confucian Classics was first promoted by the Han court as government policy, Zhougong was revered the same as Confucius.[94] In fact, his name was often given precedence, by virtue of chronological seniority. In A.D. 492, he was consecrated *wenxianwang,* "Culture Institutionalization King"; and Confucius *wenxuanwang,* "Culture Dissemination King." [95] In the mid-6th century A.D., again, he was honored with the title *xiansheng,* "Foremost Sage"; and Confucius, *xianshi,* "Foremost Teacher." [96] If subsequently the Chinese came to exclude Zhougong from such venerations, it is not because his contributions were forgotten, but because later dynastic rulers thought it was politically more desirable to have the people acclaim a commoner as the fountainhead of all wisdom rather than one so closely tied with a former imperial house not connected with their own.

But however Zhougong was venerated or not venerated, the ideas and ideals as expressed in the two books *Zhou Li* and *Yi Li* were firmly and permanently impressed upon the Chinese mind. Until China was forced, only as recently as the 19th century, to come into close contact with the West, whose culture is so different as to be a world apart, *Zhou Li* and *Yi Li* had continually shaped and dominated the Chinese way of life for some three thousand years. But despite the terrific impact that followed the initial collisions which showed China to be so much at a disadvantage, despite the many incredible and convulsive changes that have since been brought about on her, and despite the tremendous political and social ferment that is manifestly still going on within the present-day China, we are not at all sure that we have seen the end of that pervasive and lasting influence. A detailed analysis of all of those ideas and ideals is of course not possible in this book; but discussing some of their major political and social aspects, as we propose to do in the next and concluding chapter, may be of interest to students of history, government, sociology, or anthropology.

NOTES

1. *Book of History, luogao.*

2. *Historical Records, luzhougong shijia.* Also see commentaries by Sima Zhen. He was given the original place of Zhou, established by the "Ancient Duke" at the foot of Mount Qi, as his fief. Hence the name Zhougong.

3. *Historical Records, yanshaogong shijia.* The other example in this book is the Duke of Bi, Wu Wang's captain of vanguards. He was given Bi, inside the imperial domain, as his fief before Zhougong and Shaogong, but he was probably made a duke much later.

4. See above, p. 332.

5. *Historical Records, yanshaogong shijia.*

6. *Book of History, duofang.*

7. Ibid., *duoshi.*

8. By "sovereign," Zhougong meant Cheng Wang.

9. Meaning Wen Wang and Wu Wang.

10. Chengzhou is to the west of Yin.

11. The four states are Yin, Guan, Cai, and Huo.

12. The literal translation of the Chinese wording here should be, "Which is more, which is less, for you?"

13. See above, p. 316.

14. See above, p. 160.

15. *Historical Records, zhou benji.* Also see above, p. 112. *Zuozhuan,* Duke Xuan, 3rd year: "Cheng Wang settled the tripods at Jiaru." Jiaru is the name of a hill near Luo.
    In 1976, at Lintong, Shaanxi, a bronze vessel *(gui)* was discovered, bearing this description: "Wu Wang attacked Shang on the morning of *jiazi,* captured the tripods, conquered the decadent, quickly possessed all Shang. On the day *xinwei* [the eighth day counting from *jiazi*], Wang, at Lanshi, awarded Right Officer Li metal [or money], which is used to make this precious vessel for Tangong." (The translation is a combination of two versions as deciphered by Tang Lan and Yu Shenwu respectively.) See *Wen Wu,* no. 8, 1977, pp. 8–12.

16. *Shangshu Dazhuan.*

17. Ibid.

18. Both Wen Wang and Wu Wang were buried at Bi.

19. *Historical Records, luzhougong shijia; Shangshu Dazhuan.*

20. *Bamboo Chronicles.*

21. *Historical Records, luzhougong shijia.*

22. *Li Ji, fangji,* commentaries by Zheng Kang-cheng.

23. See *Book of History, shuxu* (introductory note to *biming*).

24. *Book of Poetry,* introductory note to *xiaoya: jugong.*

25. *Historical Records, zhou benji.*

26. Ibid.

27. *Historical Records, zhou benji.*

28. See above, p. 339.

29. The Chinese words are *duocai duoyi.* See *Book of History, jinteng;* and *Confucian Analects, taibo.*

30. See above, p. 342.

31. See *Zhou Bi Suanjing.* It is said that Zhougong learned this knowledge of astronomy and mathematics from one Shang Gao. We have no idea of whether Shang Gao is the full name of one person, or it means Gao of Shang. The book is listed in *Sui Shu, jingjizhi,* as *Zhou Bi;* but in *Xing Tang Shu, yiwenzhi,* as *Zhou Bi Suanjing.* Also see Joseph Needham, *Science and Civilization of China,* I, p. 213, and III, p. 21.

32. See above, p. 356.

33. This quotation and what follows in this paragraph are free translations of a passage in *Shangshu Dazhuan.*

34. *Gujinzhu.* The Chinese characters used here are *sinan zhizhi.*

35. *Lushi Chunqiu, zhongxiaji, guyue.*

36. Ibid. See above, p. 247.

37. Ban Gu, *Qian Han Shu, liyuezhi.*

38. *Jing* is better translated as "classic." But in the West, *Book of Poetry, Book of History,* and *Book of Changes* seem to have gained popular acceptance, so the common usage is here followed. In the case of *Li Jing,* however, because there are altogether four books involved, we think the translation *"Classic of Li"* is more appropriate.

39. See above, p. 263.

40. See above, p. 40. The number twenty-nine is derived from Wang Xianqian's count in his commentaries on *Qian Han Shu, yiwenzhi.* But questions have been raised about the authenticity of the document *taishi.* If that document is excluded, then there are only twenty-eight documents.

41. The ten documents are *jinteng, dagao, kanggao, jiugao, zicai, luogao, duoshi, wuyi, junshi,* and *lizheng.*

42. These were, as mentioned above, originally set to music by Zhougong.

43. The commentaries or discussions were compiled into two separate collections in the 1st century B.C., one by Dai De and the other by his nephew Dai Sheng. The first collection is known as *Dadai Liji,* and the second, *Xiaodai Liji.* The second, having become more popular, is known simply as *Li Ji.*

44. The name *Yi Li* seems to have come into usage around the time of Confucius.

45. As to *Zhou Li,* when Ban Gu enumerated all the books that obtained at his time (1st century A.D.) in *Qian Han Shu, yiwenzi,* he called the book *Zhou Guan (Zhou Government),* but listed it among the *li* books. However, as there is a document in the *Book of History* also titled *Zhouguan,* in order to avoid confusion, the book became known later as *Zhou Guan Li* (see *Sui Shu, jingjizhi*). Since the Tang dynasty, it has been called simply *Zhou Li.*

46. It is refreshing to find two eminent Western sinologues not holding this view. See Bernard Karlgren, "The Early History of the *Chou Li* and the *Tso Chuan* Texts," and Sven Broman, "Studies on the *Chou Li*."

47. See above, p. 360.

48. *Situ* is commonly translated as minister of interior, of education, or even of finance. But the Chinese word *tu* means "multitude," or "the masses," or "people," or "commonalty."

49. The five relationships are those (1) between ruler and subject, (2) between parent and offspring, (3) between husband and wife, (4) between brothers, and (5) between friends.

50. The characters used here are *jusimin*. In the past, some scholars have taken for granted that by *simin* is meant the traditional four classes of people—scholars (or officers), farmers, workers, and merchants. But dividing the people into four classes seems to have occurred at a much later date.

51. The five domains are zones outside of the imperial domain, each zone 500 *li* in width. So by "the princes of the five domains," it is meant those princes whose enfeoffments lie within 2,500 *li* of the imperial domain. A detailed description of these domains, or zones, will be given toward the close of this section.

52. About the Four Mountains, see Shun's inspection tour, above, p. 82, note 97.

53. *Book of History, zhouguan.* This is the document to avoid confusion with which the Chinese later chose to call Zhougong's book *Zhou Li.*

54. Ban Gu, *Qian Han Shu, yiwenzhi,* commentaries by Yan Sigu and Wang Xianqian. The Han court took pains to fill up the vacant sixth part with a substitute—an ancient document that describes the works of various artificers in that era, but bears no resemblance to the other parts either in design or in style.

55. The number of agencies and services as well as their personnel cannot be accurately counted. For instance, each market has two controllers and a certain number of employees; but we have no idea of how many markets there are.

56. See above, note 54. As the story goes, an imperial prince of Han, Xianwang of Hejian, was fond of acquiring ancient books, and a man by the name of Li found the book *Zhou Guan* and presented it to him. Only the sixth part of the book was lacking.

57. *Mencius, wanzhang,* II.

58. See above, p. 77, note 90.

59. See above, pp. 94–95.

60. *Mencius, lianghuiwang,* II.

61. See above, pp. 158–59.

62. See Du You, *Tongdian,* chap. 31.

63. See above, p. 309.

64. See above, pp. 159–60.

65. See above, p. 115.

66. See above, p. 158.

67. See above, p. 285.

68. Mencius himself took note of the fact that both Lu and Qi as enfeoffed states had actual possession of over five hundred *li* square each. See *Mencius, gaozi,* II.

69. *Zhou Li, diguansitu: dasitu.*

70. Ibid., *diguansitu: fengren.*

71. Ibid., *xiaguansima: zhifangshi.*

72. See, for instance, ibid., *chunguanzongbo: dazongbo* and *dianming;* and *qiuguansikou: chaodafu.*

73. See above, pp. 114–15.

74. See above, p. 151.

75. See above, p. 110.

76. *Zhou Li, xiaguansima: dasima.*

77. It is interesting to note that *Zhou Li* uses the term *guoji,* "national domain," and *wangji,* "imperial domain," alternately and interchangeably. In *dasima,* it uses *guoji;* and in *zhifangshi,* it uses *wangji.*

78. On a modern map, the distance from either Xian or Luoyang to Hanoi is something over 3,500 *li.*

79. See above, p. 373.

80. *Zhou Li, qiuguansikou: daxingren.*

81. This means all the territories known then to the ancients for certain. As related before, Yu had under Shun's orders delimited the boundaries of the nine regions by mountains and rivers (see above, p. 91). But as Yu's flood-control duties never allowed him to traverse the outer bounds of those regions, the frontiers of the empire were left in considerable vagueness. At any rate, the ancients used the term "outside the nine regions" to mean territories not definitely known to them.

82. See above, p. 163.

83. See commentaries by Zheng Kangcheng and Jia Gongyan.

84. See Xu Shen's dictionary.

85. See above, p. 376.

86. *Zhou Li, diguansitu: dasitu.*

87. Traditionally, Chinese scholars have thought that the six musical compositions were works of Yao, Shun, Yu, Tang, Wu Wang, and Zhougong himself.

88. See above, pp. 79–80.

89. According to the classification by ancient scholars, (15), (16), and (17) are Propitious Ceremonies; (11), (12), (13), and (14) are Somber Ceremonies; (3), (8), and (10) are Amicable Ceremonies; and (1), (2), (4), (5), (6), (7), and (9) are Joyous Ceremonies.

90. *Historical Records, kongzi shijia.*

91. See *Dadai Liji* and *Li Ji.*

92. *Confucian Analects, shu'er.*

93. *Confucian Analects, taibo.*

94. See Du You, *Tongdian,* chap. 53; and Zheng Qiao, *Tongzhi,* chap. 43.

95. This was done in the sixteenth year of Taihe by Emperor Xiaowen of Later Wei.

96. This was done during the years of Yonghui by Emperor Gaozong of Tang.

CHAPTER X

CONCLUSION: MAJOR ASPECTS OF THE POLITICAL AND SOCIAL HERITAGE

· 1 ·

THE CONCEPT OF THE CENTRAL NATION

In the course of the so-called opening of China by the West, one of the documents most frequently quoted by Western writers is the reply from Qianlong to George III of Great Britain, delivered through Lord Macartney, the very first British envoy ever sent to Peking and received by a Chinese emperor, in 1793. Its most celebrated passages read as follows: [1]

> As to what you have requested in your message, namely to be allowed to send one of your nationals to reside in the Celestial Court to look after your country's trade, this does not conform to the Celestial Empire's system, and definitely cannot be done. . . . The Celestial Empire ruling all within the four seas . . . there is nothing we lack, as your principal envoy and others have personally seen. We have never set much store on strange and ingenious goods.[2] Nor do we have any need of your country's manufactures.
> . . . The products of our Celestial Empire embrace all things. There is no need for imports from outside barbarous nations. But as the tea, porcelain, and silk, which the Celestial Empire produces, are necessities to the nations of the Western Ocean [3] and your nation, we have already permitted, as a signal mark of favor, the establishment of *yanghang* ("ocean companies" [4]) at Macao so that all nations may participate in our beneficence and satisfy their wants. . . . It behooves you therefore to observe this long established practice and have your traders reside at Macao. . . .

The above quotation has often been cited to exemplify China's conceit, ignorance, and arrogance at that time. But for readers of this history, it is hoped that in the mirror of Qianlong's reply, clear reflections may be also espied of the concept of China's being the Central Nation of a supposedly universal dominion, a concept which has been discussed in the preceding pages. This concept, though it had served as a practical guideline for China's conduct toward her surrounding nations for some two thousand years with varying degrees of success, was, unbeknown to the Chinese, decidedly out of date when it came to deal with the Western nations after their industrial revolution. It made her very ill prepared for their advent. The debacle of China in the 19th century is attributable to many reasons, but here we may only take note of one basic factor—the mental, or psychological, animus of the Chinese people that stems directly from that heritage. They knew nothing about nationalism or patriotism. As subjects of a universal empire, or as citizens of the world, they had seldom occupied themselves with divisive sentiments of regional devotion. If they felt any allegiance other than that to their own families, it was a sort of personal allegiance to the ruler of the Central Nation, the sovereign of the universal empire, or to his ruling house. But this personal allegiance to the ruler, or to his ruling house, could be deeply felt only by those who had benefited from the rule. So far as the people at large were concerned, there was another idea over which to muse— the idea of the Mandate of Heaven. The Mandate is not constant; what Heaven gives, Heaven can also take away. Under such an understanding, allegiance was necessarily conditioned on the ruler's ability to have and hold the Mandate. Though tradition would like the people to believe that the reward of Heaven was consistent with a diligent pursuit of virtue, history only too frequently demonstrated that possession of superior force rather than of virtue was more significant. In all events, the multitude just put their faith in the ancient saying that Wu Wang had cited: "He who cherishes us is our sovereign. He who oppresses us is our enemy." [5]

Moreover, the Chinese, as a people, never underwent experiences of racism. This is not because they are by nature freer of such bias but because the land they thought to be the whole world was peopled almost homogeneously by one race, the Mongoloid. But this does not mean that the Chinese were devoid of discriminatory prejudices geared for self-exaltation. They considered their Central Nation not only the most populous, the most affluent, and the most powerful of all nations, but also the most advanced in culture. And they viewed other nations as barbarous, or at least not as cultured as they themselves were. And, indeed, history seemed to have provided them with plausible justification. Until the West came—except for India, whose culture was oriented more toward nonaction than action—all China's neighboring peoples had been continually borrowing culture from her, paying her the sincerest flattery by imitation.[6] Thus instead of racism, the Chinese may be said to have had—if we may be permitted to coin such a word—"culturism." One would think that the entertainment of such self-conceit should have caused them to cherish a love for the Central Nation not much less than what the Westerners have called patriotism or nationalism, especially at times when they were confronted with irruptions from the so-called barbarous nations. Yet when such events occurred, history has shown too that although examples of singular devotion or heroic sacrifice were not lacking, the Chinese people by and large were rather passive and apathetic in the defense of the Central Nation—neutralized once again by their heritage. For, on the one hand, the concept of universal empire had envisaged for them an ideal that "within the four seas all are brothers"; [7] and, on the other, the "culturism" that is based on the Doctrine of the Mean and the Principle of Harmony also enjoined them to practice what they believe, even toward barbarous nations. But then how about the Mandate of Heaven? While many of them would devoutly hope that Heaven Itself might refrain from granting the Mandate to a barbarian, others simply took refuge in what Mencius had written early in the 3rd century B.C.: [8]

> Shun was born in Zhufeng, migrated to Fuxia, and died in Mingtiao [9]—he was a man of Eastern Yi.[10] Wen Wang was born in Qizhou and died in Biying [11]—he was a man of Western Yi. The distance between their two places is more than a thousand *li;* the time between the two men is more than a thousand years. Yet when they were able to carry out what they intended throughout the Central Nation, the results were alike. Although one sage was earlier and the other sage later, the principles of government they followed are the same.

Thus if the Mongols produced a Genghis or a Kublai, or the Manchus a Nurhachi or a Kangxi, most Chinese simply could find no cause not to acknowledge allegiance to them, confident however in the superiority of their own culture and trusting that sooner or later the new Sons of Heaven would follow the same principles of government as had been laid down by their former sages. And, indeed, subsequent events proved that they were right, and both the Mongols and the Manchus were so assimilated. Conditioned with such a world outlook, we can see how handicapped the Chinese people were in coping with the sudden, unexpected, and unremitting onslaughts of 19th-century European imperialism. The history of modern China is therefore a history of how her people woke up to the impracticality of the concept of theirs being the Central Nation of a universal empire in the face of drastically changed circumstances. Though a few of them may be yet clinging to the belief that eventually humanity will have to come together in "the Parliament of Man, the Federation of the World," it has taken several disastrous wars, many humiliating treaties, much loss of territory, three bloody revolutions, and a century's time for China and her people to learn to accommodate themselves to the travails and tribulations of modern nationalism.

· 2 ·
CENTRALIZATION, ABSOLUTISM, AND RESTRAINT ON ABSOLUTISM

Other ideas of the ancient Chinese heritage, however, have fared differently. In fact, some of these are still being practiced today, even though they are no longer packaged as of old and many Chinese themselves may not be aware of their true origins. Since the beginning of the 20th century, China has chosen to discourage the study of ancient classics; as a result, books like *Zhou Li* and *Yi Li* are seldom read. Moreover, with the displacement of the classical form of written language by the vernacular, even if today's Chinese student wished to read those books, he might encounter much difficulty in comprehending them fully, written as they were in an unfamiliar style and with characters that often look the same but carry different meanings.

Take government organization. The dividing of the imperial court, or the central government, into ministries is of course based on the principle of division of labor, which men of all nations alike discovered when they first attempted organization. It is therefore no wonder that this practice has been followed in various forms through all ages.[12] And as such, it may not be said to be a peculiarly Chinese heritage. The organization of local government, as described in *Zhou Li,* however, presents a different scheme. It seems to have been a genuine product of the genius of Zhou;[13] and its principles of organization are still being religiously observed in China. According to Zhougong, the imperial domain (except for a modicum of land carved out for special enfeoffments[14]) was divided into urban and rural areas. The government structure for both areas is the same, but the names of the administrative units are different. We have already given the table of organization for the urban areas before; we may now give a combination table as follows:

URBAN AREA	NUMBER OF FAMILIES	RURAL AREA
bi[15] (neighborhood)	5	*lin*
lu (village)	25	*li*
zu (clan)	100	*cuo*
dang (ward)	500	*bi*[15]
zhou (district)[15]	2,500	*xian*
xiang (department)	12,500	*sui*[16]

In connection with this organizational structure, there are two things worthy of our notice. The first is the principle of using numbers of families or households as the basis to form government units. It is to be noted that this principle is still being heavily relied upon in organizing lower-level local government. In Taiwan, ten households are grouped together to form one *lin,* and ten *lin* to form one *li.*[17] Except for a difference in the number of families involved, the whole idea, even the names, cannot but remind us of *Zhou Li.* In mainland China, though we are not certain as to how the so-called "street committees" are formed, the very appellation suggests that they are structured on the grouping of households. Then, according to *Zhou Li,* "within a neighborhood, the five families should labor for mutual protection; within a village, the twenty-five families should shelter one another in need; within a clan, the one hundred families should bury their dead together, sharing one another's grief; within a ward, the five hundred families should rescue one another in emergency; within a district, the 2,500 families should give aid and succor to one another whenever necessary; and within a department, the 12,500 families should visit with, or learn from, one another." [18] Moreover, it is stated that such local units are to be used not only to register births, deaths, and immigration and emigration,[19] nor for the whole purpose of mutual assistance, but also "to form the basis for the armed force, to work on concerted labor projects in the fields, to suppress and pursue thieves and robbers, to enforce the collection of taxes and levies." [20] From such an array of functions, one may perceive how the concept of the "people's communes" may perhaps have germinated.

The second principle is that all heads of local government, from the topmost level to the lowest, were appointed either directly by the sovereign or indirectly with his consent; and all were to hold their offices at his pleasure. Even the head of a lowest unit, be it the urban *bi* or the rural *lin,* though apparently chosen from among the heads of the five families concerned, could not have functioned without the sanction of the highest authority of the land. This is centralized government in its most straightforward and absolute form. And this is the principle of government that has been guiding China through all these centuries down to today.

And looking at Chinese history from this angle, one gains a fresh perspective. The Chinese people in general have tended to believe that it is the First Emperor of Qin who, after having conquered all China by force, abolished the feudal system and introduced this form of centralized government in the 3rd century B.C. But now, as we can see, that estimation of the First Emperor's accomplishment may have been historically not exactly accurate. The centralized form of government was probably first introduced by Wen Wang early in Zhou, when he tried to bring optimum administrative efficiency to his small nation in order to forge it into a power to challenge the might of Yin. This policy was naturally continued and reinforced by Wu Wang and Zhougong. Yet for all their determination to expand the power of the house of Zhou, because the then existing feudal system had endured through two previous dynasties, after the fall of Yin they were compelled to accept it as it was, and content themselves with setting up the kind of government they preferred only in their own enlarged imperial domain. Then Zhou declined after the irruptions of the savage tribes of Quanrong and Xiyi drove it to move its capital eastward. And not long afterward China entered into an era when, as her historians are wont to depict it, "the strong encroached upon the weak, the many terrorized over the few." [21] The process went on for some three centuries until there remained only seven states in the whole empire. And the seven vied ceaselessly with each other in applying the same policy which Wen Wang had used before, to make themselves strong and efficient in order to prepare against a final struggle for supremacy. So by the time the First Emperor conquered the whole of China, what he did was to incorporate six independent states, already centralized, with his own to form one centralized empire. Thus so far as the abolition of feudalism is concerned, he seems to have made only one decision which may be said to be crucial: When some of his advisers counseled a return to the Zhou system to set up enfeoffed states for his kith and kin "to form fences and screens" for the new dynasty, he brushed the suggestion aside contemptuously. Instead, he divided China into provinces and ruled them through his appointed governors, who, like all other officers of the empire, were made responsible to him, and to him alone.[22] And from his time down to today, though China's boundaries may have been at times expanded and at others contracted, though the number of provinces may have varied, and though the form of provincial government may have undergone many an apparent change, basically this principle of centralized government has remained the same.

Centralized government means concentration of power in the hands of the sovereign. The more centralized a government is, the more powerful the sovereign becomes. When centralization is exerted beyond restraint, absolutism comes into being. Such a prospect was probably never envisaged by Wen Wang, when he first introduced the system. For if there ever was a man endowed by nature with a strong sense of moral restraint, it was he. Even when he finally attained so much power he could have easily taken revenge on the tyrant Zou, he refrained from doing so because he thought it was not fitting and proper for a subject to overthrow his lord to whom he had sworn allegiance. Under him, the system was therefore aimed as much at strengthening Zhou as at promoting harmony and mutual assistance among his subjects, as evidenced by *Zhou Li*'s descriptions of the various duties of the lower-level government units we have just cited above. When the seven "Warring States" adopted the system later, even though their rulers were hardly ever endued with such a sense of restraint as Wen Wang's, yet there existed for them a constant pressure from outside that produced an almost similar effect. In the dire struggle for survival, each of the rulers could not but realize that he needed popular support at home; and Confucian scholars were not lacking to remind him that the best way to ensure such support was to rule his state with humanity and justice; in short, with *li,* that is, with a sense of propriety.[23] But after conquering all China, such pressure existed no longer for the conqueror. Devoid of inner restraint, the First Emperor thus became truly a man who neither knew nor recognized any limitations to his own power. What had been revered as traditions he now considered to be but hindrances to his freedom of action. What had been widely acclaimed as books of wisdom and ethics he viewed as threats to his claimed omniscience. Thus he trampled down esablished practices at will. He burned books and slaughtered scholars. And the system that Wen Wang had devised, partly at least, as a means to promote harmony and mutual assistance among the people, he now turned into a total absolutist weapon for his personal indulgence. His word was law, to be obeyed by all with alacrity, to be carried out by his officers from ministers through governors to the heads of the lowest households to its fullest extent. It was thus that even after the last of the rival states of Qin had been vanquished, even after the northern barbarian tribes had been driven away from the relatively inhabitable valleys of Ordos into the bleak deserts of Gobi in desperate straits; even though the whole empire was then pining for a moment of respite, at a word from him, he had millions of men drafted from every village or every household in his vast dominion, as far as the extreme south, and sent to the remote north to build a wall that was to stretch over some two thousand kilometers. It was absolutism carried to an ultimate extent.[24]

So long as he remained at the helm of the empire, the momentum of fear that he had generated among the people intimidated them into total submission. But the moment he was gone, that fear dissipated. Mass revolt rose almost instantly, and his dynasty was toppled scarcely three years after his death, or fourteen years after his conquest of all China. The man who succeeded in setting up a new dynasty, after defeating his rivals, was no scion of noble birth, no prodigy of learning, but a lowborn commoner of unconscionable reputation and, indeed, of rascally habits.[25] But he was quick to learn. After enthronement, he was approached by a scholar who kept talking about ancient books. The newly acknowledged Son of Heaven mocked, "I, your lord and master, have gained possession of all under heaven from horseback. What use have I for those books?" Answered the scholar, "Your majesty has gained possession of all under heaven from horseback. But can you govern it from horseback as well?" [26] The answer so stunned the mocker that the truth sank home. Empires may be won by force and violence, but they may not be ruled by force and violence for long. Thus began a fresh interest in the study of ancient books by the new dynasty, and soon, also, in a search for the burned or lost ones. By the time of the founder's great-grandson, in the second century B.C., it culminated in a firm decision to exalt the Confucian Classics above the writings of all other schools and to promote them as the official teachings of the empire.[27]

Thus, from the Han dynasty to the very end of the Qing dynasty in A.D. 1911, it may be said that through some twenty centuries, no matter what the ruling house may have been at any particular moment, the guiding principle for Chinese government was one and the same. It was the practice of absolutism. Yet, at the same time, it was a practice tempered with restraint. Since the advent of the West, many Chinese, dissatisfied with their own old system of government, are wont to blame Confucianism as the main prop of absolutism. But speaking strictly from the standpoint of history, the teachings of Confucius seem to have provided the actual practice of absolutism with more discouragement than encouragement, with more causes for restraint than support. If one studies the records of those twenty and more dynasties carefully, one cannot fail to notice that when attempts were made to exercise absolutist power, more often than not they were met with vigorous and uncompromising opposition that drew its strength from the public's knowledge and understanding of the Confucian Classics, which include, of course, Zhougong's *Zhou Li* and *Yi Li*.

Indeed, the teachings of Confucius are far from absolutist. Space does not allow us to give a full representation; but a few major precepts will suffice. Firstly, there is the time-honored belief in the Mandate of Heaven. No sovereign was supposed to be able to rule without such a Mandate, which specifically enjoined him "to be father and mother to the people. He must love what the people love, and hate what the people hate." [28] Moreover, "the Mandate is not constant;" [29] what Heaven gives, Heaven can take away. Explained Confucius, quoting from an ode written by Zhougong, "In the *Book of Poetry*, it is said, 'Before the house of Yin lost the hearts of the people, they could appear before the Lord Above. Take warning from the house of Yin! The Great Mandate is not easy to keep.' [30] When the course followed (by the sovereign) gains the people, the empire is gained; when the course followed loses the people, the empire is lost." [31]

Secondly, the continuous study of the Confucian Classics by the people has instilled in them a sort of consensus about the general standards of *li*, or of propriety, that should be observed by all humanity in their relations with one another. And the sovereign, being the first among men, should also be the first to abide by them and set himself up as an example for others to follow. He must therefore "not neglect to be careful. If he deviates from those standards, he will be denigrated by all under heaven." [32] Confucius was once asked about good government. His reply was simple: "There is good government, when the ruler acts as a ruler, and the subjects act as subjects." [33] And Mencius expounded: "When the ruler regards his subjects as his hands and feet, the subjects regard him as their belly and heart; when he regards them as his dogs and horses, they regard him as any other man; when he regards them as dirt or as grass, they regard him as a robber and an enemy." [34]

Over and above these, there are the two cardinal principles for society, laid down by Zhougong in *Zhou Li* and reaffirmed again and again by Confucius—the Principle of Harmony and the Doctrine of the Mean. The Doctrine of the Mean is succinctly defined by Confucius: "Whatever you would that men should not do to you, do not do so to them." [35] As for harmony, it is acknowledged as the supreme objective of government, of society. Said a disciple of Confucius, "In practicing *li*, harmony is the most prized of aims. In the ways prescribed by former sovereigns, this is the quality considered the most valuable. It is to be followed in all things, both small and great." [36] Just as the Doctrine of the Mean precludes the pursuit of the extreme, so the Principle of Harmony interdicts any kind of action that may conduce to discord or violence. And the emperors of Qing, the last dynasty of China, lest they themselves should forget this supreme objective, had the principal hall of the Forbidden Palace, where they maintained their dragon throne, called *taihedian,* "Hall of Great Harmony." [37]

Notwithstanding, absolutism is absolutism. Just to what an extent, or to what a degree, the practice of it was actually restrained by Confucianism, however popular and however revered, but not institutionalized in the form of legal checks and balances, is open to question. Though Chinese history is replete with instances that may be cited to demonstrate the efficacy of such restraint, until exhaustive study of the records of the past two thousand years is made, no word on this point may yet be accepted as final and conclusive. However, for skeptics who disallow the potency or the reality of this heritage, a contemporary event may be perhaps served them as food for thought.

The study of the Confucian Classics was officially discontinued in 1905. The monarchical form of government was abolished for good in 1912. Marxism-Leninism was formally proclaimed as the national cult of China in 1949, and the entire population has been indoctrinated with its dogmas and with its thought since then. Yet, despite all that, as recently as 1974, when some latter-day absolutists sought to impose their will upon the country, they still found it imperative to launch a nationwide campaign with no purpose other than to denounce Confucius and exalt the First Emperor of Qin, which, however, turned out to be short-lived and of no avail to them.

· 3 ·
LI BEFORE LAW: THE CONCEPT
AND ITS RAMIFICATIONS

In the pre-Republican days of China, that is, as recently as the turn of this century, one of the most frequently quoted sayings of Confucius was the following:

> If the people are to be guided by law, and nonobservance of law is to be corrected by punishment, they will learn to avoid punishment, but have no sense of shame. If the people are to be guided by virtue, and nonobservance of virtue is to be corrected by *li,* they will have the sense of shame, and, also, they will transform themselves into better persons.[38]

This, indeed, is the Confucian theory of *li* in a nutshell. Moreover, it may be said to represent the quintessence of the various government institutions stipulated by Zhougong in his book *Zhou Li.* Although, as we have pointed out before, Confucius may never have known about the book *Zhou Li,*[39] yet the minds of those two men seem to have been running so much in the same channels that there is scarcely a thesis found in the writings of one that does not find substantial support in the writings of the other.

However, if one should interpret the above saying of Confucius's as to imply that either he or Zhougong would have wished to displace law with *li* in government or in society, one would be grievously mistaken. For in the *Commentaries on Music*[40] (though all ancient musical compositions, including those by Zhougong, which Confucius knew so well and admired so much, are lost), the great sage is said to have also descanted: "With *li* to regulate people's minds, with music to harmonize their voices, with law to administer their affairs, and with punishment to serve as safeguards—with all of these four prevailing in the land and not working at cross-purposes, the way of a sovereign then becomes complete." Thus what Confucius wanted is clear. He wanted the four of them to co-exist and complement each other. And of the four, as later scholars appear to agree, music may be categorized under *li,* and punishment under law. So the great historian Sima Qian wrote in his *Historical Records* defining the difference between the functions of *li* and law: "To impress restraint before the fact, is *li;* to impose restraint after the fact, is law."[41] There is therefore no ground for conflict between the two. But even in an act of complementarity, a question will arise as to which will complement which. While the legalistic school that came after Confucius insisted that there need be only law and no *li,* or that, if there must be *li,* it should be subordinated to law,[42] Confucius, of course, thought differently. What he aspired after was not merely effective government, but better society. Law at best can be conducive but to the former; only *li* may lead men to the attainment of the latter. Hence, in his mind it is not law before *li*, but *li* before law; and whatever legal institutions there may be, they should all be so constituted as to further the ends of *li*. And in this, without his knowing it, he was precisely echoing the ideas expressed by Zhougong in *Zhou Li*.

However, the legal institutions as described in *Zhou Li* may not strike a reader at first glance as too different from those of many other nations. The sovereign was the fountainhead of all judicial authority; and the minister of justice, assisted by two deputy ministers, served as chief executive officer. Under the ministry there was a number of judges, of whom four were distinguished as senior judges. In addition, there were judges assigned to local jurisdictions, namely, for urban areas, for rural areas, for special distant areas, for areas carved out as enfeoffments within the imperial domain, and also for the "four directions," that is, for the enfeoffed states outside the imperial domain. The duties of the last were rather light, for apparently the power of dispensing justice in those states was largely reserved for their princes. Only when inquiries about a point of law were made by those states were the judges for the "four directions" charged to draft answers. Or when the states had adjudicated cases conspicuously contrary to the law, then those judges would be sent over to readjudicate them.[43]

As to the judicial process, whatever the area, it was about the same. The local judge would hear a case, examine the evidence and testimonies, determine the crime and punishment according to law, and make his report within a specified time; the nearer the distance to the capital, the shorter the time limit. Then the minister, or one of the deputy ministers, would hold a session to review the case, attended by all the judges concerned as well as the officer in charge of punishment, each of whom was expected to give his opinion from his point of view of the law. After a consensus was reached, a senior judge was to finalize the judgment and decide on the date for carrying out the sentence. In case the sovereign wished to grant a pardon or a reprieve, he must do so before that date.[44]

The heavier punishments, besides imprisonment and exile, were corporal. They were divided into five classes, tattooing, cutting off the nose, castration, crippling, and death.[45]

So far there does not seem to be anything setting the system apart from the heritage of other nations. But in the matter of penal code, the first note of dissimilarity may be noted. It is said in *Zhou Li*:

> The office of *dasikou*, "minister of justice," is to take charge of the three codes of the empire to assist the sovereign in administering justice throughout the states and nations and exercising corrections on the peoples of the four directions:
>
> Firstly, in administering justice within a new state, the code with light penalties is to be used;

Secondly, in administering justice within a state with normal conditions, the code with medium penalties is to be used;

Thirdly, in administering justice within a state fraught with violence and disturbance, the code with heavy penalties is to be used.[46]

As what was written in *Zhou Li* may have been only what Zhougong thought was fitting and proper, we are not certain at all whether there were indeed three codes at the time, or whether the idea of using different codes for different conditions was ever actually put into practice. But living in an age when the disease of crime seems to have grown out of proportion for society, one may well wonder if Zhougong has not provided some food for thought about a possible cure.

But then Zhougong believed in the concept that *li* should be placed before law as an instrument to deter evil and wrongdoing; and the more closely we study the book *Zhou Li,* the more this is made clear to us. To begin with, the whole system was geared to discourage litigation between individuals or private parties. As related previously, harmony is the key word that the minister of commonalty was instructed to inculcate in the people; the Doctrine of the Mean is the criterion for human conduct; and cooperation and mutual assistance is the guiding spirit for the entire popular organization.[47] Under such beliefs and under such conditions, if differences should arise between families in the same neighborhood, the neighborhood itself would be bound to have the matter resolved harmoniously; and if differences should arise between families of two neighborhoods, if the neighborhoods involved could not resolve them, surely the village as a whole could be depended upon to find for them a harmonious settlement. Conciliation and arbitration were therefore the order of the day, and no differences were expected to grow so serious as to need the adjudication of a judge. And in order to fortify this convention further, it was expressly stipulated: "To inhibit civil litigation, before a hearing can be had for a dispute, both parties involved are required to be present, each to surrender a packet of a hundred arrows to the court in advance." [48] Now, a hundred arrows was evidently a costly fee to pay at that time. Besides, this was required not just of one party but of both parties. So if either party should express a willingness to accept arbitration and refuse to pay the fee, no litigation could ever take place.

But *Zhou Li* also recognizes that there are cases which, because human emotions are heavily involved, may not be amenable to arbitration through ordinary procedures. So an office of arbitrator *(tiaoren)* was specially established to deal with them. It was placed not under the minister of justice, but under the minister of commonalty. Apparently the exercising of this authority was regarded as more disciplinary in nature than punitory. The relevant passage reads:

Arbitrator. His function is to take charge of exceedingly difficult conflicts between people and resolve them in conciliation and harmony.

In case of involuntary manslaughter, or unintentional maiming of persons, he is to settle the dispute with the assistance of the community or communities involved. Involuntary killing or injuring of birds and animals may be treated similarly.

To resolve such conflicts, if a father is killed, the killer should voluntarily exile himself as far as the frontiers of the empire. If a brother is killed, the killer should voluntarily exile himself beyond a thousand *li*. If a first cousin is killed, the killer should voluntarily exile himself by going to another state. The killing of one's prince is regarded the same as killing one's father. The killing of one's teacher or elder is regarded the same as killing one's brother. The killing of one's bosom friend is regarded the same as killing one's first cousin.

If the killer does not voluntarily exile himself, the injured party shall be given a jade insignia signifying that he is authorized to arrest him wherever he finds him.

If the killer kills a second time and flees, an order of general arrest for him shall be issued to all states.

If a killing is justifiable, the killer shall be ordered to exile himself from the state, and the injured party shall be ordered not to take revenge on him on penalty of death.

If a fight has resulted from an outburst of angry passions, the arbitrator shall do his best to seek an amicable settlement. If no settlement can be reached, the whole proceedings shall be entered into record. Thereafter, the party that strikes first shall be punished.[49]

The above passage, in itself, may not seem too important. But it goes far to show to what meticulous extent Zhougong had gone in his attempt to build up a society based on the Principle of Harmony. Thus it is to be noted that throughout the whole *Zhou Li,* though we are sure that detailed penal codes had been proclaimed, we have an impression that no civil code was enacted at all, setting thus an unequivocal example for later dynasties to follow. Even after commerce and industry had developed into far more complex and complicated stages, China continued to use the same principle. Apart from local communities, commercial and industrial guilds took it on themselves to arbitrate disputes between their members or between themselves, and their decisions were as a rule accepted as final and binding on all parties concerned. Until the presence of Westerners brought about many disputes between them and the Chinese, China, as a matter of fact, never saw any need to issue a civil code separate from her criminal code.

If it is difficult for a Western reader to understand the Chinese policy discouraging civil litigation, it may be even more puzzling to him that the Chinese ancients also deliberately discouraged people from pressing criminal charges against one another. As in the matter of civil litigation, it is again explicitly prescribed: "In order to inhibit people from pressing criminal charges, the party who wishes to do so must first file two copies of the complaint and surrender thirty *jin* of copper.[50] If after three days he still persists in filing the charge, the case shall be then referred to the court and heard." [51] The reasoning behind this stipulation is based on the concept of collective responsibility. For the Chinese believe that it is the prime responsibility of a community—be it a family, a neighborhood, or a village—to deter, to detect, to prevent, or to prosecute any criminal offense that may be happening or may have happened within its confines. So if a crime is in the process of being, or has been, committed, the community itself is expected to deal with it. Under such circumstances, if an individual should yet wish to press charges against someone, then he would be laying himself open to doublefold suspicion. Either he was harboring unwarranted malice toward the party charged, or he was entertaining sinister designs to subvert the harmony of the community. Hence the drastic requirement that he must pay such an exorbitant fee in advance.

There is, of course, the possibility that the head of a community himself may use the law to tyrannize over an individual, especially when the intended victim is poor and helpless. So *Zhou Li* makes another provision: "A reddish stone shall be placed outside the imperial court for communication with the destitute. Anyone from far or near, old or young, without brothers or without children, if he has complaints against his superiors and fears their oppression, may stand on the stone three days, whereupon a hearing shall be given him by a judge, and the findings shall be communicated to proper authorities so that the complainant's superiors may be duly punished, if found guilty." [52] Moreover, if the head, or a member, of a community is punished for some criminal offense, the community as a whole is taught to feel and endure shame and humiliation. In the case of a neighborhood (*bi*), all its five families and their members may even be penalized in consequence.[53]

Shame, in fact, is the human sense that *Zhou Li* aims to inculcate strongly in people, and then to rely upon as the principal means to deter men from committing crime and, also, to reeducate a criminal after he has committed a crime. It provides different treatments for different stages of development in a possible crime career, starting from even before a crime is committed. The officer entrusted with the initial phase of this process is called *sijiu*, "rescuer," who, like the arbitrator, is placed under the supervision of the minister of commonalty, not the minister of justice:

> Rescuer. His function is to take charge of people who exhibit evil or depraved propensities, or who commit acts of error; to rebuke and punish them; and to rescue them by restraining them with preventive proprieties.
>
> In case of a man showing an evil or depraved nature, he shall be rebuked. After having been rebuked three times, he shall be reprimanded by flogging. After having been reprimanded three times, if he continues to show the same propensity, he shall be sent to a judge, who will have his back fastened with a tablet bearing inscriptions of his offense, and also have his person exposed to shame on

the Good Rock (*jiashi*).[54] Afterward he shall be put to labor under the ministry of works.

In case of a man who, after having been rebuked three times and reprimanded three times, commits yet another open act of wrongdoing through error or carelessness, he shall be sent to the Circular Ground (*huantu*).[55]

The use of the Good Rock is explained in a later passage:

The Good Rock is to be used to straighten people who persist in depravity. In case of persons who have committed offenses harmful to their community but not covered by law, they shall be pilloried and made to sit on the Good Rock. Afterward, they shall be sent to labor under the ministry of works.

In case of the gravest offenses, the offenders shall sit thirteen days and labor a full year; the next, sit nine days and labor nine months; the next, sit seven days and labor seven months; the next, sit five days and labor five months; the least, sit three days and labor three months.

After the term of labor is over, the offender's community will be asked to guarantee his good behavior afterward. When this is done, he shall be forgiven and released.[56]

As to the Circular Ground, there is this explanation:

The Circular Ground is used to assemble and reeducate people difficult to correct.

In case of those people who have done acts injurious to others, they shall be placed inside the Circular Ground and put to various kinds of work. They shall be put to shame with wooden tablets fastened on their backs bearing inscriptions of their offenses. If they can rectify their errors during the incarceration, they shall be returned to their respective communities. But in their communities, for three years they shall not be accorded the privileges of seniority to which their age may entitle them. If they leave the Circular Ground without rectifying their errors, they shall be put to death.[57]

This is further expounded in a passage describing the functions of the officer in charge of the Circular Ground (*sihuan*):

Sihuan. His functions are to keep and educate people who are difficult to correct and who have done acts injurious to others. He shall not let them wear ordinary headgear and apparels, but shall have them wear wooden tablets on their backs, showing clearly what offenses they have committed. He shall have them assigned to various kinds of work, and educate them while in custody. If they are able to rectify themselves, in case of serious offenses, they shall be released after three years; in case of lesser offenses, they shall be released after two years; in case of still lesser offenses, they shall be released after one year. In case they leave the Circular Ground without rectifying themselves, they shall be put to death. However, even after they are released, for three years they shall not be accorded the privileges of seniority to which their age may entitle them.

Punishment shall be meted out in the Circular Ground when necessary, but it must be such as not to cause permanent injury to the body, or loss of property to the offender.[58]

We moderns are naturally disapproving of corporal punishment. But from a study of the above one can see how much emphasis *Zhou Li* has placed on preventing people who have shown propensities for wrongdoing from becoming inveterate and irredeemable criminals. Apparently it was only after an offender had gone through all the above-mentioned correctional processes and yet continued to persist in a criminal career, or because the crime he had committed was truly self-evident and unforgivable, that he was put to trial by the court and sentenced to one of the five categories of corporal punishment.

· 4 ·

THE BOOK OF THE WORTHY AND THE CAPABLE

The Chinese ancients by this time were already possessed of a long-established tradition, as has been shown in these pages, that the first and foremost duty of a good sovereign is to secure the worthiest men in the empire to help him. It goes as far back as Yao, who sought a man to control the flood and succeed him to the throne; and he found Shun. And Shun did likewise and found Yu. Since then, though succession to the throne had become hereditary, the wise emperor nonetheless considered the selection of an assistant to serve him more like a teacher than a minister a matter of supreme importance. Thus, not to mention rulers of lesser significance, Tang had Yi Yin, Wuding had Fu Yue, and Wen Wang had Taigong. Moreover, with Wen Wang, there was still another problem. At his time, Zhou was a very backward state, deficient in culture and short of talents. For his fast-expanding princedom, he had not even enough men to fill the administrative positions. To meet this difficulty, he was forced, on the one hand, to seek by every means to induce men of high caliber to come from outside; and, on the other, to train and select qualified personnel inside his own state. With a man like Wen Wang, it is therefore not only within reason but quite probable that he should have evolved a selective process for this sort of undertaking. Exactly how it was done, we are unable to tell. In *Zhou Li*, however, we have a definitive procedure for the selection of "the worthy and the capable," which must have originated with Wen Wang and which may also represent further refinements by Zhougong.

Like the other topics already discussed, the system is not spelled out in one passage or under one heading. It must be pieced together from scattered descriptions of the functions of various officers who had roles to play in the selection. Under the minister of commonalty, we find a part of his functions is defined as follows:[59]

> The department (*xiang*) administrations are to be used to teach the myriads of people three things. The interest of the people in these three things is to be

aroused and enhanced by honoring those who have excelled in them as guests in ceremonies.

The first is to teach man to cultivate six virtues: to augment his capacity to learn, to feel compassionate, to see ahead of events, to deal with all matters justly, to hold onto the Doctrine of the Mean, and to cherish a harmonious spirit that is neither too soft nor too hard.[60]

The second is to teach man to practice six types of behavior: to be filially pious, fraternally affectionate, congenial with his own bloodline as well as with his mother's and his wife's kith and kin, trustworthy to his friends, and generous to the poor and needy.

The third is to teach man to learn six arts: "proprieties" (*li*), music, archery, chariot-driving, books, and numbers.

The above is therefore a comprehensive program for the education of the people, which Zhougong also proposes to use as a basis for the selection of worthy and capable men. In order to understand the system clearly, it is best to begin with where the process takes its very first step, that is, with *luxu*, "village servitor," who had under him five neighborhoods (*bi*), or twenty-five families.

> Village servitor. Each village servitor is in charge of the conscription orders of his village. From time to time in the year he shall take count of the inhabitants of the village, distinguish who are within conscription age and who are not. He shall assemble all the people that should be assembled, for Spring and Autumn veneration ceremonies, for public works and hunting exercises, for community gatherings and activities, for funeral services. After every assemblage, he shall read the law to the people; he shall also enter into record which ones of them are conscientious of duty, which ones are quick of wit, which ones are dependable for independent projects, and which ones are compassionate toward others.[61]

Then we come to *zushi*, "clan preceptor," who had under him four villages, or one hundred families:

> Clan preceptor. Each clan preceptor is in charge of all instruction and government in his clan. On an early auspicious day of every month, he shall assemble the people and read the law to them. He shall also enter into record which ones among the people have been filially pious, fraternally affectionate, and loving and helpful toward their kith and kin, and which ones have displayed possession of learning and knowledge.
>
> In Spring and Autumn, when ceremonies are held for veneration of ancestors or worship of local deities, he shall pursue the same course.[62]

Now we ascend to *dangzheng*, "ward supervisor," who supervised five clans, or five hundred families.

> Ward supervisor. Each ward supervisor is in charge of the execution of laws and orders, of education, and of government in his ward. On an early auspicious day in the first month of every season, he shall assemble the people and read the

law to them with the purpose of leading them into righteous conduct. On occasions of Spring and Autumn veneration or worship, he shall do the same. At the end of the year, after a special ceremony is held for all deities and spirits, with a view to practicing proprieties he shall invite the people to drinks at the local school, where the whole assemblage will be ministered to strictly in accordance with seniority of age (with seats provided for those above sixty, for instance). However, in the case of an officer who has received the first Order of Honor, he shall be seated the same, but below all of those who are older than he is in age. In the case of an officer who has received the second Order of Honor, he shall be seated below only those of his own paternal relations who are older. In the case of an officer who has received the third Order of Honor, he shall be seated apart from others regardless of age.[63]

. . . Early in the year he shall instruct the people to study the law and also enter into record those of the people who have displayed moral character, intellectual accomplishment, or practical talents.[64]

And now we climb to the higher level of *zhouzhang*, "district superintendent," who controlled five wards, or 2,500 families:

District superintendent. Each district superintendent is in charge of the enforcement of laws concerning education, government, and other regulations in his district. On an auspicious day in the first month (*zheng*) of the year, he shall assemble all the people of the district and read the law to them. He shall make it his purpose to examine their individual moral character, intellectual accomplishments, and practical talents in order to encourage them to better themselves, and, also, to review their errors and wrongdoings in order to deter them from becoming worse. If ceremonies are held at the district *she* altar either annually or seasonally, he shall use the occasion to assemble the people and read the law the same as before. In Spring and Autumn, he shall invite the people to practice proprieties by asking them to join in an archery ceremony at the district school.

. . . In the middle of the year, he shall repeat the course of reading the law and instructing the people.

. . . Every three years there shall be a general review of the local government operations within the district in order to assist the *xiangdafu*, "department administrator," in deciding on what new projects to promote, or what old undertakings to discontinue.[65]

And finally we arrive at the topmost level of local government—*xiangdafu*, "department administrator," who governed five districts, or 12,500 families:

Department administrator. Each department administrator is in charge of the government, education, and enforcement of laws and decrees in his department.

On an auspicious day in the *zheng* month of the year, he shall receive instructions from the minister of commonalty about the law. Thereupon he shall return and issue the same to the officers within his department and direct them to transmit the instructions to those for whom they are responsible, that they themselves may be examined later in the process to see how much virtue or talent they have demonstrated in carrying out the orders.

In every season of the year he shall compile statistics related to the numbers of persons of all the households in the department, making a distinction between those who are subject to conscription and those who are not. In the densely populated heartland of the nation from the age of twenty to sixty, and in the thinly populated rural area from the age of fifteen to sixty-five, all are subject to conscription. The exemptions are those who occupy positions of authority; those who are recognized for virtue, for knowledge, or for talents; those who are in government employment; and those who are prematurely old or diseased. In every season he shall report same to the minister of commonalty.

In every three years, he shall hold a general review, examining all the people within the conscription-age bracket with respect to their moral character, intellectual accomplishments, and practical talents. He shall make a selection of men who are worthy and, also, of men who are capable. Then, along with the department senior adviser,[66] he shall lead the officers of the department to entertain those worthy men and capable men in a ceremony and honor them as guests.

On the very next day, the department senior adviser and the department administrator, accompanied by officers concerned, shall present the sovereign with "the Book of the Worthy and the Capable"; and the sovereign shall acknowledge the receipt of it bowing twice. Thereupon the book shall be deposited in the imperial treasury house (*tianfu*), with the internal secretary (*neishi*) [67] keeping a duplicate copy.

Upon his return, the department administrator shall invite the people to join in a department communal archery, where he will inquire of them if they still know of some men (in addition to those already listed in the Book of the Worthy and the Capable) who have impressed them with accomplishments in these fields: (1) ability to harmonize a household or a community, (2) fortitude or forbearance, (3) skill in hunting animals for fur and hide, (4) talent for making music, and (5) other signs of ingenuity or inventiveness.

All this is for the purpose of making the people themselves elevate worthy men, who may be entrusted with leadership positions externally, and also capable men, who may be charged with business management internally.[68]

The process through which officers are selected is thus very clear. As soon as a man is of age to join in adult activities such as veneration ceremonies, hunting exercises, public works, or communal festivities, he is under the constant watchful eye of his superiors. The opinion of his own immediate family or neighborhood is of course important, but it is considered not objective enough and therefore not included in the process. But from the village level on, through the clan, the ward, the district, and up to the department, how a man has conducted himself in every situation is being noted and weighed. If he shows signs of perverse or evil nature, he will be placed under the supervision of a special officer, the rescuer,[69] in the hope that he will correct himself. But if he does not, he will be heading for serious trouble which may land him eventually in pillory or in jail. On the other hand, if he displays a readiness to acquire virtue, knowledge, or talent, his merits will be not only approved but entered into record and reported from one level to another until his name finally reaches the eyes of the sovereign himself in the

Book of the Worthy and the Capable. Thereafter, if there are leadership positions to fill, or public businesses to manage, he and others like him will of course be the first to be given such opportunities.

The system suited well the Zhou society, which was agricultural and not too populous. Also, there is no question that through the adoption of this system a principle was firmly planted in the minds of the Chinese that hereditary rulers notwithstanding, government officers by and large should be chosen from among the people themselves, strictly on the basis of merit. As time went on and society grew more complex and the population more numerous, the selective system that was based mainly on judgment of men through personal contact and observation was bound to become less and less workable. A new and impersonal standard had to be set up to evaluate the many candidates for officialdom, and so the idea of putting them to test on their knowledge of the Confucian Classics came into use. This was first introduced in the second century B.C.; and by the sixth century A.D. it developed into a full-fledged examination system by which most government officers were recruited. However we may question the adequacy of the subjects on which the candidates were tested, the fact remains that it was in China that a civil-service examination system was first thought out and has since been continually practiced. It was only in the 19th century that Great Britain, confronted with the Herculean task of governing a subcontinent and deeming it necessary to have more qualified personnel in its colonial civil service, found wisdom in the Chinese idea of open competitive examination and adopted it for use in India. The system proved successful, and was later taken up in Great Britain itself, and then spread to other Western nations.

Another point we cannot fail to notice is that the book presented to the sovereign was called "the Book of the Worthy and the Capable." The ancients, therefore, were making a clear and sharp distinction between men of virtue and men of ability. Indeed, even the rewarding of the two was not the same. It is explicitly stated that the worthy men "may be entrusted with leadership positions externally" and the capable men "may be charged with business management internally." In other words, men who have shown notable talents may be put in charge of matters that are suited to their particular capabilities, at home or under supervision; but it is only men of the highest repute that should be given independent direction of the larger policies of government.

For this purpose, all local authorities, from ward supervisor up through district superintendent to department administrator, were directed especially to study and observe men with respect to "their moral character, intellectual accomplishments, and practical talents." But here the formulators of this selective process met with a problem: Practical talents are easy to recognize, and intellectual accomplishments are not too hard to distinguish, but it is quite a different matter to discern a man's true character. The ancients were long aware of this. For in one of the earliest historical documents of China, Shun's minister of justice, Gaoyao, called this matter to the attention of both Shun and Yu:

> Gaoyao said, "All lies in knowing men, in being able to give tranquillity and comfort to the people."
> Said Yu, "Verily it is as you say. For to attain that, even our Emperor Yao has found it difficult. Indeed, wise is the ruler who knows men. Then he can put the right man in the right office. And by putting right men in right offices, he will be able to give the people tranquillity and comfort, and the people will cherish him for his kindness. If he is able to be both wise and kind, what worries need he have? [70]

Thus in order to overcome this difficulty and make the task easier for the local authorities, *Zhou Li* essays to set up some concrete standards for the selective process. In the case of village servitors, they were instructed to record which ones "are conscientious of duty, which ones are quick of wit, which ones are dependable for independent projects, and which ones are compassionate toward others." And in the case of clan preceptors, they were told specifically to mark out those "who have been filially pious, fraternally affectionate, loving and helpful toward their kith and kin." So there we have the ancients' concrete ideas regarding what constitutes the highest moral quality in man. It is, in brief, his capacity to love his kind—the capacity that enables him to bring harmony among men or give tranquillity and comfort to the people; the larger the capacity, the greater the virtue, and thus the worthier the man of high positions.

One may think that there might have been an inordinate emphasis on harmonious family relationships. But in the thinking of men like Zhougong, these are the very things most noticeable to a village servitor or a clan preceptor. Moreover, if a man has been observed to have behaved atrociously toward his own parents, or toward his own brothers, how much consideration or compassion can he be expected to show to others who are not related to him at all? In this connection, to understand the mentality of the ancients better, it may behoove us to recall why Yao had raised Shun from an unknown commoner to supreme power. As the Four Mountains told Yao, Shun's father "is stupid and contumelious; his stepmother arrogant and abusive; his half brother Xiang conceited and contemptuous. But through his own filial conduct he has succeeded in making the whole family live together in harmony, leading each of them to better self-discipline so that not one of them has proceeded to open wickedness." [71] And conversely, it befits us too to recall why Yao rejected his own son Zhu for the throne. He said, "Alas! Zhu is abusive and disputatious. How can he do?" [72] In short, Shun's nature was all orchestrated toward harmony, and Zhu's toward divisiveness; Shun was a man of virtue, Zhu was not. And once such a criterion is set up, the conclusions may be easily drawn. It is only men of virtue who should be entrusted with leadership positions. As to men of ability, they should be given charge only of businesses in which they excel in expertise, but always under supervision of other leaders who have shown more virtue than they have.

This perhaps explains why the Chinese never developed, or even conceived, an election system for choosing their leaders. They devised the civil-service system and sought through tests on the Confucian Classics to promote the candidates' interest in the pursuit of virtue. They even practiced a recommendation system, from time to time, by which local authorities were required to recommend a certain number of men, "worthy, good, square, and upright." [73] But they never thought of using any elective process. Perhaps election by popular vote was, until recently, basically alien to their tradition. For virtue, in their view, consisted much more in self-abnegation than in self-assertion. Nor would they approve of partisan politics, which was to them more conducive to divisiveness than harmony. Nor would they think much of the principle of majority rule, for their idea of a stable society rested upon concerted action through formation of consensus, not upon the suppression of the opinions of one portion of people by those of a larger portion. It is only in this 20th century that the Chinese, pressured by the mounting weight of Western impact, have at last adopted an election system of sorts in their political framework. But how deeply they are converted to this concept, or whether they will seek other ways to reconcile the foreign practice with their own heritage, is a subject that may well occupy the attention of future historians.

· 5 ·

THE MARRIAGE CEREMONY AND AN UNRESOLVED ANOMALY

Our discussions so far have been confined to the influence of *Zhou Li* on latter-day government and politics. But it was equally Zhougong's intention, through his second book, *Yi Li,* to leave a standard of social proprieties to posterity. How well he succeeded in this respect we shall now endeavor to examine.

For any human society, one of the most basic problems to resolve is the one pertaining to relationship between the two sexes. Yet it is the one problem that seems forever to elude a perfect solution. While total avoidance of direction will certainly lead to promiscuity, opening up a Pandora's box of evils, any attempt at regulation, be it ever so simple or ever so complex, will never be met with complete acceptance or universal satisfaction. It is therefore in this connection, and in this connection only, that we have detected some ambiguity or ambivalence in Zhougong's two books.

China had long practiced polygamy before Zhougong's time. Not to mention anything else, Yao wedded Shun to his own two daughters.[74] As to the house of Zhou, they themselves claimed to have descended from Di Ku, who had married four wives.[75] However, Zhou was a frontier land. And in such lands, men tend to outnumber women; and women, whether native-born or brought in from outside, are likely to be hardy and determined. So the early history of the house of Zhou is replete with accounts of what splendid helpmates their women were to their men. From the Ancient Duke through Duke Ji to Wen Wang, for three consecutive generations the forebears of the new dynasty were all blessed with consorts celebrated not only for their beauty, but for their virtue and wisdom.[76] While there is no record to indicate that these men adhered strictly to monogamy, there is also no evidence that they took concubines or other wives.[77] Reared under such family tradition, and more especially under such strong maternal influence, both Wu Wang and Zhougong seem to have led exemplary marital lives. Wu Wang was married to Taigong's daughter; besides Cheng Wang, he had only four other sons.[78] Self-effacing by nature, Zhougong left little account about his private life. For all his writings, we do not even know who his wife was or how long she lived. We only know that besides the Marquis of Lu, he seems to have had at most seven other male offspring.[79] Both men, therefore, might never have indulged in the practice of polygamy. This perhaps explains why there is found in *Zhou Li* a curious set of statistics which otherwise seems to be out of place with all of the rest of its contents.

As related before, Yu divided the empire into nine regions (see Map II). This example Zhou followed, but he changed some of the names and also some of the boundaries. The book *Zhou Li* gives a description of the new nine regions; but besides terrain, plant life, animal life, and indigenous products, it also mentions the ratio between men and women in each region, from which the following table may be drawn:

RATIO BETWEEN MEN AND WOMEN [80]		
REGION	*MEN*	*WOMEN*
Yangzhou	2	5
Jingzhou	1	2
Yuzhou	2	3
Qingzhou [81]	2	2
Yanzhou	2	3
Yongzhou	3	2
Youzhou	1	3
Jizhou	5	3
Bingzhou	2	3
Total	20	26

The significance of the ratio is not shown either here in the relevant passage or anywhere else in the book. Nor are reasons given for compiling the statistics. This seems to leave us with one possible conjecture. Zhougong might have begun with the idea of taking a more positive stand on monogamy; but upon discovering the disproportionate ratio between men and women, he decided to let the matter remain as it had always been, leaving the statistics in the book as a sort of self-justification.

Thus in *Zhou Li* we find some provisions which by themselves are quite precise; but when put together with other provisions, they present a rather confused picture. To begin with, we have the office of matchmaker (*meishi*) under the ministry of commonalty, whose functions are defined as follows:

> Office of matchmaker. It is in charge of the mating of the myriads of people. For all males and females above three months old, it shall keep a record of their names and their birthdates. It shall instruct the people that men should marry at thirty years old and women at twenty. As soon as a man or a woman is married, it shall enter the fact into the record. In the middle month of every spring, it shall direct local communities to arrange meetings for those men and women who have reached the marriageable age limit and are not yet married to get together. During this month, elopement shall not be prohibited.
> The office shall also arrange to bring widows and widowers together.
> When marrying off a daughter or taking a wife, (to inhibit excessive spending) the present given by either party to the other shall not exceed ten rolls of black cloth.[82]

The language of the above certainly cannot be construed to indicate that, for the people at large, marriage other than monogamy was ever contemplated. However, in describing the composition of the imperial household, the provisions, though each of them is drawn concisely, all together are quite confusing. On the one hand, it is made abundantly clear that the empress was the emperor's one and only consort, sharing many of the imperial prerogatives and enjoying the homage of the whole court.[83] Yet, on the other hand, there is no ignoring the fact that the imperial palace was almost entirely filled with womenfolk. Besides female domestics,[84] there were three kinds of titled women, namely: *jiupin*, "nine ladyfriends," *shifu*, "generation matrons," and *nuyu*, "maids in attendance." On the surface, they were all treated in the book like other government officials, with their respective functions clearly defined.[85] The maids in attendance ranked the lowest. They were to serve as attendants to the emperor's inner chambers, and also to devote their spare time to silk work and linen work.[86] The generation matrons were given management of female domestics and also the charge of all communications with officials outside the palace.[87] The nine lady friends ranked the highest. They were entrusted with the education of all women in the palace with respect to "their virtue, their speech, their appearance, and their work."[88] And besides these functions, all the three categories of women were assigned specific duties in assisting the empress in discharging her obligations, especially in veneration ceremonies.

However, despite these definitions of their offices, history has regarded the presence of those women as a tacit acknowledgment of the practice of polygamy. Perhaps this is the manner in which an imperial household had always been composed in the ancient times,[89] long before Zhougong. Perhaps the austere duke had endeavored to assign to those ladies official functions, especially in veneration ceremonies where they must necessarily be exposed to public view, so as to make the monarchs more careful in the choice of them. In any event, it was a situation that Zhougong found impossible to change, supposing that he had wished to change it in the first place. The sovereigns were a law unto themselves. He might have exerted some influence on his imperial nephew to good effect.[90] But there was no way for him to extend his persuasive sway to Cheng Wang's heirs and successors. Moreover, besides the emperors, there were hundreds and hundreds of enfeoffed princes, each of them a minor monarch in his own princedom. Polygamy was a privilege they had long enjoyed; to restrict it in any way would surely be viewed as a sort of personal affront and might well lead to political unrest. Perhaps it was these considerations that caused Zhougong to hesitate and order instead a preliminary survey of the population to find out how the ratio stood between men and women in the empire. And upon discovery of the apparent disparity, he refrained from taking any further action.

However, if Zhougong saw futility in trying to regulate human behavior by political means, he thought that perhaps this could be better achieved through social contrivance. Thus he formulated the marriage ceremony in the book *Yi Li* with this purpose specially in mind. He gave this part of the book the title *shihunli, Marriage Ceremony for Officers,* that is, for those who had received the initial Orders of Honor from the sovereign. But what he really intended was that the ceremony would be adopted by all of the common people for their own use. For if there was any group of men who could be described as "middle-class" in those times, it was those men who had just been chosen by the court to enter into government service. A description of a marriage ceremony for enfeoffed princes, or even for administrators, might have been more glamorous in itself, but that would be undesirable from Zhougong's point of view. Such a ceremony being necessarily more pretentious and more costly, it would be difficult to induce the common people to imitate it. Besides, as the princes, and probably many administrators too, still practiced polygamy, to set forth their marriage ceremony as a model would be defeating Zhougong's own monogamous purpose. But in presenting the marriage ceremony for officers as a sort of standard, Zhougong could feel sure of two effects. Not only could the officers be trusted to put the ceremony into practice faithfully, he being the revered duke; but the ceremony would be bound to be closely watched, widely talked about, and eagerly copied by the people afterward, the officers themselves being the cynosure of their respective communities.

At the time of Zhougong, association between men and women seems to have been much freer than it later became in China. But even after the Chinese people took up a more rigid position regarding relationship between the sexes, especially after the Song dynasty, China never adopted a system of segregation of women such as purdah. In the early times of Zhou, social gatherings of mixed company were apparently not taboo; a case in point is that the office of matchmaker was specifically instructed to arrange meetings to bring together men and women who had reached the marriageable age limit but were not yet married. As a common practice, males after reaching twenty and females after reaching fifteen were considered mature enough to marry.[91] Although direct private contact between individual youths of opposite sexes was frowned upon,[92] there were plenty of chances for them to get together in public communal functions. As soon as a young man saw a girl he liked,[93] he could report the matter to his parents; or conversely, when the parents met with someone who they thought would make a suitable match for their son, they could certainly be trusted to mention it to him. And once the parents and the son reached an agreement, as is implied in *Yi Li*, the next step they would take was to submit the question respectfully to the ancestral spirits at the family altar and ask for their guidance through divination.[94] Upon receiving an auspicious answer, they would then seek out a friend, or a relation, who was also known to the family of the intended, to serve as go-between. This was important, for until the very last stage of the formal ceremony, the go-between played an indispensable role.

The formal ceremony is divided into six parts. All of them were written out in great detail by Zhougong, quite like a modern film script, complete with dialogues and descriptions of movements of everyone taking part in them. Here, however, we can present only a bare outline. The first part is called *nacai*, "declaration offering." The go-between receives final instructions from the young man's father and goes to the house of the intended. He brings an offering to her father and formally requests her hand in marriage on behalf of the prospective groom. The second part is called *wenming*, "name inquiring." After giving the family of the intended sufficient time for consideration, the go-between returns and requests to be told of the girl's name on the pretext that the young man's family is in need of it for the purpose of divination. If her father obliges, it signifies consent. Then the third part follows, which is called *naji*, "good omen offering." Since divination had already been performed even before the formal ceremony began, the go-between shortly returns to the girl's father and reports the good omen. The fourth part is the formalization of the betrothal, called *nazheng*, "token offering." According to *Zhou Li*, as we have mentioned before, "When marrying off a daughter or taking a wife, the present given by either party to the other shall not exceed ten rolls of black cloth." [95] This is the occasion when such a present will be given by the groom's family to the betrothed. The fifth part is *qingqi,* "date requesting." After receiving instructions from the groom's father, the go-between repairs for the last time to the bride-to-be's father and decides with him on a mutually satisfactory wedding date. The final part is *qinying,* "welcoming in person." The bridegroom goes to the bride's house to take her home to consummate the nuptials.

The above outline is far from exciting. But Zhougong managed to put into the ceremony so much meaningfulness, so much solemnity, so much impressiveness, that only a full literal translation of his script could do it justice. Space here, however, allows us to take note of only a few important points:

1. In ancient days, every family, however humble, had a room, or just a niche, usually in the center of their dwelling, reserved for the ancestral altar. So Zhougong prescribes that inasmuch as marriage is a matter that involves the union of two families and the continuation of the bloodlines, all the six parts of the ceremony must be held both before the groom's altar and the bride's so that the ancestral spirits of both families may bear witness to the entire proceedings.[96]

2. The Chinese ancients believed, as many modern Chinese still believe, that the cosmos is motivated by two forces—*yang,* the masculine, and *yin,* the feminine. Just as the sun and the male represent *yang,* so the moon and the female represent *yin.* For marriage of man and woman, so Zhougong regulates, the only time fitting to hold the ceremony, or any part of it, is either at daybreak or at evenfall when the two cosmic forces merge.[97] Thus, as *Yi Li* has it, the first five parts are each to begin at daybreak, with the groom's father giving his instructions to the go-between at his family altar. And the final part is to be held at the altar of the bride's house, where the groom must time his arrival by evenfall. The significance of this is self-evident. The marrying of man and woman symbolizes the merging of the masculine and the feminine forces of the cosmos. Just as there is only one sun and one moon, so there ought to be only one husband and one wife. But lest the meaning of this provision be not fully understood, Zhougong adds yet another.

3. For each of the six parts of the ceremony, the groom's family has to make an offering to the bride's family with one live wild goose.[98] The reasons for the choice are two. While one of the reasons will be explained later, the more important of the two is that the bird is known to have only one mate for life; it would die rather than mate another. And by requiring the groom's family to repeat the offering every time, it aims obviously to hammer into the mind of the prospective groom that if a bird knows how to appreciate the value of monogamy, should not man do as well?

4. Since marriage of man and woman is likened to the merging of the two cosmic forces, there can exist no possible ground for either one of the two to

claim ascendancy or superiority over the other. But Zhougong was apprehensive of the retention of such sentiments by men, especially in an age when polygamy was openly practiced. So he appears to have regulated the final part of the ceremony with particular care. Not only is the groom required to go to the bride's house to welcome her in person, but before he leaves for this purpose, while the whole family are gathered at the altar to see him off, the father is directed to give this advice to the son (which may well have been the very feelings Zhougong had felt at the time he married): "Go welcome your mate so as to carry on our bloodline. Lead her on by mutual respect, for she is to be the heir and successor to your own mother, to your own grandmother. Consider them as the standard; and respect your mate even as you respect your mother, your grandmother." And when the groom arrives at the bride's house, before taking away the bride, he has to ascend to the altar, deposit the goose at a designated spot, bow twice, fall down on his knees, and touch his head to the ground—the highest form of reverence one performs only to Heaven, to Earth, to the sovereign, or to one's own ancestors. And, again, when he leaves with the bride, even though her family has a carriage already prepared for her, he is to climb up to the driver's seat, bend down, and extend a sort of baton to her. This instrument is as a rule used by the driver, considered a servant, to help his master or mistress get up to the box seat, with himself pulling at one end and with the passenger holding fast to the other. In performing this chore, the groom is thus symbolizing his readiness to serve the bride in every way, even as her servant. This is of course declined by the bride through the matron who accompanies her. But even after the bride and the matron are seated inside the carriage, before yielding his place to the regular driver, the groom will still have to drive the carriage on for a short distance, betokening that he will nonetheless regard himself as her servant always.

Thus we can see that what Zhougong envisioned for man and woman in marriage is nothing short of one equal partnership, one unbreakable bond, one indissoluble union, not only for this life, but also for the life to come. Not only did he undertake to permeate every rite of his script with such ideals, but he also sought to disseminate them as widely as possible. For this purpose he made the whole ceremony as inexpensive as he could so that even the poorest families could take it as model. For the bride's family, except for some repasts to be served to the go-between, there were almost no expenses to speak of. And for the groom's family, the total burden consisted of only the "token offering" plus six wild geese at most.[99] And here we have the second reason why Zhougong chose that bird for the ceremonial offerings. It appears that at that time the plains of China abounded with the species; one could acquire any number of them merely for the trouble it took to capture them. As to the "token offering," black cloth was the commonest material, and a roll was only about twenty feet long.[100] As every woman knew how to weave in those days, that would not take long to make. Besides, the law had prescribed that the offering could not *exceed* ten rolls, so poorer families could come up with fewer if necessary.

And judging from the subsequent development of Chinese society in this regard, apparently Zhougong succeeded in fulfilling the task he had set for himself. Confucius was a monogamist, and so have been the overwhelming majority of the Chinese people ever since. In the later ages, though the ceremony has been frequently modified, according to the fashion of the day or according to the desires of the parties concerned, the intent of marriage which Zhougong tried so hard to imprint has always remained fresh and firm in the minds of most Chinese, remembering well the ancient saying that was a commentary on the ceremony, "Once you have measured yourselves together side by side, you shall not change throughout your lives." [101]

Yet, until only very recently, polygamy has continued in China since the days of Zhougong, though practiced by a very limited minority. But influenced again by *Zhou Li* and *Yi Li,* these Chinese at most took concubines, not wives. And inside such a house, the one wife who married her husband "under instructions of the parents and through the pledges of the go-between" [102] was still considered the undisputed mistress. She controlled the management of the house, and sometimes even the fate of the concubines. This seems to have been the rule even with emperors. The empress enjoyed a unique position inside the imperial palace and with the imperial court. It was her sons, and her sons only, who had, in the order of seniority, the prerogative to succeed to the throne. Though the emperor might dispense his favors indiscriminately among many concubines, or concentratedly upon one favorite, yet if he should wish to force the empress to abdicate in favor of another woman, he could seldom carry it off without running into the strongest possible opposition among the people and creating a political crisis of the first magnitude.[103]

The Chinese heritage on the matter of marriage is therefore, to say the least, ambivalent. Confucius, for one, never thought that any "proprieties" (or ceremonies) designed by man could be permanent. He said, "The Yin derived their proprieties from the Xia; what they took away from them and what they added to them are things that can be known. The Zhou have derived their proprieties from the Yin; what they have taken away and what they have added can be also known. Some other dynasties may follow Zhou; even though the period of time may lengthen to a hundred generations, yet we may be sure that there will still be things taken away, and things added." [104] His thinking is therefore that no social system is perfect; each is devised only to suit its time, and its shortcomings will be discovered as time rolls on, and sooner or later a new system has to be established to take its place, benefiting from the old, but lasting also only as long as it is suitable. However, he defended Zhougong's marriage system stoutly before the Duke of Lu, his liege lord, who, like his fellow princes of the period, was used to the practice of polygamy. The prince complained to him about the ritual of "welcoming in person"; he though it too demanding. Confucius said sternly, "To unite two persons into one so as to produce heirs and successors to your ancestors, who will be future rulers of your princedom—how can your lordship consider it possible for such ceremonials to be too demanding!" [105] So Confucius, though not averse to changing ceremonies by some sort of concerted popular effort, was openly opposed to any change by arbitrary, individual action. He was especially critical of cohabitation without the benefit of rules. He thought it would work only harm on the individuals who engaged in such practice. Said he, "If marriage proprieties are disregarded, then the course for man and woman to mate each other will become rough, bitter, fraught with frustration and pain." [106]

· 6 ·
MOURNING APPARELS AND THE CLOSE-KNIT FAMILY SYSTEM

The Chinese are proverbially known to the West for the closeness of their family ties. There is no doubt that they have derived this heritage from times much earlier than the Zhou. But there is also no question that it was Zhougong who gave it its finished form and enhanced its significance manifold through his book *Yi Li*—especially through a chapter titled *sangfu, Mourning Apparels.*

Mourning, in the sense of expressing grief, must have coexisted with man almost from the very beginning. The earliest record of mourning in Chinese history goes only as far back as Yao, when it mentions that at his passing, "all the people mourned for him as for a parent. And for three years the eight instruments of music were spontaneously stopped and hushed." [107] At the death of Shun, and later of Yu, the same was recorded.[108] As to the mourning of a son for his father, the clearest record is the one about Wuding, who not only mourned three years but dramatized it so singularly by speaking not so much as one word throughout that length of time.[109] It may be safely assumed, therefore, that rituals for mourning had developed long before Zhougong. Says Mencius:

> The three-year mourning, the garment of coarse cloth with lower edges unsewed and even, and the eating of meager food—these were equally prescribed by the Three Dynasties and binding on all, from the sovereign to the common people.[110]

Nevertheless, we are reasonably certain of one thing: In "institutionaliz-ing those proprieties" Zhougong was strongly influenced by a feeling of his own—the one regret he felt in his entire life, the regret over the Three Supervisors' Rebellion and the subsequent death of his older brother Guan and degradation of his younger brothers Cai and Huo. He felt only regret, not guilt, however. What he himself had done throughout the crisis had simply sprung from loyalty for Wu Wang, who was not only his sovereign but also his eldest brother. But the question remains, if he himself felt so much loyalty for Wu Wang and his son and heir Cheng Wang, why could not the three supervisors have felt the same, their relationship with Wu Wang and Cheng Wang being exactly like his own? Notwithstanding, he could also look at the matter from Prince Guan's point of view. Was not the transmission of throne from father to son a rather recent rule taken up by Zhou? Was not the Yin practice of brother succeeding to brother a much older tradition? After the death of Wu Wang, should not the throne have passed on to Prince Guan himself, he being the next in the order of seniority among the brothers? This kind of argument must have sorely troubled Zhou-gong. It was therefore with the purpose of resolving the issue once and for all that he wrote the document *Mourning Apparels,* not only to "institutionalize the proprieties" for expressing grief but also to propound a system of family structure that came later to be known as *zongfa,* "house rules." [111]

The system is one that aims firmly to establish the rule of primogeniture for dynastic succession. It divided the descendants of a common ancestry into two kinds of house—*dazong,* the "senior house," and *xiaozong,* the "junior house or houses." [112] Take the house of Zhou as an example. Wen Wang was succeeded by Wu Wang, his eldest living son by his wife. And Wu Wang was succeeded likewise by Cheng Wang, and Cheng Wang by Kang Wang, and so on. The line of succession is always from the father to the eldest son borne by the wife, not by a concubine. As such, this line forms the senior house of Zhou, to which belong the prerogatives of inheriting the empire, worshiping the Lord Above and other deities of imperial signifi-cance, venerating the Zhou ancestors, from Wen Wang through Wang Ji and Tai Wang to as far back as Houji, the famed "Prince of Agriculture," the primordial founder of their house. As to the junior houses, these consist of Wu Wang's younger brothers and their descendants. Because they are Wu Wang's younger brothers, they are invested with princedoms, which they may transmit to their descendants by the same rule of primogeniture; and within their princedoms, their descendants will venerate them as found-ers of their respective houses. But, over and above, they and their descen-dants must always yield precedence, and render loyalty, to the senior house. They cannot inherit the imperial throne. Nor can they worship Heaven and

Earth. Nor are they permitted to use imperial music. And for the veneration of their father, Wen Wang, their grandfather Wang Ji, their great-grand-father Tai Wang, and their other direct ancestors, they cannot perform independent ceremonies within their own princedoms, but can only follow in the train of the principal heir of the senior house, that is, the emperor, at the ancestral temple in the capital of Zhou. This rule does not obtain solely in the generation of Wu Wang and his younger brothers; it obtains for all generations to come. To this rule, however, Cheng Wang made an excep-tion of the junior house of Zhougong, of which the Marquis of Lu, Boqin, was the heir by virtue of primogeniture. In recognition of Zhougong's ex-ceptional services, the grateful nephew granted his house the imperial pre-rogatives to worship Heaven and Earth, to use imperial music, and to venerate Wen Wang and all the other ancestors.[113] Unique as the exception is, it serves further to strengthen the rule that the senior house is the main-stream of the bloodline, to which all junior houses owe their undivided fidelity. It is only within this general framework that, while upholding the interests of the senior house, an older brother may exercise his seniority rights over a younger brother, or a younger brother may yield to an older brother's claims.

The system was thus formulated by Zhougong clearly to justify his own conduct in suppressing the Three Supervisors' Rebellion. Yet it cannot be denied that he seems to have had also a larger political objective in view. This was explained by the Duke of Shao, Zhougong's chief lieutenant, in a poem he composed:

> The flowers of the plum tree,
> How clearly they are supported by the calyxes!
> Of all men in the world,
> There are none like brothers.
> . . .
> Brothers may squabble inside the walls,
> But together they will resist affronts from without.[114]

Thus although brothers may have small quarrels among themselves, they will all be expected always to support the senior house without fail, like the calyxes supporting the flower.

Such were then the motivations that prompted Zhougong to formulate those "house rules." And how the policy worked to the benefit of Zhou is amply demonstrated by subsequent history. After the dynasty was forced to remove its capital to Luo, it would have declined even more drastically and even more precipitately had not its prestige received a boost from the rising power of Jin, a junior house descended from a younger brother of Cheng

Wang. For more than two centuries, from 636 B.C. to 403 B.C., Jin, as hegemon, succeeded in maintaining a sort of shaky peace and order in the empire in the name of the Zhou sovereign. It was only after Jin itself became decadent and was finally partitioned by several of its powerful ministers that Zhou began to lose the last vestiges of sovereignty.

To return to *Mourning Apparels (sangfu)*, it is, as is denoted by the title itself, a document in which Zhougong drew up regulations governing what apparels to wear for the mourning of what relations, and how long to wear them. They are quite complex. Roughly speaking, mourning apparels are divided into five grades. The closer the relationship between the mourner and the mourned, the coarser and the severer the clothing. However, as the materials used for those apparels as well as the manners for using them have since undergone so many changes, it would no longer be of interest to describe what Zhougong originally prescribed. For our discussion here, an analysis of the so-called "mourning periods" may serve the purpose. These too are divided into five grades, by and large corresponding with the five grades of mourning apparels, varied once in a while with exceptions. The shortest period is three months, i.e. one full season; the next, five months, nearly two seasons; the next, seven to nine months, about three seasons; the next, a year and a month; the last and the longest, two years and a month, which is what is popularly known as the "three-year mourning." The last two periods are for one's closest relations. The reason why one month is added to each of them is to show that even after having mourned for a full year or two years, the feeling of grief is yet so strong in the mourner that he wishes to continue the mourning a little longer.

Now, when the different periods are combined, or rather supplemented, with the different apparels, one can see how varied the symbolization of the degrees of mourning can be. Suffice it to say that they cover all possible diversified blood relations one may meet with in the full length of a life span. As is explained in an ancient commentary, "In order to show a man's attachment to his kith and kin, he begins with three to form five, then with five to form nine; thus ascending or descending or going sidewise, embracing one and all to whom he may be attached." [115] To put it in less cryptic terms, the beginning three consists of the man himself, his father, and his son. From that ascending, his attachment extends from his father to his grandfather; and descending, from his son to his grandson, making altogether five. Then from grandfather to great-grandfather and great-great-grandfather, and from grandson to great-grandson and great-great-grandson, the further extension of attachment embraces a total of nine. As to "going sidewise," it means the wives, brothers, and sisters of the nine generations. However, even though there are nine generations, the mourning apparels or the mourning periods need have only five grades, for counting from oneself either upward or downward, each way there are only five generations.[116] Speaking generally, the "three-year mourning" is reserved for the closest relations. For grandparents, and for those descended from them other than one's father, the period of mourning is a year and a month. For great-grandparents, and for those descended from them other than one's grandfather, the period of mourning is three seasons. For great-great-grandparents, and for those descended from them other than one's great-grandfather, five months. And for brothers and sisters of the great-great-grandfather, three months. Beyond that, since it is seldom possible for anyone to have personal contact with either his great-great-great-grandparents or his great-great-great-grandchildren, it is considered that one's mundane attachment has come to an end. Thus five grades of mourning apparels are regarded as sufficient; and the term "within the five apparels" is used to signify one's recognized kith and kin.[117]

Like many other ancient peoples, the Chinese must have adopted the patriarchal form of family system long before Zhou. And like others again, the Chinese traditional form of patriarchy seemed to have been rather small, dominated by a father and composed of all his offspring and their descendants. But Zhougong was evidently not satisfied with that. What he envisaged in the book *Yi Li* was a much larger patriarchy, large enough to embrace all "within the five apparels" who are on the paternal side and therefore bear the same surname, divided into a senior house and as many junior houses as is necessary, each a small patriarchy in itself, but all dominated by the head of the senior house, and all working for the interests of one another, that is, for the interests of the entire house as represented by the head.

As Zhougong saw it, there is only one key word to make the system work—harmony. And in order to achieve harmony, two qualities are essential for the members to cultivate. The first is filial piety, and the second fraternal affection. And of the two, the first is the more basic. For unless a man is dedicated to serving his parents with unfailing filial piety, he cannot be expected to be unswervingly affectionate toward his brothers. And once he has acquired these two virtues, since he has already been taught what blood relations he should mourn after their death, he himself will know with what proper attachment and respect he should behave toward them while they are alive. For this reason, Zhougong sought to inculcate in the people the sense of filial piety through various funeral and veneration ceremonies, the details of which, however, we need not discuss here.[118]

Sketchy and incomplete as this outline of Zhougong's family system is, it suffices to enable us to go into some of the important political and social consequences it has wrought upon posterity. Ironically, if we measure it by Zhougong's own expectations, it must have been quite a disappointment to him. For the duke's principal motivation, as explained before, was to establish primogeniture as the rule for dynastic succession and to divide the family into senior house and junior houses in order to ensure the loyalty of all members of the same bloodline toward the one and only senior branch. But, as facts stand, while the rule of primogeniture was generally accepted by later dynasties,[119] the concept of senior house and junior houses did not last longer than the Zhou dynasty itself. No sooner had the First Emperor of Qin abolished feudalism than he made it plain that his and his direct successors' was to be the only ruling house, needing no junior houses for support. And the dynasties that came after him more or less followed his example. Oddly enough, however, while this part of the system fell into complete disuse in China, it seems to have gained acceptance as late as the 17th century A.D. and as far away as in Japan. When Tokugawa Ieyasu founded the *daimyo* system, the establishment of the *shimpan* sounds, superficially at least, like a replication of the tune of the enfeoffed junior houses long ago sung by Zhougong.

Ironically again, the rule that a person's mundane attachment is limited to five generations in either direction is the one to which least attention has been paid; yet it happens to be the rule that has been inveterately followed by successive imperial houses. This is perhaps the main reason for the lack of a large body of permanent nobility in China. Although our research has failed to find any legal statute formally promulgated at any time on this point, if we examine all biographical accounts of historical figures who are known to have sprung from imperial ancestry, we cannot but notice that if they were descendants of the sixth or a later generation of an emperor, they were always regarded by the ruling house, whose surname they still bore, just as common people, and treated no differently.[120] By and large, therefore, the principle prescribed, or rather implied, by the *Mourning Apparels* has become the unproclaimed law of the land: "By the sixth generation, the attachment relationship is exhausted." [121] And this has proved beneficial to China. For otherwise, with the ceaseless pursuit of absolutist rule by the imperial house on the one hand and the unchecked practice of concubinage by its privileged relations on the other, there would have been no end to the spawning of parasites at the country's expense. As it is, there was always a limit to the number of imperial kith and kin. Moreover, with the change of each dynasty, the entire set of old nobility would be displaced by the new. Thus, even though the history of China is much longer than that of any European nation, it never had a class of nobility that could boast of having lasted longer than one dynasty.[122] And conversely, the Chinese have never felt much fascination either for titles or for the titled. For each family, no matter how humble their present station, if they but searched back a little, would not fail to find if not an imperial ancestor at least a royal or ducal one; and as often as not, a black sheep at that.

More important, the blood relationship as detailed in the *Mourning Apparels* has formed a major basis for the provisions of legal codes proclaimed by various dynasties.[123] Ever since the 1st century B.C., astute monarchs seem to have been sensitive to the truth of a popular saying: "A loyal minister can be invariably found inside the gate that leads to a filially pious son." And by and by they have put this belief in concrete expressions. Not to mention anything else, from the 6th century A.D. down to the beginning of this 20th century, every legal code passed by the ruling dynasty would begin with a list of the so-called "Ten Cardinal Evils." Besides high treason and lese majesty, five out of the ten are related to offenses committed by a person against his own kith and kin "within the five apparels." [124] Of these, the foremost is titled "Lack of Filial Piety." A number of conditions are listed under this category, for which a man may be punished rather severely; and one of these is failure to provide for his parents or grandparents. In general, for crimes committed against one's own relations, the penalty is openly harsher than against persons unrelated; the closer the relation, the harsher the penalty. Moreover, for the same offense, if it is committed by a person of a lower generation "within the five apparels" against one of a higher generation, the penalty is appreciably increased; but if it is the other way around, the penalty is reduced. The entire purpose of these provisions is to make the people "within the five apparels" conscious of the fact that they all belong to one and the same bloodline, and they are considered by the government as one single social entity, to work harmoniously among themselves and to bear collective responsibility for their actions to the state.

And the dynasties did everything conceivable to further this end. If a member of the family attained a high rank in government service, his parents would automatically be awarded an honorable title; and if he advanced still higher, not only more honors would be piled on the parents, but new ones would be bestowed upon the grandparents. And if his services became even more valuable, his sons or grandsons would also be rewarded, less frequently with titles than with special privileges such as being permitted to join in the imperial guard or to enter the imperial academy without going through examinations.[125] And conversely, the dynasties also bent backward to show their favorable disposition toward this family system in dispensing justice. For instance, if a person has been sentenced to death for a crime which is not one of the Ten Cardinal Evils, and if his parents or grandparents are still living but badly needing support, and if no relation can be found within "the one-year-and-a-month mourning" bracket able to take care of them, the authorities concerned are directed to report the facts to the imperial court and ask for special dispensation.[126] But in the case of high treason, it is here that the dynasties revealed their iron hand inside the velvet glove. Not only those who are directly responsible are to be decapitated, but the fathers, and the sons above the age of sixteen, are to be hanged; the mothers, the wives, the daughters, the children below sixteen, the concubines, the grandparents, the grandchildren, the brothers, and the sisters are to be condemned to slavery; and even the uncles, the nephews, and their children are to be exiled beyond three thousand *li*.[127]

The interest the dynasties have taken in strengthening this kind of family system is therefore not without ulterior motive. But the Chinese people, of themselves, seem also to have pushed forward the system by their own exertions. To begin with, they evolved a vocabulary in their language giving different designations to every variation of blood relationships. When the "five apparels" were discussed in this work a few pages back, many a Western reader might well have felt confused about the jumble of "great-grand-" and "great-great-grand-." But to the Chinese, that is not a problem at all in their native tongue. For they have a name for each generation. A grandfather is *zufu*. A great-grandfather is *zengzufu*, "two-storied grandfather"; and a great-great-grandfather is *gaozufu*, "high grandfather." Nor do they have only different designations for relations of different generations; they have also separate names to distinguish an older brother from a younger brother, an older sister from a younger sister, an uncle or an aunt who is older than one's father from an uncle or an aunt who is younger, and so on and so forth. It is of interest to note that at the time Zhougong composed the *Mourning Apparels*, this kind of vocabulary might have been not yet fully developed. For in the book *Er Ya* (the earliest Chinese attempt at lexicography, whose authorship is also attributed to Zhougong[128]), there is a chapter giving these designations in full.[129] It almost seems as if Zhougong purposely put the chapter in there so that people could better understand his regulations about mourning apparels in *Yi Li*. And perhaps it is of even greater interest to observe that in addition to Zhougong's original set of designations, the Chinese have over the centuries developed another set for the same relationships. Not that they have elected to put Zhougong's set to disuse; but rather they have felt so much respect for the author of *Yi Li* that they do not wish to subject it to profanation. So a practice has evolved to reserve Zhougong's original appellations for serious and solemn usage such as are found in inscriptions on gravestones and on ancestral tablets or in veneration eulogies and requiems, and to keep the new names for daily ordinary use. Indeed, while the former may be said to be written testimonials to the creative part Zhougong contributed to the making of the Chinese family system, the latter bears unequivocal and articulate witness to the spontaneity and enthusiasm with which the Chinese people themselves have endorsed and sustained that heritage.

Thus it is along these lines that the Chinese family system developed through some thirty centuries, by and large following the principles laid down by Zhougong in *Yi Li* with the only exception of the one dividing a house into senior and junior houses. As a matter of fact, until the very beginning of the 20th century A.D. a typical Chinese family would be described as follows: It consists of three generations—an elderly couple living with their grown-up sons, and the sons' wives and children. If there is a daughter still not married at the time, she is also living with them. The sons and their wives are wedded "under the instructions of parents and through the pledges of go-betweens," [130] more or less in accordance with the ceremonies prescribed by Zhougong. And the women were always sought from families whose surnames are different from their own. For, from a time as far back as the Zhou,[131] the Chinese came upon a eugenic discovery: "When man and woman of the same surname are joined in wedlock, their offspring do not multiply or prosper." [132] As to the size of the family, it all depends on how long the aging father or mother lives. The entire society is pervaded by the spirit of filial piety. To every Chinese, as soon as he is of age, or even before that, his first concern is not to go out into the world and seek his own fortune, but to do whatever he can to help his father and brothers to enhance the family well-being. And when the father and mother grow old and feeble, it is again his bounden duty to take good care of them—to feed them, to clothe them, to minister to their every need—even as they had so taken care of him while he was still an infant or child. Thus for a son to leave the house without parental permission would be unthinkable; and as long as the father or the mother lives, the family stays together and grows. Sometimes a father or a mother lived so long that five generations were found living under one roof.[133] But more often, the parents died off before they could lay their eyes on their great-grandchildren.[134]

But some of the sons do leave home with their parents' blessing. Mostly, it is because they are engaged in trade or business which necessitates their journeying to distant places. And frequently, too, it may be because they have successfully passed through civil-service examinations and entered government service. These latter are considered the fortunate ones; and success such as theirs is what every family has been hoping for. In order to make this possible, the families who can afford the expenses hire private tutors for their children, while those who cannot still manage to send them to the less expensive clan-sponsored schools. But no matter where these sons may go, and however they may advance in the outside world, they always regard where their family dwells as their permanent home. And so long as their

parents live, they return periodically to pay them their respects; and whatever money they may have earned outside is treated by all as common
property. And in the event of the passing of either parent, even if the son
occupies a high and responsible position in government, unless he is explicitly excused from observing the "proprieties" by special dispensation of
the imperial court, he goes into temporary retirement, returns home, and
mourns through the whole period of mourning as prescribed in *Yi Li*.[135]

After the death of both parents, sometimes after the death of just the
father, the sons may by agreement dissolve the old family and set up new,
separate families. This of course entails a dividing of common properties into
shares. Each son is entitled to an equal share, with the oldest son usually
getting a slightly larger share, but seldom more than two shares, and the
unmarried daughter half a share.[136] But before they do this, usually they
donate a portion of the properties to the clan for use in its common interest.
Now, a clan is called *zu*, or *zongzu*. It automatically embraces all persons
who bear the same surname (that is, who are of the same bloodline) and live
within the same community as its members. It is run by a council consisting
of the heads of all these families and presided over by one of them, chosen by
consensus either for his seniority or for his prominence. And constituted as
such, the clan builds and manages the ancestral temple, arranges the veneration ceremonies, compiles and prints clan genealogical books,[137] administers
clan-owned properties, sponsors and supervises clan schools, mediates quarrels and arbitrates disputes among its members, provides succor and relief for
those who are in need, and sometimes goes outside the clan to distribute food
and clothing to the poor and destitute in the community.[138]

From the above, it may be seen that the Chinese concept of family is quite
different from the Western concept. Each Chinese family is not only for the
grown-ups to bring up the young, but also for the young, when grown up, to
take care of the old. And a clan is an association of those families bearing the
same surname, "within the five apparels" or even beyond, banded together
to promote their mutual interest and to look after their own needy and
helpless. A society composed of such families and clans may well be said to
have in its possession a built-in, workable social-security system. However,
the system may be suited only to an agricultural society—which China in
fact was, especially before the advent of the West. In the past century and a
half, she underwent a unique experience such as no other civilization as
ancient as hers had undergone before. With the abrupt impact of a new and
totally different culture that caught her unawares, accompanied and aggravated by her repeated discomfiture in confrontations with Western nations
that revealed more her weaknesses than her strengths, her family system,
like her other social and political institutions, was buffeted and pummeled
continuously by all kinds of hostile forces from within and without. More-

over, while the process of industrialization (though tardy in its first coming
to China, yet nonetheless inevitable and ever widening) has been ceaselessly
eroding the agrarian foundation of the system, wars and revolutions have
only too frequently uprooted millions and millions of China's sons and
daughters from their ancestral homes and cast them adrift in unfamiliar or
alien lands seeking independent fortunes or struggling for mere survival.
Thus the typical family that was has become typical no more. And for most
of the Chinese of this generation, even though they seem still to retain a
sense of obligatory filial piety as an integral part of their social consciousness
or subconsciousness, the term "within the five apparels" appears to be, if not
completely forgotten, at best only vaguely remembered and even more
vaguely understood. Under these changing conditions, this ancient "propriety" is bound to adjust itself as Confucius has long intimated, taking some
things away and adding some things new. But how this will turn out is
perhaps of more absorbing interest to a sociologist than to a historian.

· 7 ·
CEREMONIES NEGLECTED BUT NOT FORGOTTEN

There are two proprieties, or rather ceremonies (for this latter word
seems to be more appropriate in this instance), which Zhougong must
have taken great pains in composing, and from which he must have hoped
inestimable benefits would accrue to society; yet the actual effects fell far
short of his own expectations. These two ceremonies are the subjects of the
Yi Li documents *xiangyinjiuli, Communal Festivity,* and *xiangsheli, Communal Archery.*[139] From their titles, one might expect nothing of exceeding
importance. But when studied closely, these ceremonies reveal the loftiest
dream Zhougong might have cherished for humanity.

As has been noted repeatedly before, from the time of Yao and Shun on,
the Chinese people seemed to have been deeply imbued with the idea that
harmony should be the quintessence—the principle to live by, the goal to
work for—of every human organization, small or great, be it a family, a state,
or the very empire (which is what they thought was "all under heaven").
They had thus an innate aversion to conflict, an instinctive abhorrence for
war. That is why the two pacifists, Boyi and Shuqi, who vainly tried to stop
Wu Wang from marching against Yin and who afterward chose to die of
starvation rather than "eat any grain produced under Zhou rule" [140] have
been ever since so fondly yet so sadly remembered by the Chinese people,
not lost in the oblivion of some three thousand years in which countless men
who led far more eventful lives were buried and forgotten. Perhaps the
ancients owed this heritage to the tradition that originated with Yao and
Shun. There was no honor or position higher than that of the emperor. Yet,

for all that, Yao, seeking harmony in the state, gave it away to Shun with nothing more than a single salutation; and Shun gave it away in the same manner to Yu. *Yirang,* "Salute and give." [141] That is how they settled this matter of the utmost importance. And indeed, to respect an ideal and act unselfishly and pragmatically to achieve it is the only fitting and proper way for men to settle all matters among them. People in other places, or of other nations, may have had the same aversion to conflict or the same ideals about harmony; but they did not have the same tradition. To others, "salute and give" might well be an impossible dream; but to the Chinese ancients, *yirang* is reality. Yao and Shun practiced it before; why cannot others? That Yao's and Shun's circumstances were unique, that they both were a special kind of man—that is no matter. What is important is that the *yirang* of Yao and Shun is a historical fact.

Zhougong, however, had still another source of inspiration, more real, less remote, and truly personal: his own knowledge of what his granduncles Taibo and Zhongyong had done.[142] Especially what Taibo had done—Taibo, whom Confucius later would extol as the most outstanding example of "giving" (*rang*).[143] He not only gave away the dukedom of Zhou to his third brother, Zhougong's own grandfather, out of filial piety; but he also gave away the princedom of Wu to Zhongyong out of fraternal affection. He had a right to both; yet for what he thought was fitting and proper, he gave both away. If only all people could learn to follow the example of Taibo, conflict would be banished from mankind forever. But could they learn? And Zhougong was firmly convinced that they could—through education and practice, through active participation in memorable social conventions, and by setting up clear examples and patterns. Within the family, to inculcate the sense of filial piety; without, to inculcate the spirit of "giving"—these are the key to harmony for all men, and that is also the guiding principle that Zhougong held when he undertook to "institutionalize the proprieties." Here, therefore, a passage from *Zhou Li* which we already quoted once before is worth repeating:

> The department (*xiang*) administrations are to be used to teach the myriads of people three things. The interest of the people in these three things is to be aroused and enhanced by honoring those who have excelled in them as guests in ceremonies.
>
> The first is to teach man to cultivate six virtues—to augment his capacity to learn, to feel compassionate, to see ahead of events, to deal with all matters justly, to hold onto the Doctrine of the Mean, and to cherish a harmonious spirit that is neither too soft nor too hard.
>
> The second is to teach man to practice six types of behavior: to be filially pious, fraternally affectionate, congenial with his own bloodline as well as with his mother's and his wife's kith and kin, trustworthy to his friends, and generous to the poor and needy.

The third is to teach man to learn six arts: "proprieties" (*li*), music, archery, chariot-driving, books and numbers.[144]

We have already seen how Zhougong used the above as a basis for his "recommendation system" by which the worthy and the capable are selected for possible employment by the imperial court. Now we shall see how he proposed to use it as the method by which he hoped to inculcate in the people the sense of what is fitting and proper, and more especially, the spirit of "giving" (*rang*). As he explicitly stated that "the interest of the people in these three things is to be aroused and enhanced by honoring those who have excelled in them as guests in ceremonies," so he specifically formulated the ceremonies of communal festivity and communal archery with that object in view.

These ceremonies have been alluded to previously by Zhougong in the book *Zhou Li*. In our discussion on the "recommendation system," we have cited the following:[145]

> Ward supervisor (*dangzheng*, head of five hundred families). . . . At the end of the year, after a special ceremony is held for all deities and spirits, with a view to practicing proprieties he shall invite the people to drinks at the local school, where the whole assemblage will be ministered to strictly in accordance with seniority of age.

> District superintendent (*zhouzhang*, head of 2,500 families). . . . In Spring and Autumn, he shall invite the people to practice proprieties by asking them to join in an archery ceremony at the district school.

> Department Administrator (*xiangdafu*, head of 12,500 families). . . . In every three years, he shall hold a general review, examining all the people within the conscription-age bracket with respect to their moral character, intellectual accomplishments, and practical talents. He shall make a selection of men who are worthy and, also, of men who are capable. Then, along with the department senior adviser, he shall lead the officers of the department to entertain those worthy men and capable men in a ceremony and honor them as guests. . . .
> Upon his return (from presenting the Book of the Worthy and the Capable to the sovereign), the department administrator shall invite the people to join in a department communal archery, where he will inquire of them if they still know of some men (in addition to those already listed in the Book of the Worthy and the Capable) who have impressed them with accomplishments. . . .

Thus we can see that communal festivity and communal archery were ceremonies regularly practiced at different levels of local government, wherever the population was over five hundred families. Probably these were begun by Wen Wang, who used them to observe and study the character of men whom he wished to employ as officers. But it was Zhougong who refined them further for his own larger objectives. As *Yi Li* has it, the two ceremonies are closely linked to each other. In every archery ceremony, both preceding and following formal exercises of the sport, drink and food are to be served in accordance with the manners as prescribed for communal festivity. So there is no need to discuss them separately. Nor it is necessary for us to detail the ceremonies step by step. For our purpose it suffices to present the various aims Zhougong was apparently striving for through those ceremonies, and to describe how he hoped he could influence the people to join in his efforts to reach for them:

1. *Respect for Virtue.* In either ceremony, whether communal festivity or communal archery, the host is the head of the local government. Before holding the ceremony, his most important task is the selection of the guest of honor. For, though all the worthy and capable men under his jurisdiction will be invited as guests, along with elders over fifty years of age as well as government officers interested in the community, he has to single out one of the worthy men deserving of the greatest recognition as the guest of honor, and another man next to him in merit as the second guest of honor. In this matter, however, he is not to make the decisions alone. He must consult first with the so-called "earlier born" [146] in the area, which term comprises teachers of local schools as well as other government officers who have been living there in retirement.[147] Using the six virtues, six behaviors, and six arts as criteria, they will review the qualifications of all possible candidates and finally obtain a consensus. When the choices are made, the head of the local government, no matter how high his rank, will personally call upon the guest of honor, and next the second guest of honor, to extend to them the invitation. And when the ceremony is held, by previous arrangement the guest of honor, the second guest of honor, and all the other guests except government officers are to arrive together; but at every step of the many rituals that ensue, the guest of honor is to be honored first, the second guest of honor next, and then the other guests.

2. *Respect for Age.* As noted before, all elders over fifty are invited with the worthy and capable men to the communal festivity. Except for the guest of honor and the second guest of honor, and also for government administrators and officers either incumbent or retired, they are treated with all the honors due to them in the order of seniority. As is cited in a commentary:

> In the ceremony of communal festivity, the elders over sixty are supplied with seats, while those over fifty remain standing ready to minister to them or waiting for services—this is to show the difference in seniority. The elders over sixty are served with three containers of food each;[148] those over seventy, four containers; those over eighty, five; and those over ninety, six—this is to demonstrate the need of increasing tender care for the aged. It is only when people learn to respect their seniors and to care for the aged that they will be able to be filially pious and fraternally affectionate within their own households. When people are filially

pious and fraternally affectionate within, and also respectful of their seniors and willing to care for the aged without, then the aim of education is fulfilled and the tranquillity of the nation may be assured.[149]

3. *The "Giving" (rang) of the High for the Low.* To both ceremonies, incumbent administrators and officers who are in some way connected with the locality, or who are simply interested in its affairs, are as a rule invited. But if they attend either of the functions, they must not arrive at the appointed time the guest of honor, the second guest of honor, and the other guests were asked to come together. They must wait outside until the host has toasted by turns the guest of honor, the second guest of honor, and then the other guests collectively, before they make their entrance. Though the host, the guest of honor, and the other guests will all take a step forward to extend them welcome, they will not usurp the honors that are due to those guests, especially due to the guest of honor, on this occasion. Their claim to distinction is only given recognition in their seating. For they are provided with seats regardless of their age. For those of them who are lower-class officers, their seats are below the guest of honor, the second guest of honor, and all the other guests who are older than they are. For those who are middle-class officers, their seats are below those who are their paternal relations and also older. As to those who are upper-class officers or administrators, they are seated not with the other guests on the right side of the guest of honor, but on his left. But from there on the ceremony will proceed with them as simple participants, the center of attention being still the guest of honor, and next the second guest of honor.

In the case of communal archery, the "giving" of the high for the low is even more sharply drawn. Unlike communal festivity, there is only a guest of honor and not a second guest of honor. And in the exercising of the sport, all participants are divided at the behest of a master of ceremonies into pairs, with one of the pair called the "high archer" and the other the "low archer." Even though an upper-class administrator is present, who may outrank the host himself, he is not to be included in the first pair to ascend to the archery platform to try his skill with the sport. That position is reserved for the guest of honor and the host, with the former designated as the high archer and the latter as the low archer. The upper-class administrator, however, is given a place in the second pair, but only that of the low archer, as against a commoner who will act as his high archer. And the same procedure is followed with other officers.

4. *The "Giving" (rang) of the Winner for the Loser.* According to the rituals, all the high archers form one team and all the low archers form another. Each archer is given a bow and four arrows; and at every turn, the high archer shoots before the low archer. Whenever a shot hits the target, it

scores one point for the side of the archer who shot it. After all have finished shooting, then the scores are counted, and the master of ceremonies will announce which team has won. But it is not the winners who will be served with drinks, but the losers, as a token of encouragement to urge them on to greater efforts the next time.

5. *Advancement Through Self-Improvement.* The lesson that Zhougong tried to inculcate through these ceremonies is simple and direct. Men are born with competitive spirit; that is a human condition taken for granted. It is to be promoted because it is mainly through competition that one may expect to improve oneself. Yet man should not be encouraged to develop the spirit in such a way as to incline himself to compete only for personal aggrandizement. Thus as Zhougong would have it in the communal archery ceremony, there is no individual championship recognized, only team victory. Moreover, even the team formation is not of any sort of permanent nature. One who plays a part in the high archer's team at this turn may play a part in the low archer's at the next. So neither personal jealousy nor team rivalry is given a chance to grow. In short, Zhougong sought to discourage men from contending against one another just for the sake of contending. As explained by Confucius later:

> A man of culture should not contend for anything. If he must, it should be as it is in the archery ceremony. He salutes and courtesies to his competitor as he ascends the platform to shoot at the target. And if he loses, he descends and drinks his wine. This is the way to contend that befits a man of culture.[150]

But this does not mean that a man should not seek self-improvement through competition. On the contrary, it is very much desired. Explained Confucius again:

> In archery there is something resembling the way of a man of culture. When the archer misses the mark, he turns around and seeks the cause for his failure in himself.[151]

6. *Moderation Through Self-Discipline.* There is still another lesson Zhougong aimed to teach through these ceremonies. Human passions and desires being what they are, it would be calamitous to let them move freely without rein; yet it is equally impossible to keep them perpetually under tight control. Thus a commentary expatiates, comparing the matter to the stretching of a bow:

> To keep it stretched taut and not ever to let it loose, that is what neither Wen Wang nor Wu Wang could do. But to keep it loose and not stretched at all, that is also what neither Wen Wang nor Wu Wang would do. To stretch it and then

to loosen it; and to stretch it and then loosen it again—that is the way both Wen Wang and Wu Wang pursued.[152]

And in composing the ceremonies, Zhougong may well have recalled the advice Emperor Shun had once given to Yu:

> The heart of a man is ever so dangerous,
> The core of Truth is ever so small.
> Be refined in method; be undivided in purpose;
> Hold on always to the very center of the core.[153]

Apparently Zhougong formulated the rituals of communal festivity and communal archery on the basis of those principles. The people are given occasions not only to demonstrate their respect for virtue and for age, but also to enjoy themselves. Not only food and wine are served for their entertainment, but the sport of archery is exercised to provide a vent for their competitive ardor. However, Zhougong also thought fit to put the ceremonies to another use—to let the people learn to practice moderation through self-discipline, especially in the matter of drinking. As is expounded in a commentary:

> Spirits are not made to cause trouble for men. But when spirits are consumed without restraint, they have given rise to many quarrels and much trouble. Because of this, ancient rulers have devised the ceremonies for drinking. For one toast, the host and the guest have to salute and bow to each other numerous times. Thus even if the drinking continues for a whole day, none will be the worse for it.[154]

So Zhougong contrived to put all these meanings into the two ceremonies. And what effects have they had on posterity? For one thing, they did not last very long. While many of the regulations prescribed for the marriage ceremony and for mourning apparels were still religiously observed as recently as the beginning of this century, the ceremonies of communal festivity and communal archery fell completely into disuse long, long ago. Of course, they were practiced in the early Zhou dynasty. But by the time of Confucius, only some six centuries after Zhougong, popular enthusiasm for them had evidently waned so much that the Great Sage seems to have deemed it necessary to revive public interest in them by staging a communal archery ceremony himself with the help of his disciples.[155] But if this bore fruit at all, it was predestined not to endure. For China entered into the period of the Warring States shortly after. As weeds of violence grew rampant, so ceremonies bearing blossoms of harmony and "giving" were smothered out of existence. It was not until the establishment of the Later Han in the 1st century A.D. that a feeble effort was undertaken to resurrect the ceremonies.[156] But after that dynasty came to an end two centuries later, no further attempt was made to continue the practice.[157]

Notwithstanding, such ideals as envisaged by Zhougong in those ceremonies have never been completely forgotten. So long as the study of the Confucian Classics was considered to be the *sine qua non* in a Chinese scholar's training, and the mastery of them the key to advancement in government service, those ideas must have served as a source of inspiration for countless young men over tens of centuries, giving them a vision of a better society which, though they may have realized it is different from the real one they knew, they may nonetheless still have wished of themselves to obtain for the world to come.

But the study of the Confucian Classics has been officially discontinued since 1905. Beset by a new set of values in the current modern world, where progress is preferred to harmony, and self-assertion to self-abnegation, it is quite possible that this idea of "giving" *(rang)* may be one of the very first concepts of the ancient Chinese heritage doomed to extinction.

· 8 ·

IDEALISM AND REALITY

Perhaps the goal Zhougong aimed at is too high, and the instruments he designed to reach for it are not equal to the task. Perhaps he had too much faith in the goodness of man from the very outset and so his expectations were bound to be disappointed in the end. Indeed, in this respect, he seems to have made a similar miscalculation in another instance. This is the so-called *Code of Posthumous Titles,*[158] which he composed jointly with Taigong probably after the victory over Yin but before he began to "institutionalize the proprieties." Even at that early date he appears to have been directing his thoughts to the question of how to lead the world to harmony. His circumstances being what they were, they must have inclined him to think that the development of a society is vastly dependent upon the personal example of its rulers. For right before his own eyes stood two clear examples—the Yin emperor Zou and his own father, Wen Wang. As the former had abandoned himself to intoxication and to oppression, so the Yin people were given to drink and to corruption. And as the latter was bent on improving himself in learning and in virtue, so the population of the West Land became likewise transformed in his mold. But there is the rub. Now that his own house had founded a new dynasty, how could he be certain that there would not be another dissolute, worthless man like Zou born to succeed to the throne sooner or later? To be sure, he had personally witnessed, and indeed experienced, how Wen Wang had brought up his sons, especially the heir apparent his own brother Wu Wang.[159] And he knew too that, given the opportunity, he would see to it himself that Wu Wang's son and heir would be well taught to qualify for the succession. Yet what assurances could he have from the unknown generations to come? Zhougong must have worried over the matter no end; but study of Shang history suggested a new approach.

The Shang had singled out some of their most distinguished forebears for special honorable titles after their deaths. Thus Tang came to be venerated as the High Progenitor *(gaozu)*, Taijia as the Grand Ancestor *(taizong)*, Zuyi as the Middle Ancestor *(zhongzong)*, and Wuding as the High Ancestor *(gaozong)*. And after the overthrow of the Shang, Wu Wang, more or less following these precedents, had invested his own forebears with imperial titles. He consecrated his great-grandfather the Ancient Duke as Tai Wang, "Grand Emperor," and his grandfather Duke Ji as Wang Ji, "Emperor Ji." But when he came to his father, he had difficulty in finding a suitable title that would do justice to the many virtues of the real founder of the Zhou empire. Finally, after much consultation with his advisers, especially with Zhougong and Taigong, he settled on the title Wen Wang, "Cultural Emperor."

Now, Zhougong pondered, in the case of good rulers who rendered invaluable service to humanity, it was fitting and proper that posthumous tribute should be paid to them through titles. But conversely, in the case of bad rulers who had done disservice to humanity, would it not be fitting and proper to express to them posthumous censure? And believing as all the people at the time believed that men's spirits would continue to exist after death, Zhougong thought that if a system of posthumous tribute and censure should be devised, it would help encourage future rulers to do good and discourage them from doing evil. Thus, in conjunction with Taigong, he composed a *Code of Posthumous Titles,* defining what words should be used to depict what kinds of deeds. And so at the death of Wu Wang, they consecrated him as such, not only because he had been so called when alive, but because *wu* is defined in the code as "selflessly straightforward," "virtuously triumphant," and "able to bring order out of chaos." And after setting this example, Zhougong apparently intended that the system would be fully put to use by posterity.

It was—but with a sorry twist. For some ten generations following Cheng Wang, Zhougong's intentions may be said to have been faithfully carried out, as there are in fact three emperors on whom posthumous titles far from complimentary were conferred.[160] But after the Zhou were forced to move their capital eastward, the more their fortunes declined, the more they sought to make up for their rulers' lackluster reigns by dignifying them with glorious titles after their deaths. Then came the First Emperor of Qin, who declared, "To confer posthumous titles upon deceased emperors is to permit sons to criticize their fathers, and subjects to criticize their sovereigns." And he abolished the system altogether.[161] But no sooner had he passed away than his dynasty was replaced by the Han and the system was restored. And from there on the same practice was continued by every succeeding dynasty until the very end of the last one in A.D. 1911. Outwardly, they have all adhered to the principles of Zhougong's code. But as a matter of fact, there is one significant difference. All posthumous titles conferred by every one of those dynasties were designed not to convey any sense of censure but to gratify the vanity of the members of the ruling house, both dead and alive.[162]

Thus we see how the high purposes of Zhougong's schemes came to be distracted by the very weaknesses of human nature which he had essayed to correct and transform. Notwithstanding, the Chinese people have continually sung praises of those ideals in which he and the other ancient sages put their faith, and to which Confucius gave this summary expression:

> When the Great Way prevails, all the people under heaven are dedicated to public well-being. The worthy are selected for high offices, and the capable are assigned to fitting positions. Integrity is cultivated, and harmony developed. Men, therefore, do not love only their own parents; nor do they cherish only their own children. The aged are nurtured to the end of their lives, the adults are given useful employment, and the young are enabled to grow up in suitable conditions. And the orphaned, the widowed, the childless, the disabled, and the diseased are all cared for. Each man will have his share, each woman her home.
>
> Everyone will work to bring more abundance to all, not to himself alone, hating to see any resources left on the ground and not fully utilized. Each individual, if he has not exerted his utmost to that end, will feel ashamed of himself, even though the exertions may not be for his own benefit. Thus there is no room for scheming, for conspiracy; no pilfering, no thieving, no disorders, no violence. There is no need for any house to close its outer doors at any time.
>
> Such a state is called the state of the Great Commonwealth.[163]

Needless to say, China has never attained to conditions approaching such a state. Perhaps it is simply not within the realm of human capacity to realize so perfect a fulfillment. Yet, as is attested by history, after the passing of Zhougong, while his teaching and influence were still fresh and vigorous in men's minds, "for some forty years during the reigns of Cheng Wang and Kang Wang, though the penal codes were all in force, none of them were used because no occasion had arisen to require the use of any of them." [164]

NOTES

1. The following is a more or less literal translation of the original reply, which actually consists of two separate epistles. For the complete Chinese text, see Xiao Yishan, *Qingdai Tongshi*, II, pp. 815–820.

2. The reader may recall the theme of the *Hounds of Lu*, see above, pp. 313–14.

3. Some translators have translated the Chinese term as "European nations."

4. About 1535 A.D., the Ming dynasty granted the Portuguese a request to rent some land in Macao for trading purposes. Ever since then, Portuguese traders as well as those of other European nations were allowed to reside in Macao and establish what the Chinese called *yanghang*. At the same time, the term *yanghang* was also applied to Chinese business firms that were specially licensed to deal with foreign traders. Later, foreign ships were also allowed to touch at the port of Canton, but no foreigners were allowed to reside there. This was of course changed after China was defeated by Britain in the so-called Opium War and the Treaty of Nanking was concluded in 1842.

5. See above, p. 292.

6. In this connection, it may be of interest to take note of what a scholarly and judicious American sinologue has written about China (Kenneth Scott Latourette, *The Chinese: Their History and Culture*, p. 247): "In the latter part of the seventeenth and through most of the eighteenth century, indeed, it [China] was the most populous and possibly the most prosperous realm on the planet. In numbers of people it outstripped all the other great contemporary empires—the British, the Spanish, the French, the Russian, the Ottoman, and the Mogul. From the standpoint of order and justice it was probably as far advanced as any state of the time, for that was before the humanitarian movement had ameliorated the laws, the courts, and the prisons of the West. In total wealth, too, it very possibly surpassed every other nation of the period."

7. *Confucian Analects, yanyuan.*

8. *Mencius, lilou,* II.

9. These three places are not identifiable. We know however that Shun died in Jiuyi (see above, p. 101). Could Jiuyi be also called Mingtiao? We do not know.

10. *Yi* is the big barbarian with a bow. See above, p. 108. Here *yi* may mean Yi Zone (see diagram, p. 387). It is conceivable that there might have been an ancient usage dividing the zones into east and west sections.

11. *Qizhou* means "Zhou by Mount Qi"; and *biying* is Bi.

12. It may be of interest, however, to note that after many changes through three millennia, the last dynasty of China, Qing (Manchu), again divided the imperial court into six ministries, whose functions were more or less like those stated in *Zhou Li*. See *Qing Shigao, zhiguanzhi,* I.

13. See above, p. 252.

14. See *Zhou Li, qiuguansikou: chaodafu.*

15. The two *bi* are different characters. The character for *zhou* here is also different from that for the name of the dynasty.

16. For the urban divisions see *Zhou Li, diguansitu: dasitu*; for the rural divisions, see ibid., *suiren.*

17. See *Hujifa Shixingxize*, published by the Nationalist Government, June 21, 1936. In that document, the ten-household unit is called *jia*, and the ten-*jia* unit is called *bao*. But in Taiwan, for local reasons, they are called *lin* and *li* respectively.

18. *Zhou Li, diguansitu: dasitu.*

19. Ibid., *bizhang*. From experience the author knows that this is a most effective and efficient system for taking census.

20. Ibid., *xiaositu.*

21. The Chinese wording is *qiangqinruo, zhongbaogua*. See *Historical Records, qinshihuangdi benji, taishigong's* comments.

22. *Historical Records, qinshihuangdi benji.*

23. *Mencius* and *Xunzi* are examples.

24. *Historical Records, qinshihuangdi benji.*

25. *Historical Records, hangaozu benji.*

26. Ibid., *lujia liezhuan.*

27. Ban Gu, *Qian Han Shu, wudiji*. The imperial decree announcing the establishment of *wujing boshi*, "Five Classics doctors," was issued in 136 B.C.

28. *Da Xue (Great Learning)*, chap. 10. It may be of interest to the reader to know that *Great Learning* was originally not a separate book, but a chapter of *Li Ji.*

29. *Book of History, kanggao.*

30. *Book of Poetry, daya: wenwang.*

31. *Da Xue*, chap. 10.

32. Ibid.

33. *Confucian Analects, yanyuan.*

34. *Mencius, lilou,* II.

35. *Zhong Yong (Doctrine of the Mean)*, chap. 13. Originally, this book was also a chapter of *Li Ji*, like *Da Xue (Great Learning)*.

36. *Confucian Analects, xue'er.*

37. In the Ming dynasty, the gate leading to the hall was called *taihemeng*, "Gate of Great Harmony."

38. *Confucian Analects, weizheng.*

39. See above, p. 377.

40. *Li Ji, yueji.*

41. *Historical Records, taishigongzixu.*

42. Prominent examples are Shang Yang and Han Fei. See Bibliography.

43. See *Zhou Li, qiuguansikou: dasikou, xiaosikou, shishi, suishi, xiangshi, fangshi, yashi,* and *sixing.*

44. Ibid.

45. Ibid., *sixing.*

46. Ibid., *dasikou.*

47. Ibid., *diguansitu: dasitu.*

48. Ibid., *qiuguansikou: dasikou.*

49. Ibid., *diguansitu: tiaoren.*

50. A *jin* is said to be equivalent to sixteen ounces.

51. *Zhou Li, diguansitu: dasitu.*

52. Ibid.

53. Ibid., *bizhang.*

54. This is the rock on which the offenders are pilloried. *Shi* means "rock," and *jia* means "good" or "auspicious," from which two idiomatic terms are derived: *jiahui,* meaning "to benefit," and *jia-mian,* "to urge people to greater efforts with encouragement."

55. *Zhou Li, diguansitu: sijiu.*

56. Ibid., *qiuguansikou: dasikou.*

57. Ibid.

58. Ibid., *sihuan.*

59. *Zhou Li, diguansitu: dasitu.*

60. The original Chinese is too terse to translate literally. Here the translation is based on Zheng Kangcheng's commentaries.

61. *Zhou Li, diguansitu: luxu.*

62. Ibid., *zushi.*

63. The translation here is not literal, but based on commentaries of Zheng Kangcheng and others. The officer who has received the first Order of Honor is lower-class officer; the second order, middle-class officer; and the third order, upper-class officer.

64. *Zhou Li, diguansitu: dangzheng.*

65. Ibid., *zhouzhang.*

66. Ibid., *diguansitu.* It is here stipulated that for every two departments there is a *xianglao,* "senior adviser," or literally, "department elder." The position is usually filled by one of the *sangong,* or by a retired minister.

67. Ibid., *diguanzongbo. Neishi* is the chief secretary or scribe in the imperial household.

68. Ibid., *diguansitu: xiangdafu.*

69. See above, pp. 411–12.

70. *Book of History, gaoyaomo.*

71. *Book of History, yaodian.* Also see above, pp. 70–71.

72. Ibid. Also see above, p. 70.

73. This is a translation of a Chinese term which consists of four characters, *xian liang fang zheng.*

74. See above, p. 74.

75. See above, chart p. 64; also p. 233.

76. See above, p. 240.

77. See above, p. 279, note 2. Besides ten sons by Taishi, Wen Wang was known to have fathered eight or nine other sons. Wen Wang was supposed to have lived close to a hundred years. Since we do not know when Taishi died, it is possible that Wen Wang remarried after her death.

78. *Zuozhuan,* Duke Xi, 24th year.

79. Ibid. Here *Zuozhuan* mentions, besides the Marquis of Lu, six princes by the names of their investitures, not by their given names. We know, however, that Jun Chen was one of Zhougong's sons (see above, p. 370); but we do not know whether *Zuozhuan* included Jun Chen among the six or not.

80. See *Zhou Li, xiaguansima: zhifangshi.* The same may be found as a chapter in *Yi Zhou Shu,* except for a very minor difference (see the note following).

81. The *Yi Zhou Shu* version has the ratio of two men to three women in Qingzhou.

82. *Zhou Li, diguansitu: meishi.*

83. See *Zhou Li, tianguanzhongzai: shanfu, paoren, jiuzheng, waifu;* and *chunguanzongbo: dianlu,* etc.

84. The Chinese characters used here are *nugong.* According to some commentators, *gong* signifies *gong* penalty, that is, sentenced to labor in the palace.

85. In describing most offices, *Zhou Li* gives the number of officers for each office as well as their respective ranks. But the book gives no number at all about those "women officers." The exception is generation matrons. They are described—uniquely for the book—in two places, one under the office of the premier, the other under the minister of the imperial household. In the latter description, number and rank are given.

86. *Zhou Li, tianguanzhongzai: nuyu.*

87. Ibid., *shifu,* and *chunguanzongbo: shifu.*

88. Ibid., *tianguanzhongzai: jiupin.*

89. In *Li Ji, hunyi,* it is stated: "In ancient times, the emperor and empress established six palaces in which there were three *furen* (dames), nine *pin* (lady friends), twenty-seven *shifu* (generation matrons), and eighty-one *yuqi* (attendant wives)." One can imagine that a monarch like the last emperor of Yin could have well pursued this scheme to gratify his carnal appetite. If this was so, then Zhougong may be said to have made an attempt to reduce the number of such concubinage in *Zhou Li.*

90. See *Book of History, wuyi,* in which the duke counseled his nephew to think of the toils of husbandmen and not to indulge in idleness and indolence. The whole tenor of the advice, to this author, was to warn Cheng Wang of the possible danger of having his life shortened by such indulgence. See above, pp. 183 and 217.

91. Twenty is the age for the "capping ceremony" for males. And for females, see *Li Ji, neize.*

92. See *Mencius, tengwengong,* II.

93. See *Book of Poetry, zhounan: guanju.*

94. Hu Peihui, *Yi Li Zhengyi, shihunli,* commentaries.

95. *Zhou Li, diguansitu: meishi.* Also see above, p. 421.

96. *Li Ji, hunyi.*

97. Hu Peihui, *Yi Li Zhengyi, shihunli,* commentaries.

98. *Yi Li, shihunli.*

99. There is one goose for each of the six parts of the ceremony. But in the first part, that is, "declaration offering," after the go-between has made the offering and left the house, the bride's father returns the goose to him through an intermediary, signifying that he has agreed only to consider the proposal, not to accept it as yet. So this goose may be used again.

100. *Zhou Li, diguansitu: meishi,* commentaries.

101. *Li Ji, jiaotesheng.*

102. *Mencius, tengwengong,* II.

103. The one instance well known to the West is the forced abdication of the original empress of Tang Gaozong in favor of the notorious Empress Wu in 655 A.D.

104. *Confucian Analects, weizheng.*

105. *Li Ji, aigongwen.*

106. *Li Ji, jingjie.* The Chinese character *ku* means all these three things, and perhaps more.

107. *Book of History, yaodian.* See above. p. 96.

108. *Mencius, wanzhang*, I. See above, pp. 106 and 116.

109. See above, pp. 201–2. Also *Book of History, wuyi.*

110. *Mencius, tengwengong*, I.

111. *Li Ji, sangfu xiaoji* and *dazhuan.*

112. Ibid. Also see Cheng Yaotian, *Zongfa Xiaoji.*

113. *Li Ji, mingtangwei* and *jitong.*

114. *Book of Poetry, xiaoya: changdi.* Also see *Zuozhuan*, Duke Xi, 24th year.

115. *Li Ji, sangfu xiaoji.*

116. Counting upward, there are oneself, father, grandfather, great-grandfather, and great-great-grandfather, five generations in all. Downward, there are oneself, son, grandson, great-grandson, great-great-grandson, also five generations in all.

117. See Hu Peihui, *Yi Li Zhengyi.*

118. These ceremonies (see above, p. 392) are (12) death of a parent, (13) burial, (15) seasonal veneration of ancestral spirits, and (17) rites after the formal veneration.

119. The notable exceptions are the Yuan (Mongol) and Qing (Manchu) dynasties. The Mongols and the Manchus, in the matter of succession, followed their own tradition acquired while they were still nomads.

120. For notable examples, see Fan Ye, *Hou Han Shu, guangwudiji*; and Chen Shou, *Shanguozhi, shushu, xianzhubei.*

121. *Li Ji, dazhuan*; also *wenwangshizi.*

122. The exceptions are descendants of Confucius and some of his disciples, all of whom have been honored by various dynasties with titles. But the Chinese do not regard them as "nobles" in the European sense.

123. See Dai Yanhui, *Zhongguo Fazhishi*, pp. 25–28.

124. The legal code of Tang is generally hailed as the model for those of later dynasties, so we use it here to illustrate our points.

125. This is called *yin*, meaning "shade" or "shelter." It implies that a man has done so much that he resembles a big tree casting its shade, or offering shelter, for others' benefit.

126. *Tang Code, minglilu*, Article 26.

127. Ibid., *zeidaolu*, Article 1.

128. See above, p. 375.

129. *Er Ya*, chap. IV, *shiqin.*

130. *Mencius, tengwengong*, II.

131. *Li Ji, dazhuan.*

132. *Zuozhuan*, Duke Xi, 23rd year.

133. See *Ci Hai*, 1969 edition, *wushitongju.* A few instances are given here.

134. No modern statistics can be found on this matter. But in Zheng Qiao's *Tongzhi*, vol. 59, it is stated that "at the time of Dezong (780–804 A.D.) . . . in general, a house sometimes supports one hundred mouths, and sometimes ten mouths. On the average, there are no less than twenty persons for each house."

135. The mourning period for the father is two years and a month; that for the mother, if she dies after the father, is the same; but if she dies before the father, out of respect for the still-living father as the head of the house, the mourning period for her is one year and a month.

136. Daughters are usually married off with dowries around the age of twenty. So in a typical family there is, as a rule, no unmarried daughter. For legal rules regarding division of property, see Dai Yan-

hui, *Zhongguo Fazhishi*, pp. 216–19.

137. This is called *zongpu* or *zupu.*

138. See Dai Yanhui, *Zhongguo Fazhishi*, pp. 190–98.

139. The *xiang* used here literally means "department," a Zhou regional denomination. See above, p. 401. However, the ceremonies were performed also at the *zhou*, "district," and *dang*, "ward," levels. See above, pp. 415–16.

140. See above, pp. 283–84. On this point, the author in his research has diligently looked for a similar story in ancient histories of other peoples; but so far his effort has not been rewarded.

141. *Rang*, like *li*, is one of the most difficult Chinese words to render into another language. It is translated here as "give," somewhat like the "give" in the sentence "The shoe gives," or in another, "Please, give in a little." It is also interesting to note that Chinese scholars of old were fond of coupling the words *li* and *rang* together, such as *lirang weiguo*, "to govern a country with the sense of propriety and the spirit of giving."

142. See above, pp. 240–41.

143. *Confucian Analects, taibo.*

144. *Zhou Li, diguansitu: dasitu.* Also see above, p. 414.

145. See above, pp. 415–16.

146. The Chinese term is *xiansheng*, somewhat corresponding to the contemporary American term "senior citizen." In modern Chinese usage, *xiansheng* means either "mister" or "teacher."

147. See Zheng Kangcheng's commentaries on *Yi Li, xiangyinjiuli.* According to Zheng, the retirement age for Zhou officers was seventy. If they wished, they would serve in local schools as teachers, the retired *dafu* to be known as senior teacher and the retired *shi* as junior teacher.

148. The Chinese word is *dou*, a sort of covered container.

149. *Li Ji, xiangyinjiu yi.* In communal festivity, the selection of a second guest of honor is a must; but in communal archery, it is not.

150. *Confucian Analects, bayi.*

151. *Zhong Yong (Doctrine of the Mean).*

152. *Li Ji, zaji*, II.

153. *Book of History, dayumo.*

154. *Li Ji, yueji.*

155. See ibid., *sheyi.*

156. *Hou Han Shu, liyi*, I.

157. See Hu Peihui, *Yili Zhengyi*, commentaries on *Yi Li, xiangyinjiuli.*

158. *Yi Zhou Shu, shifa.* Sometimes the code is published as an appendix to Sima Qian's *Historical Records.*

159. *Li Ji, wenwangshizi.*

160. The three are Yi Wang (894–879 B.C.), *yi* signifying "government by slaughter"; Li Wang (878–828 B.C.), *li* signifying "killing the innocent"; and You Wang (781–771 B.C.), *you* signifying "blocked up without communication."

161. *Historical Records, qinshihuangdi benji.*

162. The Zhou enfeoffed states also used the system to confer posthumous titles on their deceased princes. Later on, the dynasties also conferred posthumous titles on their high officials as a sort of reward rather than censure.

163. *Li Ji, liyuan.*

164. *Historical Records, zhou benji.*

ON THE USABILITY
OF ANCIENT CHINESE
WRITINGS AS
SOURCES FOR
HISTORY

Many contemporary sinologues, both Western and Chinese, are skeptical of the authenticity of ancient Chinese writings. They maintain that a large number of these, especially the ones ascribed to remote antiquity, were actually composed, or even fabricated, at much later dates, and therefore should not be used by critical scholars as sources for history, as Chinese traditional historians had done in the past.[1] This book has not followed the traditional interpretation of these writings in many places, but has nonetheless used them as reliable sources. In order to explain the reasons for this approach, it is necessary first to discuss how these ancient writings originated, how they were transmitted through successive ages, and how they have finally arrived at their present forms.

As described above in Chapter I, Section 7, the recorded history of China began with *pudie*, "lineal tablets," and *dieji*, "tablet records." The former gave the genealogical descent of her ancient rulers; and the latter, a sort of desultory chronological narration of their doings. Both of these were recorded by the *shi* (scribes or official historians) of the ruling houses, kept by them in sacrosanct files, and passed on from generation to generation. In time, as written language advanced further, important pronouncements of rulers came to be preserved too, in the form of special documents.

Naturally, interest in these documents was wider. As they increased in number, they were separated from *pudie* and *dieji* and placed in more profane archives. Conceivably, it was from such materials that the long lost collections known as "Three Tombs, Five Canons, Eight Cords, and Nine Mounds" were formed.

Traditionally, the Chinese have believed that Confucius was the first man to disseminate such knowledge to the general public as he was able to gather from those ancient archives. From *pudie* and *dieji,* he gave the earliest account of the Five Premier Emperors in his two discourses, *wudide* and *dixing*. And from among the documents, he selected some one hundred pieces and compiled them together into what has been known as the *Book of History*. And it is mainly based on these sources, and also on a reexamination of *pudie* and *dieji,* which were still kept intact in the Han dynasty, that Sima Qian wrote the first few chapters of his famed *Historical Records*.

However, contemporary scholars have expressed doubts about Confucius being the man solely responsible for such transmittals. But from all the records we have today, there is no denying that Confucius appeared to be the only one who had both the ability and the opportunity and also the desire and the determination to do so. Laozi (Lao Tzu) may have had equal ability and opportunity, but certainly he cannot be accredited with either the desire or the determination. In any event, over centuries, not a single scholar, Chinese or non-Chinese, has been able to suggest any other person, or even one name, who could have taken the place of Confucius for what he had done.

This point, however, is not important. What is much more important is to realize the arduous and cumbersome nature of the process by which these ancient writings were transmitted to posterity, or rather, the only process by which they could have ever been transmitted. These documents spanned over some fifteen centuries, the last one predating Confucius by a century and a half. The Chinese written language, an ever-increasing aggregate of multiformed ideograms, was, and still is, complexity itself. And in the early stages of its development, changes in construction, in pronunciation, and in style of writing or carving must have been even more rapid and frequent. That these documents could have been comprehensible at all to later ages must have been due to the fact that they were orally transmitted, side by side with the inscribed tablets, by the *shi* from one generation to another. There is evidence that Confucius could read the ancient writings in the original.[2] Presumably, it is only after he had mastered that craft that he was able to translate them from the archaic language in which they were written into the one in use in his own day so as to make them understandable to the public.

Then, for those who wanted to keep the knowledge of such documents as part of their learning, there seemed to be only two ways possible. One was to commit them to memory; the other, to copy them, that is, to carve them word for word on bamboo strips or wooden blocks. Both are liable to error. Moreover, rigid discipline cannot be expected from all and sundry. In copying, each copier, affected by his own background or predilections, or just for expedience or convenience, might well choose to alter a few words, add some, or omit others in the text.

And as the documents became more popular, later-generation copiers, copying from copies, seldom had the chance to check with the originals. Thus, conceivably, further alterations, additions, and omissions were interpolated, either wittingly or unwittingly.

Then, alongside the documents, there were commentaries made, or said to have been made, by Confucius or his immediate disciples. As these were quite helpful to the understanding of the texts, they too were copied and went through the same transmission process.

And the process went on for some two centuries and a half, roughly from Confucius's death at 479 B.C. to the burning of books by the First Emperor of Qin at 213 B.C.

Thus, judging by the very nature of the process, even had all those copies prior to the 3rd century B.C. been preserved intact today, probably we would still have had endless controversies over whether any of those documents, or some passages or some words in them, were correctly translated, or correctly copied. But, as it is, the "Fires of Qin" occurred, and all or almost all of the early copies were lost, including Confucius's original translations.

As explained in Chapter I, Section 7, there were two batches of documents found later at different times. The discovery and dissemination of these two batches may serve well to illustrate the complex and hazardous nature of the process we have just outlined above. Writing about the first batch, Ban Gu wrote in *Qian Han Shu, rulin liezhuan,* as follows:

> Fu Sheng, a native of Jinan, served the Qin as a *boshi* (court-appointed doctor of philosophy). During Xiaowen's reign (179–157 B.C.), searches were made for men versed in *Shangshu* ("Ancient Writings"), but throughout the empire none was found. Then Fu Sheng was reported to be such a man. The emperor wanted to summon him to court. But Fu Sheng was already over ninety years of age, too old to travel. So order was issued to the *taichang,* minister of ceremonies, to direct Chao Cuo, an officer in charge of antiquities *(zhanggu),* to proceed to where Fu Sheng was and learn from him.
>
> When the Qin banned the "Ancient Writings," [3] Fu Sheng had them hidden inside a wall. After the outbreak of the civil war, he had to flee from home. With the restoration of peace under the Han, Fu Sheng returned and found that several tens of the documents were lost. Only twenty-nine of them were left.

About the second batch, the same historian wrote in *Qian Han Shu, yi-wenzhi:*

Guwen Shangshu ("Ancient-Language Ancient Writings") were discovered from inside Confucius's walls. Toward the close of the reign of Wudi (140–87 B.C.),[4] Prince Gong of Lu wished to demolish Confucius's former residence to enlarge his own palace. (In wrecking the walls), he found tens of volumes such as *Guwen Shangshu, Li Ji, Lunyu,* and *Xiao Jing,* all written in ancient characters. . . .

Kong Anguo, a descendant of Confucius, gained possession of all of them. Comparing the *shangshu* with the twenty-nine documents (already transmitted by Fu Sheng), he had sixteen more documents. Anguo presented them to the court. But because of the unrest of the time, they were not included in the teachings of court-appointed educators.

And Ban Gu explained further in *Qian Han Shu, rulin liezhuan,* "Kong Anguo used modern language to interpret *Guwen Shangshu.*" For this reason, the Chinese have ever since called the first-batch documents *Jinwen Shangshu* ("Modern-Language Ancient Writings") because they were transmitted by Fu Sheng in the language already in use by the Han at the time, and the second-batch documents *Guwen Shangshu* ("Ancient-Language Ancient Writings") because they were originally found written in archaic characters which had to be deciphered by Kong Anguo. But for our readers' convenience, we shall here continue designating them simply as the first-batch and the second-batch documents.

Thus throughout the Earlier Han and Later Han dynasties only the twenty-nine first-batch documents were recognized by the court and officially disseminated in the empire. Nevertheless, the second-batch documents seemed to have gained some currency among private, knowledgeable scholars, men like Ma Rong and Zheng Xuan. In the 2nd century A.D. when Zheng Xuan wrote his famed commentaries on various Confucian classics, he treated them the same as the other writings. But because they were not officially accepted by the court, they were not amply copied. Consequently, after a period of unprecedented national upheaval following the Barbarian Invasions in the early 4th century A.D., no copies of them were known to have survived. Then, shortly afterward (in fact, less than ten years after the barbarians' capture of the northern capital), one Mei Ze, a magistrate of modern Jiangxi province, claimed to have found one copy of those documents and submitted them to the then southern Jin court.

From the very beginning of their submission, doubts were raised about their authenticity. Yet, either because these documents were so skillfully compounded with indisputable ancient materials, or, perhaps even more likely, because they read or sounded so much like the originals to those who had read them previously, the court soon granted its approval. Popular acceptance ensued. And for some fourteen centuries thereafter, they were officially passed on for genuine. Nevertheless, dissension persisted until the matter was brought to a climax by a great Qing scholar Yan Ruoju, 1635–1704. Yan spent almost his whole lifetime writing the lengthy *Guwen Shangshu Shuzheng* (128 sections), and succeeded in proving, once and for all, the spuriousness of Mei Ze's documents. His favorite method is to take up each one of them, go over it paragraph by paragraph, sometimes sentence by sentence, and demonstrate which parts of it have appeared elsewhere in other books (written later than the period to which the relevant document is supposed to belong, but still quite ancient, such as *Zuozhuan, Mencius, Xunzi, Li Ji*, and others), which quotations have been quoted without adequate regard for the context, and which passages are simple interpolations. His findings, though rambling at times, are devastatingly exhaustive and conclusive.

After Yan, interest in the *Book of History* naturally intensified among Qin scholars. As Yan's studies were confined to the second-batch documents, so others now paid special attention to the first batch. However, if they had entered the field with a purpose of putting the latter to acid tests similar to Yan's with the former, they came out with apparently different results. Among these, the most notable scholar is Duan Yucai, 1734–1815, a recognized master of what the Chinese used to call "Small Studies," a sort of combination of Chinese etymology and lexicography. Having written *Shuowenjiezi Zhu*, which traced every ideogram in China's first dictionary (produced by Xu Shen in the early 2nd century A.D.) through its various forms of construction and changes of meaning back to its earliest origins, he now examined the first-batch documents document by document, line by line, character by character, and came out in the end with a book titled *Guwen Shangshu Zhuanyi*. He did not find any error in them, but gave many of their wordings clearer and sharper definitions. This book was followed by another noteworthy work, Sun Xingyan's (1752–1818) *Shangshu Jinguwen Zhushu*, giving these documents new annotations and commentaries.[5] The studies of these scholars have restored credibility to the first-batch documents. And throughout the Qing dynasty, their authenticity was never seriously challenged.

At the turn of this century, however, as a result of China's having suffered repeated humiliations from outside, her younger people began to lose faith not only in their own government but also in their own culture. Iconoclasm became the dominant mood of the day. As in politics they boldly turned to revolution, so in mentality they were recklessly bent on tearing down all ancient beliefs. Everything ancient was instantly suspect, especially ancient writings.

I myself am a product of that age. Though born in a classically trained family, and given as much classical training in my childhood as any of my forebears had been, in my teens I turned out to be an iconoclast, as fanatical as any of my fellow teenagers who had taken part together in Peking in the now so-called May Fourth Revolutionary Movement. When Gu Jiegang published his first volume of *Gushibian* in the mid-1920s, asserting that Yu, the famed controller of the Great Flood in Chinese history, was not really a man but a sort of mythical animal, I still remember vividly how I grabbed one of its very first copies and read it with gusto.

But that was some sixty years ago. For some thirty years thereafter I fruitlessly pursued the life of a revolutionary in politics. Then I was forced into retirement, and for the last quarter of a century I have had ample time to read over the old Chinese classics again and again, examining them and weighing them in the light of all the criticisms and charges that have been leveled against them in books and publications, both Chinese and Western. And slowly and gradually, and rather reluctantly at first, I have come to the conclusion that I am at variance with my former fellow iconoclasts and their present-day following, who have kept on insisting that ancient Chinese writings are not reliable sources for creditable history. Had there been enough space, I would have liked to discuss the divergences of our views book by book and document by document. But as it is, we shall have to content ourselves with some general observations. As, for example:

ITEM ONE

Variations of style in the texts of the documents have been closely studied to disprove their authenticity. But, even as some of the critical scholars themselves admit, the use of this criterion is far from satisfactory. For instance, it is asserted that the earliest first-batch documents *(yaodian, gaoyaomo,* and *yugong)* cannot be as old as they were claimed to be, circa 23rd century B.C., because their style is much more modern—closer to the time of Confucius, 5th century B.C.—than *pangeng* and some of the Zhou documents that are known to have been composed respectively in the 14th and the 12th century B.C.

But this can be easily explained by the process of transmittal outlined above. When Confucius (or, for that matter, anyone else who did the transmitting) undertook to disseminate those documents, he must have thought his first obligation was to make them comprehensible. As the earliest documents were the most archaic or the most incomprehensible, so he had to convert them into the up-to-date language of his own day. As to *pangeng* and the Zhou documents, since their times were not so remote, their wordings, though still obscure, were yet readable. Thus in order to preserve their genuine flavor, the transmitter made as few modifications as possible.

Arguments of this nature have also been used with respect to the authorship of *Zuozhuan* and *Guo Yu.* Traditionally, these two works have been attributed to one and the same author, Zuo, a *shi,* "official historian," of Lu. But now it is contended that this cannot be, because there is a noticeable difference between the styles of the two. But this dissimilarity may be explained by the sources he used for each. In the case of *Zuozhuan,* he relied mainly on the records of the state of Lu; thus his style is consistent. But in the case of *Guo Yu,* the materials he collected are from the records of seven other states. Very likely, he just edited them, leaving them each, as much as he thought fit, in its own choice of diction and writing style. As a matter of fact, for such a possibility or probability, there is an actual example. We all know and recognize that Chen Shou, A.D. 233–297, is the sole author of *Sanguozhi,* "History of the Three Kingdoms." Yet the style he used for two of the kingdoms, Wei and Shu, is markedly different from that he used for the third one, Wu. Indeed, here even the grammar sometimes differs. The simple reason for the variation is that at that time Wu's writing style was a little different from that of the rest of China, and Chen Shou just followed the style of the indigenous sources he used.

Nevertheless, scholars are not lacking to claim that judging by the style of various documents they can tell that such and such were composed in the earlier Zhou before Confucius, or in the later Zhou after Confucius, or in the Warring States, or in the Earlier or Later Han Dynasty. I am inclined to believe that most of the points they have raised to back up their contentions are based only on innocent interpolations or alterations made by copyists at different times. A good example of such ingenuous variation can be found in the two versions of *gaoyaomo:* The one is the regular version transmitted in the *Book of History;* the other, a version quoted in full by Sima Qian in his famed *Historical Records (xia benji).* The latter not only here and there omits a few words, or adds others, but also makes a number of alterations. Yet, on the whole, the gist is the same in both versions. Then, why the variations? A few simple illustrations may serve to disclose the purpose. For "yes," the former uses *yu,* the latter *ran;* for third person possessive adjectives, the former uses *jue,* the latter *qi. Yu* and *jue* are pre-Confucian, *ran* and *qi* are Han. In short, the great Han historian simply thought it best to convert the relatively archaic wordings of the document into those more in accord with the usage of the Han readers. Both Duan Yucai and Sun Xingyan, in their works, had compared the two versions word by word, and they never saw any reason to question the reliability, or authenticity, of either of the two versions.

ITEM TWO

Logical sequence in the evolution of human thought has been used as another criterion. The document *hongfan (Great Plan)* [6] has been adjudged suspect because it contains brief definitions of the "five elements" (water, fire, wood, metal, and earth) that smacks of the Yin-yang school of philosophy, which gained prominence only in the Period of the Warring States, circa 468–222 B.C.[7] It is therefore contended that the document was written toward the end of that period, not, as traditionally believed, at the time of the founding of the Zhou dynasty some nine centuries earlier.

For similar reasons, it has also been asserted that the commentaries on the *Book of Changes,* commonly known as the *Ten Wings,* and traditionally attributed to Confucius, could not have been written by either the Great Sage or his immediate disciples, but by some later scholars of the Yin-yang school.

But speaking from the standpoint of evolution of human thought by stages, it seems that one of the very earliest preoccupations of man must have been about the basic elements that make up his universe. Thus the Hindus speculated that all matter arose from four elements—earth, water, fire, and wind. The Greeks believed that the elements were five—earth, water, fire, air, and ether. The Chinese thought that the five were metal, wood, water, fire, and earth. Such speculations must have struck root in men's minds long before any school of philosophy began.

Historically, in the Chinese documents, the term *wuxing* ("five elements") appeared for the very first time in the *Gan Address,*[8] predating the *hongfan* by a thousand years, or forty-odd generations. Moreover, the hero, or rather sage, of *hongfan* is Jizi, a younger contemporary of Wen Wang. Even if Jizi had not read Wen Wang's *Book of Changes,* he, being reputed one of the most learned men of his age, must have been conversant with the materials from which Wen Wang had derived his interpretations of the sixty-four hexagrams.[9] In these, mentions of the five elements must abound as much as in Wen Wang's work, such as "in the middle of the earth is water," "on the earth is water," "within the earth wood grows," "water over wood," "fire over wood," "water over fire, and "fire over water." Only metal is less frequently mentioned. Still, we meet with such statements as "received metal arrows" and "oppressed in a metal carriage," etc. Then, it is said, rather mistakenly, that the *Book of Changes* never uses the words *yin* and *yang.* But in the hexagram *tai,* a statement attributed to Wen Wang reads, "Inside is *yang* and outside *yin."* And in the hexagram *pi,* we have the reverse, "Outside is *yang* and inside *yin."* However, all the ideas expressed either in *hongfan* or in the *Ten Wings* fall short of the theory of the Yin-yang school of the Warring States, which postulates that the five elements are mutually creative as well as mutually destructive (that is, water is creative of wood, wood of fire, fire of earth, earth of metal, and metal of water; simultaneously, water is destructive to fire, fire to metal, metal to wood, wood to earth, and earth to water).

Now, looking at the above objectively, such evolution of human thought by stages seems to have been a very natural one. Had *hongfan* or the *Ten Wings* been written during or after the Period of Warring States, doubtless the theory of mutual creativity and mutual destructiveness would have found expression in them. The total absence of such ideas appears to indicate clearly that they were written much earlier.

Also, there is an argument that Confucius could not have written the *Ten Wings* because the concepts expressed in them are nonethical and therefore non-Confucian. But for this we have a passage from Xunzi, circa 340–245 B.C.:

> Roughly modeling after the ways of former wise sovereigns but not fully under-standing their systems, confident of their own capacity and overbearing in their ambition, they have heard and seen much, but they are without discrimination. Based upon old tradition, they have invented their own theory and called it "Five Elements." Sophisticated and specious, there is nothing like it: Its meanings are abstruse and without explanation; its assumptions cut-and-dried and without ra-tionale. They have decorated it with words and treated it with every respect, saying, "This is verily what our late Master has said!" Zisi[10] proclaimed the theory first, and Meng Ke (Mencius) seconded it. And the common, purblind scholars of the day, not knowing that it is wrong, accept it and pass it on, believing that this is indeed the benefit that Confucius and (his disciple) Ziyou had wanted to confer on posterity.
> This is the crime of Zisi and Meng Ke.[11]

As we know, Xunzi is an advocate of a school of Confucian philosophy opposed to that of Mencius. So it is no surprise that he should have cast aspersions on Mencius and Mencius's mentor, Zisi, Confucius's own grand-son. But what is of interest for us here is that from this passage we know for certain that Zisi and Mencius had actually passed on the theory of "Five Elements" as part of Confucian teachings. Hence, the traditional belief that the *Ten Wings* were written by Confucius, or by his immediate disciples, cannot be said to be groundless. Of course, they were subject to the same process of transmittal as other ancient writings, with all concomitant con-tingencies of omissions, additions, or alterations. But there seems to be no reason why a philosopher who taught ethics should not be believed to have simultaneously given expression to some of his thoughts on cosmology. And judging from the contents of the *Ten Wings* themselves, certainly there does not appear to be anything in them that makes them so basically incompatible with the other teachings of Confucius.

ITEM THREE

Doubts have also been cast upon certain documents by what may be called "circumstantial evidence." The document *wuyi,* traditionally attributed to

Zhougong, may be taken as an example. (In order to maintain utmost objectivity, for quoting excerpts in this connection, I shall use only James Legge's translation.) In *wuyi*, Zhougong was recorded to have told Cheng Wang, his nephew:

> . . . Tsoo-kea (Zujia) enjoyed the throne for thirty and three years. The emperors which arose after these all their lifetime enjoyed ease. From their birth enjoying ease, they did not understand the painful toil of sowing and reaping, nor hear of the hard labors of the inferior people. They only sought after excessive pleasures. . . .[12]

But in *duoshi (Numerous Officers)*, Zhougong said:

> From T'ang the Successful down to the emperor Yih (Diyi), every sovereign sought to make his virtue illustrious, and duly attended to the sacrifices.[13]

Again, in *duofang (Numerous Regions)*, it is said:

> In the case indeed of T'ang the Successful. . . . He paid careful attention to the essential virtues of a sovereign. . . . From him down to the emperor Yih, the sovereigns all made their virtue illustrious. . . .[14]

The three statements, all attributed to Zhougong traditionally, are considered self-contradictory, and so the document *wuyi* is suspected of being spurious. But such suspicions should be allayed, if we probe deeper into the divergent circumstances under which each of the statements was made. In *wuyi (Against Luxurious Ease)*, Zhougong was giving advice to his young nephew not to abandon himself to pleasure. In fact, he was warning him that as the Yin sovereigns who had led virtuous lives had lived long years and those who had indulged in pleasure had not, unless the teen-age emperor followed the good examples, his own life might be shortened by indulgence. So the speaker was careful to name all the good examples and give them their respective years of reign, in order to set them apart from the bad Yin emperors. But in *duoshi*, the duke was addressing the "obdurate people of Yin" for the purpose of coaxing them to accept their fallen misfortunes. So he was putting the blame of their woes entirely on the person of the last ruler of Shang, deliberately avoiding blaming his predecessors. The same circumstances obtained for *duofang*.[15]

Or take the document *mushi*. It is contended that this cannot be authentic because Wu Wang could not have given such a dull, uninspiring address to his troops just before giving battle to the last emperor of Yin. However, if the reader turns to Chapter VII, Section 2 above, and reads it over again, I am confident that he may have a different view as to whether or not Wu Wang made an appropriate speech on the occasion.[16]

Attempts, of course, have been made to find harder, or rather material, evidence to prove the spuriousness of ancient documents. The most notable one is related to the word "iron" found in the text of *yugong, Yu's Levies.* The document mentions iron as an item of tribute Yu levied from the region that produced it. Skeptics have argued that this is impossible because iron came into use in China only in the Period of the Warring States, at the earliest not earlier than the Period of Spring and Autumn, 770–468 B.C.[17] And for a time all the students of Chinese history, including myself, have accepted this as indisputable proof. However, even then, collectors have been known to have collected Shang bronze swords or arrows with edges or darts made of iron.[18] Skeptics, however, have countered that these are either weaponry of later dates or counterfeits forged by fraudulent dealers. But in March 1972, a bronze battle ax *(yue)* with iron edge was excavated from Gaocheng, Henan. After examination by modern technology, it has been adjudged to be a Shang product of the 14th century B.C.[19] If this is true, and we have no reason to doubt it, then it is no longer impossible that Yu may have known about iron and ordered it to be levied as tribute.

ITEM FOUR

Some isolated instances may be cited to illustrate the achievements as well as the disappointments of modern scholarship. A notable success is related to the term *ning wang* found in the documents *junshi* and *dagao.* The ideogram *ning* has been traditionally taken to mean "pacifying." The famed commentator Zheng Kangcheng maintained in *junshi* that by *ning wang* was meant Wen Wang, because Wen Wang was the person who had pacified the empire. But in *dagao* Zheng seemed to become unsure of himself. His annotations are: "Zhougong called Wen Wang *ning wang;* Cheng Wang also called Wu Wang *ning wang.* This term was used for both men." [20] Such an explanation, to say the least, is confusing. Now, modern scholarship, by examining inscriptions on bronzes, has determined that *ning* in ancient script was so close to *wen* that *wen* could have been easily copied erroneously into *ning.*[21] This is certainly helpful in the clarification of certain texts.

However, some contemporary scholars would go beyond that. They went ahead and claimed that because of this clarification, *dagao* should be no longer regarded as a proclamation issued by Cheng Wang against the rebellion of Wugeng and the three supervisors, but as one issued by Wu Wang against Zou when the former launched his first invasion against the latter.[22] But if one should examine the document with care, one would readily find that such an assumption does not jibe at all with the text.

Indeed, similar instances of letting imagination take control over research are not lacking. My late friend and fellow iconoclast in the 1920s, Fu Sinian,

was a brilliant scholar who made great contributions in reinterpreting many
a poem in the *Book of Poetry*. However, in his overeagerness to discredit the
old, he was often too quick to give credence to the new. A case in point is
Gu Jiegang's assertion that Wen Wang was related to Zou, the last Yin
emperor, by marriage, which Fu endorsed enthusiastically.[23] Gu based his
argument on the poem *daming*, the relevant stanzas of which may be translated as follows (in this translation I have followed James Legge in the main;
but where I feel his interpretation is not literal enough for our purpose here,
I have tried to make it more so):

> ... In the early years of Wen Wang
> Heaven made for him a match,
> On the north of the Qia,
> On the banks of the Wei.
> When Wen Wang would wive,
> There was the lady in a large state.
>
> In the large state there was this lady,
> Verily like a sister of Heaven.[24]
> Having determined an auspicious date by agreement,
> (Wen Wang) went to the Wei to welcome (her) in person.
> Over it (he) made a bridge of boats;
> Was not the glory on this occasion illustrious?
>
> The Mandate came from Heaven
> To this Wen Wang at his capital in Zhou;
> And destined to renew his line was this lady of Xin,
> The eldest daughter of that state.
> Thus reverentially she gave birth to Wu Wang,
> Who was to preserve and protect the Mandate,
> And in accordance with it smote the great Shang.

This is all *daming* has said about the marriage of Wen Wang to the eldest
daughter of Xin. As the surname of the house of Xin was Si, so Wen
Wang's consort was known as Taisi.

Now, in the *Book of Changes*, in the hexagram *tai*, there is written a line,
diyi guimei, "Emperor Yi gave his sister in marriage." The same line appears
again in the hexagram *guimei*.[25] As we know, there are five emperors in the
Shang dynasty, all of whom, being born on a *yi* day, bore the given name Yi.
The first one is the very founder of the dynasty. He was sometimes called
Dayi (Senior Yi), but he was better known as Tang. Then came the thirteenth emperor, Zuyi (Ancestral Yi); the twenty-first emperor, Xiaoyi
(Junior Yi), and the twenty-seventh emperor, Wuyi (Martial Yi). Presumably, the epithets *zu, xiao,* and *wu* were added to their names so as to
distinguish them from the others. And lastly, we have the twenty-ninth

emperor, Zou's father. Presumably too, when he ascended the throne, for the same purpose he had himself simply called Diyi (Emperor Yi). But speaking loosely, each one of them could be called Diyi. Now, *diyi guimei* (Emperor Yi marrying off his sister) must have been a celebrated social event of the day, well remembered throughout the Shang dynasty. But to which one of the five emperors the event belonged is utterly lost to our knowledge. However, because several lines of the two hexagrams appear to imply that the sovereign was giving a parting admonition to his sister that an imperial princess, when married, should especially conduct herself with modesty, some traditional scholars have thought that Tang fitted the case better than others.

Until the 1920s, no one suggested that there might be a connection between the poem *daming* and the line *diyi guimei* in the *Book of Changes*. But then Gu Jiegang claimed that according to the poem, Wen Wang was married to none else than the twenty-ninth Yin emperor Diyi's sister. For proof, he pointed out that it was because the sovereign was her brother that she was said to be "verily like a sister of Heaven." But then Wen Wang's consort has been always known as Taisi, Si being the surname of the house of Xin, which is different from Zi, the surname of the house of Shang. So Gu ventured that Taisi was a lady-in-waiting sent by Diyi to accompany the princess as a would-be concubine, and Wen Wang married her after Diyi's sister's death. But then Taisi was said in the poem to be from the state of Xin "On the north of the Qia, on the banks of the Wei," a state that is known to have been in the neighborhood of Zhou. Gu insisted, however, that Taisi came from a different state of Xin, which was situated in the west of modern Shandong, quite adjacent to Anyang, the Yin capital.

Gu might be complimented on his fertile imagination, but one should be excused for not thinking his suppositions too well grounded. Yet, regretfully, some contemporary historians have taken such materials as reliable sources and duly reported that Wen Wang and Wu Wang may well have been related to Yin, or Shang, by marriage.

ITEM FIVE

The sharpest divergence between our views, however, arises from some contemporary sinologues' contention that almost all the documents in the *Book of History*, even the early first-batch ones, should not be used as sources for history because these had been doctored by Confucius, deliberately idealizing those ancient emperors so as to suit his own teachings. This allegation, obviously, is at odds with the other assertion that Confucius could not have been the man solely responsible for transmitting the documents. But leaving this point aside, we are of the opinion that, historically, it was not possible for Confucius to have altered the contents of the documents so drastically when he converted them into the language of his own day. The original tablets were still preserved in the archives of Zhou, and scholars were not yet lacking who could read them as well as Confucius.[26] Moreover, direct quotations from many of the documents are found in books that are still extant today but were written before the Fires of Qin. While the very existence of such books serves to reinforce the authenticity of those documents so quoted, it also argues well that Confucius had no monopoly on the knowledge of those ancient writings and therefore could not distort them at will.

If the first-batch documents have been so frowned upon by some contemporary sinologues, the second-batch documents have fared even worse in the hands of nearly all critical scholars. In fact, in their discussions on sources for Chinese history, they almost always ignored them. To them, Yan Ruoju has proved these documents to be forgeries; so whatever is connected with such forgeries should be regarded as fabrications. Hence, by implication, even the events which the documents are said to have been written about are suspect; and historians, in writing credible history, should shy clear from them. But Yan Ruoju, in his exhaustive studies on this subject, aimed only at proving that the present texts of these documents are not the original texts discovered in the Earlier Han dynasty, but Mei Ze's counterfeits. He never denied that such originals had existed previously. Nor did he ever doubt the actuality of those past events which had brought the original documents into existence in the first place. In fact, every evidence he adduced to prove the spuriousness of Mei Ze's version implies and supports his intrinsic belief in the historicity of those events. Take Yi Yin's banishment of Taijia. In this connection, there are four documents involved: *yixuan* and *taijia* I, II, and III. We know that their present versions are compounded of numerous passages taken from authentic ancient works, some of them stating explicitly in their own texts that they were quoting from the original documents *yixuan* and *taijia*. We know too, through *Book of History, shuxu,* and *Historical Records,* that Yi Yin had banished Taijia for three years because of his unfitness to rule, and then returned him to sovereign power after his manifest repentance. We know for certain even the very date—the year, the month, and the day—when Yi Yin delivered his first lecture to Taijia. These are the facts. Why cannot we put them forward as history? Indeed, in such cases, provided that the reader is informed of the counterfeit nature of such documents, I can see no harm in quoting them in part or in full, using them as paraphrases for the originals, so to speak.

The above represents some of the divergences between my views on this subject and those of some contemporary scholars. Notwithstanding, I believe that their "critical scholarship," as they are accustomed to calling it, has done much service to the study of Chinese history. In research, skepticism is, and should always be, welcome. And in this instance, to say the least, it has stimulated a keen interest in China to search for sources other than her ancient writings in the investigations of her antiquity, as evidenced by the increasing scale and number of archaeological explorations as well as the progressive application of modern scientific methods to the examination of bronze inscriptions and other artifacts. At the same time, however, it must be sadly pointed out that such critical scholarship is not devoid of ill effects. It has discouraged the study of ancient Chinese writings among the Chinese themselves. At the turn of this century, most educated Chinese had some classical training, and many could even recite much of the classics by rote. Thus, when Gu Jiegang came forth with his *Gushibian* publicizing his theory that Yu was not human but a mythical animal, many young men of his generation, though falling in the same iconoclastic mood as Gu, and admiring his boldness and enjoying reading his book, could yet tell from their own knowledge of the classics that Gu's thesis was far from substantiated. But as time went on, this is no longer so. In 1905, the Qing dynasty abolished the literary examination system that required the study of classics for entrance into government service. In the 1920s, the New Culture Movement gained ascendancy; and the classical style of the written language has since been replaced by the vernacular style. In consequence, the ancient Chinese classics are becoming almost as difficult for present-day Chinese to read as ancient Latin is for modern Italians. This is, of course, not the fault of contemporary scholars critical of ancient writings. Nevertheless, they have contributed to the problem. For they have helped build up an impression for the general public that Chinese ancient history, as traditionally passed on, is nothing more than a package of myths and legends. And since the present-day Chinese, generally speaking, are either unused to reading or unable to read those ancient works themselves, that impression not only has been sinking deeper and deeper in their minds, but has obtained wide currency outside China.

It seems to me, therefore, that the time has arrived to write a new history of ancient China. Yet, for all that, I would not have dared make the attempt myself, had it not been for the discovery of the oracle bones and the findings of Wang Guowei. For to write a history, events have to be sequenced. And for a credible history, the sequence has to be coherent, consistent, and confirmed beyond doubt. That is why the great historian Sima Qian, despite his own exhaustive readings and extensive travels, would not start writing the first chapters of his *Historical Records* until he became assured of his own bearings by examining the *pudie* and *dieji* that were then still stored in the Han imperial palace. But these tablets or records are long lost. What proof have I that Sima Qian's sequence is correct?

It is in this connection that the discovery of the oracle bones may be likened to a miracle. Still, had it not been for the efforts of a handful of exceptional scholars who succeeded in deciphering their inscriptions and linking them up with history, the bones would have been of little use to the historians. But to be able to do so, one must have four qualifications: (1) a complete mastery of ancient classics, (2) a profound knowledge of "Small Studies," (3) a prodigious memory, and (4) a penetrating mind. That is why though so much literature has been written on the subject, yet so little, so very little, can be cited for use in this volume. Fortunately, for China at that juncture, there was a man who fulfilled the four qualifications—Wang Guowei. Of course, he benefited from scholarship of others, from men like Liu E and Luo Zhengyu. But it was he, and he alone, who searched out and confirmed the genealogy of all of the thirty emperors of the Shang dynasty as well as the fourteen generations of their forebears as far back as Di Ku—almost the very sequence Sima Qian had taken from the lost *pudie* and *dieji*, and used for chronology in his own *Historical Records*.

Yet, even a miracle is not without limitations. Now we can safely claim all Shang history to be credible. But can we claim the same for Xia? True, we can say that the oracle bones have enabled us to trace back, through Shang ancestry, to Di Ku, who is none other than Yao's father and the Yellow Emperor's great grandson. But apart from the fact that there are still doubts being expressed about the identification of Di Ku by Wang Guowei,[27] there is no denying that the Shang ancestors did not constitute the mainstream of China's history, which happens to be represented at that period by the rulers of the Xia. True, also, we can argue that Sima Qian had taken the sequence of Xia emperors from the same lost *pudie* and *dieji* as he had taken that of Shang emperors. Since we have already found the latter to be reliable, why should we not believe the same of the former? Yet, speaking objectively, we must concede that such an argument, though plausible, is but implication, not proof. Moreover, there are documents in the *Book of History* said to be even earlier than Xia. What about them? What, especially, about the first document, *yaodian*, the *Canon of Yao*, that purports to be a factual account of Yao, of Shun, of Yu, and of the Great Flood? Is that credible?

Then, unexpectedly, we have another godsend. In the middle of the last century, Dr. W. H. Medhurst became the first Western scholar to acknowledge that the *Canon of Yao* might be carrying within its own text proofs of its antiquity.[28] In 1865, James Legge, when publishing his translation of the *Book of History*, was astute and careful enough to include Dr. Medhurst's findings in his notes. And finally, after a lapse of over a century, in 1981, Dr. H.K.C. Yee, an American-trained astrophysicist, based on Legge's translation of Chinese star names and using modern precession formulae, has reexamined the astronomical observation data mentioned in the canon and come up with this conclusion: "The period described in *yaodian* is indeed around the year 2200 B.C." [29] So now, thanks to these three men, we may reasonably assume that this very first document in the *Book of History* may be also used as source for credible history.

NOTES

1. See the following: Herrlee G. Creel, *The Origins of Statecraft in China*, I, pp. 444–86, Appendix A, "The Sources"; Cho-yun Hsu, *Ancient China in Transition*, pp. 183–92, Appendix, "Authenticity and Dating of Pre-Ch'in Texts"; and *Essays on the Sources for Chinese History*, ed. Donald D. Leslie, Colin Mackerras, and Wang Gungwu, chap. 3.

2. *Confucian Analects, shu'er:* "The Master used *yayan:* with respect to *Odes* and *Historical Documents* and in the conduct of ceremonies, he always used *yayan.*" The character *ya* is defined in Duan Yucai's *Shuowenjiezi Zhu* thus: "A small bird, with belly still white, just able to leave its mother, is called *ya.*" *Yan* means speech. So *yayan* may be translated as "early speech."

3. The original meaning of the term *shangshu* is "ancient writings." See above, p. 39; Chap. I, note 117.

4. Some scholars, especially Yan Ruoju, thought that "toward the close of the reign of Wudi" was wrong. *Wudi* should have been *Jingdi*, Wudi's father, who reigned 156–141 B.C. In that case, Kong Anguo could have gained possession of those volumes and deciphered them later.

5. These works by Yan, Duan, and Sun are not included in the discussions of the books listed in note 1. However, in this author's opinion, for a critical appraisal of the documents of the *Book of History*, a thorough study of these works is essential.

6. See above, pp. 310–11.

7. For an account of the rise of the Yin-yang school, see Dr. Fung Yu-lan, *A History of Chinese Philosophy*, tr. by Derke Bodde, I, pp. 154–69.

8. See above, pp. 117–18.

9. See above, pp. 262–63.

10. Confucius's grandson, reputed to be author of *Zhong Yong*, the *Doctrine of the Mean*.

11. *Xunzi, feishi'erzi.*

12. Legge, *The Chinese Classics*, III, pp. 467–68.

13. Ibid., pp. 456–57.

14. Ibid., p. 498.

15. Please note: In this book, *duofang* is considered to be a proclamation issued by Cheng Wang and not by Zhougong. See above, pp. 365–66.

16. See above, pp. 293–95. The motivations attributed to Wu Wang for making this address *mushi* before the battle are not the author's own invention. They were explained to him by his late father, a classical scholar in his own right, who said that they were taught him in turn by his tutor. So, it seems, there was actually a tradition of transmitting such interpretations of ancient classics by mouth from one generation to another.

17. See Qu Wanli, "Lun Yugong Zhuchengde Shidai," pp. 55–59.

18. Several samples of such weaponry are in the collections of the Freer Gallery of Art, Washington, D.C.

19. *Wen Wu*, November 1976, pp. 56–59.

20. See Sun Xingyan, *Shangshu Jinguwen Zhushu*, commentaries on *dagao*.

21. See Fu Sinian, *Quanji*, I, pp. 75–76.

22. Ibid.

23. Gu Jiegang, *Zhongguo Gushi Yanjiu*, III, pp. 11–15. Also see Fu Sinian, *Quanji*, III, pp. 990–91.

24. Legge's translation of this line is "Like a fair denizen of Heaven," which, singing figuratively of the maiden's beauty, is probably the true meaning here.

25. In *The I Ching*, tr. by Wilhelm and Baynes, Princeton, 3rd edition, 1980, this line appears under "T'ai/Peace" on p. 51 as "The sovereign I gives his daughter in marriage," and again under "Kuei Mei/The Marrying Maiden" on p. 211 as "The sovereign I gave his daughter in marriage." *Mei*, in Chinese, usually means "sister." In ancient times, it was sometimes used to mean "young maiden." Perhaps it is because of this usage that Wilhelm and Baynes have translated it into "daughter." This is mentioned here so that the reader may not get confused if he should happen to consult the Wilhelm and Baynes version on this point.

26. See *Zuozhuan*, Duke Zhao, 12th year. The man known to be able to read the "Three Tombs, Five Canons, Eight Cords, and Nine Mounds" was Yi Xiang, a *shi* of Chu. This was in the year 529 B.C., twenty-two years after Confucius was born. Conceivably, most *shi* at that time, in other states beside Chu, could also read those ancient writings.

27. Sun Haibo, "Du Wangjinganxiansheng *Gushixinzheng* Shuhou." Also see Ho, Ping-Ti, *The Cradle of the East*, p. 314, note 89.

28. See above, pp. 66–67.

29. Medhurst's findings caught my attention quite a few years ago. As I personally knew no one with astronomical expertise, I had to seek help from known institutions. Over the years, I applied to several of these, but all were of no avail. When the time came to submit my manuscript to my publisher, I had to content myself with having only Legge's translation in it without any comment. After signing the contract with my publisher, I desperately sought to have Medhurst's findings either confirmed or disproved for good. I read about a well-known astronomer, and I made bold to approach him with my request. I wrote to him thrice, and I never received a reply. Then my daughter-in-law suggested that an astronomer of Chinese descent might be more inclined to take interest. After plodding through many an astronomical journal, she came up with the name of Dr. H. K. C. Yee. I communicated with him at once, and the results are as printed in this volume.

This story is told here not to give utterance to my past frustrations, but to offer possible explanations for how and why Medhurst's findings, so important to the study of ancient China, has been left uninvestigated by astronomers for so long. It seems that astronomers are astronomers and historians are historians, and the twain shall never meet, unless they are brought together once in a long century by happy chance.

Dr. H. K. C. Yee was born in China. He is now a Canadian citizen. He received his high school and college education in Toronto, Canada, graduating from the University of Toronto with a degree in engineering science. He obtained his Ph.D. in astrophysics at the California Institute of Technology.

Dr. Yee replied to my request on February 9, 1981. An excerpt of his letter is as follows:

"So far, I have not had time to research for the primary source, i.e. *The Chinese Classics*, Vol. III, hence I can only give you a partial analysis based on the quotation (about Medhurst's findings) that you furnished me:

"The fact that the Pleiades cluster is at (or near) the point of vernal equinox in the year 2200 B.C. is correct. I have repeated the calculation using more modern precession formulae. However, I was not able to determine exactly what 'Cor Hydra' is, other than the fact that it is some stars in the Hydra cluster. But it is reasonable to assume that Medhurst did not make an error in the relative position of 'Cor Hydra' and the Pleiades, i.e. they are about six hours apart. Thus, I would conclude that the Medhurst statement is essentially correct. However, because I do not know their precise astronomical definition of 'sunset,' nor the exact position of 'Cor Hydra,' the year that can be inferred from the information 'Cor Hydra culminated at the sunset on the day of the vernal equinox' is only approximate, and 2200 B.C. is about right."

Then, after having reviewed Yao's four commands in Legge's translation, he wrote a second letter dated February 25, 1981, excerpts of which are given below along with Legge's translations and my own notations in parenthesis:

[Legge, III, pp. 18–19] (He separately commanded the second brother He to reside at Yu-e, in what was called the Bright Valley, and there respectfully to receive as a guest the rising sun, and to adjust and arrange the labors of the spring. "The day," he said, "is of the medium length, and the star is in *Neaou;* you may thus exactly determine mid-spring.")

[Dr. Yee] Vernal Equinox: There is serious doubt in my mind whether one can use this observation properly. The culminating star *"Neaou"* is open to interpretation. It seems that there were some arguments concerning which star *Neaou* represents (see Legge's notes on p. 19). . . . But regardless of that point, I shall show you the results for Cor Hydra. I will assume that the modern name for Cor Hydra is Alpha Hydra, the brightest star in the constellation Hydra. The precession formulae used are those in page 500 of K. R. Lang's *Astrophysical Formulae.* The next most important point in the calculation is the time of sunset, which is dependent on the latitude of the place of observation. For vernal equinox, this does not matter much, since sunset is the same (within a few minutes) in LST (local sidereal time) throughout the northern hemisphere. Assuming that the observation was made at a latitude of about 35°N (south of Peking, which has a latitude of 39°), the time of sunset, which can be obtained from American Ephemeris, is approximately 6h14m. Alpha Hydra is only about 10min from the meridian on the day of vernal equinox in the year 2254 B.C., that is, that was the culminating star in that time. It was exactly at the meridian at sunset around 2050 B.C.

One additional thing bothers me about the vernal equinox observation. It seems that "the second brother He" was to observe *sunrise* (either in Shantung or Korea), i.e., he was sent to the east. Is it possible that when they say star *Neaou,* they might not mean that the culminating star at *sunset* is *Neaou* but rather that it could also be interpreted as the culminating star at *sunrise?* If this is the case, *Neaou* could have been misinterpreted by all of the commentators.

[Legge, III, pp. 19–20] (He further commanded the third brother Ho to reside at Nankeaou, and arrange the transformation of the summer, and respectfully to observe the extreme limit of the shadow. "The day," said he, "is at its longest, and the star is *Ho;* you may thus exactly determine mid-summer.")

[Dr. Yee] Summer Solstice: Legge interpreted the star *Ho* as "the heart of Scorpion," which I assumed to be Alpha Scorpio (i.e. Antares), the brightest star in the constellation Scorpio. In the summertime, the time of sunset is strongly depen-

dent on the latitude of the place of observation. The text stated that it was made from Nankeaou, which was interpreted as near Annam. This is probably believable; though for someone like me, with limited knowledge of history, it seems somewhat surprising that they could travel so far south in those times. Thus, if we assume the latitude to be 20°N (i.e. about the same as Hong Kong) the LST at sunset is 12h44m, the right ascension of Antares precessed to 2254 B.C. is 12h22m, again, very close, off by only 22 minutes. If we assume that the observation is made at 10°N latitude, it would be almost right on.

[Legge, III, p. 20] (He separately commanded the second brother He to reside at the west, in what was called the Dark Valley, and there respectfully to convoy the setting sun, and to adjust and arrange the completing labors of the autumn. "The night," he said, "is of the medium length, and the star is *Heu;* you may thus exactly determine mid-autumn.")

[Dr. Yee] Autumnal Equinox: There does not seem to be too much doubt in interpreting *Heu* as Beta Aquarius, since it has the same Chinese name as one of the seven constellations in *xuanwu* (note by Wu: Dr. Yee used Chinese characters here. *Xuanwu* is the Pinyin for what Legge has translated in his notes as "The Dark Warrior.") Again, for Aquarius, the place of observation is not important. Sunset at 35°N latitude on the day of autumnal equinox is 17h59m (LST), the position for Beta Aquarius precessed to 2254 B.C. is 17h53m, almost exactly at the meridian at the time of sunset. This is the best agreement of the four observations. However, there is one minor point that can be of problem. Beta Aquarius is 3.1 magnitude in brightness; while the following statement does not rule out the authenticity of the observation, it does raise a small question mark. I believe that in sunset instances, with naked eyes, at the time of sunset, we can only see stars brighter than 2nd magnitude. Thus, Beta Aquarius may be too faint to be observed at the moment of sunset. However, the above is only a tentative objection, and can be settled by a simple actual observational test when the star is at the meridian during sunset.

[Legge, III, p. 21] (He further commanded the third brother Ho to reside in the northern region, in what was called the Sombre Capital, and there to adjust and examine the changes of the winter. "The day," said he, "is at its shortest, and the star is *Maou;* thus you may exactly determine mid-winter.")

[Dr. Yee] Winter Solstice: This represents the biggest difficulty. If we are to assume that Legge is correct, then there are two inconsistencies. First, if *Maou* is indeed the Pleiades cluster (this probably can be found out by someone with knowledge of Chinese astronomical names), and if the observation was made from a place which must be at least as far north as Peking, then sunset was about 22h40m LST, and the precessed position of the Pleiades to the year 2254 B.C. is 23h39m, we are off by a whole hour. An even bigger problem, from my experience as an observational astronomer (and I also asked other astronomers), the Pleiades are much too faint to be observed at the moment of sunset with naked eyes.

[Dr. Yee's conclusion] Thus, the above is my analysis of the four observations discussed in *yaodian.* The conclusion is: if we assume Legge's identification of the stars to be correct, the period described in *yaodian* is indeed around the year 2200 B.C. (with the exception of the observation of winter solstice).

But as you can see for yourself, there still remain quite a few questions unanswered.

BIBLIOGRAPHY

For every ancient Chinese writing, there are almost numberless editions, printed at various times, often with different paging. In many cases, because the authors are so well known, or so numerous, or so uncertain, the books are mentioned only by their titles. In other cases, they are designated simply as works of "Master So and So," usually just a surname. In referring to these, the Chinese practice is not to give the edition and the page but the headings of the relevant chapters and sections. This practice is followed in the notes of this book, with the romanized names of authors and titles of books capitalized, but with the headings of chapters and sections not capitalized, to show the difference.

The Pinyin system of romanization has been used throughout the book, and romanized titles and authors are listed here in the same way. However, the listings here also include exact or approximate dates of authors, Wade-Giles romanizations of names and titles (in parentheses), Chinese names and titles, English translations of the titles when possible, and sometimes brief explanatory notes about important works. Chapters and sections of works are listed in alphabetical order, not in their original order; and usually only Pinyin romanizations and the Chinese forms are given for them.

Bamboo Chronicles, Zhushu Jinian (Chu Shu Chi-nian), 竹書紀年
> In A.D. 281 a graverobber opened up a tomb of a king of Wei, one of the seven states in the Period of Warring States, 468–221 B.C. Many books, written or carved on bamboo tablets, were discovered. One of these is the so-called *Bamboo Chronicles,* which purported to begin with the Yellow Emperor and end with the death of the buried king, i.e., 296 B.C.

Ban Gu (Pan Ku) 班固, A.D. 33–92. *Baihu Tongyi (Pai-hu T'ung-i)* 白虎通義, "White Tiger General Understandings."
> In A.D. 79 the Later Han court assembled many well-known scholars at Baihu Guan ("White Tiger Palace") to examine the similarities and dissimilarities among the various interpretations of the Confucian Classics. Ban Gu, as the foremost scholar of his day, was directed to put the consensus on record. Hence the title of the book.
> *hao* 號, *sanjiao* 三教 *sheji* 社稷, *wuxing* 五刑.

———. *Qian Han Shu (Ch'ien Han Shu)* 前漢書 , "History of Earlier Han," 206 B.C.–A.D. 24.

This is the first "dynastic history" of China. After *Qian Han Shu,* there are twenty-three subsequent dynastic histories. In the opinion of many Chinese scholars, Ban Gu's work tops them all in style and in choice of materials. It is regarded as second only, if not equal, to Sima Qian's *Historical Records.*

Ban Gu followed Sima Qian's practice in dividing his history into *ji* or *benji,* "basic chronicles," for rulers; *zhuan* or *liezhuan,* "biographies," for individuals or outside nations; *zhi,* "records" or "discourses," on special subjects, such as *yiwenzhi,* "records on literature and the arts" (Sima Qian used the term *shu* instead of *zhi)* ; and *biao,* "table" or "chart."

baiguan gongqing biao 百官公卿表 , *dilizhi* 地理志 , *jiaosizhi* 郊祀志 , *liyuezhi* 禮樂志 , *lulizhi* 律歷志 , *minyuewang liezhuan* 閩粵王列傳 , *nanyuewang liezhuan* 南粵王列傳 , *rulin liezhuan* 儒林列傳 , *simaqian liezhuan* 司馬遷列傳 , *wudiji* 武帝紀 , *(yuanguang* 元光 , name of a reign year), *xingfazhi* 刑法志 , *xiongnu lizhuan* 匈奴列傳 , *yiwenzhi* 藝文志 ·

Book of Changes, Zhou Yi (Chou I) 周易 or *Yi Jing (I Ching)* 易經 .

ge 革 , *guimei* 歸妹 , *jiji* 既濟 , *qian* 謙 , *qián* 乾 , *sun* 損 , *tai* 泰 , *weiji* 未濟 (the preceding are hexagrams), *xici* 1 and 2 繫辭上，下 (the last are two of the ten commentaries attributed to Confucius, which are known as *shiyi* 十翼 , the *Ten Wings).*

Book of History, Shangshu (Shang Shu) 尚書 or *Shu Jing (Shu Ching)* 書經 . The name *Shangshu* was used in the time of Confucius. It means "Ancient Writings." It is still used by many modern Chinese scholars.

First-batch documents (the Chinese call these documents *jinwen shangshu* 今文尚書 , and the second-batch documents *guwen shangshu* 古文尚書 ; for their meanings, see Appendix):

dagao 大誥 , *duofang* 多方 , *duoshi* 多士 , *feishi* 費誓 , *ganshi* 甘誓 , *gaoyaomo* 皋陶謨 , *gaozong tongri* 高宗肜日 , *guming* 顧命 , *hongfan* 洪範 , *jinteng* 金縢 , *jiugao* 酒誥 , *junshi* 君奭 , *kanggao* 康誥 , *lizheng* 立政 , *luogao* 洛誥 , *luxing* 呂刑 , *mushi* 牧誓 , *pangeng* 盤庚 , *shaogao* 召誥 , *tangshi* 湯誓 , *weizi* 微子 , *wuyi* 無逸 , *xibo kanli* 西伯戡黎 , *yaodian* 堯典 , *yugong* 禹貢 , *zicai* 梓材 .

Second-batch documents:

biming 畢命 , *caizhongzhiming* 蔡仲之命 , *dayumo* 大禹謨 , *junchen* 君陳 , *lu'ao* 旅獒 , *taijia* 太甲 , *taishi* 泰誓 , *tanggao* 湯誥 , *weizizhiming* 微子之命 , *wucheng* 武成 , *wuzizhige* 五子之歌 , *xianyouyide* 咸有一德 , *yixun* 伊訓 , *yinzheng* 胤征 , *yueming* 說命 , *zhonghuizhigao* 仲虺之誥 , *zhouguan* 周官 .

shuxu 書序 (introductory notes attributed to Confucius, one for each document).

Book of Poetry, Shi Jing (Shi Ching) 詩經 . A collection of some three hundred ancient songs and odes, traditionally said to have been compiled by Confucius from various sources.

binfeng 豳風 (songs originated in Bin, ancestral home of Zhou):

chixiāo 鴟鴞 , *qiyue* 七月 .

daya 大雅 (greater odes): *daming* 大明 , *gongliu* 公劉 , *huangyi* 皇矣 , *lingtai* 靈臺 , *mian* 緜 , *shengmin* 生民 , *siqi* 思齊 , *wenwang* 文王 , *wenwangyousheng* 文王有聲 .

lusong 魯頌 (sacrificial odes of Lu, Zhougong's fief): *bigong* 閟宮 .

shangsong 商頌 (sacrificial odes of Shang): *changfa* 長發 , *liezu* 烈祖 , *yinwu* 殷武 .

shaonan 召南 (songs originated in Shao, Shaogong's fief, and spread to the south):
  gantang 甘棠.

xiaoya 小雅 (lesser odes): *changdi* 常棣.

zhounan 周南 (songs originated in Zhou and spread to the south): *guanju* 關雎.

zhousong 周頌 (sacrificial odes of Zhou): *siwen* 思文, *youke* 有客,
  yougu 有瞽, *zhenglu* 振鷺.

Broman, Sven. "Studies on the *Chou Li*," *Bulletin of the Museum of Far Eastern Antiquities* 33 (1961).

Cai Chen (Ts'ai Ch'en) 蔡沈, early 13th century A.D. *Shujing Jizhuan (Shu-ching Chi-chuan)* 書經集傳.
  (Over the centuries a great many Chinese scholars as well as Cai Chen have written commentaries on Confucian Classics, each with a title only slightly different in meaning from others. It is no use to try to differentiate them in English. So in referring to a work such as Cai Chen's, we use the simple form *"Book of History,* commentaries of Cai Chen."

Chang, Kwang-chih. *The Archaeology of Ancient China.* Yale, 1977.

Chen Shou (Ch'en Shou) 陳壽, A.D. 233–297. *Sanguozhi (San Kuo Chih)* 三國志, "History of the Three Kingdoms" (A.D. 220–280).
  shushu 蜀書: *xianzhubei* 先主備.

Cheng Te-k'un. *Archaeology in China,* II, *Shang China* (1961); III, *Chou China* (1963). Cambridge and Toronto.

Cheng Yaotian (Ch'eng Yao-t'ien) 程瑤田, 18th century A.D. *Zongfa Xiaoji (Chung-fa Hsiao-chi)* 宗法小記, "A Brief Review of House Rules (of *Yi Li*)."

China in the 16th Century, The Journals of Matthew Ricci 1583–1610, tr. by Louis J. Gallagher. New York, 1953.

Chu Ci (Chu Tz'u) 楚辭. Collection of poems by Qu Yuan (Ch'u Yuan) 屈原, d. 299 B.C., and other Chu poets.
  jiubian 九辯, *lisao* 離騷, *tianwen* 天問.

Chunqiu (Ch'un Ch'iu) 春秋, "Spring and Autumn Annals." Confucius's *Chunqiu* has three ancient commentaries, all derived from shortly after Confucius's death. They are known as *Gongyangzhuan, Guliangzhuan,* and *Zuozhuan, zhuan* meaning "as related or commented by." Each of the three is listed separately here.

Ci Hai (Tz'u Hai) 辭海, Taiwan, 1969: A modern dictionary of idioms and allusions.
  wushitongju 五世同居.

Confucian Analects, Lunyu (Lun Yu) 論語. A collection of the sayings of Confucius, and also some of the sayings of his close disciples, compiled by his disciples shortly after his death (479 B.C.).
  bayi 八佾, *gongyechang* 公冶長, *shu'er* 述而, *taibo* 泰伯, *weilinggong* 衛靈公, *weizheng* 爲政, *weizi* 微子, *xianwen* 憲問, *xue'er* 學而, *yanyuan* 顏淵, *yaoyue* 堯曰, *yongye* 雍也, *zihan* 子罕, *zizhang* 子張.

Confucian Classics. In the 2nd century B.C. the Han dynasty had court-appointed instructors to teach nationally selected students these five classics: *Book of Poetry, Book of History, Book of Changes, Li,* and *Chunqiu.* In the Tang dynasty, 618–906, the usage at first was to list *Book of Poetry, Book of History, Book of Changes, Zhou Li, Yi Li, Li Ji,* and *Chungqiu* as respectively commented upon by Gongyang, Guliang, and Zuo as "the nine classics." Later, *Xiao Jing (Book of Filial Piety,* attributed to Confucius and Zengzi), *Confucian Analects,* and *Er Ya* were added to form "the twelve classics." Then in the 10th century the Song dynasty added *Mencius,* and we have the complete list of "the thirteen classics."

   Da Xue ("Great Learning") and *Zhong Yong* ("Doctrine of the Mean") were originally two chapters in *Li Ji.* Together with *Confucian Analects* and *Mencius,* these are also called "the four books."

Creel, Herrlee G. *The Origins of Statecraft in China,* I. Chicago, 1970.

Dadai Liji (Ta-tai Li-chi) 大戴禮記 . There are two collections of commentaries and discussions on the principles and practices of Li either by Confucius himself or by his disciples, both compiled in the 1st century B.C., one by Dai De (Tai Te) 戴德 and the other by his nephew Dai Sheng (Tai Sheng) 戴聖 . The first collection is known as *Dadai Liji,* and the second *Xiaodai Liji,* which, having become the more popular of the two, is also simply called *Li Ji,* which see.

   baofu 保傅 , *dixixing* 帝繫姓 , *wudide* 五帝德 , *xiaxiaozheng* 夏小正 , *yongbing* 用兵 .

Da Xue (Ta Hsueh) 大學 , "Great Learning," attributed to Zengzi (Tzeng-tzu) 曾子 , one of Confucius's closest disciples. Originally, this was a chapter of *Li Ji.* Because of its importance to Confucianism, it was taken out to form an independent book in the 12th century.

Dai Yanhui (Tai Yen-hui) 戴炎輝 . *Zhongguo Fazhishi (Chung-kuo Fa-chih-shih)* 中國法制史, "History of Chinese Jurisprudence." Taiwan, 1971.

———. *Tanglu Tonglun (T'ang Lu T'ung Lun)* 唐律通論 , "General Review of the *Tang Code.*" Taiwan, 1964.

Dong Zuobin (Tung Tso-pin) 董作賓 . *Jiaguxue Liushinian (Chia-ku-hsueh Liu-shih-nien)* 甲骨學六十年, "Sixty Years of Shell-and-Bone Studies." Taiwan, 1965.

———. *Xinhuo Buci Xieben Houji (Hsin-huo Pu-t'zu Hsieh-pen Hou-chi)* 新獲卜辭寫本後記 , "Postscript on the Publication of Newly Discovered Divination Inscriptions." Institute of History and Philology, Academia Sinica, 1945.

———. *Yin Lipu (Yin Li-pu)* 殷歷譜 , "Yin Chronology." Institute of History and Philology, Academia Sinica, 1945.

   dixin ripu 帝辛日譜, *sipu* 祀譜, *wenwuding ripu* 文武丁日譜, *wuding ripu* 武丁日譜, *yinzhouzhiji nianlikao* 殷周之際年歷考, *zujia sipu* 祖甲祀譜 .

———. *Zhongguo Nianli Jianpu (Chung-kuo nien-li Chien-p'u)* 中國年歷簡譜 , "Simplified Chronology of China," I. Taiwan, 1960.

Du You (Tu Yu) 杜佑 , A.D.734–812. *Tongdian (T'ung-tien)* 通典 .

   This work and two others (Zheng Qiao's *Tongzhi* and Ma Duanlin's *Wenxian Tongkao,* usually simply called *Tongkao)* are known as the *Santong,* "Three Comprehensives." *Tongdian* may be literally translated as "Comprehensive Institutions," *Tongzhi* "Comprehensive Records," and *Tongkao* "Comprehensive Studies," each different from the others in the categorization of topics. *Tongdian* has 200 volumes or chapters, *Tongzhi* 200, and *Tongkao* 348. Together, they constitute an encyclopedia of

Chinese political and social institutions and traditions. See also Zheng Qiao and Ma Duanlin.

In the 18th century, under Emperor Qianlong, these three works were each brought up to date; and the new works were called respectively *Xu* ("continued") *Tongdian, Xu Tongzhi,* and *Xu Tongkao.* Then a new set for the Qing dynasty, known as *Qing Tongdian, Qing Tongzhi,* and *Qing Tongkao,* was produced.

Du Yu (Tu Yu) 杜預 , A.D. 221–284. *Chunqiu Zuoshi Jingzhuan Jijie (Ch'un Ch'iu Tzo-shih Ching-Chuan Chi-chieh)* 春秋左氏經傳集解 , "Commentaries on *Chunqiu* and *Zuozhuan.*"

Duan Yucai (Tuan Yu-ts'ai) 段玉裁 , A.D. 1734–1815. *Guwen Shangshu Zhuanyi (Ku-wen Shang-shu Chuan-I)* 古文尚書撰異 . See Appendix for further information.

———. *Shuowenjiezi Zhu (Shuo-wen Chieh-chi Chu)* 説文解字注 , "Exegeses on Xu Shen's Dictionary."

Er Ya (Erh Ya) 爾雅 . China's earliest attempt at lexicography, partly attributed to Zhougong (Chou Kung) 周公 , 12th century B.C.
    shiqin 釋親, *shitian* 釋天 .

Essays on the Sources for Chinese History, ed. Donald D. Leslie, Colin Mackerras, and Wang Gungwu. Columbia, S.C., 1975.

Fan Wenlan (Fan Wen-lan) 范文瀾 . *Zhongguo Tongshi (Chung-kuo T'ung-shih)* 中國通史 . Peking, 1978.

Fan Ye (Fan Yeh) 范曄 , A.D. 397–445. *Hou Han Shu* 後漢書 , "History of Later Han," A.D. 25–219.
    guangwudiji 光武帝紀 , *rulin liezhuan* 儒林列傳 , *xiqiang liezhuan* 西羌列傳 .

Fu Sinian (Fu Ssu-nien) 傅斯年 . *Quanji (Ch'uan-chi)* 全集 , "Complete Works." Taiwan, 1980.

Fung Yu-lan. *A History of Chinese Philosophy,* tr. by Derk Bodde, I. Princeton, 1952.

Gao You (Kao Yu) 高誘 , 2nd century A.D. *Huainanzi Zhu (Huai-nan-tzu Chu)* 淮南子注 , "Commentaries on *Huainanzi.*"

Genealogy of the Premier Emperors, dixixing. See *Dadai Liji.*

Gongyangzhuan (Kung-yang Chuan) 公羊傳 . Confucius's *Chunqiu* as related or commented on by his disciple Bu Zixia (Pu Tzu-hsia) 卜子夏 to his own disciple Gongyang Gao (Kung-yang Kao) 公羊高 .

Gu Donggao (Ku Tung-kao) 顧棟高 , A.D. 1677–1758. *Chunqiu Dashibiao (Ch'un Ch'iu Ta-shih-piao)* 春秋大事表 , "Table of Major Events in the Period of Spring and Autumn."
    songjiangyu lun 宋疆域論 .

Gu Jiegang (Ku Chieh-kang) 顧頡剛 . *Gushibian (Ku-shih-pien)* 古史辨 , "Ancient History Disputations." First published in Peking, 1925. Now published as *Zhongguo Gushi Yanjiu (Chung-kuo Ku-shih Yen-chiu)* 中國古史研究 .

Gu Yanwu (Ku Yen-wu) 顧炎武 , A.D. 1612–1682. *Rizhilu (Jih-chih-lu)* 日知錄 , "Notations of Things Learned Daily."

Guanzi (Kuan-tzu) 管子 , "Works of Master Guan," Guan meaning Guan Zhong (Kuan Chung)管仲, d. 645 B.C.
  fengchan 封禪, *dishu* 地數.

Gujinyunhui (Ku-chin Yun-hui) 古今韻會 , "Dictionary of Ancient and Modern Rhymes," attributed to Huang Gongshao (Huang Kung-shao) 黃公紹 of the Yuan dynasty, A.D. 1277–1367.

Gujinzhu (Ku-chin-chu) 古今注 , "Commentaries, Ancient and Modern." Author uncertain. Some sources attribute the work to Cui Bao (Ts'ui Pao) 崔豹 of the Jin dynasty, A.D. 265–418.

Guliangzhuan (Ku-liang Chuan) 穀梁傳 . See *Gongyangzhuan*. Bu Zixia had another disciple whose surname was Guliang, but whose given name has been variously transmitted as *xi* 喜, *chi* 赤 , or *chu* 俶 . Guliang also wrote his version of commentaries on *Chunqiu*.

Guo Moruo (Kuo Mo-jo) 郭沫若 . *Buci Tongcuan Kaoshi (Pu-tz'u T'ung-ts'uan k'ao-shih)* 卜辭通纂考釋 , "Interpretations of a Compilation of Divination Inscriptions." Tokyo, 1933.

———. *Jiaguwenzi Yanjiu (Chia-ku Wen-tzu Yen-chiu)* 甲骨文字研究 , "Study of Shell and Bone Writings." Peking, 1962.

Guo Yu (Kuo Yu) 國語 , "Lores of Nations." See *Zuozhuan*.
  chuyu 楚語, *jinyu* 晉語 , *luyu* 魯語, *zhengyu* 鄭語, *zhouyu* 周語.

Hall, John W., and Richard R. Beardsley. *Twelve Doors to Japan.* New York, 1965.

Han Yu (Han Yu) 韓愈 , A.D. 768–824. *Jinxuejie (Chin-hsueh-chieh)* 進學解 , "Essay on Advanced Education."

Hanfeizi (Han-fei-tzu) 韓非子 , "Works of Master Han Fei," d. 233 B.C.
  naner 難二 , *nanyan* 難言, *nanyi* 難一, *shixie* 飾邪, *shoulin* 說林, (34th section) *waichu shou* 外儲說, *wudu* 五蠹, *yulao* 喻老 .

Hanshi Waizhuan (Han-shih Wai-chuan) 韓詩外傳 , "Outside Commentaries on the *Book of Poetry* as Transmitted by Han." Han is Han Yin 韓嬰 (2nd century B.C.).

Historical Records, Shiji (Shih Chi) 史記 , by Sima Qian (Ssu-ma Ch'ien) 司馬遷 , circa 145–90 B.C.
  benji 本紀 (basic chronicles): *hangaozu* 漢高祖 , *qin* 秦 ,
    qinshihuangdi 秦始皇帝 , *wudi* 五帝 , *xia* 夏 , *xiangyu* 項羽 , *yin* 殷 , *zhou* 周 .
  biao 表 (charts or tables): *sandai shibiao* 三代世表 ,
    shi'er zhuhou nianbiao 十二諸侯年表 .
  liezhuan 列傳 (biographies): *boyi* 伯夷 , *dongyue* 東越 ,
    guice 龜策 , *huoqubing* 霍去病 , *laozi* 老子 , *lujia* 陸賈 , *quyuan* 屈原 .
  shijia 世家 (distinguished houses): *chu* 楚 , *guancai* 管蔡 ,
    kongzi 孔子 (Confucius), *luzhougong* 魯周公 , *qitaigong* 齊太公 , *songweizi* 宋微子 ,
    wei 魏 , *weikangshu* 衛康叔 , *wutaibo* 吳太伯 , *xiaoxiangguo* 蕭相國 , *yuewanggoujian* 越王勾踐 , *yanshaogong* 燕召公 .
  shu 書 (discourses): *fengchan* 封禪 , *li* 歷 .
  taishigong zixu 太史公自序 (Sima Qian's autobiography).

Ho, Ping-Ti. *The Cradle of the East.* Chicago, 1975.

Hsu, Cho-yun. *Ancient China in Transition.* Stanford, 1965.

Hu Peihui (Hu P'ei-hui) 胡培翬 , A.D. 1781–1849. *Yi Li Zhengyi (I Li Cheng-I)* 儀禮正義, "Commentaries on *Yi Li.*"

Huainanzi (Huai-nan-tzu) 淮南子 , "Works of Master Huainan," Huainan meaning Liu An 劉安, Prince of Huainan, d. 122 B.C. Assembling many scholars from different schools, he had a book composed known as *Huainanzi.*

 daoying xun 道應訓 (*xun* meaning discourse), *fanlun xun* 氾論訓, *lanming xun* 覽冥訓 , *qisu xun* 齊俗訓, *taizu xun* 泰族訓, *xiuwu xun* 修務訓, *yuandao xun* 原道訓, *zhushu xun* 主術訓 .

Huangfu Mi (Huang-fu Mi) 皇甫謐 , A.D. 214–282. *Diwang Shiji (Ti-wang Shih-chi)* 帝王世紀, "Chronicles of Ancient Emperors."

Hujifa Shixingxize (Hu-chi-fa shih-hsing Hsi-tse) 戶籍法施行細則, "Census Law, Executive Regulations." June 21, 1936.

Jiayi Xinshu (Chia-i Hsin-shu) 賈誼新書 , "A New Book by Jiayi," 200–168 B.C.

Jia Gongyan (Chia Kung-yen) 賈公彥, flourished in the reign of Tang Gaozong (T'ang Kao-tsung) 唐高宗 , A.D. 650–683. *Zhou Li Zhushu (Chou Li Chu-shu)* 周禮注疏 , originally named *Zhou Li Zhengyi (Chou Li Cheng-yi)* 周禮正義 , "Commentaries on Zhou Li."

Jin Shu (Chin Shu) 晉書 , "History of the Jin Dynasty," A.D. 265–418.
 taokan liezhuan 陶侃列傳 .

Kaogu (K'ao-ku) 考古 , Peking (periodical).

Karlgren, Bernard. "The Early History of the *Chou Li* and the *Tso Chuan* Texts," *Bulletin of the Museum of Far Eastern Antiquities* 3 (1931).

———. "Some Weapons and Tools of the Yin Dynasty," *Bulletin of the Museum of Far Eastern Antiquities* 17 (1945).

Kong Anguo (K'ung An-kuo) 孔安國. *Shangshuxu (Shang-shu-hsu)* 尚書序 , "Preface to the *Book of History.*" Kong was the transmitter of the original second-batch documents. See Appendix.

Kongzi Jiayu (K'ung-tzu Chia-yu) 孔子家語 (sayings of Confucius made in his residence).
 guansong 冠頌 , *liuben* 六本 .

Kuodizhi (K'uo-ti-chih) 括地志 , "Geographical Records." Li Tai (Li T'ai) 李泰 , son of the famed Tang Taizong (T'ang T'ai-tsung) 唐太宗 , A.D. 627–649, assembled a group of scholars and composed this work. It was lost, but much of it has been preserved in other books. The present version is a compilation by Sun Xingyan, whom see.

Latourette, Kenneth Scott. *The Chinese: Their History and Culture.* New York, 1963.

Legge, James. *The Chinese Classics.* Hong Kong, 1970.

Li Ji (Li Chi) 禮記 , also known as *Xiaodai Liji (Hsiao-tai Li-chi)* 小戴禮記 . See *Dadai Liji* for information on authorship.
 aigongwen 哀公問 , *biaoji* 表記 , *dazhuan* 大傳 , *fangji* 坊記 , *hunyi* 昏義 , *jiaotesheng* 郊特牲 , *jifa* 祭法 , *jingjie* 經解 , *jitong* 祭統 , *liyun* 禮運 , *mingtangwei* 明堂位 , *neize* 內則 , *sangdaji* 喪大記 , *sangfu xiaoji* 喪服小記 , *sheyi* 射義 , *tangong* 檀弓 , *wangzhi* 王制 , *wenwangshizi* 文王世子 , *xiangyinjiuyi* 鄉飲酒義 , *yueji* 樂記 , *yueling* 月令 , *zaji* 雜記 , *zengziwen* 曾子問 , *ziyi* 緇衣 .

Liezi (Lieh-tzu) 列子, "Works of Master Lie." Attributed to Lie Yukou (Lieh Yu-k'ou) 列圄寇, a senior contemporary of Zhuangzi (Chuang-tzu) 莊子, circa 365–290 B.C.
  huangdi 黃帝, *liming* 力命, *tangwen* 湯問.

Lin Chunpu (Lin Chun-pu) 林春圃. *Zhu Shu Jinian Buzheng (Chu Shu Chi-nien Pu-cheng)* 竹書紀年補證, "Commentaries on *Bamboo Chronicles.*" 1838.

Liu Shu 劉恕. *Zizhitongjian Waiji (Tzy-chih T'ung-chien Wai-chi)* 資治通鑑外紀. A pseudo-historical account of earliest China (finished before A.D. 1077).

Liu Xiang (Liu Hsiang) 劉向, 77–76 B.C. *Diwang Zhuhou Shipu (Ti-wang Chu-hou Shih-p'u)* 帝王諸侯世譜, "Chronology of Emperors and Enfeoffed Princes."

———. *Lienuzhuan (Lieh-nu-chuan)* 列女傳, "Biographies of Women."

———. *Shuoyuan (Shuo-yuan)* 說苑, "Garden of Anecdotes."

Liu Xin (Liu Hsin) 劉歆, Liu Xiang's son, d. A.D. 22. *Santongli (San-t'ung-li)* 三統歷. See Chapter I, Section 7, note 132.

Liutao (Liu-t'ao) 六韜. Attributed to Lu Shang, better known as Taigong (T'ai Kung) 太公.

Lushi Chunqiu (Lu-shih Ch'un Ch'iu) 呂氏春秋, "Spring and Autumn of the House of Lu." Written by hired scholars under the patronage of Lu Buwei (Lu Pu-wei) 呂不韋, prime minister of Qin, 249–237 B.C.
  jiqiuji 季秋記 : *shunmin* 順民,
  lisulan 離俗覽 : *yongmin* 用民,
  mengdongji 孟冬紀 : *yiyong* 異用,
  shendalan 慎大覽 : *guiyin* 貴因,
  shenfenlan 審分覽 : *shenshi* 慎勢, *junshou* 君守,
  shijunlan 恃君覽 : *xinglun* 行論,
  xianshilan 先識覽 : *xianshi* 先識,
  xiaoxinglan 孝行覽 : *benwei* 本味, *shoushi* 首時,
  zhongdongji 仲冬紀 : *dangwu* 當務,
  zhongxiaji 仲夏紀 : *guyue* 古樂.

Ma Duanlin (Ma Tuan-lin) 馬端臨, d. A.D. 1316. *Wenxian Tongkao (Wen-hsien T'ung-k'ao)* 文獻通考. See Du You.
  bingkao 兵考, *jiaoshekao* 郊社考.

Ma Rong (Ma Jung) 馬融, A.D. 78–166. Noted for his commentaries on *Lunyu, Book of History, Book of Poetry, Book of Changes, Zhou Li, Yi Li*, etc. These are now scattered among many books.

Mao Shi (Mao Shih) 毛詩. The *Book of Poetry* as transmitted by Mao Gong (Mao Kung) 毛公, 2nd century B.C.

Mencius, *Mengzi (Meng-tzu)* 孟子, "Works of Master Meng," Meng meaning Meng Ke (Meng K'o) 孟軻, 371–289 B.C.
  gaozi 告子, *gongsunchou* 公孫丑, *jinxin* 盡心, *lianghuiwang* 梁惠王, *lilou* 離婁, *tengwengong* 滕文公, *wanzhang* 萬章.

Mozi (Mo Tzu) 墨子, "Works of Master Mo," Mo meaning Mo Di (Mo Ti) 墨翟, circa 479–390 B.C.
  gengzhu 耕柱, *jianai* 兼愛, *shangxian* 尚賢.

Needham, Joseph. *Science and Civilization of China,* I (1961); III (1965). Cambridge.

Nelson (William Rockhill) Gallery of Art and Atkins (Mary) Museum. Handbook II, *Art of the Orient.* Kansas City, 1973.

Pei Yin (P'ei Yin) 裴駰 , 5th century A.D. *Shiji Jijie (Shi-chi Chi-chieh)* 史記集解 , "Commentaries on *Historical Records.*"

Qian Mu (Ch'ien Mu) 錢穆 . *Guoshi Dagang (Kuo-shih Ta-kang)* 國史大綱 , "Outline for a History of China," I. Taiwan, 1965.

Qing Shigao (Ch'ing Shih-kao) 清史稿 , "Draft for the Dynastic History of Qing," A.D. 1644–1911. Taiwan, 1961.
  zhiguanzhi 職官志 .

Qu Wanli (Ch'u Wan-li) 屈萬里 . "Lun Yugong Zhuchengde Shidai" ("Lun Yu-kung Chu-cheng ti Shih-tai") 論禹貢著成的時代 , "On the Composition Date of *yugong,*" *Bulletin of the Institute of History and Philology* 35 (1964), Academia Sinica.

———. *Shangshu Shiyi (Shang-shu Shih-i)* 尚書釋義 , "Commentaries on the *Book of History.*" Taiwan, 1980.

Ruan Yuan (Juan Yuan) 阮元 , 1763–1849. *Jiguzai Zhongdingyiqi Kuanshi (Chi-ku-tsai Chung-ting I-ch'i K'uan-shih)* 積古齋鐘鼎彝器款識 , "Inscriptions on Bronze Bells, Tripods, and Vessels in the Studio for the Accumulation of Antiquities."

Shan Hai Jing (Shan Hai Ching) 山海經 , "Book on Mountains and Seas." See Chapter II. Section 6.
  xishanjing 西山經 .

Shang Yang (Shang Yang) 商鞅 , d. 338 B.C. *Shangjun Shu (Shang Chun Shu)* 商君書 , "Book of Lord Shang." A principal exponent of the Legalist school of philosophy.

Shangshu Dazhuan (Shang-shu Ta-chuan) 尚書大傳 , "Great Commentaries on the *Book of History.*" Attributed to Fu Sheng (Fu Sheng) 伏生 , who first transmitted the "first-batch documents" in the 2nd century B.C. See Appendix.

Shiben (Shih-pen) 世本 , "Generation Roots." See Chapter I, note 135.

Sima Zhen (Ssu-ma Chen) 司馬貞 , of Tang dynasty, A.D. 618–906. *Shiji Suoyin (Shih-ch' So-yin)* 史記索隱 , "Commentaries on *Historical Records.*"

Sui Shu (Sui Shu) 隋書 , "History of the Sui Dynasty," A.D. 589–617.
  jingjizhi 經籍志 .

Sun Haibo (Sun Hai-po) 孫海波 . "Du Wangjingan Xiansheng *Gushixinzheng* Shuhou" ("Tu Wang-ching-an Hsien-sheng *Ku-shih Hsin-Cheng* Shu-hou") 讀王靜安先生 古史新證書後 , "A Review of 'Ancient History, New Proofs' by Wang Guowei," *Kaogu Shekan* (periodical) 2.

Sun Yat-sen 孫中山 . *Sanmin Zhuyi (San Min Chu-i)* 三民主義 , "Three People's Principles," I.

Sun Xingyan (Sun Hsing-yen) 孫星衍 , A.D. 1752–1818. *Shangshu Jinguwen Zhushu (Shang-shu Chin-ku-wen Chu-shu)* 尚書今古文注疏 , "Commentaries on the *Book of History.*" See Appendix.

Sunzi (Sun-tzu) 孫子 , "Works of Master Sun," Sun meaning Sun Wu 孫武 , late 6th century B.C.

Swann, Peter C. *Chinese Monumental Art.* New York, 1963.

Taiping Yulan (T'ai-p'ing Yu-lan) 太平御覽 , "Imperial Readings of Taiping." Taiping was the name chosen by Emperor Taizong of the Song dynasty to number these years of his reign—A.D. 976–983. Under his orders, excerpts from over 6,000 books were selected for his reading.

Tang Code, Tang Lu (T'ang Lu) 唐律 . The legal code issued by the Tang dynasty. *mingli lu* 名例律 , *zeidao lu* 賊盜律 .

Wang Guowei (Wang Kuo-wei) 王國維 , 1878–1927. *Gushi Xinzheng* (Ku-shih Hsin-cheng) 古史新證 , "Ancient History, New Proofs." Peking, 1925.

———. *Guantang Jilin (Kuan-t'ang Chi-lin)* 觀堂集林 , "A Collection of Works of Guantang," Guantang being a courtesy name of Wang Guowei. This is a compilation by his admirers, in which the following works may be found:
Beiboding Ba (Pei-po-ting Pa) 北伯鼎跋 , "On the Inscriptions of the Beibo Tripod."
Gaozong Tongri Shuo (Kao-tsung T'ung-jih Shuo) 高宗肜日説 , "Discussions on the Document *gaozong tongri.*"
Guifang Kunyi Yanyun Kao (Kuei-fang K'un-i Yen-yun K'ao) 鬼方昆夷玁狁考 , "A Study on the Guifang, Kunyi, and Yanyun Tribes."
Shang Sangoubing Ba (Shang San-Kou-ping Pa) 商三句兵跋 , "On the Inscriptions of Shang Sangou Weaponry."
Shuo Juepeng (Shuo Chueh-p'eng) 説珏朋 , "On the Use of Jade and Cowry" (as Shang currency).
Yin Bucizhong Suojian Xiangongxianwang Kao (Yin Pu-tz'u-chung Suo-chien Hsien-kung Hsien-wang K'ao) 殷卜辭中所見先公先王考 , "A Study of the Former Ancestors and Former Emperors of the Yin as Seen from Their Divination Inscriptions" (this was first published in 1917), *Xu Kao (Hsu K'ao)* 續考 , "A Continued Study."

Wang Mingsheng (Wang Ming-sheng) 王鳴盛 , 1721–1797. *Zhou Li Junfu Shuo (Chou Li Chun-fu Shuo)* 周禮軍賦説 , "Discussions on the *Zhou Li* System of Military Service and Taxation."

Wei Zhao (Wei Chao) 韋昭 , A.D. 203–273. *Guoyu Weishijie (Kuo-yu Wei-shih-chieh)* 國語韋氏解 , "Commentaries on *Guo Yu.*"

Wang Xianqian (Wang Hsien-ch'ien) 王先謙 , d. 1917. *Qian Han Shu Buzhu (Ch'ien Han Shu Pu-chu)* 前漢書補注 , "Commentaries on *Qian Han Shu* (of Ban Gu)."

Wen Wu 文物 , Peking (periodical).

Wuyue Chunqiu (Wu-yueh Ch'un Ch'iu) 吳越春秋 , "Annals of Wu and Yue." Attributed to Zhao Ye (Chao Yeh) 趙曄 of the Later Han dynasty, A.D. 25–219.

Xiao Yishan (Hsiao I-shan) 蕭一山 . *Qingdai Tongshi (Ch'ing-tai T'ung-shih)* 清代通史 "General History of the Qing Dynasty." Taiwan, 1967.

Xie Yunfei (Hsieh Yun-fei) 謝雲飛 . *Zhongguo Wenzixue Tonglun (Chung-kuo Wen-tsu-hsueh T'ung-lun)* 中國文字學通論 , "General Discussions on Chinese Etymology." Taiwan, 1965.

474

BIBLIOGRAPHY

Xin Tang Shu (Hsin T'ang Shu) 新唐書 , "New History of the Tang Dynasty," A.D. 618–906.
   yiwenzhi 藝文志 .

Xu Shen (Hsu Shen) 許慎 , flourished in the reign of Andi (An-Ti) 安帝 , A.D. 107–125. *Shuowen Jiezi (Shuo-wen Chieh-tzu)* 說文解字 . China's first dictionary.

Xu Tongdian (Hsu T'ung-tien) 續通典 . See Du You, *Tongdian.*

Xu Zheng (Hsu Cheng) 徐整 , of the Period of the Three Kingdoms, A.D. 220–280. *Sanwu Liji (San-wu Li-chi)* 三五歷紀 . An ancient chronology as quoted in *Taiping Yulan.*

Xun Xu (Hsun-hsu) 荀勗 , d. A.D. 289. *Mutianzi Zhuan Xu (Mu-t'ien-chi Chuan Hsu)* 穆天子傳序, "Preface to the Biography of Mu, Son of Heaven."

Xunzi (Hsun-tzu) 荀子 , "Works of Master Xun," Xun meaning Xun Kuang (Hsun K'uang) 荀況 , circa 340–245 B.C.
   dalue 大略 , *feishi'erzi* 非十二子 , *feixiang* 非相 , *jundao* 君道 , *xing'e* 性惡 , *yaowen* 堯問 .

Yan Ruoju (Yen Jo-chu) 閻若璩 , 1635–1704. *Guwen Shangshu Shuzheng (Ku-wen Shang-shu Shu-cheng)* 尚書古文疏證 . See Appendix.

Yan Sigu (Yen Ssu-ku) 顏思古 , A.D. 584–645. *Qian Han Shu Zhu (Ch'ien Han Shu Chu)* 前漢書注, "Commentaries on *Qian Han Shu* (of Ban Gu)."

Yang Rongguo (Yang Yung-kuo) 楊榮國 . *Zhongguo Gudai Sixiangshi (Chung-kuo Ku-tai Ssu-hsiang Shih)* 中國古代思想史 , "History of Ancient Chinese Thought." Peking, 1978.

Yi Li (I Li) 儀禮 , "Standard Proprieties." Attributed to Zhougong (Chou Kung) 周公 , 12th century B.C. For detailed description, see Chapter IX, Section 4.
   pinli 聘禮 *(ji* 記 *)*, *sangfu* 喪服 *(zhuan* 傳 *)*, *shiguanli* 士冠禮 , *shihunli* 士昏禮 , *shisangli* 士喪禮 *(shezong* 設重 *)*, *xiangsheli* 鄉射禮 , *xiangyinjiuli* 鄉飲酒禮 .

Ying Shao (Ying Shao) 應劭 , flourished between A.D. 180 and 200. *Fengsu Tongyi (Feng-su T'ung-i)* 風俗通義 , "Common Understanding of Customs and Traditions."

Yi Zhou Shu (I Chou Shu) 逸周書 . Originally named in Ban Gu's *Qian Han Shu, yiwenzhi,* simply as *Zhou Shu,* "Zhou Documents." But since these are outside of the historical documents chosen by Confucius for the *Book of History,* they are more commonly known as *Yi Zhou Shu,* "Unselected (or Misplaced) Zhou Documents."
   chengkai 成開 , *dakuang* 大匡 , *duyi* 度邑 , *keyin* 克殷 , *mingtang* 明堂 , *shifa* 諡法 , *shifu* 世俘 , *shixun* 時訓 , *wanghui* 王會 , *wenzheng* 文政 , *wuquan* 五權 , *zhouyue* 周月 , *zuoluo* 作雒 .

Yue Jue Shu (Yueh Chueh Shu) 越絕書 , "History of the Destruction of Yue." Anonymous. Some sources attribute it to Yuan Kang (Yuan K'ang) 袁康 of Later Han, A.D. 25–219.

Zhang Shoujie (Chang Shou-chieh) 張守節 of Tang Dynasty, A.D. 618–906. *Shiji Zhengyi (Shih-chi Cheng-i)* 史記正義 , "Commentaries on *Historical Records.*"

Zhanguoche (Chang-kuo-ch'e) 戰國策 , "Strategic Plans of the Warring States." These are documents kept by various states in the Period of the Warring States, 468–221 B.C., that dealt with their national policies or strategies. In the 1st century B.C. Liu Xiang collected them together to form this compilation. (See Liu Xiang.)
   weiche 魏策 .

Zhao Chizi (Chao Ch'ih-tzu) 趙尺子. *Meng Han Yuwen Bijiaoxue Juyu (Meng-Han Yuwen Pi-chiao-hsueh Chu-yu)* 蒙漢語文比較學舉隅 , "Examples of a Comparative Study on the Mongolian and Chinese Languages." Taiwan, 1969.

Zheng Qiao (Cheng Ch'iao) 鄭樵 , A.D. 1102–1161. *Tongzhi (T'ung-chih)* 通志. See Du You.
   wudiji 五帝紀, (vol. 59) *xuanju* (2) 選舉 , *zayilunxia* 雜議論下 .

Zheng Xuan (Cheng Hsuan) 鄭玄 , A.D. 125–199. Better known as Zheng Kangcheng (Cheng K'ang-ch'eng) 鄭康成 . He was Ma Rong's disciple, but outshone his mentor in the end. Commentaries on many classics, quoted in numerous books.

Zhong Yong (Chung Yung) 中庸 , "Doctrine of the Mean." Like *Da Xue,* it was originally a chapter in *Li Ji* but taken out later to form an independent book. Attributed to Kong Ji (K'ung Chi) 孔伋 , better known as Zisi (Tzu-ssu) 子思 , Confucius's grandson and Zengzi's disciple. See *Da Xue.*

Zhou Bi or *Zhou Bi Suanjing (Chou Pi Suan-ching)* 周髀算經 . China's earliest book on astronomy and mathematics. Attributed to Zhougong (Chou Kung) 周公 , or the Duke of Zhou, at the turn of the 12th century B.C.

Zhou Li (Chou Li) 周禮 , "Zhou Proprieties." Attributed to Zhougong. The book embodies his ideas on how the Zhou government should be organized. For detailed description, see Chapter IX, Section 3.
   chunguanzongbo (or *zongbo)* 春官宗伯 , "Minister of Imperial Household":
      dazongbo 大宗伯 , *dianlu* 典路 , *dianming* 典命 , *dianrui* 典瑞 , *neishi* 內史 , *shifu* 世婦 , *taibu* 太卜 , *taizhu* 太祝 , *waishi* 外史 , *wu* 巫 .
   diguansitu (or *situ)* 地官司徒 , "Minister of Commonalty":
      bizhang 比長 , *dasitu* 大司徒 , *fengren* 封人 , *luxu* 閭胥 , *meishi* 媒氏 , *sijiu* 司救 , *suiren* 遂人 , *tiaoren* 調人 , *xiangdafu* 鄉大夫 , *xiaositu* 小司徒 , *zhouzhang* 州長 , *zushi* 族師 .
   qiuguansikou (or *sikou)* 秋官司寇 , "Minister of Justice":
      chaodafu 朝大夫 , *dasikou* 大司寇 , *daxingren* 大行人 , *fangshi* 方士 , *shishi* 士師 , *sihuan* 司圜 , *sixing* 司刑 , *suishi* 遂士 , *xiangshi* 鄉士 , *xiaosikou* 小司寇 , *yashi* 訝士 .
   tianguanzhongzai (or *zhongzai)* 天官冢宰 , "Prime Minister":
      jiupin 九嬪 , *jiuzheng* 酒正 , *nuyu* 女御 , *paoren* 庖人 , *shanfu* 膳夫 , *shifu* 世婦 , *waifu* 外府 .
   xiaguansima (or *sima)* 夏官司馬 , "Minister of War":
      xiaosima 小司馬 , *zhifangshi* 職方氏 .

Zhuangzi (Chuang-tzu) 莊子 , "Works of Master Zhuang," Zhuang meaning Zhuang Zhou (Chuang Chou) 莊周 , circa 365–290 B.C.
   xuwugui 徐無鬼 , *tianxia* 天下 , *tianzifang* 田子方 , *waiwu* 外物 .

Zuozhuan (Tso-chuan) 左傳 . Commentaries on *Chunqiu* by Zuo Qiuming (Tso Ch'iuming) 左丘明 , a contemporary, if not a disciple, of Confucius. He was said to be a *shi* (official historian) of Lu, and also author or editor of *Guo Yu. Zuozhuan* follows the chronology of *Chunqiu,* which numbers the years by the reigns of different dukes. Thus we cite accordingly, giving the reign year.
   Duke Ai 哀公 , Duke Wen 文公 , Duke Xi 僖公 , Duke Xiang 裏公 , Duke Xuan 宣公 , Duke Yin 隱公 , Duke Zhao 昭公 .

INDEX

absolutism, 432
  centralized government and, 403–4
  Confucianism and, 405–6
Accounting Mountain (Kuaiji), 115
agricultural people (husbandmen):
  calendar used by, 113, 162, 299
  oppression of, 131–36, 238
  self-defense measures by, 136–37, 138, 150, 357–58
  tithe of, 92, 132, 134–35, 260
  xia character and, 108
agriculture:
  development of, 21–22, 36, 56, 69, 71, 92, 96, 109–10, 114, 133–34, 148, 149, 158, 160–61, 162, 183, 312, 336, 339, 381
  discouraged by Taikang, 120–21
  Ji veneration and, 8, 25, 87, 91, 233–34
  location of imperial seat and, 159–61, 180, 185, 199
  ministry of, 87, 120, 125, 235, 237
  oxen used in, 126
  prosperity and, 224
  well-field vs. simple levy systems in, 135
ancestral veneration, 16–20
  development of chronology and, 24–25
  by emperors, 18–19, 113, 153, 159, 172, 428–29
  family system and, 21, 24, 428–29
  lineal purity and, 24–25, 35
  mourning rites and. See funeral and mourning rites
  propitiating of spirits in, 16–17
  record keeping and, 35–36
  shi as surrogate in, 20
  temples for, 16–20, 153, 159, 428–29
  women in, 24, 172
  zhu used in, 20
  See also specific dynasties
Ancient Duke. See Gugong Danfu
animals:
  domesticated by Paoxi, 52
  in mythology, 5–6
animism, 62
Announcement to the Emperor (digao), 131
archaeological findings:
  at Anyang, 9, 30–31, 171, 199, 228
  See also bronzes; oracle bones
archery, 60, 120, 313, 392

inculcation of virtues and, 439–44
architecture, advances in, 228–29
astronomy, 34–35, 41, 66–67, 374

bamboo tablets as "books," 37
Ban Gu, 452–53
Batu Khan, 147
bi (jade disk), 227–28
Bi, Duke of, 297, 307
Bigan, Junior Tutor, 258, 259, 280, 286–89, 300
Bin, location of, 237
bo (hegemon; field marshal), 214–15
Bo as "Great City Shang," 153
Book of Changes (Yi Jing), 11, 26, 164, 174, 225–26, 375
  Ji Chang's contributions to, 262–64
  legends about, 51–53, 54
  lianshan and guicang schools of, 262
  Ten Wings in, 263
Book of History (Shu Jing), 39–40, 41, 375
  historical data in, 7, 18, 65–66, 88, 97, 110, 117, 121, 122, 127, 129, 182, 216, 227, 229, 272, 287–88, 292, 311, 313–14, 343–45, 349, 354–55, 364, 377–78
  historicity of, 67, 454
  loss of original documents for, 40, 71, 131, 138, 169, 176–77, 313
Book of Poetry (Shi Jing), 273–75, 336–39, 375, 405
Book of the Worthy and the Capable, 416, 417
Book on Mountains and Seas (Shan Hai Jing), 90–91
books, making of, 37
Boqin, Marquis of Lu, 323, 336, 345, 429
border states. See Four Lands
Boyi, 249–50, 283–84, 437
Bright Hall, 359, 360
bronzes, 224–27
  categories of, 225
  Shang-Yin, 30, 43, 224–27
  in verification of historical records, 30, 43, 112, 154, 182, 460, 464
Buddhism, 8, 15, 16
  idol worship and, 7
Buku, 121, 234